ROUTER HANDBOOK

PATRICK SPIELMAN

Sterling Publishing Co., Inc.   New York

*To my family—for only they understand and tolerate my obsession **with wood***

Picture Credits

The illustrations in this book display the products, creations, and photography of many people and business organizations. Represented among them are the following: Albert Constantine and Son, Inc., 234–239; Beall Tool Company, 320; Beall Woodworking, 319; Black & Decker, 9, 20–21, 41, 44–45, 47, 50–51, 89, 130–141, 143, 147, 160, 163, 167–168, 171–173, 175, 180–182, 247–248, 255–256, 290, 297, 301, 304, 308, 312, 329, 331, 396 (photo by The Holmes I. Mettee Studio), 398 (photo by J. H. Schaefer & Son); Bonville, Keith, 198, 544, 571; Bosch, 23, 34, 40, 46, 71, 75, 91, 553–554; Buckeye Tools Corp., 52; C. R. Onsrud, Inc., 472–448; Customwood, 4; David A. Keller, 411–417; Don Allen, Inc., 501–503 (photos by Greg Gretz); Dremel, 23, 33, 155, 242, 448–449; Ekstrom, Carlson & Co., 15, 18, 54–55, 57, 88, 105; E. L. Bruce Co., 216 (photo by Hedrich-Blessing); Elu, 19, 156, 226; Emperor Clock Co., 203; Eze-Lap, 131; Forest City Tool Co., 111; Hirsch Co., 338; Island Craft Shop, 497; Joseph Vernon, 392–394 (photo #393 by John Fisher); Keystone Wood Specialties, 3, 228–230; Kimball Co., 484–492 (photos by Photo Arts, Inc.); Kurt Mfg. Co., 479 (photo by Alan Forest); Larch Diamond, Inc., 60, 553–556; Laskowski Enterprises, Inc., 6, 133, 135, 504–516; Leigh Industries, Ltd., 403–406, 410; Makita, 27–28; Marlin Industries, 493–497 (photo #493 by Harry Merrick); Milwaukee, 26, 48; North American Machinery Enterprises, 5, 230, 270, 498–500; Onsrud Cutter Mfg., 85, 96; Porter-Cable, 11, 15, 19, 56, 70, 73, 106–109, 113, 340, 342–343; The Princeton Co., Inc., 183; Quality Industries, Inc., 481–483; Rockwell, 341, 470–471; Ryobi, 29, 42; Safranek Enterprises, Inc., 559; Scandia, 526; Schmidt, Jeff, 219; Sears, 7, 24–25, 47, 49, 76–77, 104, 179, 305, 307, 309–311, 313–315, 321–324, 326–328, 331–337, 339, 341, 354, 378–380, 399, 450, 549–550, 557; Shelburne Museum, Inc., 13 (photo by Einers J. Mengis); Shopsmith, Inc., 391, 451–458, 465–467; Sioux Tools, Inc., 31–32, 53; Scan Furnishings, 231; Stanley Power Tools, 14, 303, 387–388, 400–402; Vermont American, 318; Walter Hartlauer, 316, 468–469; Wisconsin Knife, 114–118; Wing, 551–552.

Edited and designed by Hannah Reich

Library of Congress Cataloging in Publication Data

Spielman, Patrick E.
  Router handbook.

  Includes index.
  1. Routers (Tools)—Handbooks, manuals, etc.
I. Title.
TT203.5.S63 1983   684′,083   83-14566
ISBN 0-8069-7776-0 (pbk)

Fifteenth Printing, 1986

Copyright © 1983 by Patrick Spielman
Published by Sterling Publishing Co., Inc.
Two Park Avenue, New York, N.Y. 10016
Distributed in Canada by Oak Tree Press Ltd.
℅ Canadian Manda Group, P.O. Box 920, Station U
Toronto, Ontario, Canada M8Z 5P9
Distributed in the United Kingdom by Blandford Press
Link House, West Street, Poole, Dorset BH15 1LL, England
Distributed in Australia by Capricorn Ltd.
P.O. Box 665, Lane Cove, NSW 2066
Manufactured in the United States of America

Contents

Acknowledgments - 4

Introduction - 5

1 Router Basics - 20

2 Router Bits - 30

3 Safety and Maintenance - 48

4 Basic Routing Operations - 52

5 Pattern and Template Routing - - - - - - - - - - - - - - - - - - 69

6 Routing Joints and Surfaces - - - - - - - - - - - - - - - - - - - 79

7 Freehand Routing - 101

8 Routing Plastic Laminates - 116

9 Purchased Router Accessories - - - - - - - - - - - - - - - - - 122

10 Router Tables - 136

11 Router Dovetailing - 150

12 Overarm and Pin–Routing Machines - - - - - - - - - - - - - 168

13 Router Carving Machines - 182

14 User-Made Jigs and Fixtures - - - - - - - - - - - - - - - - - - 196

15 Panel Routing Devices - 206

16 Project Section - 210

Index - 223

Acknowledgments

A book of this scope and magnitude is obviously impossible to assemble without generous and cooperative assistance from many experts and specialists. I've been fortunate to meet, visit, and correspond with various manufacturers and their engineers, many woodworking artists, and some terrific individuals who directed me to some spectacular ideas and illustrations. These people have put forth their best efforts to make this an informative and helpful volume.

First, thanks must go to my good friend Charlie, for providing the idea, the motivation and the "pressure." Much gratitude is expressed to my wife Patricia, our son Bob, and our assistant Mark Obernberger, for keeping the business on course during my involvement with this work.

My sincerest appreciation and respect is extended to the following individuals who were more than helpful in a multitude of ways:

Glen Davidson of Welliver and Sons for his support and "leads."

Jeff Laskowski for some outstanding photos.

Bob Bogan, President of Customwood Manufacturing, for allowing me to include some of their beautiful wood products.

Glenn Docherty of Albert Constantine & Son, Inc. for his quick help with inlaying.

Roger and Tom McIlree for the outstanding alphabets.

Vince Pax at Shopsmith for a practical router table idea and selection of photos.

Stan Seidman and Don Reno of Black & Decker for photos and technical help.

W. M. McCord of Vermont American Corp. for assistance with the accessories.

David Keller for the special pictures of his dovetail templates.

Dick Riggens of Wisconsin Knife; R. S. O'Brien, President of Onsrud Cutter; and the staff at Ekstrom, Carlson & Co., for supplying photos and technical data about router bits.

Ken Grisley for making it possible to include the Leigh dovetail jigs.

The staff people at Black & Decker, at Porter-Cable, at the Bosch headquarters, and at the Sears Tower for their illustrations of routers, bits, and accessories.

And, to all of the other individuals and companies listed elsewhere for their photographic contributions.

Finally, a very special note of thanks goes to my typist, Julie Kaczmarek, for effectively following the "arrows," and turning rough scribbles into finished copy.

Patrick Spielman
Spielmans Wood Works

Introduction

The hand-held electric router has been dubbed the wonder tool. It is incredibly simple in its design and operating functions, yet it is amazingly versatile and easy to use. The development of the router has probably done more to revolutionize home craft and professional woodworking than any other device since the invention of the wheel. With a router and some direction (such as this book), a little practice, and a touch of imagination, you will literally have an entire workshop of tools in your hands.

Making and fitting perfect joints can be a breeze with a router. Even difficult jobs, such as making through- and half-blind dovetails (Fig. 1), mortise and tenons, stopped dadoes, and grooved joints, are all a snap with the router. Making letter-perfect wood signs (Fig. 2), carving raised or incised designs in wood surfaces, creating raised panels (Fig. 3), louvred cabinet doors, or decorative architectural panels (Fig. 4) are just a few of the other jobs you can handle perfectly with a router.

With some inexpensive attachments and auxiliary devices now available you can use your router to duplicate all kinds of carvings (Figs. 5 and 6), from simple designs to very intricate shapes, such as gun stocks. You can make some unbelievable wood turnings—even router-cut spiral turnings of table legs (Fig. 7), lamps, beautiful bowls, and goblets.

Fig. 1. Perfect dovetail joints in stock up to $^{13}/_{16}$ inch (17 mm) thick are easy to make with a router and appropriate bits. Refer to Chapter 11 for the information about router dovetailing with and without commercial jigs.

Fig. 3. Routers are widely used in all phases of cabinet-making, such as shaping the edges and making the joints for this door.

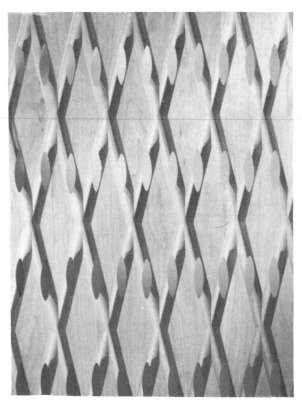

Fig. 2. The lettering on this sign was engraved with a portable router.

Fig. 4 (right). Beautiful and decorative architectural grills are router-cut.

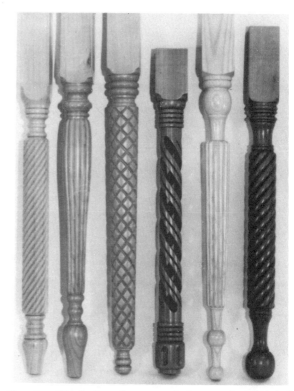

Fig. 5. Some decorative details carved with a router in a duplicating machine.

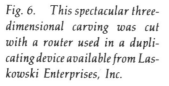

Fig. 6. This spectacular three-dimensional carving was cut with a router used in a duplicating device available from Laskowski Enterprises, Inc.

Fig. 7. Think these legs were lathe-turned and hand carved? They were cut with a router in a device called a "Router Crafter." It's illustrated on page 131.

Using your own easily made routing fixture you can "spin" out perfect dowels of various diameters in any length desired. With a special jig, the router will *even* cut wood threads.

Use of the router is not limited to cutting wood. It is widely used in industry to cut plastics of all kinds. A fairly common woodworking practice is the precise fitting and trimming of high-pressure plastic laminates for kitchen counters and overlaid furniture. With the proper bits, routers cut soft metals including aluminum, brass, and copper. I know one large industry that cuts half-inch (12-mm)-thick aluminum and smooths its welded joints with a hand-held electric router.

The router is practically an entire workshop in itself. I mean it! Think for a moment. The router can be used freehand to cut irregularly curved pieces from boards, as would a jigsaw or band saw (with some limitations—agreed). A lot of work that is normally done on these machines can also be done with a router. You can bore a hole and make a pierced cutout of a

design, for example, in one operation, without removing your hands from the router. (See Fig. 8.) Jointing the edges of boards to make them smooth and flat for gluing (normally done on an expensive jointer) can likewise be accomplished by a "crafty" person using the router. To some extent, the router can also be used to surface pieces of wood to make them uniform in thickness. This type of work is normally done on very expensive planers. Many woodworking joints conventionally made with radial and table saws can be cut as perfectly, with a router—and many joints are made faster and better.

The spindle shaper, a standard piece of expensive equipment in many mill and pattern shops, is now used less because of the router and the availability of new bit shapes. Edge-

Fig. 8. *This piercing cutout normally requiring a drill and a jigsaw or a sabre saw was done entirely with the router.*

Fig. 9. A router table is just one of many commercial and user-made accessories described in this book.

forming cuts and mouldings of various shapes are machined smoother and cleaner with the router, because of its high bit speed. A router owner who would like the convenience of a shaper can easily make or purchase a table to hold the router so it functions as a spindle shaper. (See Fig. 9.)

I have already mentioned that the router can be adapted to do some wood turning. There are, perhaps, other adaptations for router usage that you will devise yourself as special needs arise. In addition to using a router in the normal upright (vertical) position, it can also be used upside down, or sideways (horizontally). The router can be brought to the work, or it can be fixed in place and the piece of work taken to the router. The variety of jobs that can be done with the router is almost endless.

It's rather humorous if you think about it. Did you ever visit a cabinetmaker's shop or a professional woodworker's studio? Usually, hanging on the wall are some crude, jury-rigged looking apparatuses usually made from scrap or inexpensive materials. When you ask what these things are, the answer is

something like, "Oh, these are our router jigs, our fixtures for making decorative grooves in cabinet doors," or, "these are for routing a series of slots in stiles to make louvred panels." Seemingly impossible operations and special joint cuts are routinely made by the accomplished router craftsman, who uses ingenuity, know-how, and skill to turn out excellent, astonishingly well-crafted woodwork.

One of the objectives of this book is to lead you on to such ideas so that you can fully profit from the total capabilities of your router. A distinct advantage of being able to utilize the router to its fullest potential is that it simplifies and facilitates production or reproduction capabilities without expensive equipment. You can set up your own mini-factory and operate inexpensively and yet efficiently with a minimum of space. Easy-to-make patterns, templates, jigs, and fixtures (many made with the router itself) enable you

to make identical cuts or profile shapes in quantities of 2 to 20,000 pieces or more, as your needs require (Fig. 10), for example.

Today there are hundreds of different router-bit configurations in about as many different sizes to choose from. (See Fig. 11.) As new bits appear on the market, the list of the more commonly used bits becomes longer and longer. I remember when I first saw a carbide-tipped bit with a ball-bearing guide attached to it. My heart skipped several beats. I had to have one immediately, regardless of the cost, because I could see all of my problem jobs wiped out with this one bit.

I've spent plenty since then on other router bits, some wise purchases, and others not so wise. So it goes: Hound the manufacturers' distributors to see what's new. As industry develops a new product or solves a problem requiring a special bit, the word spreads Within a few years it filters down from the manufacturer to the customer. Some great new bits are shown and described in these

Fig. 10.   Pattern routing, to duplicate cuts and parts precisely. Here ¼-inch (6-mm) plastic pieces are triple-stacked and all cut together in one pass.

pages, along with many new router accessories. Some nifty gadgets will help make your router an almost limitless woodworking instrument.

The capabilities of the router are now so extensive that, whenever confronted with any woodcutting or -shaping problem, I look first to the router for the solution. Have you ever seen hand-carved wooden chain? Can you imagine the tedious effort and work involved to carve it? There is a mystifying look and certain eye appeal of it that often tempted me to try it by hand. But I never did, because I honestly lacked the time and patience. Looking to the router gave me the solution. (See Fig. 12.) I know it's not the same as hand-carved chain, but it *is* made of wood, with each link as perfect as the next. To see how it's done with the router, turn to pages 217 to 220.

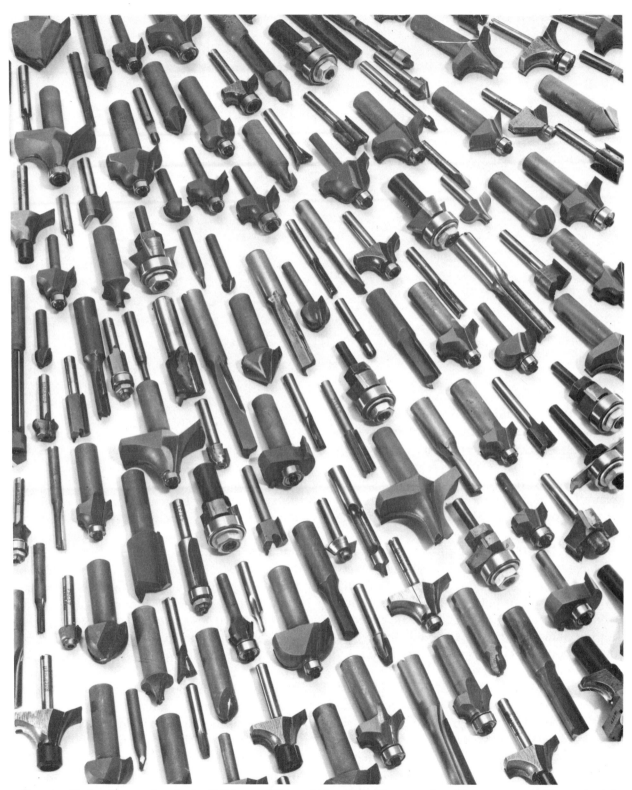

Fig. 11.   Today there are hundreds of bit types, styles, and sizes available, to match nearly every conceivable routing job. Shown here are bits of high-speed steel, carbide-tipped bits, solid carbide bits, bits comprised of various parts assembled on an arbor, and bits with guiding pilots and ball bearings.

11

Fig. 12. *This may look like hand-carved chain, but it's made with a router. Refer to pages 217 to 220.*

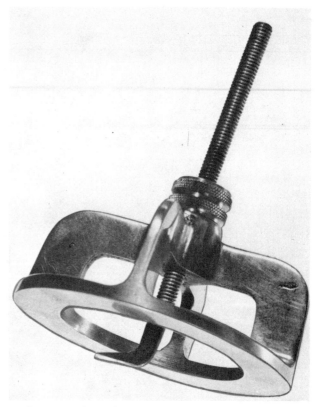

Fig. 13. *An early hand router.*

History All serious woodworkers should thank those intelligent, inventive pioneers whose genius has contributed to the development of today's modern router. The term "router" probably evolved from a specific type of early hand plane called the router plane (Fig. 13). This tool was fitted with cutters to scoop out v-shaped, round, and flat-bottom grooves.

The first portable electric router is believed to have been developed in Syracuse, New York, by patternmaker R. L. Carter, during World War I. His cutter (bit) was fashioned from the worm gear of an old electric barber's clipper. This cutter was attached directly to the shaft of an electric motor. Its efficiency was immediately noticed, and the news spread quickly. The popularity of the tool led Carter to manufacture 100,000 routers in the next 10 years. They were then called "Electric Hand Shapers," and soon they were referred to as "The Wonder Tool." The hand shaper was later improved by the addition of a base and a chuck to hold rotary tools, such as files and specially made router bits with ¼-inch (6-mm)-shank diameters.

The original Carter routers were low-performance tools with only one-quarter horsepower. The system of depth control and adjustment was much the same as that of many modern routers. The motor housing and base frame were threaded with 16 threads per inch (24 mm). A single full revolution of the motor within the frame changed the depth of the cut by ¹⁄₁₆ inch (1.5 mm).

Carter sold his business in 1929 to Stanley Electric Tools. Stanley continued to manufacture routers until the early 1980's. (See Fig. 14.) The Stanley Power Tools division was purchased by the Bosch Power Tool Corp.

The basic router idea—a cutter mounted directly onto the shaft of a high-speed motor—was applied to large, stationary, factory-type machines in the early 1900's. Today there are very sophisticated production routing machines with hydraulic and air-feed systems, and automatic computer-programmed controls. (See Figs. 15 to 18.) Most

Fig. 14. *The progressive changes in router design and manufacturing are evidenced in these old Stanley routers.*

Fig. 15. *A computerized numerical control (CNC) production routing machine with four router heads. Machines of this type have enormous capacities and are very large in size. This one weighs over 10,000 lbs (4,500 kg). Its computer has the capacity to direct the positioning of the work in any of 350,000 different locations every second.*

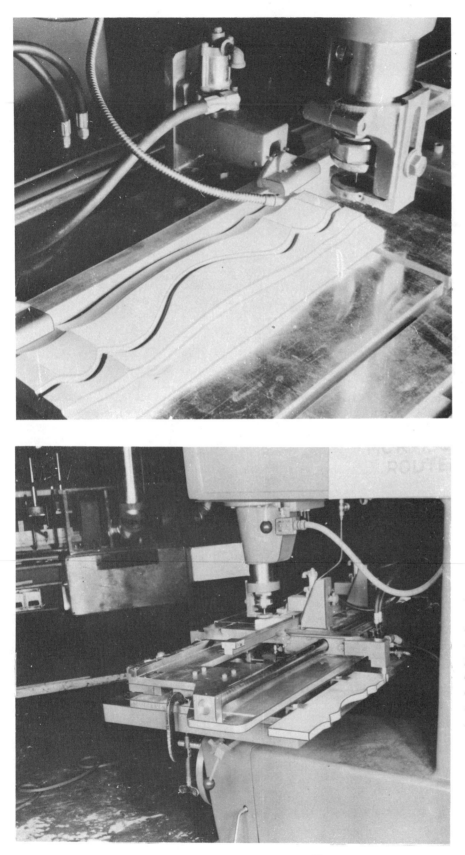

Fig. 16. A closeup view of an industrial operation called serpentine routing. The machine has an automatic feed table and an air-controlled floating router head, which changes the bit depth during the cut.

Fig. 17. A pattern fixed to an industrial machine. It guides the cutting direction of the part being made in Fig. 16. Using a portable router without hydraulics, automatic controls, or anything elaborate, it is possible to simulate pattern routing. Refer to Chapters 5 and 14.

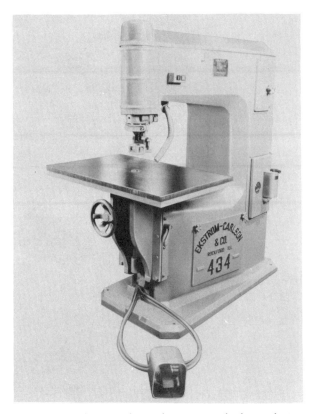

Fig. 18. *A large, industrial pneumatic high speed pin-routing machine. It has a ¾-inch (18-mm) collet capacity, 4-inch (101-mm) vertical spindle travel, turns at 20,000 RPM and weighs about 2000 lbs (908 kg).*

Fig. 19. *The Porter-Cable 1½ horsepower, 23,000 RPM, ½-inch (12-mm)-collet capacity router has a "D" handle, trigger switch, and weighs in at 14 lbs (6.3 kg).*

of these machines carry bits similar to those available to the home craftsman. With some improvisation you can simulate factory routing jobs yourself with your own router unit.

Routers Today A familiar brand name that will no longer be synonymous with router manufacturing is Rockwell. Their line has been returned to Porter-Cable, the company founded in 1906 and purchased by Rockwell in 1960. (See Fig. 19.) As of 1982, Millers Falls Electric Tools and Skil will no longer be producing routers with their label. Some other companies have also fallen by the wayside, despite the growing popularity of the electric router. U.S. Census figures indicate that the router is third in the list of tool ownership, following drills and saws.

The lineup of the more popular electric router brands available today includes the following American brands: Black & Decker (Figs. 20 and 21), Bosch (Fig. 22), Dremel (Fig. 23), Porter-Cable (Fig. 19), Sears Craftsman (Figs. 24 and 25), and Milwaukee (Fig. 26). Makita (Fig. 27), Hitachi (Fig. 28), and Ryobi (Fig. 29) are Japanese-made routers that are becoming very popular in the U.S. Elu (Fig. 30) is a German-made router well-known in Europe and England that may also be finding its way into the United States market soon.

Air-powered routers (Figs. 31 and 32), normally used only in industrial production shops, are becoming more and more popular in custom shops and small woodworking businesses. Today the woodcraft consumer has much to choose from. Each router company offers a number of models in its line to satisfy individual needs regarding purchase price, convenience, and size (horsepower and bit capacity). A vast array of specialty features includes such options as built-in dust collectors, lights, plunging mechanisms, motors controlled by electronic chips, and electronic read-out depth scales.

Fig. 20. Black & Decker's light-duty router has a 4.5 amp, ⅝ horsepower motor, 30,000 RPM speed and a ¼-inch (6-mm) collet. It is double-insulated and weighs just under 4 lbs (2 kg).

Fig. 22. The Bosch "Shop Router," 1½ horsepower, 23,-000 RPM motor, 3⁵/₁₆-inch (84-mm) diameter. It has a ¼-inch (6-mm) collet capacity, removable handles for one-hand routing, and weighs 6¼ lbs (3 kg).

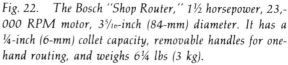

Fig. 21. This Black & Decker router has a plunging-type base, and features an electronic digital depth-of-cut read-out with a push-button reset. Other specifications: 1½ horsepower, 25,000 RPM, ¼-inch (6-mm) collet capacity, work light, double-insulated, 8 lbs (3.6 kg).

Fig. 23. The Dremel "Moto-Tool" router has a 30,000 RPM motor and collets that carry bits up to ⅛-inch (4-mm)-diameter shanks. This tool is used for modelling and delicate routing.

Fig. 24. This Sears ¼-inch (6-mm) collet, light-duty router has a ⅝ horsepower, 25,000 RPM motor, plastic housing and base, and weighs 5.6 lbs (2.4 kg).

Fig. 26. The Milwaukee line of heavy-duty routers are available in 1, 1½, and 2 horsepower models. All have ¼- and ⅜-inch (6- and 9-mm) collets. The 1½ and 2 horsepower models have ½-inch (12-mm) collet capacities. The speeds are 23,000, 24,500, and 26,000 RPMs, respectively. Weights range from between 8–8¾ lbs (3.6–3.9 kg).

Fig. 25. The Sears 1 horsepower, 25,000 RPM router has a ¼-inch (6-mm) collet capacity, trigger switch-on handle, a work light, and a weight of 8¾ lbs (3.9 kg).

Fig. 27. Hitachi makes plunging routers in ¼-inch (6-mm) and ½-inch (12-mm) collet capacities with 24,000 and 22,000 RPMs, respectively.

Fig. 28. The Makita plunging router has a ½-inch (12-mm) collet and a vertical range of 2⅜-inch (60-mm) cutting depth. It's a 22,000 RPM unit, with a net weight of 11 lbs (5 kg).

Fig. 29. The lineup of Ryobi routers. Made in Japan and distributed in the United States, they include, from left to right: 1. A 3-lb (1.3-kg), 29,000 RPM trimmer with a ¼-inch (6-mm) collet, and a 3.8 amp motor. This tool can also be used for light grooving. 2. A 1 horsepower, ¼-inch (6-mm) collet, 5.9-lb (2.7-kg) plunging router. 3. A 2 horsepower, ½-inch (12-mm) collet router weighing 13.4 lbs (6 kg). 4. The 3 horsepower, ½-inch (12-mm)-collet plunging router weighing 9.7 lbs (4.4 kg).

Fig. 30. *This plunging router is made by Elu in Germany.*

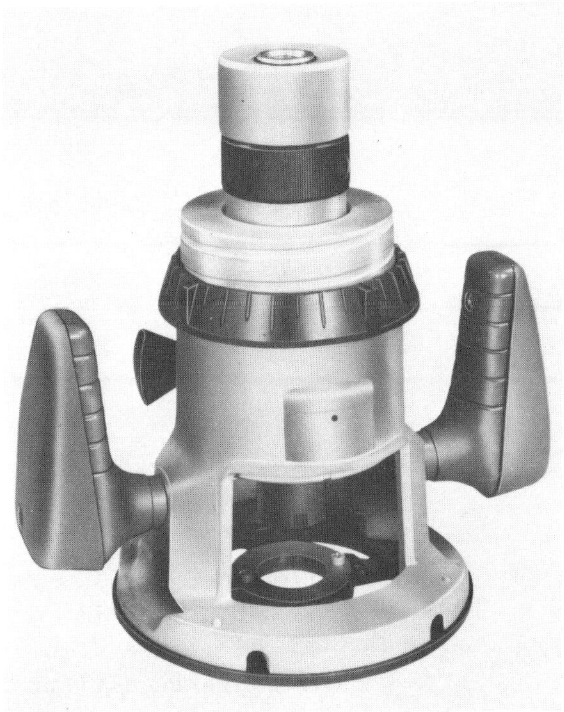

Fig. 31. *This heavy-duty air-powered router, manufactured by Sioux Tools, has a ⅜- and ½-inch (9- and 12-mm) collet capacity, turns at 20,000 RPM and weighs only 7½ lbs (3.4 kg).*

Fig. 32 (right). *Another air-powered router. This one has a ¼-inch (6-mm) collet size, 40,000 RPM, and weighs just 2 lbs (9 kg). It's also made by Sioux Tools, Inc.*

The chapters that follow will highlight some of the advantages and disadvantages of the current routers, along with the many accessory devices available. You will also see many ideas for user-made jigs and fixtures, to help you get the most from your router. Finally, to help you get into it, included are router projects. In this book I have attempted to draw together a broad cross section of standard router operations along with some very interesting illustrations of unusual approaches, to help your woodcrafting become easier, faster, better, and more individually your own by using the diverse services of the router.

Patrick Spielman

1
Router Basics

This chapter discusses and illustrates the basic types of routers available and will highlight some of their special features. This information cannot ever be regarded as the final word on the subject, because new models of routers are always being developed and tested. Innovative features can be expected in the not-too-distant future. Improvements in router performance and convenience are evident in the better models now available, as well as those soon to reach the market.

It is highly doubtful that there will ever be one "super" router that will do it all. The best router depends entirely on the range and type of woodworking it will have to do. A very small mini-router, such as the Dremel (Fig. 33), is perfect for models, miniatures, and light woodcraft. A 3¼ horsepower production router (Fig. 34) would obviously not be a

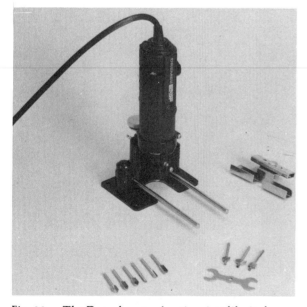

Fig. 33. The Dremel router functions just like its larger counterparts. Although limited in horsepower and bit capacity, it is useful for modelling and similar light work.

Fig. 34. This big production router made by Bosch, weighs 14 lbs (6 kg), has a 3¼ horsepower, 21,000 RPM motor, and a ½-inch (12-mm) collet capacity. With power like this, it can handle through slotting and making sink cutouts in ¾-inch (18-mm) stock.

match for this type of work, but such a heavy router might be ideal for handling the work in cabinet, furniture, and heavy-wood-project fabrication plants.

The majority of woodcrafters need routers that perform a broad range of tasks somewhere between the extremes described above. Zeroing in on the one best router is not a simple task. The most common mistake is to purchase a router based entirely on price. In a relatively short time it wears out or burns out because it was a cheaply built model. It is indeed depressing to have to admit that your router does not have the horsepower and other conveniences that make routing fun and pleasurable—thus refuting the reasons for using the router entirely.

Serious amateurs and professional woodworkers eventually purchase a second and even a third router. Each purchase should be carefully analyzed, and the router selected specifically for a particular class of work or woodworking job. There are many excellent general-purpose routers to choose from. You will probably select a router made by one of the manufacturers whose routers were illustrated in the introduction, in this chapter, or on other pages of this book. Knowing the basic parts of the router, analyzing the functions or performance of those parts, and examining the extra router features should be helpful in selecting a router that best meets your needs and preferences.

The essential parts of a typical router are illustrated in Fig. 35. Note that there are two major parts, the motor and the base. Routers are sized (designated by their power) in terms of motor horsepower or motor amps. Most routers sold today fall into a ½–1½ horsepower category. Those under ½ horsepower are for light woodcrafting, and those from 1½–3½ horsepower are more or less production tools, intended for heavy cutting and continuous operation.

Motor speeds, revolutions per minute (RPM), range from 16,000–30,000. Horsepower, more than motor speed, is required for making deep or heavy cuts in difficult-to-

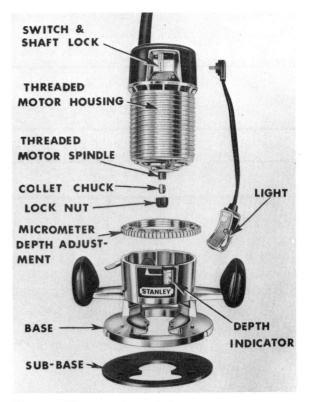

Fig. 35. The parts of a typical router.

machine materials. High motor speeds are not synonymous with increased power. In fact, the reverse is true. Usually, the lower the horsepower, the greater the RPM. Low horsepower-high RPM routers will not hold up when cutting deeply into difficult hardwoods. This is not to say that lightweight routers are not good. Lightweight routers are designed only for jobs involving shallow cuts, trimming, and the like. They should not be forced to exceed their built-in design limits.

Generally, it is safe to assume that all routers have sufficient motor speeds for the work they are designed to do. Routers have much higher speeds overall than other types of woodworking tools. A hand drill seldom exceeds 2500 RPM. Circular saws seldom rotate faster than 5500 RPM. It is the high speed of the router that produces surfaces cut so smoothly that they need only minimal sanding, if any at all.

Higher speeds, in theory, do produce smoother cuts. If you have a router operating at 20,000 RPM and one of equal horsepower rotating at 25,000 RPM, you get 25 percent more cuts per inch or foot of cut surface from the faster model. A lightweight, high speed, low horsepower router can do many of the same jobs as larger, heavier horsepower models, but with limitations and inconvenience. For example, instead of making a deep cut in one pass, the cut will have to be made in two, three, or more successive passes at shallower depths. This practice is essential as a preventative measure, to minimize the possibility of excessive strain on the motor and bearings and avoid burnout. This sort of inconvenience often taxes patience and certainly reduces the pleasure of routing. In summary, the essential benchmark for overall router performance is motor horsepower, not speed (RPM).

Most experts agree that ball bearings are indicative of the quality of a router. The bearings must endure the constant sideways forces, or thrust pressures, against the motor shaft in operation. The heavier and the larger the bearings, the longer the life of the router. (See Fig. 36). Routers must provide users with protection from possible electric shock. This means that they must be provided with a third wire, a grounded three-prong plug, or be double insulated. Exterior electrical cords should have "strain relievers" at possible sharp bends, at the motor housing, and where tension may cause premature cord wear or damage.

Most routers have similar chucks to grip the cutting tool (bit). Chucks are usually a split-collet type, which tightens around the shank of the bit when secured with a threaded lock nut. A well-built chuck-collet system is a necessity for safe operation and longer bit and router life. The collet itself should be long enough internally to grip a good length of the bit shank. This reduces collet wear, vibration, and run-out. Smaller routers have collets that will only accept ¼-inch (6-mm)-diameter bit shanks. Larger, higher-priced routers have two or more collets of different sizes, to take bits with ⅜-inch (9-mm)- and ½-inch (12-mm)-diameter shanks. This feature is of vital importance if you plan to use your router for a very broad range of operations. Owning a router that carries bits with ½-inch (12-mm)-

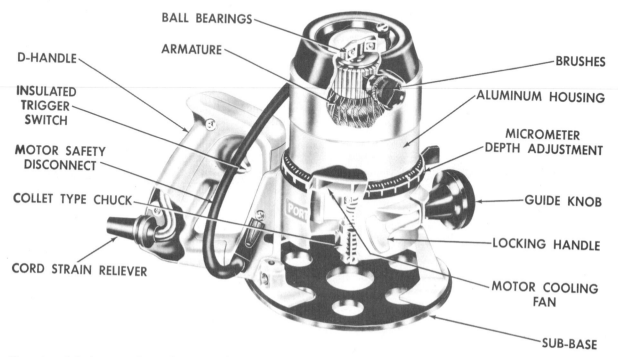

BALL BEARINGS
ARMATURE
D-HANDLE
INSULATED TRIGGER SWITCH
MOTOR SAFETY DISCONNECT
COLLET TYPE CHUCK
CORD STRAIN RELIEVER
BRUSHES
ALUMINUM HOUSING
MICROMETER DEPTH ADJUSTMENT
GUIDE KNOB
LOCKING HANDLE
MOTOR COOLING FAN
SUB-BASE

Fig. 36. A look at another style router, showing some of its internal construction.

diameter shanks permits the use of specialized production router bits. This increases the range of cutting configurations and bit-design selections that can be used in the router, and at the same time increases its overall versatility.

Most routers require two wrenches to install and remove bits. Others have motor-shaft locking devices that allow bit changes with only one wrench. Look for convenience and simplicity when making bit changes. It is surprising how often a particular job requires bit changes. There are some jobs, such as template-guided dovetailing, where the bit must be inserted without removing the router motor unit from the base. Some routers are designed so that this is practically an impossible task.

The design of the router base deserves some thought and criticism, as well. It should be designed so that it is a plus in performing work. Some bases are designed with large, open areas around the cutter, and others have small, enclosed viewing areas. If you do any freehand routing it's vital to see what's going on inside and to guide the router to follow layout lines. When work is mostly of the type where the router is guided with fences or templates, the more enclosed bases are not as much of a problem.

It is somewhat puzzling to me that router manufacturers provide an opaque, black-plastic sub-base. It's hard to see through—in fact, you can't. Some brands give little peep-holes, just big enough to tease your vision. On some there isn't even an extra peephole. One of my personal requirements is to see what I'm doing and to observe what's going on in the action area. In many cases it's possible simply to remove the sub-base entirely. However, for many jobs, particularly when working near the corners or edges of a surface, using a router without its sub-base presents support problems.

To rectify the sub-base problem, I made my own. In fact, I've made several interchangeable sub-bases for specific routing jobs. The one I use most is made of transparent plastic

Fig. 37.   View of one of my homemade, clear-plastic sub-bases. Note the large center hole and the slightly rounded edges on the plastic base.

(Fig. 37). Using the manufacturer's sub-base as a pattern for the outside diameter and the screw-hole locations, I made one of clear polycarbonate plastic (Lexon). This material is virtually scratch- and mar-proof. An occasional cleaning with a plastic-cleaning solution containing an anti-static ingredient so dust doesn't cling to it works perfectly.

Incidentally, the center hole on mine is larger than the one on the manufactured version. It's made so bits with larger cutting circles will fit through the base. The one I'm using now has been serving me well for six years. It gets plenty of use. Sometimes my router runs 30 or more hours per week. My first clear plastic base was made from an acrylic-type plastic. This one was hardly worth the effort. Acrylic scratches easily, and before long it wasn't much better than the solid black version provided by the manufacturer.

The router base is also where many accessories are attached to the router. Fences, circle-cutting devices, template-guide bushings, laminate-trimming guides, and other attachments are held to the bases by slotted or thumb screws. Check these areas out. Do they interchange and tighten easily and securely? Are they sturdy? Are the mounting areas sufficient, or will they cause stripped threads because of soft metal or plastic housings? Are the support areas thin and likely to crack from repeated use or occasional abuse?

The router base also houses the knobs or handles that are used to move and control the router. At first, you might think: "Handles are handles and knobs are knobs, so what?" Give this some additional thought. A number of router manufacturers are supplying routers with permanently affixed knobs and/or handles. Some manufacturers have the handles attached to the motor unit. (See Fig. 38.) In tight areas, knobs and handles do get in the way occasionally. A router of this type may

Fig. 38. *This router is made with the handles as an integral part of the motor housing. Note the trigger switch in one handle.*

give you headaches when you use it with accessories, such as router tables, or when you make your own attachments. I really prefer removable knobs and handles to fixed handles. Then again, there are many jobs where I prefer a "D" handle because I've grown so used to it.

Should the knobs or handles be located higher up or lower down on the router base? Each location has advantages in certain situations. Personally, I like them located low on the router base. In freehand work, this allows

me to press my wrist and forearms down on the surface of the work, which gives me better overall control. I can use my wrist as a pivot, with a compasslike manoeuvre for small, free curves or my elbow as a pivot in doing larger curves. A combination of wrist and elbow movement allows me to do reasonably well on medium-sized curved cuts. But more on freehand work later.

The disadvantage of having knobs and handles located low on the router base is their interference when guiding the router along straight edges and base-guided templates. There are some kinds of work, such as trimming, fast and light signmaking, and freehand detailed carvings, where no knobs or handles at all are often preferable. (See Figs. 39 to 42.)

Fig. 39. *Some router units are small in diameter and light in weight, which makes them useful for woodcarving and power filing with burrs rather than regular router bits.*

Fig. 40. *This Bosch ¾ horsepower, 30,000 RPM trimming router has no handles at all. Its compact size permits routing in close quarters. Motor diameter is only 2¾ inches (70 mm).*

Fig. 41. *The Porter-Cable laminate trimming router has a 3.8 amp, 28,000 RPM motor, weighs only 3.6 lbs (1.6 kg), and can also be used for general light routing jobs.*

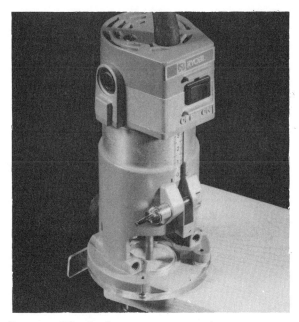

Fig. 42. The Ryobi trimming router has a 3.8 amp, 29,000 RPM motor and weighs 3 lbs (1.4 kg). It has a depth scale and is designed for rabbeting, grooving, and other light cutting jobs, in addition to trimming plastic laminates.

The router base also incorporates the mechanism that provides for the vertical adjustment of the motor unit, giving the changes in depth of the cut settings. (See Fig. 43.) There

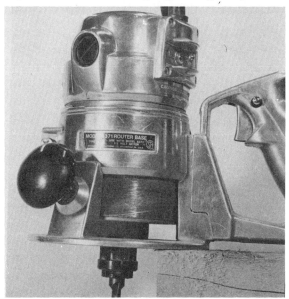

Fig. 43. The total distance of vertical adjustment is often an important feature in some special jobs. This router has a spiral-grooved depth adjustment.

Fig. 44. Black & Decker's 1½ horsepower, 25,000 RPM, ¼-inch (6-mm)-collet router has a rack-and-pinion depth-changing system. The total weight is 7¼ lbs (3.3 kg).

Fig. 45. The Ryobi plunging router weighs 5.9 lbs (3 kg), has a ¼-inch (6-mm) collet, 24,000 RPM, 1 horsepower motor. Note the three-position adjustable stops at the front left. These can be preset for three different cutting depths.

are now four different devices: 1) The system where the motor just slides vertically and is clamped. 2) The conventional threaded system—spiral grooves on the motor and inside the base. (See Fig. 43.) 3) The familiar rack-and-pinion system. (See Fig. 44.) 4) A system with a plunging device. (See Fig. 45.)

The plunging router is relatively new to the United States. However, plunging routers have been in use in some countries for almost 40 years. Their popularity appears to be growing in the United States. Before rushing to join the crowd be sure to analyze the total performance and limitations of a plunging router. Can the motor unit be removed and used independently of the base? Does it convert conveniently to work in a shaper table? What are its limits in vertical adjustment or depth of cut?

Plunging routers do have some distinct advantages. There are some operations where the plunger has no equal. Most have bases incorporating a spring-loaded system. This allows the motor unit to be pressed down or lowered to the stock with minimal exertion, so the bit enters the work at exactly 90°. The cutter is similarly retracted, with a flip of a lever, at the completion of the cut. Thus, the cut can be started and completed without lifting the base of the router off the work surface. This offers obvious safety features, as the bit projects below the base only during the actual routing operation. The bit is automatically retracted with a flip of a lever, and is out of harm's way when the job is completed. Another feature of some plungers is the turret-like depth stop, allowing for presetting to multiple cutting depths. (See Fig. 45.) This is especially handy when cuts are too deep to be made in the first single pass.

The type of on-off switch control is another item deserving vital consideration, depending upon needs and expectations. If you ever do anything bordering on a dangerous practice (which we all tend to do eventually), it is comforting to have the on-off switch convenient for a quick shutdown. Additionally, if your work requires a lot of starting and stopping such as in freehand routing, carving, and dovetailing, the seemingly unimportant matter of the location of the switch becomes more deserving of consideration. The best in these situations is a spring-loaded switch control that can be worked without removing hands from the knobs or handles.

Fig. 46. The Bosch 2¼ horsepower production router turns at 26,000 RPM. This model has a "D"-handle with trigger switch, ¼-, ⅜-, and ½-inch (6-, 9-, and 12-mm) collet capacity and weighs in at 11¾ lbs (5.3 kg).

Fig. 47. The Sears 1 horsepower router is a ¼-inch (6-mm) collet, 25,000 RPM unit with a trigger switch built into one handle.

One of the primary reasons for my preference of the "D" handle is that it also houses a spring-loaded trigger switch. (See Figs. 43, 46, and 47.) Just simply releasing my trigger finger shuts down the router. Another advantage is that I know the power is off until I pull the trigger. I think the worst switches are the toggle, flip, or sliding types, because it is accidentally possible to connect to power with the switch in the "on" position. Equally bad is a switch that requires you to reach for it. With the spring-loaded trigger I do not have to make that inconvenient visual check to determine if the router is on or off when starting up after bit changes.

Perhaps one of the best router systems is the kind with two switches. That is, one switch convenient in the knob or handle of the router base and another on the motor itself. (See Fig. 43.) Consequently, when you want to use the motor independently of the base, the router motor has its own switch. This is especially convenient when using the router motor unit in a router table, or an overarm carving, or turning machine.

It is a good idea to assess the value of the motor unit when used independently of the base. Will routers with handles attached to the motor housing give you problems? Throughout this book there are many applications of the motor unit alone. Can it easily fit and support other attachments such as the overarm carving and duplicating mechanisms now so popular? Are all capabilities of the motor as an independent tool accessory unit adequately considered? Some other features (or conveniences) offered by manufacturers include such items as built-in lights, dust pickups, flat-top motors (some people think these make bit changing easier), and micrometer depth-stop adjustments. All such extras are always well worth pondering and evaluating. (See Figs. 48 and 49.)

Fig. 48. All Milwaukee routers have flat tops for steady positioning when changing bits, removing the sub-base, and measuring the depth of cut.

Fig. 49. This Sears 1½ horsepower router features a dust-pickup system that draws up through one handle into a bag. Other specifications include: 25,000 RPM, ¼-inch (6-mm) collet, 9¾ lbs (4.4 kg) net weight, internal work light, and a trigger switch.

Fig. 50. *Black & Decker's 1½ horsepower plunging-base electronic digital-display router gives a depth-of-cut read-out with push-button reset and English-to-metric conversion. It has a 25,000 RPM motor, ¼-inch (6-mm) collet, work light, and weighs 8 lbs (3.6 kg).*

Fig. 51. *Black & Decker's newest production router has a 3½ horsepower, ½-inch (12-mm) collet, and two-speed (16,000/20,000 RPM) electronically controlled motor. It weighs 15 lbs (6.8 kg).*

Modern electronics is making some noteworthy improvements in the overall design and performance of routers. The newest feature is a digital read-out, which gives the precise depth of cut. (See Fig. 50.) Other features to look for in production routers (Fig. 51) that are here today include:

1. Speed selectors for two or more speeds. It's possible to flip a switch to slow a router, for better cutting of aluminum and some other metals and plastics and then flip it back to a conventional high-speed router.

2. Minimal-torque start-up. Most conventional routers jerk upon start-up. New routers have a slower "ramp start," which accelerates the motor smoothly to its full speed without jerking.

3. Constant selected cutting speed. This is provided through electronic controls that govern the motor.

4. Overload protection. This feature warns you if you are pushing the router too hard. The electronics will decrease the motor speed and power output. Upon reducing the load, the motor will resume normal speed and power—an essential feature in ensuring a long life for the router motor.

Air-Powered Routers These are certainly well worth considering, should you have a suitable air supply available. Air or pneumatic routers have some exclusive advantages over their electric counterparts. They are generally similar in appearance, do most of the same jobs as electric routers, and are available with some of the basic attachments such as template guides (Fig. 52) and laminate trimmers. Their distinct advantages are as follows:

1. They are, by and large, considerably lighter in overall weight when compared to electric routers of equal horsepower and speed capacities.

2. They operate at lower temperatures and are, thus, more comfortable in continuous use.

3. They are free of any electrical parts; consequently, they may be used safely in wet, damp, or explosive environments.

4. They have fewer working parts and are less expensive to maintain and repair.

5. Their motors are virtually burnout-proof. Even when overloaded to the point of full stall, air motors are not damaged. (See Fig. 53.)

On the negative side, air routers require a substantial-sized air compressor. It must provide a continuous flow of air with an output range of 20–38 cubic feet (0.5–1.0 cubic m) per minute (depending upon router horsepower size) at 90 pounds per square inch (620 kilopascals). Additionally, in-line moisture filters to dry the air supply, a lubricator, and a pressure regulator to assure that the air supply is properly conditioned and will not cause internal damage to the tool are required.

Although I have not included illustrations of every router available today, those shown in this chapter and in the introduction give an overview of what is available. Most are identified by brand or manufacturer and the essential specifications and features are noted. Costs and other factors are not given as prices change, and design additions, improvements (or omissions), and alterations are made by manufacturers frequently.

When shopping for a router be sure to take your time. Give it a mental dry run. Ask questions. One of the most important being: "Are service and parts available locally, or must these come from an out-of-town factory or service center? Ideally, before buying a router talk to someone owning the model you are considering. Better, try it out yourself. Make your decision based on your needs and work expectations. Simply going by someone else's say-so is not enough, since the other person may have entirely different uses for the router than you will.

Fig. 52.   An air-powered router fitted with a template guide.

Fig. 53.   This Air Turbine 1⅓ horsepower router has a ⅛-inch (3-mm) collet, 65,000 RPM, and weighs just over 3 lbs (1.3 kg). These tools are effective for light work, but are also capable of removing large quantities of material. These routers are used in aircraft industries, furniture factories, and are useful in working fibreglass and plastic products.

2
Router Bits

Since it is the bit that actually produces the cut surface in routing, it makes good sense to give some serious thought and consideration to the selection, use, and care of router bits. As new models of routers continue to improve, router-bit manufacturers are making great strides in perfecting better-performing cutting bits with longer-lasting cutting edges, and an ever greater selection of bits in different cutting shapes. (See Figs. 54 and 55.)

In addition to knowing the capabilities and limitations of a router, it is essential to have an understanding and appreciation of router bits in general. A productive router craftsman should know basic bit terminology, be familiar with the various special features of bits made for specific uses, and know the ins and outs of router-bit maintenance and care. It is also extremely helpful to have a visual reference illustrating a good sampling of the hun-

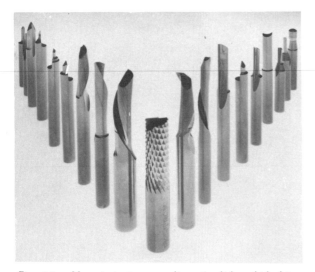

Fig. 54. Here is just a sampling of solid carbide bits, most designed for specific routing jobs. The diamond-cut one in the foreground is made especially for routing fibreglass, epoxy, and other hard, nonmetallic abrasive materials.

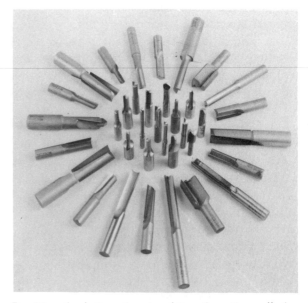

Fig. 55. A selection of various bit configurations, all of a straight-flute design for making straight cuts. Note the various cutting lengths and cutting diameters.

dreds of different bit types, styles, shapes, and sizes available today. This chapter deals with all these topics.

The amount of work actually accomplished with a good router bit is almost too impossible to comprehend. Just think of all the rapid, successive little cuts a bit makes in just an hour of use or in its entire lifetime of service. Every second it's rotating, a router bit makes an incredible number of cuts. One individual cutting edge of a typical router bit, for example, if driven at 28,000 RPM makes 467 cuts every second. If that single edge had a "helper on board," their combined effort would give over 930 cuts per second, or 55,800 identical cuts every minute. Indeed the router, due to its high turning speed, is a real slave driver to the bit it carries. (See Fig. 56.) No other woodworking tool expects as much work of its individual teeth or cutters.

Fig. 57. An industrial routing operation. Here one bit enters the wood, cuts out the profile shape, and forms the edge shape all in one operation.

Router bits often have to do more than one job, too. Although most bits are designed to do side cutting in most jobs, many times they have to work as boring tools as well. Bits are often expected to make their own entry into the routing area, so that both the end and side edges of the bit get their share of work. (See Figs. 56 and 57.) The bits must also throw out the waste chips from the cut. With all of its speed, force, engineered cutting edges and angles, a good bit is really a masterpiece of geometric wizardry.

Thus, in terms of the effort and the work it does, a good router bit is indeed one very special bargain. Still, many woodworkers expect bits to be even more perfect than they actually are. They feel that a bit should go on and on performing (often under impossible conditions), almost forever with minimal care or respect. Do not lose respect for these wonder tools. In terms of actual stock removal, a hand plane iron gets sharpened much more frequently than a router bit, as do most all other woodworking tools, and a neglected or abused router bit will fight back. It will put more wear and tear on the router; it will require more physical exertion and strain during use. The resulting cut or surface quality

Fig. 56. A craftsman freehanding a cut through tough ¾-inch (18-mm) plywood in a single pass. This requires a router of substantial horsepower, along with a bit selected for its strength and ability to cut. This bit also needs to bore its own way through and have sufficient space between the cutting edges to provide adequate chip removal.

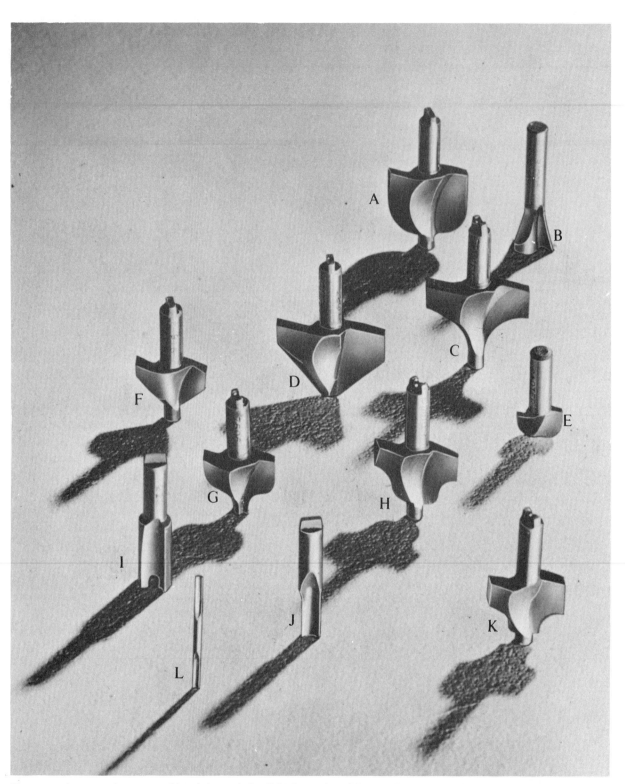

Fig. 58. *A group of one-piece, ¼-inch (6-mm)-shank high-speed-steel bits of the type usually sold as a "starting well sharpened, these less-expensive bits will make excellent cuts in most species of solid wood. Shown are: a. cove, b. dove-tail, c. corner rounding, d. v-groove, e. core box, f. chamfer, g, h. ogee, i. stair routing, i, j. straight, k. beading, and l. double-end veining bits.*

will not measure up to the standards of fine workmanship—a level we all naturally seek. Just a little respect of and care for these special tools will reap good dividends.

Select the best bit for the job at hand. This does not necessarily mean the most expensive bit, either. (See Fig. 58.) One company is now providing industry with "throwaway" bits, ¼-inch (6-mm)-diameter spirals that cost from just a little over $1.00 to under $3.00 each, in quantities of 100. In view of this, one tends to question the well-established axiom, "You get what you pay for." On the other hand, higher-priced bits generally do mean better overall quality and thus longer-lasting edges and longer service.

Router bits were first made of special metals, called high speed steel (HSS for short). (See Fig. 58.) In the 1950's came tungsten carbide. Small pieces of this hard material are brazed, to make cutting edges on a tool-steel base material. These are called carbide-tipped bits. (See Figure 59.) They have an edge life 15 to 25 times longer than conventional HSS bits. There are good carbides and cheaper carbides. Better carbide bits have more and thicker tips, allowing for more sharpenings. A good production-quality carbide-tipped bit should be able to be reground up to 15 times. Cheaper carbides must be discarded or retipped after four to six regrinds.

Fig. 59. A carbide-tipped bit with two straight flutes.

Surfaces are ground more smoothly and edges are sharper on the better carbide bits. They have better brazing and balance. Cheaper carbides are thinner, less sharp, and best thrown

away after a few sharpenings. Better carbide-tipped bits can be retipped with new carbide and reground by a qualified tool-conditioning service to like-new condition. This can often be done for much less than the cost of buying a new replacement bit. Some smaller-sized bits are made of solid carbide. (See Fig. 54.) All carbides require special diamond stones for sharpening.

The newest-type bits to arrive in industry are the diamond bits. (See Fig. 60.) These bits have a carbide base onto which man-made diamond crystals (polycrystalline diamonds) are bonded by a high-pressure, high-temperature process. Diamond router bits are said to retain their sharpness 300 to 400 times longer than carbide. The diamond bits are extremely expensive, ranging up to approximately $1,000 for a typical ½-inch (12-mm)-diameter bit. Still, despite this high price, industry finds it cost-effective in production. There is less sharpening time necessary, the quality of work improves, feed rates and cutting speeds can be increased, and so factory output jumps.

Fig. 60. The new diamond bits. These unassuming-looking industrial bits are very expensive. They have diamond crystals bonded to a carbide-base material with a high-pressure, high-temperature process. Diamond bits outperform the best carbides, with up to 300 times longer edge life.

Experts predict that because diamond is the most wear-resistant material now known, it will be the toolmaking material of the future. Diamond tools must be sharpened by experts with facilities that even large woodworking factories currently do not have. It is not economically feasible for the home craftsman even to consider diamond bits at this stage of the game. However, knowing that carbide is not the all-perfect tool material increased my respect for all it *can* do. Many weekend woodworkers can get by just fine with the conventional—and much less expensive—high-speed-steel bits. But even HSS bits can vary immensely in price, depending upon tool hardness, thickness, sharpening, balance, and finish quality. The key, as with any woodworking tool, is to keep bits sharp.

It is difficult to categorize router bits into specific groups or types. In addition to being grouped by the material they are made of (HSS, carbide-tipped, solid carbide, or diamond), they could be classified as one-piece (Fig. 58), multiple-part (Fig. 61), piloted (Fig. 62), or nonpiloted (Fig. 63), straight-cutting (Fig. 64), or forming and specialty bits. There

Fig. 64.   *Straight double-flute bit. Also available in single flute, these bits are used for general-purpose and flat-bottomed cuts. They will cut grooves, dadoes, and lap joints. Sizes range from 1/16-inch (1.5-mm) up to 1¼-inch (31-mm) cutting diameters.*

is no fine line separating such specific groups. Figs. 65, 66, and 67 identify some of the es-

Fig. 65.   *Basic parts.*

Fig. 61.   *A router arbor (shank) which accepts interchangeable edge-forming cutters. Shown here are carbide-tipped cutters.*

Fig. 62.   *A carbide-tipped ball-bearing piloted bit.*

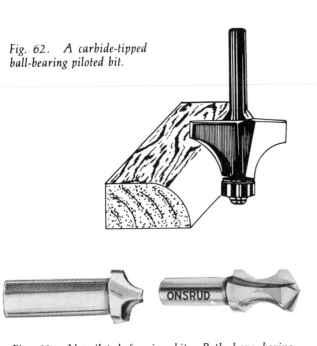

Fig. 63.   *Nonpiloted forming bits. Both have boring points.*

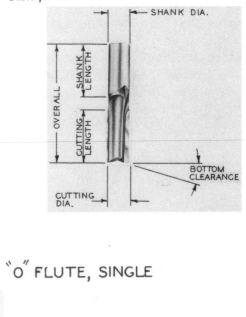

"O" FLUTE, SINGLE

"O" FLUTE, DOUBLE

"V" FLUTE, DOUBLE

Fig. 66.   *Flutes and cutting edges.*

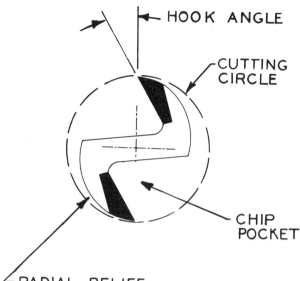

HOOK ANGLE

CUTTING CIRCLE

CHIP POCKET

RADIAL RELIEF

Fig. 67. Design provisions for easy cutting include: correct cutting angles, side-clearance relief, gullets for chip removal, and rotational balance.

sential terms associated with router bits. Figs. 68–79 illustrate some of the popularly shaped edge-forming bits commonly used by woodworkers, amateurs and professionals alike.

Fig. 68. The single-piece two-flute corner-rounding bit with integral pilot is used where guiding is necessary. It is available in sizes ranging from ³/₁₆–¾-inch (4.5–18-mm) cutting radius.

Fig. 69. A piloted rabbeting bit. Most such bits available cut a standard ⅜-inch (9-mm) rabbet width. Rabbet bits with ball-bearing guides can be converted to cut ¼-inch (6-mm) rabbets by using a larger-diameter ball bearing.

Fig. 70. A cove bit, carbide-tipped with ball-bearing pilot. The guide eliminates burning or marring the work edge. Cove-bit sizes range from ¹/₁₆–½-inch (1.5–12-mm) cutting radius.

Fig. 71. Ball-bearing chamfer bits are available in 15°, 25°, and 45° angles with ½–⅝-inch (12–15-mm) outside cutting lengths. They are used to bevel edges.

Fig. 72. A piloted HSS beading bit available in cutting radius sizes from ³/₁₆–½ inch (4.5–12 mm).

Fig. 73. A Roman ogee ball-bearing guided, carbide-tipped bit available in various sizes with 1⅜ inch (35 mm) the largest overall cutting diameter.

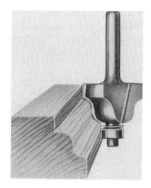

Fig. 74. *A very large ogee bit shows how different shapes may be cut with the same bit by changing the depth of cut.*

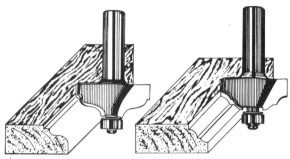

Fig. 75. *Two bits for highly decorative edge work are used to make mouldings, frames, and so on. (left) An ogee with fillet. (right) A "classical" form-cutting bit.*

Fig. 76. *A raised-panel edge-cutting bit with ball-bearing pilot. Raised-panel bits come in a variety of cutting profiles and sizes.*

Fig. 77. *Sash bead and cope bits are used for beading the inner sides of window frames. They have a ³⁄₁₆-inch (4.5 mm) cutting radius.*

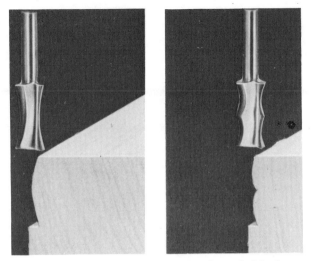

Fig. 78. *Two more edge-forming bits. (left) Large-radius edge-rounding bit. (right) A double-bead edge bit.*

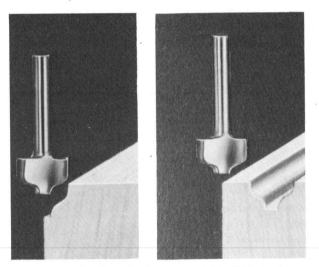

Fig. 79. *Another edge-forming ogee bit. This is also an end-cutting type that permits cutting into a surface, as shown at right.*

Straight-Flute Bits Figs. 80 through 87 show some of the straight-cutting and surface-forming bits. These bits are used for many routine jobs involving simultaneous bottom and side cutting, such as making grooves with straight sides and flat bottoms. Bits in this category are available in a variety of sizes, ranging from a ¹⁄₁₆-inch (1.5-mm) cutting diameter up to a 2½-inch (65-mm) cutting diameter (on ½-inch [12-mm] shanks), and various cutting-edge lengths are also available. Straight-flute cutters are widely used to make grooves, slots, dadoes, rabbets, laps, boxes, joints, mortise-and-tenons, dovetail pins, and for other joint-fitting work. These bits are also used to make recessed or through cutouts freehand, or to follow the straight or irregular curves of templates or other patterns with some type of router guide. Straight bits come in one- , two- , three- , and four-flute configurations, but the one- and two-flute types are the most popular.

Fig. 80. An HSS straight single O-flute, ¼-inch (6-mm) shank bit. (left) A ¹⁄₁₆-inch (1.5-mm) veining bit for decorative freehand routing, carving, and inlay work. (right) Typical single-flute ¼-inch (6-mm) diameter used for cutting softwoods quickly.

Fig. 81. An HSS straight double-end bit for general routing, strip inlay, and scroll-cutting. Sizes range from ¹⁄₁₆–¼-inch (1.5–6-mm) cutting diameters.

Fig. 82. A carbide-tipped single-flute bit with end ground for easy plunging.

Fig. 83. A double-flute carbide-tipped bit, used for smoother finished surface-cutting on medium and hard-woods, and for cutting abrasive materials, such as plywood and particle board.

Fig. 84. An HSS double O-flute production-type bit. O-flutes are stronger than V-flutes, and thus better suited to faster feed rates in solid woods.

Fig. 85. A carbide-tipped straight V-flute bit. These are available in up to 2-inch (50-mm) cutting diameters with 1¼-inch (31-mm) cutting edges and ½-inch (12-mm) shanks.

Fig. 86. A mortising bit developed for hinge butt template routing, but with various other uses. Note the deep center gullet for maximum chip removal.

Fig. 87. A double-flute carbide-tipped chip-breaker bit. This bit is made for fast cutting of abrasive and dense materials, such as chip board or particle board. The edges are designed to break up the chips at high feed rates. The flutes are ground to overlap each other, producing a straight cut.

Generally speaking, single-flute bits are stronger and allow for faster feed rates. Two-flute bits make smoother cut surfaces. Straight bits may also be designed with their own integral pilots, or they may have pilots with boring (drilling) points for easy plunging or piercing. (See Fig. 88 to 92.) Ball-bearing-guided bits as well as straight bits with non-boring pilots cannot be used for plunge-entry into the work.

Fig. 88.   A group of various piloted straight cutting bits used for trimming, and template or pattern-guided cutouts.

Fig. 89.   Panel pilot bits with drill points. (left) Single-flute HSS. (right) Double-flute carbide-tipped. Bits of this type are available in ¼-, ⅜-, and ½-inch (6-, 9-, and 12-mm) cutting diameters with up to 1¼-inch (31-mm) cutting edges.

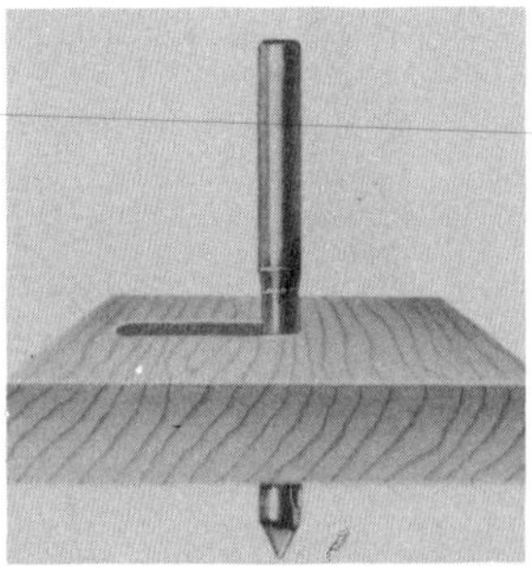

Fig. 90. Through slotting with a panel bit.

Fig. 91.   A stagger-toothed piloted panel bit with drill point. This bit is designed to give more chip clearance with higher feed rates. This is an ideal bit for cutting plywoods, hardboards, particle board, and other abrasive material. It is available in various sizes up to a 2½-inch (64-mm) cutting length with an overall length of 4¾ inches (120 mm).

Fig. 92.   The ball-bearing piloted carbide-tipped trimming bit is designed primarily for trimming plastic laminates, but it has many other uses. Due to its shallow or small flute design, it is not intended for fast-feed cutting of wood materials, as the panel bits previously illustrated are. Bits of this type are available in two and three flutes with up to 1½-inch (38-mm) cutting lengths.

A new concept involves installing a ball bearing on the shank of a bit. The bearing is set onto the shank below the area gripped by the router collet and above the cutting edges of the bit. (See Fig. 412, page 161.) This arrangement affords guided work with templates and patterns mounted above the work surface. Obviously, this technique could be applied to bits other than straight-fluted ones as well.

Spiral Bits Figs. 93 to 95 show bits that are gaining popularity with woodworkers. Spirals are designed as either upwards-cutting or downwards-cutting. Their flutes draw the shavings either up and out of the cut, or force the chips down towards the worktable or through the workpiece. Single-flute (or -edge) spiral bits allow for faster feed rates, but double cuts produce smoother cut surfaces. The spiral cutting action is somewhat different from cuts made with straight-edged or straight-fluted bits. Unlike straight bits that make one cut, revolve, make another cut, and so on, the spiral makes a continuous uninterrupted cut. It could be compared to the cutting differences between a jigsaw and a band saw. The jigsaw reciprocates up and down, cutting only on the downward stroke, whereas the blade of a band saw is always moving downwards into the wood.

Fig. 93. An HSS single-flute spiral up-cut bit. In through cutting, the down cuts are a better choice as they make the chips flow away from the router and operator.

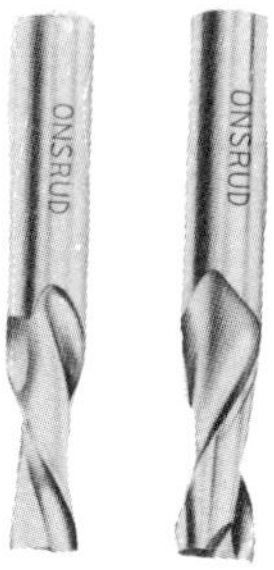

Fig. 94. HSS double-flute spirals. (left) Down cut. (right) Up cut. Double-edged bits make smoother cuts whereas single-edged bits permit faster feed rates.

Fig. 95. HSS spirals piloted down cut with boring point. These are available in ¼-, ⅜-, and ½-inch (6-, 9-, and 12-mm) cutting diameters with ¾–1¼-inch (18–31-mm) cutting edge lengths.

Spirals produce less tear-out, a clean, chip-free work surface, and are especially beneficial for plunging through cutouts, for trimming, and when routing critical materials with one good face. The only disadvantage is that spirals transmit slightly more torque back to the operator than do straight-flute bits. This makes routing more difficult for freehand work. Spirals are not as problematic for guided router jobs as long as the workpiece is securely clamped or fixtured. Incidentally, spiral bits are the choice bits for cutting aluminum. Spirals are available in several materials: HSS, carbide-tipped, or solid carbide. They can have one, two, three, or four flutes (cutting edges). Spirals are good general bits for cutting nonferrous metals, softwoods, and hardwoods; and they are ideal for profiling, slotting, and deep-plunge routing. Spirals are available in ⅛–¾-inch (3–18-mm) cutting diameters.

Fig. 96. The new "On Shear" bit offered by Onsrud Cutter Mfg. features a shearing cutting action. Onsrud makes it in HSS and carbide-tipped, in one- or two-flute designs, and in sizes from ¼–½-inch (6–12-mm) cutting diameters with up to 1¼-inch (31-mm) cutting length. Use HSS for plastics and solid woods. Carbide-tipped bits are recommended for plywood, and other tough materials.

A new bit, developed by Onsrud Cutter and gaining much attention in woodworking circles, is the "Shear Cut" configuration. (See Fig. 96.) This is closer to a straight-flute bit, but the inclined edge generates a cut that is a cross between those of a straight- and a spiral-flute bit. The manufacturer claims it is free-cutting, produces fine surface cuts on most materials, requires less horsepower, and lowers operator fatigue.

Other Groove-Forming Bits These are illustrated in Figs. 97 to 105.

Fig. 97. A round-bottom veining, double-end, single-flute bit. This one is used for grooving, freehanding decorative designs, lettering, and small cove cuts. Usual sizes are ⅛-, 3/16-, and ¼-inch (3-, 4.5-, and 6-mm) cutting diameters, and they are available in HSS and solid carbide.

Fig. 98. Core box bit. This is an HSS one-piece bit used for round-bottom cuts, fluting, carving, and sign work. Sizes range from ¼–¾-inch (6–18-mm) cutting radius.

Fig. 99. Roundnose bits are available in HSS carbide-tipped, and, in smaller sizes, solid carbide. They can also be obtained in single- or double-flute styles. Smaller versions are best in solid carbide and larger ones carbide-tipped. They are available in various cutting radius sizes from 1/16 inch (1.5 mm) to 1/2 inch (12 mm) [1 inch (24 mm) diameter] and up to 1/4-inch (6-mm) cutting lengths.

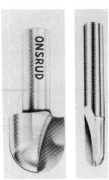

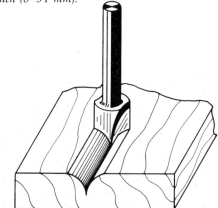

Fig. 103. Dovetail bit available in HSS and carbide-tipped with various-degree angled edge. (15° and 14° the most popular). They can be purchased in cutting heights from 1/4–7/8 inch (6–21 mm) and cutting diameters from 5/16–1 1/4 inch (8–31 mm).

Fig. 100. The V-groove bit is used in panelling, sign-making, and decorative freehand work. It is available in HSS and carbide-tipped. Most stock bits have a 90° included angle but may be ground to suit. Sizes can be obtained in up to 1 1/2-inch (38-mm) cutting diameter.

Fig. 104. The point-cutting quarter-round bit is used for surface decorating, carving, and beading. Also available are point-cutting ogee bits. Both styles come in various sizes.

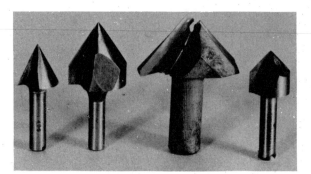

Fig. 101. Some V-bits used in sign work, including a specially ground one at left. Stock bits at right.

Fig. 102. The round-over bit with boring point is available in various sizes up to a 2-inch (50-mm) cutting diameter with a 1/4–1/2 inch (6–12 mm) boring-point diameter and radius of from 1/4–3/4 inches (6–18 mm).

Fig. 105. A two-wing HSS bit blank that can be ground to any desirable cutting edge. It is available in sizes from 1/2–2 1/2-inch (12–64 mm) cutting diameters.

Panel-Raising and Simulated-Panel-Raising Bits These are shown in Figs. 106 to 109. These can also be used to form edges or to make decorative surface and internal cuts.

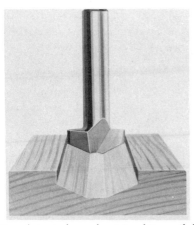

Fig. 106. A typical panel-raising bit available in HSS or carbide-tipped with up to 1⅛-inch (30-mm) cutting diameter.

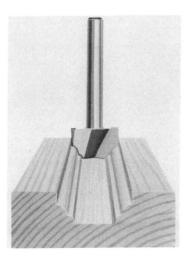

Fig. 107. A bead and fillet combination bit for traditional simulated panel designs.

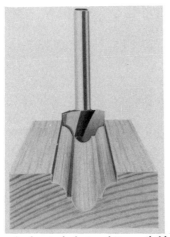

Fig. 108. A classical design bit available in HSS or carbide-tipped in various sizes.

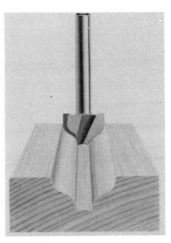

Fig. 109. Ogee bit for cut-in grooves and edge-forming.

Some bits are now available that are specially designed for edge-forming of raised panels. (See Figs. 110 and 111.)

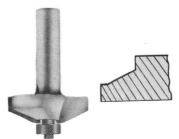

Fig. 110. Edge-forming carbide-tipped panel-raising bit with ball-bearing pilot.

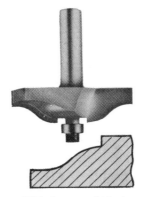

Fig. 111. This large carbide-tipped panel-raising bit of ogee fillet design with ball-bearing guide is 3⅝ inches (92 mm) in its largest cutting diameter.

Plastic-Laminate (Formica) Cutting and Trimming Bits Such bits must be of solid carbide or carbide-tipped, because the hardness of laminates quickly dulls conventional

HSS cutters. Figs. 112 to 118 illustrate and describe a number of laminate-cutting bits used in regular hand-held routers or the laminate-trimming-type routers shown on pages 24–25. Although not illustrated in this group of bits, solid carbide veining bits designed to cut round- and flat-bottom designs (such as French Provincial door borders) in and through plastic laminate are also used extensively.

Fig. 112. This solid-carbide piloted flush-trimming bit has a ¼-inch (6-mm) shank and an overall length of 1⅝ inches (42 mm). It's used to make square cuts flush to a surface with its ⁵⁄₁₆-inch (8-mm)-long cutting edge.

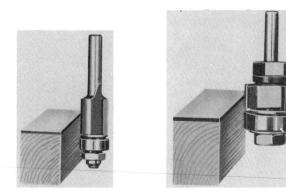

Fig. 113 (left). Two-wing and (right) three-wing carbide-tipped, ball-bearing flush-trimming bits. Four-wing versions that make even smoother cuts are also available for production work.

Fig. 114. This solid-carbide piloted-bevel trimmer bit produces a slight bevel (7°) on the finished edge of plastic-laminate covered furniture and cabinets.

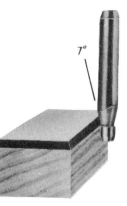

Fig. 115. A combination flush-and-7°-bevel trim bit. With the bit raised it cuts a bevel rather than a flush cut at the depth it is set to.

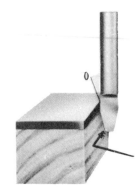

Fig. 116. A production ball-bearing bevel-cutting trim bit with four cutting edges.

Fig. 117. A special ball-bearing guided overhang cutting bit. This trims to a ³⁄₁₆-inch (5-mm) rough size overhang, to eliminate possible chipping when making a finish cut with a square flush-cutting or 7°-bevel bit.

Fig. 118. This solid-carbide boring and flush-cutting trim bit drills its own starting hole and trims flush to an edge. It's a perfect bit for cutting through plastic laminates bonded over materials that have pre-cut openings.

Slotting Cutters Fig. 119 shows this item. Slotting cutters have a number of applications, including grooving for edge joints, making kerfs for weather-stripping doors and

Fig. 119. *Slotting cutters. Available as interchangeable cutters on one arbor (shank), assembly includes a ball-bearing guide.*

windows, cutting the slots in plywoods and core materials to receive "T"-edging in plastic laminate work, and making the spline kerfs for spline mitre joints or spline butt joints. Slotting cutters are specified according to the width and depth of the kerf cut. The depth of the cut is usually ½ inch (12 mm). Interchangeable two- or three-wing carbide-tipped-teeth cutters are available for use with one shank (arbor). Slot (kerf) bits are available in many different cutting widths between 1/16 inch (1.5 mm) and ¼ inch (6 mm). Three-wing versions are stronger and last longer when cutting thin kerfs in hard materials. Two-wing versions allow faster feed rates with more room for chip removal.

A different type of slot cutter is the "Keyhole" bit. This cuts the special slots often seen on the backs of picture frames, wall-hung plaques, and mirrors. Fig. 120 shows the bit and the cut it makes.

Fig. 120. *A Keyhole slotting bit is used to make the hanger cut into the backs of picture frames, plaques, and other wall-hung objects.*

Fig. 121. *Trim saws.* (left) *Flush-cutting type with blade permanently mounted on an arbor.* (right) *Blade to install on an arbor with ball-bearing guide.*

Fig. 122. *Arbor for interchangeable cutters and ball bearings.*

Trim Saws Figs. 121 and 122 show saws in ¾–1⅝-inch (18–40-mm) diameters, permanently mounted on arbors or as individual blades for arbor mounting, are also available to trim laminates and for other applied overlay materials. These are available in HSS or solid carbide. Solid carbide is recommended for hard abrasive materials. Individual arbor or spindle assemblies (Fig. 122) for shaper-cutter components with individual ball-bearing guides (Fig. 123) and plane cutters (Fig. 124) can be adapted to the router to satisfy almost any cutting requirement. However, before loading an arbor with many combina-

Fig. 123. *A typical ball bearing and interchangeable shaper-cutters with two, three, and four flutes are available in many cutting patterns.*

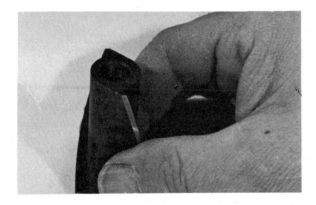

Fig. 124. *Plane cutters that fit arbors are available in HSS and carbide-tipped for edge-jointing and planning operations with routers.*

tions be sure to check with the manufacturer's representative to be sure that all components selected will operate safely on that arbor or spindle with your particular router.

Milling Cutters Fig. 125 displays the type used in metalworking machine shops. They can also be carried in the router. Ball mills are good for carving and end mills can make some smooth cuts. The major disadvantage is that end mills for metal cutting do not have as much clearance as cutters or bits designed specifically for woodcutting. However, a tool sharpener can grind additional clearance for improved cutting.

In addition to all the bits and various cutting devices previously discussed and illus-

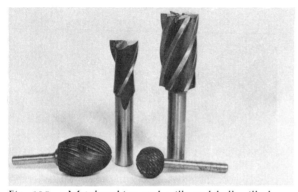

Fig. 125. *Metalworking and mills and ball mills have some applications in wood routing.*

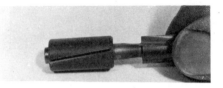

Fig. 126. *Use a shank adapter to increase bit-shank diameters.*

trated, the shank adapter is a very handy accessory to know about. (See Fig. 126.) This inexpensive item is available in·steel or hard-fibre resin. (The latter is better as it absorbs vibration.) Shank adapters allow smaller shank diameters to fit larger diameter collets, and thus increase even further the bit selections. Adapters are available in outside diameters from ¼–¾ inches (6–18 mm), and with inside openings in sizes from ⅛–½-inch (3–12-mm) diameters. This accessory also allows use of bits made for small, high-speed carving tools, such as the Dremel and Foredom carvers to be carried in the router. However, experts are quick to advise that these little bits should be used with care to prevent breakage.

Some Tips on Bit Selection Here are some miscellaneous tips for better routing performance:

1. Use larger shanks and larger-diameter bits when possible. The larger the cutting circle of the bit, the better the quality of the cut surface produced. The sharpness will also last longer, and the likelihood of chatter and breakage will be reduced. For example, using a ⅜-inch (9-mm)-diameter bit instead of a ¼-inch (6-mm) bit increases the bit strength and rigidity between 50 and 100 percent, depending upon its design and number of flutes. A ¼-inch (6-mm)-diameter bit should not be used to cut deeper than ¾ inch (18 mm). However, there are times when this is not possible. In such cases, make multiple passes or several cuts at shallower depths.

2. Bits, in order to cut right, must adequately accommodate chip removal and have sharp edges. Cutting pressure should not necessarily be proportionally increased when using bits of increased diameter.

3. Always use bits with the shortest possible cutting edge. Longer bits increase the chance of excessive vibration, chatter, collet run-out, and possible breakage. A good general rule here is that the cutting-edge length should not exceed three times the diameter of the bit. For example, a ⅜-inch (9-mm)-diameter bit should not have a cutting edge longer than 1⅛ inch (30 mm).

4. Always put as much of the shank as possible into the collet. This practice reduces collet wear, and places less strain on the motor and bearings.

5. Avoid single-flute bits of over ⅜-inch (9-mm) diameter. These tend to create out-of-balance conditions, causing bearing wear and other problems.

6. Be sure to select bits best matched to the job and the material to be cut. Even the very best HSS bit can overheat and dull in just one pass when cutting particle board or veneer-core plywood panels.

Bit Care and Sharpening There are three basic and simple, but very important, routines that dramatically aid in maintaining cutting quality and bit sharpness:

1. Store bits properly. Edges are easily nicked with careless handling and storing. (See Fig. 127.) This is especially true of carbide-tipped bits, as their edges are more brittle than HSS. A good storage system for bits not in use is well worth the little extra effort. (See Fig. 128).

2. Keep the bits clean. Many species of wood tend to cause pitch and resin tars to accumulate on the bit. The results are decreased chip clearance, increased friction and overheating, and, subsequently, additional feeding pressure, placing more

Fig. 127.   *This very poor storage system is outright bit abuse.*

Fig. 128.   *A much better idea for storing bits.*

strain on you as well as your router. Clean your bits frequently with lacquer thinner or special wood-pitch removers. If necessary, scrub with fine steel wool, but avoid working the steel wool over the cutting edges. Pilots and ball-bearing guides can also get gummed up, especially from the adhesives in plastic laminate work. Clean with appropriate cement solvent.

3. Apply a protective surface coating to your bits. Bits kept in damp or humid basements or unheated garages and workshops can get rusty and pitted surfaces. Apply a coating of light oil, spray wax, or spray lubricant to all bits periodically.

Bit Sharpening In my opinion, this category of bit maintenance should be turned over to a well-qualified expert. Bits wear and dull faster than most people realize. Even those wonderful carbides will give in sooner from cutting plywoods, resin-filled particle boards, laminates, and similar abrasive materials. Carbides require special diamond wheels for grinding and polishing. Because of the inherent geometrics involved, router bits must be expertly sharpened to ensure perfect balance and have proper relief in addition to sharp edges. Most professionals would agree that sharpening should be done by qualified experts. That's why many bit manufacturers offer resharpening services.

A properly resharpened bit should perform like new. Check the telephone book for the local expert. A good sharpening service should be equipped to handle carbide; they also should be able to retip carbides, and grind special bit shapes upon request. Should such a service not be available locally, deal directly with a reputable manufacturer providing a speedy mail-order tool-sharpening service. You may have to try a few local or mail-order services to find the best one. Use a magnifying glass to inspect cutting edges and all ground or polished surfaces. It will vividly identify dulled, chipped cutting edges and crisply sharpened ones.

What about that in-between stage? The point where bits can neither be called sharp nor classified as dull? Touch them up yourself. A number of router manufacturers offer bit-grinding attachments as router accessories. These grinding attachments use the router motor as a direct-drive grinder. A suitably formed abrasive wheel chuck is incorporated.

For that stage between like-new sharpness and distinct dullness, touch up HSS, straight-flute, "V," two-wing, and flat-edge bits with small, inexpensive slip stones. Use an aluminum oxide or an India abrasive stone. Work the flat "inside" of the cutting face of the flute, being certain to maintain the correct rake angle, as shown in Figs. 129 and 130. Straight-flutes and flat "insides" of carbide bits can be touched up in the same manner with a diamond hone. This, by the way, is not terribly

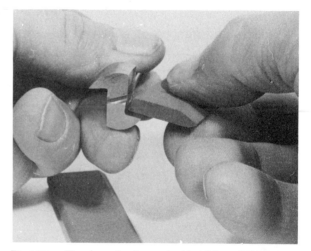

Fig.129. *Touch-up honing a double V-flute HSS bit.*

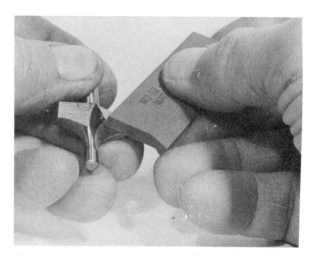

Fig. 130. *Honing a two-wing HSS piloted round-over bit is more difficult. Exercise care to avoid grooving the pilot. Only very short strokes are possible.*

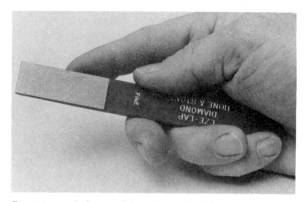

Fig. 131. *A diamond hone for carbide bits. Use it much like a file.*

expensive. (See Fig. 131.) A good choice is one with a layer of diamond 600 grit and 400 grit on an aluminum or plastic handle.

Should an HSS bit need more material removed than falls into a category of minimal honing to restore "inside" and edge sharpness, light grinding can be done in several ways. One method of grinding HSS bits that works pretty well is to use a cone-mounted stone in the drill press not exceeding 1500 RPMs. (See Fig. 132.) However, don't get carried away. Carefully grind the bit as shown, trying to remove an equal amount from each wing or flute. Remember to follow with fine honing. For the best and safest results, turn grinding and sharpening over to an outside expert! Never sharpen or grind anything on the outer surface or circumference of bits. Leave that to a professional! If bit clearance is reduced or the rake angle changed, the bit will ride the cut, burn the material, and become prematurely dull. Either condition creates exasperating problems, especially in the finishing stages. When, through repeated grindings, the web becomes thin or the carbides grind down, it may be wisest to discard the bit. Don't be afraid to dispose of a used-up bit. Probably for all of the above reasons manufacturers are starting to push the concept of disposable tooling. Initial cost is less and the tool is simply thrown away when dull.

There are a few other points concerning general maintenance which more directly relate to safety and operation. This information is covered in the next chapter.

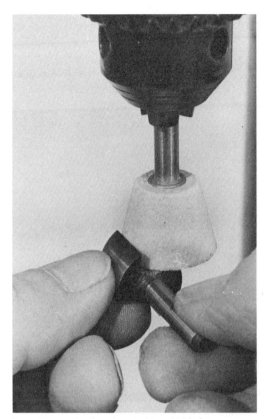

Fig. 132. Freehand grinding HSS bits using a mounted wheel in the drill press.

3
Safety and Maintenance

If you seriously value your own immediate and long-term physical well-being, secure adequate protection against these hazards associated with routing: 1. eye and sight injury, 2. hearing loss, and 3. lung/respiratory damage.

Everyone who works with wood tools has been repeatedly warned and is well schooled about the ever present hazards of flying chips, sawdust, and knots ejected from power tools. The router is certainly no exception! The chances of a bit breaking, coming loose, or fracturing during operation may be thought by some individuals to be relatively slim, but such a situation certainly deserves heeded warnings. The possibility of motor screws vibrating loose and falling into the cutting area is also slim, but then isn't it an awful surprise to strike an imbedded nail or knot unexpectedly? Such things do happen. Don't allow yourself to be exposed to such rare dangers, or to the obvious hazards of flying chips, without good eye and/or face protection (See Fig. 133.)

For those who do any amount of routing work, the continuous high-pitched "whir" of the router is far from a comforting sound. It's my opinion that this noise is eventually damaging to hearing. Router manufacturers could do a great service if they developed quieter routers. Until they do, the only alternative is to wear earplugs or protective earmuffs. (See Fig. 134.) A sign I saw in an industrial plant reads: "A ringing in the ear is the cry of a hearing cell in distress."

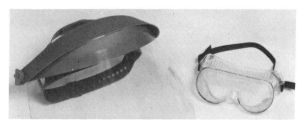

Fig. 133.   *Wear a protective face shield or safety goggles.*

Fig. 134.   *Wearing earmuffs or earplugs is also recommended during long periods of routing.*

Fig. 135. *A respirator or dust mask gives protection from dust particles.*

More and more articles are being published concerning a potential hazard for all woodworkers to be alerted to—dust. Some wood dusts are more dangerous than others, but all are being researched. The router not only throws out chips and shavings, but it also generates microscopic dust particles that remain airborne for hours after routing. Like the dust from fine sanding, it gets into the nasal passages and lungs. Clear your nose after routing and you'll have proof. So use protective armor: goggles, earmuffs, and a dust mask (See Fig. 135.)

Sears has a dust-pickup attachment for one of their routers. I really do not know how effective it is. I do know that my own vacuum system is quite effective and powerful. It's possible to incorporate into the router a hose attached directly to a shop or home vacuum cleaner. My vacuum cleaner is hung from the shop ceiling over my workbench. With extra lengths of hose, a rope, and a pulley with a counterweight, it allows for free router movement within approximately an 8-foot (2.4-m)-diameter working circle. The hose is thus always in near-vertical position and out of the way. The slack is taken up automatically by the counterweight. The hose is connected vertically alongside the router with a modified metal-pipe reducer—an inverted funnellike shape. (See Fig. 136.) This part was cut to fit as

Fig. 136. *A homemade vacuum attachment connected directly to the router. It is seldom in the way and is efficient for many otherwise dirty routing jobs.*

closely as possible into and alongside one of the "webbed" or bridged openings of the router base where other guides are normally secured or attached.

To make a better air seal, use epoxy paste (from an auto-body repair shop) and putty in the cracks and crevices. Before doing this, prepare the surfaces on the router, to release the cured epoxy. This is accomplished by first covering all areas with a generous coating of paste wax. As a secondary release measure I used thin clear-plastic wrap. I also imbedded into the epoxy a metal-fastening lug, so the vacuum attachment could be held securely in position on the router with one of the base knobs. This entire attachment can be removed simply by unscrewing one knob. (See Fig. 137.)

I also found it advantageous to close in the remaining openings under the "bridges" of the base. This was accomplished by using clear-plastic lens material from safety goggles.

Fig. 137. *A view of the vacuum attachment disconnected from the router. One of the base knobs is all that is needed to reattach it to the router.*

Cut the plastic to fit, and secure it directly to the router bridging and lower base area with a generous bead of hot-melt glue. This lens material must be cleaned occasionally, as the air static tends to attract dust particles onto its surface. Use a plastic cleaner with an antistatic ingredient and you will pretty well minimize that problem.

This dust-collecting attachment has made my routing immensely more pleasurable, and it keeps the shop and air much cleaner. It has also improved my routing craftsmanship. Without the vacuum, chips and slivers that would otherwise get partially knocked out of the cut often get stuck in the hole opening in the sub-base and send the router in a wrong direction. The inside vision is much better, too, with chips and dust sucked away from layout lines. Without the vacuum, the router also tends to crawl over chips, changing the depth of cut when surface routing. Chips become lodged between the base and the guide, affecting the straightness of the cut.

A powerful vacuum setup really does the trick. Perhaps someday a manufacturer will make such an attachment available with routers designed to accept them. There are some jobs where the vacuum is not too efficient, particularly edge-forming jobs (chips get away), but, overall, the vacuum catches a good share of chips, along with a good portion of microscopic dust particles.

In addition to protection from the hazards of flying chips, noise, and dust, there are a number of additional safety precautions important to heed:

1. Read the router operator's manual.
2. Be certain that the router horsepower, bit selected (shank strength and cutting diameter), and planned cutting depth are all matched up to handle the cutting characteristics of the material.
3. Know the limits of your tools, and do not exceed them with force.
4. Do not use dull cutters or bits with chipped or cracked cutting edges.
5. Dress properly. Wear short sleeves or be sure to button cuffs on long-sleeve shirts.
6. Disconnect power when changing bits or mounting attachments.
7. Do not be victimized by an accidental start-up. Always be sure that the switch is off before connecting the router.
8. Be sure that bits, attachments, clamps, and locking devices are secured before start-up.
9. Keep children and observers at a safe distance.
10. Make sure that pieces are securely clamped or held well.
11. Be especially cautious when working small pieces.
12. Keep hands and fingers away from revolving bits and cutters.
13. Do not operate electric routers in moist or wet areas.
14. Always grip the tool tightly. Be prepared at start-up to resist the motor torque.
15. Develop the habit of intermittent start-up switching. In other words, immediately after switch-starting, shut the

router off. As the motor starts to coast down, observe with sight, sound, and by feel, any unfamiliar conditions and irregularities. If all looks and sounds good, start up again. Shut down immediately at the first indication of any unfamiliar noise or vibration, and locate the problem.

16. Never start up the router with the bit in contact with the material. Be sure that the bit will rotate freely, well away from the work, before turning on the power.

17. Always feed in the proper direction, against the direction of bit rotation. Refer to page 53.

18. Maintain equipment carefully. Replace worn parts, discard worn-out bits, and check the router periodically.

Some Maintenance Tips Keep all mating areas of collet, threads, bit shanks, and spindle clean and free of dust, resin, pitch accumulation, and grit. Clean with appropriate solvents or pitch remover, and protect surfaces with a coating of light machine oil. If there are any unusual vibrations, first check the bit. It may be bent, chipped, or running off-center. It may also be improperly ground, without adequate relief clearance, or be carrying an excessive chip load, due to an excessive feed rate, or it may just be the wrong bit design for the job.

Check bearings frequently. Routers place great strain on their bearings. At any sign of deteriorated bearings they should be replaced immediately. If there is still any sign of vibration, disconnect power, remove bit collet and collet lock nut. Turn the motor shaft (spindle) slowly, feeling for rough or irregular rotation. Attempt to push the spindle side to side and then up and down, to detect any movement. There shouldn't be any such movement at all. If there is, it's likely that the ball bearings are rough and should be replaced.

Check the collet. Collets do wear, particularly if they are made from lower grades of steel. Vibrations also indicate collet wear, which causes bit run-out. That is, a tool or bit

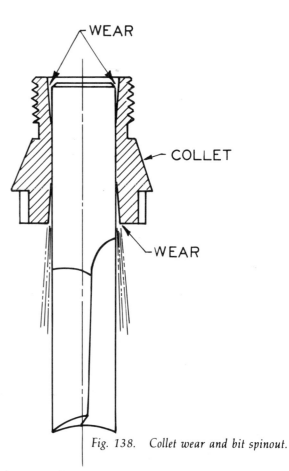

Fig. 138.   Collet wear and bit spinout.

is not spinning or rotating on its center axis. (See Fig. 138.) Get into the habit of inspecting bit shanks as they are removed from the collet. Collet markings on the shank indicate that the collet may be worn. To make a preliminary check for a worn collet, disconnect the power, insert a fairly long bit, and tighten the collet and lock nut with hand pressure only (without wrenches). Then apply sideways pressure to the extreme lower end of the bit. If the bit appears to move inside the collet, the collet is worn. Get a replacement collet immediately. If vibration still exists, send the router to an expert or back to the factory repair center for appraisal and possible repair or replacement.

Finally, from time to time blow out the dust from the motor, switch housings, and other areas where it may accumulate. Tighten all screws, and, if necessary, replace worn motor brushes, frayed electrical cords, plugs, and switches.

4

Basic Routing Operations

The owner's manual that accompanies each router provides the essential instructions for installing and changing bits (Fig. 139), assembling the base and motor unit, and making adjustments for depth of cut. (See Figs. 140 and 141.) A couple of pointers here: 1) Always disconnect the power before making any adjustments. 2) When installing a bit, insert the shank all the way and then withdraw it about $\frac{1}{16}$–$\frac{1}{8}$ inch (1.5–3 mm) before tightening.

Should the bit have a round fillet, or radius between the shank and the cutting edge, be sure not to insert this area into the collet. After setting the depth of cut (the amount of bit protruding below the sub-base), ensure that all necessary clamps or lock knobs are securely tightened. Plunging routers will require presetting of the depth scale or stops.

Refer to the previous chapter for safety precautions. Once again, wear appropriate safety attire and goggles. Be sure that your stock is securely clamped. Hold the router firmly in both hands. Be prepared for the jolt at start-up created by the starting torque of the motor. With the router held so that the bit is off the surface, switch on the power and immediately switch it off. This only takes a second. Developing this routine as a habit affords a quick check as the router starts to coast down. If all sounds, feels, and looks all right, switch it on again and begin routing.

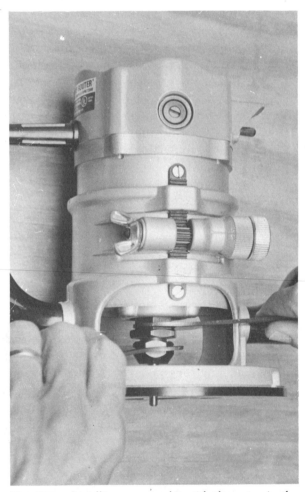

Fig. 139. Installing a router bit with the motor in the base. With some routers it may be easier to make bit changes with the motor removed from the base.

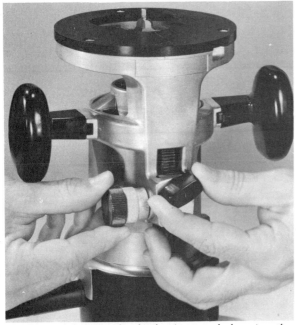

Fig. 140. *Adjusting the depth of cut and clamping the motor in the base.*

First-time router users: Begin by making some shallow practice cuts on scrap of the same kind of material you intend to work with. Upon completing a cut, switch off the router and set it on the workbench, placing it on its side with the bit facing away. Hold the router steady until the bit coasts to a complete stop.

Feeds and Speeds These are two aspects of router crafting that must be mastered in order to handle a router really effectively. The router must be fed (advanced) in the most opportune direction. That is the direction which counters the force (or torque) of the router and cuts the smoothest and cleanest. The speed at which the router is advanced into a cut is just as important as the proper feed direction. However, there are a number of variables that influence that one optimum feed rate.

Consider the direction of the bit rotation with regard to the nature and type of cut to determine the best feed direction for the router. The bit rotates clockwise, as viewed from above the router, so the feed direction should be against the rotation of the bit, as shown in Figs. 142, 143, and 144. In this direction the working forces transferred to the bit from the router tend to feed or pull the bit itself into the work. Fig. 144 illustrates this for edge-routing all around the perimeter of a board. Here the feed direction, viewed from above the router, is counterclockwise. Incidentally, always rout end grains first. If there is any splintering at the corners, this can be cleaned up when making the remaining passes, which are cut in line with the grain direction of the board.

When routing the inside edges of openings (such as those shown in Fig. 144), the router should be fed clockwise. Essentially, proper feed directions can be remembered as follows: For outside (perimeter) routing, move the router counterclockwise. For inside openings, move the router clockwise.

With feed direction established, determine the best rate of feed, or the optimum feeding

Fig. 141. *Some routers have a micro vertical-adjustment ring, as shown. This device can serve as a final depth-setting stop when it's necessary to make multiple passes at various depths to complete duplicate cuts, and so on. Check the owner's manual for specific instructions.*

53

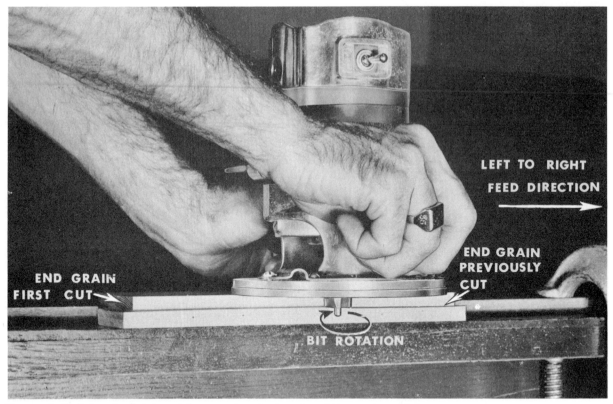

LEFT TO RIGHT
FEED DIRECTION

END GRAIN
PREVIOUSLY
CUT

END GRAIN
FIRST CUT

BIT ROTATION

Fig. 142. Feed direction is left to right, or against the direction of bit rotation, as shown.

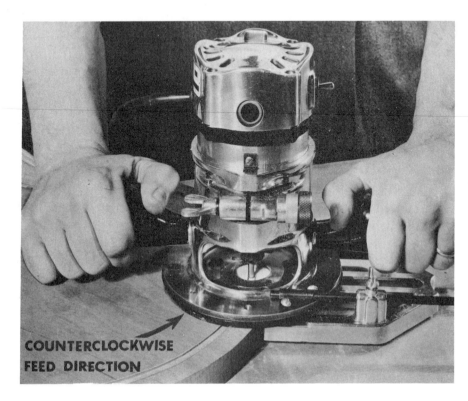

COUNTERCLOCKWISE
FEED DIRECTION

Fig. 143. Routing a groove parallel to the edge of a circle with the aid of a base guide. Here, the feed direction is counterclockwise so the torque, or force of the bit entering uncut wood, pulls the guide and router against the work, rather than pushing it away.

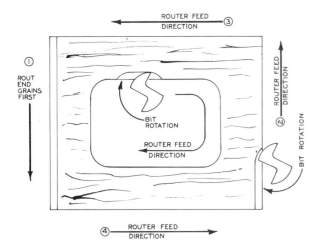

Fig. 144. *A diagram clarifying proper feed directions for outside and inside routing. Note the sequence of cuts for routing around all four edges of a rectangle or square board.*

Fig. 145. *Effects of various cross-grain feed rates in hardwood (maple at left) and softwood (willow at right). Cuts are ⅜-inch (9-mm)-radius coves made in one pass using a 1½ horsepower, 23,000 RPM router. The top cut was made at the correct feed rate. The center cut was made at too fast a feed rate. Note the torn fibres—especially in the willow. The bottom cut was made with the slowest feed. This caused some burn on the maple, but the willow cut is almost totally burnished.*

speed. The ideal feed rate is somewhere between too fast (forcing it) and too slow (the cut surface becomes burnished). (See Fig. 145.) Knowing exactly the best feed rate at which to advance the router is primarily determined by experience, instinct, feel, and the sound of the router. Concessions must be made for these variables:

1. Motor horsepower
2. Machining qualities of the material (hardness, softness, grain direction)
3. Bit characteristics (diameter, sharpness, number of flutes)
4. Established depth of cut

It is possible to use a powerful router with a dull, small-diameter bit, and to force a deep cut through hard material fairly rapidly, but the finished surface will not be high quality. Besides, this sort of practice is both foolish and dangerous. A small bit can snap under such stress.

The primary objective in most jobs is to allow the cutting edges of the bit to make clean, sharply severed chips with each rota-

tion. The router must be moved with just the right amount of forward feeding pressure. When it is just right, the bit will not choke on huge chips or—because the feed is too slow—burn and create dust rather than shavings. This means that there must be some degree of load on the motor. The sound of a free-running router should be the recognizable reference from which to identify the sound of a proper feed rate. A small-diameter, sharp-veining bit set to a shallow depth will hardly put any load at all on most routers. The sound does not change much, so it is possible to cut practically as fast as you are able to advance the router. In making either a deeper cut or using a larger diameter bit, the feed rate will have to be proportionally slowed. This will change the sound of the router, because it is working harder. Cutting across the grain will require a slower feed rate than will the exact same cut when made with the grain on the same stock.

It is somewhat easier to become familiar with the proper feed rates in freehand routing than in jobs where controlling the router is aided by a pilot, straightedge, or other guide. If the router is fed too slowly in freehand cutting, it is more difficult to control as the bit tends to jiggle around in the cut or jerk along in the cut, with some burning in evidence. (See Fig. 146.) By gradually increasing the feed rate, it is possible to reach the speed where the router will go along its intended path in a smoother, more easily controlled line. Watch for these signs of feeding too fast:

1. The motor will slow down.
2. It will have a laboring sound.
3. It will overheat.
4. The job will require more physical exertion.
5. The resulting cut will have torn fibres rather than cleanly cut surfaces. (See Fig. 145.)

When edge-routing, the base of the router should be level and should ride flat over the surface. Complete or end the cut by lifting the

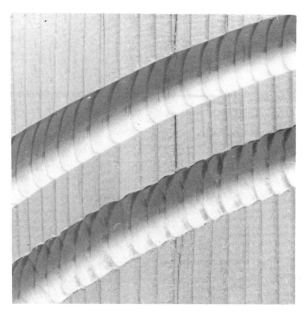

Fig. 146. Freehand cuts in Douglas fir, a difficult wood to machine because of its alternating hard and soft growth rings. The bottom cut shows a wobbly cut, resulting from too slow a rate of feed. The smooth top cut was made with the same bit and router, but with a faster feed rate.

router, to remove the bit with the power on. The same technique applies when making grooves or forming cuts in a surface. It is not recommended for the beginner to stop the feed and shut off the power while the bit coasts down still in contact with a cut or against the work. The slightest movement of the router could cause the bit to grab, kick back the router, and ruin the cut. Similarly, it is not a good practice to start up the router again with the bit reinserted into an existing cut. The starting torque will jerk the router, causing the bit to grab.

Using Guides There are only two ways of controlling the movement of the router along the desired path or line of cut:

1. With a mechanical aid or a device of some sort to support or assist the router direction.
2. Freehand, following a line.

Router control is provided only by the operator's eyesight, instincts, and steady hands.

It is almost impossible to make absolutely straight line cuts of any real length or to make large, smooth, gradual curves or true circular cuts freehand.

There are many devices available to guide the router. Most do a satisfactory job, but many times they do not have the reach, convenience, or capacity to handle special jobs. In such cases, determine if the job warrants the time required to make a special jig or fixture to handle the job safely and accurately.

Using Pilot-Guided Bits This is the simplest and easiest way to control the horizontal direction of a cut. Bits with self-contained pilots or ball-bearing guides are perfect for edge-forming cuts along straight, circular, and irregularly curved work edges. (See Fig. 142.) Remember that any irregularities in the edges will automatically be transferred to the cuts, because the pilot just as easily follows imperfections as clean, smooth edges. So prepare and smooth edges well before edge routing.

Bits with ball-bearing guides are easier to use than the self-contained, rub-type pilots. With rub pilots, care must be exercised not to put too much horizontal pressure against the bit. You must not dwell in feedings, especially on end grains, where burning is more likely. Rub-type pilots also tend to burnish or work-harden the wood surfaces contacted, making sanding and particularly staining more problematic. It is usually best to make edge-forming cuts in light, multiple passes of varying depths, with the final pass a shallow finish cut. Less horizontal pressure is required and less rubbing friction is thereby produced by the pilot.

Holding Small Pieces Edge-routing requires a simple, secure way to prevent work from slipping and minimize the possibility of hazardous kickback. One of the best and quickest ways to hold pieces too small to secure conveniently or safely with clamps is simply to glue them down with hot-melt glue. Hot melts do not really make for difficult releases if short beads of glue are applied, and their holding strengths are sufficient. (See Figs. 147–150, which illustrate the solution to the inside rabbeting procedure for a small, difficult-to-secure, heart-shaped picture frame.)

Fig. 147. ¼–½-inch (6–12-mm) beads of hot-melt glue will temporarily secure small and difficult-to-clamp pieces for routing. Spot-glue the project to a larger piece of scrap plywood clamped to the workbench.

Fig. 148. Routing an inside rabbet in this difficult-to-hold workpiece is quick and easy as it is held fast temporarily with hot-melt glue. Remember the feed direction is clockwise on inside cuts.

Fig. 149. With the rabbeted routing complete, a chisel is used to carefully release the work from its spot-glued position.

Fig. 150. A sharp chisel removes the remaining hot-melt glue. Since hot melts have minimal penetration, this creates little problem with subsequent sanding or staining.

Sometimes the shape of the piece is such that a holding fixture is fairly easy to make. (See Fig. 151.) The routed chain link shown in Fig. 152 is a good example. Other work-holding systems involving pointed nails and some other adaptations are shown in subsequent chapters. In most cases, the routing is safe and easy once an adequate fixturing method has been devised.

Fig. 151. *This work-holding fixture for making chain links can be applied to other similar small work for inside routing. This fixture also serves as a pattern. Here, a ball-bearing trimming bit is used to clean up the inside opening, which had most of the material previously drilled out.*

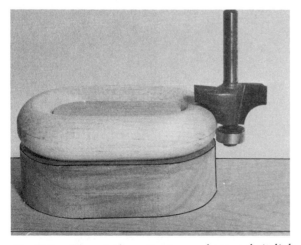

Fig. 152. *The outside routing to round over a chain link. The link is fixtured with an internal plug glued to a larger base, which in turn is clamped to the bench.*

The pilot needs at least 1/16 inch (1.5 mm) of uncut surface to guide the router effectively. Should it be desirable to shape an entire edge—meaning to produce a formed edge extending from one surface to the opposite face—it can be done with an auxiliary pattern placed below the work for the pilot to follow. (See Fig. 153.) The pattern must be made to conform exactly to the profile of the workpiece. It can be fastened to the work with clamps or nails, or spot glued with hot-melt adhesive. (Refer to Chapter 5 for more on pattern routing.)

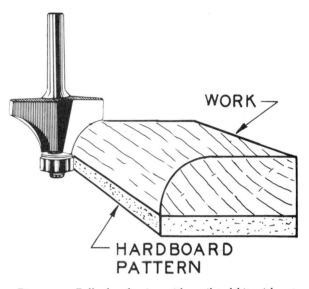

Fig. 153. *Full edge shaping with a piloted bit with pattern underneath the workpiece.*

The Router Edge Guide This is a useful and inexpensive accessory. The edge guide is used to cut grooves, dadoes, and decorative cuts parallel to the edge of the work. (See Figs. 143, 154, 155, and 156.) This attachment also allows edge-forming cuts to be made with bits without using pilots. (Typical examples are illustrated in Figs. 154, and 155.) Routers are made with provisions for mounting edge guides and other accessories. It is best to purchase such guides from the same manufacturer as the router to assure a proper fit. Most guides are comprised of two guide rods and adjustable plates or bars of various configurations. (See Figs. 157, 158, and 159.) These are all easy to set up and use. Fig. 160 shows how the guide works for routing around an outside circular shape such as a tabletop.

If a job is of a production nature and one that will be duplicated exactly in the future, it may be worth the effort to make a special guide. Fig. 161 shows two examples of hand-made edge guides. These can be made of ¼-inch (6-mm) plywood using the pattern of the plastic sub-base. In fact, it's a good idea to stack-cut several wood sub-bases at one time, to have extras on hand when needed. Special edge guides can be made up at one time and used to duplicate the cuts exactly any time required.

Fig. 156. The Elu plunging router with an edge guide attached. Note the extended length of the guide and the work with cuts made parallel to the work edges.

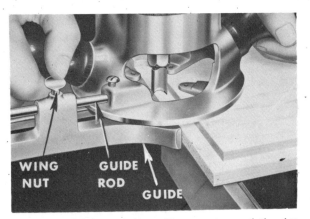

Fig. 154. Making an edge rabbet cut using a pilotless bit and an edge guide.

Fig. 155. A guide on the little Dremel router provides a decorative edge cut.

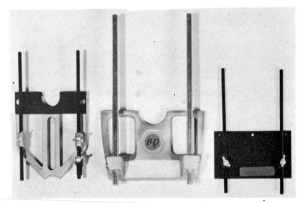

Fig. 157. Various styles of edge guides.

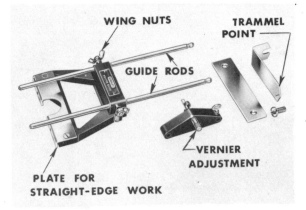

Fig. 158. A guide kit does both straight and circular work.

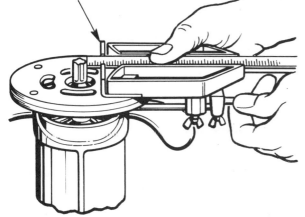

REMOVE STRAIGHT-EDGE FOR CIRCULAR
CUTS PARALLEL TO AN EDGE

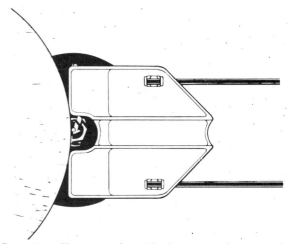

*Fig. 159.   Adjusting the edge guide to make a surface cut
parallel to an edge.*

*Fig. 160.   To accurately guide the router along curved
edges; use two points of contact against the edge of the
stock. This shows the operating position for making a decorative edge around a circular tabletop.*

*Fig. 161.   Special user-made, permanently set edge guides. The center shows a guide for making cuts parallel to a
straightedge. Note its extra length. The right shows a guide to follow along a workpiece having an irregular or inside curved
edge.*

Straightedge Guides These are used to
make various joint-fitting cuts, such as
straight grooves, dadoes, dovetail dadoes,
wide tenons, and all other types of straight-
line surface cuts. A simple straightedge is
used when commercially made edge guides
do not reach, or when the cuts are not parallel
to the work edge. The straightedge is clamped
or tacked securely to the surface. It is
positioned in the proper location so the desired cut can be made with the router base
bearing against it. The straightedge must be
held securely in a position that is exactly
parallel to the intended line of cut. It must
also be offset at a distance equal to the mea-

surement from the cutting edge of the bit to
the outside edge of the router base. (See Fig.
162.) Remember to feed in the direction that is
against the rotation of the bit, so the thrust of
the router pulls itself towards the straightedge. Stops can be located appropriately to facilitate making blind cuts and stopped dadoes,
as shown in Fig. 163.

A "spacer stick" (Fig. 164) makes locating
the offset position of the straightedge much
faster than measuring. The spacer stick is a
piece of ⅛-inch (3-mm) hardboard (or other
similar material) in a suitable length, ripped to
a width that equals the offset measurement.
That is, the distance from the cutting edge of

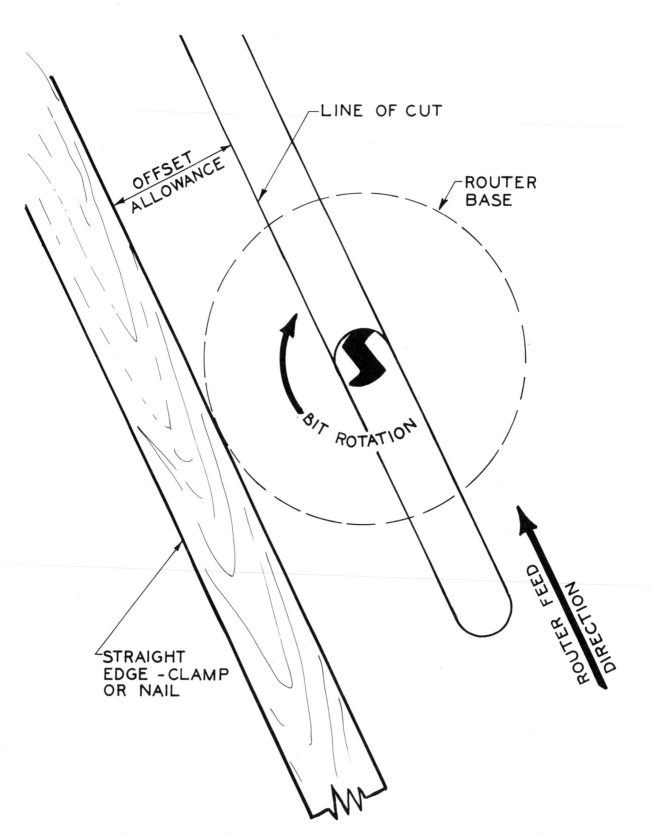

LINE OF CUT

OFFSET ALLOWANCE

ROUTER BASE

BIT ROTATION

STRAIGHT EDGE - CLAMP OR NAIL

ROUTER FEED DIRECTION

Fig. 162.   Routing against a straightedge. Note the location of the line of cut and the recommended feed direction.

62

Fig. 163. *Above shows a through dado cut just completed with the straightedge clamped in the position shown. A blind cut and a stopped dado cut as made with a straightedge along with the use of stops clamped appropriately to end the cuts.*

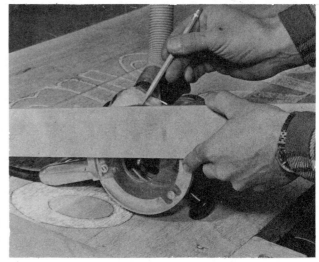

Fig. 164. *A spacer stick is a length of ⅛-inch (4-mm) hardboard ripped to a width that equals the exact distance between the cutting edge of the bit and the router base.*

the bit to the edge of the router base. (See Figs. 163, 164, 165, and 166.) Rip spacer sticks for bits of various diameters. Then, with a soft-tipped pen, mark the bit size on each of the spacer sticks so they will all be made up and on hand.

Fig. 165. *The spacer stick eliminates the need for repeated measuring when securing the straightedge at its appropriate location.*

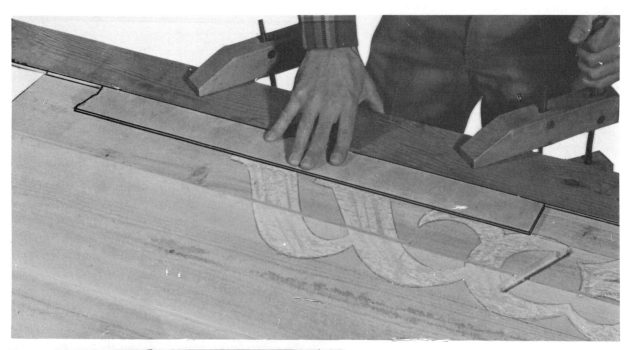

Fig. 166. *Here a nailed down straightedge is used to cut the straight bottomed letter strokes in routing of engraved wood signs. All letters will be uniformly straight and the same height.*

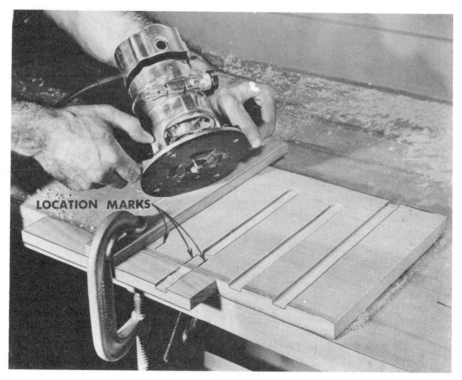

Fig. 167. This homemade routing T-square is an adaptation of the straightedge.

LOCATION MARKS

Fig. 168. The frame guide consists of two parallel straightedges spaced (with two cross members) to a distance exactly equal to the diameter of the router sub-base.

The T-Square (See Fig. 167.) This is a very simple device to make, with many obvious uses for guided router cuts. It is especially handy for making dado and other cross-grained cuts. It can be made in any convenient size, with the head and blade lengths to suit special requirements. However, if the blade length exceeds 12–16 inches (300–410 mm), both parts should be made wider, or an extra clamp should be used to secure the blade end opposite the head. (The torque, or rotational force of the router, will bend narrow-bladed T-squares during the cut if they are clamped only at the head.) With the T-square head positioned firmly against the work, splintering at the edges is reduced. When a router cut is made through the head it also makes positioning the T-square easy.

The Frame Guide Fig. 168 shows another adaptation of a straightedge. This homemade device is also simple to construct and extremely useful for accomplishing many routine and unusual routing jobs. This fixture is something of a combination double straightedge (that cradles the router base), with the

Fig. 169. *A frame guide with a T-square-like head at 90° to the parallels. When used with a spacer stick quick positioning is easy. Clamp securely.*

Fig. 170. *Here the frame guide is used to outline the vertical straight cuts of routed sign letters.*

Fig. 171. *When securely clamped, the frame guide also makes easy work of straight cuts at any oblique angle.*

advantages of the T-square head set at 90° for cuts perpendicular to a trued-up edge. Figs. 169 to 171 show some applications for the frame guide.

Circular and Slot-Cutting Guides Attach these to the base of the router much like the router edge guides discussed previously. Many straight-cutting guides incorporate trammel points for circular cutting in addition to the conventional router edge guides. They are very useful for cutting out perfectly round discs, making round holes, or making surface designs with concentric, decorative cuts. Most guides will make circular cuts from a ½-inch (12-mm) radius up to almost 24-inch (600-mm) diameters. Fig. 172 shows a disc cutout with a counterclockwise feed direction. When making such cutouts, secure the work over a scrap piece of stock to prevent cutting into the workbench. A temporary tack with hot-melt glue to secure the work to the scrap is another good idea.

Fig. 173 illustrates an example of some interesting designs that can be produced by using a combination of different bit-cutting shapes with the guide set to cut various diameters.

Cutting-diameter capacities of such commercially made guides can be increased by substituting longer steel rods. Or make a do-it-yourself version as illustrated in Fig. 174. This is simply a piece of hardboard attached to the bottom of the router in place of the sub-base. Make it of ¼-inch (6-mm) hardboard or plywood in any suitable length. Cut a hole for a bit opening, and use a nail pivot driven through at the desired radius location.

The Parallel-Slot-Cutting Guide This is a device to guide the router for making evenly spaced or parallel dadoes and grooves. This attachment is often an accessory to the commercially available circular cutting guide or the router edge-cutting guide. Fig. 175 shows a typical application of its use. This device can also be handmade. Again, simply make a plywood base of suitable size and glue a wood strip to it the desired distance from the bit.

Fig. 172 (above). A disc and through cutout made in ¾-inch (18-mm) stock with a circular cutting attachment. The arrow shows the recommended feed direction. Through cuts such as this often must be done with multiple passes of increasing depths, depending upon horsepower and other factors.

Fig. 173. The circular cutting guide can be creatively applied to make interesting surface decorations, as shown here.

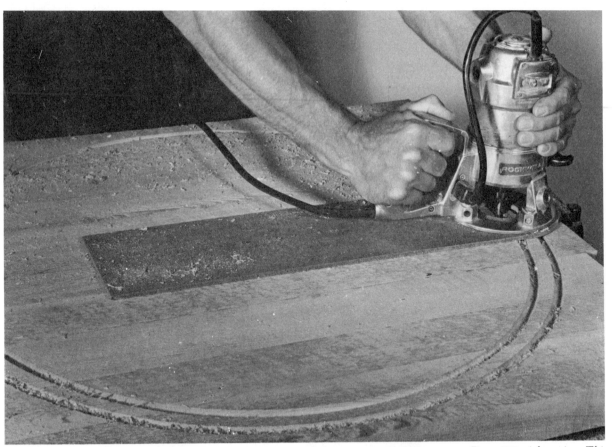

Fig. 174 (above). This homemade circular guide is attached in place of the router sub-base. A nail is used at the pivot point.

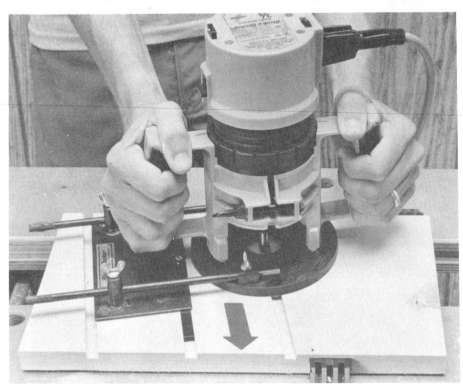

Fig. 175. This device for cutting parallel grooves and dadoes is called a slot-cutting guide.

5

Pattern and Template Routing

Pattern- or template-guided routing is one of the most dramatic and satisfying areas of router crafting. It affords the opportunity to challenge and express creative and inventive talents. Once you get into it, your imagination will soar with new and unique ideas. Before you finish one project, new ones will occur to you. The major advantage of routing parts and designs from templates and patterns is that you can easily carry your creations over to a production basis. Once the design is developed and the template made, you can duplicate precisely cut after cut and project after project with each exhibiting your expert woodworking skills. Should you need only to make that one tricky part for your own special project or to duplicate one in large quantities, employing the techniques of pattern and template routing will undoubtedly prove to be incredibly valuable. And—the best part of all—it isn't really complicated or difficult.

To avoid confusion, the terms *pattern* and *template* will be used interchangeably. Technically, a pattern is an original part or object from which another part or object is precisely traced or copied in exact shape, size, and detail. A template can be described as a guide (or pattern) which is used to duplicate and/or guide routing cuts. (See Figs. 176, 177, and 178.) As Fig. 176 shows, a template is made of a suitable material, such as plywood. Hard-

board, lumber, aluminum, and plastic are also used for patterns and templates. Generally, the durability or hardness of the template material is determined by convenience, availability, and desired length of service required. Thickness of templates can vary from ⅛ inch (3 mm) to ¾ inch (18 mm), depending upon the type of guide attachment fitted to the router base, the depth of the cut required, and the bit length selected for the job. Generally, ¼ inch (6 mm) is a thickness suitable for the majority of jobs. It is a good idea to make templates of thinner materials when possible, as they are easier to cut, for example, when using the router to make a template for duplicating irregular or intricate shapes and designs. Cut templates freehand with the router if a jigsaw or band saw is not available. Refer to Chapter 7 for information about freehand routing.

There are some templates commercially available. These include lettering templates for sign work (Fig. 179), templates for recessing butt hinges in doors, and templates for making dovetail joints. (These are discussed in Chapter 11.)

In pattern routing (as shown in Fig. 178), use straight-cutting, piloted, or ball-bearing-guided bits. To rout with the aid of a "template" it is possible to use a wide variety of bits, but generally not those with pilots. Pat-

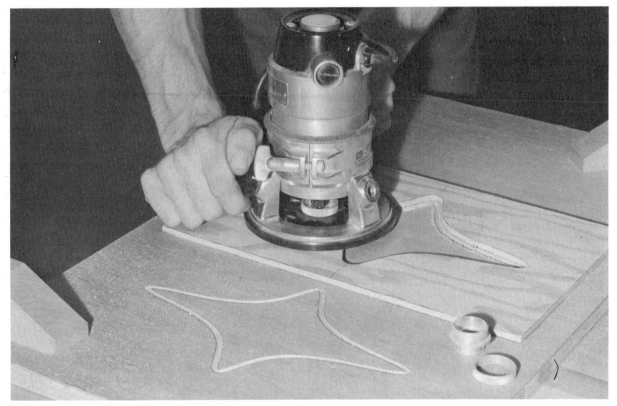

Fig. 176. *Template-guided routing makes it easy to duplicate precisely router cuts of any desired design or pattern.*

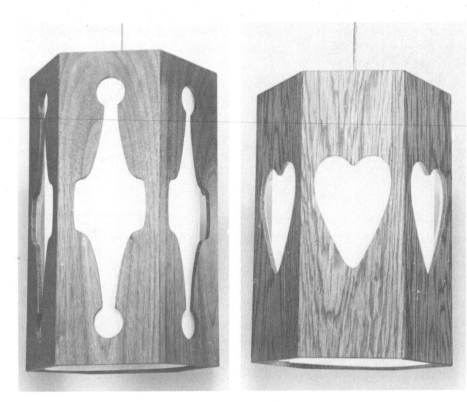

Fig. 177. *Pattern (or template) routing was employed to pierce-cut the identical segments for these hexagonal box lamps.*

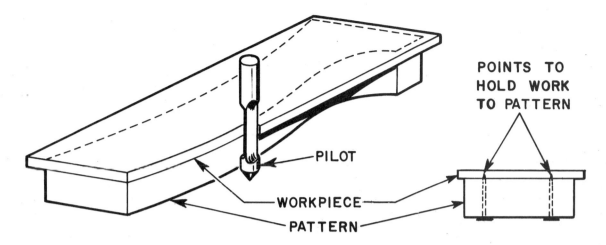

Fig. 178. Routing to a pattern with a piloted panel bit.

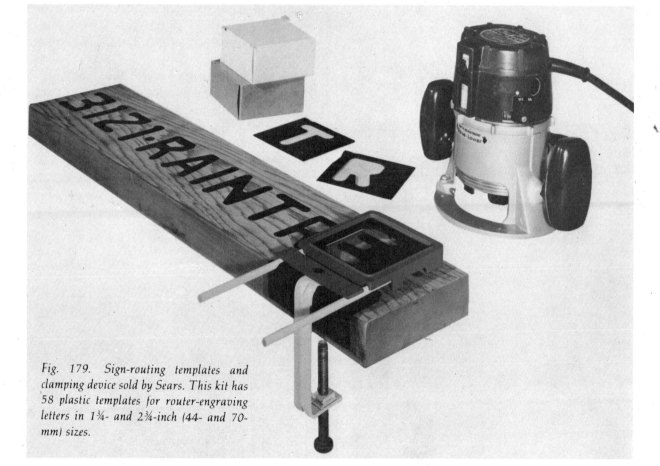

Fig. 179. Sign-routing templates and clamping device sold by Sears. This kit has 58 plastic templates for router-engraving letters in 1¾- and 2¾-inch (44- and 70-mm) sizes.

terns designed to be reproduced and cut with piloted bits are cut so that their profile shape is exactly the same size as is desired for the copied part. (Refer again to Fig. 178.)

Template routing is usually performed with a special tubelike attachment fitted to the center of the router sub-base. This is a template guide. Two popular types are shown in Figs. 180, 181, and 182. Template guides are specified according to the inside diameters as well

Fig.180. *The template guide (lower portion of illustration) is available in many sizes. Each attaches to the router sub-base with a common lock-nut (above portion of illustration).*

Fig. 181. *Another style template guide. Also available in many sizes, this one is fastened to the sub-base with screws.*

Fig. 182. *Mounting a template guide to the router sub base.*

as their outside diameters. There is a broad range of sizes available, but it's my opinion that there still are not enough sizes to select from. It would be great if the center holes of router sub-bases were larger, and larger-diameter templates were available to accommodate bits with larger cutting diameters. I have one or two of every size template guide available, but I still find myself boring the inside hole a touch larger or cutting to reduce the length protruding below the router base.

In use, the router bit protrudes through the hole in the template guide and the side of the template guide bears against the edges of the template when making the desired cut. There is one minor problem associated with the use of templates and template guides. Because the bit is encircled at the router base by the template guide, the template or pattern size must be adjusted to allow for the distance between the cutting edge of the bit and the outside diameter of the template guide. This allowance is graphically illustrated in Figs. 184 and 185.

Obviously, the bit must clear the inside of the template guide. So in planning a job get the correct combination of bit diameter as well as a template guide with a suitable inside diameter. Remember, too, that the larger the

Fig. 183. *This universal sub-base kit has a roller edge guide and several popular-sized template guides.*

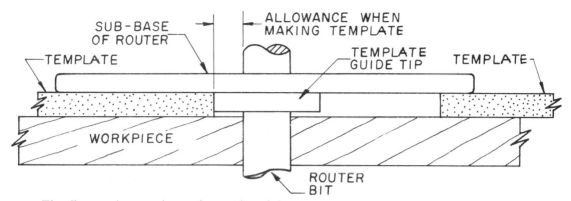

Fig. 184. *The allowance between the template guide and the cutting edge of the bit. This distance must be subtracted all along the contoured edges of the template.*

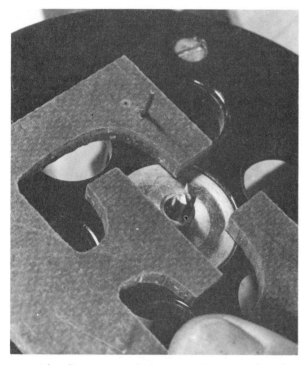

Fig. 186 (above). *Individual-letter templates nailed in place will facilitate easy outline routing with the template guide to make raised letters.*

Fig. 185 (left). *A user-made letter template. This shows the relationship between the template size and the cutting line of the bit. In this case the template guide will reproduce a pattern larger than the template.*

outside diameter of the template guide, the less intricate the detail it will be able to reproduce. The edges of the template should be cut smooth and be without defects. Just as in routing with piloted bits, any error or miscut along the working edge of the template will automatically be transferred to the work.

Another thing to consider is the relationship between the thickness of the template material and the distance that the template guide extends below the router base. Consider these two dimensions and make a mental run-through. It's usually easier to start a cut

holding the template guide against the template edge without the router bit already in contact with the work. Here is where plunging routers have great advantage. They can be held so that the template guide is bearing against the edge of the template before lowering the bit into the work.

Draw upon your own resources for ways to hold or secure patterns and templates to the workpieces. They may be nailed, if nail holes are not objectionable in the finished product. (See Fig. 178 and Figs. 184 to 188.) They can also be spot glued with hot-melt (as shown in

Fig. 187.   A pattern for routing the profiles of wooden switch plates. Short, pointed nails will hold the work in position during routing.

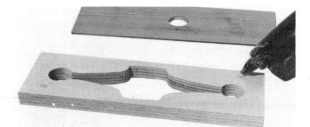

Fig. 190.   Two spots of hot-melt glue will hold the work to the pattern to pierce-rout one of the hanging lamp segments shown in Fig. 177. Notice that the work has a pre-bored hole. For demonstration purposes, this part will be pattern-routed with a ball-bearing guided bit.

Fig. 188.   The piece is cut slightly oversize. The pattern is pressed to the work and held by the nail points. The extra block (with holes) is glued to the pattern and serves to hold the entire assembly in a vise during routing.

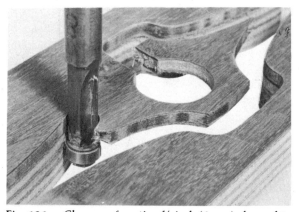

Fig. 191.   Close-up of routing ¼-inch (6-mm) plywood to a pattern using a ball-bearing guided straight trimming bit.

Fig. 189.   The routing operation, using a ¼-inch (6-mm) piloted panel bit with a boring point.

Figs. 190 and 200.) (This technique was previously discussed and illustrated on page 57.) Clamping the template to the work is the easiest method. If the nature of the planned cut or work allows for template material that can facilitate clamping, that's the way to go. (See Fig. 192.)

Another idea useful for many jobs is the hinged template fixture, shown in Fig. 193. This combination holding device and template is an especially good system for routing surface designs, through-routing as in piercing jobs, or for cutting recesses, such as is done to the backs of switch plates. (See Fig. 194.) It can also be applied to cut narrow recesses for making trays. (See Fig. 195.)

Fig. 192. A template guide designed to cut the stock butt sockets for a gun cabinet. Note that the template is tilted and has a location stop at one edge. The resulting routed surface will be inclined, making a perfect stock-holding socket to keep the guns from tipping.

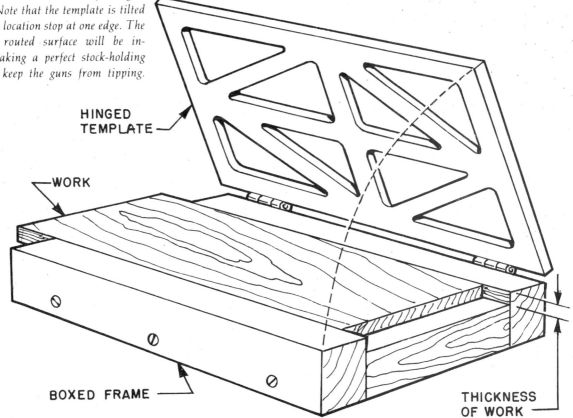

HINGED TEMPLATE

WORK

BOXED FRAME

THICKNESS OF WORK

Fig. 193. This hinged-box-type template has the advantage of quick positioning of the work for routing. The work is held secure with pointed nails in the bottom of the jig.

Fig. 194 (left). A hinged box jig is perfect to fixture the work for jobs such as routing this recess in the backs of switch plates.

Fig. 195 (below). The recess of this little tray is another item routed with a hinged box template.

A saddle template (Fig. 196) is one more idea incorporating a positioning technique and a template. The saddle template provides a good opportunity to pass along a cutting technique for confronting the problem of making a deeply cut recess or through-opening, such as that one. The capacity a good router can actually handle is amazing. But first of all, be warned that deep cutting, or cutting completely through 4-inch (100 mm) rough-sawn timber, should not be attempted without a heavy-duty router. And even with such extra power, many passes of slightly increasing depths must be made, in order not to put any strain on the bit or router.

Here is the step-by-step procedure:

1. Using a drill, bore out as much excess material as possible.
2. Use the template with a template guide that can handle a ½-inch (12-mm)-diameter straight or spiral bit. Make many successive passes with the router, gradually increasing the depth with each pass.

Fig. 196. A saddle template is not only designed to guide the router, but, like the box template, it also locates where the cut should be made in the work.

3. When the full length of the cutting edge is used up, remove the template and template guide.
4. Reset the bit depth, so that the part of the shank not in the collet but above the cutting edges can be used as the pilot to follow the previous cuts. Remove the sub-base, if necessary, to gain another ¼ inch (6 mm) in depth.

Fig. 197. *This is the result of a very careful and systematic approach to making a very deep cut (in this case entirely through the work) that was started with a template.*

Fig. 198. *This cutting block with an inclined cutting surface presented some interesting challenges that were essentially solved utilizing template-routing techniques.*

Caution: Do not attempt to extend the cutting length by chucking less shank in the collet. Should it not be possible to reach clear through with the original bit—and this is most likely—flip the work over and finish the cut with a bottom-piloted straight cutting bit. The pilot then follows the surfaces of the previous cuts made from the first side. (See Fig. 197.)

Some projects present problems that require much extensive thinking, planning, and experimenting to solve. One such project was the large cutting board illustrated in Fig. 198. The problem here was to determine how to cut a very large recess with a portable router, and how to cut the bottom surface of the recess flat and on a slant so that meat juices would drain to the back.

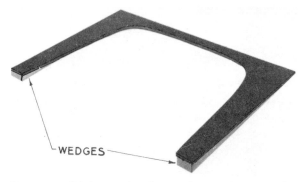

Fig. 199. *Wedges under the template used to rout the inclined cutting surface of the cutting block shown in Fig. 198.*

A template was obviously needed to cut the outline of the recessed area. Wedges (Fig. 199) placed under the template automatically made a progressively deeper cut from front to back. Hot-melt glue held the template secure (Fig. 200) as clamping was nearly impossible, and nail holes—no thanks! The first inside cut had to be made with a large-radius bit, larger than could be used with any commercially available template guide. The router base also had to be enlarged or extended so that it could ride on top of the template throughout the entire recessed-surface cutting operation.

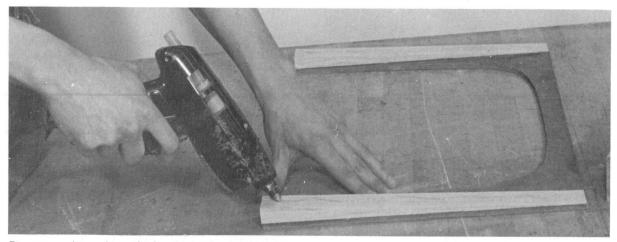

Fig. 200. *Again, hot-melt glue (in thin beads) is used to secure the template to the work for routing.*

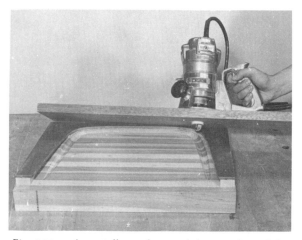

Fig. 201. *A specially made extended router base. It has its own integral template guide that is simply a short length of plastic pipe fitted tightly into a bored hole.*

Fig. 202. *A closeup view of the extended router base and the template guide made from plastic pipe.*

The solution was to use a sufficiently long board screwed to the bottom of the router base in place of the usual sub-base. Additionally, this board had to have an integral template guide. (See Figs. 201 and 202.) Longer screws had to be substituted for those that normally attach a regular ¼-inch (6-mm) plastic sub-base. The hole for the template guide was precisely drilled.

With the board sub-base attached, a v-bit was installed in the router. It was clamped so that the point of the bit transferred a mark indicating the exact center for the hole to be bored to receive a plastic-pipe template guide. The hole was then bored, and the length of plastic pipe was glued in position. This made the template guide perfectly concentric with the center axis of the collet or bit. With a large round-bottom bit installed, the inside outline of the slanted recessed area was cut to the desired depth. (See Fig. 201.) A flat-bottomed bit was then used to remove the remaining stock, and the flat, inclined surface originally desired resulted.

Other similar problems will require the application of many techniques. Often, various routing techniques are combined to create some very unusual woodworking operations. Pattern-and-template routing is one of those areas to consider and analyze when confronted with a totally new and difficult woodworking problem. Additional applications of template routing will also appear in subsequent chapters.

6
Routing Joints and Surfaces

Many popular woodworking joints and a variety of construction details are presented here. These joints can be made with the router by employing several of the techniques illustrated in previous chapters. (See Fig. 203.) This chapter also includes some ideas for making decorative moulding and fluting, for cutting designs in surfaces, for routing veneer inlay, and for levelling chunks of wood. Dovetailing is not included, because Chapter 11 is devoted entirely to all phases of dovetailing. Joint-making and surface-cutting operations are also covered in the chapters discussing commercial accessories, router machines, and user-made jigs and fixtures.

A great majority of woodworking joints (Fig. 204) can in one way or another be cut with the router. On first thought, the basic and widely used dowel joint might be excluded. However, with a plunging router, it is a simple task to make a guide fixture to align the tool for boring dowel holes precisely at the desired locations. This job could be handled with a conventional router perhaps, but would require a suitable guiding fixture. In deciding whether or not to make a specialized jig, consider the time, need, and feasibility. If you own a good dowel jig, why bother? Determine what is the easiest, best, and most practical for a project and consider the operations required to complete it.

Fig. 203. This clock project involves lots of joinery and router-cut mouldings.

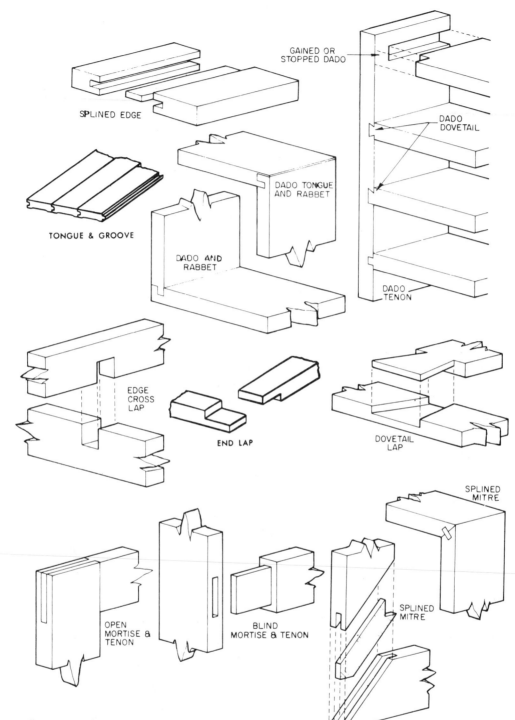

SPLINED EDGE

GAINED OR STOPPED DADO

DADO DOVETAIL

TONGUE & GROOVE

DADO TONGUE AND RABBET

DADO AND RABBET

DADO TENON

EDGE CROSS LAP

END LAP

DOVETAIL LAP

SPLINED MITRE

OPEN MORTISE & TENON

BLIND MORTISE & TENON

SPLINED MITRE

Fig. 204.   *Some joints that can be made with a router.*

The basic joinery cuts, particularly the rabbet, dado, and groove (Figs. 205 and 206) can often be cut more quickly and more cleanly with the router than with a table saw. Most other joints are an adaptation of the basic cuts involved in cutting dadoes and rabbets. The tongue cut (Fig. 206) is simply a rabbet cut from both surfaces along a common edge. A

Fig. 205.   The basic cabinet joints are the dado and rabbet.

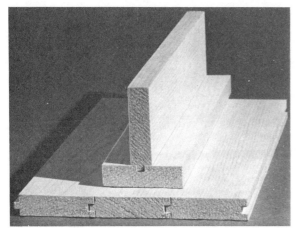

Fig. 206.   The tongue and groove joint.

Fig. 207.

Fig. 208.   Routing a center mortise. This cut is best made in two passes with the router guide riding against each side. The resulting cut will then be in the exact center of the workpiece.

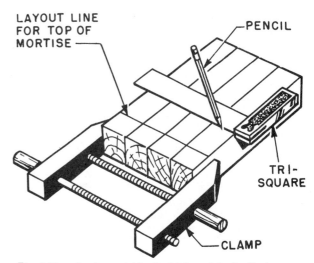

Fig. 209.   Laying out identical joints. Mark all pieces at the same time.

tenon of the mortise-and-tenon joint (Fig. 207) is simply a rabbet cut around the end of one member.

Edge grooves and slots, such as the mortise opening in Fig. 207, can be cut in several ways. The way shown in Fig. 208 requires a straight guide mounted on the router base. Incidentally, when making two or more identical pieces with the same joint, lay them all out at the same time, as shown in Fig. 209. Don't forget that slotting bits (Chapter 2, Fig. 119), are very useful for cutting slots and for spline cuts in joint-making.

Fig. 210 illustrates a splined mitre joint. Obviously, cutting 45° mitres is best and easiest done with a saw. Cutting the spline kerf can be done very accurately and quickly using the router and a slotting cutter, as shown in Fig. 211. Observe closely in the photos that the kerf for the spline can easily be a "stopped cut" concealing the spline in the assembled joint.

Lap joints (Figs. 212 and 213) are easily cut using the T-square guide. Simply use a straight bit to make the shoulder cuts to the appropriate depth, as in dadoing. Then clean up between the cuts to get the exact lap width. Fig. 214 shows a good gift-shop project using scrap material.

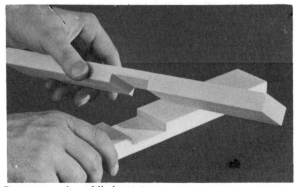

Fig. 212. A middle-lap joint.

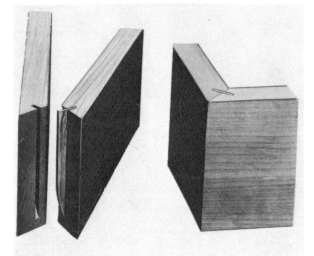

Fig. 210. Splined mitre joint. The pieces at left; the assembled joint at right.

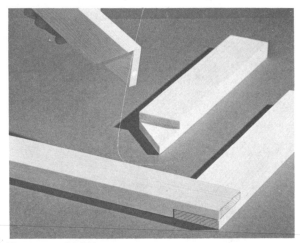

Fig. 213. Half-lap joints.

Fig. 211. Making a splined mitre joint using a ⅛-inch (3-mm) slotting cutter with ball-bearing guide. The spline kerf can be stopped, to make a blind splined mitre.

Fig. 214. This cross is made with an edge cross-lap joint. After assembly the edges are router-shaped.

Making wall panelling (Fig. 215) and wood flooring (Fig. 216) can prove to be cost-saving and very practical applications for the router. In order to save material, I used edge spline joints to make my wall panelling (shown in Fig. 215). A ⅛ × ⅝-inch (3 × 15-mm) length of hardboard formed the spline. Use a slotting cutter or a straight bit with a base guide to cut the kerf for the spline if a table saw is not available. The edges were bevelled slightly with a ball-bearing chamfer bit. Construction details for making solid wood panelling are shown in Fig. 217. Note that splines can also be used to "end match." This allows for the use of boards of random length as well as width to produce panelling.

Fig. 215.   Making wall panelling is a good job to do with a router.

Fig. 216.   The router can also be used to make tongue-and-grooved flooring. Making cuts in the ends (end matching) allows the use of short pieces in random lengths.

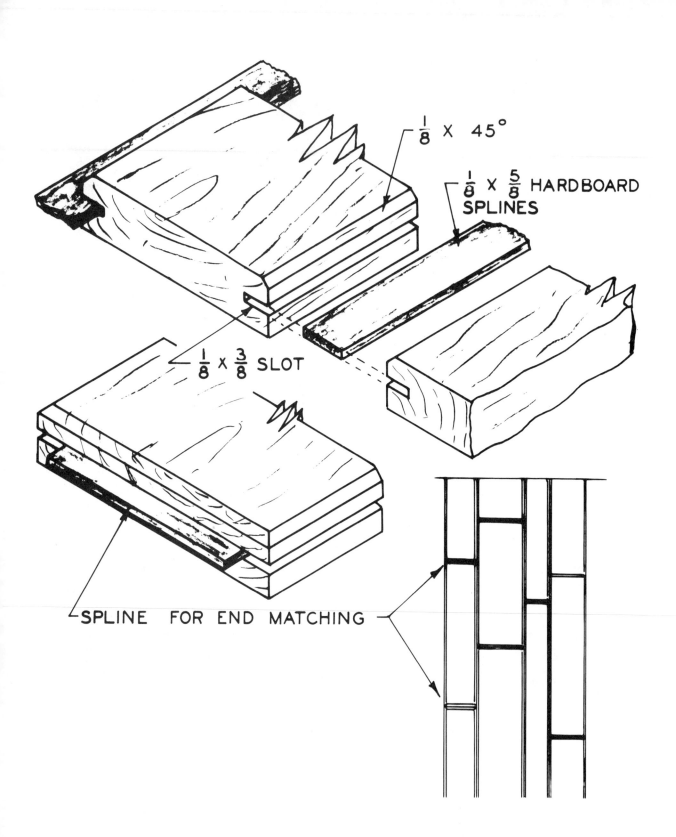

$\frac{1}{8}$ × 45°

$\frac{1}{8}$ × $\frac{5}{8}$ HARDBOARD SPLINES

$\frac{1}{8}$ × $\frac{3}{8}$ SLOT

SPLINE FOR END MATCHING

Fig. 217. *Machining and assembly details for making splined wall panelling.*

The router has many applications in cabinetmaking. Furniture can be given that professional look using a router with the appropriate bits. Simple mouldings (Fig. 218) and those with complex profile sections have many uses for the woodworker. Picture frames, trim around doors and windows, and decorative trim on furniture are all applications of user-made mouldings. To make mouldings is quite simple. It is best to make narrow mouldings, first shaping the edge of a wider board with the router and then ripping off the moulding using a table saw.

Picture frames are made other ways besides using narrow moulding. Figs. 219 to 221 illustrate some interesting applications of the router in picture framing. More ideas and designs for picture frames are shown on pages 210–212.

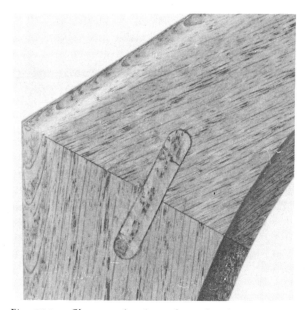

Fig. 220. *Close-up of a face inlet, splined mitre joint. Note the router-shaped edges.*

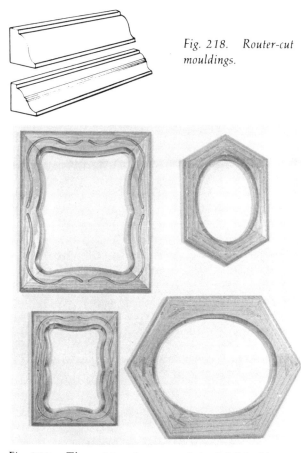

Fig. 218. *Router-cut mouldings.*

Fig. 219. *These picture frames made by Jeff Schmidt are good examples of router joinery and surface-routed decorative effects.*

Fig. 221. *The rabbeted back of a picture frame. The same cut can be used for making glass or panel cabinet doors.*

The serious cabinetmaker puts the router to good use in machining many joints and construction details. Basic case and box construction (Figs. 222 and 223) involves various rabbet joints. A lot of times in conventional woodworking practices stopped rabbets must be made and cut before the assembly of the component parts. I have found that for many jobs I can make the rabbet cuts after assembly. It saves time and energy to cut a rabbet that will receive box bottoms and cabinet backs after assembly. (See Fig. 224). I use a ball-bearing-guided rabbeting bit, which of

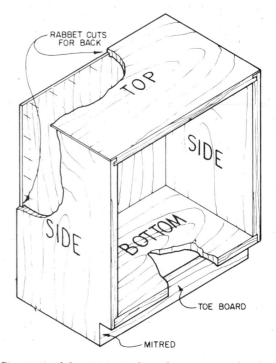

Fig. 223. Most joints in this cabinet case can be router-cut. Note the rabbeted-in back.

course leaves the rounded inside corner. This can be chiselled square if the rabbet is left as router and the corner of the panel rounded to fit, as shown in Fig. 224.

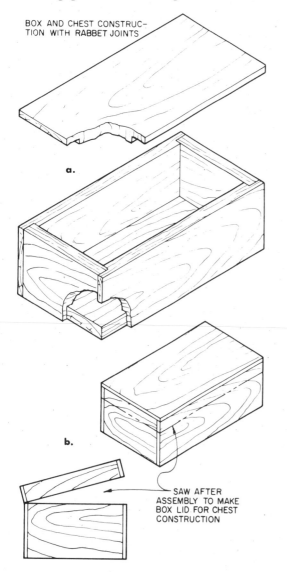

Fig. 222. Box and chest detail shown here with the simple rabbet joint.

Fig. 224. Routing rabbet cuts after assembly (using a piloted bit) eliminates the setup and machining of stopped rabbets. This technique saves time and is useful when rabbets are needed for cabinet and case backs, box and chest bottoms, and picture-frame rabbeting. The corner may be left with a radius (as shown here) or chiselled square.

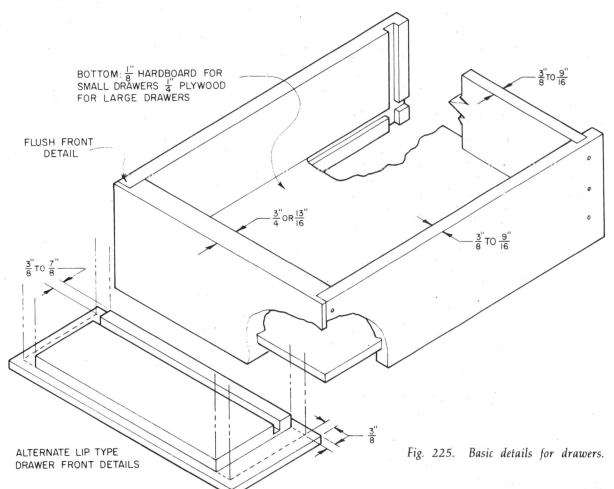

BOTTOM: $\frac{1}{8}''$ HARDBOARD FOR SMALL DRAWERS $\frac{1}{4}''$ PLYWOOD FOR LARGE DRAWERS

FLUSH FRONT DETAIL

$\frac{3}{8}''$ TO $\frac{9}{16}''$

$\frac{3}{4}''$ OR $\frac{13}{16}''$

$\frac{3}{8}''$ TO $\frac{9}{16}''$

$\frac{3}{8}''$ TO $\frac{7}{8}''$

$\frac{3}{8}''$

ALTERNATE LIP TYPE DRAWER FRONT DETAILS

Fig. 225. Basic details for drawers.

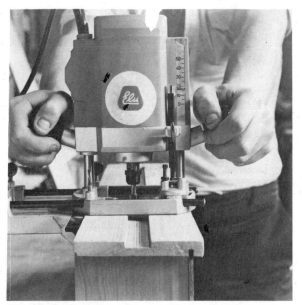

Fig. 226. Grooving a drawer side for a guide.

Rabbet cuts and grooving operations are also necessary for drawer and door construction in furniture and cabinetry. Fig. 225 gives basic specifications and assembly details for typical lip- and flush-type drawers. Again, a straightedge cutting guide and a straight bit are used to cut the grooves for the drawer bottoms, the dadoes for the drawer backs, and the grooves in the sides for slides. (See Fig. 226.)

Cabinet doors are made in many different styles and with many various decorative touches. I have included some basic types, to illustrate fundamental construction details and design suggestions. (See Figs. 227, 228, and 229.) Looking through cabinet and furniture catalogues will give other design ideas. (See Fig. 230.) Most can be fabricated by employing the joints and assembly methods given in this chapter. Refer to Chapter 2 for

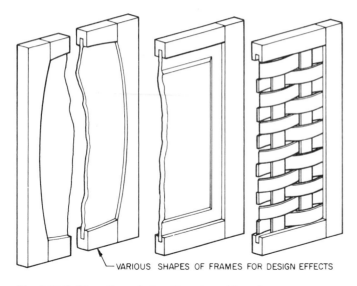

VARIOUS SHAPES OF FRAMES FOR DESIGN EFFECTS

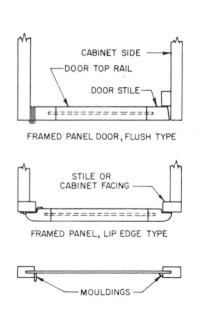

CABINET SIDE

DOOR TOP RAIL

DOOR STILE

FRAMED PANEL DOOR, FLUSH TYPE

STILE OR
CABINET FACING

FRAMED PANEL, LIP EDGE TYPE

MOULDINGS

*Fig. 227 (left).   Some design ideas for cabinet doors.
(right) Top view of basic panel doors.*

Fig. 228.   Raised panel door. Refer to Chapter 2 for special panel-raising bits.

Fig. 229.   Glass panel doors also require mortise-and-tenon joints, rabbeting, and edge-forming operations.

Fig. 230. Custom door, drawer, and decorative mouldings add that professional touch to your furniture and cabinets.

various router bits for making moulding cuts and panel raising of cabinet doors. Refer to Chapter 15 for more ideas and designs, as well as information about panel routing accessories.

In much of today's fine furniture and cabinetry, plywoods or other sheet materials covered with beautiful veneers are used, as shown in Fig. 231. Fig. 232 illustrates some ways of covering the edges of veneer-faced plywoods and other sheet materials. Most applications are some form of a tongue or groove cut into a solid edging. Once a solid edge is applied, almost any shape can then be routed to the edge.

The drop leaf table joint (Fig. 233) is popu-

Fig. 231. This handsome teak dining table by Scan Furniture features wood-sheltered hinges and veneer-faced material with solid wood edging and legs.

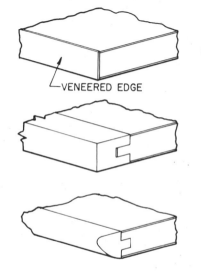

VENEERED EDGE

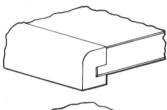

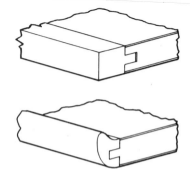

Fig. 232. Some ways of dealing with the edges of plywood or veneered particle board.

lar for making a hinged table leaf. A cove bit is used to make the cut in the leaf. A rounding-over bit of the same radius set to the proper depth makes the cut in the tabletop. A small core-box bit is used to mortise the underside of the tabletop for the hinge barrels. Do not attempt to mortise the hinge itself into the work. It is best to make practice cuts on scrap stock of the same thickness as the finished table will be. It is essential that the distance of line AB be exactly the same as that of line BC in Fig. 233. Make practice cuts and mount hinges to scrap pieces to check all cuts. To make the full edge-shaped cut use the piloted rounding-over bit with a straight-edged board clamped under the work for the pilot to ride against. Set the core box bit about 1/32 inch (0.75mm) deeper than required to obtain clearance between the leaf and the top.

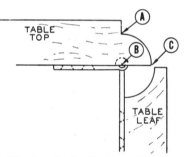

Fig. 233. *The drop leaf table joint. Distance AB must equal BC. Note that only the barrel of the hinge is mortised in, not the leaves.*

Making inlays (Fig. 234) Inlays require shallow recesses to be cut into a surface—a job perfectly suited to the router. The popu-

Fig. 234. *A sunburst design inlay adds a professional touch to tabletops, box lids, and similar pieces.*

larity of inserting inlays on projects is growing among do-it-yourselfers. Inlays are inexpensive, the technique of inlaying is surprisingly simple, and the results are always dramatic. Inlays are available by mail order in hundreds of designs, including flowers, birds, zodiac, fraternal, and sports symbols, and many other stylish designs and motifs in delicately fitted small pieces. Most inlays are taped on the face as a means for holding the parts intact until the inlay is glued down. To make an inlay, the following procedure can be applied to most jobs:

1. Trim the inlay (if necessary) with a craft knife (Fig. 235).

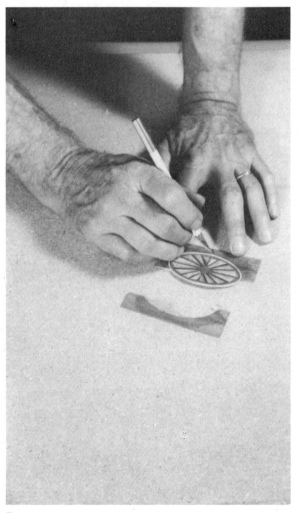

Fig. 235. *Trimming the waste veneer.*

2. With paper side up, pencil a light location or reference mark identifying the position of the inlay. With the knife, cut an incision around the inlay, as shown in Fig. 236.

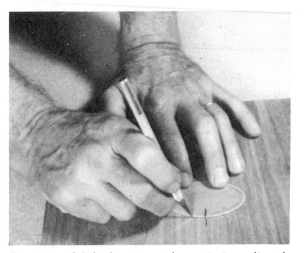

Fig. 236. With the paper side up, incise-outline the inlay with a sharp knife. Note the pencil line reference mark.

3. With a router and small (1/16-inch) (1.5-mm) bit deepen the incised line (Fig. 237) to equal the thickness of the veneer inlay. Outline around the incised line. Install a 1/4-inch (6-mm) or larger bit set to the same depth, and clean out the inside. Assure that the bottom is level and smooth.

Fig. 238. Glue in the inlay with the paper side up.

4. Glue the inlay in place with the paper side up and still on the inlay. Use yellow glue and let it get tacky (about 3 to 5 minutes), to reduce squeeze-out. (See Fig. 238.) Press in the inlay and allow the glue to dry completely. Remove the paper with a moist (not dripping wet) rag. After a couple of minutes the moistened paper will peel off. Do not try to sand off the paper. If it's difficult to get the paper off, moisten it some more or loosen it carefully with a square chisel. When clean and dry, the inlaid surface is ready for sanding and finishing.

Incidentally, professionals use an inexpensive little hand-router plane as shown in Figs. 239 and 240 to true up surfaces and to square corners of router cuts. Figs. 241 and 242 show two other router recessing operations done in preparation for inlays.

Fig. 237. Routing for inlay. Cut carefully to the knife-cut incision.

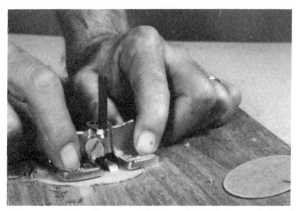

Fig. 239. Levelling an inlay recess with a small hand router plane.

Fig. 240. *Work in progress on a center inlaid panel with border inlays.*

Fig. 241. *Routing a tabletop for a checkerboard inlay. Note the use of the straightedge for outlining. The inside is removed freehand.*

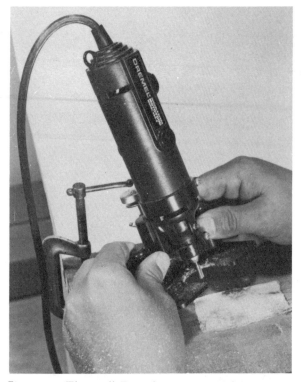

Fig. 242. *The small Dremel router is useful for cutting shallow recesses for veneer inlays.*

Fig. 243. *The single template/pattern shown at the left was used to create all the router cut designs in the board at the right. The pattern was shifted horizontally and vertically with successive cuts.*

Routing surface designs Giving texture and interest to wood panels is limited only by the imagination and the surface-cutting bits available. Routing surface designs can be done freehand. Some techniques and examples are illustrated and discussed in Chapter 7. Here are a few of the hundreds of possibilities that can be created using a simple straightedge and pattern or template guides. Fig. 243 illustrates a template with an irregular curved edge that was used to create the incised router designs cut into the surface of the board shown. Simply shifting the position of the same template (pattern) for each successive cut can produce some very interesting designs.

Surface bead cuts parallel to each other, as shown in Fig. 244, create a textured effect. Using a point-cutting ogee and a point-cutting quarter-round bit (available from Sears) along with any straight router-guiding system will produce the results shown in Fig. 244. Surface

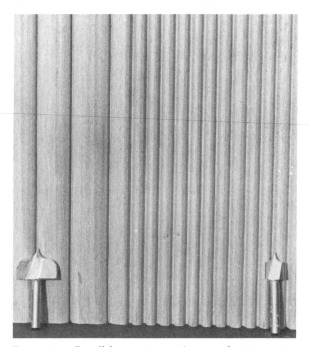

Fig. 244. *Parallel cuts in surfaces make interesting panels.*

94

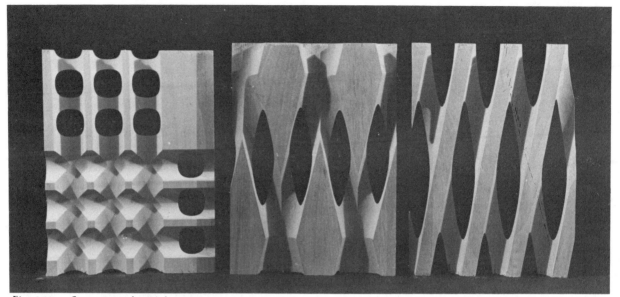

Fig. 245. Some examples of decorative surface cuts and grill work produced with the router.

cuts made parallel and at right angles or at oblique angles can carry this same surface-designing concept even further. The cuts can all be made into the surface from one side or cut from both surfaces, as shown in Fig. 245. Notice that the decorative grill effect is achieved by routing into both sides to a depth that is more than half the thickness of the stock. By varying the depth of the cuts, the direction (or angle) of the cuts, and the shape of

the bit used to make the cuts, a multitude of design possibilities come into existence.

Fluting Fig. 246 shows fluting, the use of grooving for decoration on flat and turned round surfaces. This is still another job well suited to the router. Various cove-cutting, v-groove, or veining bits are commonly used. The more complex the shape of the surface to be fluted, the more involved will be the jig or

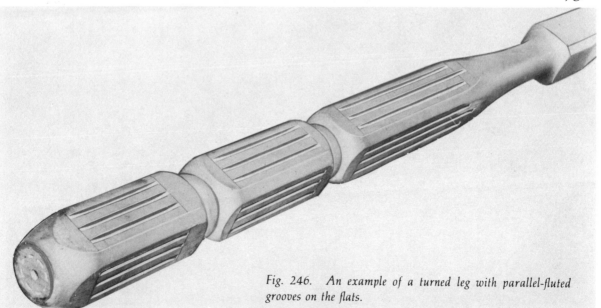

Fig. 246. An example of a turned leg with parallel-fluted grooves on the flats.

95

Fig. 247.   *A box fixture for fluting turned cylindrical shapes.*

Fig. 248.   *A closeup view of fluting a turning.*

fixturing device necessary to handle the job. The straightedge guide can be used to handle fluting on flat and parallel legs, such as the sample shown in Fig. 246. If the leg is of a square taper, the straight-edge guide can still be used, but the flute will be cut parallel to the tapered edge.

Fluting lathe-turned work with the router is a fairly common practice among woodworkers. The problems to overcome are:

1. Layout—indexing the location of the flutes so they end up equally spaced.
2. Devising a fixture or support to guide the router to effect the fluting operation.

Some lathes have an indexing-lock-pin device on the spindle or spindle pulley, which makes locating the spacing and holding the work rigid for routing easy. Without such a device, work out the flute spacing on a length of flat paper equalling the circumference of the surface to be fluted. Tape the paper pattern to the work, and pencil-transfer each flute-cut location. The work can be held rigid

and prevented from turning by clamping the belt to a block of wood held against a pulley.

Fig. 247 illustrates a box fixture set over the lathe for guiding the router in fluting parallel, straight-turned cylinders. It has two guides to accommodate the diameter of the router base. (See Fig. 248.) Stops (blocks nailed across from rail to rail) can be used to limit the travel of the router, making all flutes uniform in length. Should the turning be round and also tapered, then the rails supporting the router must be cut to conform to the contour of the desired fluted area. Just about any conceivable fluting job can be handled with a router, given some imagination along with basic fixturing or router-guiding techniques.

Surfacing This can be done on a limited basis with the portable router. Levelling rough-cut slabs, for example, can be handled in a box or frame fixture using an extended router base. The setup for this operation is shown in Fig. 249. The box keeps the router travel at a uniform level above the work. The work can be secured with hot-melt glue or

Fig. 249. Levelling or router-surfacing a wood slab to even thickness.

Fig. 250. *Some boards used to extend router bases. The top two have integral template guides; one is made of aluminum tubing and the other* (center) *plastic pipe. The lower one is used for general surfacing, as is done in Fig. 249.*

Fig. 251. *Truing the end of a log held in a framed stand.*

nails, or wedged so it doesn't slip or move while being cut. In surfacing work, use the widest straight bit possible that can be carried in the router. Fig. 250 shows some of the boards used for extending router bases. Fig. 251 shows another application of a surfacing or truing operation. In much of my work I need to make the end surfaces of rough-cut logs perfectly flat and exactly parallel. This is done with the router by using a box frame on a stand and the extended router base. Fig. 252 shows a close-up of the cutting operation. I also use the same methods and equipment for truing surfaces of thick slabs in preparation for turning them into wood bowls. (See Figs. 253 and 254).

Another router operation somewhat related to a surfacing process is tapering. Taper-cut surfaces—required in making square, tapered table legs—can be router-cut with the aid of a suitable wedge work-supporting fixture. An example of such a device is shown in Fig. 255. The small end of the leg should be marked with layout lines, to indicate the amount of stock that needs to be removed. The work is wedged up until the bit lines up appropriately at both ends of the tapered surface. With the work clamped securely, the router is worked

Fig. 252. A close-up of a log end being levelled.

Fig. 253. Using blocks to support a thick chunk of rough-cut wood to be levelled with a router prior to being turned into a bowl on the lathe.

Fig. 254. Router levelling makes a flat surface for mounting to the lathe faceplate.

over the surface to cut one of the four tapered surfaces. The work is repeated, to cut each tapered surface on each leg until the job is completed and all the legs (four or more) are identical. The same device can be used to cut flutes into the tapered surfaces. (See Fig. 256.)

Fig. 255 (left). *A homemade device for router cutting the slanted surfaces in making square, tapered furniture legs.*

Fig. 256 (below). *The same jig may be used to hold the tapered leg for fluting (shown) or other surface-decorating jobs.*

7

Freehand Routing

Freehand routing involves any class of work where the router is guided or controlled exclusively by the eye and hand of the operator. Skillfully executed freehand router work borders on artistry. The ability to carve sign letters and other exacting cuts in smooth, flowing curves (Fig. 257) with quickness and simplicity, like that of an artist making a brush stroke on canvas, does not come overnight. It takes practice to develop the experienced eye-and-hand coordination necessary. The router artist must also know materials and the way a particular kind of material will react to the chosen bit and depth of cut. Some woods such as redwood cut like butter with a sharp bit, regardless of grain direction. This is why many professional sign carvers prefer redwood. Douglas fir and some other woods are much more difficult to work freehand because their fibre and grain structure, hardness, or alternating hard and soft growth rings create problems for the beginner. Chapter 4, (page 53), discusses feeds and speeds, which are of much importance to freehand routing success.

There are so many applications and jobs where freehanding is the only possible and practical solution. Being able to freehand fairly well increases confidence to the point where many templates and patterns can be thrown away. And, for production jobs, it is

Fig. 257. *A typical freehand routing job. A small veining bit and a shallow depth give little resistance for a smooth execution.*

Fig. 258.   Freehand routing. This engraved design in rough-sawed wood is good practice for the beginner.

possible to make templates and patterns freehand. Take the incised profile of the duck shown in Fig. 258, for example. Normally, this could be outlined with a no-fail template and template guide. If it is necessary to cut a hundred pieces like this, then employ the template-guided technique. But, suppose it is necessary to make only one such design? It is not profitable and certainly not as satisfying to go through all of the effort to make the template and setup as it is to "zip" out the job freehand in just a matter of minutes. Projects such as the one shown in Fig. 258 provide be-

ginners with good practice and experience in handling freehand work. Starting right out immediately to freehand single-stroke letters for a sign may be disappointing. First, prepare scrap pieces and learn where the router wants to go by itself, more or less, in relation to the direction of the grain and the desired line of cut.

As mentioned earlier, remove as many obstacles as possible, so that freehanding is easier. First of all, have good vision to the bit and the area around the cut. After all, it's crucial to be able to see the layout line and enough of

Fig. 259.   Sub-bases for freehand routing. The one at the far left is a factory-made base used for a pattern. The others were made by the author. The best one for general work is the second from the right, of clear plastic. The large one at the far right is used as an extended base to support the router over large cut-away areas.

the line in advance of the cut to anticipate when changes of direction will be coming. Remove the sub-base to open up the viewing area, or use the clear plastic sub-base described in Chapter 1, Fig. 37 (page 23).

Fig. 260. *Poor freehand routing position for the beginner. The work is too close to the edge of the bench to allow for arm support, reducing router control.*

The next thing to do to ensure better and more comfortable control of the router is to get the best possible position for routing. This is accomplished by clamping the work down onto the workbench well in from the edge. In other words, the work should be secured at a location that requires reaching for it. This forces the operator to place his arms on the bench and/or work (if it's a large size). The sign router in Figure 260 is in the wrong position, especially for a beginner. A stool or bench to sit on at the correct height should give an almost level line or a very low angle of vision to the work with minimum neck or back bending. (Refer to Figs. 264 and 274.)

The following is a step-by-step illustrated demonstration of a typical freehand job. The job is to cut a recessed design into the side of a shelf or mantel-supporting bracket, shown laid out in Fig. 261. Since this is a small-sized, difficult-to-clamp workpiece, it will be tack glued to a larger piece of scrap board (particle board). The scrap piece is clamped to a location well onto the workbench, as shown. Fig. 262 shows the transparent router base. Fig. 263 shows the location where the bit will first

Fig. 261. *The job laid out and clamped well onto the workbench ready for a freehand routing demonstration.*

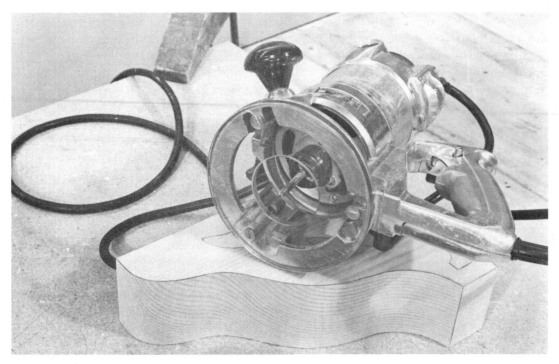

Fig. 262.   A view of the transparent sub-base recommended for freehand work.

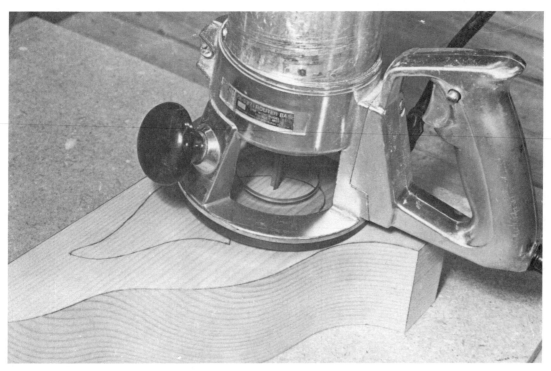

Fig. 263.   Note the good view of the layout line and bit. Here is where the bit will first enter the work—well inside and safely away from the layout line.

enter the work. Notice that it is well inside and safely away from the layout line. The over-the-shoulder photo, Fig. 264, illustrates good operator position. His eye level is low, his forearms are spread and pressing down on the bench, and essentially his wrists will ma-

nipulate the router to make the short curved cuts required.

Rout away the center area with clockwise circular cuts, working outwards towards the layout line. (See Fig. 265.) Note that the bit is set to a shallow depth, and the bit selected has

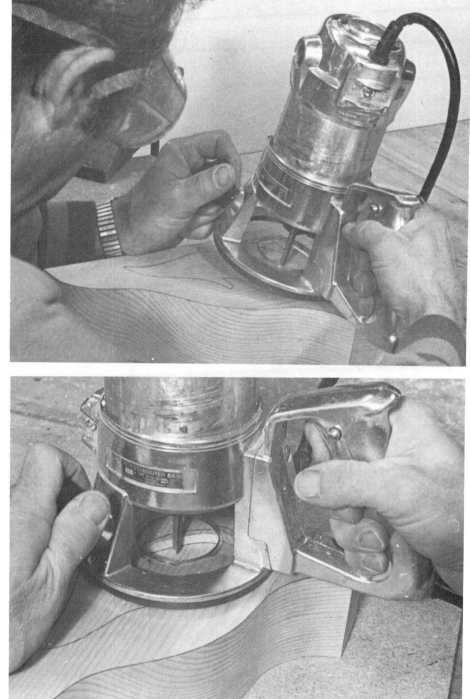

Fig. 264. Good fundamental operator positioning for freehand routing. Eye level is low, forearms are spread out and pressing down to the bench for extra anchorage and better control.

Fig. 265. The first cuts are in a clockwise-feed direction, working from the center outward towards the layout line.

Fig. 266.   The final trimming cut next to the layout line. Note that this last cut removes a minimum of stock—slightly less than one-half the bit diameter. Also note the feed direction for this finished cut. It is counterclockwise, with the router being pulled towards the operator.

a fairly small cutting diameter. Fig. 266 shows a closeup view working the router bit right up to the layout line. There are a couple of things to note about this finish-cut operation. First of all, the last cut is removing stock less than half the diameter of the bit. The second point to observe is the feed direction. In the finishing cut, the feed is counterclockwise, cutting towards the operator. This is so that the bit, due to its rotation, does not grab and pull the router further horizontally, or beyond the line of cut. The last photo, Fig. 267, illustrates the completed cutout design in smooth-flowing curves with the layout lines remaining. Should the operator slip and go beyond or into the layout line, the cut line can often be touched up. Simply, feather out the curve very carefully, using the recommended coun-

terclockwise feed direction. In most cases, no one will be able to identify the repaired, recut piece.

Fig. 267.   The completed job with smooth flowing curves and layout lines still visible.

Take a piece of wood, draw some lines on it in different directions from the grain, and practice following the lines as closely as possible. Make a vertical straight cut across the grain. Use a pulling stroke, cutting in a direction from the above edge down towards the lower one (the edge nearest you). Notice that the router has a tendency to pull itself to the right. It will be necessary to learn how much to press against the router throughout the cut so it makes a reasonably straight line. Do the same in routing right to left with the grain of the wood.

Next, practice angled cuts to the left and to the right obliquely across the grain. Then practice curves. Do some flowing left and right to get the feel of the router's reaction to grain directions. In all practice cuts begin with a shallow depth and a slow feed rate. There will be some burning and puffs of smoke floating up at the start, but this is only practice. Increase the speed of feed to the point where you still feel comfortably in control of the router and the burning or smoking ceases. If necessary, set the bit shallower. It is always possible to increase the depth for a second pass. The second, deeper cut will more easily keep the bit following the layout line. Also in the first practice sessions, attempt to simplify the feed directions. Make most vertical cuts across the grain with a pulling feed direction—that is, in the direction from the far edge of the board downwards, towards yourself. Make horizontal cuts with the grain in a right-to-left feed.

With more experience you will be able to feed the router in almost any direction and know which way to apply counterpressure so that the router will stay on its intended course regardless of grain direction. Slow the feed when going through or near knots and wild grain. Wide and deep cuts also require slower feeds coupled with more downward pressure applied against the base of the router.

Freehand routing opens the door to an endless array of ideas for artistic expression. Designs can be engraved into the wood (as in Figs. 261 to 267) or backgrounds cut away so the pattern or design stands up in relief. (See Figs. 268, 269, and 270.) Routing freehand designs, when done in conjunction with other routing guides and duplicating devices, further widens the opportunity for creative router crafting. (See Fig. 270.) Fig. 271 illustrates a picture-frame project which, if not decorated with some freehand decoration, would be considerably less appealing. Ideas for freehand applications are endless.

Fig. 268.   Designs and lettering in relief.

Fig. 270.   Some interesting design ideas.

Fig. 269.   Backgrounds of relief work can be routed smooth with a flat-bottom bit or made textured as shown above. Here the background was removed with a core-box or roundnose bit, simulating hand-carved texturing.

Fig. 271.   The freehand routed design on this picture frame adds an artistic touch.

An area of freehand routing that receives considerable interest among router owners is sign work. (See Fig. 272.) My book, *Making Wood Signs* (Sterling Publishing Co., 1981), covers all aspects of sign routing and many other sign-fabricating techniques as well. Some of the illustrations have been selected for republication in this and other chapters.

The photos and captions of Fig. 273 through 277 give an overview and some essential tips for freehand-routed sign work.

Fig. 272.   Routed sign done freehand in single-stroke lettering with a roundnose or core-box bit. This bit and this nonrigid lettering style is recommended for beginners.

Fig. 273.   All our signs are first laid out with chalk, then outlined in pencil to a width approximating the desired bit diameter.

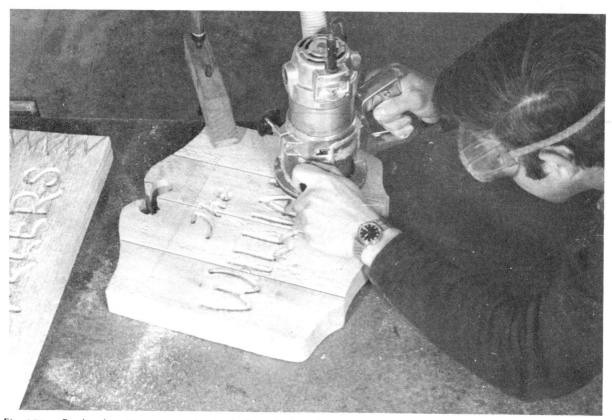

Fig. 274.   *Freehand routing a name sign in single-stroke lettering.*

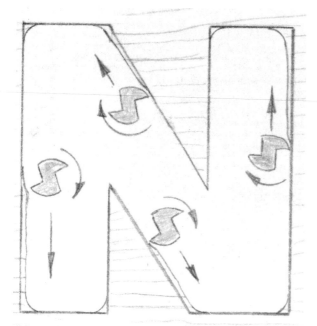

Fig. 275.   *Some of the recommended feed directions for trimming to the line in engraved letter routing.*

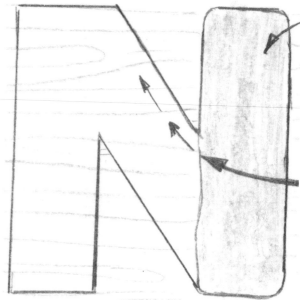

Fig. 276.   *Here is a tip to reduce splintering: Rout towards new wood when possible, not towards or into a previously cut area.*

Fig. 277. *After gaining experience you will be able to make outlining cuts directly following the layout line. For deep cuts it's best to use a guide for straight line work.*

Fig. 278. *The author begins freehand work on an extremely large sign. Notice the vacuum connection and chalked layout.*

Real craftsmanship in routed sign work is the ability to make an Old English or modified Old English lettered sign, as shown in Fig. 279. A complete alphabet, developed just for this book by professional sign carver Tom McIlree, is illustrated in Fig. 280. The first thought of attempting to master this alphabet might cause some gasps of fright, but with practice and the letters broken down to individual strokes, it will turn out to be much easier than it looks. The best results will be achieved by selecting the easiest wood to rout—clear redwood. Select a few pieces for practice first, since the investment in the wood for the sign itself probably will not be small.

The bit for this work should be an HSS v-bit specially ground to an included angle of approximately 60°. A small, lightweight router is the easiest to use. (See Fig. 281.) Most professionals prefer a small-diameter

Fig. 279.   *A name engraved in this modified Old English style is dignified and appeals to friends and potential customers.*

Fig. 280.   *This complete alphabet routed by Tom McIlree will serve as a guide for copy and practice.*

router motor without any handles. In fact, one that can be held and controlled comfortably with one hand is even better.

Look closely and study the individual letters in Figs. 279 and 280. An analysis of the letters reveals that most of the strokes consist of a combination of straight vertical or inclined cuts at various depths. These strokes are ended with sweeping serifs. Most serif cuts are made by smoothly lifting the router towards the end of the cut, so the lines converge at the conclusion of the cutting stroke. (See Figs. 281 and 282.) Practice making the sweeping, pointed serif cuts first. The straight lines are easy and will be dealt with a little later. With the bit set to a suitable depth,

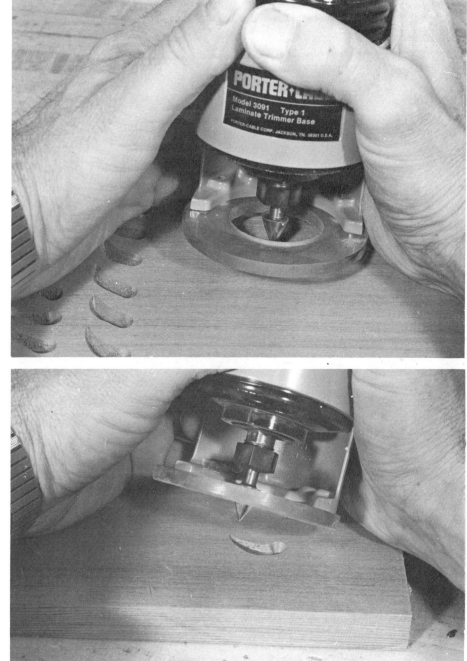

Fig. 281. Holding the router ready to make a sweeping serif cut. Note that the router is tipped back, with the routing resting on the rear edge of the base. Note, too, that the sub-base is a homemade version of clear plastic.

Fig. 282. A completed serif practice stroke.

lower it into the surface to full depth. Then with a curved stroke, simultaneously lift the router so the bit cuts more shallowly as it is moved to the point where it exits from the wood. If necessary, do the first cuts with a layout line marked on the wood to outline the curved teardrop cut that will be produced.

However, with practice such assistance will not be necessary. (See Fig. 283.)

Between horizontal and parallel pencil layout lines for letter heights, chalk in the letters, copying the shapes of the desired letters from Fig. 280 as closely as possible. Use a small homemade T-square (hand-held, not

Fig. 283. A filled board with practice strokes made right to left. Left to right and sweeping vertical directions get you ready to put it all together into a sign.

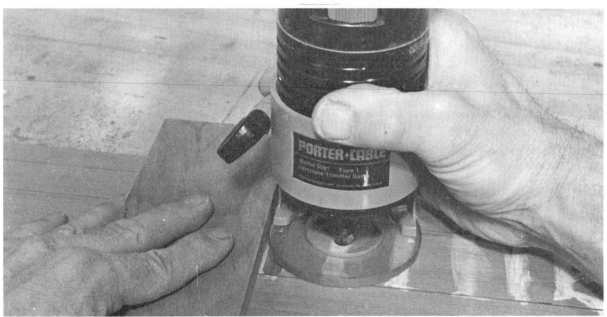

Fig. 284. All vertical strokes are made first with the assistance of a small T-square guide. Try top-to-bottom and then bottom-to-top feed strokes to determine which is best for you.

clamped) and cut all verticals with a top-to-bottom feed stroke. See Figs. 284, 285, and 286. Some sideways pressure will be necessary as the router will tend to move away from the T-square edge. If slippage becomes a problem, glue a piece of 60 grit sandpaper under the blade. If it is more comfortable and less awkward, use a vertical bottom-to-top feed direction for making the vertical letter strokes.

Practice and concentration regarding feed and router resistance in various grain directions are essential to becoming skilful at free-hand work. All the effort and practice will be well invested. So often small jobs—not just signs, but tasks such as hinge mortise routing, carving out lock recesses, inlay work and cut-outs normally made with a jigsaw or scroll saw, and numerous other jobs—can all be handled quickly and accurately with a router.

Fig. 285. The straight strokes are easy. Good layout spacing is important for good-looking results.

Fig. 286. Once all vertical strokes are finished, add the serifs.

8

Routing Plastic Laminates

Because of their durability, plastic laminates are widely used to cover countertops, edgings and facings of furniture, and cabinets. They are also applied to doors and walls, shower stalls, and even window sills. This material is available in a variety of different colors and in various decorative patterns, such as slate, marble, and wood grains. It can be ordered with a polished high-gloss finish, or in satin, suede, or sculptured designs that have a textured, three-dimensional effect. Slate and weathered-wood patterns are examples of sculptured finishes. One of the newest developments by the Formica Corporation is their "color core." In solid-color patterns the color runs through the full thickness of the Formica.

Most general-purpose laminates are a standard 1/16 inch (1.5 mm) thick. "V-32" is 1/32 inch (.75 mm) thick and is used for vertical applications, such as on walls and other surfaces where wear is not as severe. There are other special types of laminates: backing or balance sheets and cabinet-liner grades. These are thin, less-expensive materials that usually have a plain, nondecorative face. Core materials (or substrates) to which decorative laminates are applied include particle board, plywood, hardboard, metal, and solid lumber. Solid lumber over 4 inches (100 mm) in width is likely to warp. Suitable glues include white

liquid, urea resin, Resorcinal, and contact cements. All except the contacts require extensive clamping, which makes contact cements the most popular choice.

The basic process involves three easy steps: 1. cut, 2. adhere or glue, and 3. trim. The router is used for the first and last steps. The whole process is relatively easy and professional results are almost immediate. One distinct advantage is that not much is needed to get into working with decorative plastic laminates. Small lightweight routers are preferred over larger and heavier ones, but any router will do most of the basic cuts. And one or two fairly inexpensive bits will go a long way. (See Fig. 287.)

Often, smaller-diameter bits allow cutting inside corners and in other tight areas that can not be cut with the larger and more expensive bits. (Refer to Chapter 2, page 41 for more information about bits for cutting and trimming plastic laminates.) A good practice project for plastic laminates is the overlaid clock shown in Figs. 288 and 289.

When cutting plastic laminate to cover a particular surface always leave at least 1/4 inch (6 mm) extra on all overlapping sides and edges. Fig. 290 shows a good way to cut laminates to rough sizes with the router. Use a small piloted carbide bit. The line of cut is aligned with a straightedge clamped under the

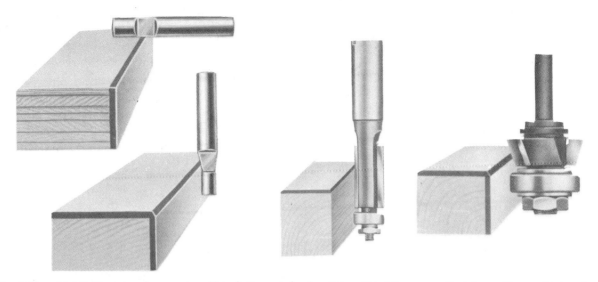

Fig. 287.   At left, these two inexpensive, ¼-inch (6-mm)-shank solid carbide bits are excellent for cutting and trimming plastic laminates. At right, two of the more expensive ½-inch (12-mm)-shank professional bits that make the same type of cuts.

Fig. 288.   These clocks with overlaid decorative plastic laminates are good practice projects. The one at left is 10 inches (250 mm) square. The one at right is 12 inches (300 mm) square. Both are 1½ inches (37 mm) thick.

Fig. 289.   Make-your-own-clock kit by cutting all pieces before bonding and trimming. The core is comprised of five pieces of ¾-inch (18-mm) particle board (or plywood) cut and assembled as shown. Markers may be purchased or, as shown here, lengths of dowels set into holes can be bored through the bonded laminate.

Fig. 290.   Cutting edge strips of laminate for a clock project or self-edged counter or table.

laminate, and the router is simply guided with the pilot bearing against the straightedge. Plastic laminates are very brittle and care should be exercised so that pieces are well supported during cutting to prevent accidental cracking or breaking. It's best to cut all the pieces at one time. When making the clock or a kitchen counter with laminate on the vertical edge (called a self-edge), it's best to bond that edge first. (See Fig. 291.)

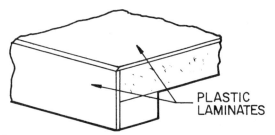

Fig. 291. *The arrangement of parts for a countertop with a self edge. Note that the countertop laminate overlaps the vertical laminate of the self edge.*

Contact cement is applied to both the laminate and the substrate (core) material and both are allowed to dry before bonding. When the two coated surfaces meet or make contact with each other, the bond takes place. Very porous particle board edges and plywood edges may need a second coat of contact cement. Apply contact cement in accordance with the manufacturer's directions. Laminates receive bonding pressure from narrow rollers or from taps with a hammer onto a small block of hardwood as the block is moved over the laminated surfaces.

Once the first piece of laminate is applied and pressure-bonded, trimming can begin immediately. Contacts do not require cure times as do other glues. Trim the self-edge square and flush to the top of the larger surface, using the appropriate bit. (See Fig. 287.) Remember, it is essential that carbide or carbide-tipped bits are used. (See Fig. 292.) The hardness of the laminate will quickly dull even the best HSS bits. Feed directions should be the same as in conventional edge routing.

After the edge is trimmed, cut and bond the top piece, overlapping the self-edge in much

the same manner as described above. Trimming the top may be done with one of the bevel-cutting bits that are pilot- or ball-bearing-guided. These put a slight bevel on the edge, reducing the sharpness of the corner. For my own work I use a straight bit, as shown in Fig. 292, and round the edge slightly with a fine mill file. It's a good idea to file the corner even if a bevel-trim bit is used.

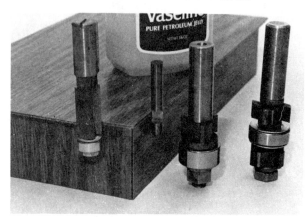

Fig. 292. *Some straight bits for trimming overhangs. The pilot bit requires a lubricant (like petroleum jelly) to prevent marring where the pilot bears against the laminate surface. The ball-bearing bit, at right, is a double-cutting production bit.*

If piloted bits will bear against the laminate during trimming, a lubricant such as wax or petroleum jelly should be used to prevent marring. If ball-bearing trim bits are used, be sure to exert sufficient pressure against the ball bearing so that it does not spin freely, which could also mar the work.

At this point, I'm tempted to say that that's all there is to the plastic-laminate process, but there are some other tips and tools that should be included here to make this a more complete router handbook.

One thing to keep in mind when working with plastic laminates is that it is often necessary to make overlaid panels with balanced construction to prevent warping. Tabletops, for example, will warp, unless securely fastened all around the edges, the way a kitchen counter is fastened to the base cabinets. Thus either apply laminate to both surfaces or use the special, less expensive balance sheet on the underside. (See Figs. 293 and 294.) This material can often be purchased from suppliers or from cabinet shops.

Fig. 293. A balance or backing sheet is essential to prevent overlaid panels from warping.

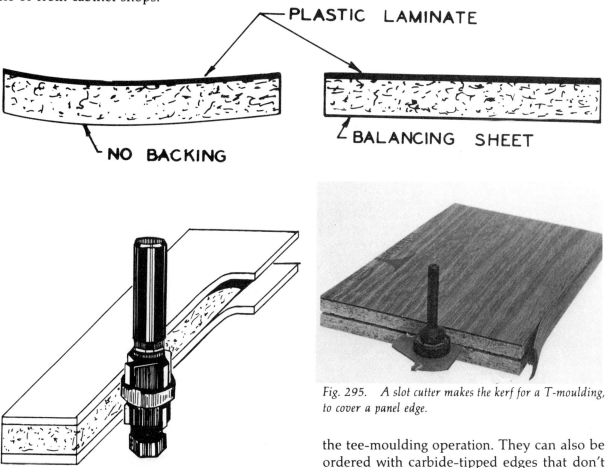

PLASTIC LAMINATE

NO BACKING

BALANCING SHEET

Fig. 294. Double-cutting bits are production tools for trimming faces and backing laminates for doors and tables in one pass.

Fig. 295. A slot cutter makes the kerf for a T-moulding, to cover a panel edge.

There are many other ways of treating edges in addition to the self-edge method. Solid wood can be splined or tongue-and-groove-fitted flush with the top surface. Then these solid wood edgings can be edge-formed using any bit-cutting configuration desired. One edge often found on factory-produced laminate products is the plastic (or metal) "T" moulding. (See Fig. 295.) Some mail-order houses now offer tee mouldings of various sizes, colors, and wood grains in small quantities for the handyman. Remember, slotting cutters come in a wide range of cutter widths, so it's not much of a problem to get set up for

the tee-moulding operation. They can also be ordered with carbide-tipped edges that don't dull in particle boards and plywoods.

A router, a table saw, and a carbide blade are all the necessary tools for making the unusual raised-edge panel shown in Fig. 296. In this case, the top-surface laminate is applied first in the usual manner. The kerf is sawed, glued fast with yellow glue, and allowed to dry. The edge is then trimmed flush. Laminate is applied to the edge and is finished off by softening the sharp corners with a file.

Custom shops, cabinetmakers, and production shops involved in the application and trimming of plastic laminates use various router trimming attachments or special routers called laminate trimmers. Figs. 297 and 298 illustrate one such tool. For those who have a conventional router, a kit is available to convert the router into a laminate trimmer.

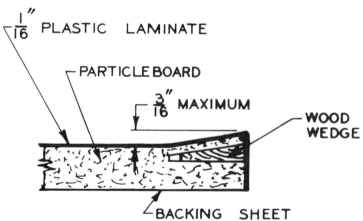

$\frac{1}{16}$" PLASTIC LAMINATE

PARTICLEBOARD

$\frac{3}{16}$" MAXIMUM

WOOD WEDGE

BACKING SHEET

Fig. 296. Details for making a raised-edge panel.

Fig. 297. Black & Decker's ⅝ horsepower, 27,000 RPM, ¼-inch (6-mm) laminate trimmer weighs just 4 pounds (1.8 kg). Note the adjustable ball-bearing guide.

Fig. 298. A power trimmer is similar to a router but usually smaller in size. Here it is used one-handed to trim a surface overhang.

These accessories are shown in Figs. 299 and 300. I seriously question their practicality. If the purchase cost of these kits were applied to buy the now widely used ball-bearing carbide bits instead, it wouldn't be necessary to buy this attachment.

Fig. 299. *A veneer and laminate trimming accessory attaches to the router base.*

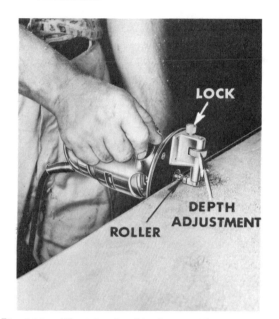

Fig. 300. *The trimming kit shown with its parts and adjustment for flush trimming.*

9
Purchased Router Accessories

In addition to the accessories previously discussed and illustrated (straight and circular cutting guides, template guides, and laminate trimmers), there are a growing number of handy and useful devices available. These ingenious gadgets enable the router to perform some astonishing operations. Most of the items illustrated in this chapter are sold with step-by-step instructions and replacement-part lists. Consequently, I will not give specific, detailed operating instructions. The objective here is to introduce these accessories and, where possible, to illustrate and preview their capabilities.

The power-plane attachment Figs. 301 and 302 show an attachment that is a very useful addition to the router's motor unit. The power and high speed of the motor produces a very smoothly cut surface. Most plane attachments are easily adjusted to change the depth of cut from heavy to very shallow. This device is especially useful to finish carpenters. Its portability makes fitting trim and doors faster and easier than sawing and hand-planing fits. Other woodworkers who do not have conventional jointers will find this accessory extremely helpful in planing boards square for gluing edge to edge to increase width dimensions.

Fig. 301. Black & Decker's attachment converts a router to a power plane.

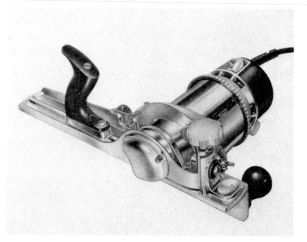

Fig. 302. A plane attachment with the motor unit installed ready for edge-jointing jobs.

Power-plane attachments have adjustable fences, assuring that cuts are made square to the face. And, obviously, they can be adjusted to various angles for bevel planing. Spiral cutters (see Chapter 2), which fit special arbors, make smooth, shearing cuts even on difficult grains. One disadvantage of this type of power plane is that large, flat surfaces, such as those involved in levelling a large tabletop cannot be planed. Not all router motors fit all plane attachments. It is best to purchase the planing attachment from the manufacturer of the router to be assured of a proper match.

Door/butt-hinge mortising templates

These are widely used by full-time, professional builders and contractors. These templates and kits are made in various styles by a number of different manufacturers. (See Figs. 303 to 305.) Essentially, they are adjustable templates that permit fast, accurate placement and mortising for installing hinges on doors and door frames (jambs). Once adjusted for the size of hinges and the location, built-in nails hold the template secure to the door as it is being routed. The router is guided by an appropriate size base-mounted template guide. The adjustment of the template unit remains unchanged as it is removed from the door. It is then transferred to the door frame (jamb), to cut the mating recesses, and thus assure a perfectly accurate alignment and fit every time. The router will cut recesses with rounded corners. These areas will need to be chiselled away by hand if hinges with square corners are being installed.

Those who hang doors just occasionally or just want to have templates on hand may find it advantageous to purchase individual templates in 3½- and 4-inch (88- and 101-mm) sizes (Fig. 305). Or, make hinge templates similar to the one shown in Fig. 306. With just one door to hang it's just as fast to pencil-trace around the hinge and rout the recess away freehand, cutting close to the layout line at the proper depth. Then use a sharp chisel to clean up the cut, enlarging the recess precisely to the layout line.

Fig. 303. *View showing door-hinge mortising. Note the template guide and straight mortising bit.*

Fig. 304. *Another view of a door being routed for hinges.*

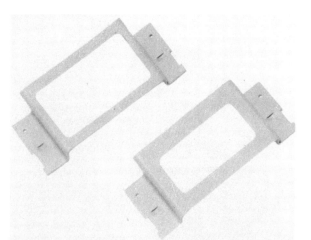

Fig. 305. *Sears sells the individual butt-hinge templates shown here in 3½- and 4-inch (89- and 105-mm) sizes. These also require a base-mounted template guide (bushing).*

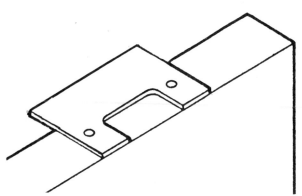

Fig. 306. *A homemade hinge-recessing template.*

Letter-routing templates Holding devices assure perfect, uniformly styled letters right from the first attempt. The sets (Figs. 307 and 308) produce only simple, block-style letters. Various effects, however, can be obtained using differently styled router bits. A guided letter-routing set consists of a frame and a clamping device that holds various interchangeable templates during routing. The router must be fitted with a base-installed template guide (bushing) to limit router travel to the inside opening of the template.

Always exercise care to avoid accidentally hitting the template with the cutting bit at entry. It's best to wait for the router to stop revolving before lifting it off the template frame. Plunging routers greatly reduce the need for these precautions. Most brands of router may be used with the sets shown in Figs. 307 and 308. Incidentally, it is possible to make templates of plastic or hardboard to fit the frames of these sets.

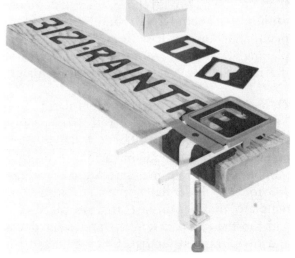

Fig. 307. *The Sears letter template set includes a clamping device with 58 plastic block letter templates 3½ inches (89 mm) square that cut letters 1¾ and 2¾ inches (44 and 70 mm) in height.*

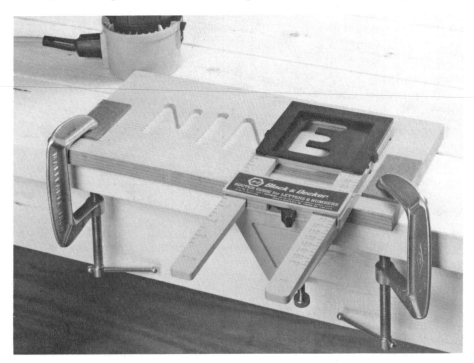

Fig. 308. *Black & Decker's letter-routing set is similar to Sears's, cutting 1¾- and 2½-inch (44- and 64-mm) letter heights.*

The Sears Rout-A-Signer Fig. 309 shows a more versatile sign-routing guide than those previously described. Almost every kind of router can be mounted to power this machine without any modification. A router unit (with base) is simply mounted to a plastic adapter plate with thumbscrews. The system uses templates similar to those mentioned earlier. However, the router is controlled by guiding a stylus following in the template. This in turn directs the movement of the router. Base-mounted template guides (or bushings) are not used at all.

With the proper adjustment, letters can be carved in vertical strokes or made so that they slant to the right, inclining at an angle of about 28°. The unit will carve letters in any size between ¾ inch (18 mm) and 4½ inches (114 mm) in height. Letter height is determined by bit diameter, template size, and the setting of an adjustable tie bar. There is no limit to sign lengths the Rout-A-Signer will

handle, but it is limited to routing boards under 10 inches (255 mm) in width and not greater than 2 inches (50 mm) in thickness. The Rout-A-Signer comes with 58 templates in a plastic storage carousel. It is constructed of steel with some plastic and weighs nearly 10 pounds (4.5 kg). The overall assembled size is 22 × 30 inches (560 × 765 mm) and it is only 2½ inches (64 mm) high without the router mounted to it.

Pantographs Pantographs (Figs. 310 to 312) are used to copy and duplicate signs, artwork, and thin relief carvings. The concept of mounting a router to a pantograph, which is nothing more than four rigid arms with movable joints or connections forming a parallelogram, suggests the great potential for using the router as a copying tool. The system can be used to trace flat work and even full three-dimensional sculpted pieces. Some of these latter devices are discussed in Chapter 13.

Fig. 309. The Sears "Rout-A-Signer." At right is a round carousel which holds plastic letter and number templates.

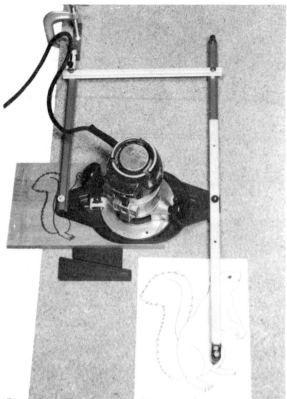

Fig. 310. *The Sears two-dimensional router pantograph shown with a paper pattern and its reduced copy in wood.*

Fig. 311. *The Sears pantograph making raised letters from a stylus-followed paper pattern.*

Fig. 312. *The Black & Decker router pantograph can be used with any router having a 6-inch (150-mm) diameter or smaller base. Note that this unit is mounted to a plywood base, but can be mounted directly to the workbench as well.*

Typical of the simplest home-craft router pantographs are the Sears and Black & Decker models. (See Figs. 311 and 312.) In examining both routing pantographs, notice that the router is mounted on one of the four connecting arms comprising the basic parallelogram. One corner is the major pivoting point, which is also where the unit is fastened to the workbench. Diagonally opposite this point is the stylus. The stylus is at the end of one extended arm. This extension allows room for seeing and following a paper pattern or stencil with the stylus. Because the stylus is extended, the pantograph does not copy in a size equal to the original. The resulting design cut by the router is smaller than the original pattern. The Black & Decker unit offers reduction ratios of 40, 50, and 60 percent. Sears's reductions are 42, 50, and 58 percent. The further away the stylus is located from the arm-pivot joint, the smaller the reproduction will be. To use, hold only the stylus, not the router. Lifting the stylus arm removes the router bit from the cut. Straight-line cuts are best, made by guiding the stylus along a straightedge held securely over the line on the pattern.

Apart from the distinct disadvantage that the pantographs do not make same-size copies, they do have good applications. They are useful for making shallow, incised cuts in the reduced reproduction of flat designs from any source. Signs, plaques, and other decorative effects are just some of the possibilities.

The Sears three-dimensional router pantograph This is illustrated in Figs 313 through 315. This device can be used for engraving designs of animals, sign letters (Fig. 313), and work similarly handled with the pantographs described previously. In addition, this unit will handle on a limited basis three-dimensional carving. It successfully reproduces contoured surfaces of carvings that have a flat back. As with the other pantograph routers, this unit has three settings, which give reduction ratios of 40, 50, and 60 percent. This unit will fit all routers having 6-inch (152-mm) diameters or smaller bases. (See Fig. 152.) The machine's capacity for three-dimensional carving is limited to a maximum pattern size of 1¼ inches (31 mm) thick × 13 inches (330 mm) wide × 24 inches (600 mm long). Any fairly durable item within these size restrictions can be used for master patterns.

There are many inexpensive items of plaster, plastic, or cast metal that can be purchased at most hardware and variety stores and that make good patterns and nice products when carved in wood. (See Fig. 315.) The process is not especially fast because small bits, such as a ⅛-inch (3-mm) veining bit must be used to get good, detailed reproduction. The stylus must touch every point on the sur-

Fig. 314. *A close-up showing the router on the styrene plastic base held with mounting clips and wing nuts. Note the use of wedges to secure the workpiece.*

Fig. 313. *A full view of the Sears three-dimensional routing pantograph.*

Fig. 315. *Full view of three-dimensional carving with the Sears router pantograph.*

face of the pattern. The manufacturer's manual states: "A 6-inch × 6-inch [152-mm × 152-mm] 3-D pattern will take a couple of hours to complete."

Walter Hartlauer of Eugene, Oregon, provides the sign industry with large, commercial routing pantographs. Various models have the capability to both enlarge and reduce. In addition to making a cutout as shown in Fig. 316, the machines can do engraved routing from a pattern into the surface of the wood. Needless to say, there are many applications of various pantograph systems for copying and reproduction that go far beyond just the realm of sign work.

Fig. 316. One of Walter Hartlauer's large router pantographs used for commercial sign work. His machines both enlarge and reduce. Here a number 24 inches (600 mm) high is enlarged to 48 inches (1200 mm).

Radial router guides Figs. 317 and 318 show guides that are available from a number of mail-order sources. Notice that any router can be attached to a universal mounting device. This router guide is ideal for multiple-groove operations, as shown in Fig. 318. With various bits, very decorative panels and grills may be cut with ease. The base swivels much like that of a power-saw mitre box, which can be adjusted and locked at any desired angle up to 45°, left or right. Guide rails are connected to pivoting support legs at each end. This hinged feature allows the unit to adjust itself automatically to various thicknesses. It rests upon the surface of the work and holds the work in place throughout the cut.

The unit in Fig. 318 has an opening capacity of 17½ inches (445 mm) in stock width and can handle wood up to 3¾ inches (97 mm) in thickness. Incidentally, some of these radial guides will also accept portable circular saws mounted to the carriage assembly.

Fig. 317. This radial router guide carries a router on a straight-line carriage. This device has many uses: making various mouldings and cuts, such as rabbets, dadoes, and lap joints. It can also make angle cuts and trim, decorative panels, and wood grill.

Fig. 318. A radial guide illustrating angled, decorative panel grooving. This unit has a locking device allowing the work to be fed under the carriage for grooving, slotting, and moulding operations. The rails also lock in the raised position at any desired height up to approximately 4 inches (105 mm).

Router-cut wood threads Fig. 319 shows these. On round dowels, threads can be cut in several ways. Some very complicated jigs with

Fig. 319. This wood "Pillow Block" clock shows one of many unusual projects that can be made incorporating router-cut wooden threads.

thread box guides can be concocted using the router with specially ground bits to cut both internal and external threads. One such user-made device with plans and instructions was published in an article by R. J. Harrigan in the March/April 1983 issue of *Fine Woodworking*. In the same issue are plans for a router-table wood-thread box by Andrew Henwood. This one cuts external threads. Anyone considering making a wood thread-cutting accessory should refer to these articles.

The Beall Tool Company of Newark, Ohio, is on the verge of making available a commercially produced wood threader, as shown in Fig. 320. The Beall people produce a line of wood products requiring parts with external wood threads. Not finding any tool available satisfying their needs, they invented one. The Beall wood-threader router attachment will cut external threads in hardwoods and soft-

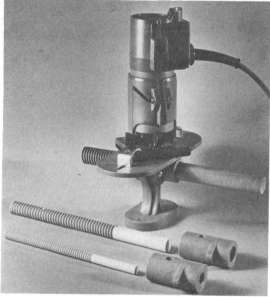

Fig. 320. The Beall commercial wood threader cuts three sizes of external threads (½-, ¾-, and 1-inch [12-, 18-, and 24- mm] diameters) with any router and a special three-fluted, 60° spiral bit.

woods, as well as some plastics. Any router may be used. The Beall attachment currently features interchangeable lead inserts in the following sizes: 1-inch (24-mm) and ¾-inch (18-mm) diameters × 6 threads per inch (24 mm) and ½-inch (12-mm) diameter × 8 threads per inch (24 mm). Other sizes and even lefthanded cutting guides may also be available in the future. The unit is said to be relatively easy to set up.

The router is accurately positioned with the aid of an indexing sleeve. The bit cutting depth is set by trial and error, using the router's own depth-adjustment mechanism. Once set, the device is durable enough for continuous production work with only occasional replacement of the special router bit required. The bit is an HSS three-flute spiral-cut, 60°, double-ended veiner bit—and it is surprisingly low-priced.

The Bowl Crafter Fig. 321 shows one of the newest items in the growing line of Sears's router accessories. This incredible attachment takes almost any router of ¾ horsepower or larger with a 6-inch (152-mm) diameter base and converts it into an unusual machine for making a variety of turned wood products. (See Figs. 321 and 322.) Some of the possibilities include: large and small salad bowls, plates, goblets, candle holders, salt-and-pepper-shaker sets, egg cups, candy dishes, turned lidded boxes.

This accessory comes with its own 110V motor-driven headstock which turns the work very slowly—only 4 RPMs. As the piece rotates, a plastic guide on the bottom of the aluminum router carriage follows a precut template (Figs. 323 and 324). One of the three special router bits (one each for convex, concave, and straight surfaces) cuts the shape of the template pattern into the wood. (See Fig. 325.) This remarkable attachment will turn pieces up to 10 inches (255 mm) in diameter and up to 5 inches (127 mm) in thickness (or length). The unit comes unassembled and without bits or router, but it does include an excellent owner's manual that also contains

Fig. 321. The Sears Bowl Crafter with some samples of projects that can be router-turned using special arbor mounted bits.

Fig. 322. More projects made with the Bowl Crafter.

numerous project template plans, along with guidelines for designing projects.

Fig. 323. *Routing the outside surface of a large salad bowl. Note the template pattern below the workpiece.*

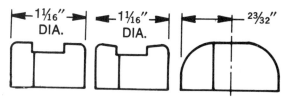

Fig. 325. *The three profile shapes of the bits used with the Bowl Crafter. These thread onto the end of a special arbor support of the router carriage. Left to right: straight bit, outside bit, inside-concave bit.*

The router lathe Fig. 326 shows a router lathe, or as Sears calls their unit, Router Crafter. This is a fairly new attachment that in the truest sense of the word gives a router versatility. Aside from turning bowls and similar faceplate work, this attachment will do more than an ordinary turning lathe. It is possible to make turned lamps, table legs (Figs. 327 and 328), posts, and hundreds of other turned carvings of almost any conceivable design. And it is easy to duplicate pieces exactly. There are four basic categories of operation that can be done on this machine. They are:

1. Straight beading and fluting. This includes cuts made lengthwise or parallel to the workpiece. They may be of a straight, tapered, or contoured style.
2. "Roping" or spiralling in both the right and left hand. These cuts may also be on straight (Fig. 329) or tapered surfaces.

Fig. 324. *Making the inside cut in the large salad bowl. Again note the template limiting the router.*

Fig. 326 (below). *The Sears Router Crafter uses the router to do the work of an ornamental turning lathe.*

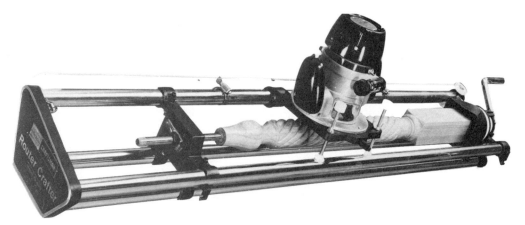

Fig. 327. This "turned" lamp and these elegant table legs are typical Router Crafter projects.

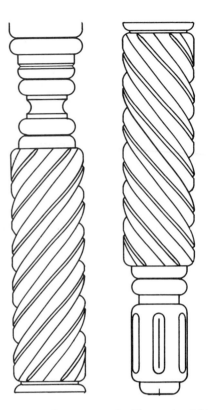

Fig. 328. Router cut spiralling to the right or left on straight or tapered turnings is just one of the many operations handled with the Sears Router Crafter.

Fig. 329. A straight bit is used to "turn" down a square blank to a round cylinder.

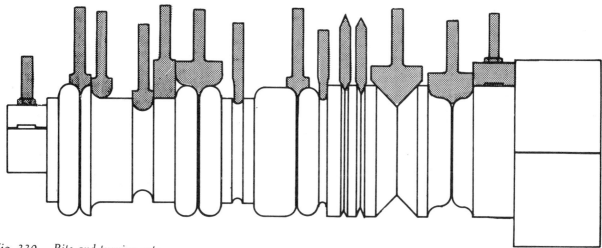

Fig. 330.   Bits and turning cuts.

3. Turn beads, coves, and flats around the work. These cuts are determined by the cutting shape of the router bit used. (See Fig. 330.)

4. "Contour template turning," in which the router follows a template attached to the front of the machine.

These four basic types of cutting used in combination with one another will result in hundreds of different design configurations.

Essentially, the router lathe consists of a headstock and tailstock connected by four heavy steel tubes. A carriage, which a router is mounted to, travels along these tubes. Also included is a system incorporating cables, drums, an indexing mechanism, and a hand crank which through cable connections synchronizes the carriage travel and workpiece rotation. The work stock capacity is 3 inches (76 mm) square by 36 inches (900 mm) in length.

The router lathe can also do simple turnings starting from square stock (Fig. 329). A straight bit is used for the initial roughing cut. First, the router travels back and forth length-

Fig. 331.   A closeup view of spiralling using an ogee point-cutting bit.

wise with the stock held stationary for each pass. This is continued until a series of flat cuts makes it nearly round. Then the piece is turned as the router travels lengthwise, producing a perfectly round cylinder.

Almost any turning profile consisting of flats, steps, beads, or coves can be made by selecting the appropriate bit. When set to make lengthwise flutes and beads, the stock is held stationary and the carriage feeds the router parallel and lengthwise along the work. This operation is done in conjunction with suitable settings of the 1 to 24 indexing posi-

In spiralling, or roping, the operation involves cutting beads (or flutes) spiralled around the piece. In this case, the carriage

moves simultaneously with the work as it is rotated with the hand crank. (See Figs. 331 and 332.) By making shallow cuts in both righthand and lefthand spirals, the machine produces the diamond or "pineapple" effect, shown in Figs. 333 and 334.

Figs. 335 and 336 are reprinted from the Sears owner's manual, which is very complete. These drawings illustrate some of the many contoured profile shapes that can be duplicated with the aid of a template. In this operation a follower on the router carriage raises and lowers the router as it is moved over the length of the template. The drawings also vividly illustrate the overall capabilities of the remarkable Router Crafter.

Fig. 332. A work sample showing the spiral carving capability of the Router Crafter.

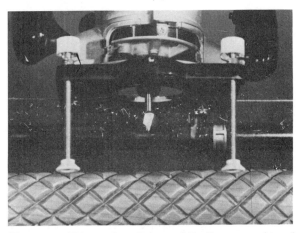

Fig. 333. Diamond or "pineapple" effects are achieved by employing both righthand and lefthand spiralling techniques.

Fig. 334. A combination of different cuts creates this "factory-made" look. Note the clean transition cut from square to round.

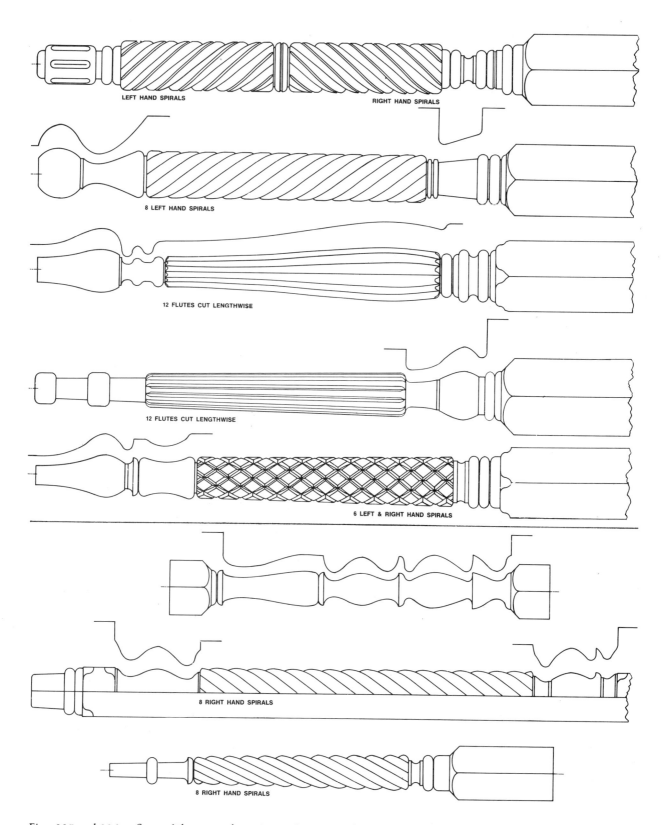

LEFT HAND SPIRALS   RIGHT HAND SPIRALS

8 LEFT HAND SPIRALS

12 FLUTES CUT LENGTHWISE

12 FLUTES CUT LENGTHWISE

6 LEFT & RIGHT HAND SPIRALS

8 RIGHT HAND SPIRALS

8 RIGHT HAND SPIRALS

Figs. 335 and 336. Some of the unusual turning configurations that can be produced with the Router Crafter. Those with lines next to the profile indicate the need of templates for duplication.

10

Router Tables

The router table is another accessory that is practically a must for the serious router craftsman. A router table is any arrangement where the router (or motor unit alone) is hung upside down under a flat surface with the bit protruding through that surface. In operation, the router is held stationary and the work is passed over or along the rotating bit. Most operations are performed with a fence secured to the table to assist in guiding the work.

With any sort of router-table setup added to the shop come all the capabilities comparable to a light-industrial spindle shaper. There is an endless list of different operations possible with a router table. Obvious jobs include: straight-line dadoing, rabbeting, edge-forming, jointing, smoothing edges, mortising, grooving, slotting, spline cutting, tenoning, and shaping irregular edges. Template reproduction of profiled cutouts can also be adapted to some extent. It is impossible to present every conceivable router-table operation. This subject alone could fill a book. Refer to the operating procedures for spindle shapers in a good general woodworking text, since most shaper techniques can be applied to a router table.

This chapter will examine commercially made router tables and also provide some ideas for user-made ones. Some basic operations will be presented, along with some un-

usual ones to show the value and versatility of the router table. One special operation that is not included in this chapter, but that utilizes the router table, is making large, through dovetail-joint cuts. Refer to pages 162 to 167 for this illustrated application.

Commercial router tables Figs. 337 to 339 show tables designed to accept the entire router unit with its base. Some have clamped-on housings that take just the motor unit alone. There is a variety of different router tables available. Most, as shown in the accompanying photos, are relatively small and primarily intended for and limited to the hobbyist woodworker. These are fine, except that they are likely to be quickly outgrown. Light-duty router tables are priced so reasonably that anyone can afford one. However, if they don't meet long-term expectations they can be a distinct waste of money. Be sure to look at the construction features closely. Most are made of moulded plastic or stamped sheet metal. The net weight should give a good clue. Such tables are certainly suitable for some individuals' needs. It just depends on the potential use and the overall service expected from it. For anyone planning on only doing light work on small parts, any of these lightweight router tables should suffice for some time.

Some years ago, several router tables were

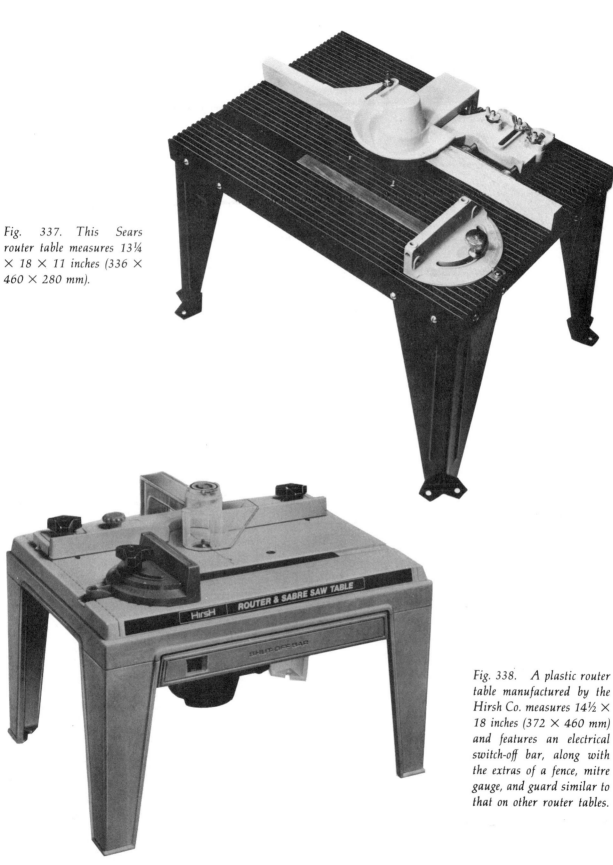

Fig. 337. This Sears router table measures 13¼ × 18 × 11 inches (336 × 460 × 280 mm).

Fig. 338. A plastic router table manufactured by the Hirsh Co. measures 14½ × 18 inches (372 × 460 mm) and features an electrical switch-off bar, along with the extras of a fence, mitre gauge, and guard similar to that on other router tables.

Fig. 339. *Sears die-cast aluminum router table with vacuum hook-up.*

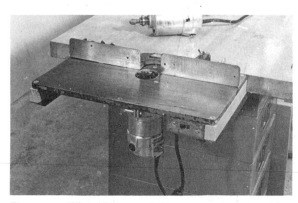

Fig. 340. *The old Porter-Cable router table of cast iron has been in use for 25 years. Notice how it is mounted (with angle iron) flush to the surface at the end of a workbench.*

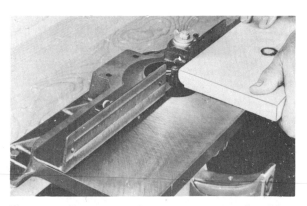

Fig. 341. *Forming an edge on a router table. Both fence halves are aligned as a straightedge.*

available made of heavy cast iron. Two such tables are illustrated in Figs. 340 and 341. Although they have small-sized table surfaces, like the light-duty models available today, they are very durable, sturdy, and just well made. When mounted so the table is flush to another work surface (as when set into a workbench surface), their capacity is thereby increased. Wood board extensions can be

screwed to the fences, increasing their accuracy and capacity.

Years ago, Stanley Power Tools and the Porter-Cable Company manufactured excellent router-shaper tables designed specifically to carry the motor units for their own lines of routers. Stanley's unit mounted into a bench top. Porter-Cable's table (Figs. 340, 342, and 343) could likewise be installed or secured to a specially user-made supporting bench. These old router-shaper table units were per-

Fig. 342. A close-up view showing the adjustable infeed section on the fence.

Fig. 343. The recommended mounting of a router table is flush to another surface. Thus, fence-to-bit capacity can be increased by clamping a straightedge to the adjoining workbench.

fect for serious woodworkers and professionals alike. They had sturdy motor-mounting housings that even adjusted from 0° to 45°. When the tilting feature was used in combination with various bits, a great number of new cutting forms (shapes) resulted. Sadly, these excellent router tables are no longer being manufactured. Stanley Power Tools is currently out of the router business. And Porter-Cable has no future plans to bring back their router table. My search did not locate any products currently available of comparable construction quality.

Fences On the better commercial router tables fences should be of durable construction. This is especially true if the shaper table will be used as a jointer to make accurate, straight line cuts. (See Figs. 344 to 346.) Fences

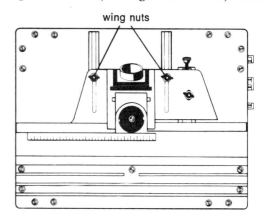

Fig. 344. The entire fence unit is adjusted laterally to accommodate bits of various diameters and to locate surface cuts.

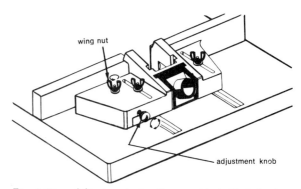

Fig. 345. Adjustments for the movable half of the fence unit.

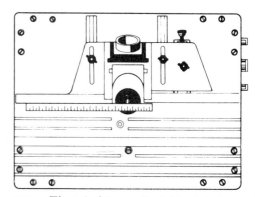

Fig. 346. The infeed fence adjusted for jointing or full-edge shaping. Note closely that the two fences are not aligned as a straightedge.

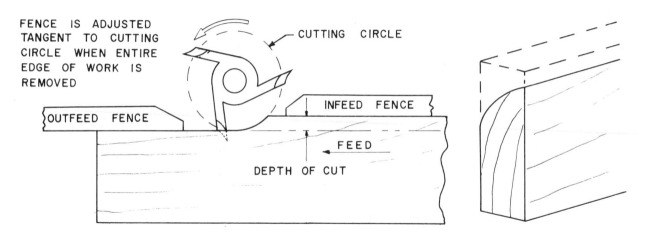

FENCE IS ADJUSTED
TANGENT TO CUTTING
CIRCLE WHEN ENTIRE
EDGE OF WORK IS
REMOVED

CUTTING CIRCLE

OUTFEED FENCE

INFEED FENCE

FEED

DEPTH OF CUT

Fig. 347.   The infeed fence as adjusted for full-edge shaping (as for the piece at the right) or for jointing.

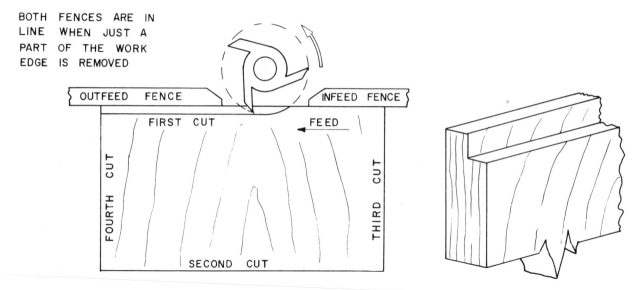

BOTH FENCES ARE IN
LINE WHEN JUST A
PART OF THE WORK
EDGE IS REMOVED

OUTFEED FENCE

INFEED FENCE

FIRST CUT

FEED

FOURTH CUT

THIRD CUT

SECOND CUT

Fig. 348.   The basics of edge forming with the halves of the fence aligned. When cutting all four edges around a board, do the end grains first.

have one independently adjustable or movable section. When adjusted properly the fence functions just like the infeed and outfeed tables on a jointer. (See Fig. 347.) The two sections can be aligned with each other so the fence serves as a work-guiding straightedge. (Refer to Figs. 341 and 348.)

One of the convenient advantages of a router table is that it is just as easy to feed a piece on its flat, larger face (Figs. 341 and 349) as it is to feed it on its edge (Fig. 350). Should extensions or a higher fence be necessary for

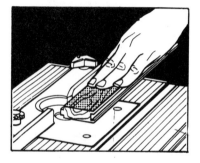

Fig. 349.   Feeding a workpiece flat on its face surface to make a tongue cut using a straight or rabbeting bit.

Fig. 350. Feeding stock on edge in this grooving operation.

special jobs, devise them and clamp them to the worktable. Figs. 351 and 352 illustrate two examples. When routing narrow pieces, as in

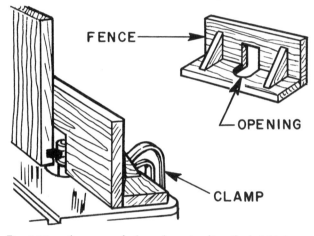

Fig. 351. A user-made fence for extending the height to achieve better support in vertical feeding.

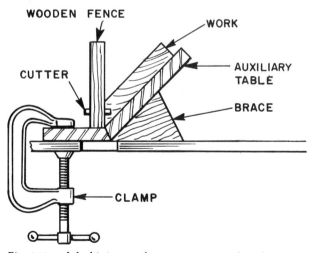

Fig. 352. Machining a spline mitre joint with a slotting cutter. The work is guided by this combination fence and angled work support.

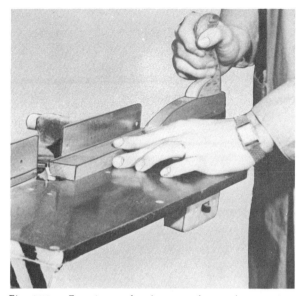

Fig. 353. Exercise good safety procedures when routing narrow and other small pieces.

making strip mouldings, be sure to take appropriate safety measures, as shown in Fig. 353. Some commercial router tables also feature table slots which permit the use of a mitre gauge like those used on a table saw. These are especially useful for dadoing and supporting narrow or small pieces during the cut. (See Fig. 354.)

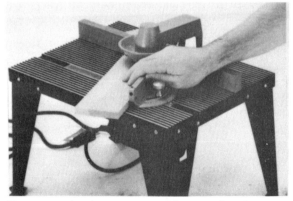

Fig. 354. A mitre gauge provides control and support when routing small pieces.

With piloted or ball-bearing-guided bits, the router table can also be used to shape either straight or irregular work edges. Feeding direction must always be against the rotational direction of the bit, as shown in Fig. 355. (See Fig. 356.)

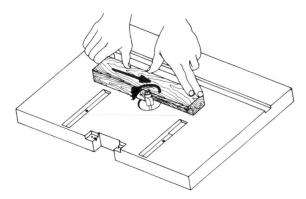

Fig. 355. *Edge shaping with piloted or ball-bearing bits. Note that the feed direction is against the bit rotation.*

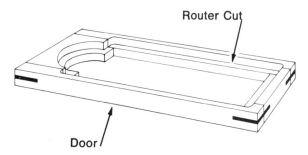

Router Cut

Door

Fig. 356. *The inside rabbet for a panel is cut into this door frame with a piloted rabbeting bit.*

User-made router tables These are designed to be very simple or very elaborate, made to be temporarily or permanently mounted, or made large or small in size. Whatever way one is made, it should be designed and constructed in accordance with individual needs. I know of a custom cabinet shop (with minimal space and equipment) that simply used a piece of plywood temporarily tacked to two sawhorses. The router was bolted through the base and the bit opening was a bored hole through the plywood. A piece of scrap with one straight edge was nailed to the plywood for a guiding fence. The cabinet shop used this fundamental router table for years to make rabbet and round-over cuts for their lipped doors. Fig. 357 gives suggested details for an inexpensive easy-to-make router table that can be mounted in several different ways.

On the other side of the coin, there have been a good number of published articles along with plans for do-it-yourself router tables. Check woodcraft magazines such as *Fine Woodworking, Woodsmith, The Woodworker's Journal,* and *Workbench,* which have featured some pretty fancy router-table plans in the past. Of all those that I've seen and read about, there are only two that I believe are worth considering. First, and obviously, is my own router table, and second, I like the idea of fitting a router into a wing or extension of a table-saw table. The latter idea has a number of distinct advantages. First, if a shop is cramped for space, the table-saw router table adds to the line of stationary equipment without consuming additional floor space. The second advantage of this arrangement is the ability to utilize the fence and mitre gauge in conjunction with the router. The only disadvantage is not being able to leave a routing setup and use the table saw for sawing.

A number of table saws can be fitted with table extensions (and some have extra-long fence rails available) of plywood or similar material. This should make the construction of a router table a distinct possibility and a relatively easy task. Even with extensions or table-saw wings of cast or pressed metal, it can still be done. Simply remove the part in question from the saw, and with router in hand, take it to a machine shop for the boring, tapping, and other necessary metalwork. The cost should be minimal when figured in terms of increased shop versatility from this new, dual-purpose machine.

My own router table is not at all elaborate or even pretty to look at. It was easy and inexpensive to make, but more important, it is very functional for my particular needs. It is sturdy, as I often have large pieces of work that must be cut with substantial fence-to-bit adjustment capacity. I use powerful routers that take bits with ½-inch (12-mm) shanks, to make fast, deep cuts when grooving large timbers and panels. Thus, this table was designed for rugged use, but is still refined enough in its construction to do precise joint-making cuts. My shop is large, but still I did not want to devote an entire 4 × 8-foot (1.2 × 2.4-m) space just to a router table. So I placed it at the

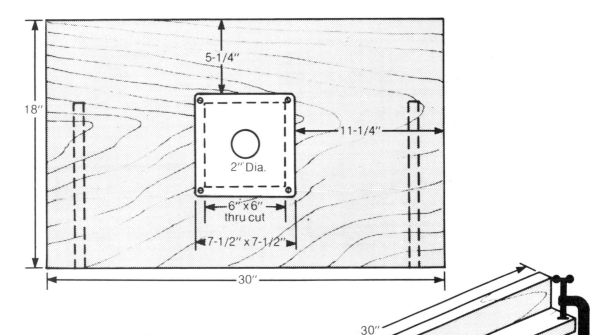

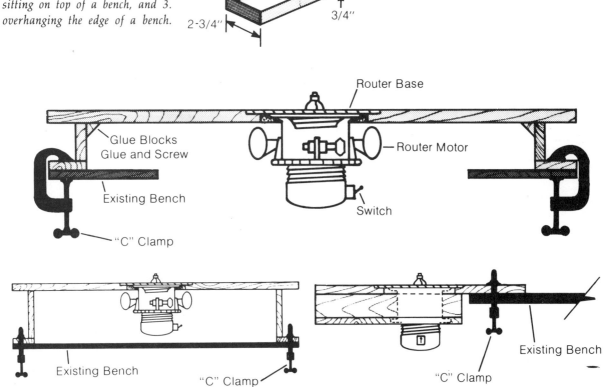

Fig. 357. A simple router table and fence plan provided by Shopsmith, Inc. It is made from ¾-inch (18-mm) plywood with a ⅛-inch (4-mm) thick metal insert. The ways it can be mounted are: 1. bridging two existing benches, 2. sitting on top of a bench, and 3. overhanging the edge of a bench.

18″

5-1/4″

11-1/4″

2″ Dia.

6″ x 6″
thru cut

7-1/2″ x 7-1/2″

30″

30″

2″

Rout for bit clearance

3/4″

2-3/4″

Router Base

Glue Blocks
Glue and Screw

Router Motor

Existing Bench

Switch

"C" Clamp

Existing Bench

"C" Clamp

"C" Clamp

Existing Bench

corner of the 4 × 8-foot (1.2 × 2.4-m) assembly bench, which has a flat and true work surface. Figs. 358 and 359 show two views of the router table. It is made to match the thickness of my assembly workbench. The laminated construction consists of two layers of ¾-inch (18-mm)-dense particle board sandwiched by two pieces of ¼-inch (6-mm) tempered hardboard for balanced buildup.

Fig. 358. *A sturdy, user-made router table is corner-mounted flush to the surface of an assembly bench.*

Fig. 359. *Another view. If more fence-to-bit capacity is needed, a longer straightedge can be clamped directly to the adjoining workbench.*

I purchased a second base for the router and mounted it permanently under the router table. In fact, I purchased only what I needed—no handles, knobs, or sub-base. Then, using the router itself, I very carefully and accurately inlaid a prepared square of ¼-inch (6-mm)-thick tempered aluminum. This was set in exactly flush and was secured with

Fig. 360. *An extra router base (without handles) is mounted directly to a ¼-inch (6-mm) aluminum plate precisely inlaid flush to the top surface.*

flathead machine screws through the laminated table. The extra base is hung with flathead screws directly to the holes in the base which are normally used to attach a sub-base. (See Fig. 360.) All exposed wood and edges were sealed, varnished, and waxed.

My router table is virtually warp-proof and has little movement with changes in humidity. Some user-made router tables are surfaced with plastic laminate (Formica), which is a good idea if it's "balanced," to minimize possible warpage. Any suitable straight material used for a fence is secured to the table with two clamps. If extra capacity is required, clamp a longer straightedge across the assembly bench, thus utilizing the full 4 × 8-foot (1.2 × 2.4-m) bench when necessary. This arrangement is particularly advantageous when it is necessary to support the leading end of long workpieces.

To convert a router table to a vertical-cutting jointer requires only a simply devised jointing fence. This is a non-split or non-adjusting variety, but it works. Shown in Figs. 361 and 362, the jointing fence is simply a straightedge with one half faced with a piece of ¹⁄₁₆-inch (1.5-mm)-thick plastic laminate. It is bonded to the outfeed part of the fence. To use, simply line up this part of the fence so its surface is exactly tangent to the cutting circle of the bit. A straight metal rule works fine. (See Fig. 361.) The fence is clamped in position, and it is checked again after clamping.

Fig. 361. *A jointing fence is simply a straight-edged, 2-inch (24-mm) board with ¹⁄₁₆-inch (1.5-mm) plastic laminate bonded to the outfeed half. Shown here is a custom relief-ground, large-diameter, spiral-milling cutter which gives a smooth cut.*

Fig. 362. *The jointing fence in use.*

With this basic set up every jointing cut will be exactly ¹⁄₁₆ inch (1.5 mm) in depth, which is suitable for most jobs. (See Fig. 362.)

By now the great potential of a good router table should be pretty clear. For a number of routing jobs, it is easier and faster to set up and do the job on the router table than to use the router in its usual portable operation. Cutting stopped dadoes and grooves on the router table are good examples.

The only problem in doing them on the router table is that the work must be done blind—meaning you don't see the cut being made because it's done from the underside with the work fed to the bit upside down. One of the best and most convenient jobs to do with the router table is cutting open mortises, such as would be cut on a furniture leg to receive the tenons of the horizontal apron pieces. The primary steps of the procedure are

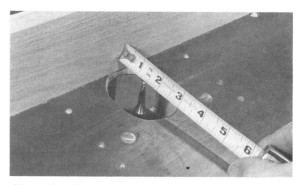

Fig. 363. *One of the first steps in making a stopped slot or open mortise is to set the fence to the bit.*

Fig. 364. *Transfer a registration mark from the infeed side of the bit to the fence and then extend it vertically on the fence beyond the thickness of the material to be cut.*

illustrated in Figs. 363 to 366. First the fence and depth of cut must be adjusted or set. A registration pencil line must be transferred to the fence, to indicate later where to stop the feed. A mark indicating where the cut is to end will need to be laid out, and transferred square to the top of the workpiece. (See Fig. 365.)

Fig. 365. *A line transferred to the top of the workpiece indicates where the feed must stop to end the cut. This is when the registration mark on the fence and the mark on the work meet.*

Fig. 366. *Completed cuts of open mortises or stopped grooves.*

Fig. 369. *The work is advanced until the second pair of reference marks meet, indicating the end of the cut, as shown here.*

To make totally blind cuts (those that neither begin nor exit at an edge or end), the basic procedure described above can be applied with just one or two additional steps. First, two registration or reference marks must be drawn on the fence. These lines are equal to the cutting diameter of the bit. Incidentally, the bit must be an end-cutting type. (See Fig. 367.) Two lines must now be transferred square to the top of the work, one to indicate the start and the other to indicate the end of the cut. The workpiece must be lowered onto a revolving bit (Fig. 368) and then advanced, as in Fig. 369.

With fairly large workpieces, this is not especially dangerous. However, the smaller the work, the more hazardous this becomes. Exercise judgment. Stop blocks can be clamped to the fence in appropriate locations. One stop block for the start of the cut—to keep the work from kicking back—is recommended, especially when machining small pieces. Another stop block can be secured to the outfeed side of the fence so that there's no possibility of inadvertently overfeeding and going beyond the length of the desired cut. The use of stop blocks is recommended, especially when doing monotonous production jobs. (See Figs. 370 and 371.)

Fig. 367. *For completely blind slotting, grooving, or mortise cuts, two lines must be drawn on the fence equal to the cutting diameter of the bit.*

Fig. 370. *Optional use of a stop block. As shown here, it is located to stop the cut. A stop can similarly be located to support work for starting the cut. Stops are recommended for production jobs.*

Fig. 368 (left). *Starting position for making the blind cut. Here the forward marks are aligned as the work is held above the bit and against the fence. The work is then carefully lowered onto the revolving bit.*

Fig. 371.   *A completed stopped groove or blind mortise cut.*

Round tenoning and shaping   On the router table round tenoning and shaping are novel, but often very useful, operations. Some typical work samples are shown in Fig. 372. All the cuts illustrated were made with the aid of a simple v-block setup, as shown in Fig. 373. This fixture consists of a v-block (with a bored hole for the bit), glue, or a screw fastened to a

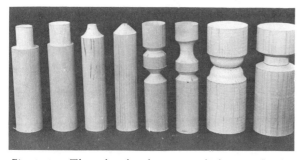

Fig. 372.   *These dowel ends were not lathe-turned. They were machined on a router table. The round tenons are shown at the left. The other decorative cuts have good applications for wood toys and chess sets.*

Fig. 373.   *The fixture for round tenoning and decorative dowel shaping is simply a V-block with a bored hole. A fence or other stop limits the length of the tenon or it locates decorative cuts.*

suitable sheet of ⅛-inch (3-mm)-thick hardboard. This fixture is clamped to the router table. An independent fence is set, clamped, and used as a stop to limit the length of the tenon (Fig. 374), or to locate other cuts. Piloted bits and ball-bearing-guided bits can be used to cut decorative dowel ends, as shown in Figs. 375 and 376.

Fig. 374.   *A close-up look at the round tenoning setup. Note how the fence acts as a stop.*

Fig. 375.   *Chamfering a dowel end with a ball-bearing guided bit.*

Fig. 376.   *A ball-bearing guided cove bit makes this decorative cut.*

To form the edges of circular-cut discs and for similar work with the router, a simple board fence with a v-cut in it will handle the job nicely. (See Fig. 377.) This trick allows the use of any of pilotless bits for edging round lamp bases and tabletops with the router table. This technique is much faster than setting up the router for portable use, plus, with this technique, it isn't necessary to clamp the piece down.

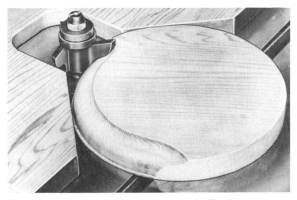

Fig. 377. *Although this shows a spindle shaper operation, the same setup can be utilized on the router table for circular edge-forming with pilotless bits.*

The Sears Edge Crafter Fig. 378 shows a tool that extends the capabilities of their router table. However, with some slight modifica-

tion, it could be adapted to work on other router tables and user-made versions. The Edge Crafter makes it possible to rout pie-crust-edged tabletops and round or oval picture frames with a wide variety of decorative edges on projects up to 30 inches (760 mm) in diameter. (See Figs. 379 and 380.) In operation, the work is cut in an upside-down posi-

Fig. 379 (above). *A completed table with its top having inside and outside scalloped or contoured edges machined on the Edge Crafter.*

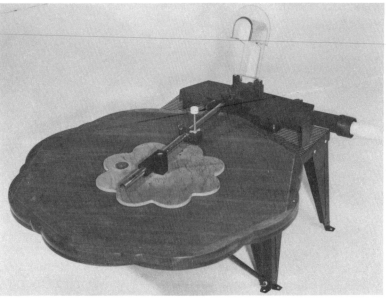

Fig. 378 (left). *The Sears Edge Crafter routing the inside of a raised table edge. Note the top is upside down and the template is fastened to the work.*

Fig. 380. The inside and outside profiles of this oval mirror frame were cut with the Edge Crafter.

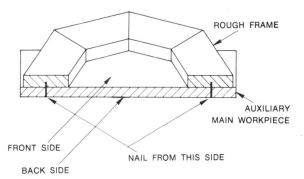

ROUGH FRAME

AUXILIARY
MAIN WORKPIECE

FRONT SIDE

BACK SIDE

NAIL FROM THIS SIDE

Fig. 382. Built-up segmented edges. If a frame, the rough frame is nailed to a temporary work panel for routing as in the machining of table edges.

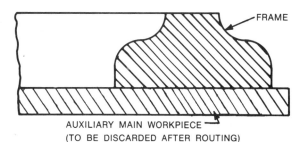

FRAME

AUXILIARY MAIN WORKPIECE
(TO BE DISCARDED AFTER ROUTING)

Fig. 383. Picture and mirror frames are routed nailed to an auxiliary workpiece, such as ¼- or ⅜-inch (6- or 8-mm) plywood.

tion. The work is appropriately guided in or out with an overarm slide as the work is rotated into the cutting bit. A roller assembly bears against a work-mounted template (pattern). This traces and simultaneously controls the direction of cut in accordance with the contoured edge of the template.

The Edge Crafter is used to make tabletops with raised and sculpted edges or borders. The border to be routed is normally built-up, solid-wood construction consisting of segmented blocks glued around the perimeter of the workpiece. This is shown in Figs. 381 and

The variety of shapes that can be cut on inside and outside profiles is only restricted by the bit-cutting shapes available and the range of variable vertical settings they are used at. (See Fig. 384.)

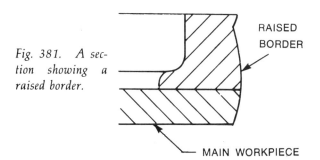

RAISED
BORDER

Fig. 381. A section showing a raised border.

MAIN WORKPIECE

382. When making an oval or round frame (such as a mirror or picture frame), glue it together with splined or dowelled segments. Then after the glue has cured, the rough-sized, assembled frame is tacked/nailed to an auxiliary piece of plywood for the routing operation on the Edge Crafter. After routing, this auxiliary piece of plywood is discarded. (See Fig. 383.)

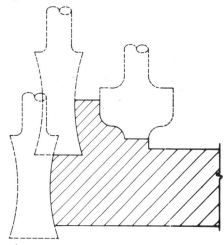

Fig. 384. The number of shapes possible on the inside and outside of the raised edge is limited only by the cutting profiles of the bits available and their positions of vertical adjustment.

149

11
Router Dovetailing

Fig. 385. This through dovetail joint, in ¾-inch (18-mm) stock, is a router-assisted, hand-fitted joint made without any commercial fixturing devices.

Sharply executed and perfectly fitting dovetail joints are unquestionably the hallmark of high-level craftsmanship. (See Fig. 385.) Dovetail joints attract the eye of everyone. Woodworkers particularly scrutinize the quality of a joint and pass judgment on the maker's expertise and woodworking capabilities. This chapter will help you get to the top of the heap. With a little practice and assistance from new, better cutting, and larger bits, along with some excellent, easy-to-use jigs and fixtures, it's easy to become a dovetailing expert.

In addition to making the two popular dovetail joints (with commercial fixturing), this chapter will cover some other applications for basic dovetail cuts, and will finish up with an easy, step-by-step procedure for making router-assisted, hand-fitted, through dovetail joints all without the use of any commercial fixturing devices. (See Fig. 385.)

Bits for dovetailing As discussed in Chapter 2, bits come in a variety of sizes. When ordering bits, specify the shank size, the angle desired (14° and 15° are common), the largest cutting diameter, the cutting height, and HSS or carbide-tipped. Fig. 386 shows a comparison of bit sizes available. They range from ⁵⁄₁₆–1¼-inch (8–31-mm) cutting diameter and ¼–⅞-inch (6–21-mm) cutting height. For a

Fig. 386. *Comparative sizes of dovetail bits. The smaller one was used to cut the tails on the right. The large one was used to cut the tails for the joint in Fig. 385.*

broad range of dovetailing, it is necessary to have at least two sizes of bits. I suggest getting one of the largest available. Have a smaller one for cutting thinner materials and the big one for the heavier, massive dovetail-joint cuts. It is difficult to recommend exact sizes or other bit specifications because for bits used with commercial fixtures, the router manufacturer recommends the bit needed. Big bits do require routers with ½-inch (12-mm) collets.

Before getting into routing the through and half-blind dovetails (the most popular ones), here, briefly, are some other applications of basic router dovetailing:

Dovetailed dadoes and grooves Using the router is the only practical way to make long, straight-line dovetail cuts in any direction. Such cuts, with matching dovetailed tongues, are used for panel joints in fine furniture and cabinetry. It is relatively easy to figure out how to cut them. Any of the router guiding methods discussed in previous chapters can be used: employing straightedges, T-squares, frame guides, or fence guides on a router table.

The open-ended mortises, or slots in leg and rail construction (for tables, when cut with a dovetail bit and fitted with matched dovetails on the tenons), make very strong joints. Joints of this type are used a good deal for furniture kits, for some "knocked-down" furniture, and in the construction of wooden household accessories. All such joints are easiest to make on the router table. However,

Fig. 387. *Making the female dovetail cut. Note the blocks clamped to each side to give support to the router base.*

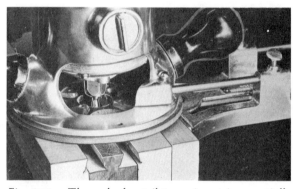

Fig. 388. *The male dovetail tenon is cut in essentially the same way.*

Figs. 387 and 388 show how male and female dovetail cuts are made using the portable router with a straight guide. Fig. 389 shows another application of a dovetail joint used on a signpost. The female cut is made with the portable router and the arm (male cut) is sawed to fit.

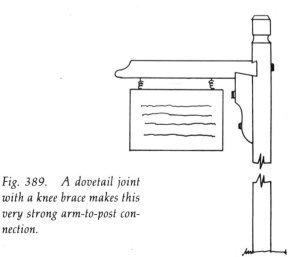

Fig. 389. *A dovetail joint with a knee brace makes this very strong arm-to-post connection.*

Sliding dovetails These have a number of applications of interest to the creative wood-worker. Obviously, the fit of the matching members is less exact with sufficient clearance intentionally provided to effect smooth movement of the mating parts. A few ideas for sliding dovetails include: box covers (Fig. 390), drawer slides and glides, adjustable shelving, adjustable track lighting, adjustable book and record holders, and various adjustable tooling and work-guiding fixtures used for woodworking.

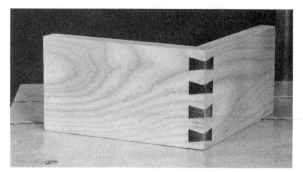

Fig. 391.   *The dovetail-keyed mitre joint.*

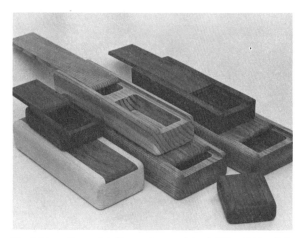

Fig. 390.   *Boxes totally router machined. The sliding lids are dovetail cuts made on the router table. Openings were cut with saddle templates (page 76) and corners were rounded over with a piloted bit.*

The dovetail-keyed mitre joint Fig. 391 shows a rather unusual joint that is being seen a lot. This dovetailing simultaneously provides a good way to decorate, strengthen, and add creative spice to the conventional edge mitre joint. This joint is especially advantageous when using plywoods and other veneer-faced panel materials. Conventional through dovetails are seldom used on projects made of plywood or similar materials. First, cut and glue the mitre joint in the usual manner and allow the glue to dry. There are several ways to rout the dovetail key cuts across the assembled joint. You can devise a slotted guide with a v-block fixture that cradles the joint to support and guide the portable router. Another way is to make the key cuts on the

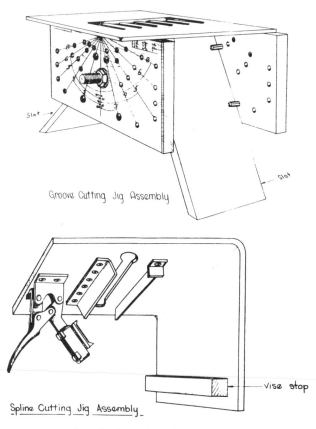

Groove Cutting Jig Assembly

Spline Cutting Jig Assembly

Fig. 392.   *Joseph Vernon's tooling for routing the dovetail-keyed mitre joint. Above: the jig for routing the key slots will take boards up to 9 inches (225 mm) wide. Below: the jig for router-machining the key inserts.*

router table. Use the fence to guide the work while it is held in a supporting fixture.

Joseph Vernon of Tazewell, Virginia, manufactures a template-jig assembly designed specifically for making the dovetail-keyed mitre joint. Shown in Fig. 392, this tooling is adjustable, permitting pieces to be joined at any of five angles relative to the component joints of triangles, squares (Fig. 393), pentagons, hexagons, and octagons (Fig. 394). The Vernon kit even comes with a jig for router-machining the wood keys, which otherwise would be bevel-ripped on the table saw.

Fig. 393. *Keys are solid wood of contrasting color, cut slightly longer, glued in, and sanded flush.*

Fig. 394. *A dovetail-keyed joint in an octagonal corner assembly.*

Commercial dovetailing jigs and fixtures These are available to make the two most popular dovetail joints (half-blind and through). Most come with understandable instruction manuals, but sometimes they assume that you know all the dovetailing jargon. For the beginner, I will identify joints and their component parts. Terminology will be kept as simple as possible. Here and in the remaining sections of this chapter I will deal only with two kinds of dovetail joints, the through dovetail, which is illustrated in Figs. 385, 386, and 395, and the half-blind dovetail, which is illustrated in Fig. 396.

Fig. 395. *Through dovetails. Left: the assembled joint has been rounded over.*

Fig. 396. *Half-blind dovetails are cut to make flush (left) and lipped (right) drawers with a commercial finger template fixture.*

The two terms used to identify the different parts (cuts) of a dovetail joint are a little more difficult to keep straight. These are *tails* and *pins*. The tails are cut on the piece shown at the right in Fig. 386. A close observation of a dovetail joint shows that the tails taper with the face grain. The pins are shown at the left in Fig. 386. A close observation reveals that the pins taper across the end grain.

Can you identify the tails and pins in the joints shown in Figs. 395 and 396?

Fixture-routing half-blind dovetails Commercial dovetailing fixtures for cutting the half-blind dovetails have been around for several decades. They are not new ideas, but those currently on the market are somewhat improved over their earlier counterparts. So, anyone who tried one some time ago and wasn't satisfied may find the end results produced on one of the new and better ones a pleasant surprise. Set up properly, it's possible to cut dovetails all day, making a complete joint every couple of minutes. Setting up the fixtures for dovetailing does require considerable time, patience, and some trial-and-error work to get the combinations of bit depth, shims, stops, template location, and similar adjustments all just right.

The best-known companies providing half-blind template fixtures include Black & Decker, Bosch, Sears, and Porter-Cable. Recent shop tests indicate that they all cut good dovetails, but some require substantially more setup time than others. Prices vary, as do construction features and size capacities. The basic sizes in board-width capacities range from 8 inches (205 mm) to 16 inches (410 mm) (the largest available). Don't buy the smallest or cheapest.

Most router-dovetailing fixtures for making half-blind dovetails come with a standard-plastic finger template (Figs. 397 and 398) designed to machine ½-inch (12-mm) dovetails, the largest size that can be cut. These are used to cut dovetails in stock from ⁷⁄₁₆–1 inch (11–24 mm) thick. Also be sure to have a router-base-mounted template guide (bush-

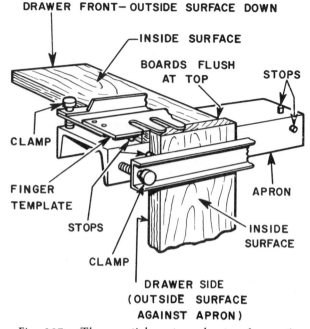

Fig. 397. *The essential parts and setup for routing half-blind dovetails. Note that the pieces are routed with their inside surfaces facing out.*

Fig. 398. *Routing a test piece. A template guide (bushing) mounted to the router base guides the router in and out of the template to effect the cut.*

ing) that has a ⁷⁄₁₆-inch (11-mm) outside diameter and a ½-inch (12-mm) dovetail bit with a ¼-inch (6-mm) shank. This setup is used to cut dovetails in the most popular sizes of drawers for furniture and cabinets. (See Figs. 399 and 400.) There are a good number of adjustments that are necessary to get everything working just right. Refer to the owner's manual for specific instructions. For example, various guide pins have to be set when changing from flush to lip-type drawer dovetailing. If fits are too loose the bit needs to be raised; if

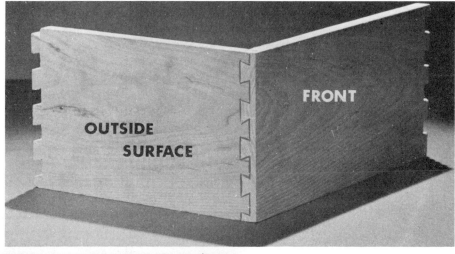

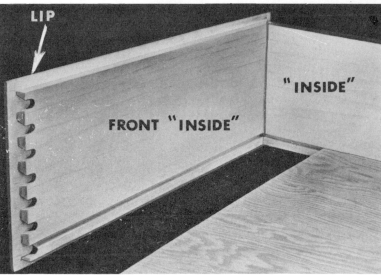

Fig. 399. Two pieces assembled for a drawer with a flush-type front.

Fig. 400. Details showing a lipped drawer front. Note the dovetail pins cut into the front.

Fig 401 (below). A close-up of the cutting operation.

too tight, the bit should be lowered. The finger template is also adjustable in or out, to correct cuts that are too shallow or too deep.

Incidentally, it's possible to purchase an optional, second interchangeable finger template for routing smaller, ¼-inch (6-mm) dovetails in thinner stock (⁵⁄₁₆–⅝-inch [8–16-mm] thick). This is used with a router-base-mounted template guide (bushing) that has a ⁵⁄₁₆-inch (8-mm) outside diameter and is used with a ¼-inch (6-mm) dovetail bit.

The really neat feature of these fixtures is that once set up and adjusted properly, both the pins and tails of the joint are machined at the same time. Both members of the joint are clamped together on the fixture. The router is

carefully moved in a left-to-right direction in and out, between and along the fingers of the template (Fig. 401), cutting the pins and tails simultaneously in one operation.

Fig. 402. Carefully following the template fingers feeding left to right and then back again (right to left, here) assures that all cuts are clean and complete.

Most owners' manuals suggest that a return cut be made by following the template fingers a second time (Fig. 402), feeding in the opposite (returning) direction to assure that all areas are cut cleanly. One special word of caution (also stressed in the owners' manual): It is so easy to inadvertently lift the router when completing a cut, because this is a normal router movement in many other router operations. *Don't* do it in dovetail routing with fixture templates, because it's easy to strike the finger template with the rotating bit and completely ruin it. The router must be slid away in a perfectly level and horizontal direction. It's best to shut down the router, wait for the bit to stop revolving, and then slide the router off the template without any lifting.

In spite of all the fussing associated with using these fixtures, the end results are well worth the trouble. The finished dovetails will fit absolutely perfectly, and they are strong, enduring, and professional-looking joints. Best of all, they can be quickly executed when all the little bugs are worked out.

Commercial devices for through dovetailing

These are the newest types of accessories available. They are rapidly gaining acceptance by woodworkers at all levels because they are durable and well engineered. Most importantly, they make routing functional and decorative dovetails a snap. Yes, there are some preliminary adjustments necessary in order to get the fits just right. However, these devices for making the through type of dovetail joints are much easier to set up than are the jigs for half-blind dovetailing discussed previously. In fact, after making several practice cuts it's easy to know all the little shifts or adjustments that are necessary to get perfect cuts every time.

Once the jigs are set up, the routing and assembly of through dovetails is a sheer delight. Everything goes smoothly in cutting and fitting. Cost is the only drawback. To get into this involves a fairly sizable investment depending upon the type of device and size capacity. However, anyone considering production or working in production may well find these devices cost-effective when compared to hand cutting or using user-made templates. The two devices getting good reviews today are the Leigh dovetail jigs and the Keller large dovetail templates.

The Leigh dovetail jigs

Figs. 403 and 404 show the invention of Ken Grisley, an English boat builder. Manufactured in Canada by Leigh Industries Ltd., this jig is available from a host of dealers and mail-order suppliers in Canada and the United States. The first model of the Leigh jigs has a board-width capacity of 12 inches (300 mm), but the manufacturer has recently developed a larger unit providing the ability to cut dovetails along the ends of stock up to 24 inches (600 mm) in width.

The Leigh jigs are the only adjustable devices currently available that allow for variable spacing of the pins and tails along the ends of workpieces in any width that can be clamped in the jig. (See Fig. 405.) Essentially the jig consists of two sets of template fingers separated by a slide bar. (See Fig. 404.) In actuality, the fingers are one-piece adjustable parts that extend from one side to the other under the removable top slide bar. One end of the fingers is pointed with an angular face, and the other end is straight with a square guiding face. (See Fig. 406.)

Fig. 403.　An overall view showing the Leigh jig in use. Both tail and pin pieces are cut while clamped vertically in the jig. The pins are cut under the pointed fingers, shown on this side of the slide bar. The operator is cutting the tails of a workpiece clamped under the straight fingers.

Fig. 404.　A top view showing the fingers covered by the guide bar. Though this device looks complicated, it is very easy to set up and use. To make fits tighter or looser, paper shims are used to shift the stock in or out on the pin-cutting side.

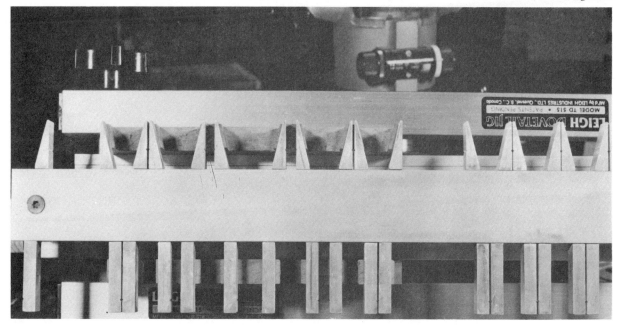

The cutting bit—straight for the pins, dovetail for the tails—with a router-base-mounted template guide is used to follow along, in, and out of the fingers. The workpieces are both cut while held in vertical positions, one clamped to each side of the jig. Both pieces are not cut together simultaneously as they are in jigs for half-blind dovetailing. One pass must be made with the router (carrying a dovetail bit), to cut the tails as shown in Fig. 407. Another router setup and separate pass must be

Fig. 405. Variable spaced dovetails as shown here are cut with the Leigh jig. The tails are at the right, and pins are cut in the piece at the left.

Fig. 406. The Leigh jig showing its basic parts. The fingers are independently adjustable by removing the top slide bar. When a finger is moved, the tail and pin cuts are simultaneously relocated and remain aligned to each other.

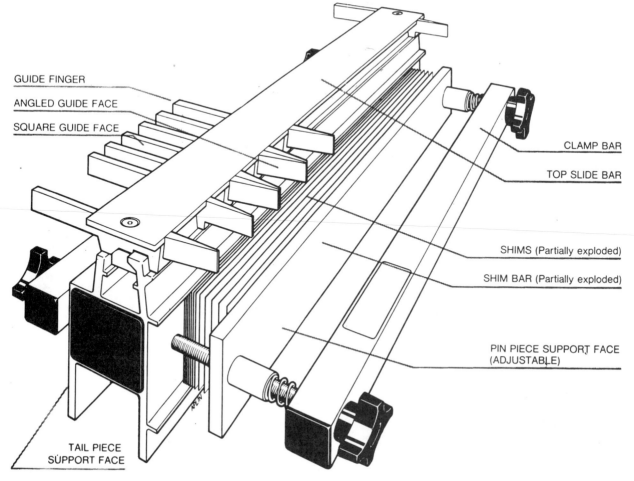

GUIDE FINGER

ANGLED GUIDE FACE

SQUARE GUIDE FACE

CLAMP BAR

TOP SLIDE BAR

SHIMS (Partially exploded)

SHIM BAR (Partially exploded)

PIN PIECE SUPPORT FACE (ADJUSTABLE)

TAIL PIECE SUPPORT FACE

Fig. 407. *Cutting the tails. The template guide follows the straight fingers. Note here how the carbide-tipped bit has cut cleanly through a hard knot.*

made using a straight cutting bit, to cut the pins as shown in Fig. 408. Having two routers makes the job much more convenient—especially for small production runs. (See Fig. 409.) Set one router up for tail cutting and another for routing the pins.

Fig. 408. *Cutting the pins in ½-inch (12-mm) stock. Note how the template guide follows the pointed fingers.*

Fig. 409. *Some of the author's small boxes and tissue holders, all made of ½-inch (12-mm) stock with through dovetails cut on the Leigh jig.*

I've found that my small trimming router will even handle work up to ½ inch (12 mm) thick, thus making cuts to ½ inch (12 mm) in depth. (See Fig. 408.) The feed needs to be a little slower, of course, but cutting the pin end grains in dovetailing does not require as much horsepower as is needed for routing into face grains. Obviously, when using just one router all cuts for either the pins or tails would be cut first, and then the router changed over to cut the other part. Once the jig is set, it makes no difference if the pins or the tails are cut first.

Fourteen-degree carbide-tipped dovetail router bits are specified for use with the Leigh jig. Their 12-inch (300-mm) model will cut tails in stock up to 1 inch (24 mm) thick, but pin cuts are limited to stock ½ inch (12 mm) in thickness. The new 24-inch (600-mm) model will cut tails in stock up to 1 inch (24 mm) in thickness and pins in stock up to ¾ inch (18 mm) in thickness.

Bits and template-guide specifications are included in the instructions accompanying the Leigh jig. The 24-inch (600-mm) model comes with the appropriate tail-cutting bit, which is a ¾-inch (18-mm), 14°, two-flute, carbide-tipped dovetail bit. Both models require a user-made beam or support for mounting the jig. With one made as shown in Fig. 410, it's possible to mount the total assembly sturdily in a bench vise for dovetailing and then conveniently remove it for safe storage when not in use.

Fig. 410.   The Leigh jig vise mounted for portability.

The Keller large dovetail templates   Fig. 411 shows another system for through dovetailing in cabinet and furniture construction. Designed, manufactured, and distributed by David A. Keller of Bolinas, California, these dovetail templates, with special ½-inch (12-mm) shank ball-bearing-guided bits (Fig. 412), will cut standard, true through dovetails in stock up to ⅞ inch (21 mm) in thickness. The initial setup is relatively easy, and tightness of fit can be controlled by positioning the templates appropriately on mounting blocks (user-provided). (See Figs. 413 and 414.) Keller's template set is designed to handle stock up to ⅞ inches (21 mm) in thickness, but with a change to the mounting blocks, pins can be cut into stock 1¼ inches (31 mm) thick.

The standard joint produced is shown in Fig. 415. This has 1-inch-wide (24-mm-wide) pins uniformly spaced on 3-inch (76-mm) centers. Optional variable spacing can be achieved by shifting the templates after each cut, but keeping the alignment is a little tricky. The templates are big enough to handle almost any joint width. They, will handle stock up to 36 inches (900 mm) wide at one setting, but this capacity can even be increased infinitely by shifting the templates along the work. Figs. 416 and 417 show "action" close-ups of making the tail and pin cuts respectively.

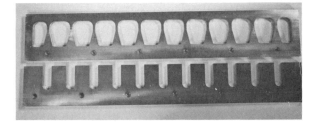

Fig. 411. The Keller large dovetail templates are made of ½-inch (12-mm) aluminum plate. With these templates, it is possible to make through dovetail joints in pieces up to 36 inches (900 mm) wide at one setting.

Fig. 412. The shank-mounted ball-bearing bits used with the Keller templates. Left: a ¾ × 1-inch (18 × 24-mm) diameter-cutting-length straight bit for cutting the pins. Right: a 14° × ⅞-inch (22-mm) cutting-height dovetail bit used for cutting the tails.

Fig. 413. The Keller template in use for tail routing. Note that the template is screwed to a user-provided heavy mounting block which in turn is clamped to the workpiece.

Fig. 415. Standard through dovetails cut with the Keller templates have pins 1 inch (24 mm) wide spaced 3 inches (36 mm) apart.

Fig. 416. Cutting the tails with the Keller template. Notice that the router is not fitted with a base-mounted template guide. Instead, the router is controlled by the bearing mounted on the bit's shank.

Fig. 417. A straight cutting bit is similarly guided along the Keller template with the shank-mounted ball bearing to produce the tails.

Fig. 414 (left). The pin-routing template in use.

Router-assisted hand-fitted dovetails I have developed a system for jobs requiring through dovetails. The procedures given here can be applied to making dovetails in stock of any thickness with any pin and tail spacing. This procedure, by and large, enables anyone to design and produce perfect pin and tail cuts on workpieces, for professional-looking joints of any width. The resulting joints will be so good they will appear to be made with the expensive jigs described earlier. The major advantage of this process is that the dovetails are made without using chisels. Especially in soft woods, these are difficult to use with proficiency. Some samples of these router-assisted, hand-fitted dovetail joints are shown in Figs. 385, 395, and 418.

Fig. 418. *A contemporary stool with router-assisted, hand-fit through dovetails. The dimensions are 8½ inches (212 mm) wide, 15 inches (375 mm) long and 7½ inches (190 mm) high with a 1½ × 4½-inch (37 × 112-mm) hand slot.*

Essentially the process involves a minimum of handwork coupled with a combination of router-table and controlled freehand-routing techniques. Although the number of detailed step-by-step photos included here describing the total procedure may appear at first to make this look like a long, involved, tedious technique, it really isn't. After making the necessary fixturing and two or three practice joints, it's easy to zip through the job quite rapidly from there on.

The illustrations that follow show large dovetails being cut in ¾-inch (18-mm) stock using a large bit with a ⅞-inch (21-mm) cutting height capacity. This bit can be used to cut various through dovetails in stock from ½–⅞ inch (12–21 mm) thick. The process can be applied exactly the same way with smaller bits intended for dovetailing thinner stock. The cutting height of the dovetail bit determines the maximum thickness of stock that can be cut.

First, design and lay out the tails of the joint directly onto one piece of work. Simply make a paper or template pattern of a pin and use it to draw the tails wherever desired (Fig. 419). The joint should be laid out so the spacing between the tails is at least ⅛ inch (4 mm)

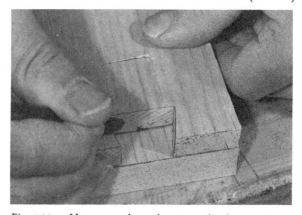

Fig. 419. *Here a wood template is used to lay out the pin openings on the tail piece.*

wider than the cutting diameter of the dovetail bit. Tails will be cut on the router table. With the dovetail bit installed, set the cutting depth exactly equal to the thickness of the pin workpiece, as shown in Fig. 420. All the tail cuts will be made first, before cutting any pins.

Set (clamp) the fence (Figs. 421 and 422), to locate the first cut so it is made approximately the desired distance from the edge of the workpiece as initially designed and laid out. Super accuracy in the fence location is not critical. As many identical pieces as can be conveniently clamped together should be cut at the same time. This operation requires a support fixture similar to the one shown in

Fig. 420. *In the router table, the bit is set to equal the stock thickness.*

Fig. 421. *Set the fence approximately to the distance desired for the first cut.*

Fig. 422. *A straightedge can be clamped to increase the fence-to-bit capacity, if needed.*

Figs. 423 and 424. Notice in Fig. 423 that an auxiliary backup board is inserted between the workpieces and the support fixture. This extra backup eliminates any splintering or tearing as the bit exits from the last cut.

Fig. 423. *Making the first cuts in the tail pieces. The workpieces are supported vertically on a user-made sliding fixture and guided against the fence. The board between the two workpieces and the support is not part of a joint. These back-up pieces are used to eliminate splintering as the bit exits from the cut pieces.*

Fig. 424. *Dimensions for the support fixture are as follows: Base is 11 × 13½ inches (275 × 340 mm), vertical piece is 11 × 6¼ inches (275 × 155 mm), and the two runners are 1 × 1¼ × 12¼ inches (25 × 31 × 306 mm) set in 1¼ inches (31 mm) from each edge. These sizes are only suggestions. Check or change them to accommodate individual needs.*

Complete the routing of all of the tail pieces on the router table, as shown in Fig. 425. Now all the tails are cut and should be identical in depth. Absolutely identical tails are not critical. Thus, tails can be large (wide) or small (narrow) as desired.

Fig. 425.   Make all the tail cuts on the router table.

Fig. 426.   Use a very sharp pencil and lay out the pin cuts using the tail piece as a pattern.

Next saw-cut the verticals for the pins. The location for each vertical saw-cut will need to be marked onto the work, as shown in Fig. 426. Cutting the tails is tricky, but certainly not a difficult step. There will be less confusion during cutting if "hash marks" are used to identify the waste areas where stock must be removed. (See Fig. 427.) A simple but carefully made guide block will help with sawing the pin verticals. (See Figs. 428 and 429.) It's

Fig. 427.   Hash marking clarifies which areas need to be cut away. Note that the layout is done only on the end grain.

Fig. 428.   In addition to the router, here is what's needed. The wood blocks are used to guide the handsaw when making the sizing cuts in the pins.

Fig. 429.   Block clamped to the work guides the dovetail saw. Accuracy when making the block is critical. It is cut to the same angle as the dovetail bit used. Clamp the block so it just covers the layout line.

best to make the guide blocks with a table saw for absolute accuracy. The angle on the block must be exactly equal to the angle cut by the dovetail bit.

The guide block can also be made so it functions as a depth stop; that is, so the distance from the work surface to its upper surface is such that the back reinforcement of the saw will strike it when the desired depth is reached. If made properly, no layout line to indicate the depth or termination point of the cuts will be needed. To assure that joint fits will neither be too tight nor too loose when assembled, the block is precisely clamped to the work so it just covers the layout line. (See Fig. 429.) The verticals are now cut with a

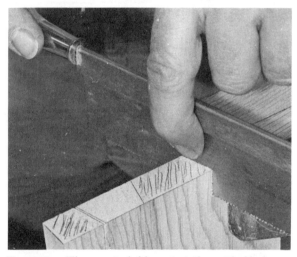

Fig. 430. *The saw is held against the guide block, assuring true vertical cuts. The guide block can also function as a depth stop, eliminating the need for layout lines.*

dovetail or other fine-toothed saw, as shown in Fig. 430. If the guide block is made so it is not of a stop-block type, use a soft-tipped pen line marked on the saw blade to indicate approximately where the cut should stop. The saw cuts do not need to be cut precisely to finished depths. In fact, it's best to stop these cuts about ⅛ inch (4 mm) short of full depth.

The next step is to clean most of the waste from between the pins and make a true and finished bottoming cut. Both of these jobs can be handled simultaneously with the portable router and a straight bit. Install the straight cutting bit and adjust the depth of cut so it equals the thickness of a previously made tail-cut member. (See Fig. 431.) Two or more pieces can be clamped together for the pin-

Fig. 431. *Adjusting the bit for routing the pins.*

Fig. 432. *Two pin pieces (with hand-sawed kerfs) held together in a vise. An extra board is clamped flush to provide additional support for the router.*

routing operation. Fig. 432 shows two pieces held together in a vise. An extra square and flat-edged board should be clamped flush to the work surfaces to help support the router base. Remove the waste material between the saw kerfs using freehand-routing techniques. Stay safely away from the pin stock. If it feels more comfortable, cut only to within ⅛ inch (4 mm) or 1/16 inch (2 mm) of the pin's saw kerfs. (See Figs. 433 to 435.)

Fig. 433. One view of freehanding the waste away from between the pins.

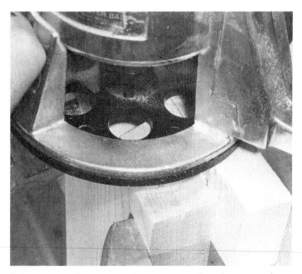

Fig. 434. The operator's view of freehand routing dovetail pins.

Fig. 436 shows how to use a sharp knife to remove any remaining waste. With some practice using the router, it is possible to free-hand-rout into the kerf and still exercise sufficient router control so the bit doesn't touch the sawed surfaces of the pins. *Voilà!* Make a test fit of the mating joint pieces, as shown in Fig. 437. They should require a little extra force to get started. If necessary (but it shouldn't be), trim a pin or two as needed with a chisel. When all signs are go, apply

Fig. 436. One or two quick slicing strokes with a sharp knife will clean up the cuts. Chiselling should not be necessary.

Fig. 437. A little force should be needed to fit the joint together.

Fig. 435 (left). The freehand waste removal completed. Note that cuts must be made into the support piece and that the cuts are made only fairly close to the pins.

some glue and drive the joint home with a hammer and scrap block, as shown in Fig. 438. Clamping is not required if the joint is precisely cut.

Fig. 438.   Driving the joint home.

Boxes (Fig. 439), cases, and similar projects can all be made employing the above router-assisted, hand-fitted dovetailing procedures. In addition to being much faster than by hand, it is much more accurate and predictable. Furthermore, it's gratifying to the ego (and pocketbook) that it can be done without the use of expensive, commercially made jigs.

Fig. 439.   Assembling a small box with through dovetails.

Incidentally, the box joint shown in Fig. 440 can also be made on the router table using the fence and work-support fixture. Use a straight cutting bit and index the operation, so that the male pins and female openings are exactly equal in width. However, the dovetail joint is much more attractive and as easy, if not easier, to fabricate.

Fig. 440.   Box joint.

12
Overarm and Pin-Routing Machines

Overarm and pin-routing machines are extremely flexible pieces of equipment. They are used to make all sorts of different router cuts, including practically everything with the exception of three-dimensional carving. Essentially, the machine's rotating bit is in a stationary position and the work is moved either under, over, or alongside the bit with various kinds of guiding devices. (See Fig. 441.) Machines of this type are also used to make internal or piercing cuts. They have the capability to combine into one operation the work normally done on band or jigsaws, and shapers or routers. (See Fig. 442.)

Fig. 442 (above). *Some work samples produced by overarm and pin routing methods.*

Fig. 441 (left). *Fence-guided straight-line grooving on a Rockwell overarm shaper. Note that the feed direction is away from the operator, against the bit rotation.*

Machines of this type, with all their unlimited potential, would fall exclusively into the category of very expensive, heavy, industrial production machines. However, in recent years a number of scaled-down versions have become available that are marketed directly towards the home-craft and light-production woodworking markets. Arm attachments are even available to convert the drill press into a light-production overarm router. And, in Chapter 14 I will discuss some other easy-to-make jigs and user-made accessories that will allow the home craftsman to do many of the same jobs done on machines that cost thousands of dollars.

This chapter will look at a very broad range of machine-routing principles and techniques which to some extent may be applied to home shop machines, arm attachments, and some of the homemade devices discussed in Chapter 14. I will take a look at some of the equipment available today that falls into the general category of overarm and pin routers. I will not discuss safety precautions, how-to-do-it instructions, or detailed step-by-step operating procedures. The purpose here is to present a brief overview illustrating a sampling of the various attachments and machines available today.

Basic overarm and pin-routing applications These include the following operating techniques:

1. Straight-line work (Fig. 443).
2. Edge-forming with piloted bits (Fig. 444).
3. Pin-routing of contours with and without templates or patterns (Fig. 445).
4. Forming internal openings and piercing with patterns (Fig. 446).
5. Freehand routing (Figs. 457 and 459).

As these illustrations show, the applications can create an endless variety of different profiling and shaping cuts. Overarm and pin routing have some distinct advantages over

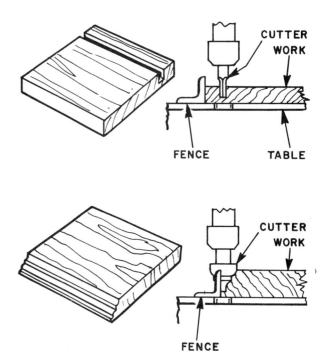

Fig. 443.   Two set-ups for straight-line routing with the fence.

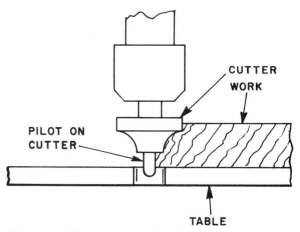

Fig. 444.   Edge forming with a piloted bit.

conventional table-routing operations discussed in Chapter 10. The essential advantage is that, unlike table routing, the routing is done with the operator's full view of the cutting action. This allows stopped grooving, mortising, dadoing, and other similar jobs to be done much faster with less setup time and inconvenience involved. Another important advantage is that with the cutting done above

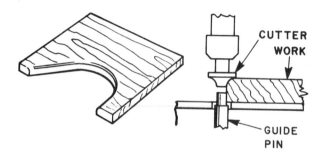

Fig. 445. *Above: pin routing without a template pattern. Below: contoured edge-forming with a template pattern.*

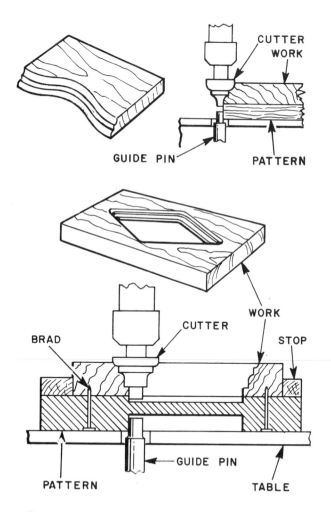

Fig. 446. *Pattern-template routing with a table pin to produce an inside opening.*

the work, it simplifies machine-template-routing techniques, which are otherwise more problematic on router tables.

With pin and overarm work the template is fastened under the blank workpiece and the operator can easily see where the cutting is and see when the job is completed. Overall, fixturing is just a lot easier too, though not for all jobs. More intricate and complicated routing jobs can, by and large, be handled much more effectively on this equipment. Fig. 447 is a good example. Industry makes very good use of overarm and pin-routing machines. As mentioned earlier, some are very large, heavy, high-production machines. See pages 13 to 15. Many are computer controlled, with a variety of automatic accessory devices, and even robot feeders. Space just does not allow me to discuss or illustrate all these important and interesting high-production processes. However, I will look at a few machines ranging from very small to those bigger ones that might be found in well-equipped home shops, custom shops, and light-production woodworking facilities.

One of the smallest units that falls into this category is the Dremel Drill Press-Routing accessory, shown in Figs. 448 and 449. This unit is of course intended for very small and light work. The small, high-speed Dremel motor unit is mounted to a column with operating mechanisms. A table supports the work with a lift knob that raises the table, with a 1-inch (24-mm) feed carrying the work to the spinning bit. The table can be locked in any position, and a fence can also be attached for guided routing and shaping. This unit is ideal for model building, miniature making, and other very light-duty work. Even though the Dremel attachment is very small in size, many of the principles of overarm and pin-routing can be performed on it, on a very small scale, of course.

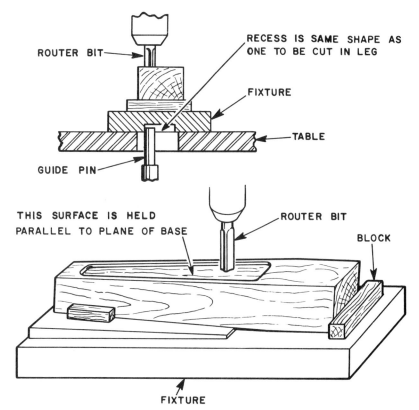

ROUTER BIT

RECESS IS SAME SHAPE AS ONE TO BE CUT IN LEG

FIXTURE

TABLE

GUIDE PIN

Fig. 447. Fixturing can handle unusual jobs like this tapered leg.

THIS SURFACE IS HELD PARALLEL TO PLANE OF BASE

ROUTER BIT

BLOCK

FIXTURE

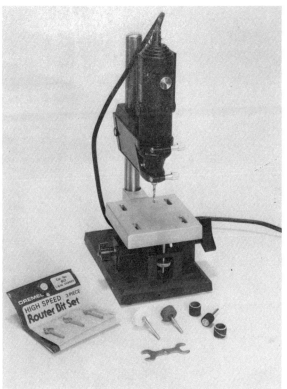

Fig. 448. The Dremel drill press/routing accessory is ideal for miniatures and modelling.

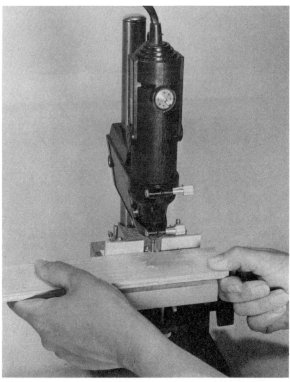

Fig. 449. Fence-guided overarm routing with the Dremel tool. Note the small size of this unit compared to the operator's hands.

The Sears pin router Fig. 450 shows a router that mounts almost any hand-held router in a cast-aluminum carriage located over a table. The carriage is attached to a welded steel overarm extending over a 1½ × 20 × 27-inch (38 × 510 × 685-mm) work-table. The router-carriage mechanism is operated with a lever providing the vertical-feed travel and depth-of-cut adjustment. It even has a depth indicator and depth-stop gauge for control and accurate plunging cuts. This accessory also has a table pin providing additional operating versatility. The table pin makes it possible to do template-guided reproduction work like that done on larger production machines. (See Figs. 445 to 447.)

Template routing is easy. A template is secured to a blank workpiece with nails or screws. The template is placed over the table guide pin. The router is lowered into the work and locked, and the template is moved over or along the pin. The pin will follow only the contour of the template, so the workpiece is moved under the router bit in the same cutting pattern as the template. In addition to template routing, straight line cuts, such as grooving and mortising, can be done by clamping a guiding fence to the table.

The router-arm attachment Shown in Fig. 451, this excellent router attachment currently marketed by Shopsmith Incorporated, and originally marketed by Bryco Inc., was invented, manufactured, and sold by Norman Bryden of Champaign, Illinois, until a few years ago when he turned it over to the Shopsmith organization. The router arm works like a drill press. In fact, it is designed to attach to the vertical column of a drill press. Simply loosen the head on the drill press and rotate it out of the way, right or left, as shown in Fig. 452, or just swing the table to the side

Fig. 450. *The Sears pin router has a vertical-travel router carriage mounted to an overarm. Almost any hand-held router can be used on this accessory machine.*

Fig. 451. The Bryco router arm attachment, now sold by Shopsmith, Inc.

Fig. 452. Swing either the head or the table of the drill press to the side to make room for the router arm attachment. Note the auxiliary wood table.

Fig. 453. The Bryco overarm pin routing machine carries your own router.

Fig. 454. The Shopsmith overarm pin router is changed very little from the earlier Bryco version.

and mount the arm above the drill press table—more or less using the drill press side-saddle. An auxiliary table of any size (usually of plywood) is bolted or clamped over the existing table of the drill press. For anyone who does not own a drill press, it's possible to purchase a complete bench-mount assembly as shown in Figs. 453 and 454. This unit has a metal base that supports its own worktable and a vertical column.

Any conventional motor unit of a portable hand-held router between 3 inches (76 mm) and 4¼ inches (107 mm) in diameter is clamped rigidly to the overarm, to provide the power source. This entire motor-mount as-

sembly has a vertical travel of 3½ inches (89 mm) on a rack-and-pinion slide. It is operated by the large quill-feed lever that locks in any position with a simple twist of its knob. The Shopsmith overarm pin router is equipped with an adjustable depth-stop that limits the vertical movement of the router motor. It also has a safety shield. The complete unit comes with an 18 × 30-inch (460 × 760-mm) work-

173

table with premachined slots for mounting fences and other fixtures. The entire table assembly is adjustable in or out, and it has a metal insert to accommodate pins of various sizes. The unit has a generous clearance capacity of approximately 15 inches (380 mm) between the column and the bit.

Fig. 455. *The samples illustrate the range of projects and types of cuts made with Shopsmith's overarm pin router.*

Fig. 455 shows a number of typical products and cuts that can be made with Shopsmith's overarm pin router. Figs. 456 to 467 show and describe a number of operations that can be applied to pin and overarm routing machines in general, as well as to some of the user-made accessories described in Chapter 14. Figs. 465 to 467 illustrate some basic ideas for using the pin router to make a template pattern from another part. This copied pattern is then used to copy or reproduce that part again and again, as many times as desired. Obviously, the photos here do not illustrate all the capabilities of pin routing machines. They can also be used to drill holes, machine mouldings, raise panels, and cut recesses of all types, such as hollowing out boxes and trays. They can be set up with a planing fence to function as a vertical jointer or full-edge shaper and can handle many other operations, including trimming plastic laminates and making delicate inlays. Anyone getting into a production operation will find

that it is a good idea to rig up a foot-operated switch connected to the router motor, hold the work at all times with both hands, and maintain control should it be necessary to shut down in a hurry.

Fig. 456. *Fence-guided mortising and grooving. Remember, feed is left to right, against the bit rotation.*

Fig. 457. *Making piercing cutouts freehand.*

Fig. 458. Raised-letter sign work as done here involves fence-guided work for the long straight-border cuts and freehand feeding.

Fig. 459. Surfacing a rough slab to uniform thickness is a job perfectly suited to an overarm router.

Fig. 460. A setup for pin routing. At left is a bottom view of a pattern for making oval cutouts. Note that the pin and bit diameters are equal and perfectly aligned one over the other.

Fig. 461. *A close-up showing a cutaway of the pattern and workpiece, revealing the pin groove of the pattern and the reproduced cut made by the bit. Note that the pattern is "boxed" (cradling the workpiece which is also clamped securely to the pattern).*

Fig. 463. *A pattern mounted under this cabinet door is pin guided to effect this decorative groove cut.*

Fig. 464. *A different pattern setup for production grooving of doors all the same size requiring the same design. This pattern boxes in the workpiece for quick positioning for each successive door panel.*

Fig. 462 (left). *Another cradle-type pattern permits the work to be shifted, to repeat identical cuts within the same workpiece.*

176

Fig. 465. *An original part being copied and converted into a pattern, which in turn will be used to produce more parts. Here the router is grooving into particle board faced with plastic laminate to make an accurate, durable template-pattern.*

Fig. 466. *The pattern is converted into a work-holding fixture. Here the profile is reproduced as the pattern now under the workpiece guides the cut and the pin follows the grooves of the pattern made in Fig. 465.*

Fig. 467. *The completed project is a lamp with all four identical side pieces cut by pattern on the overarm pin router.*

The Duz-Awl Manufactured by Walter Hartlauer of Eugene, Oregon, this is a somewhat different version of the pin router. On this machine (Fig. 468) the router motor unit is mounted under the table and the guide pin extends down from the overarm directly over the cutting bit. This machine is designed for routing letter profiles from wood, plastic, and aluminum, but potentially it has many other applications. One special advantage of this concept is that chips and shavings can be picked up with its vacuum hookup. (See Fig. 469.) Duz-Awl machines are available in various sizes ranging from 15–24-inch (380–600-mm) throat capacities. They all have foot peddles that when depressed lower the bit below the table and lift the arm and guide pin. In operation the work is cut while a top-mounted pattern follows the guide pin. This is essentially the same principle as other pin routers.

Fig. 468. Hartlauer's "Duz-Awl" machine has the router motor mounted under the table and the pin extending from the arm.

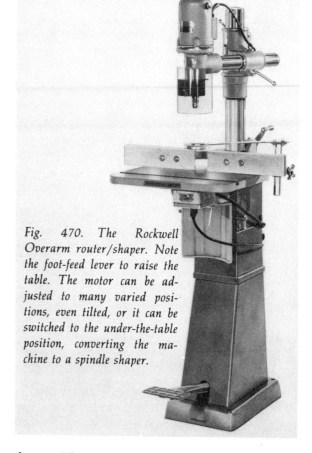

Fig. 470. The Rockwell Overarm router/shaper. Note the foot-feed lever to raise the table. The motor can be adjusted to many varied positions, even tilted, or it can be switched to the under-the-table position, converting the machine to a spindle shaper.

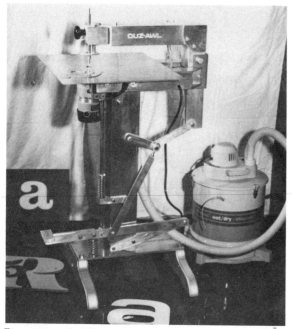

Fig. 469. A full view of the "Duz-Awl" pin-routing machine. Note the foot-operated control and vacuum hookup.

The Rockwell Overarm Router Shaper Fig. 470 shows a machine that combines the best features of an overarm router and a spindle shaper. The special versatility of this machine is that it can be used either as an overarm routing machine, shown in Figs. 470 and 471, or it can be converted to a spindle shaper. This is achieved by switching the motor from the overarm position to the under-the-table position. When used with the head in the above-the-table position for routing, it will perform any of the standard routing operations. (Refer to Figs. 441, 442, and see Fig. 471.) The work is carried into the revolving bit with a foot-lever action; stops can be set to limit the table travel and hence control the depth of cut. A unique feature of this machine is its facility for a variety of head-position adjustments. The head can be moved and fixed at any point in or out, up or down, anywhere within the full 360° around the vertical column. Not only that, but it can also be tilted right or left or rotated 360° on its horizontal overarm.

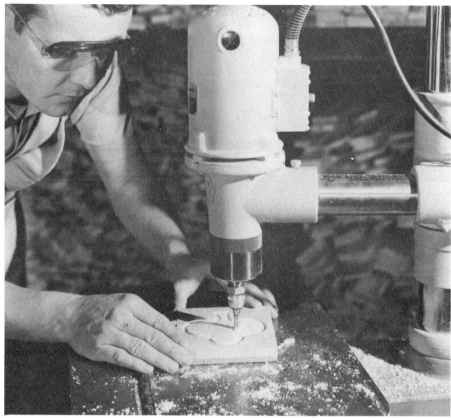

Fig. 471. *The Rockwell over-arm router/shaper in use.*

The basic specifications include: a 2 horse-power, 20,000 RPM power unit with a ½-inch (12-mm) chuck, a 14 × 18-inch (360 × 460-mm) table with a slot for a mitre gauge, a split fence, and a weight of 300 pounds (136 kg).

There are a number of companies that manufacture larger industrial production overarm and pin routing machines. The list of names well known in the industry includes: Ekstrom Carlson & Co. (refer to page 15), Onsrud Division of Danly Machine Corp., Porter Machinery Co., Powermatic, Wesflex, Rockwell, and C. R. Onsrud, Inc. Since it is impossible to illustrate and describe them all, I have selected two machines that somewhat bridge the gap between those used for home-craft or light industrial applications and the more automated machines designed for high-production factory installations.

C. R. Onsrud's Inverted Router Fig. 472 shows a light-to-medium-duty machine that has its power unit under the table with the

Fig. 472. *C. R. Onsrud's Model 2003 Inverted Router.*

guide pin mounted on the overarm. The model in Fig. 472 is actually a scaled-down version of one of their larger routers. In fact, it is available specially tooled, to accept most portable hand-router motors or special high-cycle motors up to 6 horsepower and 21,000 RPM. However, its standard motorized spindle is a 3¼ horsepower, 22,000 RPM commercial-duty production router motor. The motor is raised or lowered mechanically by a foot pedal with adjustable upper and lower depth stops to limit spindle travel. The guide pin is retractable and is activated automatically either by a pneumatic (air) or electrical cylinder controlled by the spindle foot pedal. Thus, a great safety feature exists as the operator controls the cutter: It's either below the table or buried in the workpiece. Another feature of this machine is its dust- and chip-removal system built into the 24 × 36-inch (600 × 900-mm) table. The vacuum system can also be coupled to make vacuum-mounted templates that adhere themselves to the work, without any screws, nails, or other fastenings required. (See Fig. 473.)

Fig. 474. *C. R. Onsrud's Model 2427 Intri-Shaper has a 7½ horsepower motor driving a 25,000 RPM spindle, with up to ¾-inch (18-mm) collet capacity. The unique feature of this machine is its capability to make cuts like those made with a narrow-bladed band saw. Its special small-diameter spiral bit has tension at both ends. Note the sample workpiece shown here.*

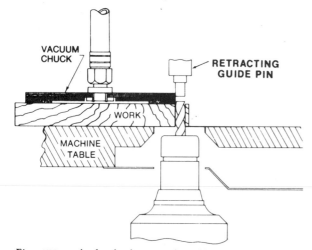

Fig. 473. *A sketch showing the table vacuum opening and a top-mounted vacuum chuck template.*

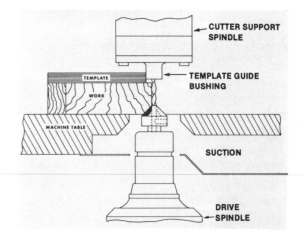

Fig. 475. *A section view showing the basic features of the "Intri-Shaper" machine.*

A much larger version of C. R. Onsrud's Model 2003 is an interesting machine they call the Intri-Shaper. (See Fig. 474.) This unit has a 25,000 RPM spindle speed-driven by a 7½ horsepower motor with a collet capacity up to ¾ inch (18 mm). Its 24 × 36-inch (600 × 900-mm) table also has a built-in vacuum. (See Fig. 475.) The unique feature of this machine

is its band-sawing capabilities, achieved through the use of a small-diameter, high-helical spiral bit secured under tension at both ends. It literally has a 360° sawing-shaping capability to an inside radius as little as 3/32 inch (3 mm). (See Figs. 476 and 477.) Its downward-cutting action, coupled with the vacuum-suction draws dust and chips through

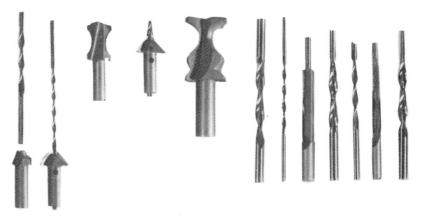

Fig. 476. Some of the bits, including the special high helical spirals, that permit 360° sawing/shaping to very small inside radius cuts (as little as ³/₃₂ inch [5 mm]), on the Intri-Shaper.

Fig. 477. A close-up showing the small-diameter spiral bit (with tension at both ends) and the table vacuum grill. Chips and dust are removed by both the downward cutting action and the vacuum suction.

Fig. 478. The safety feature of C.R. Onsrud's inverted routing machines is that, as shown here, the operator's fingers are near a non-rotating pin instead of dangerously close to a rotating cutter.

the opening in the table. The machine can obviously perform many template-guided and other routing and shaping operations. One special advantage, not common to most overarm routers with their cutters mounted above the table is the inherent safety feature of this machine. Conventional overhead routers expose the operator to the rotating bit unless it is very well guarded. On this machine the cutter is either retracted under the table or in the cut. As shown in Fig. 478, the operator's fingers are on top of the template near the

nonrotating guide pin, instead of on top of the work closely exposed to the dangerous rotating bit. The Intri-Shaper has various standard and optional electrical and pneumatic controls and other safety features. Two such standard features are that the cutter will not engage the work until the guide pin is in its full down position, and that the foot pedal retracts the guide pin and the cutter, keeping dangerous cutters safely away while the operator positions the part or moves to a new cut.

Although these large industrial machines are certainly far beyond the needs of the hobbyist woodworker, a basic understanding of their features, mechanical functions, and operating capabilities is helpful when solving production problems on a smaller scale.

13

Router Carving Machines

Production carving machines are fairly simple in their operating concept. Still, they remain very fascinating pieces of equipment. Industrial carving machines have been around since the 1850's. Only in recent years, however, have a number of carving machines become available for home shops and serious woodworkers. Most carry a high-speed router motor as the power source or carving head. These are generally light-duty, inexpensive machines compared to those used in high-production factories for making multiple carvings in large quantities of table legs, gun stocks, and similar items.

Carving machines are a great attraction for most woodworkers—especially "router crafters." It's an interesting experience to see a rough chunk of wood turn into a three-dimensional form amid a growing pile of aromatic wood chips. It is not even necessary to be artistic or creative to make some fantastic carvings with these machines. Most carving machines today are primarily used to copy or reproduce master patterns. These machines are very easy to set up and use; they require no special skills. The crucial requirement is patience—even machine-carving takes time. However, it is still much faster and more accurate to machine-carve an object by tracing a pattern or another carving than it is to do it all by hand, from scratch. Many experienced hand carvers use carving machines to duplicate their originals.

Most machines have the ability to reproduce very fine details. Some have greater carving-size capacities, more reach, and overall convenience than others. The quality seems to improve as the purchase price increases. But this is not always the case. Anyone who intends to carve just for fun or for profit, would do well to check the various types of router carving machines illustrated in this chapter. Before purchasing any specific machine, it is a good idea to contact several manufacturers. Product improvements and new models are occasionally introduced. Also prices change rather regularly, and it's good to know in advance what the bill will be.

Some of the machines described here are simply larger versions of the router pantographs and carving devices listed as acccessories in Chapter 9. Consequently, not all those described on the following pages are capable of reproducing or copying fully rounded contours of true three-dimensional shapes. Some only do two-dimensional work, such as flat wood signs. The reason they are included here is because they are generally larger than those devices normally labelled accessories.

The Hobbi-Carver Fig. 479 shows one of the two models manufactured by Kurt Mfg. Co. of Minneapolis, Minnesota, one of the recognized companies in the industry that also manufactures a complete line of larger multiple-spindle production carving machines. Only this model is designed to have a router mounted to it. It will take any router with a 6-inch (152-mm)-diameter base or smaller. The operator must provide a work surface. The Hobbi-Carver machines operate on a two-level table arrangement, as shown in Fig. 479. This model will reproduce contoured objects, but the pattern must have a flat-backed surface. (See Fig. 480.) The maximum carving size is 2 × 10 × 12 inches (50 × 255 × 300 mm). A stylus traces the pattern on the lower table while the router makes corresponding cuts on the upper table. The unit is of cast aluminum and comes with three matching sets of bits and styluses. Shipping weight is approximately 19 pounds (9 kg).

Fig. 480.   These flat-backed shelves and mirror frame typify the carving capabilities of the Kurt Hobbi-Carver.

Fig. 481.   A bird's eye view of the Rout-A-Sign machine (Patent No. 4,221,052).

The Rout-A-Sign Just as its name implies, this is a machine designed for the guided router carving of wood signs. (See Fig. 481.) This unit is manufactured by Quality Industries, Inc., of Hillsdale, Michigan. This is no toy. Its listed weight is 960 pounds (436 kg). It can rout a 7-foot (2.1-m)-long sign in one setting with 4-inch (101-mm) and 6-inch (152-mm) cast-aluminum alphabets and letter templates (Fig. 482) that come with the machine. The routing is stylus-controlled, with carving reproduction transferred from template to router through an aluminum pantograph as-

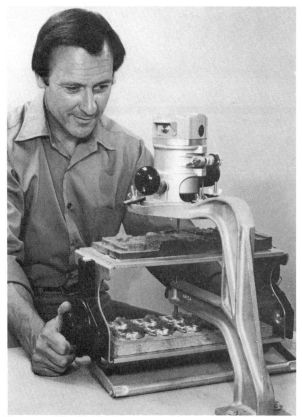

Fig. 479: The Hobbi-Carver, by Kurt Manufacturing Co.

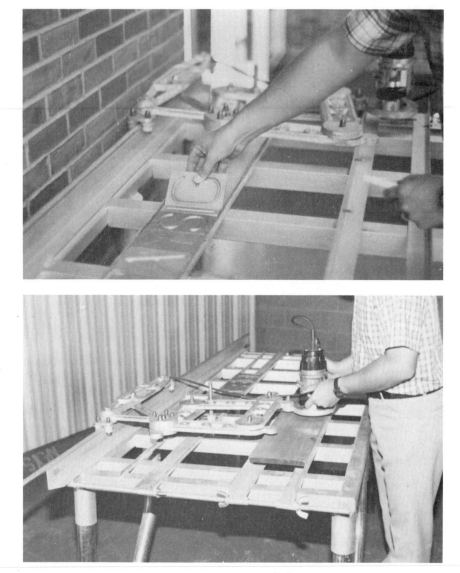

Fig. 482. Standard cast aluminum and number templates come with the Rout-A-Sign machine.

Fig. 483. The Rout-A-Sign machine works on the pantograph principle, with router movement stylus controlled from the templates.

sembly. (See Fig. 483.) One particular feature of this machine is its ability to produce various letter styles from slanted to gothic using the same set of templates, simply by changing the pivot points and stylus locations.

The Kimball Woodcarvers Figs. 484 and 485 show machines essentially designed for the signmaking industry. As is true of all these machines, however, they have other capabilities, given the restrictions of their work-size capacities. The Kimball machines are tabletop units which a hand-held router is mounted to. The manufacturer recommends that the unit be connected to a shop vacuum and provides

a plastic exhaust port and vacuum-dust-line, which draws directly from the router for a clean operation. The other structural parts are essentially of cast-aluminum and steel-rod construction. The machines copy on a one-to-one ratio, can handle stock up to 2 inches (50 mm) thick in any length, and in widths from 16–27 inches (410–685 mm). Fig. 486 illustrates the machine repeating the profile of a large letter cutout from the stylus-followed template. Figs. 487 to 492 illustrate some of the kinds of work it can do and the range of sizes that can be handled. The Kimball Woodcarvers are manufactured by the Kimball Company, Savannah, Georgia.

Fig. 484. Kimball's Model K-2 woodcarving machine.

Fig. 485. The Kimball K-3 machine. Note the plastic templates in the holder under the stylus.

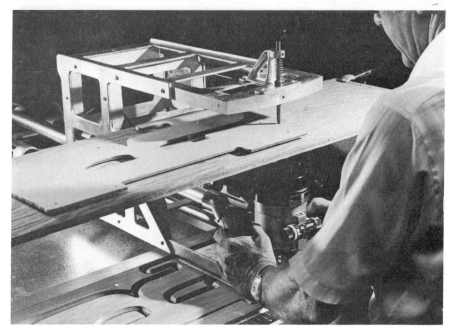

Fig. 486. A Kimball carving machine in operation.

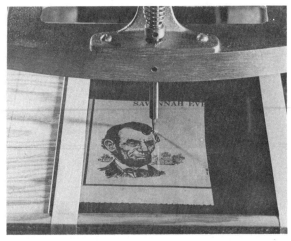

Fig. 487. *This small printed illustration provides the pattern for the completed, finely detailed wood engraving in Fig. 488.*

Fig. 488. *A delicate and intricate wood engraving copied from a paper pattern.*

Fig. 489. *The one-to-one reproduction ratio of the Kimball carvers is ideally suited to matched inlay work, as illustrated by these letter samples.*

Fig. 490. *Engraved art created with the Kimball carving machine.*

Fig. 491. *Small or large parts (of any profile) can be router-carved on the Kimball machines.*

Fig. 492. *Producing identical parts in any quantity is a feature of carving machines.*

The Marlin carving machine Shown in Fig. 493, this is one of three different models manufactured by Marlin Industries of Long Beach, California. All operate on the pantograph principle. The largest model can carve an area covering 22 × 28 inches (560 × 720 mm). However, for big signs simply reposition the work for unlimited lengths. All models have a 3-inch (75-mm) depth-of-cut capacity and can reproduce contoured and carved surfaces as illustrated in Fig. 494. This machine, like the others previously described, is widely used to carve wood signs. Figs. 495 to 497 show some actual carving operations and a sample sign.

Fig. 493 (below). *The Marlin Carving Machine.*

Fig. 494. *An original plaster casting is the pattern for the partially carved wood copy.*

Fig. 495. *Close-up of the outlining operation for a raised letter on a Marlin carving machine using ⅛-inch (3-mm) straight bit. Note the operator "working" the stylus as the router follows its every move.*

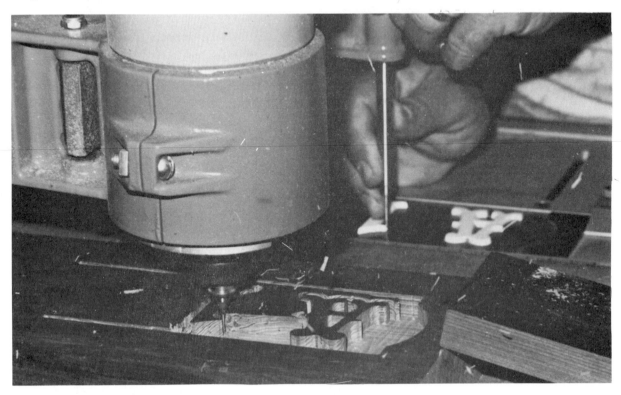

Fig. 496. *Removing the background to complete the raised letters.*

Fig. 497. *A 24 x 30-inch (600 x 750-mm) sign produced with the Marlin Carving Machine. Note the textured background.*

The X-Y Routermatic machine Formerly CarvAgraph, this is a product of North American Machinery Enterprise, based in Tallahassee, Florida. This machine (Fig. 498), like a number of the others described here, is also designed primarily for carving wood signs, but is not limited to this application. Work-size capacity of the X-Y Routermatic ranges up to 5-foot (1.5-m) widths and 10-foot (3-m) and longer lengths, in multiple settings. Otherwise, the carving capacity is limited to 12 × 24 inches (300 × 600 mm) or 12 × 36 inches (300 × 900 mm) at one setting. Material can be up to 2¼ inches (57 mm) thick. A 1½-horsepower, 25,000 RPM motor is mounted above the worktable. It is vertically adjustable only, and is controlled by a foot pedal. The power unit will cut most materials to a ¾-inch (18-mm) depth.

The X-Y Routermatic machine has a one-to-one reproduction ratio. The work is guided under the cutter by a manually controlled stylus that traces a stationary master pattern. The piece is clamped to a worktable carriage and moved into the stationary rotating bit. The table carries the work in or out and right or left as necessary to complete the carving. When all routing has been completed, the foot pedal is released and the cutter raises, withdrawing itself from the work by the action of a return spring. The X-Y Routermatic machine requires a 3 × 4-foot (.9 × 1.2-m) space and weighs about 160 pounds (72 kg). In addition to carved wood signs (Fig. 499), the X-Y Routermatic machine can make shallow relief carvings for chair backs, wood mouldings, picture frames, cabinet drawer-and-door fronts, as well as custom-carved boxes, jewelry chests, carved entrance doors, and similar detailed decorative carvings. (See Figs. 499 and 500.)

Fig. 498. The X-Y Routermatic in operation. The operator moves the stylus over the pattern manually as the cut is made into the work clamped onto a movable table located under the stationary cutting head.

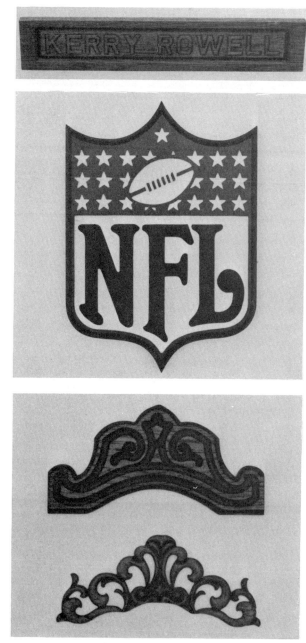

Fig. 499. The X-Y Routermatic makes signs and decorative carvings.

Fig. 500. More examples of panels with decorative carvings produced on the X-Y Routermatic machine.

The Allen duplicating machine Fig. 501 shows a one-to-one, two-spindle, manually controlled, high-precision, three-dimensional milling-type carver. This equipment is especially suited to reproducing the outside contours of gun stocks (Fig. 502), and it has the engineering necessary to hold the extremely rigid tolerances required for the stock inletting or interior machining. (See Fig. 503.) The manufacturer, Don Allen, Inc. of Northfield, Minnesota, claims that they have no difficulty reproducing to tolerances within a range of ±.002–1 inch (.05–25 mm)—remarkable for wood carving. Although a machine of this ca-

Fig. 501.   The Allen Duplicating Machine is engineered for very sensitive reproduction, such as for the extreme accuracy milling gun stocks requires.

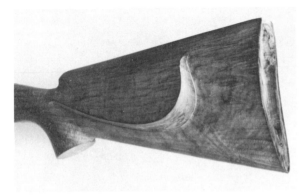

Fig. 502 (left).   The contoured surfaces of this gun stock were carved on the Allen Duplicating Machine.

Fig. 503.   Internal carving or inletting requires a high degree of accurate router carving.

pability is obviously built with the precision necessary for copy milling gun stocks (Figs. 502 and 503), it is not limited just to such use.

The unit shown will handle work up to 46 inches (1170 mm) in length but with special equipment this capacity is extended to 66 inches (1680 mm). The standard machine requires 34 × 78 inches (860 × 1980 mm) of floor space and has a listed shipping weight of 1100 pounds (500 kg). The large welded-steel base is designed so it can be filled with sand or concrete, to give it more weight and thus add to its overall rigidity.

The intergral movements of the bit, stylus, pattern, and workpiece are achieved through a system incorporating a "six-point parallelogram" with a built-in balancing device. The work head consists of a 1¼ horsepower, 18,000 RPM motor and the stylus. Both are rigidly mounted together on a common plane or faceplate. This arrangement is unusual. On most other machines, these two components are individually mounted on or at different parts or locations of the machine. The head and stylus move together vertically and side-to-side, as well as moving as a unit lengthwise, or in a direction that is parallel to the work.

The workpiece and pattern are mounted on centers that rotate in unison within a complete range of 360°. Thus, all surfaces and cavities can be reached by the stylus and cutting bit. The machine is advertised as the Don Allen five-axis, one-to-one duplicating machine, because it incorporates a fifth axis that allows the operator to adjust the angle at which the cutter contacts the work. This feature permits accurate holes to be drilled into the work at any angle.

The Dupli-Carver machines Figs. 504 and 505 show machines manufactured by Laskowski Enterprises, Inc., of Indianapolis, Indiana. They offer a full line of special router-type carving machines designed to do a wide variety of special carving jobs. In addition to those made for true three-dimensional carvings in various model types and work size capacities, Laskowski Enterprises makes spe-

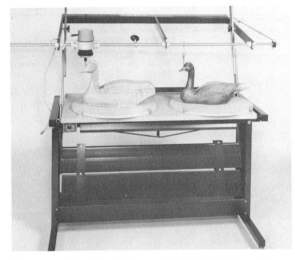

Fig. 504. The Dupli-Carver, Model F480, has the capacity to carve 3-dimensional objects up to 20 inches (500 mm) in diameter by 40 inches (1000 mm) tall.

Fig. 505. A close-up look at a carving in process. Note the exceptional detail achieved with just a ⅝ horsepower router and the small, pointed detail cutting bit.

cial carvers to handle specific jobs such as making relief carvings in doors, panels, and signs, as well as carving gun stocks. They also have versions of carvers that function as an overhead router-shaper and a spindle carver. Fig. 506 shows the various carving actions

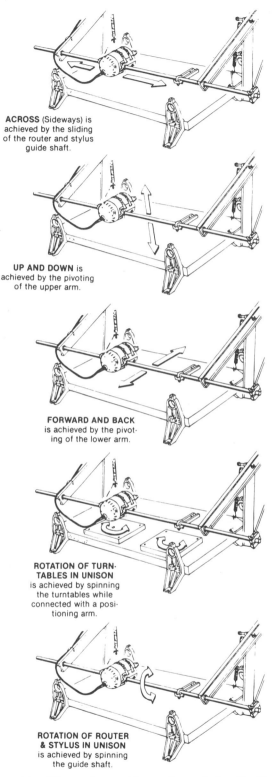

ACROSS (Sideways) is achieved by the sliding of the router and stylus guide shaft.

UP AND DOWN is achieved by the pivoting of the upper arm.

FORWARD AND BACK is achieved by the pivoting of the lower arm.

ROTATION OF TURNTABLES IN UNISON is achieved by spinning the turntables while connected with a positioning arm.

ROTATION OF ROUTER & STYLUS IN UNISON is achieved by spinning the guide shaft.

Fig. 506. The various cutting actions of the Dupli-Carving machines permit reproduction of three-dimensionally carved objects, including those with hard-to-reach undercuts and intricate contours.

possible. The machines are provided with a speed control for their ⅝ horsepower standard-line router. The speed control reduces machine noise and turns the bit at a slower RPM, which prevents overheating and increases the life of their HSS cutters.

Their oldest machine is F200, shown in Fig. 507. The manufacturer also has a tandem kit available for this machine, which enables two

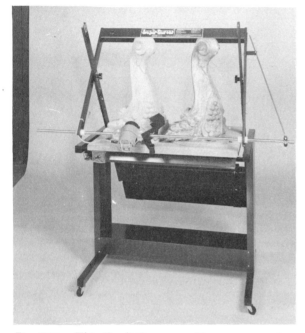

Fig. 507. This Dupli-Carver machine can carve pieces 14 inches (360 mm) in diameter by 40 inches (1000 mm) tall.

machines to be linked together. Thus, with the appropriate attachments it becomes a four-station carver that carries four individual router-carving heads (all linked together and operating in unison). This setup offers the ability to produce four identical carvings at a time from one master pattern, using a single stylus. Figs. 508, 509, and 510 illustrate relief carving with a Dupli-Carver. Figs. 511 and 512 show the machine set up for sign carving.

Just like the large multiple-spindle carving machines used in industry, the model T-110 Dupli-Carver does similar reproduction on a 1-to-1 scale. The work and pattern are mounted horizontally on centers (turntables) that are linked together and rotate in unison

Fig. 508. A Dupli-Carver reproducing in relief from a plaster master.

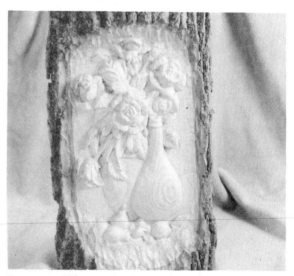

Fig. 509. The completed example of relief carving.

Fig. 510. Some other examples of carved projects produced on a Dupli-Carver.

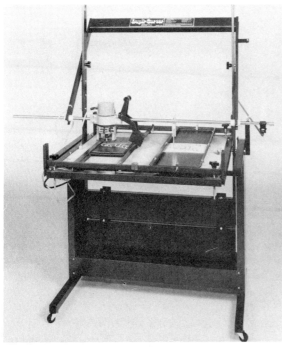

Fig. 511. *A Dupli-Carver set up for sign work.*

Fig. 512. *A sign carving in process. Note the router-textured surface.*

through 360°. Figs. 513 and 514 illustrate roughing and finish-cutting steps involved in router-spindle-carving detailed surfaces of carved table legs. Fig. 515 clearly illustrates the three-dimensional capabilities of the Dupli-Carver equipment. The manufacturer provides a number of optional accessory attachments that are designed to increase work size capacities or to convert the machine to function as an overhead-spindle router-shaper. In the latter situation, the only accessory required is a fence with a clamping de-

vice to hold the router in a fixed position. Thus, the Dupli-Carver can be used to perform the operations of an overarm or pin-routing machine like those described in Chapter 12.

Fig. 513. *Reproducing a carved table leg on spindle carver manufactured by Laskowski Enterprises. This shows a roughing operation. Notice the simple bar arrangement linking the turntables so they rotate in unison.*

Fig. 514. *Finish cuts are made with a small pointed bit and stylus of an identical shape.*

Fig. 515. *A detailed carving produced on a Laskowski Dupli-Carver.*

14

User-Made Jigs and Fixtures

In addition to those various user-made templates and patterns, extended router bases, straight cutting guides, router tables, and various work supports illustrated in earlier chapters, there are a few more easy-to-make devices to ice the cake. This chapter illustrates a number of uncomplicated and inexpensive items to make in a short time. They will permit some unusual but practical routing operations. More importantly, they can save the operator lots of money. A couple of the devices shown here cost only a few dollars to make and enable the user to do many of the same operations performed on the expensive overarm and pin routers described in Chapter 12. It's also possible to use the router with table-saw scraps or edgings to spin out free wood dowels of any variety and size.

Serpentine routing Fig. 516 shows routing into a contoured surface. The simple fixture in the photo shows how to make grooves or flutes that wind in one direction and then another. Hence, this class of work is labelled serpentine routing. The construction details of the fixture are fairly straightforward. A wood v-block or band-sawed cradle holds the router motor in a horizontal position. Cut a large hose clamp in half and screw each end to the motor mounting block.

The guide pin or follower is simply a ¼-inch (6-mm)-diameter machine bolt with its head cut off and bolted through a counterbored hole in the bottom of the base. Notice that in Fig. 516 the workpiece is raised with some scrap boards so that the cut is made at the desired location.

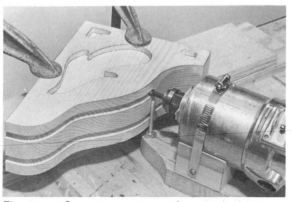

Fig. 516. Serpentine routing with a simple device supporting the router horizontally. Note the guide pin follower assuring uniform depth of cut.

Fig. 517 takes the serpentine routing concept a step further, combining the horizontal router action with a template guide. The template can be any configuration. This principle may be applied to machining decorative grooving into the surfaces of flat or gradually contoured surfaces. In both instances (Figs. 516 and 517), either the workpiece or the

196

Fig. 517. *Template-guided routing produces tapered grooves in a flat surface. Note the template and pointed follower at the base of the fixture and the shims between the template and the work.*

Fig. 518. *A horizontally mounted router permits freehand smoothing with rotary files.*

Fig. 519. *Cleaning out the prebored hollow for a carved spoon.*

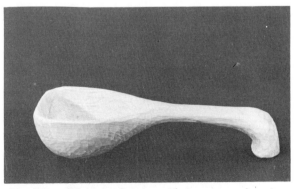

Fig. 520. *The carved spoon with its contoured surfaces worked with the router.*

router-supporting fixture can be shimmed with pieces of plywood to position the work in relation to the bit so the cut can be made exactly where desired. The work is clamped in position and the router fixture slid along on the surface of the workbench to make the cut. Fancier versions of this fixture and operating techniques can be worked out to satisfy individual needs. To serve production work, a ball bearing can be mounted to the guide pin or attached to the pointed follower. A combination workpiece-positioning fixture with stops, integral clamps, and a template or pattern can be added as desired.

Freehand carving With the router held stationary and horizontal near the edge of a workbench, it is possible to do some good wood carving. (See Figs. 518 and 519.) Suitable metal cutting burrs, rotary files, or ball mills can be used. Be sure the cutters are designed for high RPMs and sized according to the router's horsepower. Do not use standard two-wing or single-flute router bits. These could be dangerous, as they may dig in and throw the work. Burrs and files have many cutting edges with small flutes that limit excessively deep cutting, unless forced by the operator. (See Fig. 520 for a typical application of this process.)

Preparing large, rough turnings With the router this is a technique I use occasionally when turning heavy green chunks of wood. Due to the weight of such turnings, they must be well balanced in advance of actual lathe turning, to eliminate excessive and often dangerous vibration. The simple fixture shown in Fig. 521 facilitates router removal of protruding knots, unevenness, or other bumps that create out-of-balance turnings. A router with a large bit and extended base is passed over the workpiece until true. The log (or whatever) is simply rotated on nail centers at intervals during this routing operation.

Fig. 522. *Radial router accessory. Note the spacing block under the clamp and board supporting the router slide. This device will handle work 2 inches (50 mm) thick. Thinner stock can be raised with other stock (shims) to reduce the reach of the router.*

Fig. 521. *A router with an extended base, as shown at left, is used to true and balance heavy green logs prior to their being mounted in the turning lathe.*

A radial router This is a versatile, easy-to-make accessory. This device consists simply of a parallel tracked base or guided router slide that is slotted for the bit. It is raised and pivoted on one end with a single flathead wood screw driven into a work fence. Fig. 522 clearly shows its construction details. The base of the one shown here is approximately 4 feet (1.1 mm) at its largest dimension, 35 inches (890 mm) wide, and has a radius cut along one side to facilitate clamping the 35-inch (890-mm)-long router slide to any angle with the 2-inch (50-mm)-thick work fence.

A little imagination will reveal numerous job applications for this homemade routing guide. Panel grooving, dadoing, or decorative routing as done to make the slotted grills in Figs. 523 to 525 can all be performed with this

Fig. 523. *The radial router as used with a secondary 90° fence facilitates work support for many angle routing jobs. See Fig. 527.*

Fig. 524. *Right-angled grooves cut into both surfaces create this interesting grill pattern.*

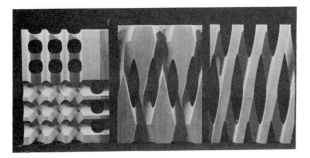

Fig. 525. *More decorative routing ideas for the radial routing device.*

device. The possibilities increase further by combining the use of a plunging-type router with stop blocks clamped to the router slide to limit horizontal router travel. With this combination it is possible to make stopped dadoes, stopped grooves, and so on. With a little experimentation, make grillwork cuts similar to the trivets shown in Fig. 526. A

Fig. 526. *These commercially made trivets by Scandia are created by routing from both sides to one half the stock thickness.*

plunging router is also ideal where deep multiple or identical cuts are necessary. Most plunging routers can be set with multiple depth stops. Thus, when several passes are required to make a deep cut, the final pass will always result in exactly the same depth as the preceding cuts.

One problem is slippage of the workpiece during routing. Various jury-rigged clamping methods have to be devised, especially when routing short pieces. Small workpieces can be tack-glued with hot-melt or nailed to larger and longer support boards that in turn are clamped to one side of the base. Pointed nails extending through the fence will hold the stock, too, but they make holes in the edge of the workpiece. A secondary fence (Fig. 527) is often helpful for many jobs, especially cuts that are sharply angled to the edge of the workpiece. (See Fig. 523.)

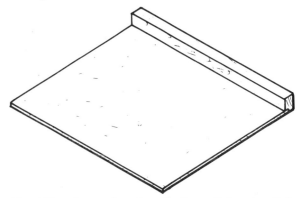

Fig. 527. *A secondary fence for the radial router. It is clamped to the base to make another work fence that is 90° to the primary fence.*

Radial-saw routing attachment A very simple accessory can be custom-made to combine the high speed of the router with all the motions or actions of the radial arm saw, which in itself is very versatile, but essentially just for sawing jobs. For a marriage of the best features that each of these power tools have to offer, remove the saw blade and make (or have made) a router-mounting device similar to the one shown in Figs. 528 through 531. This accessory has received considerable praise and even raves from everyone who has seen it in operation or has used it.

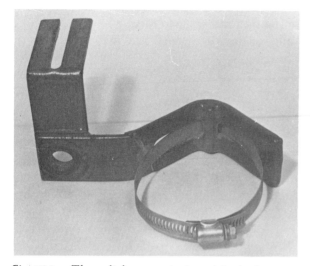

Fig. 528. *The radial saw router mount is simply made of flat bar stock with a slot for a large hose clamp.*

Fig. 530. *The radial saw mount will accept most types of router motors—even those with awkward handles fixed to their motor housings, as shown.*

Fig. 529. *The radial arm router mount on the saw arbor secured at the saw guard pin on the motor.*

Fig. 531. *View from a different angle showing a conventional 1½-horsepower router motor in the mount.*

The radial-saw router mount is simply made from ⅛-inch (3-mm) flat steel with a bored hole so it slips over the arbor of the radial-arm saw motor. (See Fig. 529.) It is kept rigid with a secondary anchor to the blade-guard pin, found on the motor housing of most radial saws. A slot in the bent area of the arm permits a large hose clamp to be inserted to secure the router vertically. To have one made, make a mock-up of stiff cardboard to

assure that it will fit the saw. Then take it to a metal shop and have one made. A little bend or twist in a vise, with leverage from an adjustable wrench, may be necessary to get the router in a true vertical position. The one shown in the photos (particularly Fig. 530) was dipped in liquid plastic to protect the router motor housing.

Any of the operations performed with the homemade, wood radial router discussed in the previous section can also be performed with this attachment. Just a few of the obvious, basic radial saw/router operations are illustrated in Figs. 532 to 534. Figs. 535 to 537 give some ideas for routing workpieces supported on inclined surfaces.

Fig. 532. *The radial saw motor mount demonstrating 90° and angular cuts, through and stopped.*

Fig. 533. *Indexed grooving to make a decorative moulding pattern. The fence is shifted after the first cut so successive cuts are made without pencil layouts. Each previous cut is aligned with the cut made in the fence, assuring perfect spacing.*

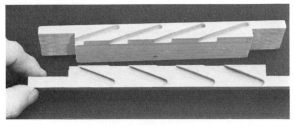

Fig. 534. *A stop clamp on the saw's arm track and a work-holding fixture assisted in making stopped slot cuts for louvers in these door stiles.*

Fig. 535. *Inclined work supports facilitate bevel-routing jobs as done here to make raised door panels.*

Fig. 536. *With a wedge supporting the work, a nail pivot, indexing or reference marks, and a stop clamped to the saw arm, these interesting cuts are possible.*

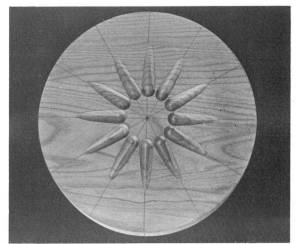

Fig. 537. *This will be a clock face.*

Remember that the carriage (yoke) of the radial arm saw can be clamped at any point along its arm track. Thus, the router can be held vertically and suspended in a stationary position over the worktable. With this setup, the router can be used in conjunction with the guide fence for various jobs in which the work is moved under the stationary, revolving cutter. In essence this arrangement allows you to do most of the operations done with expensive overarm routers. Refer to the operations illustrated in Chapter 12. It doesn't take too much effort to drop a dowel or short aluminum rod into the worktable to do all the pin-routing operations and template-reproduction work described in the same chapter. And, don't forget that the blade on the radial saw can be tilted for compound mitring and bevel-sawing operations. This means that with the radial saw router mount, the router can likewise be tilted. All the various cuts that can be made, all the jobs it will do, and all the unusual projects that can be made by employing the numerous combinations of various router bits, coupled with all the adjustment capabilities of a radial saw, make it just incredible.

Drill-press overarm accessories These can also be homemade. The ones shown here are somewhat crude in appearance and mechanical functioning. However, within certain limitations they can do many of the jobs done with the overarm and pin-routing machines. One such fixture is shown in Fig. 538, and a typical setup for fence-guided routing is shown in Fig. 539. The arm is simply a flat steel bar ended with a column clamp. This column clamp is actually a part taken from a commercially available drill-press clamp manufactured by the Wetzler Clamp Co., of Long Island City, New York. The arm attaches directly to the chuck of the drill press. The quill of the drill press must always be in the locked position. The overarm device does not accurately permit vertical entry into a workpiece, and it is best *not* used for such operations. However, for jobs requiring overarm vertical routing and some pin applications it

works just great. It makes a rigid overarm hookup. (See Fig. 540.)

Fig. 538. *This homemade accessory converts a drill press to an overarm routing machine. The cast-iron column clamp is from a commercially manufactured drill-press clamp.*

Fig. 539. *The overarm works well for fence-guided operations and similar jobs not requiring vertical entry into the work. Note that the arm is clamped into the drill chuck. The quill is locked to prevent vertical movement.*

Fig. 540. *Surfacing a rough slab.*

Another version of this same idea, made entirely of metal, is shown in Figs. 541 and 542. It will do the same jobs as the one discussed above. This one is made from a short length of large-diameter pipe to make the motor housing. Set screws hold and adjust the router to a true vertical position. (See Figs. 543 and 544.)

Fig. 541. *Another version of a drill-press overarm routing attachment. This one of large pipe has two welded rods for a choice of bit-to-column capacities. Either rod may be chucked in the drill press.*

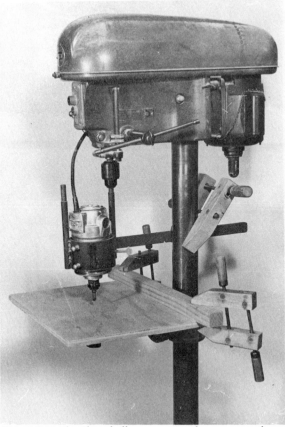

Fig. 542. *Another drill press setup for overarm fence-guided routing. Note the clamp holding the arm against the column.*

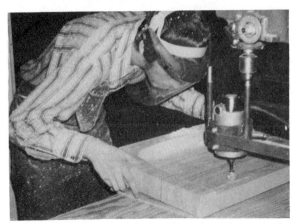

Fig. 543. *A large auxiliary table with guide pin facilitates routing this cutting board with a slanted surface. Wedges between the work and template tilt the work so the resulting surface is slanted. See Fig. 544.*

Fig. 544. *This cutting board made by Keith Bonville employed the setup shown in Fig. 543.*

A dowel-making fixture Figs. 545 to 548 show a fairly efficient device. When set up just right, it aids in spinning out router-cut dowels with amazing speed and accuracy. The one in the accompanying photos is made from three pieces of ¾-inch (18-mm) Northern hard maple 5½ × 20 inches (140 × 510 mm). Two of the pieces are laminated together face to face. This thicker, built-up member makes the die or exit block. In this piece, holes will be bored that are the same diameter as the prospective dowels.

Fig. 546. *A square blank is fed under a rotating router bit with drive provided by an electric drill.*

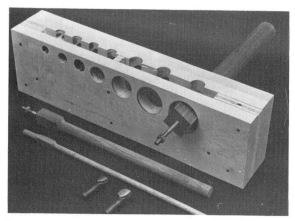

Fig. 545. *A jig for making router-cut dowels.*

An entry work-guiding block is an aid in obtaining a straight starting feed of the square blank into the rotating bit. Bore larger holes in this piece of hardwood, each a size that will permit a workpiece of square cross-sectional shape to just spin and be fed into this hole. The chart below gives the finished dowel size, the large-hole diameter for the blank-entry guide block, and the approximate cross-sectional size for rip-sawing the square dowel blanks.

Fig. 547. *Close-up showing the square blank at entry and the dowel at the exit side. Note the hanger bolt for gripping the workpiece in the drill chuck.*

Finished Dowel Diameter	Large Engry Hole Diameter	Approximate Square Blank Size
¼″ (6 mm)	½″ (12 mm)	⅜ × ⅜″ (9 × 9 mm)
⅜″ (9 mm)	¾″ (18 mm)	½ × ½″ (12 × 12 mm)
½″ (12 mm)	⅞″ (21 mm)	⅝ × ⅝″ (16 × 16 mm)
¾″ (18 mm)	1¼″ (31 mm)	⅞ × ⅞″ (21 × 21 mm)
1″ (24 mm)	1⅝″ (40 mm)	1⅛ × 1⅛″ (29 × 29 mm)
1¼″ (31 mm)	1⅞″ (45 mm)	1⅜ × 1⅜″ (35 × 35 mm)
1½″ (38 mm)	2⅜″ (60 mm)	1⅝ × 1⅝″ (40 × 40 mm)

The holes in the entry block and the die block must be perfectly aligned to each other on their centers. A close look at Fig. 547 shows a ¾-inch (18-mm) plywood spacer inserted between the entry block and the die block. This allows room for chips to fall through during cutting.

As noted previously in the chart, approximate sizes are given for ripping the square blanks. Depending upon hard or soft wood, it is best to have the squares sawed a touch oversize, so only the very outer corners of the blank will be knocked off as the workpiece spins in the large hole of the entry block. This will take some experimentation to get it just right. Small blank pieces can be sanded or carved round at one end to fit the chuck of the electric hand drill used to feed. Fig. 547 shows a ¼-inch (6-mm) or ⁵⁄₁₆-inch (8-mm) hanger bolt screwed into the end of the blank. This is then chucked in a portable electric drill. It's important that the hanger bolt be inserted straight into the blank or the workpiece will wobble, making feeding more difficult.

Use a ⅜–½-inch (9–12-mm) roundnose bit for cutting dowels up to ¾ inch (18 mm) in diameter and a ⅝-, ¾-, or 1-inch (16-, 18-, or 24-mm) roundnose bit to cut the larger size dowels. The router is clamped on top of the jig (Fig. 546) and lined up so the vertical axis of the router bit aligns with the front surface of the die block on the entry side. Use the router's own vertical adjustment. By trial and error, set the best depth-of-cut adjustment. When the depth of cut is properly set, the dowel will spin through the die hole. The cut surface of the dowel should come out surprisingly smooth. When working just right, the surfaces become slightly burnished from spinning against the inside surfaces of the die hole as the dowel is fed through. If the bit is set too shallow, there will be resistance in the feed and a burned surface will result. If the bit is set too deeply, the work will tend to feed too fast and the dowel will have rough spiral grooves on the surface. (See Fig. 548.)

Fig. 548. Examples of router-cut dowels, from top to bottom: ¼-inch (6-mm) oak and walnut, ⅜-inch (8-mm) butternut, ½-inch (12-mm) oak, ¾-inch (12-mm) butternut, 1-inch (25-mm) pine, 1¼-inch (30-mm) and 1½-inch (37-mm) dowels in butternut.

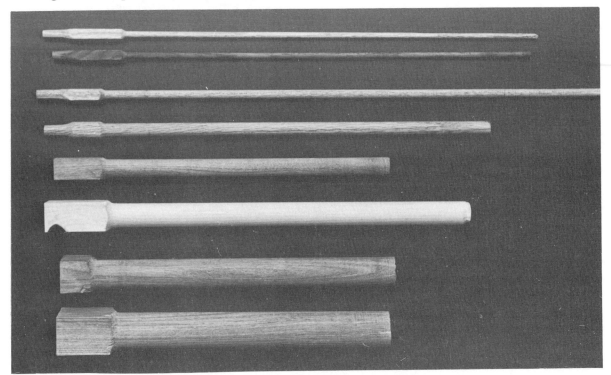

15

Panel Routing Devices

There are several different types of router accessories and machines available designed specifically for making decorative designs and joint-fitting cuts in panels. These devices are primarily used by professional cabinetmakers for machining cabinet ends, drawer fronts, doors, and similar work. The different pieces of equipment illustrated in this chapter range greatly in their purchase price and work capacities. The largest machine will handle panels up to 62 inches (1550 mm) wide of unlimited length. Most of the devices operate with the workpiece positioned horizontally, but the larger units machine the panels supported in a vertical position, to save floor space and facilitate easier handling of the large panels.

The least expensive units are designed for making decorative grooves in the drawer fronts and doors of kitchen cabinets and similar cabinetry. These employ basic template- and straight-line routing operations. They consist of four adjustable guide rails and interchangeable corner templates of various designs. In use, the router (with a base-mounted-template guide [bushing]) is moved along the rails and corner templates to effect the cut.

The Sears door and panel decorator Fig. 549 shows a device that will make a variety of designs in panels up to 36 × 36 inches (900 × 900 mm) in size. The kit comes with seven sets of different corner templates that simply

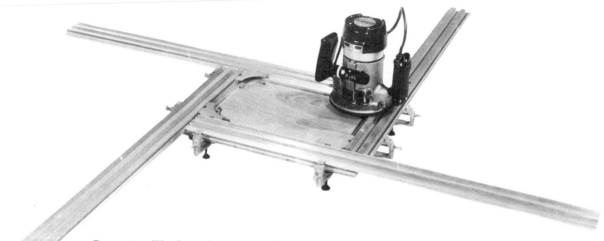

Fig. 549. The Sears door and panel decorator.

snap in and out of the straight extruded aluminum guide rails. Clamps hold the assembly to the panel. Repetitive cuts in various pieces are easy to make without further adjustment, as long as each panel is the same size. The Sears door and panel decorating kit also comes with an adjustable radius arm for cutting arcs, as shown in Fig. 550.

Fig. 550.   A radius cutting arm is part of the Sears door and panel decorator kit.

The Wing router templates   Fig. 551 shows a similar device used to make ornamental border designs in doors or drawers. It is manufactured of steel tubing and die-cast aluminum. The Wing unit adjusts to fit any square or rectangular workpiece from 3½ × 3½ inches (89 × 89 mm) up to 24 × 36 inches (600 × 900 mm). Extension bars are available to increase panel size capacity to 84 by 84 inches (2140 × 2140 mm). Wing Sales and

Fig. 551.   The Wing door and drawer routing template.

Distributing Co. of Payson, Arizona, has 16 basic border and corner template design sets available. Four come with the purchase of the accessory. When their various templates are used in combination with each other, a great

Fig. 552.   The Wing arc design attachment.

number of new design configurations become possible. An optional arc design attachment (Fig. 552) is also available from this manufacturer.

The Bosch cabinet door template system   Figs. 553 and 554 show a different operating system from those described above. The router base rides directly on the door surface, so no template guide or bushing is

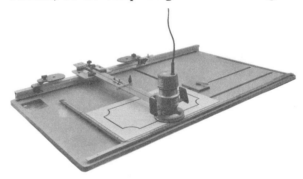

Fig. 553.   The Bosch cabinet door machine. Note that the router rides directly on the surface of the door panel.

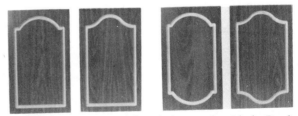

Fig. 554.   Some typical door designs made with the Bosch cabinet door template system.

required. The straight line cutting is accomplished through a carriage-and-rail system. This also permits straight line grooving, to make vertical or cross planking design effects. (See Fig. 555). The Bosch system has many accessories available, such as their variable arc routing attachment (Fig. 556), which makes a science of decorative door routing. Their corner templates are made of phenolic plastic. One special feature of their basic machine is that the distance from the edge of the door to the cut can be varied on all four sides or set to be cut the same. This unit will handle door panels up to 2 inches (50 mm) thick, and up to 36 × 60 inches (900 × 1500 mm).

The Sears Decorout-or-Planer Fig. 557 shows a router-guide carriage assembly that rides on rails over any point on an area up to 21 × 42 inches (535 × 1070 mm). It will accept stock up to 1⅜ inches (35 mm) in thickness. With a wide, flat cutting bit, this device can be used to plane or level to uniform thickness work such as glued-up boards. Subsequent sanding is necessary to obtain smooth, flat surfaces. This router accessory comes without the worktable, which must be constructed. The tubular rails require approximately 39 × 67 inches (990 × 1704 mm) of

Fig. 555. A straight-line grooving accessory for the Bosch system has stops on the bar which control the location of the grooves cut into the door.

Fig. 556. A unique variable-arc cutting guide for the Bosch unit employs dual movable pivots that allow the radius of the arc to be varied through the length of the cut.

Fig. 557. The Sears Decorout-or Planer.

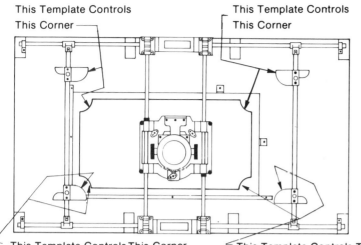

This Template Controls This Corner

This Template Controls This Corner

This Template Controls This Corner

This Template Controls This Corner

Fig. 558.   Top view showing how templates control the corner cuts for routing a provincial design. The carriage has rollers at each corner that ride against the corner templates.

space for mounting the unit. Various templates are available or can be user-made to do door and panel decorative grooving. Fig. 558 shows how corner designs are control-cut. The unit comes with four different size templates in two styles (provincial and reverse-provincial), along with an operator's manual.

Large panel routers   Fig. 559 shows big units that require 2½ × 10 feet (.8 × 3 m) of floor space and stand 7 feet (2.1 m) high. The machine shown here is basically intended for routing dadoes, grooves, and rabbet cuts of all types, as required in the fabrication of residential and institutional cabinetry. The router, on a tracked carriage, moves very easily vertically with counterweight assistance. Even though track guided, the router is mounted so

it actually rides on the surface of the work. It has a crowned router base, which assures that the cut will be of uniform depth throughout—even if the workpiece is warped. Vertical cuts are made by the vertically tracked guided router, and horizontal cuts are made by feeding the workpiece while the router is locked in a stationary position.

The manufacturer, Safranek Enterprises, Inc. of Atascadero, California, makes a complete line of panel routers in various models and with numerous optional features. Air clamps, air vacuums, air routers, automatic feeds and various other fixturing, and special bits are available independently or in combination, to make a customized machine for particular production requirements.

Fig. 559.   The Her-Saf panel routing machine is used for production of cabinetry requiring grooves, dadoes, rabbets, and various stopped cuts in panel components.

16
Project Section

Throughout the pages of this book are a number of projects developed especially for the router. This section contains illustrations and drawings showing the construction details for many of these projects, but in some cases it will be necessary to refer to other chapters for the operating illustrations or photographs of the completed project.

The dimensions and other specifications provided here are only suggestions. They may be changed or modified to accommodate the materials available, changed so the project matches the operator's router capacity or the bit limitations, and they can be changed to improve, personalize, or modify the overall design. Directions and other information are given in the captions and text accompanying the project drawing and photos.

Basic routing techniques are employed to make the projects shown in Fig. 560. Refer to Figs. 561, 562, and 563 for essential details. Turn to page 85 for some other design ideas for picture frames.

Fig. 560.   Some projects that involve basic routing techniques.

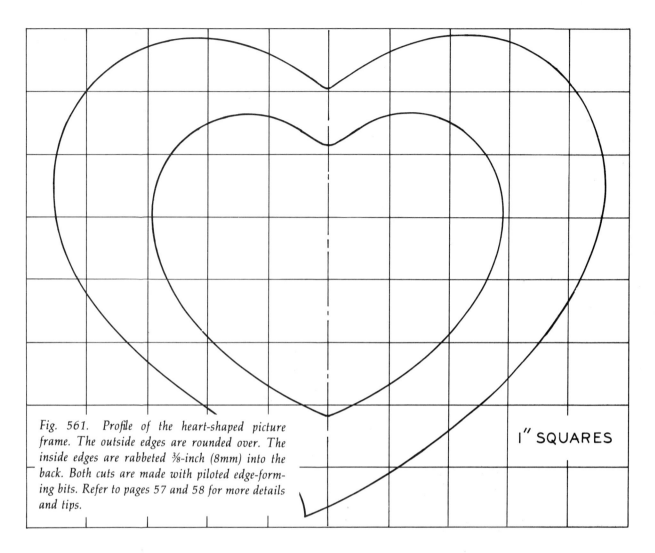

Fig. 561. *Profile of the heart-shaped picture frame. The outside edges are rounded over. The inside edges are rabbeted ⅜-inch (8mm) into the back. Both cuts are made with piloted edge-forming bits. Refer to pages 57 and 58 for more details and tips.*

1″ SQUARES

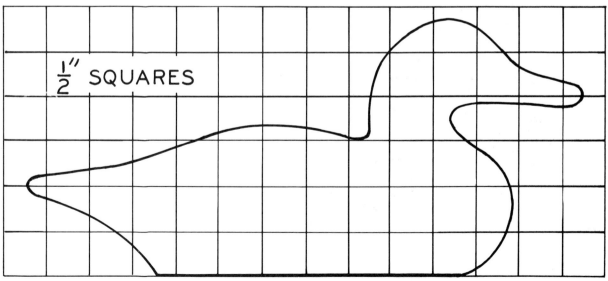

½″ SQUARES

Fig. 562. *A pattern such as this is good for practicing freehand engraving.*

Fig. 563. *This double-oval picture frame involves freehand incised routing. Inside ovals are rabbeted, and all edges are rounded over.*

Wood switch plates are ideal projects that involve basic template routing. (See Figs. 564 and 565.) Fig. 566 shows a close-up of a recess cut into the back of a plate. This is an optional operation. Refer to pages 74 and 76.

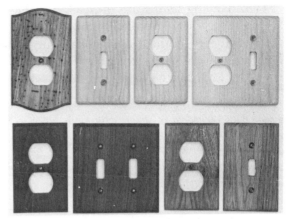

Fig. 564. *Wood switch plates (of any profile) are good "little" production jobs using patterns and templates.*

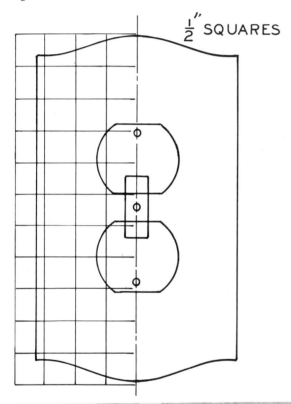

½" SQUARES

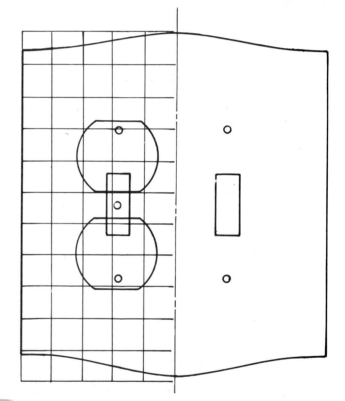

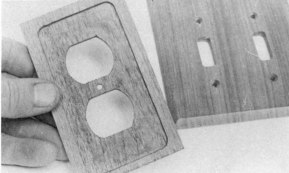

Fig. 565 (above). *A composite drawing of switch and receptacle plates. Stock thickness can vary between ¼ and ⅜ inches (6 and 8 mm).*

Fig. 566 (left). *Back view, showing a recess which allows the plates to fit closer to the wall.*

Two hanging lamps are illustrated in Figs. 567 and 568. Decorative chain can be added to convert these to the popular hanging-style lamps. Such chain is available from hobby shops and hardware dealers.

Fig. 567 (right). *Hanging lamps of ¼-inch (6-mm) plywood. Both hexagonal in shape, with joints glued using tape or large rubber bands for clamping. Thin, rigid sheets of fiberglass shade material rolled into interior cylinders are available from crafts stores and mail-order houses specializing in plastic materials.*

Fig. 568 (below). *Half pattern details for the hanging lamp. Refer to pages 72 and 74 for more information.*

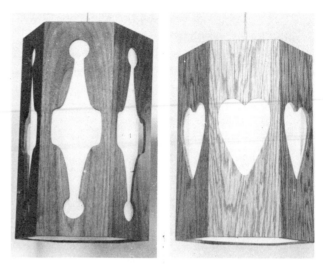

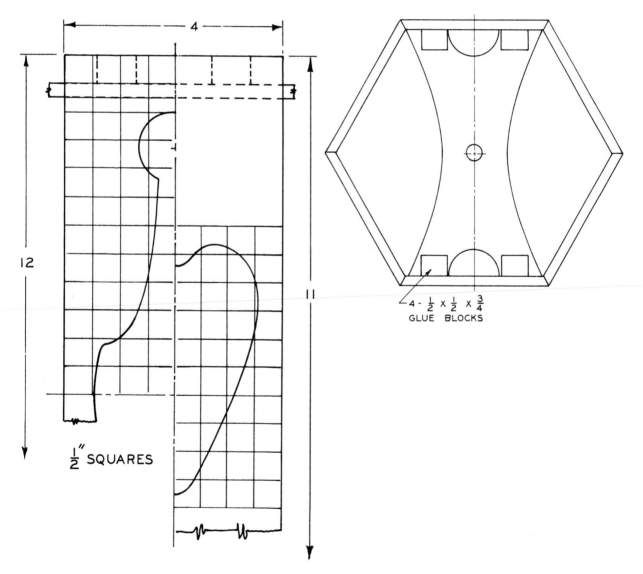

½" SQUARES

$4 - \frac{1}{2} \times \frac{1}{2} \times \frac{3}{4}$
GLUE BLOCKS

Fig. 569 is the drawing of the shelf or mantel bracket, used as a freehand routing demonstration on page 103. Turn to page 196, which shows how to rout the grooves into the front edge.

Turn to page 196, which shows how to rout the grooves into the front edge.

Fig. 569.   Details of a bracket for a fireplace mantel or a support for a heavy shelf.

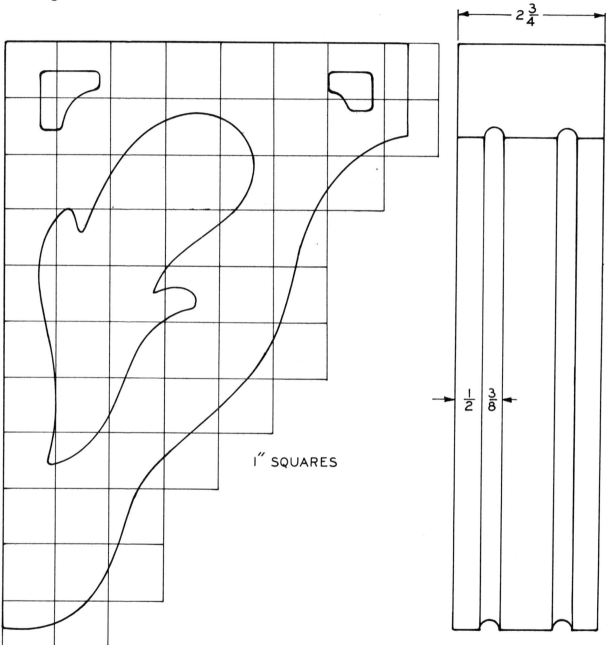

1" SQUARES

Figs. 570–572 show projects that involve similar router cuts. Fig. 570 gives the details for making a small, narrow tray from a 1 × 4-inch board (24 × 104-mm) board. The details and dimensions are easily modified to make serving trays of larger sizes. Incidentally, trays and cutting boards require cuts with flat bottoms and a radius to the inside wall (or vertical) surface. Anyone who intends to do much of this type of work should have a special bit ground just for this class of cutting jobs. A bit of this type can easily be ground from any conventional straight cutting bit. Otherwise, such jobs require two bits—a roundnose to outline the inside perimeter, and another bit to cut a flat bottom. The latter bit is used to remove all stock on the flat surface and to clean it to the point where the radius cut by the roundnose bit starts to turn up the wall.

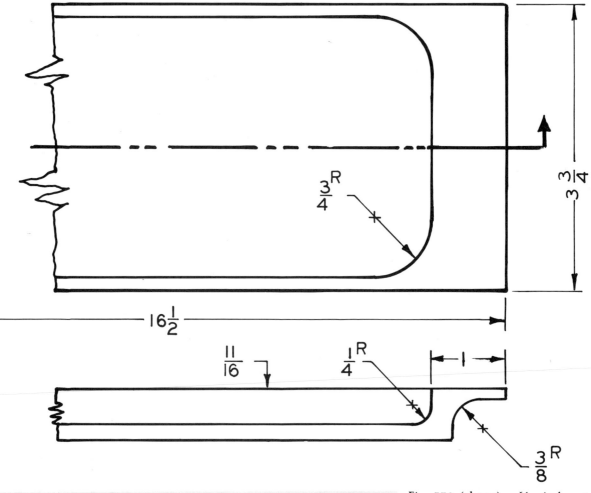

Fig. 570 (above). Here's how to rout a tray from a 1 x 4 (25–100). Change width and length dimensions to make larger as desired.

Fig. 571 (left). Essentially the same cuts are involved to make this cutting board as to make the small tray. The pattern is shown in Fig. 572.

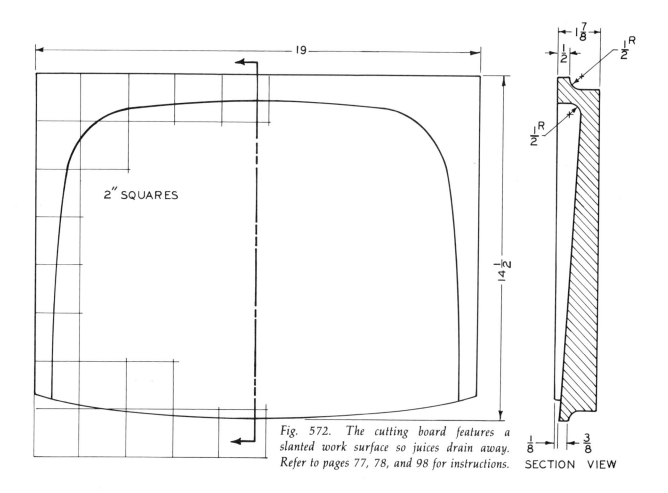

19

2" SQUARES

14 1/2

1 7/8

1/2

1/2 R

1/2 R

1/8

3/8

SECTION VIEW

Fig. 572. *The cutting board features a slanted work surface so juices drain away. Refer to pages 77, 78, and 98 for instructions.*

Wooden chain (Fig. 573), without dispute, is unique and fun to make. A choice of two suggested sizes is detailed in Fig. 574. To make the chain links, a box-type and a plug-type workpiece-holding fixture/pattern must be accurately made for each size chain link. Make the box fixture/pattern first (left, Fig. 575). Then make the plug so it fits snugly (without too much clearance) into the female pattern. A little trial-and-error fitting may be necessary. If the inside opening of the link is cut too large, the work can be shimmed with paper when set onto the plug. However, for production of links, it's best to get the combination of fits just right—it makes the job faster and more fun. Other people will want you to make chains for them once they see yours, so prepare yourself appropriately. Refer to pages 12 and 59 for more information and other illustrations pertaining to this project. The majority of steps involved are illustrated in Figs. 576–583. You'll like this project!

Fig. 573. *Chain can be made in large or small sizes.*

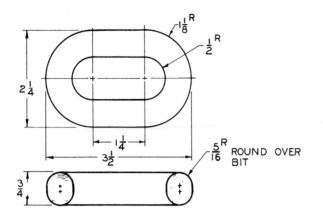

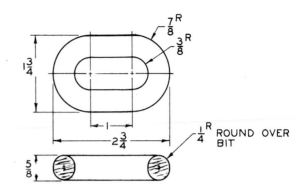

Fig. 574. This drawing gives the details for making chain in two different sizes.

Fig. 575. Make work-holding fixtures as shown to match the chain link size.

Fig. 576. Prepare the blocks to finished size. Remove most of the inside waste by boring. Use a ball-bearing trimming bit to clean up the inside opening with the block held in the box-pattern fixture.

Fig. 579. *Rounding over the inside in the "box" fixture.*

Fig. 577. *Here's how the inside opening is cleaned and trimmed to size. Note that the ball bearing rides on the pattern part of the fixture.*

Fig. 580. *Rounding over on the "plug" fixture. When rounding over, set the depth so a small "flat" remains uncut providing a surface for the ball bearing or pilot to ride on. Use minimal horizontal pressure.*

Fig. 578. *The outside profile can be worked to shape using the trimming bit. Feed counterclockwise. To prevent chipping, cut only the two opposite corners, as shown. Then flip the workpiece over and cut the two remaining corners. This procedure allows you to cut all the corners, working with the grain. A piloted spiral bit works best for this job—or the corners can be sawed to rough size and then trimmed using the setup shown here.*

Fig. 581. Following sanding split open every other link. If it does not snap easily with hand pressure, use a thin-bladed knife and split one end open, cutting from the inside. Incidentally, a flap wheel speeds sanding.

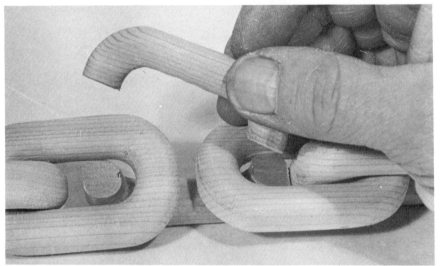

Fig. 582. Here's how the links go together to make a length of chain.

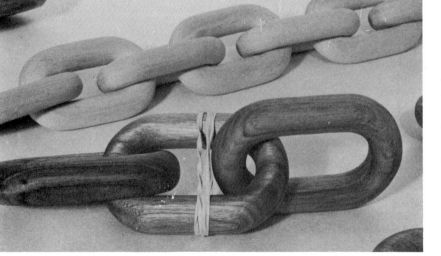

Fig. 583. Gluing in sets of threes with rubber band clamping pressure. Small hand screws, C-clamps, and a vise can be used for assembling the sets into long chain.

A nifty project designed to give some experience in making interesting wood grills with the router is the hanging lamp, shown in Fig. 584. (See also Figs. 585 and 586.)

Fig. 584 (left). *Grills of router-cut boards are assembled to make this lamp.*

Fig. 585 (above). *A close-up showing one of the grill cut boards before mitering the vertical edges to make the lamp in Fig. 584.*

Fig. 586 (below). *Layout for the cove cuts. This is only one of hundreds of different design patterns possible. Refer to pages 6, 95, 198, and 199.*

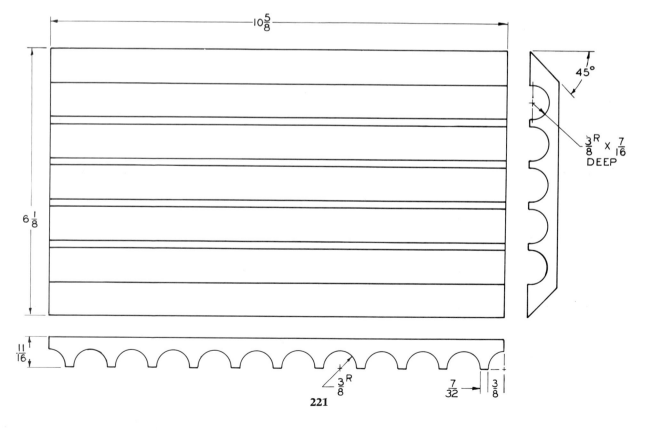

Fig. 587 shows a carving project. Fig. 588 gives some suggested sizes. This project was not totally shaped with the router. First it was band-sawed to a compound shape by sawing the profile of the side view and then turned 90° to saw the top-view profile. The hollow was bored with several holes at varying depths to remove excess material and then power-filed to its inside and outside contours with the router, as shown on page 197.

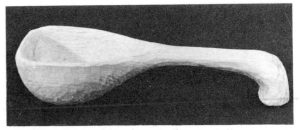

Fig. 587. *A carved spoon (ladle). Its hollow, concave surface was worked with router assistance.*

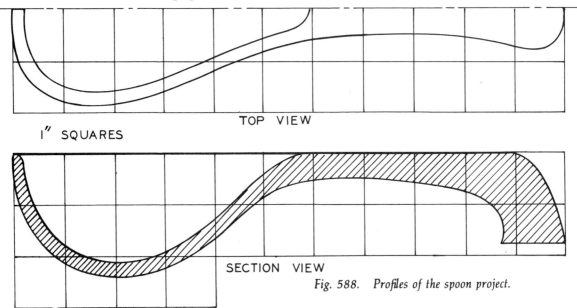

TOP VIEW

1″ SQUARES

SECTION VIEW

Fig. 588. *Profiles of the spoon project.*

Many other projects for router work are also found throughout this book. Drawings and other specifications are not included here for projects that are very fundamental or basic in design or construction when details are easy for the router craftsman to figure out. A plastic laminated clock is shown on page 117; examples and techniques for routing wood signs are given on pages 64, 73, and 109–115. A number of dovetailing projects, such as various boxes (Fig. 589) and a stool, are illustrated in Chapter 11, page 162.

The above projects show the extensive variety of work that can be performed with the router. These examples are only a small number compared to the many router projects appearing regularly in woodcraft magazines.

The router is definitely the "in" tool today. Its potential as a woodworking instrument is just beginning to be put to the test. For to-

Fig. 589. *Drawings are not really needed for all router projects. Refer to Fig. 390, page 152.*

morrow, who knows? It's not unreasonable to expect that, along with new routers and cutting tools, many new uses and projects will arrive on the scene. After all, what else can happen when a tool of this capability is put into the hands of today's talented and creative woodworkers—a group whose numbers are increasing daily?

Index

A
Air-powered routers, 15, 19, 28–29
Allen Duplicating Machine, 192
Alphabet, 112

B
Ball bearings, 22, 38, 51
Basic information, 20–29
Basic operations, 52–68
Beall Tool Co., 129–130
Bevel planing, 123
Bits, 11, 30–47, 116, 133, 150–151, 159, 161, 181
Blind cuts, 146
Bosch cabinet door template system, 207–208
Bowl Crafter, 130
Bracket, 103–196, 215

C
Cabinetmaking, 6, 85–91, 206–209
Carbide-tipped bits, 33
Chainmaking, 12, 59, 217–220
Clocks, 7, 79, 117, 129, 201
Collet, 51
Contact cement, 118
Cutting board, 77–78, 216–217

D
Dado, 81
Doors, cabinet, 88–89
Douglas fir, 56, 101
Dovetail joints, 5, 150–167
Dowel-making fixture, 204–205
Drawer assembly, 87
Dremel Drill Press-Routing accessory, 170–171
Drill-press overarm accessories, 202–203
Drop-leaf table joint, 89–91

Dupli-Carver, 193–195
Dust, 49–50
Duz-Awl, 177–178

E
Edge Crafter, 148–149
Edge guides, 59–64
Edges, of plastic laminate, 118, 119

F
Feed direction, 53
Fences, 139–141, 152
Finish carpenters, 122
Fluting, 95–97
Frame guide, 65–66
Freehand routing, 101–115, 197, 211, 212, 215

G
Goggles, 48
Grillwork, 6, 95, 198–199, 221
Guides, 56–68

H
Hartlauer, Walter, 128, 177, 178
Her-Saf panel routing machine, 209
High-speed steel, see HSS
Hinge mortise routing, 115
History, 12
Hobbi-Carver, 183
Horsepower, and function, 21–22
Hot-melt glue, 57, 73, 74, 78, 97
HSS, 33

I
Inlay making, 91–94

J
Joint routing, 79–100

K
Keller, David A., templates, 160–161
"Keyhole" bit, 43
Kimball Woodcarvers, 184–186

L
Laminate trimmers, 119–121
Lamps, 70, 214, 221
Lap joints, 82
Leigh dovetail jigs, 156–160
Letter-routing templates, 124–125

M
Maintenance of router, 48–51
Marlin Carving Machine, 187–189
Mortise-and-tenon joint, 81
Mortising templates, 123

Mc
McIlree, Tom, 112

O
On-off switch, 26–27
Onsrud, C. R., routers, 179–181
Overarm routing machines, 168–181

P
Panel-raising bits, 40–41
Panel routing devices, 206–209
Pantographs, 125–128, 183–184, 187
Particle board, 118
Pattern routing, 10, 69–78
Picture frames, 85, 107, 198, 210–212
Pin-routing machines, 168–181
Plastic laminates, 116–121
Plunging router, 26, 79
Power-plane attachment, 122–123
Projects, 210–222

R
Rabbet, 81, 86
Radial router, 198–199
Radial saw, 199–202
Redwood, 101, 112
Resorcinal, 116
Rockwell Overarm Router Shaper, 178–179

"Roping," 131, 134, 135
Round tenoning, 147
Rout-A-Sign, 183–184
Router carving machines, 182–195
"Router Crafter," 7, 131–135
Router lathe, 131–135
Router table, 9, 136–149
Rub pilots, 57

S
Saddle template, 76
Safety, 48–51
Sears Decorout-or-Planer, 208–209
Sears door and panel decorator, 206–207
Sears pin router, 172
Self-edge, 118

Serpentine routing, 14, 196–197
Shank adapter, 44
Shopsmith, router-arm attachment, 172–174
Signmaking, 6, 40, 109–115, 183–195 *passim*
Slot-cutting guides, 66–68
Spiral bits, 38–39, 123
Spoon, 197, 222
Stop blocks, 146
Sub-base, 23, 72, 78, 102, 103, 113
Surfacing, 97–100
Switch plates, 74, 76, 213

T
Tapering, 98, 100
Template routing, 69–78, 123–125, 154–161, 183–185, 197, 207
Trim saws, 43–44
Trivets, 199
T-square, 65, 114

V
vacuum attachment, 49–50, 64 138, 178
Vernon, Joseph, 152–153

W
Wall panelling, 83
Wing router templates, 207
Wood flooring, 83
Wood threads, 128–130

X
X-Y Routermatic, 190–191

Contemporary Issues in Healthcare Law and Ethics

Edited by

Austen Garwood-Gowers LLB PhD
Senior Lecturer in Law, Nottingham Law School, Nottingham Trent University, Nottingham, UK

John Tingle BA (Hons) CertEd MEd Barrister
Reader in Health Law, Director of the Centre for Health Law, Nottingham Law School, Nottingham Trent University, Nottingham, UK

Kay Wheat BA Solicitor
Reader in Health Law, Nottingham Law School, Nottingham Trent University, Nottingham, UK

ELSEVIER
BUTTERWORTH
HEINEMANN

EDINBURGH LONDON NEW YORK OXFORD PHILADELPHIA ST LOUIS SYDNEY TORONTO 2005

ELSEVIER

BUTTERWORTH
HEINEMANN

An imprint of Elsevier Limited

W 32

© 2005, Elsevier Limited. All rights reserved.

First published 2005

ISBN 0 7506 8832 7

British Library Cataloguing in Publication Data
A catalogue record for this book is available from the British Library

Library of Congress Cataloging in Publication Data
A catalog record for this book is available from the Library of Congress

Notice
Knowledge and best practice in this field are constantly changing. As new research and experience broaden our knowledge, changes in practice, treatment and drug therapy may become necessary or appropriate. Readers are advised to check the most current information provided (i) on procedures featured or (ii) by the manufacturer of each product to be administered, to verify the recommended dose or formula, the method and duration of administration, and contraindications. It is the responsibility of the practitioner, relying on their own experience and knowledge of the patient, to make diagnoses, to determine dosages and the best treatment for each individual patient, and to take all appropriate safety precautions. To the fullest extent of the law, neither the publisher nor the editors assume any liability for any injury and/or damage.

The Publisher

Working together to grow
libraries in developing countries

www.elsevier.com | www.bookaid.org | www.sabre.org

ELSEVIER   BOOK AID International   Sabre Foundation

ELSEVIER   your source for books, journals and multimedia in the health sciences

www.elsevierhealth.com

The publisher's policy is to use paper manufactured from sustainable forests

Printed in China

Contents

Contributors   vii

Table of cases   ix

Table of statutes   xiii

Table of conventions and international instruments   xvi

Table of statutory instruments   xvii

Table of abbreviations   xviii

Introduction   1

SECTION 1 – Regulating healthcare

1.   The social creation of health law and health in the USA   15
     F. Dale Parent

2.   Does it pay to be NICE? Resolving the 'legitimacy problem' in the allocation of
     healthcare resources   37
     Keith Syrett

3.   The ownership of clinical risk in acute hospitals in England – an historical perspec-
     tive   55
     Claire Strickland

4.   Does the *Bolam* Principle still reign in medical negligence cases in Malaysia?   79
     Puteri Nemie Jahn Kassim

5.   Medico-crime in the UK: an introduction   93
     Wendy Hesketh

SECTION 2 – Reproductive technologies

6. New reproductive technologies – discourse and dilemma   115
   Susan C. Johnson

7. Pre-implantation genetic diagnosis – towards a principled construction of law?   133
   Thérèse Callus

SECTION 3 – Bodies and body parts

8. Human bodies, inhuman uses: public reactions and legislative responses to the scandals of bodysnatching   151
   M.E. Rodgers

9. *Nemo censetur ignorare legem?* Presumed consent to organ donation in France, from Parliament to hospitals   173
   Graciela Nowenstein

SECTION 4 – Questionable interventions during life

10. The proper limits for medical intervention that harms the therapeutic interests of incompetents   191
    Austen Garwood-Gowers

11. Infant vaccination: a conflict of ethical imperatives?   213
    Stephanie Pywell

12. Cyberwoman and her surgeon in the twenty-first century   233
    Melanie Latham

SECTION 5 – The end of life

13. Legal recognition of the right to die   253
    Heleen Weyers

14. Regulating active voluntary euthanasia: what can England and Wales learn from Belgium and the Netherlands?   269
    Samantha Halliday

Index   303

Contributors

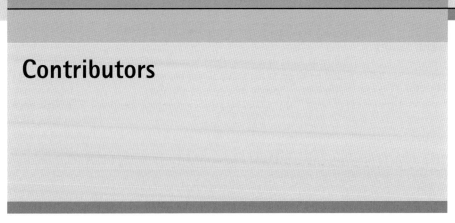

Thérèse Callus LLB(Hons) DEA(Droit Privé) PhD(Docteur en Droit Privé)
Lecturer, School of Law, University of Reading, Reading, UK

Austen Garwood-Gowers LLB PhD
Senior Lecturer in Law, Nottingham Law School, Nottingham Trent University, Nottingham, UK

Samantha Halliday LLB(Hons)
Senior Lecturer in Law, Liverpool Law School, University of Liverpool, Liverpool, UK

Wendy Hesketh LLB(Hons) PGDipLP PGCE
Department of Employment & Learning (DEL) Award Doctoral Researcher in Medical Law, School of Law, University of Ulster, UK

Susan C. Johnson RGN BSc(Hons) PhD
Lecturer, University of Nottingham, Nottingham, UK

Puteri Nemie Jahn Kassim LLB(Hons) MCL PhD(Law)
Assistant Professor, Ahmad Ibrahim Kulliyyah of Laws, International Islamic University Malaysia, Kuala Lumpur, Malaysia

Melanie Latham BSc(Hons) PhD PGCE
Reader in Law, School of Law, Manchester Metropolitan University, Manchester, UK
Graciela Nowenstein BA MA
Currently completing PhD (Sociology), European University Institute of Florence, Italy

F. Dale Parent BS(Rural Sociology) MA(Sociology) PhD(Sociology)
Professor of Sociology, Department of Sociology and Criminal Justice, Southeastern Louisiana University, Louisiana, USA

Stephanie Pywell BA LLB(Hons) PhD
Assistant Editorial Manager, ILEX Tutorial College, Bedford, UK*

M.E. Rodgers BA LLB(Hons) DipAppSS
Senior Lecturer, Nottingham Trent University, Nottingham, UK

Claire Strickland MPhil MA(Hons) PGCE
Senior Lecturer, Northumbria University, UK

Keith Syrett BA MA PhD Solicitor
Lecturer, School of Law, University of Bristol, UK

Heleen Weyers PhD(Sociology of Law)
Lecturer, Department of Legal Theory, University of Groningen, Groningen, The Netherlands

*The views of Stephanie Pywell do not necessarily represent the views of the Institute of Legal Executives or its members.

Table of cases

United Kingdom

A (Children) (Conjoined Twins: Surgical Separation), Re [2001] Fam 147
    272

Airedale NHS Trust v Bland [1993] AC 789; [1993] 1 All ER 821 (HL); [1993] 1 All ER 806
    199–201, 202, 237, 270, 271, 272–273

Attorney General's Reference [No. 6 of 1980] 2 All ER 1057
    202

B (Consent to Treatment: Capacity), Re [2002] EWHC 429 (Fam), [2002] 1 FLR 1090
    1

Blyth v Bloomsbury Health Authority [1993] Med LR 151
    235

Bolam v Friern Hospital Management Committee [1957] 2 All ER 118; [1957] 1 WLR 582
    59, 71, 79–92, 235, 236, 239

Bolitho v City & Hackney Health Authority [1997] 4 All ER 771; [1997] 3 WLR 1151
    4, 66, 70–71, 82, 83, 235, 236

B v An NHS Hospital Trust [2002] 2 All ER 449
    270

Chatterton v Gerson [1981] QB 432
    5

Chester v Afshar [2004] UKHL 41
    4

Christine Williamson v East London and the City Health Authority & Others [1998] 41 BMLR 85
    238

C (Refusal of medical treatment), Re [1994] 1 FLR 31
    237

Fairchild v Glenhaven Funeral Services [2002] UKHL 22
    4

F (in utero), Re [1998] Fam 122, 138
    121

F (Mental Patient: Sterilisation), Re [1990] 2 AC 1, [1989] 2 WLR 1025
    198

Gascoine v Ian Sheridan & Co [1994] 5 Med LR 437
    82

Gillick v Wisbech AHA [1986] AC 112
    293

Gold v Haringey Health Authority [1987] 2 All ER 888
    235

H (A Minor) (Blood Tests: Parental Rights), Re [1996] 4 All ER 28
    196

Hucks v Cole (1968), *The Times*, 9 May
    81–82

J (A Minor) (Wardship: Medical Treatment), Re [1991] Fam 33
    271

Joyce v Merton, Sutton and Wandsworth Health Authority [1995] 6 Med LR 60
  82
Leeds Teaching Hospitals NHS Trust v Mr and Mrs A and Others [2003] 1 FLR 412
  1
MB (Medical Treatment), Re [1997] 2 FLR 426
  270
Natallie Evans v Amicus Healthcare Ltd and Others [2004] 3 WLR 681
  1
NHS Trust A v M; NHS Trust B v H [2001] Fam. 348
  278
Norfolk and Norwich Healthcare Trust v W [1996] 2 FLR 613
  126
Norton v General Medical Council [2002] UKPC 6, 68 BMLR 169
  236, 238
O'Keefe v Harvey-Kemble [1999] 45 BMLR 74
  238–239
Paton v Trustees of the British Pregnancy Advisory Service and Another [1978] 2 All ER 987
  121
Pearce v United Bristol Healthcare NHS Trust [1998] 48 BMLR 118
  235–236
Penney, Palmer and Cannon v East Kent Health Authority [2001] Lloyd's Law Report (Medical) 41
  83
R (Assisted Reproduction and Gynaecology Centre) v Human Fertilisation and Embryology Authority [2002] EWCA Civ 20 (15)
  119, 125
R (On application of Bruno Quintavalle (On Behalf of Pro-Life Alliance) v Secretary of State for Health) [2003] UKHL 13
  1

R (On the Application of Pretty) v Director of Public Prosecutions [2002] 1 AC 800; [2002] 1 All ER 1, HL
  1, 9, 273, 274
R (Quintavalle on behalf of Comment on Reproductive Ethics) v Human Fertilisation & Embryology Authority [2003] EWCA Civ 667, CA; [2003] 2 All ER 105, QBD
  138, 139, 142
R v Adams, H. Palmer, Dr Adams' Trial for Murder [1957] Crim LR 365
  271
R v Arthur (1981) 12 BMLR 1
  272
R v Brown (Anthony) [1993] 2 All ER 75
  202, 237
R v Cambridge HA, ex parte B (a minor) [1995] 2 All ER 129
  39
R v Human Fertilisation and Embryology Authority ex parte Josephine Quintavalle [2003] EWCA Civ 667; [2002] EWHC 2785
  1, 119, 120
R v North Derbyshire HA, ex parte Fisher [1997] 8 Med LR 327
  39, 45
R v North West Lancashire HA, ex parte A, D and G
  39
R v Secretary of State for Foreign and Commonwealth Affairs, ex parte World Development Movement Ltd [1995] 1 WLR 386 (Pergau Dam affair)
  138
R v Secretary of State for Health, ex parte Pfizer Ltd [1999] Lloyd's Rep Med 289
  39
R v Woollin [1999] 1 AC 82; [1998] 4 All ER 103
  202, 272
S (A Child), Re [2004] UKHL 47
  196

S (Adult: refusal of medical treatment), Re [1992] 4 All ER 671
126
St George's Healthcare NHS Trust v S [1998] 3 All ER 673
270
Sidaway v Board of Governors of the Bethlem Royal and the Maudsley Hospital [1985] 1 All ER 643; [1985] 1 AC 871; [1985] 2 WLR 480
81, 82, 88, 89, 235, 237
Smith v Tunbridge Wells Health Authority [1994] 5 Med LR 334
235
South Glamorgan County Council v W and B [1993] 1 FLR 574
293
S v S, W v Official Solicitor [1970] 3 All ER 107 (HL)
196
T (Adult: refusal of medical treatment), Re [1992] 3 WLR 782
237–238, 270
W (A Minor) (Medical Treatment: Court's Jurisdiction), Re [1992] 4 All ER 627
293
Wilsher v Essex Area Health Authority [1987] QB 730
4
X (A Minor), Re [1975] 1 All ER 697
196

Australia
Chappel v Hart (1998) 195 CLR 232
4
F v R (1982) 33 SASR 189
84
Naxakis v Western General Hospital (1999) 83 ALJR 782
84–86
Rogers, Christopher v Whitaker, Maree Lynette (1992) CLR 479; (1992) 109 ALR 625 (HC of Aust)
84, 86, 89, 90, 236

Canada
Malette v Shulman (1990) 67 DLR (4th) 321 (Ont CA)
199
Reibl v Hughes (1980) 114 DLR (3d) 1
236
Winnipeg Child and Family Services (Northwest Area) v G (DF) [1997] 2 SCR 925
126

European Commission and Court of Human Rights
Airey v Ireland A 32, (1979) 2 EHRR 305
121
Pretty v UK (2002) 35 EHRR 1
1, 9
X v Austria (1980) 18 DR 154
270

Malaysia
Asiah bte Kamsah v Dr Rajinder Singh & Ors [2002] 1 MLJ 484
86
Chin Keow v Government of Malaysia [1967] 2 MLJ 45
87
Elizabeth Choo v Government of Malaysia [1970] 2 MLJ 171
87–88
Foo Fio Na v Hospital Assunta & Anor [1999] 6 MLJ 738
90, 91
Hong Chuan Lay v Dr Eddie Soo Fook Mun [1998] 5 CLJ 251
89, 91
Inderjeet Singh a/l Piara Singh v Mazlan bin Jasman & Ptrs [1995] 2 MLJ 646
86
Kamalam a/p & Ors v Eastern Plantation Agency & Anor [1996] 4 MLJ 674
90, 91
Kow Nan Seng v Nagamah & Ors [1982] 1 MLJ 128
88

Liew Sin Kiong v Dr Sharon M Paulraj [1996] 2 AMR 1403
  88–89
Mariah bte Mohamad (Administratix of the estate of Wan Salleh bin Wan Ibrahim, deceased) v Abdullah bin Daud (Dr Lim Kok Eng & Anor, Third Parties) [1990] 1 MLJ 240
  86
Roe v Minister of Health [1954] 2 WLR 915
  87
Soo Fook Mun, Dr v Foo Fio Na & Anor and Another Appeal [2001] 2 CLJ 457
  90–91
Swamy v Mathews [1968] 1 MLJ 138
  86–87

Netherlands

Admiraal case, *Nederlandse Jurisprudentie* 1985, no. 709
  280
Chabot case, *Nederlandse Jurisprudentie* 1994, no. 656 (Hoge Raad)
  275, 277–278, 279
Pols case, *Nederlandse Jurisprudentie* 1987, no. 607 (Hoge Raad)
  275
Postma case, *Nederlandse Jurisprudentie* 1973, no. 183
  254

Prins case, *Nederlandse Jurisprudentie* 1996, no. 113
  277
Schoonheim case, *Nederlandse Jurisprudentie* 1985, no. 106 (Hoge Raad)
  275, 278, 279, 280
Sutorius case HR 00797/02, 24/12/2002; (2003) 326 *BMJ* 71
  278, 287
Wertheim case, *Nederlandse Jurisprudentie* 1982, no. 63 (District Court of Rotterdam)
  275

United States

AC 533 A 2d 611, Re (DC 1987)
  126
Cruzan v Director, Missouri Department of Health 110 S. Ct. 2841 (1990)
  270
Eisenstadt v Baird US Supreme Court 405 US 438 (1972): 453
  121
McFall v Shimp (1978) 10 Pa D & C (3d) (Ct Common Pl, Pa)
  195–196
Roe v Wade 410 US 113 (1973)
  121, 264
Superintendent of Belchertown State School v Saikewicz (1977) 370 NE 2d 417
  200

Table of statutes

United Kingdom

Abortion Act 1967
  122
  s.1(1)(d)   122, 134
Anatomy Act 1832
  164–167, 169
Anatomy Act 1984
  166
Assisted Dying for the Terminally Ill Bill 2004
  1
Care Standards Act 2000
  234, 236, 239–240, 241, 247
  s.2(4)   240
  s.30   240
  Part I, Section 6   240
Children Act 1989
  s.1(1)   197
Consumer Protection Act 1987
  239
Coroners Act 1988
  167
Crown Proceedings Act 1947
  60
Family Law Reform Act 1969
  293
Health Act 1999
  s.18(1)   68
Health and Safety at Work Act 1974
  59
Human Fertilisation and Embryology Act 1990 (HFE Act)
  133, 134, 135, 136, 138, 140, 141, 143, 144, 145

  s.2(1)   136
  s.3(1)(b)   136
  s.13   122, 128
  s.13(5)   137
  s.37   122
  Sch. 2
    para 1   139
    para 1(1)(d)   136
    para 1(4)   119
    para 3   136
    para 3(2)   137
    para 3(4)   138
Human Fertilisation and Embryology Act 1991
125
  s.9(7)   120
  s.9(8)   120
Human Reproductive Cloning Act 2001
  128
Human Rights Act 1998
  ss.3.4   210
  s.19(1)(a)   209
Human Tissue Act 1961
  163, 164, 166, 167–169
Human Tissue Act 2004
  1, 168
Medical Act 1858
  57
Medical (Professional Performance) Act 1995
  236
Mental Capacity Act 2005
  1, 7, 193, 206, 210

s.1(5)	210
s.3	237
s.4	205
ss.26–29	205–206
s.30(3)	206
s.30(4)	206
s.31	206
s.31(1)	206
s.32	206–7
s.33	206–7

National Health Service Act 1977

s.11	40

National Health Service (Amendment) Act 1986

	60
s.1	60, 61
s.2	60, 61

National Health Service and Community Care Act 1990

	39, 63
s.5(1)	61
s.21	64
s.60	61
s.66(2)	61

Offences Against the Person Act 1861
236

Registered Homes Act 1984, Part II
240

Sale and Supply of Goods Act 1994, s.1
239

Sexual Offences Act 2003
106

Suicide Act 1961, s.2
274

Supply of Goods and Services Act 1982
239

Unfair Contract Terms Act 1977
239

Australia
Northern Territory's Rights of the Terminally Ill Act (1995)
294

Belgium
Belgian Penal Code
284

Art. 393	284
Art. 394	284
Art. 397	284
Art. 422	284

Law Relating to Euthanasia 2002
283, 284, 286, 288, 294, 296, 298

Art. 2	285
Art. 3	284, 289
Art. 3(1)(a)	285
Art. 3 §1	285, 287
Art. 3 §1(1)	287
Art. 3 §2(1)	285
Art. 3 §2(2)	285
Art. 3 §2(3)	287
Art. 3 §4	286
Art. 3 §5	285, 286
Art. 4 §1	289
Art. 5	289–290
Art. 14	290
Chapter II	285
Chapter V	
Arts. 6-9	290

Law Relating to Palliative Care 2001

Art. 2	285

Law Relating to the Rights of the Patient (2002)

	288
Art. 8 §4	270
Art. 12 §1	286
Art. 12 §2	286

Canada
Assisted Human Reproductive Act, s.5(1)(a)
128

Canada Health Act 2002
27–28

Denmark
Danish Criminal Code

Art. 239   258
Art. 240   258
Patients' Rights Act 1998
    258

France
Lois de bioéthique 1994
    175, 176, 182

Netherlands
Burial & Cremation Act
    ss. 7-10   282
Dutch Civil Code
    255
    Art. 450   269, 270
    Art. 476   286
Dutch Criminal Code
    Art. 40   255
    Art. 293   254, 256
    Art. 294   254, 256
Dutch Penal Code
    284
    Art. 10   282
    Art. 40   275
    Art. 289   274
    Art. 293   273, 274
    Art. 293(1)   276

Art. 293(2)   282
Art. 294   275
Dutch Termination of Life on Request
and Assisted Suicide Act (Review
Procedures) Act 2001
    275, 277, 281, 282, 283, 285,
    286, 287, 288, 294, 296, 298
    Art. 2   276
    Art. 2(1)(f)   289
    Art. 2(2)   277
    Art. 2(3)   276
    Art. 2(4)   276
    Art. 9   282
    Art. 20   275–276
Dutch Termination of Life on Request
and Assisted Suicide Act (Review
Procedures) Bill, Clause 2(4), TK
1998–1999, 26691 no. 2
    276–277

United States
Oregon Death with Dignity Act 1994
    294
Personal Responsibility and Work
Opportunity Reconciliation Act 1996
    18

Table of conventions and international instruments

Constitution of the World Health
Organization
   217
Convention for the Protection of
Human Rights and Dignity of the
Human Being with Regard to the
Application of Biology and Medicine:
Convention on Human Rights and
Biomedicine (ECHRB) (Council of
Europe) 1997
   Art. 2   195
   Art. 5   194, 270
   Art. 6   194
   Art. 16
      sub-paragraphs i to iv   194
   Art. 17   194, 195
   Art. 17(2)(i)   195
Convention on the Rights of the Child
   217
Council Directive 03/12/EC on the
conformity of breast implants to
European safety standards
   239

European Convention on Human
Rights
Preamble   121
   Art.3   121
   Art.8   121,210,270
   Art.12   121
   Art.14   210
Declaration of Helsinki
(World Medical Association)
   207
   Introduction, Principle 5   195
   Principles 24–26   195
International Covenant on Economic,
Social and Cultural Rights   218
   Art.15(1)(6)   121
International Covenant on
Elimination of All Forms of
Discrimination against Women
   Art.1   121
Universal Declaration of Human
Rights (1948)
   217
   Art.3   121

Table of statutory instruments

Medical Act (Amendment) Order 2000
    238
Medical Devices (Amendment)
Regulation 2003
    239
NHS (Liabilities to Third Parties Scheme)
Regulations 1999 (SI 1999 No. 873)
    65

NHS Litigation (Establishment and
Constitution) Order (SI 1995 No. 2800)
    65
NHS (Property Expenses Scheme)
Regulations 1999 (SI 1999 No. 874)
    65

Table of abbreviations

AFCH	French association of hospital coordinators
ALJR	Australian Law Journal Reports 1958
All ER	All England Law Reports
AMA	American Medical Association
AMR	All Malaysian Reports
AVE	active voluntary euthanasia
BAAPs	British Association of Aesthetic Plastic Surgeons
BAPs	British Association of Plastic Surgeons
BSE	bovine spongiform encephalopathy
CHA	Canada Health Act
CHAI	Commission of Healthcare Audit and Inspection
CHI	Commission for Health Improvement
CHST	Canada Health and Social Transfer
CLJ	Current Law Journal
CLR	Commonwealth Law Reports
CMO	Chief Medical Officer
CNST	Clinical Negligence Scheme for Trusts
CORE	Comment on Reproductive Ethics
CPS	Crown Prosecution Service
CRS	congenital rubella syndrome
ECT	electroconvulsive therapy
FCCE	Federal Commission of Control and Evaluation (Belgium)
GDP	gross domestic product
GIFT	gamete intra-fallopian transfer
GM	genetically modified
GMC	General Medical Council
HC	hospital coordinators
HFEA	Human Fertilisation and Embryology Authority
HGAC	Human Genetics Advisory Commission
HLA	human leukocyte antigen
ICSI	intracytoplasmic sperm injection
ICU	intensive care unit
IVF	in vitro fertilisation

KNMG	Royal Dutch Medical Association
Med LR	Medical Law Reports
MMR	measles, mumps and rubella
NAO	National Audit Office
NCAA	National Clinical Assessment Authority
NCSC	National Care Standards Commission
NHSLA	NHS Litigation Authority
NICE	National Institute for Clinical Excellence
NPSA	National Patient Safety Agency
NSF	National Service Framework
ODMB	Ordre des médecins
PAS	physician-assisted suicide
PGD	preimplantation genetic diagnosis
PVS	persistent vegetative state
QALY	quality adjusted life year
RCGP	Royal College of General Practitioners
RCT	randomised controlled trial
RPST	Risk Pooling Scheme for Trusts
SASR	South Australian State Reports 1971
SCEN	Support and Consultation on Euthanasia in the Netherlands
TQM	total quality management
vCJD	variant-Creutzfeldt-Jakob disease
WHO	World Health Organization
WLR	Weekly Law Reports

Introduction

Austen Garwood-Gowers, John Tingle and Kay Wheat

The landscape of healthcare provision has changed unimaginably in most industrialised countries over the last century: systems of provision have become more formal, complex and centralised; technology has profoundly altered the boundaries of what is possible; the allocation of resources is increasingly coming under the microscope; and provision has been affected by an increasing tendency for individuals to litigate and societies to regulate. Changes such as these have increased the pace of development and overall importance of healthcare law and ethics.

In the last few years alone the English courts have had to deal with many diverse and fundamental healthcare issues such as competent persons wishing to, respectively, have active assistance to end their own life (*R (On the Application of Pretty) v DPP* [2002] 1 All ER 1, HL (Lords Bingham, Steyn, Hope, Hobhouse and Scott) subsequently heard in the European Court of Human Rights as *Pretty v UK* (2002) 35 EHRR 1) and discontinue life-maintaining treatment in order to die (*Re B (Consent to Treatment: Capacity)* [2002] EWHC 429 (Fam), [2002] 1 FLR 1090). The courts have also had to rule on paternity dilemmas as a result of children being born following a sperm mix-up at an IVF clinic (*Leeds Teaching Hospitals NHS Trust v Mr and Mrs A and Others* [2003] 1 FLR 412), and a woman seeking the court's permission for the implantation of an embryo against the wishes of her (by then former) partner (*Natallie Evans v Amicus Healthcare Ltd and Others* [2004] 3 WLR 681). Judicial minds have been exercised by the wishes of couples trying to use IVF combined with preimplantation genetic diagnosis (PGD) to create saviour siblings (*R v Human Fertilisation and Embryology Authority ex parte Josephine Quintavalle* [2003] EWCA Civ 667), and a decision declaring the lawfulness of the creation of cloned pre-embryos through a technique called cell nuclear replacement (*R (On application of Bruno Quintavalle (On Behalf of Pro-Life Alliance)) v Secretary of State for Health* [2003] UKHL 13 (Lord Bingham of Cornhill, Lord Steyn, Lord Hoffmann, Lord Millett, Lord Scott of Foscote)).

Meanwhile the UK Parliament has considered reform and codification of several areas of healthcare law including mental incapacity (The Mental Capacity Act 2005), and active voluntary euthanasia (Assisted Dying For the Terminally Ill Bill 2004). The Human Tissue Act 2004 reforms the law concerning the removal, storage and use of human tissues. The second to fifth parts of this book give a strong flavour of issues that have been arising in these and several other areas of healthcare law, ethics and practice. Meanwhile the first part is devoted to the more overarching issue of healthcare quality.

The first part begins with Dale Parent's chapter 'The social creation of health law and health in the United States'. In his sociological analysis of healthcare in the United States, Parent reminds us of some of the essential functions of sociology. He sees it as a tool that is 'holistic in its examination of elements of society, stressing the importance of the interrelationship of society's component parts' (see p. 16). The emphasis of a sociological study of law is on understanding the development and implementation of the law as 'not simply the outcome of rational and deliberate thought and reasoning, but rather a product of the structure and culture of the social order' (see p. 15). Sociology is also concerned with the distribution of power within specific structures of social organisation within society as a whole and the way in which these concerns may have an impact on the nature of the other. Indeed Parent goes as far as suggesting that the 'business of sociology' is to see through the façade to understand how the system 'really works' (see p. 16). Understanding this can prove deeply challenging not just to those whom the status quo benefits but to all persons who find it difficult to face up to issues in their society or are fatalistic about the possibility of change. Parent suggests that Americans especially tend to fall into the first category because they tend 'to view their way of life as not only different from others, but the best way, the natural way, the way things should be' (see p. 16).

He goes on to examine the social construction of health laws and policies in the United States, the resulting healthcare system and the general health status of the country's population. His timing in doing so is impeccable for a number of reasons. Firstly, many industrialised nations are toying with, and in some cases moving towards, 'the "American model" of privatising public services' in the (false) belief that this is the most efficient and economical way to provide these services. Secondly, as Parent states, the US system which has its roots in 'competitive individualism in a capitalist economy' is widely accepted to be in a state of crisis, with staggering costs and inequities in its distribution, including significant inequities relating to race and ethnicity (see p. 16). His advocacy of change is in line with his view that sociologists should regard their role as initiators of social change, not simply as detached evaluators. Parent also gives the UK a gentle warning. He acknowledges that there is a difference between the USA, where there has never been a comprehensive system of publicly funded healthcare, and the UK which has a well-developed system, but nevertheless in the context of a move toward managed competition, although this might have its benefits, we should bear in mind the way in which healthcare has developed in the USA.

Parent's chapter is followed by Keith Syrett's examination of the role of the National Institute for Clinical Excellence (NICE) and whether it has solved the 'legitimacy' problem arising from healthcare rationing in the NHS. Syrett adopts Maynard's definition of rationing: 'a failure to offer care, or the denial of care, from which patients would benefit' (see p. 38) and wisely does not try to argue against rationing per se, acknowledging that most people regard it as inevitable. The 'legitimacy problem' he regards as having arisen following the moves in the early 1990s to introduce an internal market into the NHS, which rendered 'rationing' decisions explicit and which resulted in the NHS being perceived as lacking transparency and fairness (see pp. 40–42). Syrett's analysis takes place in the context of two controversial drugs: zanamivir (treatment for influenza) and beta-interferon (multiple sclerosis). His purpose is to illustrate how 'deeply political' is the nature of the decisions that NICE has to take (e.g. when zanamivir was first rejected by NICE the pharmaceutical industry reacted in melodramatic fashion, and when NICE subsequently chose to recommend zanamivir, this again provoked strong reactions from those opposed to the drug's use). Whilst saluting the objectifying attempts being made by NICE, this means, argues Syrett, that a legitimacy problem still remains, and that public lawyers need to undertake further critical analysis of the state processes involved in dealing with this ethically and politically controversial area.

Claire Strickland's chapter moves the discussion to the management of clinical risk in the UK. This has become an increasingly important topic, not least because of the increasing levels of complaints (every year the Health Service Ombudsman reveals a record number of complaints made to the office[1]) and the increasing tendency toward litigation. The number of legal claims has also increased over the years. According to the National Audit Office (NAO),[2] 'The rate of new claims per thousand finished consultant episodes rose by 72 per cent between 1990–1998. In 1999–2000 the NHS received some 10 000 new claims and cleared 9600.' The NAO report in the latest NHS annual accounts that the indications are that the number of claims is increasing.[3]

Strickland provides an insightful history of the concept of risk and allied concepts such as medical autonomy. One of her key observations is that since 1948 the provision of NHS services has moved from the 'reflective practice model' to the 'scientific bureaucratic model' (see p. 72). The former model involves 'maximum clinical autonomy where ownership of clinical risk resides with the doctor and to a lesser degree with the patient, with no transparency' (see p. 72). The latter model 'reduced clinical autonomy due to the rise of evidence-based practice, models for service delivery and externally driven strategies for implementation. In this model clinical risk is owned by not only the doctor and patient, but by a plethora of inspection and review bodies, Chief Executives and managers, the media and the public' (see p. 72). Doctors, trained to take more personal responsibility, are not surprisingly finding it difficult to adjust to the emphasis on the latter. The latter model seems in part to reflect and encourage a breakdown of trust between the relevant parties and it is notable that, since devolution, Scotland has been rejecting it in favour of the former model.

Whilst prevention is the watchword for management of risk in today's society, the complexity of healthcare systems and the fallibility of 'human nature' makes it inevitable that even the most well-funded and diligently operated system healthcare will run into some problems. Accordingly the hard law of medical malpractice remains an important issue. Puteri Kassim's chapter, 'Does the *Bolam* principle still reign in medical negligence cases in Malaysia?', provides an intriguing picture of the evolution of Malaysian law on breach of duty in medical negligence cases. Kassim contextualises her piece with an analysis of how English and Australian approaches to the problem have evolved. The case law in both jurisdictions, she notes, has had an influence on the Malaysian approach though ultimately the courts have swayed in favour of the English approach rather than its more patient-centred Australian alternative. However, the English approach has at least assumed a less self-regulatory character through the reinterpretation or reworking of the *Bolam* principle in cases such as *Bolitho v City & Hackney Health Authority* [1997] 4 All ER 771.

The impression that the Malaysian courts may end up with something with an Australian flavour even if it is from an English source is also confirmed by the approach to causation in relation to non-disclosure by the House of Lords in *Chester v Afshar* [2004] UKHL 41. Here their Lordships decided by a 3 to 2 majority (Lords Hope, Walker and Steyn with Lords Hoffman and Bingham dissenting) that a breach through non-disclosure of small risk of a serious adverse result (cauda equina syndrome in disc surgery) should give rise to compensation when that serious adverse result materialises even when its doing so is not attributable to careless 'technical performance' on the doctor's part and the claimant cannot prove, on the balance of probabilities, that she would have refused to go ahead with the procedure had the risk been disclosed. The House based its approach partly on its earlier decision in *Fairchild v Glenhaven Funeral Services* [2002] UKHL 22. However, the policy justification in that case was to ensure that those breaching a duty by allowing exposure to a harmful agent did not escape liability when the same harmful agent caused injury merely because it was impossible to scientifically verify whether or not this particular exposure had even materially contributed to the injury. *Chester* evidently goes much further in that liability is being imposed in spite of the fact that it is clear, on the balance of probabilities, that the breach of duty did not cause the injury. In this sense the case can be seen as allowing a loss of chance argument and, even more radically, one in which the compensation awarded is not for the amount of chance lost but for the whole damage. In this sense it must either be read as a radical new departure from previous case law, such as *Wilsher v Essex Area Health Authority* [1987] QB 730 or restricted to its context of disclosure. If the latter is so, which seems likely, it must be seen as based on the idea that breach of 'the right to know' through unreasonable non-disclosure is of itself something that should be compensated – an approach that, as their Lordships noted, has already been adopted in Australian case of *Chappel v Hart* (1998) 195 CLR 232.

However, what is then at issue is the level of compensation: both cases award compensation not for the violation of the right itself but for injury that, on a reasonable analysis of causation, was arguably nothing more than a vicissitude of life. In this respect the claimant must be seen as obtaining something of a windfall. Such a result may be acceptable in relation to the defendant from a policy perspective in as much as it gives a short, sharp, shock. Intellectually, the law would have a better shape if we simply said that unreasonable non-disclosures were actionable in trespass. Continuing to shunt non-disclosure cases through negligence is nothing but a policy device (e.g. to avoid the possibility of criminal liability for trespass or troublesome precedents like *Chatterton v Gerson* [1981] QB 432). If one reaches the conclusion that autonomy is so important then conceptually the better approach is to regard an unreasonable failure to disclose as actionable without proof – in any normal sense – of damage.

The first part of the book is completed by Wendy Hesketh's chapter on medico-legal crime. Hesketh argues that medico-legal crime is a relatively unexplored area of healthcare law. Clearly, it has only been brought to public attention by recent high profile cases such as Harold Shipman and Rodney Ledward. Hesketh argues that not only do doctors have unique opportunities to commit crime (via their licence to invade bodily integrity and access to drugs etc.), but they also have the means of concealing that crime that is not available to other wrong-doers. She argues that another exacerbating drawback is the tendency of the police to regard the area as one of professional misconduct, and puts forward various proposals for reform of the area, such as making clear dividing lines between doctors who have failures of competence and those who have stepped beyond this into the criminal arena. The state, she argues, wishes to maintain professional regulation so that the profession can retain its responsibility for resource allocation. A clear dichotomy between competence and crime, therefore, would satisfy the state's requirements. While Hesketh takes a commendably measured and proportionate response to the problem, recent experience has shown that medical 'scandals' have a habit of exciting the press and in turn influencing public opinion in ways that many would consider unhelpful. Two recent examples are the reduction of MMR vaccine uptake following controversy over its health implications and the reduction in both organ transplants and autopsy rates following organ retention and removal scandals.[4] The sharp reduction in autopsy rates sits very uncomfortably with the need perceived by Hesketh to be vigilant as to the possibility of medico-legal crime.

Some of the chapters in this book deal with questions of what we mean when we talk about concepts like 'health' and 'therapy'. The World Health Organization defines health as a state of 'complete physical, mental and social well-being, and not merely the absence of disease or infirmity'.[5] Yet in practice what is normatively meant by the terms 'healthcare provision' and 'a healthcare system' can be seen as simultaneously exclusive of some things that are conducive to well-being and inclusive of some things that are not. Increased focus and coherent thinking is required in relation to the roles of things like quality housing, transport, job and leisure opportunities. Equally, we ought to become somewhat more critical of provision that does not serve well-being either because it does not represent value for money or because it is incapable of producing benefit or harmful. Social norms about what is good for us are not something we should automatically reject but neither are they something we should automatically accept. This is illustrated very clearly by Melanie Latham's chapter, entitled 'Cyberwoman and her surgeon in the twenty-first century', which deals with the thorny issues of elective 'beauty enhancement' through cosmetic surgery. Latham's essentially feminist critique is, not surprisingly, ambivalent toward such interventions. On the one hand she is dubious about their actual value and questioning as to whether or to what extent they are actually chosen from a place of what one might call 'psychological autonomy'. On the other hand, she does not want to dismiss feminist views which talk in positive terms about the potentiality of women to make use of technology to physically, and ultimately non-physically, transform themselves. Thus, whilst her critique not surprisingly deplores the pressure under which women are placed by aesthetic cultural norms she ultimately thinks that women could make true and thus liberating choices to use surgery. These choices would not necessarily be confined to using surgery in a manner that matches with aesthetic cultural norms but also in a manner that is against these norms. Inevitably, the question with the latter use is whether action could be defined as truly subversive or whether it would merely amount to cutting off one's nose to spite one's face.

The debate over what is and is not good for a person's health continues in Austen Garwood-Gowers' chapter 'The proper limits for medical intervention that harms the therapeutic interests of incompetents'. Garwood-Gowers notes that the norm has been for therapy to be equated with interventions having the prospect of producing direct benefit. Of course this approach allows for some interventions to be described as therapeutic when they harm a person's therapeutic interests because they are less than optimal. Equally, it means that an intervention may be classed as sub-optimally therapeutic or non-therapeutic and yet still be the best option for a person overall. 'Distortions' have arisen in the ethico-legal discourse partly as a result of failures to take these factors into account. Much of Garwood-Gowers' piece is devoted to unravelling these distortions and providing a structure for assessing when interventions are consistent with a person's interests overall. Of particular note is his critique of analyses which seek to limit conceptions of benefit to that which conveys mental or physical benefit. He asserts that in order to respect a person we should treat their wishes as an end in their own right. This is of particular importance when considering the scope to perform interventions on people who are insentient and dying and therefore have no apparent prospect of deriving mental or physical benefit from interventions that are performed on them to facilitate use of their body materials after death.

Conceptions of what interventions are good for health are also brought under the miscroscope in Stephanie Pywell's chapter 'Infant vaccination: a conflict of ethical imperatives?'. Part of the role of this chapter is to question whether vaccinations on infants and young children are consistent with their interests when the primary object of vaccination is not to protect the individual who has received the vaccine, but to protect the population as a whole from the disease (see p. 214).

The chapters of both Pywell and Garwood-Gowers raise the conflict between protecting the interests of the individual and those of society. Pywell's take on the issues is to question why, when vaccination is not compulsory, '(c)urrent vaccination practices give greater weight to the societal aim of eradicating diseases than to the principles which should prevail within individual doctor–patient relationships' (see p. 229). Garwood-Gowers' take on the issues is that we must distinguish societal interests which are mere needs from those that are rights. Elsewhere he suggests that society has no right to make use of an individual's body to fulfil its needs at the cost of respect for the individual.[6] Here he builds on that by noting that proposals to dilute the protection of bodily security of one class of person – usually the incompetent – are by their nature discriminatory. This had implications for, amongst other things, the Mental Capacity Act which allows intrusive research on the incompetent adult under criteria that appear not to necessitate protection of best interests. The chapters of M.E. Rodgers ('Human bodies, inhuman uses: public reactions and legislative responses to the scandals of bodysnatching') and Graciela Nowenstein ('*Nemo censetur ignorare legem?* Presumed consent to organ donation in France, from Parliament to hospitals') provide a sociological analysis of the 'same respect for the individual versus needs of society' debate – this time largely in the context of use of material from deceased persons.

Nowenstein's fascinating chapter traces the evolution of presumed consent in law and practice in France since 1976. Using both paper research and data gathered from in-depth interviews with relevant professionals she exposes conflicting values and priorities at stake in the donation process, and she argues that the specific position occupied by the law (among other normative spheres) informs the situation and the actions of those in the legislative and political fields. She concludes that political and legal authorities are unwilling to force professionals to impose the presumed consent position that is contained within the law.

Rodgers' chapter compares 'bodysnatching' scandals between two different time frames – the early nineteenth century and the late twentieth century. Rodgers notes that although public panic and outrage ensued in both eras, reverence for the medical professional tended to result in criticism of it being muted. In both scandals there was a marked reluctance to name and shame individual practitioners. Dr Knox, the surgeon who knowingly received murdered and resurrected bodies, was seen in some quarters as being as much a butcher as Burke and Hare but 'the general approach was to do nothing more than to allude to his involvement' (see p. 157). Of the modern scandals, Alder Hey was the only scenario where the blame was particularly attached to one individual, this being Professor van Velzen who had routinely retained organs without consent. Rodgers argues that criticism in both scandals was less than it might have been because of an underlying sympathy with what practitioners were trying to achieve and an acceptance that in most cases they were not aware of the legal problem with what they were doing. Without a different attitude, removing what Rodgers calls the excuses of 'we didn't understand' and 'medical science necessitated our actions' will not prevent history repeating itself. In this regard, the situation in France is worth examining. French medical professionals almost routinely ignore their presumed consent law which suggests that they have a greater respect for the bodily security of deceased persons. However, appearances can be deceptive. It turns out that the 'French professional approach' is actually conditioned by the wish to be sensitive to the needs of surviving relatives, a point that Nowenstein evidences by the fact that they tend to have no compunction about enforcing the law when it comes to 'hoboes' (see p. 184). The limited focus on the deceased person as having rights over his or her own body seems to be practically ubiquitous in countries that have hit upon medical uses for the human body.

The issue of respect in the context of *potential persons* is illustrated in Thérèse Callus's chapter, 'Preimplantation genetic diagnosis – towards a principled construction of law?'. Callus notes that we are in 'an era where scientific prowess is equated with liberated individuals; where technical capabilities are transformed into individual rights'(see p. 133). She questions whether this trend is necessarily a liberative one. Indeed, she argues that, as far as preimplantation genetic diagnosis (PGD) is concerned, the law becomes subservient to science, and that 'we are experiencing a "biocracy" rather than a democracy when it comes to assessing the validity and viability of new reproductive techniques and their application' (see p. 143).

Medical technologies can be universally dressed as beneficent but they can be detrimental to human well-being with their emphasis on the treatment of symptoms with expensive solutions much more than one based on prevention and cure. Amongst the topics in this book, reproduction technologies, transplantation, research and elective cosmetic surgery are all 'ripe' for such a critique. However, out of all the areas in which medical technology continues its onward march it is undoubtedly the reproductive context which by its very nature raises the most concern. In the case of in vitro fertilisation (IVF) technology has been used to change the nature of how we are produced and in the cases of PGD and embryo research we have started to change the nature of why we are produced. Finally, through cloning and genetic modification of the embryo, we have reached the point of changing what is produced.

When human beings have such control in relation to their own genesis it naturally generates concern over the future direction of our race. Taking up this theme, Susan Johnson's chapter, 'New reproductive technologies – discourse and dilemma', notes more specifically that 'issues surrounding human genetic modification and selection should not be seen as a consideration of issues *only* applicable to this topic. Instead, human genetic modification is the end point of our scientific inquiry and, as the extreme, it epitomises and clarifies these issues and focuses our vision of what we want to achieve, and simplifies the judgements we make' (see p. 115). Johnson's take on the use of reproduction technology is, however, quite different overall to that of Callus. She notes that whilst the Human Fertilisation and Embryology Authority

(HFEA) has been accused of unethical decision-making and acting outside its remit, its credibility and legitimacy 'do not appear to have been damaged by the recent challenges to its decision-making capabilities' (see p. 128). Her own empirical research with women demonstrates that adopting the pattern of regulation with which the women were most confident would necessitate a body such as the HFEA. Like Melanie Latham, Johnson defends the importance of women's role in decision-making. The issue for Johnson is about promoting 'autonomous reproductive decision-making within a framework that espouses regulated autonomy' (see p. 128). Compared with Callus, who focuses significantly on the threats of reproductive technology to society, Johnson, like Latham in the cosmetic surgery context, perceives the issues more in terms of women's autonomy versus state paternalism.

The tension between autonomy and paternalism is also a feature of the two euthanasia chapters: Heleen Weyers, 'Legal recognition of the right to die' and Sam Halliday, 'Regulating active voluntary euthanasia: what can England and Wales learn from Belgium and the Netherlands?'. The former is largely devoted to a sociological and political examination of the relationship between the development of laws allowing active voluntary euthanasia and the prevalence of liberalist views; the latter, in this context, is a defence of liberalism itself. Halliday's approach (like that of Latham and Johnson) is what has traditionally been described as soft paternalism. Soft paternalism emphasises the autonomy of people to engage in significantly harmful and/or risky activities but sees a strong role for the state in, for example, ensuring not just that consent has been given but also that appropriate safety measures are in place to reduce harm and/or risk and that 'participants' are well informed of the dangers. It is an approach that, for example, is often advocated in relation to professional boxing as an alternative to an outright ban.[7]

Of course active euthanasia has an important feature that separates it from elective cosmetic surgery, professional boxing and (at least some) uses of reproductive technology: it is a life-ending decision. This feature takes away one of the normal and important benefits of respecting autonomy: that of the person in the future having benefited from having experienced that respect and a sense of control when the decision was made. Indeed, in one sense to allow active voluntary euthanasia is to allow autonomy to be extinguished. This point was used by Lord Bingham in the House of Lords in *R (On the Application of Pretty) v DPP* [2002] 1 All ER 1, HL in his argument that Diane Pretty's Article 8 right of private life was not engaged. It was a perspective rejected by the European Court of Human Rights; clearly in part because to allow it would have meant that decisions to reject life-maintaining treatment would also not have engaged the Article (*Pretty v UK* (2002) 35 EHRR 1). It is also obvious that although decisions in favour of ending life extinguish autonomy in one sense they vindicate it in the sense of respect for persons' control over one of the most important things in their life: their dying processes. Halliday uses such thinking to support her proposition that active voluntary euthanasia should be lawful under certain conditions. One of the most liberal features of her approach to legalisation is that as well as applying to competent adults it applies to competent minors of 15 years and above, subject to there having been consultation with those who have parental responsibility. Another is the way in which she envisages it applying to people experiencing unbearable suffering that has a somatic rather than simply existential basis even when their condition is not terminal.

Although autonomy is at the centre of Halliday's thinking she also argues that the current law should be changed because it is widely ignored, not widely supported by society and likely to lead to greater incidence of involuntary euthanasia than in an approach where active voluntary euthanasia is allowed under a well-controlled and transparent system. Whilst valuable in its own right, her illuminating discussion of the evolution of Dutch and Belgian law and practice is also useful for building up a detailed picture of how the English system might operate were it reformed.

There are, of course, counter-arguments to Halliday's approach. It is not necessarily the case that the fact that a law is widely disrespected is reason enough to change it. Similarly, there are arguments as to the effect of legalisation on levels of involuntary euthanasia. In addition, the case for legalisation must take into account more subtle potential effects. These include effects on the individuals who are administering the 'mercy' killings and/or assisting suicides and on the systems in which they operate. They also loop back to the intrinsic ethics of active voluntary euthanasia itself. Whilst ending-of-life decisions involve autonomy the doing of harmful acts by one person to another, even with their voluntary agreement, is something that most societies have traditionally sought to restrict. The restriction may indirectly restrict autonomy but its motivation is to resist society developing to the extent that people are permitted to show more serious forms of disrespect to each other. It is somewhat hard to argue that the mere fact that someone consents to such an act automatically neutralises any disrespect. For example, if an otherwise healthy person wants to be asphyxiated with a plastic bag, it is hard to say that the person who does this to them is acting with anything but disrespect. The intrinsic ethics of active voluntary euthanasia is thus more than a question of autonomy; it is a question of whether or when it would not be seriously disrespectful for one person to kill another or actively assist in their suicide.

The suggestion that legalisation of active voluntary euthanasia is not just about autonomy or liberalism is also confirmed by Heleen Weyers' chapter. Weyers focuses on the reasons for the more liberal approach to the subject in The Netherlands, Belgium and Denmark where the role of the Christian Democrat parties appears to have been influential, but not decisive. Weyers uses data extracted from a number of European values studies to show that the degree of liberalism in these countries on issues such as abortion, homosexuality, and divorce does not correlate in all respects with their approach to euthanasia. For example, she recognises that, on the basis of European value scores, it could not have been predicted that Belgium would have introduced a law permitting euthanasia. Interestingly, she argues that geography might be the crucial factor in predicting change; on this basis she suggests that

Luxembourg might be the next European country to liberalise its laws on euthanasia given its close proximity to Belgium.

REFERENCES

1. The Health Service Ombudsman for England. Annual Report 2003–2004. London: Stationery Office.
2. NAO. Handling clinical negligence claims in England. London: Stationery Office; 3 May 2001.
3. NHS (England). Summarised accounts, 2002–2003. London: Stationery Office.
4. Bennett JR. The organ retention furore. Clinical Medicine 2001; 167.
5. Constitution of The World Health Organization. Online. Available: http://www.who. int/about/en/.
6. Garwood-Gowers A. The right to bodily security vis-à-vis the needs of others. In: Weisstub DN, Pintos GD, eds. Autonomy and human rights in healthcare. Kluwer Academic Publishing, forthcoming, Ch 27, Introduction.
7. Gunn M, Ormerod D. Despite the law: prize fighting and professional boxing. In: Greenfield S, Osborn G, eds. Law and sport in contemporary society. London: Frank Cass; 2000.

SECTION ONE

Regulating healthcare

SECTION CONTENTS

1. The social creation of health law and health in the USA   15

2. Does it pay to be NICE? Resolving the 'legitimacy problem' in the allocation of healthcare resources   37

3. The ownership of clinical risk in acute hospitals in England – an historical perspective   55

4. Does the *Bolam* principle still reign in medical negligence cases in Malaysia?   79

5. Medico-crime in the UK: an introduction   93

Chapter 1

The social creation of health law and health in the USA

F. Dale Parent

CHAPTER CONTENTS

Introduction   15
The social context of the
   USA   17
Complexity and the façade of
   democracy   17
Structured inequality and the
   maintenance of the status
   quo   18
A system in crisis   20
The US healthcare
   system   20
Health as a commodity   21
Staggering cost   22

Health and healthcare
   inequity   23
Health as a public issue: the
   social content and social
   change   27
Changing health laws and health
   policies in the USA   29
The role of sociologists   29
Establishing a foundation for
   social change   30
Implementing social change   30
Conclusion   31
References   32

INTRODUCTION

It is crucially important, for both public and private entities, to scrutinise, challenge, and attempt to refine the merits of any nation's legal system, and its specific laws and policies. The minor details of any legal decree can potentially affect numerous groups and individuals within society.[1] Unfortunately, a narrow analysis of law is more widely recognised and focused upon than an objective and critical evaluation of the broader sociological factors that ultimately determine the procedures that form, maintain, change and interpret all legal issues.

There is an inseparable bond between law and the structure and culture of a society. The development and implementation of law is not simply the outcome of rational and deliberate thought and reasoning, but rather a product of the structure and culture of the social order. 'Law is social. Human beings create laws and do so within the context of their times and societies.'[2] Thus, the use of the sociological perspective is essential to gain a complete understanding of laws within a particular locale. Sociology is holistic in its examination of elements of society, stressing the importance of the interrelationship of society's component parts. The sociological approach, as used in this chapter, also emphasises the complexity and unequal distribution of power that exists within all societies and its effect on the structure of social organisation.

Sociology must examine all social factors with cautious and broad viewing eyes, particularly as many of these are commonly viewed as natural or as simple 'common sense'. As noted by Stimpson and Stimpson[3] sociology creates a new awareness of society and aids in a deeper understanding of its structural and cultural elements. Nothing in society, including law, is isolated or as straightforward as it is often perceived. Peter Berger states this notion clearly: 'the sociological perspective involves a process of "seeing through" the facades of social structures'[4] and thus revealing how the system 'really works', who really has power, who benefits and who loses from the existing status quo. This is the business of sociology. Unfortunately, the dominant structure and culture of a society is often overlooked or explained away as something that is beyond our control or impossible to change. Incorporating a sociological view can be very uncomfortable for many people, especially Americans, who view their way of life as not only different from others, but the best way, the natural way, the way things should be. Sociology often challenges our strongly held beliefs and forces us to look at the 'big picture', and to face the inconsistencies of our society's context.

The specific purpose of this chapter is to examine the social construction of health laws and policies in the USA, and the resulting healthcare system, and the general health status of the country's population. This is an especially important topic at this point in history for several reasons. First, the conceptualisation and treatment of health, illness and healthcare delivery in the USA is probably unique among industrialised nations since it has never had any form of universal governmental sponsored healthcare system.[5] In fact, it is characterised by basically the opposite situation. 'It lacks consistency and often encompasses a mishmash of programs involving conflicting values. It is not surprising that the American healthcare system is often described as scandalous and wasteful.'[6] In addition, in the USA quality health and reasonable access to healthcare are highly correlated with social status or class.[5] The right to high-quality healthcare continues to be debated at an extremely basic level in the USA, with many viewing it as a privilege or economic commodity rather than any type of right of citizenship.

Secondly, most industrial countries are currently debating changes and making changes in healthcare and other social service programmes. Privatisation has become a major force in many of these countries as governments reorder priorities so as to lessen their responsibility and shift it to other entities and ultimately to the individual.[7,8] In other words they are moving toward the 'American model' of privatising social services with the stated notion that this is the most efficient and economical way to provide these services. The potential negative consequences of this type of approach are illustrated in the present chapter.

Finally, the USA represents an industrial nation that epitomises a lack of understanding, by the general population, of the impact of society's social structures and cultural values on specific laws, policies and other social issues. The specific social characteristics of the nation and the reason for the public's general unawareness will be discussed in greater detail below.

THE SOCIAL CONTEXT OF THE USA

The structure of the political and economic systems, and dominant cultural values of the USA have produced vast inequalities in health status among members of its population. Cultural values have emerged from the country's institutional structure that emphasises rugged individualism and the superiority of a free-market economy as the primary weapon to solve most social ills. This is coupled with a distrust of government intervention as a solution to personal troubles. These beliefs are deeply held and provide ample justification for the enormous amount of inequality and the extremely narrow and very conservative political spectrum that maintains this state of affairs. Finally, the complex fragmented and decentralised political system in the USA makes large-scale, meaningful change almost impossible to accomplish.

COMPLEXITY AND THE FAÇADE OF DEMOCRACY

The USA has a federalist system government as opposed to a unitary system or a confederation. The federal government shares power with different units within the federal government. This is in contrast to a unitary system of government in which power rests solely in the domain of the national government or a confederation of states. It is also different from a confederation of states in which the states exercise power over the central government. To Americans the latter two arrangements may appear much less democratic and responsive to the will of the people than federalism. However, this is certainly not necessarily the case.

'. . . the fragmented and constrained system of government carefully crafted by the Founding Fathers led to a relatively small federal government that is easily entered and influenced by wealthy and well-organized private citizens, whether through Congress, the separate department of the executive branch, or a myriad of regulatory agencies. The net result is that the owners and managers of large income-producing properties score very high on all three power indicators: who benefits, who governs, and who wins. They have a greater proportion of wealth and income than their counterparts in any other capitalist democracy, and through the power elite they are vastly over represented in key government positions and decision-making groups.'[9]

Within the USA federalism has gone through a series of forms, usually moving toward greater decentralisation that typically benefits the wealthy at the expense of the poor. The most recent form of federalism is known as representational federalism. This type of federalism means that the federal government has placed more responsibility for the design, financing and administration of social programmes on individual states. One of the most recent and far-reaching examples of this increasing federalism was the passage of the Personal Responsibility and Work Opportunity Reconciliation Act of 1996 by the US Congress. This legislation is commonly referred to as 'welfare reform'. The bottom line is that spending for social programmes in general were cut and this has been accompanied in part by tighter restrictions mandated by the federal government that limited the scope of the programmes development by individual states.[10]

Currently, laws can originate, be interpreted and implemented from 87 453 different governmental units in the USA.[11] Most of these units have the authority to levy taxes.

STRUCTURED INEQUALITY AND THE MAINTENANCE OF THE STATUS QUO

'The US healthcare system did not develop and does not exist in a vacuum. It is a part of the larger society and is shaped by both its structure and cultural values. The health inequities that exist are a microcosm of the inequity that exists in every other institution in the US.'[12] Within the USA wide disparities occur in income, wealth, job security, health, diet, transportation, housing, legal services and education.[13–19] Even more dramatic, the gap between the rich and poor continues to widen.[19] This is taking place in a country that already has the greatest income and wealth inequality of any Western industrial nation.

For the most part, American citizens consider their society as the world's beacon of democracy and free-market economics.[20,21] However, the astonishing concentration of corporate and individual wealth, income and power runs directly counter to this mythology. Over 82% of total corporate assets are controlled by less than 1% of US corporations. Three US corporations, Exxon-Mobil, General Motors and Ford, have revenues greater than 184 of the 191 nations of the world.[22]

Looking at individual income and wealth, the richest 20% of households received 49.7% of the nation's income in 1999, while the lowest fifth shared only 3.6% of the total.[23] Personal wealth is even more unequally distributed throughout the population. Only 1% of households in the USA control over 38% of all wealth in the nation. The richest 10% own 75% of the total and the top 20% hold 84% of the nation's personal assets. This means that the bottom 80% of household share in only 16% of all wealth.[24]

This type of economic concentration has dire consequences for large numbers of Americans, many of whom embrace the system as fair and just. As Parenti explains, 'The ability to control the definition of interests is the ability to define the agenda of issues, a capacity tantamount to winning battles without having to fight them.'[25] He continues, 'The interests of an economically dominant class never stand naked. They are enshrouded in the flag, fortified by the law, protected by the police, nurtured by the media, taught by the schools, and blessed by the church.'[26] American sociologist C. Wright Mills,[27] writing in the mid twentieth century, clearly presents (as do many before and after him) why many in the general public are unaware and confused as to what actions are in their best interest. The ability of the wealthy few to control the major societal institutions enables them to define what is 'best' for the general public. Consequently, many individuals support ideologies and policies that limit their own life chances.

This has contributed to a majority of Americans possessing an almost religious fervour for laissez-faire economics and rugged individualism. The pervasiveness of these two ideals serves the wealthy by preventing any real threat to the status quo. It provides the structure and the cultural justification for the unequal distribution of resources in general, and healthcare in particular. The market is generally seen as the most fair and efficient way to allocate all commodities, including medical care. Thus, cultural beliefs stress individual responsibility over government support to solve social problems. Unfortunately, it is quite regular for public issues – problems over which individuals have little or no control – to be interpreted solely as personal troubles.

'Whether or not competitive individualism in a capitalist economy really works to produce a higher standard of living for a greater number of people is an empirical question. The United States is not an adequate test case of this theory because truly open competition has never been practiced. There have always been protectionist strategies designed and promoted to advantage one group or another. What does seem to be the case is that Americans are less aware of the strategies that protect the very rich, but are suspicious of policies aimed at improving the opportunities for the very poor. A failure to understand structural inequality may perpetuate this mind-set. The ideal of meritocracy leads us to believe that those who are at the top have earned their position, and those who are at the bottom are there because of their own shortcomings and lack of effort.'[28]

These ideas are clearly reflected in the nation's laws, policies and programmes that construct the nation's healthcare system and its approach to combating most other social problems. The USA has historically developed social programmes and policies that:

- are some of the least generous among similar nations
- do not reflect any notion of the interrelationship among the causes and consequences of different social problems
- are limited in scope and piecemeal in nature, especially since many are now designed, administered and financed by individual states

- are not comprehensive, well integrated, or directed toward solving a broad spectrum of social ills
- very rarely address the systemic causes of social problems, and instead are typically aimed at changing individuals' behaviours.

Recent social policies and programmes that affect health-related and other social problems have ignored the lower real wages and reduced job security produced by a post-industrial economy. In fact, current political policies continue to favour the wealthy over other members of society.[29] In recent years the nation has actually moved even more than in the past to social programmes that fault the individual for social factors that are beyond their control, and therefore are aimed primarily at changing the individual.

A SYSTEM IN CRISIS

The US healthcare system

Many scholars today question using the term 'healthcare system' in the USA because of the organisational fragmentation that is a prime feature of health-care delivery in the nation. 'Rather, it has an agglomeration of public and private healthcare providers functioning autonomously in myriad and often competing ways.'[30] In the USA healthcare is basically synonymous with medical care and seldom incorporates the broad array of issues that can affect health, especially at the community level (i.e., nutrition, pollution, working conditions).[31] In addition, the 'medical model' is overwhelmingly accepted by healthcare providers and focuses specifically on biological factors within the individual as the cause of health problems and therefore stresses the use of curative rather than preventive medicine.[32] This is in contrast to many views of health and illness that are much more holistic in nature, including that of the World Health Organization (WHO), which continues to use the first definition it published in 1948: 'Health is a state of complete physical, mental and social well-being and not merely the absence of disease or infirmity.'[33] 'US social policies have not conceptualised – much less accommodated – the total healthcare system.'[34] Light[35] classifies a nation's healthcare system according to the amount of government control that is involved in the system. He places the USA at the most decentralised end of the spectrum and describes it as dominated by private insurance with private, entrepreneurial services. To add more complexity to the issue, as mentioned above, health policy is created at three different governmental levels: federal, state and local:[36]

'The campaign for some form of universal government-funded health care has stretched for nearly a century in the US. On several occasions, advocates believed they were on the verge of success; yet each time they faced defeat. The evolution of these efforts and the reasons for their failure make for an intriguing lesson in American history, ideology, and character.'[37]

The American Medical Association (AMA) was founded in 1847 to protect the interests of physicians.[38] It has been a powerful force in defeating any attempts to establish universal healthcare coverage in the USA.[39] Business leaders in general have consistently been in opposition to broad forms of social insurance, except when they felt it would have a direct positive effect for them by maintaining a healthy workforce. An example of this was the establishment of many public health departments in the early 1990s.[40]

During the Great Depression, when there was a substantial reduction in the use of medical services, healthcare inequities became even worse. This threatened the income of many hospitals and physicians. At that time labour unions initially preferred some type of government-sponsored universal healthcare system, but eventually settled for supporting Blue Cross, a non-profit private hospital insurance system. Later, Blue Shield, a private non-profit insurance, was established for physician fees. For both Blue Cross and Blue Shield, prices were established using a community-based rating system, thereby holding the average cost down for participants. Almost immediately after the creation of the 'Blues', commercial for-profit insurance companies saw an opportunity for big profits, and began offering lower premiums to low-risk people. This eventually drove Blue Cross and Blue Shield to use the same practices.[41]

Today, as has been the case since the 1940s, the 'system' is primarily employer/insurer based, with an individual's access to care dependent on his/her being employed, and then dependent on whether the employer provides insurance, and the quality of that coverage. Persons not following the employer/insurer route to care must rely on underfunded public facilities or request (often unsuccessfully) that private clinics or physicians accept the variable and limited payment received from the government-sponsored insurance programmes. Prescription drugs are priced via monopolised markets, and are often very expensive. Insurance offers coverage of these drugs with co-payments and deductibles required of the patients in most cases. The extent of coverage again varies per the insurance plan with which the patient is insured.

In addition to the fragmentation of government entities in the USA, there is also little coordination among the three basic components of healthcare: government, insurers and providers. Healthcare providers themselves are able to develop practices and facilities that benefit them without necessarily taking community needs into account. 'If you're uninsured in America, the care you get depends on chance: how old you are, what county you live in, what piecemeal programs exist, your diagnosis, how much money you can scrape together. And it depends on your perceived worthiness.'[42]

Health as a commodity

Most citizens in the USA agree that the healthcare system is in a state of crisis.[43,44] 'The USA has had a long history of tinkering with the provision of healthcare, but has yet to overhaul the system in such a way that would begin to make an equitable distribution of health and healthcare possible.'[12]

Healthcare is considered a commodity to be purchased like all other goods and services in the economy. Therefore, those that can afford it receive some of the best healthcare in the world. Those that cannot afford it typically receive substandard care that is often critically delayed. Many among the working poor may receive no care at all.[45]

> 'The US system has been portrayed in political rhetoric as an open market of competing providers that (in theory) would lower prices if only patients would be more savvy consumers. In reality, however, the patient is in an inherently weak position as a consumer, primarily because medicine has become so sophisticated that the patient typically lacks the expertise to evaluate services (from doctor or hospital) and products (pharmaceuticals or ethnological devices, for example).'[46]

For several decades large corporations have been controlling more and more of the provision of healthcare in the USA. This is true in general and specifically within the hospital industry. Prior to the 1970s most hospitals were free standing, with community service as a top priority. The formation of oligopolies within most other sectors of the US economy has been a common occurrence throughout the twentieth century. However, many people assumed that the hospital industry would escape these monopolistic tendencies. However, this is not the case.[47] A study of nearly 500 hospitals during the 1990s found that when not-for-profit or public hospitals became for-profit there was a clear drop in uncompensated care.[48] Further, these profit-driven corporations have for years been engaged in vertical integration and diversification. In one national study, it was found that most multi-hospital systems are involved in other medical related activities (often selecting the most profitable and dropping the money losers) and also in tangentially related fields, such as office-building management, credit collection, real-estate development and insurance.[49]

Staggering cost

The provision of high-quality medical care to the general population is a topic that very seldom receives serious discourse among policy-makers, nor is it part of legislative action. Controlling costs has been the overwhelming healthcare issue of the past 35 years. It is true that the cost of healthcare for both the nation and its citizens is astonishingly high. In the year 2001, 14.1% of the nation's gross domestic product (GDP) was consumed by healthcare, more than any other industrial nation.[50] This amounts to about 1.42 trillion US dollars, averaging about 5000 US dollars per person. The USA has experienced double-digit increases in national healthcare cost for 25 years. During the 1980s the annual growth rate averaged 11%. Expenditures continued to grow during the 1990s, but at a lower level. However, by the end of the decade the pace of healthcare inflation began to resume its rapid increase.[50]

Medical inflation has outpaced the cost of other goods and services in the economy for decades.[51] In 1960 the overall cost of healthcare was 5.3% of GDP. National healthcare expenditures accounted for 7.3% of the nation's GDP in 1970, and for 8.9% in 1980. In 1998, the US figure was 13.0%, and the countries with the next highest percentage of GDP spent on healthcare in 1998 were Switzerland, with 10.7%; Germany, 10.6%; France, 9.5%; and Canada, 9.5%.

While several reasons are commonly given for the rising cost of healthcare in the USA, Paul Starr[52] refers to most of them as popular myths. He lists four basic myths. First, people in the USA expect more care compared to people in other countries. Yet, according to Starr, evidence reveals that the opposite is true in most cases. The second myth is that Americans file an inordinate amount of malpractice lawsuits. However, only about 1% of malpractice insurance contributes to medical cost. Starr's third myth is concerned with the ageing population. The popular assumption is that an older population requires more medical care. However, the population in the USA is no older than that of other industrialised nations.[53] Advanced medical technology is often cited positively for its contribution to the diagnosis and treatment of disease and other medical disorders. However, it is readily noted as a culprit in rising healthcare cost. Starr again notes that sophisticated technology contributes to only a small portion of the total cost of American medicine. In addition, advanced technology exists in other industrialised nations without producing undue inflation.

Starr blames the high and rising cost of healthcare in the USA on three factors: administrative cost, doctors' fees, and hospital cost. In a fee-for-service system the cost of the last two factors are controlled primarily by whatever the market will bear. The first factor, administrative cost, is a product of the complicated, multiple billing and third party payment system. Finally, according to the Agency for Healthcare Research and Quality, pharmaceutical companies are at liberty to set their prices according to demand. As a result prescription drug prices have been increasing between 15 and 19% per year for the past several decades.[54]

Health and healthcare inequity

As stated, the USA spends more money per capita and a larger share of its national income on healthcare than any other industrial nation. It has an abundance of well-trained healthcare professionals and is well supplied with highly sophisticated medical technology. Thus, it would be reasonable to think that the nation's healthcare system would be superior to most other nations in providing high-quality care for all that live within its borders. However, this is far from reality as millions of Americans have little access to even basic care. Healthcare in the USA is rationed by ability to pay. 'Profit drives the US system, and what is most profitable for hospitals, insurance companies, or drug companies is not most effective at producing good health.'[55]

Most citizens rely heavily on a market-based system in which healthcare can be expensive with insurance coverage, and prohibitively expensive without coverage. Unfortunately many people among both the employed and the unemployed do not have insurance. The number of uninsured Americans is over 43 million, or 15.2% of the population. Thirty per cent of the uninsured lived below the poverty line and 23.5% of households with incomes of less than 50 000 US dollars did not have *any* health insurance during the entire year of 2002.[56]

Whereas we cannot state a direct causal relationship between the US healthcare system and the population's health status, the following facts provide support for such an assumption. The USA has the highest infant mortality rate and percentages of low birth-weight infants of any major industrialised nation and ranks 15th in life expectancy. Within the USA, the 1990s were a decade of limited improvement. In 1999, the nation's overall life expectancy at birth rose to nearly 77 years. Both black and white males achieved record highs in life expectancies of 67.8 and 74.6 years, respectively.[57] The infant mortality rate fell to a record low of approximately 7.0 deaths per 1000 live births.[57] At the end of the century mortality from heart disease remained the leading cause of death in the USA, although it has continued to decline. Mortality from heart disease was followed by death from cancer, stroke and chronic lower respiratory diseases. Death due to the first two diseases has declined, while death from chronic respiratory diseases increased nearly 13% during the decade.[58]

Although the past decade showed overall improvement in the health status of the US population, glaring discrepancies remain. Referring again to the low life expectancy for black males, in 1999 it was 67.8 years compared to 74.7 for white males. For females, the figures were 80.2% for whites and 75.4% for blacks. This continuing general health gap exists between whites and other racial and ethnic minorities in the country. 'Even when [non-white racial and ethnic] groups saw improvements in the 1990s, whites in some cases saw stronger advances.'[57] The infant mortality rate for blacks (14.3) remained more than double that of whites (6.0).[57] The overall infant mortality rate for Hispanics was 7.0 with Puerto Ricans bearing a much higher rate, at 8.3.[57] Overall mortality in the USA was one-third higher for blacks than for whites in 1999. 'Preliminary age-adjusted death rates for the black population exceeded those for the white population by 38% for stroke, 28% for heart disease, 27% for cancer, and more than 700% for HIV disease.'[59] While some differences in the health status among racial and ethnic groups may be ascribed to hereditary factors, most are a product of social factors. 'Racial and ethnic minority populations are among the fastest growing of all communities in the USA. Yet, these populations in many respects have poor health and remain chronically under-served by the healthcare system.'[60] While African-Americans and Hispanics often rely on emergency room care or other inconsistent sources of care, whites more typically have a regular source of healthcare. These two ethnic groups (African-American and Hispanics) also have much less access to healthcare and fewer visits to community health centres than whites.[61] 'The combination of years of racial oppression, poverty, and physically demanding occupations probably works to generate more stress in the lives of blacks than other racial groups at the same SES [socio-economic status] level. The stress, in turn produces greater susceptibility to disease.'[62] One study revealed that blacks were less likely than whites to receive kidney transplants and even less likely to be referred for evaluation, regardless of the clinical appropriateness.[63] Blacks continue to report that they are less satisfied with their healthcare provider than whites and frequently report that they feel a 'social distance' with doctors.[54]

The USA has a long history of racial and ethnic prejudice and discrimination toward many different groups.[64] Even though there has been improvement, today Hispanics and African-Americans remain the primary victims of discrimination.[64] This no doubt has a negative impact on their general health and well-being. However, much of the racial and ethnic variation found in health status is most likely a product of social class, rather than ethnicity. Nevertheless, as the most common victims of discrimination, African-Americans and Hispanics are also disproportionately poor. In the year 2000, the total poverty rate in the USA was 11.3%. At this time, 22% of Blacks and 21% of Hispanics lived in poverty. Only 7.5% of the white population fell below the poverty line.[60]

Members of the lower classes have less access to high-quality healthcare and are more likely to live in areas that are polluted; they have inadequate housing, labour under poor working conditions, and have poorer diets, compared to those with greater financial resources. Therefore, a myriad of factors exacerbates the health problems of low-income persons in the USA. Moran and Simpkin provide the following comment on the United Kingdom's Black Report of 1980 and subsequent studies of inequality in the UK. 'Because the explanation of health inequalities was multi-factorial, policy interventions needed to be similarly broad-ranging, extending well beyond changes to healthcare systems to include improvements in areas such as housing, transport, environment, working conditions, social security and other benefits.'[65] As noted above, this is in direct opposition to the approach utilised in the USA.

In the USA, equity and quality of care take a distant second place to 'market efficiency', which is assumed to be superior to any comprehensive governmental intervention. Today, the irony is that both wealthy consumers of healthcare and physicians, while historically weary of government intrusion into medical care, are now, in many cases, both severely limited by corporate medicine.[41]

The laws, policies and goals governing the US healthcare system are a result of its political economy.[31] Wealth and big businesses exercise their influence to ensure that the system represents their interests, not those of the general population.

'The medical care system is a major part of the larger system of economics production and consumption. It is structured to allow various interest groups to make significant profits and to control considerable resources in medical production ... The powerful economic interests involved in medical businesses – insurance companies, hospital corporations, pharmaceutical companies, medical technology corporations, and so on – often supersede the interests of both sick people and healthcare workers.'[66]

The systemic interaction of these economic interests that form the US healthcare system has come to be known as the medical-industrial complex.[67] Within this system, healthcare is managed as a business (not a service) and healthcare is seen as a privilege, rather than a basic human right. Because of this, significant numbers of persons suffer from woefully inadequate healthcare services.

Vincent Navarro discusses reasons why the US Congress failed to secure comprehensive healthcare reform in the early 1990s:

'The staggering power of the capitalist class and the enormous weakness of the working class explains why health care reform failed again. The United States, the only major capitalist country without government-guaranteed universal health care coverage, is also the only nation without a social-democratic or labor party that serves as the political instrument of the working class and other popular classes. These two facts are related. In most advanced countries, the establishment of universal entitlement programs has been based on the political alliances of the working class with the middle classes, through the election of social-democratic governments or through their pressure on non-social-democratic government.'[68]

Ironically, the government does spend an enormous amount of public tax money on healthcare. The two largest programmes are Medicaid (aid to the qualifying poor) and Medicare (health insurance for the elderly receiving social security). Neither programme provides full medical coverage and both are becoming less comprehensive. Many physicians simply will not accept Medicaid patients because of the low government payments, and the problem is growing. 'Despite the economic downturn that is affecting most areas of the country, the proportion of Medicaid costs that the federal government bears is declining in more than half the states in fiscal year 2002, which began on October 1.'[69] Medicare recipients are also finding it more difficult to find healthcare providers that will accept them as patients. Again, this is a product of lower government reimbursements. 'Average annual out-of-pocket expenditures for services not covered by Medicare were $3142 (about one-fifth of seniors' income) in 2000 and are expected to rise to $5248 (one-third of income) by 2005, according to the Urban Institute.'[70]

Many conclude that it was the creation of these two programmes that began the rapid increase in medical inflation. The federal government developed these programmes within an economic and political system that allowed private healthcare entities to prosper by exploiting government payments. The government's efforts to control costs have, as stated, negatively impacted on those who depend on Medicare and Medicaid as their healthcare insurance.

HEALTH AS A PUBLIC ISSUE: THE SOCIAL CONTENT AND SOCIAL CHANGE

Our proposed solution to the current healthcare crisis in the USA may appear greatly naive given the above discussion and the changes occurring in other industrialised nations. We suggest the creation of some type of national health insurance system similar to that found in Canada.

Currently the Canadian national health insurance system is undergoing serious problems. The Canadian economy has endured over ten years of recession that has affected most Canadian institutions. 'The Canadian system, flawed and threatened though it is, is nonetheless an enormous achievement, and light-years ahead of the wildly expensive, out-of-control, profit laden non-system in the USA.'[71] In addition, many of the problems that now face healthcare in Canada can much more easily be overcome in the USA. The USA has the resources, both existing medical technology, personnel, and infrastructure, and the general wealth to sustain a viable national health insurance system through much worse times than Canada's present situation.[72] However, this would take a reordering of priorities in the USA. The commonly known 'wealthfare' system would have to be modified to redistribute resources more evenly in the nation. 'Wealthfare' consists of an array of government policies and laws that shift a much larger portion of the nation's resources to the wealthy rather than the public at large.

Below is a brief description of the Canadian system as presented by the government's Canada Health Act 2002.

'The five principles of the Canada Health Act (CHA) are the cornerstone of the Canadian health care system. The Act ensures that all residents of Canada have access to medically necessary hospital and physician services based on need, not on ability to pay, by setting the criteria and conditions that provinces and territories must satisfy to qualify for their full cash transfers under the Canada Health and Social Transfer (CHST).

The five criteria of the Canada Health Act are:

- public administration: the administration of the health care insurance plan of a province or territory must be carried out on a non-profit basis by a public authority;
- comprehensiveness: all medically necessary services provided by hospitals and doctors must be insured;
- universality: all insured persons in the province or territory must be entitled to public health insurance coverage on uniform terms and conditions;

- portability: coverage for insured services must be maintained when an insured person moves or travels within Canada or travels outside the country; and
- accessibility: reasonable access by insured persons to medically necessary hospital and physician services must be unimpeded by financial or other barriers.

The Canada Health Act also contains provisions that ban extra-billing and user charges:

- no extra-billing by medical practitioners or dentists for insured health services under the terms of the health care insurance plan of the province or territory;
- no user charges for insured health services by hospitals or other providers under the terms of the health care insurance plan of the province or territory.'[73]

Some appealing aspects the Canadian system to many Americans would be that it allows freedom of choice in selecting primary care physicians. This is something that many Americans have already lost to private insurers. It also includes the involvement of state and local entities in the financing and administration of the system, again an appealing notion to most Americans.

It is concluded that the USA must develop some type of government-sponsored universal system. Ideally this would be part of a larger comprehensive social welfare system designed to reduce inequities throughout society and provide a high standard of living for the total population. The great wealth in the USA makes it a nation where this is clearly possibly. However, based on the arguments presented earlier in the chapter, it is highly unlikely at this time.

Over the past two decades government has allowed more and more control by the market of healthcare provision. This same trend has taken hold in European countries, but the USA has never had the same commitment to ensuring basic healthcare services as these nations.[74] The sociopolitical context of the USA makes any type of fundamental change in the system appear improbable. However, a successful campaign for some type of universal healthcare system sponsored by the government remains a legitimate possibility. The civil rights and the women's movements in the USA during the twentieth century provide significant illustrations that basic social change can occur. As recent as the early 1990s national healthcare was at least on the public agenda in the USA.

As sociologists, it is our task to focus public debate once again on this crucial issue. Healthcare appears to be one area in which the strong cultural bias toward individualism and limited government involvement can be penetrated. Among the general public, according to national polls since World War II, there has been a majority who favour some type of universal government-subsidised healthcare system. This is one of the few areas in which US citizens have not overwhelmingly disapproved of comprehensive government-sponsored social programmes.

Support for a comprehensive government-sponsored national healthcare plan has lost some of its appeal in the past few years, but still held considerable support as most other social programmes were under vicious attack by the public and policy-makers. This provides a spark of optimism from which to build a renewed movement.[75]

The USA is unlikely to undergo any type of substantial move toward a more egalitarian society in the near future, including changes in healthcare. However, change is always possible. Humans create the social structures of society and therefore humans can change them. 'Humans form groups, and groups form humans; losing sight of either side loses the essential nature of humanity.'[76] Unfortunately, most Americans have little comprehension of this link.[76] This makes the task of creating more equity in society difficult, but a task that sociologists in the USA must actively undertake.

CHANGING HEALTH LAWS AND HEALTH POLICIES IN THE USA

The role of sociologists

To begin this work, sociologists in the USA must themselves fully understand the complex systemic causes of the current social order. This may sound obvious to citizens of other nations. However, the magnitude and pervasiveness of the doctrine of individualism in US society is so great that it is difficult to escape, even among many sociologists. Secondly, they must also be aware of attempts at change that have failed in the past, and recognise and work with the current and ongoing efforts by other groups. There is a small but persistent presence of non-governmental organisations and progressive foundations that are attempting to institute change (Families USA, National Physicians for National Health Plans, Robert Wood Johnson Foundation, and others). These organisations work at the national level to promote change and offer services and funds to state-based efforts, where much action must take place. Thirdly, there have always been some sociologists in the USA that, to some degree, have put theory and research into action, but in the USA the discipline has always been dominated by a non-action orientation. Peter Berger wrote an excellent book, *Invitation to Sociology*, in which he defines the nature of sociological thinking.[77] However, Du Bois is correct in his criticism of Berger, when he states the following:

> 'Peter Berger had it wrong in Invitation to Sociology. He invited people into the field on the premise that even if we can't change our conditions, we can use science to explain our situations. However, it is not enough for creatures caught in a trap to look up with some measure of understanding of their plight. The invitation that actually gets people involved in sociology is the invitation to change the world. Sociology is not just about analysis or description or even understanding. Sociology is about transforming the world.'[78]

What can sociologists do to contribute to the realisation of a fair and just health system in USA? Most importantly sociologists must emphasise, relentlessly, the impact of the social structure and culture on health and illness.[79] Secondly, as stated above, there must be a broader infusion into the discipline of the idea that as sociologists our goal should be to initiate social change and not simply to act as detached evaluators of the problem.[80-82] Thirdly, sociologists must convey to others the comprehensive nature of sociology and its ability to conduct a holistic analysis of society, including relationships with other institutions and individuals, and the forces that make social change possible.[83] Unfortunately (at least in the USA), compared to topics studied by many other professionals, many people simply do not know what sociology is or what sociologists do. This is a serious problem in that it creates a credibility dilemma that many other social and natural scientists do not face.

Fourthly, sociologists are obligated to collect accurate, valid and comprehensive data that presents the multidimensionality of the issue and the implication of change for society and individuals. Alternative and workable solutions to the status quo must always be developed. Finally, significant energy must be expended on efforts to disseminate our knowledge so that it is utilised to influence the policy-makers who have the power to make the needed changes.

Establishing a foundation for social change

The involvement of large and diverse segments of the population is essential in any effort to produce positive change to improve the health conditions of all who live in the USA. This requires change-oriented research sociologists with a real impact on social policy (something that is very limited at this time). Many private, not-for-profit organisations and communities are willing to fund the work of sociologists in research studies that provide high-quality data, evaluation and social action strategies (i.e. Physicians for a National Health Program, the Alliance for Democracy, many state-level healthcare organisations, and several other state and international organisations).

The continuing efforts at examining and utilising new theoretical and methodological approaches in sociology (i.e. chaos/complexity theories, participatory action methods) that can effectively initiate change should be intensified. Sociology must be at the forefront of adapting (not compromising) its work to the changes taking place at all levels of social reality.

Implementing social change

Changing laws and policies that would improve the health of the general population of the USA is not an easy task. The overwhelming inequality and power of the wealthy in combination with an almost total lack of class consciousness among others in society create significant challenges for those seeking a more egalitarian society.

'Profound ambivalence toward the victims of social problems has existed in American society since the colonial period. On the one hand, Americans have exhibited compassion toward those who are hungry, destitute, ill, and transient, as illustrated by a host of ameliorative public policies and a rich tradition of private philanthropy. On the other, they have demonstrated a callous disregard for persons in need.'[84]

People in the USA make great distinctions between the deserving and undeserving poor.[85] For this reason, any attempt to establish universal health-care coverage must articulate its advantages to the general public. In the USA, many of the problems of the working and middle classes are caused by the wealthy, but the blame is most often directed toward the poor. This is one of the most significant issues that must be overcome before the establishment of any true reform.

Byrne, in suggesting solutions to social exclusion and inequality in the UK, states: 'Attractive as the notion might be of watering the fields with the blood of the superclass, practically the way to deal with them is through . . . other forms of bloodletting . . .'[86] To reduce the health inequities within the USA we agree with his general notion. Dramatic change will not occur overnight, but the crisis has touched enough citizens for the social context within the USA to have reached a point where noteworthy changes in laws and policies that govern the healthcare system may reverse course and become more egalitarian.

CONCLUSION

During the 1980s and 1990s private 'managed' care dominated healthcare policy discussion throughout many industrialised nations. This of course went beyond healthcare and affected several aspects of welfare systems. For a variety of reasons some countries have moved faster than others to privatise healthcare as well as other sectors of the economy. 'The first leading nation to embrace managed competition, and to become an exemplar for other nations, was the United Kingdom.'[87] The slow economic growth beginning in the early 1970s and the pronouncements to 'trim the fat' to enable successful competition in a global economy led (or justified) governments to minimise their welfare states.[87] At the same time and today still it seems like the rational thing to do.

The purpose of this paper is not to analyse or criticise any country with a well-developed welfare state that would decide to move toward privatisation of social services as an answer to an economic downturn. Reasons for change in any of these nations may be valid, effective and the best alternative available at this time. However, the author is firmly opposed to the components of the social structure and culture of the USA that have been used to produce the following. Firstly, an economic system that gives big business and wealthy individuals an enormous amount of power so that they are able to direct public sentiment and public policy to benefit them, often at the expense of the general population. This of course includes health laws and policies. The information presented above is a clear indication that the social context of society, defined primarily by the wealthy, has created a healthcare environment that has negative consequences for many in the population. Policy-makers created health laws and policies within the political parameters set by those in power. In the USA those in power are the corporate rich who benefit from the existing healthcare system. Secondly, an unbridled market economy, extreme individualism, ethnocentrism, and the idea that competition is the only viable method to achieve progress in society and in ones personal life.

Unfortunately, these factors are viewed by many as 'natural' and positive in nature and the factors that have made America 'great'. However, the USA provides a perfect model of structured inequality among industrial nations and a social system that produces great inequalities among the population. Laws in general and health law in particular unquestionably favour the upper and corporate classes. Therefore, as many countries turn toward market-oriented solutions with reduced spending on social programmes in order to provide citizens with basic life necessities, including high-quality health, they should look closely at the results that this approach has produced in the USA.

References

1. Koppel, R. American public policy: formation and implementation. In: Straus RA, ed. Using sociology: an introduction from the applied and clinical perspectives. New York: Rowman and Littlefield; 2002:265–288.
2. Grana SJ, Ollenburger JC, Nicholas M. The social context of law. Upper Saddle River, NJ: Prentice Hall; 2002:1.
3. Stimpson J, Stimpson A. Sociology: contemporary readings. 2nd edn. Itasca, MN: Peacock; 1987.
4. Berger P. Invitation to sociology: a humanistic perspective. Garden City, NY: Doubleday; 1963:31.
5. Hellander I. Review of data on the health sector of the United States. International Journal of Health Services 2003; 33:825–855.
6. Partel K, Rushefsky ME. Health care politics and policy in America. Armonk, NY: Sharpe; 1999:2.
7. Teeple G. Globalization and the decline of social reform: into the twenty-first century. Aurora, Ontario: Garamond; 2000.
8. Sepehri A, Chernomas R, Akram-Lodhi H. If they get sick, they are in trouble: health care restructuring, user charges, and equity in Vietnam. International Journal of Health Services 2003; 33:137–161.
9. Domhoff W. Who rules America? Power and politics. Boston: McGraw Hill; 2002:182.
10. Janssen, BS. The reluctant welfare state. 4th edn. Belmont, Calf: Wadsworth; 2001.
11. USA Census Bureau. Statistical abstract of the USA. Washington, DC: USA Government Printing Office; 2002.
12. Lewis BL, Parent FD. Healthcare equity. In: Rebach H, Bruhn J, eds. Handbook of clinical sociology. New York: Plenum; 2001:293–311, at 295.

13. Braun D. The rich get richer: the rise of income inequality in the United States and the world. Chicago: Nelson-Hall; 1991.

14. Danziger S, Golkschalk P. America unequal. New York: Sage; 1995.

15. Galbraith JK. Created unequal: the crisis in American pay. New York: Free Press; 1998.

16. Blau J. Illusions of prosperity: America's working families in an age of economic insecurity. New York: Oxford; 1999.

17. Findeis JL, Jensen L, Qiuyan W. Underemployment prevalence and transitions in the US Non-metropolitan south. Southern Rural Sociology 2000; 16:125–147.

18. Lewis BL, Petrakis PA. Legal services in the United States: an application of a model for evaluating legal service access. Journal of Applied Sociology 2000; 17:118–133.

19. Greenstein R, et al. Poverty rates fell in 2000 as unemployment reached 31 year low: upturn in unemployment combined with weaknesses in safety net raise red flag for 2001. Washington, DC: Center on Budget and Policy Priorities.

20. O'Brien J. Social prisms: reflections on everyday myths and paradoxes. Thousand Oaks, CA: Pine Forge; 1999.

21. Parenti M. Land of idols: political mythology in America. New York: St Martin's; 1994.

22. Gray C. Corporate Goliaths: sizing up corporations and governments. Multinational Monitor. 1999; 20:26–27.

23. USA National Center for Health Statistics. 2001. Vital Statistics of the United States. 2001; Washington, DC: USA Census Bureau.

24. Lawrence M, Bernstein J, Schmitt J. The state of working America, 1998–1999. Ithaca, NY: Cornell University; 1998.

25. Parenti, M. Power and the powerless. New York: St Martin's; 1978:71.

26. Parenti, M. Power and the powerless. New York: St Martin's; 1978:84.

27. Mills CW. The power elite. New York: Oxford; 1956.

28. O'Brien J. Social prisms: reflections on everyday myths and paradoxes. Thousand Oaks, CA: Pine Forge; 1999:158.

29. O'Connor A. Poverty research and policy for the post-welfare era. Annual Review of Sociology 2000; 26:547–562.

30. Weitz R. The sociology of health, illness, and health care: a critical approach. New York: Wadsworth; 2004:224.

31. Freund PE, McGuire MB, Podhurst S. Health, illness and the social body. 4th edn. Upper Saddle River, NJ: Prentice Hall; 2003.

32. Mishler EG. Viewpoint: critical perspectives on the biomedical model. In: Mishler MG, ed. Social contexts of health, illness, and patient care. Cambridge: Cambridge; 1981:1–23.

33. World Health Organization. Official records of the World Health Organization. 1948; 2:100. Online. Available: http://www.who.int/about/definition/en/ 21 April 2004.

34. Freund PE, McGuire MB, Podhurst S. Health illness and the social body. 4th edn. Upper Saddle River, NJ: Prentice Hall; 2003:256.

35. Light DW. Cost containment and the backdraft of competition policies. Journal of Health Services 2003; 31:681–704.

36. Aday L, Begley CE, Lairson DR, et al. Evaluating the healthcare system: effectiveness, efficiency, and equity. Chicago: Health Adm.; 1998.

37. Palmer KS. A brief history: universal health care efforts in the US: late 1800's to medicare. Physicians for a National Health Program; 2003. Online. Available: http://www.pnhp.org/facts/a_brief_history_universal_health_care_efforts_in_the_us.php 21 April 2004.

38. Rothman D. Beginnings count: the technological imperative in American health care. New York: Oxford; 1997.

39. Lassey M. William L. Lassey R, et al. 1997. Health care systems around the world: characteristics, issues, reforms. Upper Saddle River, NJ: Prentice Hall; 1997.

40. Duffy J. From humors to medical science: a history of American medicine. Urbana: University of Illinois; 1993.

41. Weitz R. The sociology of health, illness, and health care: a critical approach. New York: Wadsworth; 2004.

42. Consumers Union. Second-class medicine. Consumers Union. Org. Sept 2000. Online. Available: www.consumersunion.org/health/i-affordability.htm 21 April 2004.

43. Starfield B. Primary care and health: a cross-national comparison. In: Eitzen DS, Leedham GS, eds. Solutions to social problems: lessons from other societies. Boston: Allyn and Bacon; 2001:155–162.

44. Geyman JP. Myths as barriers to health care reform in the United States. Journal of Health Services 2003; 33:315–329.

45. Blank RE. The price of life: the future of American health care. New York: Columbia University; 1997.

46. Freund PE, McGuire MB, Podhurst S. Health illness and the social body. 4th edn. Upper Saddle River, NJ: Prentice Hall; 2003:265.

47. Edwards RC. The centralization of economic power. In: Edwards RC, Reich M, Weisskopf TE, eds. The capitalist system. Englewood Cliffs, NJ: Prentice Hall; 1986: 66–67.

48. Hellander I. Review of data on the health sector of the United States. International Journal of Health Services 2001; 31:823–846.

49. Parent FD. Vertical integration and diversification among multihospital systems: a for-profit, nonprofit comparison. Sociological Spectrum 1991; 11:81–91.

50. National Center for Health Statistics. Health, United States. Washington, DC: Census Bureau; 2002.

51. Light DW. Cost containment and the backdraft of competition policies. International Journal of Health Services 2001; 31:681–704.

52. Starr P. The logic of health care reform: why and how the President's plan will work. New York: Penguin; 1994.

53. USA Census Bureau. World population data sheet. Washington, DC: Population Reference Bureau; 1998.

54. [Anonymous]. Blacks often are less satisfied with their health care, perhaps because they feel 'socially distant' from their doctors. Agency for Healthcare Research and Quality 2002; 260:9–10.

55. Baxandall, P. Spending #1, performance #37: how US health care stacks up internationally. Dollars & Sense 2001; 235:38–40.

56. Mills RJ, Bhandari S. Health insurance coverage in the United States: 2002. Washington, DC: Current Population Reports; 2003:1.

57. National Center for Health Statistics. Health, United States: 2001. Hyattsville, MD: Public Health Service; 2002: 49:1.

58. Associated Press. Racial inequality remains as US fights disease. 25 January 2002. Online. Available: http://www.usatoday.com/news/health/2002-01-25-overall-health.htm.

59. National Center for Health Statistics. Health, United States: 2001. Hyattsville, MD: Public Health Service; 2002: 49:6.

60. Forrest CB, Whelan EM. Primary care safety-net providers in the United States: a comparison of federally qualified health centers, hospital outpatient departments,

and physicians' offices. Journal of the American Medical Association 2000; 284:2077–2083.

61.   Sullivan TJ. Introduction to social problems. 6th edn. Boston: Allyn and Bacon; 2003.

62.   Hellander I. Review of data on the health sector of the United States. International Journal of Health Services 2001; 31:823–846, at 827.

63.   Feigin JR, Feigin CB. Racial and ethnic relations. 6th edn. Upper Saddle River, NJ: Prentice Hall; 1999.

64.   Parent FD, Parent W. Benign neglect: the realpolitic of race and ethnicity. In: Davies PJ, ed. An American Quarter Century: US Politics from Vietnam to Clinton. Manchester: Manchester University; 1995:159–175.

65.   Moran G, Simpkin M. Social exclusion and health. In: Percy-Smith J, ed. Policy responses to social exclusion: toward inclusion? Buckingham: Open University; 2000:84–106.

66.   Freund PE, McGuire MB, Podhurst S. Health illness and the social body. 4th edn. Upper Saddle River, NJ: Prentice Hall; 2003:279.

67.   Rellman AS. The new medical-industrial complex. New England Journal of Medicine 1980; 303(33):963–970.

68.   Navarro V. Why congress did not enact health care reform. Journal of Health Politics, Policy and Law 1995; 20(2):455–462; at 455.

69.   Ku, L, Park E. Federal aid to state Medicaid programs is falling while the economy weakens. Washington, DC: Center on Budget and Policy Priorities; 2001:1.

70.   Hellander I. Review of data on the health sector of the United States. International Journal of Health Services 2001; 31:823–846, at 827.

71.   Livingston M. Update on health care in Canada: what's right, what's wrong, what's left. Journal of Public Health Policy 1998; 19:267–288, at 267.

72.   McCanne D, Woolhandler S. How to achieve health care for all. Physicians for a National Health Program. 2001. Online. Available: http://www.pnhp.org/basicinfo/health_care_for_all.htm.

73.   Health Canada. Canada Health Act. 2002. Online. Available: http://www.hc-sc.gc.ca/medicare/home.htm 21 April 2004.

74.   Blau J. Illusions of prosperity: America's working families in an age of economic insecurity. New York: Oxford University; 1999.

75.   Blendon RJ, Benson JM, Mollyann B, et al. Voters and health care in the 1998 election. Journal of the American Medical Association 2000; (282):189.

76.   Sernau S. Critical choices: applying sociological insight in your life, family, and community. Los Angeles: Roxbury; 1997:1.

77.   Berger P. Invitation to sociology: a humanistic perspective. Garden City, NY: Doubleday; 1963

78.   DuBois W 2001. A Framework for doing applied sociology. In: Du Bois W, Wright RD, eds. Applying sociology: making a better world. Boston: Allyn and Bacon; 2001:1–17, at 1.

79.   Weiss GL, Lonnquist LE. The sociology of health, healing, and illness. 4th edn. Upper Saddle River, NJ: Prentice Hall; 2003.

80.   Byrne D. Interpreting quantitative data. London: Sage; 2002.

81.   Perrucci R. Inventing social justice: SSSP and the twenty-first century. Social Problems 2001; 48:159–71.

82.   Walton J. Sociology and critical inquiry: the work, tradition, and purpose. 3rd edn. Belmont, CA: Wadsworth; 1993.

83.   Johnson AG. The forest for the trees: an introduction to sociological thinking. San Diego: Harcourt; 1991.

84. Janssen BS. The reluctant welfare state. 4th edn. Belmont, CA: Wadsworth; 2001:2.

85. Katz MB. The undeserving poor: from the war on poverty to the war on welfare. New York: Pantheon; 1989.

86. Byrne D. Social exclusion. Buckingham: Open University; 1999:137.

87. Light DW. Comparative models of health care systems. In: Conrad P, Kern R, eds. The sociology of health and illness. New York: St Martin's; 1994:455–470.

Chapter **2**

Does it pay to be NICE? Resolving the 'legitimacy problem' in the allocation of healthcare resources

Keith Syrett

CHAPTER CONTENTS

Introduction   37
Modes of rationing in the
   NHS   38
The establishment of
   NICE: addressing the
   'legitimacy problem'   40
Legitimacy and due process   42
Evaluating NICE   44
Reform: making NICE
   nicer?   47
Conclusion   50
References   51

INTRODUCTION

In recent years, governments worldwide have been forced to respond to the growing pressures exerted upon limited budgets for healthcare. Social and demographic factors such as a more informed and engaged public and an ageing population have combined with advances in medical technology to expose the finite nature of resources. The consequence has been that rationing, which has, in fact, existed since the inception of publicly funded health services, has changed in character, becoming more explicit and systematic than was previously the case.

While many commentators have welcomed this development as indicative of greater 'honesty' in allocative decision-making, it has, however, brought with it further difficulties. In particular, a 'legitimacy problem' has emerged: namely, 'under what conditions should authority over priority-setting decisions be placed in the hands of a particular organisation, group or person'?[1] This issue renders this field of policy-making of especial interest to public lawyers, given that critical analysis of strategies of legitimation lies at the core of their work.[2]

This chapter examines the innovative and influential effort made to address this problem in the UK's National Health Service (NHS). By setting up the National Institute for Clinical Excellence (NICE), the Blair Government has sought to apply rationalist methodologies to priority-setting in healthcare, with a view to objectifying and depoliticising rationing choices.

However, the deficiencies of this approach have also been recognised, resulting in the adoption of procedural mechanisms by the Institute which are intended to legitimate decision-making by rendering it more transparent and participatory in nature.

It will be argued that, while NICE has received praise from several quarters, certain significant defects remain apparent, as evidenced by the controversy generated by a number of its recommendations. The final section of this chapter will, therefore, consider means by which these shortcomings might be resolved.

MODES OF RATIONING IN THE NHS

It is now widely acknowledged that rationing of healthcare, which may be defined as 'a failure to offer care, or the denial of care, from which patients would benefit',[3] is inevitable. This follows from the simple fact that demand exceeds supply: both the physical (hospitals, doctors) and monetary resources which are in place to meet the demand for treatment are finite in nature. In private healthcare systems, such as that in the United States, some degree of equalisation between demand and supply is achieved through the inability of certain patients to pay for treatment. In contrast, in publicly funded systems, such as the NHS, which is free at the point of use, the criterion of medical 'need' operates to reduce excess demand.

The 'need' factor functions as a rationing principle in that services are not provided simply because an individual considers himself to require medical care. Rather, a professional judgement of 'need' takes place. Typically, this judgement has been exercised by physicians trained in the Hippocratic tradition to act as dedicated advocates of their patients, attempting to secure all resources necessary for treatment.[4] However, in reaching a decision on 'need', the physician will take account not only of the patient's capacity to benefit medically from the allocation of resources to fund the treatment, but also whether provision of services can be socially justified, in terms of the cost of treatment and facilities measured against the clinical effect upon the patient. If the physician reaches the conclusion that there is no such justification, then rationing has taken place: the individual is being denied medical services which would have been beneficial and which she wished to receive.

The decision to prioritise social needs over those of the individual is, of course, ethically highly controversial, particularly for those who lose out as a consequence. It might be expected, therefore, that there would be significant challenges to the moral authority of the physicians charged with making such choices. Nevertheless, rationing of this type did not tend to give rise to significant problems of legitimacy, for two related reasons. First, such decisions were presented to the patient as if they were clinical in nature: justification was provided on medical grounds (e.g. 'I'm afraid that there is nothing we can do for you, given your condition'), upon which the clinician was regarded as having expertise. This fed into the second factor. The existence of high levels of trust between doctors and patients, rooted in the Hippocratic tradition, defused any suspicion that decisions to refuse care were dictated by resource considerations.[4] Rationing was therefore *implicit*, in that 'the [cost-based] reasoning involved [wa]s not clearly stated to anyone except ... the person making the decision',[5] and this served to 'render the process of rationing as it were politically invisible, by fragmenting it across space and time into individualised and private transactions between doctors and patients. The result was that the NHS was able to maintain the fiction of meeting everyone's needs.'[6]

Difficulties began to emerge, however, when the Conservative Government sought to enhance supply-side efficiency in the NHS by separating out the roles of purchaser and provider by means of the 'internal market' established as a result of the National Health Service and Community Care Act 1990. Health authorities were required to publish plans and to enter into contracts that specified which services were to be provided to their local populations. In consequence, a number of interventions (albeit mostly those of a somewhat 'marginal' nature, such as sterilisation/vasectomy reversal, tattoo removal and gender reassignment surgery) were excluded from the 'packages of care' provided by certain authorities. In other cases, guidelines and protocols, which specified the conditions of eligibility in individual cases, were developed in negotiation with local clinicians.[7]

These developments exposed to public visibility the fact that decisions were being taken to deny access to certain treatments, on grounds of cost. Media interest in rationing also increased, with instances of 'postcode prescribing', in which availability of care depended upon geographical location, being especially highlighted. Furthermore, the process of judicial review offered a mechanism through which patients who were denied care could challenge rationing decisions. While this proved to be ineffective in the leading case of *R v Cambridge HA, ex parte B* [1995] 2 All ER 129 (albeit that the publicity which the case attracted led to private funding being offered for the patient's treatment), legal challenges to geographical inequities in treatment were upheld in the subsequent cases of *R v North Derbyshire HA, ex parte Fisher* [1997] 8 Med LR 327 (failure to provide beta-interferon for multiple sclerosis) and in *R v North West Lancashire HA, ex parte A, D and G* [2000] 1 WLR 977 (refusal to offer gender reassignment surgery). A drug manufacturer also successfully challenged the process by which the Department of Health implemented the rationing decision that Viagra should not be available on the NHS (*R v Secretary of State for Health, ex parte Pfizer Ltd* [1999] Lloyd's Rep Med 289).

In sum, many elements of healthcare rationing had now become *explicit*, in that clear attempts were being made to specify who was to receive (and importantly 'who was not to receive) certain treatments. The ethical controversies entailed in priority-setting, notably the potential inconsistency between considerations of individual welfare and a utilitarian calculus of the social good, in turn emerged as clearly visible. As they did so, those who lost out as a result of the allocative choices made (and on occasion, the wider public) began to call into question the basis of those decisions, whether the decision-maker had applied appropriate criteria, and, more generally, whether it possessed the requisite moral authority to limit or deny access to a benefit which was seen as fundamental to the individual's well-being. Consequently, at least in respect of its mechanisms for the allocation of resources, the NHS appeared to be experiencing a 'legitimacy problem' of the type identified by theorists of health policy who have pointed to the 'suspicion, distrust and even resistance [which] often greet[s] efforts to set limits on access to medical services'.[8] Given the widely recognised connection between the legitimacy and effectiveness of a political institution,[9] this was a problem to which a new government would need to respond.

THE ESTABLISHMENT OF NICE: ADDRESSING THE 'LEGITIMACY PROBLEM'

The Blair Government's reforms to the NHS were outlined in two policy documents, *The New NHS: Modern, Dependable* (1997) and *A First Class Service: Quality in the new NHS* (1998), and were given legislative effect by the Health Act 1999 and related secondary legislation. In addition to measures that reformed the 'internal market', the Government attempted to respond to a perceived public lack of confidence in the NHS, which, it argued, had been undermined by the 'lottery in care' which arose as a result of 'postcode prescribing' and the failure to match public expectations of rapid access to high-quality services, as well as by a number of serious clinical failures (such as that involving paediatric cardiac services at Bristol Royal Infirmary).[10] Consequently, it sought to introduce quality assurance mechanisms into the NHS. Standardisation of good medical practice was to be achieved through the introduction of National Service Frameworks to provide models for the provision of services in particular areas of care, backed by a regime of 'clinical governance' at local level, with monitoring of performance undertaken by a new inspectorate, the Commission for Health Improvement.

Also central to this objective was a new agency, the National Institute for Clinical Excellence (NICE). Formally constituted as a Special Health Authority under s.11 of the National Health Service Act 1977, and as such accountable for its work to the Secretary of State for Health and the Welsh Assembly, this is a relatively small institution which possesses a core staff of just 60 people and a current annual budget of £12.5 million. Indeed, its chairman has described it as a 'virtual' organisation, in that much of its work is actually carried out by researchers in academic centres across England and Wales.[11] The Institute has expressed its role as being 'to produce clear national guidance, as part of the process for improving the quality of healthcare across England and Wales'.[12] To this end, it produces and disseminates guidance to the NHS in England and Wales in three fields of healthcare: guidelines on whether interventional procedures for diagnosis and treatment are safe and effective for routine use, clinical guidelines on the appropriate treatment and care of people with specific diseases and conditions, and technology appraisals of new and existing medicines and treatments.

NICE therefore contributes to the quality assurance objective through its position as a source of 'best practice'. However, it also plays a fundamental (if less openly acknowledged) role in regulating the rationing of healthcare within the NHS. This can be discerned from the statutory instruments that established the Institute: the initial obligation to 'perform such functions in connection with the promotion of clinical excellence in the health service as the Secretary of State may direct' was subsequently amended to make clear that consideration of 'the effective use of available resources' was also required.[13]

Although some clinical guidelines have the potential to have a significant impact upon the allocation of resources, it is mainly in the context of technology appraisals that NICE's role in rationing becomes apparent. Here, the Institute's Appraisal Committee draws upon evidence submitted by drug manufacturers, professionals and patient groups and commissions an independent technology assessment report which evaluates the clinical and cost-effectiveness of a treatment and, where relevant, its overall impact on the NHS and social services. This forms the basis of guidance as to whether or not the technology is recommended for routine use on the NHS, or whether its availability is to be restricted to certain categories of patients or within the context of an appropriately designed clinical trial. While this guidance is not legally binding upon clinicians, all health authorities and primary care trusts in England and Wales have been statutorily obliged to provide funding for treatments that NICE has recommended since January 2002.[14] The consequence is that a positive determination by the Institute should automatically lead to a treatment being made available on the NHS (although a clinician may choose not to provide it in an individual case), while a negative appraisal furnishes the perfect justification for a health authority to withhold funding. Hence, notwithstanding that decisions on the affordability of particular treatments formally remain with the government, in practice the impression has been created that 'because it is likely that NICE recommendations will be implemented whatever the cost, NICE is essentially making decisions about how money is spent in the NHS'.[15] It is this which lends credence to the view of the editor of the *British Medical Journal*, that the Institute is 'an instrument for rationing health care'.[16]

NICE may therefore be said to make a significant contribution to the process of rationing within the NHS, albeit within the limited, though financially significant, field of the evaluation of (mainly) new technologies and drugs. It is important, therefore, to identify the manner in which the establishment of the Institute represents a response to the problem of legitimacy to which explicit rationing gives rise.

The methodological approach adopted by the Institute may be seen as an attempt to resolve this issue through formal rationality, in which problems are solved through quantitative calculation and the application of technical factors.[17,18] NICE's recommendations draw upon the techniques (notably of evidence-based medicine and health economics) which are fundamental to the relatively new research activity of health technology assessment. This seeks to offer a systematic evaluation of the short- and long-term consequences of a health technology from a wide variety of perspectives, including all or any of clinical effectiveness, social and ethical issues and cost-effectiveness.[19] The application of ostensibly neutral and technical scientific and social-scientific criteria is intended to produce decisions that can scientifically and objectively be demonstrated as maximising benefits and minimising costs. The intention, therefore, is to depoliticise the process of rationing by means of an 'explicit, objective approach to priority-setting which, because of its objectivity, can be insulated from unnecessary interference from stakeholders with vested interests and politicians with populist agendas'.[20]

NICE can thus lay claim to legitimacy on the basis of its exercise of expert judgement, while the controversy to which priority-setting inevitably gives rise is defused as 'essentially political questions and choices become transformed into technical ones which nicely lets politicians and managers "off the hook". They can take shelter behind the evidence which, they will opine, has been objectively and independently assembled.'[21] In this respect, the creation of the Institute may be seen as a manifestation of the 'technocratic wish', defined as 'the expectation and hope that contentious issues in public life can be resolved by appeal to scientific measures and procedures rather than by the wise judgement of selected individuals'.[22]

LEGITIMACY AND DUE PROCESS

It is highly questionable, however, whether an approach rooted in formal rationality can actually resolve the 'legitimacy problem' once and for all. While decision-making based upon fuller scientific and social-scientific evidence appears intuitively easier to justify than 'what were often perceived to be the idiosyncratic and extravagant practices of doctors',[23] especially as it facilitates consistency between similar cases and thus contributes to equality of treatment, it would be mistaken to assume that 'one right answer' exists to the questions raised by the rationing of healthcare.

The fundamental difficulty lies in the fact that rationing of healthcare is not reducible solely to 'technical' factors: it is, rather, 'inescapably a political process'.[24] As outlined above, any priority-setting decision is likely to engage deep-seated ethical and social values. Although various health systems have made attempts to establish frameworks of general principles or moral standards which might be followed when making decisions on the allocation of healthcare resources, these have generally proved unsuccessful, simply because 'in a pluralist society, it may be impossible to achieve meaningful consensus on many substantive issues'.[25] Utilitarian, egalitarian, libertarian and communitarian approaches all command varying degrees of support as modes of distributive justice applicable in the healthcare context, and these are frequently in conflict: for example, the pursuit of equity may be at the cost of efficiency. Consequently, any attempt to define rationing issues as technical and apolitical risks delegitimising priority-setting as observers perceive decision-makers such as NICE to be guilty of 'failures with honesty' by:

'giv[ing] the impression that if the evidence supports a treatment then it's made available and if it doesn't it isn't. In other words, the whole messy problem of deciding which interventions to make available can be decided with some data and a computer. It's a technical problem. This lie corrupts the concept of evidence-based medicine . . . The evidence supports decision-making, but the evidence can't make the decision. The values of the patient or the community must be part of the decision.'[26]

Given these difficulties, it is important to pay attention to the 'fundamental role of process in the legitimisation of government decisions',[27] especially the values of participation and accountability (inherent in which are notions of transparency and reason-giving) which have been identified as central organising concepts of a 'critical' approach to public law.[2] Explanations for decisions should be provided, all considerations and perspectives should be properly weighed, and no single interest should be permitted to dominate the decision-making process. The goal, once again, is not to produce 'right' answers, but rather decisions that are 'socially acceptable' or 'morally defensible', allowing those who are affected by them to understand why they were reached and to agree that appropriate criteria have been applied, even if the ultimate decision is not in their favour.[28]

Several facets of the institutional design of NICE evidence a commitment to achieving legitimacy through due process in this manner. Firstly, the Institute is required to have regard to the need to 'endeavour to conduct its business in an open and transparent manner'.[29] To this end it publishes policies, procedures and decisions on a comprehensive website, holds board meetings in public, makes publicly available interim and final recommendations together with the reasoning and (where possible) the evidence upon which these are based, and operates a communication strategy to facilitate the publication and dissemination of its objectives and decisions to stakeholders. Secondly, various opportunities exist for the articulation of differing perspectives on the Institute's decision-making. These include 'lay' representation on its Partners' Council, Appraisals Committee and Appeal Panel, the opportunity for interested parties to submit evidence during the technology appraisal process, and, perhaps most significantly, the recently created Citizens Council, whose role is discussed further below. Finally, there is an internal process by means of which interested parties may appeal a decision reached by the Institute on grounds that it has acted in excess of power, perversely in the light of the evidence submitted, or unfairly, although there is no mechanism for an appeal on the merits.

These features suggest that NICE is best regarded as representing a synthesis of approaches. It bases its legitimacy both upon rationality (in the form of its gathering of information and application of technical expertise) and upon its observance of proceduralist or reflexive requirements, the latter being defined as 'the use of law not to impose substantive ends but to structure decision-making processes to ensure that the result achieved is acceptable'.[30] However, the question remains of whether this dual strategy has genuinely succeeded in addressing the 'legitimacy problem'. In order to analyse this issue, it is necessary to consider the nature of NICE's work to date and some of the responses to it.

EVALUATING NICE

A useful starting point in an assessment of the success of NICE is to consider the major reviews of the organisation which have been carried out by the World Health Organization (WHO) and the parliamentary Select Committee on Health. The former concludes that 'in only four years, NICE has developed a well-deserved reputation for innovation and methodological development', singling out for praise the Institute's achievements in transparency, participation and inclusiveness, its commitment to the use of best available evidence and the dedication of its staff.[31] It also comments that the Institute has become an 'important model for technology appraisals internationally',[31] a fact confirmed by the chairman of the Institute, who has indicated that sixty governments have examined the NICE model with a view to adoption.[32] The Select Committee is somewhat more circumspect, welcoming the creation of the Institute, recognising that it represented 'an improvement on the previous situation' and expressing confidence in its ability to learn from its early experiences and to develop its processes accordingly.[33]

In part, the generally favourable response to NICE, which has been echoed by some leading commentators on health policy,[34–36] may be attributed to an avoidance of controversy on the Institute's part: put simply, 'it's easier to say yes than no'.[26] It is notable that of the first fifty appraisals completed by October 2002, NICE recommended routine or selective use of the technology in 46 cases,[37] and that its guidance has resulted in a net *increase* in NHS spending of £640 million.[32] On the basis of these figures, it might be queried whether NICE really functions as a rationing body at all.

It should be noted, however, that the majority of these appraisals have not resulted in unrestricted availability throughout the NHS. Rather, most recommendations have been for use *only within restricted classes of patient*, with the consequence that the treatments are effectively rationed for those who do not fall within the specified categories. Such individuals may still have cause to challenge the moral authority of the body that has denied them access to treatment. Moreover, there have been a number of high-profile appraisals 'conducted in the face of articulate and often vociferous scrutiny from the clinical professions, the NHS, patient organisations, national and international pharmaceutical companies and the media',[38] which illustrate vividly the strength of feeling to which the Institute's work gives rise. In such circumstances, it remains necessary for NICE to work to establish its legitimacy so that the decision-making regime remains credible and effective.

The most controversial appraisals conducted to date by NICE have been those of drugs for the treatment of influenza (zanamivir) and multiple sclerosis (beta-interferon). In the former instance, the Institute initially refused to recommend the treatment for routine use on the NHS on the basis that it was not satisfied that it was clinically effective. This decision provoked anger from the pharmaceutical industry, with three leading drug companies writing a letter to the Prime Minister warning that it had 'potentially devastating consequences for the future of the British-based pharmaceutical industry', while the manufacturer threatened a judicial review challenge.[39] A year later, NICE reversed its decision and recommended the treatment. This, too, provoked discontent, as a group of GPs refused to prescribe the drug on the grounds that it was too expensive,[40] while the influential *Drugs and Therapeutics Bulletin*, whose editor described the recommendation as 'perverse', published an article rejecting the NICE guidance as based upon insufficient evidence.[41]

However, it is the evaluation of beta-interferon that has generated the widest interest in, and public debate upon, the work of NICE. This treatment had, in fact, been a matter of political concern since late 1995.[42] It was estimated at that date that its routine availability would consume some 10% of the overall drug budget of the NHS. This fact, coupled with the controversy that had attended previous attempts to limit access to the treatment (apparent from the successful legal challenge in *R v North Derbyshire HA, ex parte Fisher*), made it unsurprising that the drug was one of the first to be referred to NICE, in August 1999.

Appraisal of the treatment took some thirty months (more than twice the usual length of the process), as a result of a decision by NICE to recommence appraisal on the basis of revised economic modelling. This followed a successful internal appeal against the preliminary decision not to recommend the treatment, led by the Multiple Sclerosis Society (but supported by other patient groups, consultant neurologists, the Royal College of Nursing and drug manufacturers), whose campaign also involved letter-writing, questions in Parliament and threats of litigation. Nonetheless, the Institute's final decision remained that the treatment should not be recommended on the grounds that it was not cost-effective. The political uproar to which this decision might well have given rise was, however, significantly mitigated as a result of the Department of Health's announcement that it would provide funding for beta-interferon for approximately 10 000 patients on a 'risk-sharing' basis whereby the cost of the drug would be adjusted downwards by the drug manufacturers if, after an agreed time span had elapsed, the net cost of the treatment exceeded the expected clinical benefit.[43]

These episodes provide a clear indication of the scope and level of opposition that may be generated by rationing decisions, which makes it vital for NICE to establish its legitimacy. But they also reveal certain key shortcomings in the Institute's pursuit of that objective by means of the rationalist and reflexive strategies outlined above. First, it is apparent from both cases that basing decisions upon evidence may not necessarily be sufficient to defuse conflict. This is, perhaps, less surprising where the evidence in question relates to cost-effectiveness, as in the case of beta-interferon, since health economics is a 'much criticised'[44] and a 'new and imprecise' science.[45]

In particular, the 'quality adjusted life year' (QALY), which forms the primary measure of cost-effectiveness, has been viewed as 'a crude statistical relationship' which prioritises physical functionality over the material and emotional costs associated with living with a chronic illness.[46] However, the response to the zanamivir appraisal demonstrates that evidence on clinical effectiveness may also be subject to contention, particularly in a situation in which an initial decision is reversed without any apparently significant change in the evidence base.

The evaluation of zanamivir also casts light on an issue that has seriously imperilled NICE's efforts to achieve legitimacy: a perceived lack of independence. The Institute's reversal of its initial recommendation of this drug was seen as suggestive of capture by the pharmaceutical industry, especially within the medical profession. Thus, the Select Committee reports evidence of a belief that NICE had been 'got at',[47] while the British Medical Association commented that the decision demonstrated that the Institute was 'influenced by the need for political solutions' and that such perceptions 'inevitably call[ed] into question the credibility of the guidance issued by NICE and ultimately of the organisation itself'.[48] In the beta-interferon case, the position was somewhat different: through its refusal to recommend the drug notwithstanding opposition, notably from the Multiple Sclerosis Society, the Institute could be seen as asserting its independence from external pressure. Nevertheless, it might be argued that the length of time taken to evaluate the treatment reflected the influence of 'political' factors; in this case, a simple desire to avoid the attribution of blame. More damagingly, the Government's ultimate 'risk-sharing' policy significantly undermined the overall credibility of NICE, substituting its rationalist methodology for a 'scientifically unsound' solution in order to appease various powerful organised interest groupings, which favoured use of the drug.[49] One might conclude from this example that, in the final analysis, political preferences are likely to trump scientific and social-scientific evidence. It might therefore seem that it would be more realistic and 'honest' of NICE to take account of such political factors when formulating its recommendations. Yet, if it does so, it stands to be accused of privileging certain interests over others, as occurred in the zanamivir case.

A third problem is also evident from the zanamivir and beta-interferon appraisals. Notwithstanding the procedural mechanisms outlined in the previous section, NICE may be criticised for a lack of transparency in certain aspects of its decision-making process. The central concerns in this regard are two-fold. First, analysis of the Institute's decisions and documentation has indicated that it is, in practice, applying an informal 'threshold' of £30 000 per QALY above which it is very unlikely to recommend the funding of a treatment. The fact that beta-interferon exceeded this limit was therefore decisive.[50,51] For its part, NICE has denied that a threshold of this type exists, although its chairman has acknowledged the application of a 'curve' such that higher-cost technologies require more convincing evidence in support.[52] Secondly, and more broadly, both WHO and the Select Committee have identified a lack of understanding of the criteria employed by the Institute in its appraisal process as a factor which may threaten its credibility. Both bodies have therefore called upon NICE to publish and explain the criteria it uses in decision-making and to identify the relative weighting it gives to clinical and economic evidence and other factors such as equity and social values, as well as justifying any thresholds that are applied.[53,54] As the Select Committee observes, transparency on such issues might well have been of assistance in reassuring the medical profession in the zanamivir case.[55]

The picture which emerges from the above analysis of the responses to the appraisals of zanamivir and beta-interferon is of the deeply political nature of the function that NICE has been asked to undertake. It is clear that defining priority-setting questions in terms of 'objective' evidence does not, in fact, depoliticise them, simply because 'evidence becomes an instrument of politics rather than a substitute for it'.[56] The resulting mode of decision-making is not a rationalist form based upon dispassionate, scientific evaluation of objective and technical evidence: rather it more closely resembles classic interest group pluralism, in which decisions amount to compromises reached as a result of bargaining between various stakeholders. Thus, the powerful organised interests which operate within this field of public policy, whether of manufacturers, patients or politicians, will contest both the evidence itself and the methodological assumptions upon which the Institute's recommendations are based, in an attempt to sway the final decision in their favour. In turn, those who disagree with or who lose out as a result of the guidance will perceive NICE to have been unduly influenced by external pressures, especially if the Institute fails to be fully transparent as to the factors which impacted upon its judgement. In such circumstances, they are unlikely to accept that the Institute has the requisite moral authority to deny access to treatment. The 'legitimacy problem' therefore remains unresolved.

REFORM: MAKING NICE NICER?

At the very least, therefore, there is likely to be a continued problem in securing legitimacy in instances in which high-profile treatments are being evaluated, especially where the cost-effectiveness of these is in question. How might NICE's structure and procedural mechanisms be further enhanced, so as to minimise the dissension and distrust to which such decisions may give rise?

One proposal, advanced most persuasively in the 'Kennedy' Report of the Inquiry into events at Bristol Royal Infirmary, is to strengthen the Institute's independence by separating it from the Department of Health, so that it is 'at one remove from party political debate . . . seen to have a life and status of [its] own, free from changes in political fashion'.[57] On this basis, the role of the Government would be restricted to establishing the initial regulatory structure and monitoring its continuing operation. However, both the Government and Institute have rejected this recommendation, arguing that the authority of NICE's guidance would be weakened if it were no longer an

NHS body.[58] It might also be queried how far such a development would protect the Institute against accusations of capture by *manufacturer* and *patient* interests. As discussed previously, the key difficulty arises from the inherently political nature of the choices that NICE makes, which makes them highly susceptible to contestation by organised interests. It is unlikely that independence from government will reduce such external pressures: moreover, it raises additional problems of accountability which, as Prosser observes, is also a critical component of any strategy of legitimation.[2]

Other recommendations focus upon improvements to the Institute's procedures, with a view to achieving greater transparency and inclusiveness. In this regard, important suggestions made by WHO and the Select Committee include preventing drug manufacturers from submitting data to NICE subject to confidentiality, declaring interests of members of the Appraisal Committee at the beginning of an evaluation, clarifying the respective roles of the Institute and government on cost-effectiveness and affordability, enabling greater involvement of 'frontline' NHS staff in the appraisal process, affording wider opportunities for patient input on quality of life questions, and enhancement of the appeals mechanism.[59,60] When taken together with the key proposal outlined in the previous section (that the Institute should be clearer in its articulation of the grounds upon which a decision is based and the weighting given to various factors), these recommendations, if implemented, would assist in the realisation of legitimacy. Those affected by NICE decisions should at least be able to understand the criteria upon which they are based and appreciate that all relevant considerations and stakeholder views had been taken into account during the appraisal process.

From consideration of these recommendations, it is possible to detect the germs of an even more radical procedural strategy which the Institute might adopt. Commentators on health policy have identified rationing as an area of public policy that is particularly suited to a *deliberative* approach to decision-making, in which debate and discussion on difficult moral and political choices generates reasoning and argumentation which can be accepted by citizens as mutually justifiable, even if reasonable disagreement persists and no consensus can be obtained.[61-63] From this perspective, legitimacy arises from the process of intersubjective reasoning and justification among individuals who seek fair terms of cooperation and are prepared to reflect upon their preferences, rather than simply pursuing fixed and self-interested goals. Thus, the focus of reforms to structure and procedure should be upon measures which can inform physicians and the public about the need for rationing, providing the basis for a debate in which interested parties and the public as a whole can deliberate about how best to use health resources fairly to meet the needs of the population. The most prominent example of such a process being put into practice to date has occurred in Oregon, where the state Health Services Commission drew up a list of priorities for public funding based, in part, upon input derived from community meetings.[64]

While publication of clear criteria for decision-making and explanation of the weighting attached to the various factors impacting upon recommendations can contribute to a 'culture of openness about rationales [which] would facilitate learning . . . about the need for limits [on access to healthcare]',[65] it can be argued that further steps are required if a broader process of public deliberation on healthcare rationing is to be initiated. In particular, 'choices need to be informed by an understanding of community preferences if they are to gain acceptance among those affected'.[66] Consequently, it is necessary to devise mechanisms through which members of the public can engage in discussion upon the principles that should underpin priority-setting decisions.

NICE, in fact, already possesses a body with the potential to perform a role of this type. The Citizens Council was established in 2002 'to ensure that the judgments that underpin [NICE's] evaluation of clinical and cost-effectiveness reflect, more clearly, the values held by people living in England and Wales'.[67] Its thirty members, who are selected to be representative of the overall population, consider questions of a general ethical nature which are referred to it by the Institute. Examples have included the factors which the Institute should take into account when assessing clinical need (e.g. effect on life expectancy, quality of life, impact of family responsibilities etc.) and the relevance of patient age as a consideration in NICE recommendations.[68]

In view of the centrality of ethical issues to questions of rationing, the establishment of the Citizens Council is clearly a welcome development. Proper consideration by NICE of the values articulated by the members of the Council should mitigate the danger that its decision-making becomes de-legitimised as a result of a downplaying of the social, ethical and political dimensions of rationing in favour of objective, scientific and social-scientific criteria. Nevertheless, the extent to which the Council, at least as presently constituted, can function as a mechanism for bringing about broad public deliberation on the rationing of healthcare may be queried. It meets only twice a year (for some six days in total), has no power to initiate its own investigations, does not contribute to evaluations of particular treatments and, perhaps most tellingly, is merely an advisory body: the Institute is not bound to act upon its recommendations.[69]

Any or all of these deficiencies could be addressed: for example, it would be possible for the Council to have a direct consultative input upon all technology appraisals conducted by the Institute. However, it remains doubtful whether a more developed deliberative approach to rationing questions is, at present, feasible. Deliberative forms of decision-making have been viewed as impracticable simply because of the demands they make upon individuals' time,[70] and the problem is exacerbated in this context because the public are notoriously 'reluctant rationers' who are disinclined to become involved in decisions that might result in others being denied treatment.[71] Moreover, the Government and Institute persist in refusing to acknowledge that rationing of healthcare is in fact taking place, sheltering instead behind the more neutral discourse of 'priority-setting' in an attempt to avoid the attribution of blame for politically unpopular choices.[72] Such opacity about the true nature of the decisions being taken renders it difficult to embark upon any process of broad public deliberation upon rationing choices and the principles that should underpin these. And, finally, while policy-makers remain committed to some degree of rationalist methodology as a basis for allocative decision-making, public discussion and involvement is likely to be minimal, merely because the technical knowledge required to form a judgement on evidence of clinical and cost-effectiveness is well beyond the capabilities of most citizens.[73] The technocratic approach apparent in the establishment of a body such as NICE is, in this sense, fundamentally at odds with democratic participation.

CONCLUSION

In creating NICE, the Blair Government has attempted to introduce consistency and rationality into an area of public policy which, at least during the early 1990s, had apparently become characterised by inequity and arbitrariness. Simultaneously, it has sought to reduce political controversy by objectifying the process of decision-making and relying upon expert judgement.

In many respects, it is difficult to take issue with these goals and, to that extent, one might concur with the somewhat guarded welcome given to NICE by the Select Committee, as an advance upon the previous position. Nonetheless, it does not follow from this that there is no scope for further improvement and, to this end, this chapter has sought to critically evaluate the regulatory regime and to identify areas in which the Institute's structure and procedures might be enhanced.

From the perspective of a public lawyer, the most interesting issue is whether NICE can be said to represent a solution to the problem of legitimacy to which explicit rationing gives rise. The analysis presented here suggests that it is not yet possible to give an unqualified positive answer to this question. While the pursuit of proceduralist strategies has, to some degree, made up for the shortcomings inherent in a purely rationalist approach, there exists strong evidence (particularly in high-profile, controversial evaluations) that NICE is perceived as unduly influenced by external influences, and that this significantly compromises its legitimacy. Implementation of proposals for greater transparency and inclusiveness may improve the situation, but it remains highly probable that the Institute's decision-making will continue to exhibit the bargaining and compromise characteristic of interest group pluralism, which will tend to cause those who lose out to become disaffected, thus weakening legitimacy still further. The likelihood of this scenario is increased as a result of the difficulty of giving effect to the alternative, more radical, procedural model based around deliberation.

It has been argued that many choices in social policy, including those involving the rationing of healthcare resources, are 'unwinnable' in nature.[74] Recent experience in the UK would seem to bear out the validity of this assessment. The innovative attempt to address the 'legitimacy problem' through regulatory means has, seemingly, not provided a final resolution. It is therefore likely to remain necessary to undertake further critical analysis of the strategies, processes and institutions developed by the state to legitimate the ethically and politically controversial decisions that are required in this field. With the prospect of continued technological innovation in healthcare techniques and treatments and no end in sight to the crisis of funding afflicting the NHS, this evaluative task appears certain to occupy the attention of public lawyers, and especially those who are concerned with the regulation of healthcare, for some time to come.

References

1. Gibson J, Martin D, Singer P. Priority-setting for new technologies in medicine: a transdisciplinary study. BMC Health Services Research 2002; 2:14. Online. Available http://www.biomedcentral.com/1472-6963/2/14 30 April 2004.
2. Prosser T. Towards a critical public law. Journal of Law and Society 1982; 9:1–19.
3. Maynard A. Rationing health care: an exploration. Health Policy 1999; 49:5–11, at 5.
4. Mechanic D. The functions and limitations of trust in the provision of medical care. Journal of Health Politics, Policy and Law 1998; 23:661–686.
5. Locock L. The changing nature of rationing in the UK National Health Service. Public Administration 2000; 78:91–109, at 93.
6. Harrison S. The politics of evidence-based medicine in the United Kingdom. Policy and Politics 1998; 26:15–31, at 18.
7. Klein R, Day P, Redmayne S. Managing scarcity. Buckingham: Open University Press; 1996: Ch 6.
8. Daniels N. Accountability for reasonableness in private and public health insurance. In: Coulter A, Ham C, eds. The global challenge of health care rationing. Buckingham: Open University Press; 2000:89–106, at 89.
9. Weber M. The theory of social and economic organisation. New York: Free Press; 1964:130–132.
10. Department of Health. A first class service: Quality in the new NHS. London: HMSO; 1998: para 1.4.
11. Rawlins M. In pursuit of quality: the National Institute for Clinical Excellence. Lancet 1999; 353:1079–1082, at 1081.
12. NICE. A guide to NICE. London: NICE; 2003:5.
13. National Institute for Clinical Excellence (Establishment and Constitution) Amendment Order SI 1999 No. 2219, amending SI 1999 No. 220.
14. Directions to Primary Care Trusts and NHS Trusts in England concerning arrangements for the funding of technology appraisal guidance from the National Institute for Clinical Excellence, 1 July 2003.
15. Health Select Committee. Second Report. National Institute for Clinical Excellence. London: HMSO; HC 515-I (2001–02), para 106.
16. Smith R. The failings of NICE. British Medical Journal 2000; 321:1363–1364, at 1363.
17. Weber M. The theory of social and economic organisation. New York: Free Press; 1964:184–185.
18. Harrison S. New Labour, modernisation and the medical labour process. Journal of Social Policy 2002; 31:465–485, at 474–476.
19. Jonsson E. Development of health technology assessment in Europe: a personal perspective. International Journal of Technology Assessment in Health Care 2002; 18:171–183.
20. Tenbensel T. Health prioritisation as rationalist policy making: problems, prognoses and prospects. Policy and Politics 2000; 28:425–440, at 428.

21. Hunter D. Desperately seeking solutions. London: Longman; 1997:78.

22. Belkin G. The technocratic wish: making sense and finding power in the managed medical market place. Journal of Health Politics, Policy and Law 1997; 22:509–532, at 518.

23. Klein R, Day P, Redmayne S. Managing scarcity. Buckingham: Open University Press; 1996:100.

24. Klein R. Puzzling out priorities. British Medical Journal 1998; 317:959–960, at 959.

25. Williams J, Yeo M. The ethics of decentralizing health care priority setting in Canada. In: Coulter A, Ham C, eds. The global challenge of health care rationing. Buckingham: Open University Press; 2000:123–132.

26. Smith R. The failings of NICE. British Medical Journal 2000; 321:1363–1364, at 1364.

27. Richardson G. The legal regulation of process. In: Richardson G, Genn H, eds. Administrative law and government action. Oxford: Oxford University Press; 1994:105–130, at 128.

28. Klein R, Williams A. Setting priorities: what is holding us back – inadequate information or inadequate institutions? In: Coulter A, Ham C, eds. The global challenge of health care rationing. Buckingham: Open University Press; 2000:15–26, at 21.

29. Directions to the National Institute for Clinical Excellence, dir. 2.

30. Black J. Proceduralizing regulation: Part I. Oxford Journal of Legal Studies 2000; 20:597–614, at 601.

31. Hill S, Garattini S, van Loenhout J, et al. Technology appraisal programme of the National Institute for Clinical Excellence: a Review by WHO. Copenhagen: WHO; 2003:3.

32. Wright O. NICE man with a reason to smile. The Times 2 December 2003.

33. Health Select Committee, Second Report. National Institute for Clinical Excellence. London: HMSO; HC 515-I (2001–02), paras 6, 136.

34. Daniels N. Accountability for reasonableness in private and public health insurance. In: Coulter A, Ham C, eds. The global challenge of health care rationing. Buckingham: Open University Press; 2000:89–106.

35. Coulter A, Ham C. Explicit and implicit rationing: taking responsibility and avoiding blame for health care choices. Journal of Health Services Research and Policy 2001; 6:163–169.

36. Robert G. In: Ham C, Robert G, eds. Rational rationing. Buckingham: Open University Press; 2003: Ch 5.

37. NICE, Press Release 2002/052 16 October 2002.

38. Health Select Committee. Second Report. National Institute for Clinical Excellence. London: HMSO; HC 515-I (2001–02), para 7.

39. [Anonymous]. Drug companies join flu protest. BBC News 6 October 1999. Online. Available: http://news.bbc.co.uk/1/hi/business/the_company_file/466563.stm 30 April 2004.

40. Boseley S. GPs rebel against flu drug advice. The Guardian 11 December 2000.

41. [Anonymous]. Why not zanamivir? Drug and Therapeutics Bulletin 2000; 39:9–10.

42. Crinson I. The politics of regulation within the 'modernized' NHS: the case of beta-interferon and the 'cost-effective' treatment of multiple sclerosis. Critical Social Policy 2004; 24:30–49, at 34.

43. Department of Health, Press Release 2002/0056 4 February 2002.

44. Jones M, Irvine B. NICE or Nasty: Has NICE eliminated the 'postcode lottery' in the NHS? Civitas Health Briefing 2003, 25. Online. Available: http://www.civitas.org.uk/pdf/NICE.pdf 30 April 2004.

45. Health Select Committee. Second Report. National Institute for Clinical Excellence. London: HMSO; HC 515-I (2001–02), para 102.
46. Crinson I. The politics of regulation within the 'modernized' NHS: the case of beta-interferon and the 'cost-effective' treatment of multiple sclerosis. Critical Social Policy 2004; 24:30–49, at 38–39.
47. Health Select Committee. Second Report. National Institute for Clinical Excellence. London: HMSO; HC 515-I (2001–02), para 19.
48. British Medical Association. Memorandum of Evidence to Health Select Committee, Second Report. National Institute for Clinical Excellence (Vol. II). London: HMSO; Appendix 3, para 4.
49. Sudlow C, Counsell C. Problems with UK Government's risk-sharing scheme for assessing drugs for multiple sclerosis. British Medical Journal 2003; 326:388–392.
50. Hill S, Garattini S, van Loenhout J, et al. Technology appraisal programme of the National Institute for Clinical Excellence: a Review by WHO. Copenhagen: WHO; 2003:31.
51. Towse A, Pritchard C. NICE: Is economic appraisal working? Pharmacoeconomics 2002; 20:95–106, at 99–100.
52. Rawlins M. NICE: still advancing the excellence curve. British Journal of Health Care Management 2002; 8:92–95, at 93.
53. Hill S, Garattini S, van Loenhout J, et al. Technology appraisal programme of the National Institute for Clinical Excellence: a Review by WHO. Copenhagen: WHO; 2003:31–32.
54. Health Select Committee. Second Report. National Institute for Clinical Excellence. London: HMSO; HC 515-I (2001–02), paras 103–104.
55. Health Select Committee. Second Report. National Institute for Clinical Excellence. London: HMSO; HC 515-I (2001–02), para 39.
56. Rodwin M. The politics of evidence-based medicine. Journal of Health Politics, Policy and Law 2001; 26:439–446, at 442.
57. Bristol Royal Infirmary Inquiry. The report of the public inquiry into children's heart surgery at the Bristol Royal Infirmary 1984–1995: Learning from Bristol. London: HMSO; 2001, para 24.38.
58. NICE. Response to the report of the Bristol Royal Infirmary Inquiry. London: NICE; 2001:3.
59. Hill S, Garattini S, van Loenhout J, et al. Technology appraisal programme of the National Institute for Clinical Excellence: a Review by WHO. Copenhagen: WHO; 2003:5–9.
60. Health Select Committee. Second Report. National Institute for Clinical Excellence. London: HMSO; HC 515-I (2001–02), paras 31, 36, 40, 43, 45, 94, 107.
61. Daniels N, Sabin J. Limits to health care: fair procedures, democratic deliberation, and the legitimacy problem for insurers. Philosophy and Public Affairs 1997; 26: 303–350.
62. Daniels N. Enabling democratic deliberation. In: Macedo S, ed. Deliberative politics. New York: Oxford University Press; 1999:198–210.
63. Gutmann A, Thompson D. Deliberative democracy: beyond process. Journal of Political Philosophy 2002; 10:153–174.
64. Blumstein J. The Oregon experiment: the role of cost–benefit analysis in the allocation of Medicaid funds. Social Sciences and Medicine 1997; 45:545–554.
65. Daniels N, Sabin J. The ethics of accountability in managed care reform. Health Affairs 1998; 17:50–64, at 58.

66. Coulter A, Ham C. Explicit and implicit rationing: taking responsibility and avoiding blame for health care choices. Journal of Health Services Research and Policy 2001; 6:163–169, at 164.

67. NICE. Memorandum of Evidence to Health Select Committee, Second Report. National Institute for Clinical Excellence (Vol. II). London: HMSO; Ev. 120, para 1.9.

68. NICE Citizens Council. Determining 'clinical need'. 20 Dec 2002; Report on Age. 21 Jan 2004. Online. Available: http://www.nice.org.uk 30 April 2004.

69. NICE. Common questions and answers on the Citizens Council. Online. Available: http://www.nice.org.uk/article.asp?a=35546 30 April 2004.

70. Hardin R. Deliberation: method, not theory. In: Macedo S, ed. Deliberative politics. New York: Oxford University Press; 1999:103–119, at 112.

71. Lomas J. Reluctant rationers: public input into health care priorities. Journal of Health Services Research and Policy 1997; 2:103–111.

72. Rawlins M. In pursuit of quality: the National Institute for Clinical Excellence. Lancet 1999; 353:1079–1082, at 1082.

73. Hunter D. Desperately seeking solutions. London: Longman; 1997:147.

74. Heclo, H. Social politics and policy impacts. In: Holden, M, Dresang D, eds. What government does. Beverley Hills: Sage; 1975:151–176, at 152.

Chapter 3

The ownership of clinical risk in acute hospitals in England – an historical perspective

Claire Strickland

CHAPTER CONTENTS

Introduction   55
The rise of hospital care
   and clinical autonomy
   in England up to
   1948   56
Attention paid to risks in the
   NHS from 1948 to the early
   1990s   58

History of risk in other
   sectors   62
Progress towards risk awareness
   in the 1990s   63
What has happened from
   2000 onwards   71
Some reflections   72
References   75

INTRODUCTION

Whenever a healthcare professional, especially a doctor, compromises the bodily/mental integrity of a patient, there is a risk that clinically the outcome may be less than optimal, that the patient may be harmed as a result of the clinical intervention. Whilst this truism remains constant, barring huge leaps in scientific and technological advancement, what changes is the spectrum of stakeholders claiming 'ownership' of the truism. When the NHS was created in 1948 the risk of harm from clinical intervention was owned by the doctor and the patient, with attendant rights and responsibilities, and should harm materialise, then the doctor would 'manage' it whether or not the patient was aware of it. However, as the clinical autonomy of the doctor has been eroded over the intervening years by politically driven managerial and quality imperatives, by scandals and by the adoption of less deferential attitudes to doctors by both patients and the judiciary, sub-optimal clinical outcomes are now highly visible to a wide audience and are owned not just by the doctor and patient but by the employing NHS trust, external inspection and review agencies, the media, the patient's legal advisers, and the judiciary, to name but a few. Thus, where once it might have been possible to talk of clinical risk in isolation and in private, it is contended that this is no longer the case; clinical risk now has to be assimilated into the wider, generic portfolio of risks that chief executives of NHS trusts are responsible for. To fully appreciate this position, it is necessary to examine the ownership of clinical risk in hospitals from an historical perspective, a perspective that will reveal how the attention afforded to clinical risk over the years has been inextricably linked to attention afforded to non-clinical risk.

THE RISE OF HOSPITAL CARE AND CLINICAL AUTONOMY IN ENGLAND UP TO 1948

The Egyptians developed an interest in looking after the sick from the time of the healer Imhotep and their use of hospitals (official houses where the poor received free treatment) spread to Western civilisations through the Greeks and ultimately the Romans. However, after the fall of the Roman Empire, hospitals only continued to exist in monasteries and churches. In England in the thirteenth century, hospitals known as lazar-houses existed to segregate lepers from the rest of the population. During this time of hospitals, little if any attention was paid to the medical needs of the sick. In the fourteenth and fifteenth centuries, when leprosy subsided, these hospitals fell into decline such that there was a general lack of hospitals in England in the sixteenth and seventeenth centuries. There existed the five Royal Hospitals but of these only St Bartholemew's and St Thomas's were for the sick as the other three were specialist establishments dealing with vagabonds, orphans and the insane.[1] Outside of London the picture was particularly dire and Dainton notes:

> 'The few small hospitals which existed in the provinces probably did as much harm as good. The nurses for the most part were ignorant and often dirty, and if a patient recovered it was not usually due to the care he received but because his constitution was sufficiently strong to withstand the rough treatment. Consequently a sick person preferred to be nursed at home, and people only went to hospital when poverty or lack of friends absolutely forced them to do so. A patient often had to share a bed with at least one other person; the wards were never properly cleaned; and infectious patients were not isolated.'[2]

At this time then there was great risk of physical harm from admission to hospital that was an amalgam of what we now call clinical and non-clinical risk. Fortunately, due to philanthropic adventure and the establishment of voluntary hospitals, the eighteenth century can be hailed as 'The Age of Hospitals'. The social elite sponsored hospitals and in return became governors or trustees of them, wielding considerable influence over who was admitted to hospital and which physician or surgeon was appointed. The medical profession gave their services freely to such hospitals, using their enhanced status to develop lucrative private practices. However, even at this time the treatment was still very poor as doctors relied mainly on the use of leeches, operations were performed without anaesthesia or antiseptic, cross-infection was rife and the main source of lighting was generally candlelight. Thus, in 1800 there were only about 3000 people in hospitals throughout

England and it was not until the late nineteenth century that hospitals offered an outcome more positive than negative.[3] It is probably fair to say that the risk of harm from admission to hospital was passively owned in more or less equal measure by both the sick person and doctor in the sense that neither could do much about the illness.

From around the mid nineteenth century, momentum for nursing reform in hospitals gathered pace due to the reforming zeal of Mrs Elizabeth Fry and Miss Florence Nightingale. In 1859 the latter published *Notes on Hospitals* and stated:

> 'It may seem a strange principle to enunciate as the very first require-ment in a Hospital that it should do the sick no harm. It is quite neces-sary nevertheless to lay down such a principle, because the actual mortality in hospitals, especially for those of large crowded cities, is very much higher than any calculation founded on the mortality of the same class of patient treated out of hospital would lead us to expect.'[4]

Although antiseptic surgery became available from 1865, anaesthetics from 1846 and X-rays from 1896, such clinical methods to reduce the risk of harm to patients were often received with hostility because of the inconvenience it caused to both doctors and nurses.[5] Improvements in the non-clinical aspects of care also came at the end of the nineteenth century when electric lighting was introduced and attention was paid to furniture and equipment. Thus, by the start of the twentieth century hospitals were marginally less risky places than they had been hitherto, and started to attract people who had previously paid for home consultations, but they were a hotchpotch mixture of volun-tary hospitals, home hospitals, workhouse infirmaries and some remaining religious hospitals. However, given the fact that the doctor was now able to have an impact on the clinical outcome, it is possible to see how ownership of risk was moving from the shared passive ownership of doctor and sick per-son to active ownership by the doctor and passive ownership by the *patient*. Jewson states:

> 'the new occupational standing of the clinician was matched by the emergence of a new role for the sick man, that of patient. As such he was designated a passive and uncritical role in the consultative relationship, his main function being to endure and wait.'[6]

Of enormous significance in the history of the ownership of clinical risk was the 1858 Medical Act that established the General Medical Council and gave the medical profession the right to self-regulation. The medical profes-sion emerged as the monopoly provider of medical care and the notion of clinical autonomy was born. Salter states, '[clinical autonomy] is the doctor's right to use his unique access to medical knowledge to make his clinical judgements purely in the patient's interests uninfluenced by anything other than the opinion of his peers.'[7] It is the concept of clinical autonomy that allowed clinical risk to be shielded from view and thus scrutiny by any stake-holders other than the doctors themselves. Although ownership of clinical risk did widen in 1885 to include the Medical Defence Union, which was established to defend the reputation of doctors following the wrongful conviction and imprisonment of Dr David Bradley for assaulting a woman in his surgery, this was only a passive ownership.

Impetus for hospital reform gained ground after the Second World War when many London hospitals were bombed. The key stakeholders in the reform debate were the voluntary hospitals, the local authorities, the medical profession and the politicians, each coming to the debate with their own agenda. The medical profession was vehemently opposed to the introduction of a *national* health service because of the impact it would have on their opportunities for lucrative private practice. Indeed in the *British Medical Journal* Supplement 1943 it was stated that 'If this happens, then doctors will no longer constitute an independent learned and liberal profession, but will instead form a service of technicians controlled by bureaucrats and by local men and women entirely ignorant of medical matters.'[8] Under the new Minister of Health, Aneurin Bevan, a White Paper was published in 1946 that led to the creation of the National Health Service on 5 July 1948. Given the power the medical profession had in the existing hospitals the National Health Service came at a price and Bevan is quoted as having said that he had '. . . stuffed their mouths with gold.'[9] Sir Donald Irvine CBE has stated: 'There was virtually no accountability or strings attached, and the public perception of specialists as omnipotent soon became virtually institutionalised in a steeply pyramidal career structure. This made it more difficult for consultants to admit to fallibility and error, all the more important because they were the teachers and thus modelled the culture. Inevitably, the model has become self-perpetuating.'[10] The clinical autonomy granted to doctors in 1858 now paved the way for their political and economic autonomy in the new concordat with the state. Politically they had the right to ration NHS resources in accordance with their clinical judgement and economically they were secure as either salaried hospital doctors or funded general practitioners.[11] Over subsequent years it can be seen how the ability of a wider range of stakeholders to own clinical risk in hospitals is dependent on the rise of the concept of risk per se and inroads into the clinical, political and economic autonomy of hospital doctors.

ATTENTION PAID TO RISKS IN THE NHS FROM 1948 TO THE EARLY 1990s

From its inception in 1948 up to 1983, the prevailing culture of the NHS remained unchallenged – it was a service administered by government but run by the doctors. This was thus a time of 'bureau-professionalism' – a combination of bureaucratic administration and professional discretion.[12] Ham and Alberti refer to an implicit compact between the government (guaranteeing free healthcare for citizens at the point of need financed through taxation), the medical profession (delivering the healthcare and taking responsibility for the maintenance of clinical standards) and the public (accepting the package of free healthcare based on taxation).[13] This culture of medical dom-inance survived the administrative reorganisations of 1974 (which intro-duced, inter alia, consensus management) and that of 1982 (which removed the administrative tier of Area Health Authorities) and the 1979 White Paper *Patients First*. One might have thought that the Health and Safety at Work Act 1974 would impact on the attention given to risks in the NHS because this was the first piece of health and safety legislation that applied to all work places, including hospitals. However, due to Crown Immunity from criminal prosecution very little attention was paid to health and safety risks in hospi-tals. Up to the mid-1980s, then, it seems extremely unlikely that the language of risk, clinical or non-clinical, was spoken in hospitals. Any notion of clinical risk was clearly owned by the doctor, the Medical Defence Union that since 1924 indemnified doctors for all payments made in respect of medical negli-gence in addition to legal fees, and by the patient, though only to the degree afforded by the doctor. The gulf between the doctor and patient in terms of ownership of risk was ever widening due to advances in science and tech-nology; the patient simply had to trust the doctor, the professional, the expert. Clinical risk in the NHS was thus largely invisible to external scrutiny, a posi-tion reinforced by the prevailing deference to the medical profession in the courts entrenched by the case of *Bolam v Friern Hospital Management Committee* [1957] 1 WLR 582.

However, the cultural dominance of the doctors came under a more focused attack after the 1983 Griffiths inquiry into NHS management.[14] The proposals of the inquiry, implemented in 1984, saw the demise of consensus management and the introduction of general management with clear lines of accountability – 'new managerialism'.[12] Consensus management, as a decision-making mechanism, had been very slow because it had given doc-tors and nurses in management teams the power to veto change. New man-agerialism involved the appointment of general managers from outside the NHS for the first time and doctors and nurses in management teams lost their power of veto. Against this backdrop it was perhaps no surprise that man-agement concepts from the private sector were gradually infiltrated into the NHS, most notably that of total quality management (TQM). Here at last in the mid-1980s we might have expected that attention would be paid to risk in hospitals as surely the language of risk was part of the language of quality? With regard to clinical risk this certainly was not the case because in the NHS TQM did not actually honour the word total; the quality of clinical care was not to be included. This was clearly stated by the NHS Management Executive in 1993 in their publication *The Quality Journey: A Guide to Total Quality Management in the NHS*.[15] Thus, clinical autonomy and professional ownership of clinical risk persisted. In addition, although an attempt had been made to reduce the political autonomy of hospital doctors, by making them corporately more accountable for the allocation of finite resources through their clinical decisions, it is unlikely that their political autonomy was seriously eroded in the 1980s, not least because their clinical autonomy was still intact.[16] However, in the late 1980s notions of both non-clinical and clinical risk began to emerge from behind their cloaks of invisibility, the former due to the serious outbreak of food poisoning at the Stanley Royd hospital in the Wakefield district and the latter due to the introduction of medical audit.

In August 1984 a total of 19 elderly patients died and 300 patients and staff were taken ill after a serious outbreak of food poisoning that arose due to the appalling conditions in the kitchens of the 900-bed Stanley Royd psychiatric hospital that was built in 1818. In contrast to previous inquiries into the standard of care provided at Ely Hospital in 1969 and Normansfield Hospital in 1978, the inquiry into what went wrong at Stanley Royd was for the first time a 'public' inquiry.[17] It was chaired by J Hugill QC and reported in 1986.[18] Walsh and Higgins make the point that inquiries into health services have no formal powers or authority and thus have to rely on their credibility and powers of persuasion to make a difference.[19] The Stanley Royd inquiry report had a tremendous impact because it led to the enactment of the National Health Service (Amendment) Act 1986, which effected partial removal of Crown Immunity from health authorities and thus hospitals. In the original Bill the aim had been to remove Crown Immunity for 'all' purposes but this could not be agreed upon in either House. The compromise position agreed was such that Crown Immunity was removed with regard to food legislation under Section 1 and with regard to health and safety legislation under Section 2. In the debate on the Bill in the House of Commons, Mr Frank Dobson (Holborn and St Pancras) noted that Crown Immunity only applied to hospitals after the inception of the NHS on 5 July 1948. He further noted that since the Crown Proceedings Act 1947 only removed Crown Immunity in relation to the ability to sue the Crown for damages, Crown Immunity remained in relation to the ability to bring criminal charges against Crown servants or agents.[20] Although concerned with an essentially non-clinical risk issue, it is interesting that Mr Frank Dobson commented:

> 'When patients go into hospital they assume that they will be made better, that their lives will be saved and that their pain will be eased. Patients are entrusted to the National Health Service on those grounds, but many of our hospitals are breaching that trust . . . There has been a 14 per cent increase in post-operative infection since 1979 . . . Many hospital buildings are of poor design and many are in a poor state of repair. There are poor standards of cleanliness and hospitals are full of dangers to staff and patients . . . There is an assumption, which history suggests is wholly false, that people running hospitals know about health and safety and about how to keep people in hospitals healthy and safe. All the evidence suggests that outside the specialist fields in which they operate few people in hospitals know how to do that.'[21]

It is quite alarming that such a sentiment should be expressed over 100 years on from similar sentiments expressed by Florence Nightingale. One might have expected that henceforth much greater attention would be paid to food safety and health and safety in acute hospitals as a result of this Act and the potential threat of criminal prosecution. However, this was not the case. Health and safety issues in hospitals only began to creep onto the management agenda following the National Health Service and Community Care Act 1990, Section 5(1) of which empowered the Secretary of State to establish corporate bodies known as NHS trusts. As corporate bodies NHS trusts slowly began to realise that health and safety issues had to be considered more seriously, not just from the harm and financial perspectives, but from the public image perspective. However, most chief executives of NHS trusts still did not, and indeed still do not, put sufficient effort into proper ownership of health and safety, non-clinical, risks despite their clear accountability.[22] This was despite the fact that Section 60 of the 1990 Act removed 'all' Crown Immunity for NHS bodies, thus widening the scope for potential criminal prosecutions.[i]

Although medical audit was introduced into hospitals in 1989 following publication of *Working for Patients*[23] it made little impact. It did not really widen ownership of the notion of clinical risk because it was a confidential process led by the doctors; managers merely had to make sure that the process happened. A King's Fund study into medical audit in four hospitals during 1991–1992 highlighted the resistance of doctors to the process and the poor implementation of the process.[24] Progress was made in 1993 when the audit process changed from medical to clinical audit such that it involved not just doctors but the wider clinical team. In addition, although still led by the doctors, the hospital managers were given more involvement. In this way the audit process was made more visible with wider ownership. However, given that it was led by the doctors and given that the prevailing culture in hospitals was, and still is, a mixture of role and person cultures whereby doctors hold key positions in the hospital hierarchy and drive things, it is probably fair to say that real clinical risk issues may not have been addressed.

At the start of the 1990s it was thus the case that in NHS acute trusts little explicit attention was given to the concept of risk, whether clinical or non-clinical. Clinical risk was still, more or less, exclusively owned by the doctors albeit in a team setting and chief executives were paying lip-service to ownership of non-clinical risks, other than financial ones. As the 1990s unfolded the increasing threat of clinical negligence claims widened the ownership of clinical risk, in large part due to the introduction of NHS indemnity in 1990, rather than fear of criminal prosecution due to loss of Crown Immunity. NHS indemnity means that NHS bodies are vicariously liable for the negligent acts and omissions of their employees and have to make arrangements to meet such liabilities.[25] The indemnity aspect of ownership of clinical risk thus transferred from the Medical Defence Union to NHS bodies, most notably NHS acute trusts. In order to discuss whether more attention should have been afforded to risk per se at this time in hospitals, it is necessary to consider the extent to which risk was being addressed in other sectors.

---

[i] Sections 1 and 2 of the NHS (Amendment) Act 1986 were repealed by Section 66(2) of the NHS and Community Care Act 1990.

HISTORY OF RISK IN OTHER SECTORS

When the word risk first appeared in the English language in the seventeenth century, deriving from the French word risque, it was used both as a noun and a verb. In the nineteenth century it was also used as an adjective.

'In contemporary everyday English the word "risk" indicates the possibility of unintended and negative consequences of decisions or actions. This combination of probability and consequence has been implicit in the word since it entered the English language in the seventeenth century, with the main emphasis on negative outcomes – although it is also possible to identify some usage in which positive and negative outcomes are compared or balanced.'[26]

Thus, up to the early 1990s a sick person, subjectively, would have been able to express and own his or her perception of the risk of entering hospital. This is of course true today. However, this early adoption and use of the word risk at individual level was not matched at scientific or government level. In the preface to the 1977 Report of a Working Party set up by the Council for Science and Society, the chairman of the council, Michael Swan, states 'Risks have been largely neglected as a field of social or historical research. Comprehensive, reliable surveys simply do not exist. The reports of official inquiries into particular accidents, excellent in their own way, do not provide the breadth and general relevance that we need.'[27] This report made reference to and relied heavily on the 1976 work of Lowrance in the USA since it is acknowledged as being one of the first attempts at a wide-ranging investigation into risk acceptance.[28] Thus, not until the late 1970s did the scientific community begin to take a serious interest in risk issues. However, the 1977 Report is remarkably advanced in its thinking. It seeks a conceptual framework for the analysis of risk beyond discrete industry-specific analyses, fraught as they are with technical jargon, and offers definitions of key terms such as hazard and risk. In addition, it realises the complexity of the task of risk assessment in that it is a composite of the scientific, objective, quantitative approach and the subjective, qualitative, perception approach. In an age of rapid technological advancement it is realised that the government has to address the issue of the acceptability of risk. Whereas hitherto people were exposed to high occurrence, low impact risk (from illness and disease) now people were exposed to low occurrence, high impact risk (from failure of technological structures). This early work was followed by the 1983 report of the Royal Society Study Group, which championed the objective, quantitative approach to risk assessment over the subjective, qualitative approach because: 'The government decision will be essentially political, although informed scientifically . . . Awareness of public fears can be influential and lead to over-reaction and thus to excessive control.'[29] It was further stated that: 'A remarkably high proportion of accidents and misjudgements could have been avoided if lessons had been learnt from the past experiences of those concerned and of others.'[30]

The literature on risk proliferated in the 1980s and 1990s and a seminal work is the report published in 1992 by the Royal Society (the 1992 report).[31] This report differs from the 1983 report in that much more attention is devoted to subjective risk perception since it was part of the working group's terms of reference to consider and help to bridge the gap between the objective and subjective approaches to risk. Whilst this gap was not narrowed by the working group, nevertheless Chapter 6 of the report on risk management is particularly interesting. It is noted at the outset that risk management has no single meaning. If considered from the technological/scientific stance the definition will be narrow (as it was in the 1983 report). If considered from the commercial stance the definition will centre on finances and if considered in the political sense it probably relates to the handling of issues that could affect the electoral fortunes of the government.[32] Thus, a definition of risk management is adopted that denotes regulatory measures (both in public policy and corporate practice) intended to shape 'who' can take 'what risks' and 'how'. Risk management is explored from the perspective of 'institutional design' and the important point is made that not much attention has been given to considering risk management in the institutional sense because 'the notion of institutional design (as opposed to the design of safe products or structures) has only recently begun seriously to penetrate discussion of risk management' and because 'the risk management debate has become heavily politicised'.[33]

In the light of the above it is surely not surprising that risk as a concept was not explicitly an issue in NHS hospitals by the early 1990s. For one thing the NHS has to be regarded as an institution in the sense that it is composed of people and systems and the point has been made that until the early 1990s the concept of risk management was not applied to institutions. Secondly, the prevailing culture in the hospitals was still by and large one of deference to the medical profession who were still seen as the professionals, the experts, who could be trusted.

PROGRESS TOWARDS RISK AWARENESS IN THE 1990s

The concept of the internal market was introduced into the NHS under the NHS and Community Care Act 1990, which came into force in April 1991. Central to this market notion was the creation of corporate bodies, NHS trusts, and the purchasing of services from these trusts by GP fundholders, although it was not until 1994 that most hospitals had acquired trust status. Whilst the contracts that were used by purchasers specified things like waiting times, patient satisfaction and a requirement to undertake medical audit, hardly any attention was paid to the standards of clinical care.[34] This is not surprising given the focus of the Conservative Government on 'cost-containment' rather than quality.[35] It is no surprise then that clinical autonomy persisted essentially intact and with it unfettered professional ownership of clinical risk despite the new corporate agenda. Although doctors could be exhorted to reflect corporate priorities in the exercise of their clinical judgement, the reality of the situation was that the trusts had no powers to insist on this.[36]

However, from 1993 onwards, the language of risk became more explicit in the NHS when the NHS Executive published a *Risk Management Manual* under cover of Executive Letter (93)111,[37] 'commissioned' by the NHS Executive from Merrett Health Risk Management Limited. In the foreword Sir Duncan Nichol, Chief Executive, states that 'Risk management is an important activity for all parts of the NHS. With all the changes in recent years, including the loss of Crown Immunity, it is no longer an optional extra. I believe risk management has two major contributions to make. It can play a valuable role in ensuring that we provide a high quality, safe service to our patients. It can also help towards the provision of a more cost effective service by eliminating, or reducing, unnecessary costs.' The focus of the manual is unashamedly 'risk management' with 'quality' and 'safety' introduced as by-products along with 'cost effectiveness'. It is targeted at 'managers' rather than clinicians, reflecting 'new-managerialism' and TQM. The incentive for managers to implement the guidance in the manual is the avoidance of the negatives of clinical negligence claims, trial by media and possible sanctions for non-compliance with legislation. Had the manual been more targeted at doctors then arguably it might have been more widely embraced. Unfortunately, lingering medical paternalism can be read between the lines. Thus, when doctors are addressed it is in the context of the 'positive' aspects of risk management. For instance, it states 'Indeed, doctors and other health professionals should not be discouraged from taking some risks in developing more effective methods of treatment and care for patients and clients . . . Risk management is not a negative concept. It should not lead to "defensive medicine" and it is not about interfering with clinical freedom although it can and should be used to pin point deficiencies in clinical *systems* which may need to be improved.'[37] Far from integrating clinical and non-clinical risk, the manual sows the seed of this division in the NHS and for managers the avoidance of negative factors is paramount. The manual thus seems to leave the ownership of clinical risk in the hands of the doctors and the clinical team, not least when it iterates the principle of the Bolam test.[38] That the manual had little impact on incorporation of risk strategies into NHS trusts is not surprising given the timing of the manual. In the first half of the 1990s most hospital units were struggling to cope with the transition to trust status. Amid such turbulence and financial imperatives it is not too surprising that a concept such as risk, only just making itself known in the industrial sector, should be either understood or given much prominence in NHS trusts.

However, in the mid-1990s, risk management was again brought to the specific attention of trusts due to the rising costs of clinical negligence claims and the impact such claims could have on trusts due to the introduction of NHS indemnity in 1990. Under Section 21 of the NHS and Community Care Act 1990 the Secretary of State was empowered to create a scheme for NHS trusts and other health service bodies to meet expenses for any loss or damage arising to their property and liabilities to third parties for loss, damage or injury whilst carrying out their functions. This was necessary because of the loss of Crown Immunity and the introduction of NHS indemnity. The Secretary of State used his powers in 1995 to establish the NHS Litigation Authority (NHSLA) by virtue of the NHS Litigation (Establishment and Constitution) Order (SI 1995 No. 2800), which came into force on 20 November 1995. In 1996 the Secretary of State established the Clinical Negligence Scheme for Trusts (CNST) (SI 1996 No. 251), which came into force on 1 March 1996. At this stage the emphasis was on addressing the costs of clinical negligence claims and clinical risk. Non-clinical risk became the poor relation as the Risk Pooling Scheme for Trusts (RPST), incorporating the Liabilities to Third Parties Scheme and Property Expenses Scheme, was not established until 1 April 1999.[ii] The CNST published its first set of risk management standards and procedures in August 1997.[39] The reactionary, indemnity aspect of ownership of clinical risk, for participating NHS trusts, was thus transferred from them to the NHSLA. From the point of view of proactive clinical risk management in NHS acute trusts it is a shame that claims handling, the reactive indemnity-based response to an incidence of clinical harm to a patient, was, and still is, given prominence. Most chief executives of NHS acute trusts are likely to regard membership of CNST as equivalent to an insurance policy to cover clinical negligence claims, despite the fact that the scheme is a not-for-profit risk-pooling scheme. This attitude is understandable given the fact that the NHSLA itself manages claims and the bulk of their staff in this respect come from an insurance background, including the chief executive Steve Walker. The second arm of the NHSLA, which promotes proactive adherence to the clinical risk management standards, is not managed by the NHSLA itself but by a private company, Willis Ltd. The 1997 clinical risk management standards were sold to NHS trusts on the basis that achievement of level 1 for the 10 core standards would lead to a discount on their contributions to the scheme. Member trusts were originally only expected to attain level 1 in the assessment process and this merely required the putting into place of arrangements that could support a clinical risk management strategy. Since level 1 was easily attainable (*CNST Risk Management Manual*,[39] para 3.8), and core standard 10, which required clinical risk management standards and processes to be in place and operational (10.2.1), was not assessed at level 1 only at level 2, it is no wonder that most chief executives and boards would regard the attainment of level 1 as financially desirable and feasible. This attitude is still the prevailing one not least because the financial incentive to improve is not huge; members get a 10% discount on their contributions for attaining level 1 and 20% for attaining level 2. Statistics from the NHSLA reveal that at 31 March 2002, from a total of 324 NHS trusts 51 were at level 0, 229 at level 1, 42 at level 2 and 2 at level 3. Furthermore, that as at 29 February 2004 from a total of 269 NHS trusts 25 were at level 0, 190 at level 1,

---

[ii] NHS (Liabilities to Third Parties Scheme) Regulations 1999 SI 1999 No. 873 and NHS (Property Expenses Scheme) Regulations 1999 SI 1999 No. 874.

46 at level 2, 4 at level 3 and 4 at a new level 4.[40] For the RPST the statistics reveal that as at 31 March 2003 from a total of 277 NHS trusts 156 were at level 0, 97 at level 1 and 24 were not assessed. As at 29 February 2004 from a total of 269 trusts 112 were at level 0, 149 at level 1, 3 were not assessed and 5 were new trusts.[40] These statistics reveal a lot about the attitude of chief executives and boards to the ownership of both clinical and non-clinical risk. Clearly the priority is clinical risk but ownership seems to be more reactive than proactive given the bunching of trusts at level 1. However, the statistics also reveal that the initial turbulence during trust establishment was followed by further turbulence due to a series of trust mergers. Mergers necessitate the focusing of attention at board level on issues such as leadership, finances, staffing, the management of organisational change and so forth. There may be differences in the history and culture of the trusts and the nature of the estates may bring additional problems. It is thus, again, not too surprising that for chief executives and boards the issue of indemnity for clinical negligence claims could easily be resolved, and maybe forgotten about, simply by attaining level 1 of the CNST standards.

The real lack of interplay between the two arms of the CNST scheme and the dominance of the claims arm has fostered the reactionary ownership of clinical risk by NHS trust chief executives and boards. This approach has no doubt filtered down the organisations to staff at the sharp end who should be taking a more proactive approach to clinical risk management and thus ownership of clinical risk. It is arguable that the NHSLA should only handle claims, the language of litigation being adversarial, fault based and financially driven. The promotion of a culture of positive clinical risk management, proactive clinical risk ownership, might be better served either as a distinct enterprise or linked to similar proactive, more altruistic schemes.

The year 1997 is a landmark year in the history of ownership of clinical risk in acute hospitals because several things happened that made inroads into the clinical autonomy of doctors and hence spread the ownership of clinical risk. First, a new Labour Government came into office, second, corporate governance was introduced into the NHS, third, NHS Estates published the document 'An exemplar operational risk management strategy' and finally, there was the landmark House of Lords case, *Bolitho v City and Hackney Health Authority* [1997] 3 WLR 1151.

The new Labour Government came into office in May promising a new NHS that would be modern and dependable and in which the internal market would be replaced with integrated care.[41] Key aspects of their 'third way' were to put the patient at the centre of the NHS and to have a focus on the 'quality' of care provided. Quality of care is defined quite broadly as:

> '... doing the right things, at the right time, for the right people and doing them right – first time. And it must be the quality of the patient's experience as well as the clinical result – quality measured in terms of prompt access, good relationships and efficient administration.'[42]

Such a definition is too broad to be really meaningful, so it is useful that the three actions necessary to drive quality into all parts of the NHS are outlined.[43] At national level we are informed that new evidence-based National Service Frameworks (NSFs) are to be introduced along with the new National Institute for Clinical Excellence (NICE) to give a strong lead on clinical and cost-effectiveness. At local level we are told that new Primary Care Groups are to be created and that a new system of clinical governance in NHS trusts and primary care will be introduced to ensure that clinical standards are met. Finally, we are informed that a new Commission for Health Improvement (CHI) will be established to support and oversee the quality of clinical services at local level and to tackle shortcomings. Furthermore, that such quality initiatives are to be linked with efficiency and that together these will be the subject of performance measurement. It is interesting, and probably significant, that the words risk and risk management are nowhere to be found in this document. It is contended that these words were deliberately absent from the document because of their traditional negative connotations and their use in the 1993 NHS Executive *Risk Management Manual* and CNST risk management standards. Quite cleverly the government seems to have latched on to the language of quality with all its positive connotations rather than the language of risk which hitherto had not had a warm reception in NHS acute trusts. That the language of quality is being used to mask clinical risk management issues and the standard of performance of individual doctors can be seen, for example, in the following:

> 'Together, these arrangements should ensure that there are stronger systematic measures to monitor, maintain and improve quality. In the rare instances of serious service difficulty, there will now be the capacity for prompt and effective intervention. But the Government will continue to look to individual health professionals to be responsible for the quality of their own clinical practice. Professional self-regulation must remain an essential element in the delivery of quality patient services. It is crucial that the professional standards developed nationally continue to be responsive to changing service needs and to legitimate public expectations.'[44]

A rolling programme of NSFs was introduced in April 1998, NICE was established as a Special Health Authority on 1 April 1999 and CHI became operational from 1 April 2000, though from 1 April 2004 it has been superseded by CHAI (Commission of Healthcare Audit and Inspection, known as the Healthcare Commission). NSFs and NICE guidance impact not only on the clinical autonomy of hospital doctors but also on their political autonomy in the sense that the decision on the rationing of services is no longer completely in the domain of the doctor as it was under the original 1948 concordat. The ownership of clinical risk has thus been spread to these new bodies. Clinical governance is a term coined in 1997 by Liam Donaldson, now Sir Liam and Chief Medical Officer (CMO), to focus attention on the 'quality' of care provided in the NHS. Sir Liam defines clinical governance as 'the way in which NHS organisations quality assure their services and create the conditions for quality improvement year on year.'[45] No definition is given of quality but it is clear that what is being challenged as substandard is the clinical output of doctors, especially those in NHS acute trusts. Clinical governance is thus a direct challenge to the clinical autonomy of hospital doctors and a way of spreading the ownership of, and accountability for, clinical risk. This can be seen when the CMO states:

> 'For most of its first 40 years, the NHS worked on the understanding that high quality healthcare was a *logical* consequence of the provision of well-trained staff, good facilities and equipment. The quality initiatives that followed, such as medical and clinical audit, took a more systematic approach. However, they were often criticised as professionally dominated and somewhat distant from everyday healthcare activities whose benefits were not really apparent to the Health Service or to patients. Many doctors and nurses had criticised the over emphasis of health service management on workload and financial targets at the expense of quality. It was argued that the quality of care delivered by a health organisation is what matters most to its patients and its staff. For quality not to have an equal place alongside activity and resources in boardroom discussions is to fail to recognise the central purpose of healthcare – to provide the best possible outcome of care for every patient who comes through the doors of the hospital or health centre concerned.'(Emphasis added)[45]

The CMO further states that the notion of clinical governance is necessary due to the series of scandals in the NHS that occurred during the late 1980s and early 1990s, most notably that at the Bristol Royal Infirmary. These highlighted sub-optimal clinical performance by individual consultants and fed the public's increasing loss of confidence and trust in the services provided by the NHS, fuelled by massive media attention. These scandals have sown the seed for greater public ownership of clinical risk evidenced by the new third way that puts the patient at the centre of the NHS. It is generally accepted that it is through implementation of clinical governance systems that the statutory duty of quality imposed by Section 18(1) of the Health Act 1999 can be facilitated. A major problem with clinical governance, however, is that there is no working definition of what it is. This is probably due to the fact that it is merely a term that describes a process, the implementation of which is supposed to foster quality of care, whatever that is. The components of this process are evidenced in CHI/CHAI clinical governance reviews of NHS acute trusts. It is probably fair to say that the two key components are clinical audit and clinical risk management. Thus, it is not until we get down to this level of the quality agenda that we find the words risk and risk management. One has to wonder whether the contended subterfuge of the Labour Government in avoiding the language of risk by using the language of quality has made a difference in NHS acute trusts; have chief executives and NHS boards inadvertently embraced ownership of clinical risk?

It seems that despite the statutory duty to do so, under the quality agenda, on the whole they have not done so.[46] This is endorsed in CHI's first annual report on the NHS in 2003.[47] It is thus the case that chief executives and boards are still more concerned with ownership of financial and workload targets than clinical risk. This only serves to perpetuate the dominance of ownership of clinical risk by the doctors who on the whole are probably quite happy to hide it from external scrutiny. Thus, whilst clinical governance is supposed to encourage a culture change, quite clearly this will not happen in many NHS acute trusts whilst those at the top are not willing to change.

Such intransigence by chief executives and boards of NHS acute trusts with regard to ownership of clinical risk has to be seen in the context of the broader picture painted by the corporate governance agenda in the NHS, implemented through controls assurance initiatives from 1997. The first Statements of Internal Control that were required from chief executives were concerned with assurances about financial internal control.[48] In subsequent reporting periods Statements of Internal Control were additionally required for organisational controls including risk management.[49] Controls assurance is described as:

'. . . a holistic concept based on best governance practice. It is a process designed to provide evidence that NHS organisations are doing their "reasonable best" to manage themselves so as to meet their objectives and protect patients, staff, the public and other stakeholders against risks of all kinds. Fundamental to the process is the effective involvement of people and functions within the organisation through application of self-assessment techniques to ensure objectives are met and risks are properly controlled.' (HSC 1999/123,[49] para 5)

The phrases 'reasonable best' and 'self-assessment' allow chief executives leeway in their level of accomplishment in the controls assurance process despite the aspirations of the NHS Executive that by 31 March 2005 they should be able to comply with level 3 of the 'control and risk maturity matrix'.[50] At level 3 chief executives should be able to sign a statement verifying that 'risk management and internal control are part of the vocabulary throughout the organisation' and that there is 'convergence between clinical governance and controls assurance'. This is unlikely given the fact that the NHS Executive noted in 2001 that many organisations are confused at how the controls assurance initiative fits in with other internal control and risk management initiatives (HSC 2001/005,[50] para 12). Although in the controls assurance documents the words risk, risk management and quality are used, their subordinate place to the ethos of financial controls seems clear. First, the process of controls assurance is diagrammatically represented by a pyramid that places financial controls at the base, representing a solid bedrock that supports organisational controls and clinical governance (HSC 1999/123,[49] para 7). Second, the key role of financial assurance is demonstrated when it is stated that:

'The NHS Litigation Authority now administers, in addition to the existing Clinical Negligence Scheme for Trusts, two new non-clinical risk pooling schemes . . . Compliance with risk management and organisational controls standards . . . will help member NHS Trusts to minimise their future financial contributions to the schemes.' (HSC 1999/123,[49] para 7)

It can be seen how chief executives might perceive themselves to be doing their reasonable best for controls assurance by focusing on financial issues in the hope that clinical and other non-financial risk issues will be taken care of by others. Chief executives seem unwilling to seize upon the opportunity for greater corporate ownership of clinical risk. Maybe they are not yet ready to embark upon this particular buy-in as undoubtedly it would bring them into conflict with the doctors whom chief executives maybe do see as the real owners of clinical risk. Indeed, in 'A Commitment to Quality, a Quest for Excellence',[51] a joint statement on behalf of the government, the medical profession and the NHS, it is stated that, 'cases of failure in standards of care in the NHS have hit the headlines . . . it is right that they came to public attention . . . what is not right is that they should be thought of as the tip of an iceberg beneath which poor quality lies. Serious failures in standards of care are in fact very uncommon in relation to the huge number of patients helped by the NHS every year.' Thus, it is probably true that in many NHS acute trusts, middle managers, tasked with implementation of clinical governance systems, find themselves between a rock and a hard place. The explicit corporate stance is to embrace clinical risk ownership, enshrined in the controls assurance documents, yet the implicit corporate stance is to leave ownership of clinical risk with the doctors.

In October 1997 NHS Estates published 'An exemplar operational risk management strategy'.[52] In the foreword to this document it is stated that the risk exemplar provided builds on the 1993 *Risk Management Manual*. The document provides an exemplar operational risk management strategy for a hypothetical NHS acute trust and the approach taken is to adopt three risk categories: direct patient risks (essentially clinical risks), user risks (essentially non-clinical risks) and financial risks. This categorisation matches the three-tiered approach to the management of risks in NHS acute trusts taken in the controls assurance model. The basic tenets of controls assurance were thus presented to NHS acute trusts in 1997 yet this document is not well known in the NHS, not least perhaps because it was issued by NHS Estates. It is questionable whether it was ever seen by chief executives. What is perhaps significant is the headline language on the document, the language of risk. It is arguable that had the advice in the document been acted upon, the imperative for the corporate governance agenda might have been greatly reduced. Indeed, the emphasis in the 1997 document is very similar to that of controls assurance.

Finally in 1997, there was the landmark case of *Bolitho v City and Hackney Health Authority* [1997] 4 All ER 771 in the House of Lords. The impact of this case with regard to the ownership of clinical risk is the challenge it is perceived to have on the Bolam case (*Bolam v Friern Hospital Management Committee* [1957] 1 WLR 582). In the latter case McNair J stated that a doctor is not guilty of negligence if he has acted in accordance with a practice accepted as proper by a responsible body of medical men skilled in that particular art. This judgment has been interpreted as confirming the clinical autonomy of doctors, subject to scrutiny by their peers. However, in *Bolitho*, this close ownership of clinical risk by doctors may have been weakened. The essence of the *Bolitho* judgment is that the court may choose to ignore the views of a group of doctors if their views are such that no reasonable body of doctors could have held them, that their views do not withstand logical analysis. Whether or not such a principle was already a part of the *Bolam* test of negligence, which incorporates the word responsible, is perhaps of less significance than the fact that the idea of challenge is now more explicit in the courts. It could thus be argued that the judiciary is more openly prepared to accept some ownership of clinical risk. This shift in emphasis mirrors that effected by the CMO when he challenges the fact that quality healthcare is a logical consequence of well-trained staff, good facilities and equipment. What seems to be acknowledged then is that optimal clinical outcomes do not logically always follow from a consensus medical opinion or from NHS provision of healthcare.

WHAT HAS HAPPENED FROM 2000 ONWARDS

In 1997 and the years that followed, it can thus be seen that the 1948 concordat between the government, the medical profession and the public has been changing. In particular, the clinical autonomy of doctors is open to increasing external scrutiny and the public is increasingly becoming empowered to express concerns about the quality of care provided. Clinical risk and patient safety are high on the government agenda, witnessed by the creation of the National Patient Safety Agency (NPSA) as a Special Authority in July 2001. The NPSA became operational in March 2002 and since then has received much government funding and publicity. This initiative grew out of recommendations put forward by the CMO in 'An Organisation with a Memory'.[53] Steps towards implementation of the NPSA were set out in May 2001 in 'Building a Safer NHS for Patients'[54] and in 2003 the online National Reporting and Learning System was introduced. The emphasis here is to learn from past clinical errors using a system that allows local incidents to be fed into a national data bank from which information can be disseminated to avoid repetition of the incident anywhere in the NHS. However, the NPSA has not had as warm a reception by NHS staff as might have been expected. Although reporting of incidents to the NPSA is confidential, the attempt to promote an open and blame-free culture is an uphill task in an environment where rising clinical negligence claims breed a closed, blame-oriented culture. In addition, the risk assessment process promoted by the NPSA may be confusing for staff who have to carry out risk assessments for health and safety purposes, for controls assurance purposes, for the risk-pooling schemes, for clinical governance purposes and so forth. The NPSA is explicitly focused on widening the ownership of clinical risk, not just at corporate level, but at national level. It has already been demonstrated that chief executives of NHS acute trusts are not actively seeking to corporately own clinical risk and it would seem that NHS staff are not actively seeking to help the national ownership of clinical risk.

SOME REFLECTIONS

Edwards and Marshall make the point that the tensions between doctors and managers have come to the fore due to the negotiations over the new NHS consultants' contract,[55] which was seen as a direct attack on professional autonomy demonstrating a lack of trust.[56] They suggest that these underlying tensions are in large part due to the different professional cultures of managers and doctors that shape the way in which the two groups approach guidelines, targets and finance issues. Degeling et al point to surveys of clinicians and managers in 26 hospitals in England, Wales, Australia and New Zealand that support this view.[57] They suggest that the 'modernisation' agenda in the NHS behoves both clinicians and managers to accept the fact that clinical decisions have resource implications, that there is a need to balance clinical autonomy with transparent accountability, that clinical work has to be systemised and that there has to be a team-based approach to clinical work. The results of the surveys reveal that whereas general managers support a 'systemised' approach to clinical work and favour transparent accountability, medical clinicians support 'individualist' conceptions of clinical work and are equivocal regarding transparent accountability.

The way that provision of healthcare services has developed in the NHS since 1948 has moved from the 'reflective practice model' to the 'scientific bureaucratic model'.[56] The former model reflects maximum clinical autonomy where ownership of clinical risk resides with the doctor and to a lesser degree with the patient, with no transparency. The latter model reflects reduced clinical autonomy due to the rise of evidence-based practice, models for service delivery and externally driven strategies for implementation. This model reflects a 'systems' approach to the delivery of healthcare in the NHS and 'emphasises robust evidence over personal professional expertise, with patterns of care driven more by managerial processes than through professional motivation'. In this model clinical risk is owned by not only the doctor and patient, but by a plethora of inspection and review bodies, chief executives and managers, the media and the public. That doctors are struggling to come to terms with this new model is not surprising since the training of doctors has been 'based on a model in which doctors are trained to deal with individuals, not organisations; to take personal responsibility rather than delegate; and to do their best for each patient rather than make trade-offs in a resource constrained environment'.[58]

It is contended that until risk as a concept was applicable to institutions, such as the NHS, there was no real reason to challenge the clinicians' predominate ownership of clinical risk. As the concept of risk management has gradually infiltrated government policy towards the NHS, through the quality agenda, it has been introduced into the NHS on a 'systems' basis. As this systematic modernisation agenda unfurls, the clinical autonomy of doctors and their ownership of clinical risk will necessarily be eroded and chief executives of NHS acute trusts may be forced into increasing corporate ownership. Ham and Alberti suggest that a new compact between the government, the medical profession and the public can only work if they trust one another.[13] They state:

> 'Trust has been strained by failures in clinical performance and the perception on the part of the profession that government has been too ready on some occasions to blame doctors when things go wrong. The trust of the public has been undermined by the tendency of government to promise more than it can deliver, a tendency that has at the same time led doctors to feel that politicians are raising public expectations to levels that cannot be met.'

To put these issues into a broader context it should be noted that the policy of healthcare delivery in Scotland has taken an increasingly different approach to that in England, especially since devolution. In Scotland, policy is not built on the scientific bureaucratic model. Rather, it is built on a model that emphasises and respects the ownership of clinical risk by doctors. Greer states:

> 'Scotland's health politics are increasingly built around the professional structure of medicine rather than around the use of management. Reflecting the strength and policy skills of its medical elites, Scottish policy builds on their analyses of how medicine does and will work. This entails greater reliance on professionals, efforts to align formal structures with professional ways of working, decreased reliance on managers to operate the system, a focus on quality improvement led from within the professions, and the elimination of the quasi-autonomous units (trusts) that form one of Thatcher's most important legacies and the building blocks of any contract-based system.'[59]

Would chief executives of NHS acute trusts in England prefer to take a stance on healthcare delivery more akin to this model, albeit in the NHS trust setting? Are some of them taking this stance already? Table 3.1 highlights who or what is at risk and from what in an NHS acute trust or NHS foundation trust. It draws attention to the fact that the ownership of clinical and non-clinical risk is the subject of shifting paradigms, the 1990s being a watershed decade for change. What has remained constant throughout the history of the NHS, however, is the fact that the patient bears the risk of clinical harm, whether or not they exclusively own it and whether or not such ownership is passive or active. The bulk of non-clinical risk in NHS organisations stems

Table 3.1 The complexity of risk in acute hospitals showing the shifting paradigms of active and passive ownership

Who/what is at risk?	At risk from what?	Clinical/non-clinical risk	Active/passive ownership of the risk/s
Patient	i. Physical/mental harm due to admission/clinical intervention	Clinical	i. From passive to increasingly active
	ii. Physical harm from non-clinical intervention	Non-clinical	ii. From passive to increasingly active
Doctor/other healthcare professionals	i. Professional censure/dismissal/ clinical negligence claims	Non-clinical	i. From active to increasingly passive
	ii. Physical harm	Non-clinical	ii. From passive to increasingly active
Non-healthcare staff	Physical harm/ dismissal	Non-clinical	From passive to increasingly active
Public	Physical harm Non-involvement	Non-clinical	From passive to increasingly active
Acute NHS trust/NHS foundation trust	Financial failure Organisational failure Loss of reputation Negative media attention Clinical negligence claims Criminal prosecution	Non-clinical	From passive to increasingly active
Government	Unsustainable NHS model based on 1948 core values	Non-clinical	From passive to increasingly active
GMC	Loss of credibility Transfer of functions	Non-clinical	Active

directly from clinical harm to a patient. If, altruistically, the aim of government initiatives for the NHS since 1997 has been to reduce the incidence of clinical harm to patients, does it matter what the overriding driver is, does it matter what label is attached to risk and does it matter who owns it? The rapidly evolving changing ownership of clinical risk in the NHS requires a similarly rapid and evolving culture change by doctors and chief executives of NHS acute trusts; presently this is not happening.

References

1.   Dainton C. The story of England's hospitals. London: Museum Press; 1961:34.
2.   Dainton C. The story of England's hospitals. London: Museum Press; 1961:35.
3.   Abel-Smith B. The hospitals 1800–1948. London: Heinemann; 1964:1–2.
4.   Dainton C. The story of England's hospitals. London: Museum Press; 1961:117.
5.   Dainton C. The story of England's hospitals. London: Museum Press; 1961:121.
6.   Jewson ND. The disappearance of the sick man from medical cosmology 1770–1870. Sociology 1976; 90:225–244.
7.   Salter B. The politics of change in the health service. London: Macmillan Press; 1998:99.
8.   The British Medical Journal Supplement. 29 May 1943.
9.   Campbell J. Nye Bevan and the mirage of British socialism. London: Weidenfeld and Nicolson; 1987:168.
10. Sir Donald Irvine CBE, President of the GMC. The changing relationship between the public and medical profession. The Lloyd Roberts Lecture at the Royal Society of Medicine 16 January 2001. Online. Available: http://www.gmc-uk.org/news/lloyd_roberts_lecture.htm.
11. Salter B. The politics of change in the health service. London: Macmillan Press; 1998:100–101.
12. Wai-Ching Leung. Managers and professionals: competing ideologies. BMJ Career Focus 2000; 321:7266.
13. Ham C, Alberti KGMM. The medical profession, the public and the government. BMJ (London) 2002; 324:838–842.
14. Department of Health. NHS management enquiry (the Griffiths Report). London: Department of Health; 1983.
15. Department of Health. NHS Management Executive, The quality journey: A guide to total quality management in the NHS. Leeds: Department of Health NHS Management Executive; 1993.
16. Salter B. The politics of change in the health service. London: Macmillan Press; 1998:103.
17. Deer B. Food poison deaths probe may reveal NHS flaws. Sunday Times, 24 February 1985.
18. Department for Health and Social Security. Report of the Committee of Inquiry into an outbreak of food poisoning at Stanley Royd Hospital. London: HMSO; 1986.
19. Walshe K, Higgins J. The use and impact of inquiries in the NHS. BMJ (London) 2002; 325:895–900.
20. Hansard HC, 9 June 1986: col. 27.
21. Hansard HC, 9 June 1986: col. 30.
22. National Audit Office. A safer place to work: improving the management of health and safety risks to staff in NHS trusts. London: National Audit Office; 2003. Online. Available: http://www.nao.gov.uk.
23. Department of Health. Working for patients (Cm 555). London: HMSO; 1989.
24. Kerrison S, Packwood T, Buxton M. Medical audit: taking stock. London: King's Fund Centre; 1993.
25. Department of Health. HC (89)34 and HSG (96)48. NHS indemnity arrangements for handling clinical negligence claims against NHS staff. Leeds: Department of Health; 1996.
26. Alaszewski A, Harrison L, Manthorpe J. Risk, health and welfare. Buckingham: Open University Press; 1998.

27. The Council for Science and Society. The acceptability of risks. London: Barry Rose in association with the Council for Science and Society; 1977:8.

28. Lowrance W. Of acceptable risk. Los Altos, CA: William Kaufman; 1976.

29. Royal Society Study Group. Risk assessment. London: The Royal Society; 1983:176.

30. Royal Society Study Group. Risk assessment. London: The Royal Society; 1983:177.

31. The Royal Society. Risk: analysis, perception, management. London: The Royal Society; 1992.

32. The Royal Society. Risk: analysis, perception, management. London: The Royal Society; 1992:136.

33. The Royal Society. Risk: analysis, perception, management. London: The Royal Society; 1992:153.

34. Ham C. Management and competition in the new NHS. Oxford: Radcliffe Medical Press; 1995.

35. Sir Donald Irvine CBE, President of the GMC. The changing relationship between the public and medical profession. The Lloyd Roberts Lecture at the Royal Society of Medicine 16 January 2001. Online. Available: http://www.gmc-uk.org/news/lloyd_roberts_lecture.htm.

36. Salter B. The politics of change in the health service. London: Macmillan Press; 1998:126.

37. NHSME. Risk management manual. London: HMSO; 1993. Online. Available: http://www.dh.gov.uk/riskman.htm.

38. NHSME. Risk management manual. London: HMSO; 1993:17. Online. Available: http://www.dh.gov.uk/riskman.htm.

39. NHS Litigation Authority. CNST risk management standards and procedures manual of guidance version 1. London: NHS Litigation Authority; 1997.

40. Symons R (Assistant risk manager). NHSLA presentation at Northumbria University. 13 March 2004.

41. Department of Health. The new NHS: modern, dependable. London: The Stationery Office; 1997.

42. Department of Health. The new NHS: modern, dependable. London: The Stationery Office; 1997: para 3.2.

43. Department of Health. The new NHS: modern, dependable. London: The Stationery Office; 1997: paras 3.4–3.7.

44. Department of Health. The new NHS: modern, dependable. London: The Stationery Office; 1997: para 7.15.

45. Sir Liam Donaldson. Making a difference: progress in implementing policies to improve health and health care. Department of Health. Online. Available: http://www.dh.gov.uk.

46. National Audit Office. Achieving improvements through clinical governance – a progress report on implementation by trusts. London: National Audit Office; 2003. Online. Available: http://www.nao.gov.uk.

47. Commission for Health Improvement. Getting better? Commission for Health Improvement. 2003. Online. Available: http://www.chi.gov.uk.

48. Department of Health. HSG (97)17 Corporate governance in the NHS: Controls assurance statements. Online. Available: http://www.dh.gov.uk.

49. Department of Health. HSC 1999/123 Governance in the new NHS. Online. Available: http://www.dh.gov.uk.

50. Department of Health. HSC 2001/005 Governance in the new NHS. Online. Available: http://www.dh.gov.uk.

51. Department of Health. A commitment to quality, a quest for excellence. 2001. Online. Available: http://www.dh.gov.uk.
52. Department of Health. An exemplar operational risk management strategy. London: HMSO. 1997.
53. Department of Health. An organisation with a memory. 2000. Online. Available: http://www.dh.gov.uk.
54. Department of Health. Building a safer NHS for patients. 2001. Online. Available: http://www.dh.gov.uk.
55. Edwards N, Marshall M. Doctors and managers. BMJ (London) 2003; 326:116–117.
56. Davies HTO, Harrison S. Trends in doctor–manager relationships. BMJ (London) 2003; 326:646–649.
57. Degeling P, Maxwell S, Kennedy J, Coyle B. Medicine, management and modernisation: a 'danse macabre'? BMJ (London) 2003; 326:649–652.
58. Edwards N, Kornacki M J, Silversin J. BMJ (London) 2002; 324:835–838.
59. Greer SL. Four way bet: how devolution has led to four different models for the NHS. London: The Constitution Unit; 2004:10.

Chapter **4**

Does the *Bolam* principle still reign in medical negligence cases in Malaysia?

Puteri Nemie Jahn Kassim

CHAPTER CONTENTS

Introduction   79
The standard of care   79
The *Bolam* principle   80
A change of attitude   81
The rejection of the *Bolam*
  principle in Australia   84

The *Bolam* principle in
  Malaysia   86
Conclusion   91
Bibliography   91

INTRODUCTION

Since it was introduced in 1957, the *Bolam* principle has been routinely applied to medical negligence cases in determining whether the doctor's acts fell below the required standard of care. However, in its original context, the principle has been criticised as being over-protective of the medical profession and allowing the standard of care for doctors to be a matter of medical judgement. In recent years, the principle has been subjected to intense discussion throughout the common law jurisdictions. The English courts tried to restore the principle to its proper limits and correct the misinterpretation of what was originally intended. The Australian jurisdiction, on the other hand, has taken the more drastic step of refusing to apply the *Bolam* principle to a doctor's duty to warn, and later on abandoning the principle completely. The Malaysian courts, however, have always been quite conservative in the area of medical negligence. Although the trend of the cases shows that the Malaysian courts are much more heavily influenced by English decisions than by the Commonwealth ones, some decisions indicate a shift in emphasis towards the Commonwealth jurisdictions.

THE STANDARD OF CARE

The standard of care that the law demands of a person in a normal negligence case has been established to be the standard of 'reasonable care'. If a person achieves the standard satisfied by the hypothetical reasonable man, then he will not be adjudged negligent at common law. However, the formulations of the standard of care required by the medical profession have been a matter of controversy for many years, particularly, with regard to the reference point for the standard. This difficulty stems from the fact that, unlike a typical negligence case, a medical negligence one involves intricacies that are not, generally speaking, within judicial knowledge. Hence, in relation to medical conduct, it is hard for the courts to arrive at their own assessment of reasonableness.

THE *BOLAM* PRINCIPLE

The test to determine what is the standard of care demanded of a doctor was established by McNair J in *Bolam v Friern Hospital Management Committee* [1957] 1 WLR 582, which subsequently became known as the *Bolam* principle. In *Bolam*, the plaintiff, John Bolam, was a psychiatric patient suffering depressive illness. He was advised by Dr de Bastarrechea, a consultant psychiatrist attached to Friern Hospital, to undergo electroconvulsive therapy (ECT). He signed a consent form but was not alerted to the risk of fracture that can occur because of fit-like convulsions that such treatment induces. In due course, he received this treatment but was not given any relaxant drugs. As a consequence, he suffered several injuries. These included dislocation of hip joints and fractures to the pelvis on both sides caused by the femur being driven through the cup of the pelvis.

The plaintiff claimed that the doctor was negligent in not giving him relaxant drugs. By not doing so, the doctor also failed to provide adequate physical restraints to prevent the injury. He also claimed that the doctor had failed to warn him of the risks involved in the treatment. The judge, however, found the doctor not guilty of negligence as he had acted in accordance with a practice accepted as proper by a responsible body of medical men skilled in that particular area. Expert witness called by either side gave evidence as to the different techniques they adopted in giving ECT treatment; some used relaxant drugs, some used restraining sheets and some used manual control, but all agreed that there was a firm body of medical specialists who opposed the use of relaxant drugs. Further, a number of competent practitioners considered that the less manual restraint there was, the less likely would be the risk of fracture ([1957] 1 WLR 582 at pp. 589–593). With regard to failure to warn of the risks involved, the defendants' doctor opined that the risk involved was a very slight risk and it was a common practice that they would not have warned their patients of such risk. In order for the plaintiff to succeed on his allegation of failure to warn, the court held that the plaintiff had to prove to the court's satisfaction that if the plaintiff had been warned of the risk, he would not have undergone the treatment. Unfortunately, the plaintiff failed to discharge the burden of proof required of him. In his judgment, McNair J formulated a test, known as the *Bolam* principle, to determine whether the doctor's act fell below the required standard of care ([1957] 1 WLR 582 at pp. 586-587):

'The test is the standard of the ordinary skilled man exercising and professing to have that special skill. A man need not possess the highest
expert skill; it is well established law that it is sufficient if he exercises
the ordinary skill of an ordinary competent man exercising that particular art . . . in the case of a medical man, negligence means failure to act
in accordance with the standards of reasonably competent medical men
at the time . . . I myself would prefer to put it this way, that he is not
guilty of negligence if he has acted in accordance with a practice
accepted as proper by a responsible body of medical men skilled in that
particular art. . . . . Putting it the other way round, a man is not negligent, if he is acting in accordance with such a practice, merely because
there is a body of opinion who would take a contrary view.'

From the principle above, it can be seen that a doctor is not negligent if he
has acted according to a practice accepted as proper by a body of medical
men who possess similar skills to the doctor in question. It is immaterial that
there exists another body of opinion that would not have adopted the
approach taken by the said doctor. As long as there exists a 'responsible body
of medical opinion' that approves the actions of the doctor, the doctor escapes
liability. In other words, the test allows doctors to escape liability by calling
experts to testify that the procedure adopted was consistent with practices
accepted by a responsible body of medical opinion. Medical expert opinion,
thus, plays a vital role in the determination of a doctor's liability. This test can
be seen as being over-protective of the medical profession and allows little
opportunity for the court to assess the adequacy of the accepted practices. In
Sidaway v Bethlem Royal Hospital Governors [1985] 1 All ER 643, Lord Scarman
said (p. 649):

'The *Bolam* principle may be formulated as a rule that a doctor is not
negligent if he acts in accordance with a practice accepted at the time
as proper by a responsible body of medical opinion even though other
doctors adopt a different practice. *In short, the law imposes the duty of
care; but the standard of care is a matter of medical judgment.'* (Emphasis
added.)

A CHANGE OF ATTITUDE

Almost two decades before *Sidaway*, the Court of Appeal in *Hucks v Cole*
(1968) The Times, 9 May held that it was appropriate for the judge to reject
medical expert evidence if it did not really stand up to analysis. In this case,
the defendant was a general practitioner in Somerset who possessed a
diploma in obstetrics. Mrs Hucks had been a patient in a maternity hospital
when after giving birth to her child, she had suffered from a fulminating
septicaemia, which caused various sores and yellow spots to appear on her
fingers and toes. She brought them to the attention of Dr Cole, who put her
on a 5-day course of tetracycline. However, at the end of the 5-day course

he took her off the antibiotics as the sores were improving. The next day Mrs Hucks contracted septicaemia, and puerperal fever, a condition that had been extremely common before the Second World War but was very rare in the 1960s. She sued Dr Cole for negligence, alleging that he should have treated her with penicillin as soon as he read the bacteriologist's report. The defendant said he had acted in accordance with the reasonable practice of other doctors with obstetric experience. However, Lawton J found Dr Cole to have been negligent, and the Court of Appeal upheld his finding. Although the court could understand that Dr Cole was lulled into a false sense of security, as other general practitioners might have been by the normal effect of antibiotics, the court was willing to apply the test of reasonable care, in the sense of taking care to adopt that method of action which would probably lead to the least danger in preference to deciding the case in accordance with expert evidence as to whether the defendant acted in accordance with approved practice. Thus, Dr Cole was negligent because he did not take 'every precaution' to prevent an outbreak of puerperal fever and it mattered not if other doctors would have acted as he did. Sachs LJ said (p. 397):

> 'Where the evidence shows that a lacuna in professional practice exists by which risks of grave danger are knowingly taken, then, however small the risks, the courts must anxiously examine that lacuna – particularly if the risks can be easily and inexpensively avoided. If the court finds on analysis of the reasons given for not taking those precautions that, in the light of current professional knowledge, there is no proper basis for the lacuna, and that it is definitely not reasonable that those risks should have been taken, its function is to state that fact and where necessary to state that it constitutes negligence. In such a case the practice will no doubt thereafter be altered to the benefit of the patients.'

Hucks was a virtually invisible precedent until it was widely reported in the early 1990s (see, for example, [1993] 4 Med LR 393). Its approach was then adopted in a few cases, including *Gascoine v Ian Sheridan & Co* [1994] 5 Med LR 437 and *Joyce v Wandsworth Health Authority* [1995] 6 Med LR 60. In *Gascoine*, Mitchell J said that it was common sense that merely because a number of doctors gave evidence to the same effect, it did not automatically imply that these views formed an established and alternative 'school of thought' of medical opinion. In *Joyce*, Overend J commented that the medical practice must stand up to analysis and not be unreasonable in the light of medical knowledge at that time. Whilst the majority of cases decided around this time were still closely following the principles stated in *Sidaway* this all changed when the House of Lords reviewed the position in *Bolitho v City & Hackney Health Authority* [1997] 4 All ER 771. Here Lord Browne-Wilkinson drew on *Hucks v Cole* to hold that the court is not bound to hold that a defendant doctor escapes liability for negligent treatment or diagnosis just because he leads evidence from a number of medical experts who are genuinely of the opinion that the defendant's treatment and diagnosis accorded with sound medical practice (p. 778). His Lordship held that the word 'responsible' used by McNair J in *Bolam* 'show[s] that the court has to be satisfied that the exponents of the body of opinion relied on can demonstrate that such opinion has a logical basis' (p. 778). He went on to explain that before a judge can accept a body of opinion as being 'responsible', the judge will have to be satisfied that '. . . in forming their views, the experts have directed their minds to the question of comparative risks and benefits and have reached a defensible conclusion on the matter' (p. 778).

The House of Lords' decision in *Bolitho* appears to do away with the usual 'rubber-stamping' of expert medical opinion. Expert opinion now has to withstand rigorous scrutiny from the judiciary. However, one of the issues raised by this approach is how judges are supposed to conclude that a medical opinion does not withstand logical analysis when they are not themselves expert evaluators of medical opinion. Lord Browne-Wilkinson's conclusions seem to accept this problem. He stated that (p. 779):

> '. . . it will seldom be right for a judge to reach the conclusion that views genuinely held by a competent medical expert are unreasonable. The assessment of medical risks and benefits is a matter of clinical judgment, which a judge would not normally be able to make without expert evidence.'

Bolitho was cited with approval in the Court of Appeal's decision in *Penney, Palmer and Cannon v East Kent Health Authority* [2000] Lloyd's Rep Med 41. In this case, the plaintiffs claimed damages for negligent screening of cervical smears by the defendant's cytology department between 1989 and 1992. The plaintiffs alleged that the smears were negligently reported as negative, depriving them of the opportunity of obtaining early treatment which would have prevented the development of endocervical carcinoma. Screening was carried out by qualified biomedical scientists or qualified cytology screeners (cytoscreeners). Cytoscreeners are not qualified to diagnose. Their task is limited to distinguishing between smears with normal appearances and those that are or might be abnormal. In cases of abnormality or possible abnormality, the cytoscreener was obliged to refer the smear to more highly qualified individuals such as the pathologist. On the issue of whether the cytoscreeners were negligent in reporting the tests as negative, five eminent pathologists were called to give their testimony, three of whom were called by the defendants. The defendants claimed that their witnesses constituted a respectable and responsible body of opinion, thus providing them a defence under the *Bolam* principle. On this issue, Lord Woolf MR applied the *Bolam* principle as further explained and interpreted in *Bolitho*. After the expert witnesses had offered their evidence, 'the judge had to make his own findings on balance of probabilities on this issue of fact in order to proceed to the next step in answering the question of negligence or no negligence' (p. 46).

THE REJECTION OF THE *BOLAM* PRINCIPLE IN AUSTRALIA

Australian judges have subjected expert evidence to close scrutiny by checking whether a conforming practice is reasonable or not. As King CJ stated in *F v R* (1982) 33 SASR 189 (p. 194):

'... professions may adopt unreasonable practices ... The court has an obligation to scrutinise professional practices to ensure that they accord with the standard of reasonableness imposed by the law ... The ultimate question, however, is not whether the defendant's conduct accords with the practices of his profession or some part of it, but whether it conforms to the standard of care demanded by the law. That is a question for the court and the duty of deciding it cannot be delegated to any profession or group in the community.'

This view was approved by the Australian High Court in *Rogers v Whitaker* [1992] CLR 479, where it was accepted that the question of how much information should be imparted by a doctor cannot be determined by 'any profession or group in the community' (p. 488) but should be determined upon consideration of complex factors, namely, 'the nature of the matter to be disclosed; the nature of the treatment; the desire of the patient for information; the temperament and health of the patient; and the general surrounding circumstances' (p. 488). Thus, the High Court felt that opinions of medical witnesses should not be decisive at this point. In other words, it was for the courts, having regard to the 'paramount consideration' that a person is entitled to make decisions about his own life, to set the appropriate standard of care. Applying this standard to the case, the High Court found that Mr Rogers had failed in his duty by omitting to tell Mrs Whitaker of the risk of contracting sympathetic ophthalmia, for the following reasons: Firstly, Mrs Whitaker had questioned him about the possible complications involved in the procedure; secondly, she had expressed a great deal of concern about protecting her left eye, even though she had not asked specifically about whether the operation on her right eye could lead to her developing a debilitating inflammation of her left eye; and, finally, the materialisation of the risk had disastrous consequences for her.

Doubts as to whether the approach in *Rogers v Whitaker* extended beyond non-disclosure cases were laid to rest by the Australian High Court in *Naxakis v Western General Hospital* (1999) 73 ALJR 782, which held that it applied to the doctor's duty to advise, diagnose and treat. In *Naxakis*, the appellant, 12-year-old Paraskevas Naxakis, was struck twice on the head by his schoolmate's school bag. He collapsed and was admitted by a general practitioner to the Western General Hospital for head injury. At the hospital, the appellant fell into a deep non-arousable unconsciousness for 5 minutes and was unresponsive to painful stimuli. There were traces of vomit around the corners of his mouth and he began to exhibit signs of opisthotonos, that is, spasm in the muscles of the neck, back and legs and backward contortions of the body. A preliminary diagnosis was made of a subarachnoid haemorrhage caused by a blow to the head. He remained in the hospital for 9 days under the supervision of the second respondent, Mr Jensen, a senior neurosurgeon at the hospital. A CAT scan was carried out and the result indicated that he was suffering from a subarachnoid (traumatically caused) haemorrhage near the fourth ventricle. However, his condition gradually improved without further treatment and he was later discharged from the hospital. Two days later, the appellant collapsed at home and was taken to the Royal Children's Hospital, where he was attended by Mr Klug, director of neurosurgery. An angiogram was conducted which showed that the appellant had suffered a major intracranial bleed from a burst aneurysm. An operation was performed to insert a ventricular peritoneal shunt to drain cerebrospinal fluid and a craniotomy was performed to clip the aneurysm. However, the appellant suffered serious and permanent physical and intellectual impairment as a consequence of the bursting of the aneurysm. The appellant brought an action in the Supreme Court against the hospital and the senior neurosurgeon for failure to properly diagnose, as a result of which he had suffered serious and permanent physical and intellectual impairment. At the trial in the Supreme Court of Victoria, the judge accepted a no case to answer submission and then directed the jury to return a verdict in favour of the defendants. The appellant appealed unsuccessfully to the Court of Appeal, which held that there was no basis for the claim that the neurosurgeon failed to consider the possibility of an aneurysm since there was no evidence that he did not consider that possibility. The appellant appealed to the Australian High Court.

The thrust of the case against the hospital and Mr Jensen was that alternative diagnoses should have been considered and an angiogram performed to establish the cause of the appellant's condition. Thus, failure to order an angiogram showed a breach of duty on the part of the neurosurgeon. Three closely related claims were: failure to consider alternative diagnoses; failure to conduct an angiogram; and discharging the appellant without considering other possible diagnoses. The High Court applied its own previous reasoning in Rogers to conclude that '[the standard of care] is not determined solely or even primarily by reference to the practice, followed or supported by a responsible body of opinion in the relevant profession or trade' ((1999) 73 ALJR 782 per Gaudron J at p. 785), adding that it has to be decided 'whether it was reasonable for one or more of the steps to be taken . . . [and this] was not for expert medical witnesses to say whether those steps were or were not reasonable' (p. 785). Furthermore, it observed that in some situations, 'questions as to the reasonableness of particular precautionary measures are . . . matters of commonsense' (p. 785). From the evidence present, there was suspicion that a subarachnoid haemorrhage could result from other causes than trauma or blow to the head. There was undisputed evidence that the appellant did not progress as hoped and experienced neck retraction, which was considered unusual. Therefore, the logical thing to do when such symptoms arose was to conduct a cerebral angiogram, which the respondent failed to do. If the angiogram had been undertaken, the appellant could have undergone surgery 2 days prior to the bursting of the aneurysm and his present condition would have been avoided. McHugh J stated that even if there is a respectable body of opinion that would not have conducted an angiogram, this was not decisive that there was no negligence as '[t]o allow that body of opinion to be decisive would re-introduce the *Bolam test* into Australian law' ((1999) 73 ALJR 782 p. 791). As long as there exists a respectable body of medical opinion that would have conducted an angiogram, 'the issue is one for the jury, provided . . . the evidence is reasonably capable of supporting all elements of a cause of action in negligence' (p. 791). Therefore, although there was evidence by other practitioners that they would not have conducted an angiogram, it was reasonably open for the jury to consider and accept the evidence of Mr Klug, a neurosurgeon at the Royal Children's Hospital that only by performing a cerebral angiogram was there 'a way of defining whether or not there was another intracranial abnormality such as an aneurysm or other vascular malformation' (p. 791).

Kirby J agreed with McHugh J. His Honour opined that it was left to the jury to decide whether to accept expert opinion of a fellow medical practitioner. Expert opinion of a fellow practitioner should not be determinative on the issue of whether or not the defendant is negligent as such evidence may stem 'from professional courtesy or collegial sympathy' (p. 797) for the defendant. Kirby J reiterated the principle decided in *Rogers v Whitaker*, where the court pointed out that the standard of care owed by persons possessing special skills is not determined 'solely or even primarily by reference to the practice followed or supported by a responsible body of opinion in the relevant profession or trade' (p. 798). Instead, whilst evidence of acceptable medical practice is a useful guide for the courts in adjudicating on the appropriate standard of care, the standard to be applied is nonetheless that of 'ordinary skilled person exercising and professing to have that special skill' (p. 798). Therefore, the direct suggestion by Mr Klug that Mr Jensen was not negligent could not be regarded as determinative.

THE *BOLAM* PRINCIPLE IN MALAYSIA

The *Bolam* principle so formulated has been routinely applied by the Malaysian courts to the relevant cases such as *Mariah bte Mohamad (Administratrix of the estate of Wan Salleh bin Wan Ibrahim, deceased) v Abdullah bin Daud (Dr Lim Kok Eng & Anor, Third Parties)* [1990] 1 MLJ 240, *Inderjeet Singh a/l Piara Singh v Mazlan bin Jasman & Prs* [1995] 2 MLJ 646 and *Asiah bte Kamsah v Dr Rajinder Singh & Ors* [2002] 1 MLJ 484 in determining the doctor's standard of care. Amongst the earliest cases in the Malaysian jurisdiction in which the *Bolam* principle was applied is *Swamy v Mathews* [1968] 1 MLJ 138. The plaintiff in *Swamy* was an estate worker and he visited the defendant doctor for an itch on his hands. The doctor diagnosed the ailment as either ringworm or psoriasis and injected the plaintiff with doses of Acetylarsan, an arsenical compound. The plaintiff's limbs subsequently became paralysed and he claimed that this was caused by the drug. There were different opinions presented to the court as to what was the proper treatment and the procedure in giving such treatment to the plaintiff. The majority judgment accepted the testimony of the defendant doctor and his explanation that the prescription and the dosage given to the plaintiff, although at variance with the manufacturer's recommendation, was made based on personal experience. The majority judgment in discounting the contrary evidence emphasises the classic doctor-centric approach. The court did not examine the reasonableness of the treatment. The court found that the medical practitioner was not negligent because medical practitioners need not have the highest degree of skill. Mr Justice Ismail Khan cited *Roe v Minister of Health* [1954] 2 WLR 915, stating:

> 'But we should be doing a disservice to the community at large if we were to impose liability on hospitals and doctors for everything that happens to go wrong. Doctors would be led to think more of their own safety than of the good of their patients. Initiative would be stifled and confidence shaken. A proper sense of proportion requires us to have regard to the conditions in which hospitals and doctors have to work. We must insist on due care for the patient at every point, but we must not condemn as negligence that which is only a misadventure.'

Soon after this decision, the Privy Council applied the *Bolam* principle in *Chin Keow v Government of Malaysia* [1967] 2 MLJ 45. In this case, an amah in a government venereal disease clinic spoke to the staff nurse about an ulcer on her right ankle and swollen glands in her thigh. The nurse took her to see Dr Devadason, the Medical Officer in charge of the clinic. The doctor examined her but did not ask about her medical history. The doctor prescribed an injection of procaine penicillin and she died within an hour of receiving the injection. The trial judge, Ong J, adopted the *Bolam* principle and found the doctor to be negligent for prescribing a penicillin injection as a routine treatment for the patient and that he did so without asking one simple question to attempt to discover whether she was sensitive to the drug. Such practice would not be accepted as proper by a responsible body of medical opinion. The Federal Court, however, rejected Ong J's finding of negligence but on further appeal, the Privy Council adopted Ong J's decision.

In *Elizabeth Choo v Government of Malaysia* [1970] 2 MLJ 171, the plaintiff claimed that the anaesthetist was negligent during the preoperative sigmoid-oscopic examination, which had resulted in perforation of the colon. One of the issues discussed in this case was whether it was proper for the anaesthetist to perform sigmoidoscopic examination under general anaesthesia. On this issue, several medical experts gave conflicting opinions. One expert expressed the view that it is better to perform sigmoidoscopy without anaesthesia as the patient could forewarn the anaesthetist of any pain. The court, however, observed that the anaesthetist had previously successfully performed hundreds of sigmoidoscopic examinations under general anaesthesia. This technique had been in use in his unit since 1956 and the technique had not earned the condemnation of medical opinion generally (p. 172). Thus, applying the *Bolam* principle to this issue, the court held that the anaesthetist was not negligent as he had followed the general and approved practice in the situation he was facing. The technique that he adopted had been approved by a responsible body of medical men since 1956. Therefore, it did not matter if there was another body of opinion that would have taken a contrary view. Raja Azlan Shah J stated (p. 173):

'The anaesthetist had done hundreds of endoscopic examinations including sigmoidoscopy ... and had encountered no trouble except this particular mishap ... There is evidence that the greatest care is required to ensure free passage when the instrument is introduced in the rectum and the procedure required a high degree of concentration. The anaesthetist said he exercised all care and caution he possessed at the time ... at no time did he lift his sight from the mirror.'

The judicial decision in *Elizabeth Choo* was further approved in *Kow Nan Seng v Nagamah & Ors* [1982] 1 MLJ 128. In this case, the doctor applied a complete plaster cast on to the leg of the plaintiff. This resulted in insufficient blood circulation, which led to gangrene setting in and, later, amputation of the plaintiff's leg. There were conflicting opinions as to whether a complete plaster cast or a plaster slab should have been used. Again, applying the *Bolam* principle the court held that there might be differences of opinion as to the types of plaster casts to be applied in the treatment but this did not mean that choosing a type of plaster cast was in itself negligence. To be negligent, the doctor must have departed from the reasonable standard of care and skill of an ordinary competent doctor.

In *Liew Sin Kiong v Dr Sharon M Paulraj* [1996] 2 AMR 1403, the plaintiff was a patient of Dr Molly Elizabeth Matthew, a government ophthalmologist. Dr Matthew had been treating the plaintiff for juvenile glaucoma, including two operations under general anaesthesia – a trabeculectomy on each eye – in 1990. The operations were done in order to create an outflow of intraocular fluid so as to reduce the intraocular pressure. The operation was a success, with the plaintiff retaining his vision and the intraocular pressure was controlled with medication. However, about 2 years later, even with medication, the intraocular pressure could not be controlled. At that time Dr Matthew recommended that the plaintiff go for an operation in Kuala Lumpur as the required treatment was not available in Sabah. The plaintiff did not heed the recommendation; instead he sought treatment from the defendant, who is an ophthalmologist practising in a private clinic in Sabah. After conducting an examination, the defendant prescribed some medication and further operation on both eyes. The plaintiff was asked to sign a consent form. After the operation, the plaintiff suffered severe pain in his eyes. He was admitted to the Queen Elizabeth Hospital in Kota Kinabalu but as a result of infection from the operation, he lost the sight of his right eye. Ian Chin J applied *Sidaway* (pp. 1418–1419) and found the defendant not liable as the plaintiff had failed to prove that the defendant had not acted in accordance with the standards of a competent ophthalmologist. The learned judge said that although the consent form did not state that the defendant had informed the plaintiff of the risk of infection, it did not mean that the risk was not explained. Further, the court held that if a doctor was of the view that a patient was in need of an operation, then such benefit outweighed a remote risk as the doctor should be allowed the 'therapeutic privilege' in deciding whether or not to disclose the risk. However, it should be noted that even though Ian Chin J did not follow the principles established in *Rogers v Whitaker*, he commented that (p. 1420): '[t]he issue here is not what risks are material for disclosure and therefore it does not call for my decision as to whether to follow *Sidaway* or *Rogers* regarding deferring to medical expert evidence'.

However, the case of *Hong Chuan Lay v Dr Eddie Soo Fook Mun* [1998] 5 CLJ 251 shows the court's preference for the Australian decision in *Rogers v Whitaker*. In this case, the defendant doctor was found not liable for the injuries suffered by the plaintiff as there was no evidence produced to show that the defendant had performed an aspect of the surgery unreasonably. The defendant was at all material times a qualified and experienced orthopaedic surgeon and the method and procedure adopted by him were accepted in the medical field for operations of this nature. In this case, the plaintiff, a 63-year-old man, was suffering from wear and tear of the neck bone and bone growth around the vertebra. He underwent a surgical operation on his cervical spine which was performed by the defendant who was an orthopaedic surgeon attached to the Sentosa Clinic. Three weeks after the operation the plaintiff experienced paralysis of both his lower and upper limbs and incontinence. As he was not prepared to continue the postoperative treatment provided by the defendant, he sought advice from other doctors and underwent three more operations conducted by three different doctors. Even after these operations, his condition only improved marginally. The plaintiff claimed that the defendant had negligently caused damage to his spinal nerve during the first operation resulting in the present residue. The court applied the *Bolam* principle and Mr Justice James Foong found that there was no evidence to prove that the defendant had conducted the operation negligently as he had not in any way departed from the approved practice. The only indication of spinal cord injury was the clinical diagnosis of the presence of oedema. But the presence of oedema was not a conclusive pronouncement of a permanent injury to the cord as it is a common occurrence in such operations. The plaintiff also claimed that the defendant failed to inform him of the possibility of paralysis after the operation. In dealing with this claim, the court abandoned the *Bolam* principle and applied the approach used by the Australian courts in *Rogers v Whitaker*. Mr Justice Foong stated that (pp. 267–268):

> 'For sometime, the *Bolam* test i.e., the test expounded by McNair J in *Bolam v Friern Hospital Committee (supra)* was accepted to be applicable to all provisions of a doctor's duty to his patient. But by a series of cases in the United States of America, Canada and Australia, the *Bolam* test is rejected as regards to the doctor's duty to disclose information and advice to the patient. In order to explain the arguments against it, and

the new test proposed as its substitution, I shall follow the approach adopted by the justices in the High Court of Australia in their judgment of *Christopher Rogers v Maree Lynette Whitaker (supra)*. I must proclaim my highest respect to the honourable Justices of this Australian High Court for their clarity, conciseness and comprehensibility in explaining the distinction of the *Bolam* test from the new approach.'

The rejection of the *Bolam* principle became apparent in *Kamalam a/p & Ors v Eastern Plantation Agency & Anor* [1996] 4 MLJ 674. In *Kamalam*, the defendant doctor failed to diagnose the plaintiff's ailment, which turned out to be a stroke, thereby causing his death. The court found the doctor had fallen below the standard of care required of him. The court chose to accept the opinion of experts called by the plaintiff who considered that the defendant should have referred the deceased to a hospital because he manifested symptoms of an impending stroke. Giving judgment, Richard Talalla J concluded that he was not bound to find for the defendant even if there is a body of medical opinion that approved the doctor's practice. He stated (p. 691):

'. . . while due regard will be had to the evidence of medical experts, I do not accept myself as being restricted by the establishment in evidence of a practice accepted as proper by a responsible body of medical men skilled in that particular art to finding a doctor is not guilty of negligence if he had acted in accordance with that practice. *In short I am not bound by the Bolam* principle.' (Emphasis added.)

Further, in *Foo Fio Na v Hospital Assunta & Anor* [1999] 6 MLJ 738, the plaintiff, who suffered total paralysis of the upper and lower limbs, claimed that the defendant failed to inform her of the risk of paralysis that is inherent in a spinal cord operation. In dealing with this issue, Mokhtar Sidin JCA applied the principles in *Rogers v Whitaker* and considered that the risk of paralysis was considered to be a *material* risk of which the plaintiff should have been warned. According to the evidence, the plaintiff did not know that she consented to a spinal cord operation and was not told it would be a major one, which might lead to paralysis. She was only assured by the defendant that the operation was a minor one. The judge commented (p. 765):

'The question of giving proper warning was further emphasized in the Australian case of *Rogers v Whitaker* . . . It is clear from the . . . principle [in that case] that the court itself has to decide on the doctor's negligence after weighing the standard of skill practiced by the relevant profession or trade and also the fact that a person is entitled to make his own decision on his life.'

From the above cited cases, it can be seen that the decisions made by the Malaysian courts on whether the straightforward application of the *Bolam* principle or the approach taken by the Australian courts is to be preferred have been very inconsistent. However, the judgment given by Gopal Sri Ram JCA in *Dr Soo Fook Mun v Foo Fio Na & Anor and Another Appeal* [2001] 2 CLJ

457 indicates the reluctance of the courts to follow the developments in Australia and depart from the straightforward application of the *Bolam* principle. In *Dr Soo*, Gopal Sri Ram JCA overruled *Foo Fio Na v Hospital Assunta & Anor* by allowing Dr Soo's appeals. His Lordship stated that 'the *Bolam* test places a fairly high threshold for a plaintiff to cross in an action for medical negligence . . . [and] [i]f the law played too interventionist a role in the field of medical negligence, it will lead to the practice of defensive medicine [and] [t]he cost of medical care for the man on the street would become prohibitive without being necessarily beneficial' (p. 472). Further, His Lordship was of the opinion that allowing doctors to be judged by their own peers would 'maintain a fair balance between law and medicine' (p. 472). However, Dr Soo's case is currently being discussed in the Federal Court (see [2002] 2 MLJ 129) where the Federal Court has granted leave to reconsider whether the *Bolam* principle should apply to all aspects of medical negligence, particularly with regard to duty to warn of inherent risks in medical treatment. The outcome of the Federal Court's decision would be determinative on whether the Australian approach is to be preferred in determining liability in medical negligence.

CONCLUSION

Although some decisions show a departure from the straightforward application of the *Bolam* principle, decisions in medical negligence cases by the Malaysian courts have been inconsistent. The common trend seems to be that the Malaysian courts are much more influenced by English decisions than by Commonwealth ones. It can be seen that the departures from the straightforward application of the *Bolam* principle in *Kamalam*, *Hong Chuan Lay* and *Foo Fio Na* were only High Court decisions. The Court of Appeal decision of *Dr Soo Fook Mun* emphasised the view that medical practitioners are not negligent if they follow the common practice, regardless of the existence of contrary opinions. Further, neither the Court of Appeal nor the Federal Court of Malaysia has made any policy statement either in support of, or against, the departure from the *Bolam* principle. Thus, the *Bolam* principle in its original context still reigns in medical negligence cases in Malaysia.

BIBLIOGRAPHY

Brazier M, Miola J. Bye-bye Bolam: A medical litigation revolution? Medical Law Review 2000; 8:85–114.

Chalmers D. Australia and the *Bolam* principle after the Naxakis decision. Second National Medico-Legal Conference, Kuala Lumpur, Malaysia, 2000; 1–19.

Davies M. The 'New Bolam': Another false dawn for medical negligence? Professional Negligence 1996; 12(4):120–125.

Harpwood V. Medical negligence: a chink in the armour of the Bolam test? Medico-Legal Journal 1996; 64(4):179–185.

Khan M. What's to become of medical negligence in England? Malayan Law Journal 1995; 3:1ix–1xiv.

Lewis CJ. Bolitho revisited by Joyce. Medico-Legal Journal 1996; 64(4):174–178.

Malcolm DK. The High Court and informed consent: the *Bolam* principle abandoned. Tort Law Review 1994; 7:81–98.

Norrie KM. Medical negligence: who sets the standard? Journal of Medical Ethics 1985; 11(3):135–137.

Stauch MS, Tingle J, Wheat K. Sourcebook on medical law. 2nd edn. London: Cavendish Publishing; 2002.

Teff H. Standard of care in medical negligence – moving on from Bolam? Oxford Journal of Legal Studies 1998; 18:473–484.

Tickner K. Rogers v Whitaker – giving patients a meaningful choice. Oxford Journal of Legal Studies 1995; 15:109–118.

Yeo S. The standard of care in medical negligence cases. Malayan Law Review 1993; 25:30–49.

Chapter 5

Medico-crime in the UK: an introduction

Wendy Hesketh

CHAPTER CONTENTS

Definition of medico-crime 94

Reasons why medico-crime occurs 95

The current confusion between professional incompetence and medico-crime 98

Managing problem doctors 99

Resistance to change in self-regulation 100

Why preserve the status quo? 102

Recommendations for change 104

Statistics and monitoring 104

Involving the police 105

Police–health professions–CPS protocol 105

National Framework for Medico-crime 106

Public re-education/crime prevention 106

Specific legislation 106

The use of chaperones 107

Revalidation and its limitations 107

Conclusion 108

References 109

Further reading 110

A number of recent high profile cases have forced into public debate the issue of crimes committed by health professionals, but although new cases of *medico-crime* are reported regularly in the press, there is insufficient academic debate on the issue in the UK at present. Medico-crime is an important yet understudied area. The overall aim of this chapter then is to introduce the subject of medico-crime in the UK as a new topic in health law for the first time. Although many of the case examples used in this chapter involve doctors (mostly GPs, who are the most regulated in the whole of the medical profession), it should be remembered that all health professionals have, to more or less a degree, the means to commit medico-crime. Thus, this chapter should be of interest to anyone working in healthcare or the law relating to healthcare.

This chapter provides an introduction to the subject of medico-crime in the UK. The concept of medico-crime is defined and the reasons why medico-crime occurs are highlighted. There is a brief discussion of the current confusion between professional incompetence and medico-crime, with comment on how professional self-regulation has been expected to address both. This is followed by discussion of the current aims of health regulation. From this debate on self-regulation, it becomes apparent that the government is facing a dilemma: it is now being expected to reform medical self-regulation in light of a series of scandals. However, it may be reluctant to do so because this would alter the traditional contract between the state and medical profession (which has worked well for decades). A third option is advocated: differentiating criminal doctors from clinically incompetent doctors, in order to address the problem of medico-crime without altering too drastically the health-regulation landscape. This is followed by some practical examples as to how this could be achieved.

DEFINITION OF MEDICO-CRIME

A definition of the term *medico-crime* as introduced in this chapter is essential in an attempt at conceptual clarity. As with members of the general public, there are a huge variety of crimes that health professionals can commit. Crime committed by members of the medical profession can be divided into two categories. These are: 'everyday crime', committed by doctors as committed by any other citizen; and 'medical crime', committed by doctors as facilitated by their professional status.[1] In the second category, which is herein termed *medico-crime*, two distinct sub-categories are hereby established: medico-crime committed by health professionals against patients directly (*medico-patient crime*); and medico-crime which relates to the unlawful use of the health professional status to commit crimes within the medical context *other than* those that chiefly involve direct harm against specific patient victims (*medico-professional crime*): such as altering patient records; completing official documents required by a health professional (in order to pursue/conceal other medico-crimes); NHS funding fraud; misuse of prescription drugs; organ trafficking etc.

Although it will not be unusual for both medico-patient crime and medico-professional crime to be committed in conjunction with one another, perhaps even concurrently (for example, Shipman not only murdered patients by lethal doses of diamorphine, he also falsified their medical records, falsified patient visiting books, unlawfully obtained and used controlled drugs, stole items of his victims' jewellery and falsified his last victim's will), it is important to the development of an overall theory of medico-crime that its constituent elements can be distinguished. That noted, the cases that are most often reported in the media (some of which will be mentioned briefly later in this chapter) are at first glance essentially examples of medico-patient crime, in that there are a number of specific patients who are the victims of the most serious types of crime committed in the medical context. However, it will be seen during later discussion of why medico-crime occurs that medico-patient crimes tend to be *facilitated by* the medico-professional crimes underpinning them. The professional status of the role therefore clearly provides not simply 'opportunities', but *facilitates* the commission of such crimes and conceals them afterwards.

REASONS WHY MEDICO-CRIME OCCURS

The notion of opportunity, which, in the generally held consensus, creates the circumstances that criminal doctors rely on in order to commit crime, relies on *chance*. However, it is argued here that doctors do not exploit *chances* in order to commit medico-patient crime, their role frees them from any impediment in committing those crimes. This point is *the* distinguisher: the professional status does not simply create chance/opportunity to commit medico-crime, it makes medico-crime *possible*, to an extent that goes beyond mere chance. Such lack of impediment ('free-from-restraint' access) afforded by the professional status is *the* factor which differentiates the health professional and the lay criminal and is thus a major consideration of crime in the medical context (for further discussion of opportunity in the medical context, see Stark et al[2]).

The ability to commit and conceal crime due to professional status within the medical context is explicable by a number of factors (evidence that the role has an important organisational/cultural dimension; is multifaceted and not simply a 'job' which creates opportunistic circumstances). These factors include: the intimate nature of the doctor–patient relationship;[1] the vulnerability of patients connected with their requiring medical treatment, as well as being vulnerable for other reasons such as mental health or age (which are well-accepted features of vulnerability in the capacity to consent to medical treatment discourse); the access afforded to such professionals; the tradition of allowing the medical profession to self-regulate; and, crucially, the fact that certain, normally illegal, pursuits are *made lawful* when carried out by health professionals.[3]

Firstly, it is well accepted in the traditional doctor–patient relationship discourse and medical law texts that doctors have an institutionalised dominance over patients.[4] This form of paternalism, where doctors act *on behalf* of patients' interests (see, for example, texts or cases relating to consent to medical treatment), creates an imbalance of power which is regarded as proper in this instance, but which is perhaps uncommon in other, one-to-one adult relationships. Another aspect of the doctor–patient relationship that is uncommon is that it is both private (even personal), yet not marked by the usual familiarity or acquaintance of other private relationships: doctors and patients are often essentially strangers who are obliged to be intimate. Yet, essentially, this obligation of stranger intimacy is marked by an imbalance of power, highlighting the scope for potential abuse.

Secondly, the term 'patient' in the archaic sense means 'one who suffers'.[5] Patients, even in the modern sense, are seeking treatment or care *from* the doctor or other health professional. Such patients might be children or adults, have no mental impairment or have a mental disorder, they may be self-assured or emotionally vulnerable in some way. Whatever their particular circumstances, however, they present themselves to a doctor for treatment or care. The doctor or other health professional therefore has something that the patient *needs*. This factor also renders patients susceptible to abuse. See, for example, patient Jacqui Godden's experience.[6] Allegedly, Ms Godden was obliged to submit to intimate examinations fortnightly for three years if she wanted her repeat prescription for tranquillisers renewed by Dr Clifford Ayling.

Thirdly, in order to carry out their role effectively, health professionals are expected to take their skills and equipment into a variety of locations, extending the 'medical context' parameters from institutions such as hospitals and GP surgeries to clinics, health centres and even patients' homes. In fact, anywhere that health professionals ostensibly carry out their role creates a 'medical context'. Essentially, given the above, patients rely on doctors and other health professionals for care, which means that patients are obliged to accept unprecedented intimacy with an institutionally more dominant stranger (a dominance that extends to patients' homes and even their minds, in the case of mental health patients). There is therefore clearly scope for an abuse in this type of relationship.

The fourth problem, in terms of scope for abuse within the doctor–patient relationship, is that the medical profession has traditionally been expected to regulate itself.[7] In practice, professional bodies, such as the General Medical Council (GMC) and the Royal College of General Practitioners (RCGP), for example, create and enforce professional regulation. They do this by restricting who gets to practise medicine, issuing professional codes of conduct and disciplining members who breach these professional codes. Professional self-regulation is accepted mainly because the medical profession alone possess the technical knowledge of medicine, an understanding of the medical environment (made unique by the profession's technical monopoly and attendant ethical codes) and, as appointed, seemingly intelligent and ethical professionals can be expected to act *responsibly*.[8]

Fifthly, although professional institutions such as the GMC and RCGP are responsible for ensuring standards and disciplining members, the main feature of professionalism is autonomy. This means that the majority of health professionals undertake various tasks unassisted. For example, general practitioners are responsible for their own patient lists, even when they are one of several partners in a large, modern practice.

This professional independence on a daily basis is heightened (from a medico-crime perspective) by the tendency of the law to make doctors a 'special case'.[7] Doctors, for example, are permitted by law to handle and administer otherwise dangerous drugs (even if this means administering lethal doses with the intention of 'alleviating pain'), to pierce strangers' skin, to penetrate strangers' bodies with their fingers, and to record details of such acts and other confidential facts about strangers. Doctors are also expected to establish cause of deaths and opine on whether a person has been sexually assaulted etc. These are just some examples where doctors have the legally recognised and accepted autonomy to carry out and record acts which, outside of the medical context, are normally associated with the most serious crimes in our society. Essentially, this means that doctors are allowed to act in ways that, for lay people, would be contravening the law, which of course raises the possibility that doctors have the means not only to commit the most heinous of crimes, but also to pass them off as lawful (realised with horrific consequences in the Shipman case, see above).

Thus, when combined, these various factors suggest that professional privilege creates an intimate relationship that has an inherent imbalance of power and allows doctors to undertake otherwise illegal activities and to document them as lawful, which introduces the possibility of an abuse of that professional power. Unfortunately, this notion (of the possibility of the abuse of professional power vested in the medical profession) is not merely hypothetical: there are a number of decided criminal cases involving health professionals who have murdered, raped and sexually assaulted high numbers of their patients (e.g. doctors Harold Shipman, Clifford Ayling, Timothy Healy, Michael Haslam and David Baillie and nurses Ronald Mason, Paul Cobb and Beverly Allitt).

To summarise, medico-patient crime is crime committed against patients by doctors (which could be committed by a lay person against any victim), but is committed and concealed *because* it is facilitated by the 'special case' approach of the law (and society) to doctors. By being committed *in conjunction with* medico-professional crime(s) (that is, doctors abusing the special treatment afforded to them by using their powers for illegal purposes) medico-patient crime is therefore dependent upon medico-professional crime being committed. Medico-patient crime causes the same *type* of harm as crime committed by the lay criminal, but what differentiates the medico-criminal from the lay criminal is what is generally termed 'opportunity' (and has been discussed in criminological theory as such, (see, for example, Friedrichs[9]).

Thus, the 'professional' aspect of the role (within the medical context), and its attendant privileges that put a doctor above the law, is nothing to do with chance. Such privileges create a distinction between lay crime and medico-crime, regardless if the harm done (i.e. the ultimate result is rape, murder etc.) is the same as that of lay criminals'. In any event, although the *type* of crime might be the same, the 'harm done' aspect is usually substantially greater in the case of medico-criminals because they have the opportunity to commit the harm much more frequently and remain undetected for far longer than other criminals simply due to their ability to conceal their crimes. Patient victims and their families might also be considered to suffer more harm as the result of medico-crime than lay crime, because they will most likely be faced with having to assume the patient role again in future (albeit with another doctor).

The professional privileges that facilitate medico-crime (when abused) should therefore be a major theme of any proposals for change geared to protecting patients from medico-crime. This chapter, however, is only a first step to introduce the problem of medico-crime: an initial attempt at prompting a cultural shift by acknowledging that a problem exists. As a result, suggested proposals for change later in this chapter will concentrate principally on those creating a cultural shift through public education and state recognition of the problem, whereas additional specific recommendations, to address medico-professional crime through sophisticated monitoring procedures (as a mechanism for ensuring patient safety), will be the result of future work.

What has been highlighted here, so far, is that doctors have a privileged position both legally and culturally and that this renders patients vulnerable to abuse. The major point to be deduced thus far is a simple one: in order to prevent medico-patient crime, medico-professional crime has to be addressed. That is, how to stop health professionals from abusing their privileged position and/or how to allow them to work, without affording them such privileges per se. Before such questions can be addressed, it is necessary to examine in more detail some of the problems associated with professional self-regulation that have allowed some of the worst cases of serial offending the UK has ever known to arise within the medical profession.

THE CURRENT CONFUSION BETWEEN PROFESSIONAL INCOMPETENCE AND MEDICO-CRIME

Although it seems almost banal once indicated, one major point that seems to have been overlooked to date is that professional self-regulation was designed to deal with professional misconduct, not medico-crime. That is, medical self-regulation was designed to detect and discipline members who fail to act in a *professional* manner. Although committing acts of medico-crime can be considered as acting 'unprofessionally', it is hardly a logical extension (or indeed a fair expectation) that self-regulatory bodies are expected to take responsibility for the criminal actions of some doctors.

Arguably, it is unfair to criticise the GMC or to expect it, or any other regulatory body, to attempt to control crime. Crime is traditionally the realm of the criminal justice system, yet (as has been apparent after e.g. the Shipman and Ayling cases), the GMC has been criticised because its regulatory procedures have not dealt effectively with medico-crime. This seems to beg the question, 'does such criticism amount to an expectation that criminal medical professionals are to be treated *separately* from other criminals who are dealt with by the criminal justice system?' Indeed, this assumption, that doctors are *different* and should be treated separately from other criminals, is evidenced by the furore that followed the case of GP Harold Shipman, who was found by a public inquiry to have murdered at least 215 of his patients (the last victim's death being in 1998). It would seem, from that furore, that there was a state (and perhaps public) expectation that self-regulation should have controlled Shipman (and thus, medico-crime in general). See, for example, the view taken by Henry Palin, Treasury Solicitor to The Shipman Inquiry, in a leaked 'salmon' letter regarding the GMC for its policies pre- and post-Shipman (i.e. a letter which gives organisations advance warning of criticisms likely to be levelled against them).[10]

Yet, despite the view implied by the criticisms levelled at the GMC (and the medical profession in general) post-Shipman, self-regulation should never have been expected to tackle medico-crime. Further, if this point had been reflected upon in any depth, it is unlikely that there would be a general consensus that medico-criminals should be dealt with *outside* the criminal justice system. It therefore seems pertinent to discuss how such a confusion (that is, in the expectation that the GMC should have prevented/detected criminal doctors such as Shipman) ever arose.

Managing problem doctors

It is fair to say that self-regulation was designed to manage 'problem doctors'. However, the moot point is that there are actually two issues here: two completely different types of problem doctor. The first issue concerns *clinically incompetent* doctors. They might be incompetent for a number of reasons: ill health, drug or alcohol abuse, lack of interest or lack of up-to-date skills. The other issue is doctors who *commit crime* in their job role, for example doctors like Shipman or Ayling, who have murdered or sexually assaulted their patients.

These two issues (criminal and incompetent doctors) tend to get confused because they are lumped together when policies are set up or procedures refined to catch such 'problem doctors'. For example, the Channel 4 documentary report on the Ayling case showed not only interviews with victims who claimed to have been sexually assaulted by Ayling, but also a victim who experienced a brutal delivery of her baby by forceps, resulting in her baby's death.[11] Regrettably, no-one seems to have taken the required objective view that the incompetent doctor and the criminal doctor are two very separate issues that cannot be dealt with by the same procedures. Instead, there has been the misguided assumption that incompetence and crime can be detected in the same way. Not only does this cause confusion to patient victims who do not know how to alert the relevant authority to incidents of medico-crime, but neither the medical profession nor the criminal justice agencies are quite sure who should take responsibility for preventing or detecting such cases. Moreover, in the wake of the Shipman (and other medico-crime) scandals, the majority of trustworthy, hardworking doctors are being overburdened by an increase in professional self-regulation that seeks to both monitor professional incompetence and medico-crime. Some of these problems arising from this current confusion will now be examined.

Victims do not seem to realise (see, for example, the witnesses' testimonies in the Ayling case reports, details above), especially when sexually assaulted by a doctor, that they should go to the police directly. If patient victims *do* go to the police, the police might decide that it is a matter for the medical profession to deal with and direct the patient back to the medical profession. If, however, the police actually decide to investigate, they tread very carefully because they risk damaging the medical professional's career. See, for example, the testimony of DI Smith concerning the initial police investigation into the Shipman murders.[12] If the police decide to undertake a rigorous investigation of any allegations of medico-crime, they have to seek the help of medical professionals. As can be seen from the original Shipman investigation, the police need help to obtain and decipher medical records and medical jargon. At the moment, this sort of reciprocal liaison between the local police and the medical profession is done on an ad hoc basis.

Medico-crime does not feature in policing plans (despite the UK's most prolific serial killer being a doctor and there being other examples of doctors who have sexually assaulted large numbers of patients repeatedly for many years). Moreover, the GMC has been criticised for failing to prevent, for example, Shipman's murders. This suggests that it is not just victims who get confused between crime and professional misconduct by doctors, even the professionals and legal system are confused about who should bear responsibility in cases involving medico-crime.

Obviously, therefore, there should be a clear definition of types of incompetence and types of medico-crime. This should allow the creation of two separate tracks for dealing with these distinct problems. Clinical incompetence should be dealt with by the medical profession, which is the best body for recognising poor performance, but crime (even when committed by doctors) should not be left up to the medical profession, unsupported, to deal with. Medico-crime should be the preserve of the criminal justice system.

Complaints procedures, annual appraisals, revalidation and professional guides are sound ways of detecting professional incompetence, but they are not designed to catch criminals. Nor should such self-regulation systems be criticised for failing to detect criminal doctors. Clearly, the criminal justice system needs to take a more proactive involvement in catching criminal doctors. This point will be returned to later in the chapter under 'Recommendations for change'. Before discussing proposals for change, however, it is necessary to evaluate why professional self-regulation has been acceptable thus far, in an attempt to glean potential resistance to any new proposals.

Resistance to change in self-regulation

Much of the prevalent health regulation discourse (see for example, Salter[13]) focuses on allocation: the 'demand–supply conundrum', and analysing the resultant *triangular relationship* between the state, the profession and the citizen (as patient). Basically, by providing a National Health Service, the state fulfils its welfare duty in relation to the citizen (thus satisfying voters, in the hope of re-election) and relies on the profession to manage the demand–supply tension by doctors making treatment decisions on an individual basis at the 'front line'. The medical profession ensures that the appropriate standard of care is delivered by its members and in return receives the trust of citizens and the privilege from the state to regulate itself, gaining social and economic advantages. The citizen receives the right to free medical treatment of the appropriate standard (in the UK) in return for relinquishing control to government and for paying taxes out of earnings. This trilateral relationship is complicated by the fact that standard of care is dependent upon the skill of the individual doctor and also upon the availability of resources on a national level.[13]

Although it is accepted that the demand–supply dilemma at national or local level, or the appropriateness of standards or skill in relation to medical treatment, do not have much relevance in relation to medico-crime per se, this trilateral arrangement and what the parties get from it is nevertheless important in understanding the challenge of adding medico-crime to the equation.

Fundamentally, regulation is a mechanism for controlling perceived markets. The relevant market here being the healthcare market. Regulation of the healthcare market includes regulation of health professionals who are the suppliers of a service within that market. There are different forms of regulation: the NHS is an example of state-administered regulation and the doctor occupation itself is a form of professional self-regulation, which operates with state approval.

There are many examples of medico-crime which fit under the two main heads (professional/patient crime) discussed earlier in this chapter. Those crimes that have financial and/or obviously political implications that might directly affect the state can reasonably be expected to be identified for centralised control by the state, using quite restrictive legislation. Similarly, clinical incompetence, an activity that could potentially damage the reputation of the profession, could justly be expected to be dealt with as a routine regulatory task (the task of market entry and exit) by the profession itself, with state approval. The profession achieves this by using a range of regulatory styles, from the permissive in the form of ethical guidance, to techniques such as discretion in market entry and ranging to the more restrictive form of discipline for existing practitioners. An example of the latter would be professional conduct procedures and sanctions such as dismissal from practice.

Any conduct issues amounting to crime (especially against patients directly) that cannot be dealt with by the profession, perhaps because they are so serious and publicly controversial as to threaten the reputation of the profession as a whole (despite the attempted self-regulatory action), might also potentially threaten the state politically. Once *made public*, such serious medico-crime (the Shipman case is a prime example) would therefore compel state-administered regulation through the criminal justice system, invoking formal legal mechanisms and criminal sanctions in order to preserve the status quo (both within and outwith the healthcare market). In exceptionally serious (that is, politically sensitive) cases, government might set up an institution, an Inquiry usually, in order to deal with the task of appearing, in the eyes of the public, to regain control of the situation. It should be noted, however, that the response of the state is *reactive*: the detection/prevention of a 'problem' (even criminal) doctor like Shipman was expected to have been achieved by the self-regulation process. It was only when the case became public and the enormity (and politically sensitive nature) of the case revealed, that the state stepped in to regain control. This suggests that the state expects the profession to deal with 'problem doctors' as a whole, even detecting criminal actions, but that the state will act to regain control if a case threatens to affect the government politically.

One final point here, relating again to the current reactive approach of the state to medico-crime, is that although there have now been a number of private and public inquiries set up to examine medico-crime cases (e.g. the circumstances surrounding the crimes committed by Harold Shipman, Michael Haslam, William Kerr, Clifford Ayling and Peter Green), there has been no agency set up to examine the cross-findings of these cases. Setting up some sort of committee, perhaps, to investigate a number of medico-crime cases, in order to look for a commonality of systems failures that allowed these doctors' criminal actions to go undetected for so long, does not even seem to have been considered to date.

WHY PRESERVE THE STATUS QUO?

There has been much discussion in the media recently (see Clennell)[10] resulting in changes to self-regulation (see, for example, new revalidation policies introduced by the GMC post-Shipman). However, it must be remembered that the traditional triangular relationship between the state, the medical profession and the citizen has had benefits for all parties to the relationship. The reason why the state might be reluctant to completely abolish professional self-regulation in relation to the medical profession is that the state continues to want the medical profession to take (at least ostensible) responsibility for resource allocation. It is also useful for the state (from a voters' appeasement perspective) to allow citizens to believe that the medical profession is responsible for dealing with all 'problem doctors' so that when things do go wrong, citizens turn their criticism on the medical profession rather than the Government. This only works, however, if the problem can reasonably be expected to be contained within the profession itself. If a problem (for example, the Shipman case) becomes a major public concern, the state can step into the forefront and the public view of the state as the 'protector' (rather than the defaulter) is enhanced. The problem with the recent *series* of scandals reported in the media, involving the medical profession in the past five to ten years in the UK, is that such scandals seem likely to erode public confidence in self-regulation as a *whole*. There is arguably now an expectation that the Government should address the concept of medical self-regulation in light of a series of 'failures' of the profession to control problem doctors. This expectation is hardly surprising, given that the confusion relating to what self-regulation was designed for has been allowed to flourish. However, this situation is now beginning to backfire.

Self-regulation was designed to root out clinical incompetence and, crucially, it also benefits Government to allow citizens to believe that the medical profession is in control of resource allocation within the NHS (in the hope that citizens blame individual doctors rather than the Government when their access to treatment is restricted). By not even considering the possibility that 'problem doctors' involves two distinct issues (clinically incompetent and criminal doctors), however, the state has been caught off-guard by the recent series of medico-crime scandals. In self-preservation mode, the Government is on the defensive (see, for example, the Shipman Inquiry's criticisms of the GMC and other agencies). The major problem is that now the Government is expected to increase its central control of the medical profession by reforming professional self-regulation, in order to restore public confidence in patient safety. However, any change to self-regulation will obviously impact upon the public perception of doctors as resource allocators (a situation that the government will want to resist). The solution lies in making a distinction between clinical incompetence and medico-crime (a fact that seems to have been overlooked by Government and the profession). In any event, it might be argued that the major concern of the Government is not how to protect patients against these two distinct types of problem doctors (which it is attempting by generic reform of self-regulation), but how to retain the ostensible resource allocation role of doctors on the front line. That is, the state is more intent on the dilemma of how to allow the medical profession enough autonomy to be perceived by the public as resource allocators within the NHS, whilst at the same time taking control in order to prevent any further public scandals.

To summarise, the state's main concern in the self-regulation debate is the continued public perception of doctors as resource allocators within the NHS. This role requires autonomy. The notion of the medical profession as autonomous resource allocators is, however, incongruous with the control that the state is now expected (in light of a series of medical scandals; see Further reading for examples) to exert in relation to 'problem doctors'. The state is aware that in relation to clinical incompetence, the profession itself is the best body to determine and address incompetence (see earlier comments on the profession's monopoly over medicine). However, there has been a misguided assumption that the profession should also address criminal doctors as 'problem doctors'. From a medico-crime perspective, the answer is a simple one: make a distinction between clinical incompetence and medico-crime and delegate responsibility accordingly (to the medical profession and criminal justice system respectively). This suggestion would satisfy all parties to the current triangular relationship and would surely be preferable to a complete overhaul of self-regulation. Thus, the medical profession retains autonomy in relation to clinical incompetence, the state increases central control of criminal doctors via the criminal justice system. Patient safety is increased by reducing patient-victim confusion about medico-crime complaints and, most importantly for the state, this idea would satisfy the state requirement of keeping doctors as ostensible resource allocators. This last point is important when considering proposals for reform.

A major proposal (as discussed in more detail later in this chapter) to effect a cultural shift in how we view the problem of medico-crime might involve public re-education. Any education that increases the public's knowledge of how doctors work, or which encourages patients to question a doctor's authority, might be suspected (by the state) of encouraging patients to have more of a say in their medical treatment. The suspicion that any increase in patient knowledge might close the doctor–patient knowledge gap will be resisted unless reassurance can be given that public re-education will not extend to patients beginning to question the suitability or availability of medical treatment.

Again, this is associated with the confusion surrounding the current lack of distinction between clinical incompetence and medico-crime. Public re-education, to teach patients the signs of medico-crime and how to report it, is not the same as giving patients the knowledge to question the quality or availability of treatment on offer (clinical competence/allocation issues). It must be conceded, however, that giving patients a voice, *any voice* (i.e. in relation to medico-crime as opposed to in relation to clinical competence issues) marks a change in the balance of power within the doctor–patient relationship. Some might argue that it would result in the erosion of trust in that relationship. In anticipation of those concerns, it should be remembered that the media has already begun to give patients a voice[14] by reporting a series of medical scandals in the last decade and that these scandals, especially the Shipman case, have eroded that once-implicit trust patients might have had in doctors anyway. In light of this, the Government might be receptive to proposals for change in how medico-crime is addressed, including proposals involving public education. This and other proposals for change will now be considered in more detail.

RECOMMENDATIONS FOR CHANGE

Statistics and monitoring

Primarily, too little is known about the problem of medico-crime. It is such a novel idea in the UK that even the scope and dimensions of the problem are not properly understood. Although the GMC is routinely informed by the police each time a doctor is charged with a criminal offence, the GMC does not keep a database containing this information. There are also no criminal statistics that illustrate numbers of crimes committed by doctors (despite the fact that Shipman's crimes radically altered the homicide rate in the UK for two decades). A better understanding of the problem could be achieved in the following ways: firstly, a committee could be set up by the Government to investigate a number of decided medico-crime cases, in order to look for a commonality of systems failures. This would allow a proactive approach to addressing the problem in future. Secondly, a medico-crime database could be established in order to generate statistics illustrating the scope of the problem.

At present, the responsibility for managing 'problem doctors' (undistinguished) lies with the organisation that holds the doctors' contract. Currently, health authorities hold the contracts for GPs. Problem doctors come to management attention in a number of ways: reactively (by complaints or concerns raised by other health professionals or patients); or proactively, by monitoring systems. When a problem doctor comes to the attention of a local management panel, a decision has to be made whether they investigate, report the case to the National Clinical Assessment Authority (NCAA) or the General Medical Council (GMC).

Involving the police

Those cases reported which involve medico-crime should always involve the GMC to some extent. However, this depends at present on the local management team investigating initial complaints and recognising that a criminal offence (or a serious risk to patient safety) has actually been committed. This means that the reporting of crime committed by doctors currently depends on the efficiency of local management procedures in the first instance. The GMC only becomes involved when the matter is alerted to its attention and might rely on the initial investigation by the local management team to decide how to proceed. The possibility of police involvement is sometimes therefore a last option.

Police–health professions–CPS protocol

At present, crimes such as sexual assault committed by doctors are often referred to as 'professional misconduct' or 'professional abuse' and not reported directly to the police. Victims wrongly believe that the correct action is to use NHS complaints procedures. The police often think that NHS complaints procedures should be used in some of these cases too. When the police do investigate, they have no training to decipher medical records or question a doctor's conduct rigorously enough: they have to rely on help from other medical professionals. Understandably, these medical professionals might feel uncomfortable being asked to help convict a colleague of a crime.

Medico-crime is evidently difficult to detect without specialist training in the medical context (the initial police investigation into the Shipman murders is a case in point). Sexual assault and rape cases, for example, are always difficult to prove because they often hinge upon the victim's word against that of the accused. This fact is exacerbated when committed in the medical context because doctors (who are pillars of the community) can claim to have been carrying out a legitimate breast check or internal examination and they can write this in the patient's notes to back up their defence. The police need specific training therefore to allow them to investigate properly allegations of crime in the medical context. This would require training in, for example, what legitimate intimate medical procedures should consist of and how to understand the main medical documentation etc. Specialist officers, with enhanced training in investigation techniques in the medical context, could develop a working relationship with appointed medical experts in the NHS who would take full-time responsibility for helping to investigate medical crime. The Crown Prosecution Service (CPS) could also provide training in medical issues to its case assessors. This system of working could be worked out in a formal protocol.

National Framework for Medico-crime

A National Framework for Medico-crime could provide a forum for discussion of problems and possible solutions by health experts and patient groups. This might determine, for example, the investigatory process into allegations of crimes against patients. Additionally, police should keep a record of allegations (rather than rely on professional records kept by the GMC) and these records should be kept for a minimum of 40 years. The keeping of records would allow for cross-checking of that doctor's history of criminal allegations, even if the doctor moves to a new post. If more than one allegation is made against a doctor at any time, this would hopefully instigate a full and immediate review of that doctor's practice, including scrutiny of patient records, regardless of the time period between the allegations. A National Framework for Medico-Crime Advisory Committee could set up and analyse the success of the police–health professions–CPS protocol.

Public re-education/crime prevention

Patients could be protected by public re-education: informing the public (perhaps by public broadcasts, poster and leaflets etc.) that if they think a doctor has committed a criminal offence against them, then this is a matter for the police. The police and medical profession should also take this view. The form of public education here would be more akin to traditional crime prevention advice (e.g. of the type provided by the Suzy Lamplugh Trust[15]), which might dispel concerns about possible increased patients' demands for medical treatment.

Specific legislation

The medico-professional crimes that doctors can commit, such as breaches of their professional regulations that involve keeping of records, the administering of controlled drugs etc., should be made more specific, in one piece of legislation. Additionally, medico-patient crime (those crimes that are committed against patients directly) should also be formally acknowledged in new or existing legislation. For example, The Sexual Offences Act 2003[16] specifically makes it illegal for people in a position of trust, including doctors, to engage in sexual activity with a child or persons with a mental disorder. This legislation should be extended to make it a specific offence for doctors to engage in sexual activity with *any* patient, because (as has been shown in the Ayling case) even competent adults are vulnerable in the doctor–patient relationship.

The use of chaperones

It is clear from the Ayling case (Clifford Ayling was charged with 13 assaults on 10 women patients) that an untrained chaperone can offer no more protection than no chaperone at all; Ayling continued to sexually assault patients with a chaperone present. The chaperone was his sister-in-law, who stood with her back to the patient and Ayling whenever the so-called examinations took place. Even if she had witnessed what Ayling was doing with his hands on the patient's body, it is doubtful whether she would have been able to distinguish between touching for clinical purposes and sexual assault (this point, distinguishing between touching of a sexual nature and a legitimate clinical examination, is an important one and highlights the need for public and police education on such procedures). Clearly, properly trained and independent chaperones, who have the time to speak with the patient in private and make notes after any intimate examination, are urgently required.

Revalidation and its limitations

The Government had planned to introduce relicensing and revalidation in 2005 but, with the agreement of the GMC, has postponed this until completion of a review of issues raised by Dame Janet Smith in the fifth report of the Shipman Inquiry. Nonetheless, valuable insight into what may be in store can be gained from examining the proposals that were about to be put in place. At the centre of these is the idea that doctors would have to have a licence to practise which would be up for review every five years. If doctors are in a multi-partner practice, revalidation material can be collected through (government-introduced) annual appraisal schemes. If in a sole practice, or e.g. a company doctor, a doctor will have to collect the information for revalidation individually, based on the Guide to Good Medical Practice (for GPs, this is based on the Royal College of Practitioners' guide[17]).

The GMC says that it is also developing a patient satisfaction questionnaire and a professional colleague survey and that these documents will help doctors provide information under the headings of 'Relationships with patients' and 'Working with colleagues'). These questionnaires are a good idea, *if* they are confidential and are used as a way of allowing other doctors and patients to express their views about a doctor's performance. What needs to be clear, however, is whether these questionnaires will focus on clinical competence only, or whether they will ask questions directly about crime doctors can commit. And if so, whether any information collected from these confidential questionnaires filled in about doctors by their colleagues and patients will be passed on to the police, so that the GMC and the police can work together. This raises a confidentiality issue: it seems helpful if surveys are conducted by anonymous questionnaire so that people will be open about the answers they give, but this causes a problem with how to investigate claims in order to substantiate any allegations of crime. If there are allegations of crime, *how* are such allegations to be investigated and what triggers an investigation: one allegation of a serious crime, or more than one?

This is an example of where a definite police–health professions protocol would be invaluable.

Revalidation is simply a *competence-based* approach to assessing a doctor's practice. Evidence is likely to be made up of various components, including self-evaluation, peer evaluation and observation by others (e.g. practice partners, patients and managers). The evidence is likely to be collected by the doctor, who thus has to decide what is included in the portfolio. Doctors will obviously want to renew their licences, therefore they are obviously going to ensure that they include the 'good' evidence that will get them revalidated. Clearly, in the case of a criminal doctor (for example, Ayling), who had sexually assaulted patients, that doctor's records would not show 'assaults'; they would instead provide evidence that 'examinations' took place. The same doctor might request a chaperone on a few occasions whilst carrying out intimate examinations and put that evidence into the portfolio (perhaps leaving out all the instances where no chaperone was present).

The main problem with competence-based systems, therefore, is that there is a huge amount of information-gathering because evidence is required for each outcome to be tested and this has to be assessed. Where the doctor (in this case) has to provide, for example, witness statements or records to show that something has been done in a particular way, it is important to take heed of the fact that the doctor could have carried out tasks in a certain way for a short period of time, just to provide evidence of good practice. That gives a false picture of the doctor's practice. However, expecting to collect every piece of documentary evidence for every outcome of practice, for *every doctor* in the country, and then assess the *whole of each* doctor's practice, would be a huge, if not impossible task for the new revalidation procedures.

It is doubtful, therefore, whether revalidation, which is a test of a doctor's competence, will be effective in catching doctors who commit crime. Nevertheless, some evidence could prove useful in addressing medico-crime. For example, the evidence of relations with patients and colleagues, by way of confidential questionnaires or surveys of colleagues and patients, might be a useful tool to indicate criminal activity. Nevertheless, the confidentiality aspect remains problematic, as does the likelihood of such surveys being collected by doctors themselves as evidence of their own competence. Surveys and questionnaires would work best if there was an agreed procedure for using the results to investigate allegations of crime, by involving the police at an early stage. Consequently, the proposed revalidation procedures are likely to be effective as a test for clinical competence, but not in controlling medico-crime (unless that aim is made more specific from the outset).

CONCLUSION

Essentially, what should be apparent from this chapter is that there is an urgent need for a cultural shift. Medico-crime is *not* the same as professional incompetence: a new approach is required. Self-regulation should not be criticised for failing to prevent or detect medico-crime. The control of medico-crime is more appropriately a task for the criminal justice system (with more traditional, proactive crime prevention and detection techniques and specific legislation underpinning public awareness of the problem). This would allow the health profession to concentrate on what they do best (by self-regulation): dealing with clinical competence issues. Patient trust could then be restored, when their safety is more assured.

Acknowledgements

With thanks to Dr Gordon Marnoch, of the University of Ulster, for discussions on how an increase in patient knowledge might close the doctor–patient knowledge asymmetry gap, Grainne McKeever, also of Ulster, for discussions on medical ethics issues and Dr Dave Whyte, of the University of Leeds, for his comments that a police–CPS–health professions protocol would be akin to the one currently in place between the HSE–CPS–police in relation to Workplace Deaths. My original idea for a police–health professions protocol was published in The Police Journal.[3] With thanks to Mr Brian Dennehey of the GMC, who provided information by email to the effect that although the GMC is routinely informed by the police each time a doctor is charged with a criminal offence, the GMC does not keep a database containing numbers of GPs who commit criminal offences.

References

1. Dix A. Crime and misconduct in the medical profession. In: Smith RG, ed. Crime in the professions: Conference Proceedings of the Australian Institute of Criminology, 21–22 February 2000, University of Melbourne. Aldershot: Ashgate Publishing; 2002:67–78.
2. Stark C, Paterson B, Kidd B. Opportunity may be more important than profession in serial homicide. BMJ (London) 2001; 322:993.
3. Hesketh W. Medico-crime: Time for a police–health professions protocol? Channel Islands; The Police Journal 2003; 76(2):121–134.
4. Parsons T. Social structure and personality. London and New York: Free Press of Glencoe and Collier Macmillan; 1964.
5. Dictionary.com Definition of 'Patient' (noun 3). Available: http://dictionary.reference.com/search?q=patient 29 April 2004.
6. Bosley S. How did he get away with it for so long? The Guardian. Guardian Unlimited online 29 Apr 2002. Available: http://society.guardian.co.uk/primarycare/ story/0,8150,723198,00.html 29 April 2004.
7. Montgomery J. Professional regulation. Health care law. Oxford: Oxford University Press; 1997:135–163
8. Rosenthal M. The incompetent doctor behind closed doors. Buckingham: Open University Press; 1995:41–70.
9. Friedrichs DO. Trusted criminals: white collar crime in contemporary society. The Wadsworth Contemporary Issues in Crime and Justice Series. Belmont: Wadsworth; 2004.

10. Clennell A. Shipman Inquiry set to rebuke GPs' watchdog. Times Online 28 February 2004.

11. MacDonald V. Patients Unprotected. Channel 4 News Report on Clifford Ayling (online 4 March 2004). Available http://www.channel4.com/news/2004/03/week_1/04_doctor.html 29 April 2004.

12. Guardian Unlimited. Senior policeman admits being 'baffled' by Shipman case. [Internet – online news edition of newspaper], (27 May 2002). http://society.guardian.co.uk/nhsperformance/story/0,8150,723158,00.html 29 April 2004.

13. Salter B. Medical regulation and public trust: an international review. London: King's Fund; 2000:1–36

14. Williamson C. Whose standards? Consumer and professional standards in health care. Buckingham: Open University Press; 1992:1–39

15. The Suzy Lamplugh Trust. The leading authority on personal safety. Online. Available: http://www.suzylamplugh.org/home/index.shtml 29 April 2004.

16. The Sexual Offences Act 2003 Chapter 42. London: The Stationery Office; 2003. Online. Available http://www.legislation.hmso.gov.uk/acts/acts2003/20030042.htm 29 April 2004.

17. General Practitioners' Committee of the Royal College of General Practitioners. Good medical practice for general practitioners. September 2002. Online. Available: http://www.rcgp.org.uk/corporate/position/good_med_prac/GMP06.pdf 29 April 2004.

Further reading

Ananova. Ayling victims awarded damages. [Electronic news article, internet], 2002. Available: http://www.ananova.com/news/story/sm_564660.html?menu= 29 April 2004.

Ananova. Dirty doctor jailed for attacks on women, 2002. Online. Available: http://www.ananova.com/news/story/sm_150371.html?menu= 29 April 2004.

Ananova. Gynaecologist faces 33 sex charges. 11 Oct 2002. Online. Available: http://www.ananova.com/news/story/sm_205983.html?menu= 29 April 2004.

Ananova. Sex case doctor ordered struck off. [Electronic news article, internet], 2003. Available: http://www.ananova.com/news/story/sm_626153.html 29 April 2004.

BBC GMC: Guiding doctors. 19 November 2002. Online. Available: http://news.bbc.co.uk/1/hi/health/background_briefings/871484.stm 29 April 2004.

BBC News England. Detective 'struggled' with Shipman case. 27 May 2002. Online. Available: http://news.bbc.co.uk/1/hi/england/2010823.stm 29 April 2004

BBC News England. GP faces life for sex attacks. 2 August 2002. Online. Available: http://news.bbc.co.uk/1/hi/england/2168693.stm 29 April 2004.

BBC News England. GP on child porn charges. 17 June 2002. Online. Available: http://news.bbc.co.uk/1/hi/england/2050307.stm 29 April 2004.

BBC News England. Sex attack doctor jailed. 4 July 2002. Online. Available: http://news.bbc.co.uk/1/hi/england/2093610.stm.

Commission for Health Improvement. CHI investigation into Leicestershire Health Authority: issues arising from the case of Loughborough GP Peter Green, Executive summary. [Internet, website copy of report], August 2001. Available: http://www.chi.nhs.uk/eng/organisations/trent/leics_ha/2001/loughboro.pdf 29 April 2004.

Davis C A. 'Killer on the Ward'. [Internet magazine] (12 Oct 2002). Available: http://www.shotsmag.co.uk/Issue%2014%20index.htm#TOP 29 April 2004.

Friedrichs DO. Occupational crime, occupational deviance, and workplace crime: sorting out the difference. Criminal Justice: The International Journal of Policy and Practice 2002; 2(3):243–256.

General Medical Council. Revalidating doctors: ensuring standards, securing the future. London: GMC; 2000.

General Medical Council. Licence to practise and revalidation. London: GMC. Online. Available: http://www.gmc-uk.org/revalidation/licence_to_practice/questions_answered.htm 29 April 2004.

Guardian Unlimited. Sex case GP to face inquiry. (6 September 2002). Online. Available: http://society.guardian.co.uk/nhsperformance/story/0,8150,787580,00.html 29 April 2004

Hospital Doctor Online. GMC Committee Chair faces call to resign. [Internet edition of newspaper article], 28 November 2002. Available: http://www.hospitaldoctor.net/hd_news/hd_news_article.asp?ID=8647&Section=News 29 April 2004.

HSE, ACPO, and CPS. Work-related deaths: a protocol for liaison. 1999. Online. Available http://www.hse.gov.uk/pubns/misc491.pdf 29 April 2004.

Kelso P. Male nurse used sedative to kill and rape. Guardian 18 May 2000. Online. Available: http://www.guardian.co.uk/Archive/Article/0,4273,4019340,00.html 29 April 2004.

Matthews K. Nurse jailed for abusing patients. Brighton & Hove 10 August 2002. Online. Available: http://www.thisisbrighton.co.uk/brighton__hove/archive/2002/08/10/NEWS140ZM.html 29 April 2004.

Metropolitan Police. Policing & performance plan 2003 (12 March 2002). Online. Available: http://www.mpa.gov.uk/downloads/mpa-020321-06-appendix03.pdf 29 April 2004.

Montgomery J. Time for a paradigm shift? Medical law in transition. In: Freeman MDA, ed. Current legal problems, vol. 53. Oxford: Oxford University Press; 2000:363–407.

National Service Framework Zones. NHS online. Available: http://www.nelh.nhs.uk/nsf/29 April 2004.

Stark C, Sloan, D. Murder in the NHS: audit critical incidents in patients at risk. British Medical Journal 1994; 308:477.

The Shipman Inquiry. Smith, Dame Janet (Chairwoman), Transcript for Hearing Day 96. [Online transcript from public inquiry], 07 November 2002. Available: http://www.the-shipman-inquiry.org.uk/transcript.asp?from=a&day=96 29 April 2004.

SECTION TWO

Reproductive technologies

SECTION CONTENTS

6. New reproductive technologies – discourse and dilemma   115

7. Preimplantation genetic diagnosis – towards a principled construction of law?   133

Chapter 6

New reproductive technologies – discourse and dilemma

Susan C. Johnson

CHAPTER CONTENTS

Introduction   115
Dominant discourses   116
Situating women in the
   debate   117
Regulating reproduction   119

Designer babies – a case for
   regulating intimacy?   120
Empirical evidence   122
Regulating autonomy   126
Conclusions   128
References   128

INTRODUCTION

With the exponential rise in the discovery and use of reproductive genetic technologies, questions have been raised about how they are used. Although scientists have been able to modify the genes of other mammals for approximately a decade,[1,2] designing babies – the deliberate genetic modification of human beings – is not yet a scientific possibility. It should also be recognised that human genetic modification may never become a feasible intervention. Despite this, the idea that parents may one day be able to determine the physical, mental and social characteristics of their children before birth represents a dystopian future for many. This is true even though many of the issues raised in the pursuit of healthier children, better lives and increased opportunities are similar whatever means are used in achieving these goals. Consequently, the consideration of the issues surrounding human genetic modification and selection should not be seen as a consideration of issues *only* applicable to this topic. Instead human genetic modification is the end point of our scientific inquiry and, as the extreme, it epitomises and clarifies these issues and focuses our vision of what we want to achieve, and simplifies the judgements we make.

In October 2000, the prospect of 'designer babies' appeared to be one step closer with news of the birth of a baby boy in the United States.[3] Following in vitro fertilisation (IVF) treatment, the embryos produced were subject to preimplantation genetic diagnosis (PGD) in order to select an embryo that would not carry the disease-causing gene that affected the family's existing child. The embryos were also tissue-typed to ensure that the embryo used would become a child whose bone marrow would be suitable for treating his sister's condition. Although more accurately a 'donor baby' rather than a 'designer baby', the case of Adam Nash highlighted the ethical and legal questions that innovative reproductive genetic technologies could, and would, raise.

DOMINANT DISCOURSES

The rationale for tight controls to be maintained over assisted repro-genetic technologies hinges around the notion of genetic exceptionalism – genetic information is somehow 'special' and rather powerful. Genetic exceptionalism does not necessarily imply that genetic information is malignant per se, but that its *use* needs to be closely monitored and controlled. The prospect of the widespread use of human genetic modification and selection techniques has initiated a wide-ranging debate with contributions from scientific and medical professionals, policy-makers, ethicists, philosophers and pressure groups. Amongst these, three groups of discourses are dominant.[4]

Medical discourses are full of hype and hope about what may be achieved in reproductive genetics in years to come. The estimates of when human genetic modification may be achieved efficiently and safely vary depending on the optimism of the commentator concerned and may range from 'a decade or two'[5] down to 5 years.[6] In reality the time scale could well be much greater even than the former estimate. However, scientific breakthroughs may occur suddenly as was the case with somatic cell nuclear transfer (cloning) in 1997.[7] The optimism in medical discourses arises from a belief that genetic technologies will remove suffering caused by, and inherent in, all kinds of genetic disorders. They will enable medicine to remove the threat of debilitating diseases from families so that the spectre of a diagnosis of Huntington's disease, retinopathy, cystic fibrosis or muscular dystrophy will be eliminated – and society will be better for it. These discourses herald a time when mothers will no longer be faced with difficult decisions of whether to abort an affected pregnancy. Nor will their lives be 'blighted' through having to provide full time, life-long care for a child born with such a condition. In addition, the public purse will no longer have to provide services, day care, special schools and respite care for these people. The children themselves will be born happy, healthy and whole.

In contrast, disability discourses, while still buying into the medical discourse of great reproductive genetic potential, describe a very different world. Disabled people are secondary to their impairment[8] and will be subject to genetic cleansing. They face the threat of being eliminated from the gene pool. Affected embryos – future people – will be destroyed in an attempt to 'perfect' society. Those people already affected by impairment will be reviled and marginalised for being less than perfect;[9] for being a drain on the financial resources of society;[10,11] for being displeasing to the eye – a tragedy to be avoided at all cost.[12] The new genetics becomes the new eugenics.[13,14]

Closely allied with the disability discourses are those of feminists. Feminist discourses purport to recognise the problems faced by disabled people in a geneticised society.[15,16] Yet feminist discourses also describe a picture of vilification and blame for women who choose to ignore the dominant medical discourses and subsequently give birth to an affected child.[17] In these discourses women are passive victims of patriarchal medicalisation of reproductive processes,[18] or 'supermums' who suffer for their resistance against these interventions.

Of course, the risks of using genetic modification techniques are not confined to their societal effects, but may also be influenced by whether or not they meet the accepted standards of safety and efficacy. While there is some recognition that the prospects of human genetic modification are great, and the benefits may be manifold, the most important objections to interventions in the human genome are that they are either unsafe, or their consequences unpredictable. The current state of scientific knowledge and technology means that safety and efficacy cannot be guaranteed at this time; even conventional assisted reproductive techniques may carry the risk of some imprinting disorders.[19] When innovative technologies are introduced, questions of safety are the most important factors in assessing acceptability. Many of the arguments against human reproductive cloning, for example, reflect the low rate of success for the procedure.[20,21] To proceed with an intervention that is inherently unsafe is unethical practice, and even where a procedure may appear to be safe, there may be non-immediate and unforeseen dangers. It is also important to recognise that the ethical debate at a time when safety and uncertainty are issues is very different from the debate that arises once experimental procedures become clinically possible.

SITUATING WOMEN IN THE DEBATE

The dominant discourses – those that are most often heard and most widely supported – originate from academic debate, and are perpetuated in popular culture and media.[22] Despite this, there is very little evidence of public engagement with the debates surrounding genetic technologies. The Human Genetics Advisory Commission (HGAC), in collaboration with the Human Fertilisation and Embryology Authority, stressed the need for public information and debate in this area in order to legitimise the development of new genetic technologies.[23] Yet, when the House of Commons Science and Technology Committee opened up the debate on human reproductive technologies to 'the public', this sparked controversy.[24] Among the objections raised was the suggestion that the public should not be involved where they are 'coming cold to a topic' because it is difficult for them to 'understand the issues and how these translate into practicalities in terms of drawing lines in clinical practice or the law'.[25]

Yet I have carried out research that suggests that women are not 'coming cold' to the subject, but have followed the debates, assimilated the information, and situated themselves within the debate. This research, funded by the Economic and Social Research Council, and conducted in association with the Institute for the Study of Genetics, Biorisks and Society, involved 121 women in the early stage of pregnancy completing a short questionnaire about their own views on human genetic modification and selection techniques. The women's ages ranged from 16 to 41 years and they were from all socioeconomic and ethnic groups. They were also evenly divided between those who were expecting their first child and those who already had children. Twenty of the original respondents agreed to a further in-depth interview, and, from within this wide range of experiences, the women demonstrated an understanding of the potential problems and promises of genetic technologies.

Many of the women in this study articulated concerns about the impact the widespread acceptance of genetic modification and selection techniques could have on the lives of disabled people. They identified that there might develop an increased intolerance for difference, a reduction in special services, and a growth in the perception of disabled lives as lives not worth living. They were also cognisant of the impact society's judgements could have on themselves as women. Their narratives described the idealised picture of women as mothers, and what this actually meant in practice. One woman explained:

> 'It could be very hard for parents. Parents could be put in very difficult positions in the future if [genetic modification] becomes much more common, particularly if they know they are going to have a child with genetic problems and have chosen not to have genetic modification. Possibly they might be judged by others to have done the wrong thing. I guess if the culture became one where genetic modification was the norm, I guess people could feel blamed.' (Elizabeth)

All of the women were main or sole carers of their children, even where those children were particularly emotionally and physically demanding because of severe illness or disability. The possibility that genetic modification could eliminate the most distressing and debilitating genetic conditions was widely welcomed by the women, and, in this reaction, they also embraced the optimistic medical discourses.

Thus, women's own discourses recognised the dominant discourses, but they became something other than 'disablist', 'medical' or 'feminist' discourses. Instead, these dominant discourses became incorporated within 'family-centric' discourses, where wider societal issues were respected, but where the family, at whose centre the women were positioned, became the subject and the object of the women's concerns. Jackson tells us that our reproductive decisions are 'shaped by multiple external influences, but they are the only choices we have, and they are therefore of critical importance to our sense of self. Even if we recognise that social forces may shape and constrain our choices, our sense of being the author of our own actions, especially when they pertain to something as personal as reproduction, is profoundly valuable to us.'[26]

In the context of the dominant discourses, the force of family-centricity caused women to face dilemmas in how they reacted to genetic modification and selection; in how they made the 'right' decision for themselves, their child, and wider society. We can learn from women's responses to the possibility of human genetic modification, and draw on women's discourses to inform our future regulation of women's role in decision-making. It may be that the role of professionals in the future control and use of genetic technologies is strengthened, while that of a regulatory authority such as the Human Fertilisation and Embryology Authority (HFEA) comes into question. But it should also be recognised that women's own role in reproductive decision-making is critical for their sense of self, and therefore of tremendous importance within this critique.

REGULATING REPRODUCTION

Even though human genetic modification is not a scientific possibility, the legislature has already prohibited its use in the UK. Under the Human Fertilisation and Embryology Act 1990 (hereafter the HFE Act), Schedule 2, paragraph 1(4) prevents a licence being issued that would authorise altering the genetic structure of any cell while it forms part of the embryo. Most of the assisted reproduction techniques that exist short of genetic modification are regulated by the HFEA, whose remit is also to license and inspect clinics and other premises where embryos are created and stored, and to monitor research into assisted reproductive technologies.

When the HFEA was asked to grant a licence for PGD to be carried out in conjunction with tissue typing to save the life of a young boy with thalassaemia, the regulatory system in the UK came under scrutiny. The HFEA agreed to grant the licence in the first instance, although it was stated at this time that 'We would see this happening only in very rare circumstances and under strict controls'.[27] Following a legal challenge by the anti-abortion group Comment on Reproductive Ethics (CORE) (*R v Human Fertilisation and Embryology Authority, ex parte Josephine Quintavalle* [2002] EWHC 2785), this decision was found to be ultra vires by the High Court – outside of the HFEA's sphere of control:

'Like any public body, the board is open to challenge by way of judicial review, but only if it exceeds its powers or abuses the powers and responsibilities given to it by Parliament.' (*R (Assisted Reproduction and Gynaecology Centre) v Human Fertilisation and Embryology Authority* [2002] EWCA Civ 20 (15))

Although this decision has been overturned once again in the HFEA's favour and the licence granted on 8 April 2003 (*R v Human Fertilisation and Embryology Authority, ex parte Josephine Quintavalle*. Skeleton argument, 12 July 2002, claim no. CO/1162/02), CORE's challenge has highlighted the problems raised when regulatory provisions are unable to keep pace with scientific innovation. Indeed, although the challenge raised by *Quintavalle* on behalf of CORE questioned the *legality* of the decision, it was 'motivated by the conviction that the Authority had erred in its ethics' (*R v Human Fertilisation and Embryology Authority, ex parte Josephine Quintavalle* [2003] EWCA Civ 667). Where new technologies raise novel legal and ethical questions that were not anticipated by the enabling Act of Parliament, there is separation between the use of these technologies and the democratic process. CORE's objective was therefore to prompt a public debate into the use of PGD for the purposes of creating a tissue match for an existing child – thus forcing Parliament to act to tighten controls on assisted reproductive technologies generally.

The existing regulatory framework has been subject to criticism on different grounds since it came into existence in 1991.[28] The first of these originates from the obligation placed on the HFEA by the Human Fertilisation and Embryology Act 1991, Sections 9(7) and 9(8), to inspect clinics and storage facilities where assisted reproduction techniques are carried out and gametes stored. In order to discharge this duty, the HFEA appoints part-time inspectors from within the ranks of the practitioners themselves. This has led to some commentators questioning the efficacy of such an arrangement, and indeed, to suggest that it has created 'the first beginnings of a serious conflict within the regulatory framework'.[29] The perception of such a system of inspection is that it will necessarily lack sufficient objectivity to guarantee impartiality in its work, and therefore that the inspectorate is flawed at its inception. Another criticism is that the HFEA only regulates for certain interventions, while leaving others, such as gamete intra-fallopian transfer (GIFT) or intracytoplasmic sperm injection (ICSI), to clinical freedom and professional self-regulation.[30] This means that certain, potentially harmful, interventions are virtually unregulated, while more reliable techniques are strictly controlled.

The consequence of CORE's action against the HFEA is that they have once again exposed the existing system of reproductive regulation in the UK as vulnerable to criticism and legal challenge. While they have raised questions about the process of decision-making in this field, they have also raised questions about the *level* of control to which individuals are subject.

DESIGNER BABIES – A CASE FOR REGULATING INTIMACY?

Jackson describes reproductive decision-making as 'the very intimacy of reproduction'[31] and questions whether such a private and personal area of women's lives is protected by concepts of reproductive freedom. Intimate aspects of life include domestic partnerships and sexuality as well as reproduction. The understanding of reproduction as an area of intimacy, and therefore an area of *privacy*, supports reproductive freedom as a concept that is legitimately protected against outside interference. In the United States, the Supreme Court held that:

> 'if the right of privacy means anything, it is the right of the individual, married or single, to be *free from unwarranted governmental intrusion into matters so fundamentally affecting a person as the decision whether to bear or beget a child.*' (*Eisenstadt v Baird* US Supreme Court 405 US 438 (1972):453; emphasis added)

Reproductive rights generally are supported by a collection of rights that includes the right to found a family (European Convention on Human Rights, Article 12), the right to respect for dignity (European Convention on Human Rights preamble; also European Convention on Human Rights, Article 3, which prohibits inhuman and degrading treatment), the right to integrity (Universal Declaration of Human Rights, Article 3), right to the benefits of science (International Covenant on Economic, Social and Cultural Rights, Article 15(1)(b)), the right to privacy (European Convention on Human Rights, Article 8), and women's rights (Convention on the Elimination of All Forms of Discrimination Against Women, Article 1). Thus the US and UK courts have recognised the right of a mother to an abortion (*Paton v Trustees of the British Pregnancy Advisory Service and Another* [1978] 2 All ER 987; *Roe v Wade* 410 US 113 (1972)) and the right to access to contraception (*Airey v Ireland* A 32, (1979) 2 EHRR 305; *Eisenstadt v Baird* US Supreme Court 405 US 438 (1972):453). These rights, along with the notion of reproductive freedom, have their foundation in the belief that autonomous decision-making may enrich an individual's life by affording her the 'capacity to direct the course of her own life according to her own values'.[32] However, the presumption of autonomy in intimacy is rebutted where vulnerable people are subject to violation within the sphere of intimacy, such as domestic violence (particularly against women within a relationship) and child abuse. Yet, even in this situation, the state does not interfere at the inception of the intimate relationship, but only where there is evidence of mistreatment and abuse within the established relationship. Even where a child in utero is vulnerable due to its mother's lifestyle, the courts have been reluctant to intervene (*In Re F (in utero)* [1998] Fam 122, 138). Thus, provided that others are not harmed, there is a prima facie assumption that each individual should be entitled to follow their own life plan in the light of their beliefs and convictions. Further, when it comes to creating children, at the time that an individual makes a reproductive decision, there is no vulnerable party for the state to protect since it is yet to be conceived.

The question then remains as to whether the protection afforded to parents of naturally conceived children extends to those parents who choose to have children with particular characteristics through the use of assisted reproductive technologies.

Intrinsic within the decision of whether to bear children is when to have a child, and what kind of child that individual wants. With the HFEA's decision to allow preimplantation genetic diagnosis to choose a disease-free, tissue-compatible child that is a suitable donor for its sick elder sibling, recognition was given to a parent's interest in controlling the *quality* of children as well as the quantity.[33] There is also recognition of the right to make decisions about one's child's health in the Abortion Act 1967. The Abortion Act allows for termination of pregnancy where there is a 'substantial risk that, if the child were born, it would suffer from such physical or mental abnormalities as to be severely handicapped' (Abortion Act 1967, Section 1(1)(d), as amended by the Human Fertilisation and Embryology Act 1990, Section 37).

Despite the apparent presumption of a right to reproductive autonomy and the acceptance of the principle of 'quality control', the sphere of intimacy is not protected from outside surveillance and control where parents need to use assisted reproduction techniques. The 'welfare principle' within the Human Fertilisation and Embryology Act 1990, Section 13, effectively subjects potential parents to scrutiny by clinicians as to their suitability as parents, even though their prime objective is to bear a child, rather than a child with specific characteristics. The 'welfare of the child' is not taken into consideration before conception where parents are able to conceive naturally, yet parents who need assistance with reproduction are judged on their ability to parent the child before they are able to commence treatment for infertility.[34] The decision by the HFEA in permitting tissue typing in conjunction with PGD is also conditional on approval of each individual case by the Authority. Thus, parents seeking the same intervention for apparently similar conditions and under similar circumstances have been denied access to PGD and tissue typing.[35] Similarly, although women seeking termination of pregnancy under Section 1(1)(d) of the Abortion Act are making an individual decision about their own ability to cope with a child with a disability, and their own desire for a non-disabled child, what constitutes a 'severe handicap' for the purposes of the Act is dependent on a subjective judgement by the diagnosing clinician.

It can be seen, then, that the perception of genetic information as powerful, combined with the discernment of risks expressed in the dominant discourses, actually leads to a presumption against reproductive autonomy, so that women's decision-making is routinely scrutinised, judged and controlled. However, if the role of the HFEA as a democratic, accountable, *ethical* arbiter of assisted reproduction generally is questioned, then what alternatives are available and, perhaps more importantly, are acceptable, for wider society and specifically for women as major reproductive decision-makers?

EMPIRICAL EVIDENCE

There are five suggested alternatives for regulating assisted reproduction:

1. A private ordering approach, based upon individual control, responsibility and power.
2. Professional self-regulation and control through the medical profession, local research and institutional review committees, which has been a hallmark of medical regulation for centuries.

3. Community control, through national ethics committees and the courts.
4. Legislative and regulatory control.
5. A combination or blending of one or more of these approaches.[36]

The model that is chosen in any jurisdiction will depend on what is seen to be the appropriate level of state intervention in women's reproductive decision-making. With this in mind, the questionnaire asked women to express their views on the regulation of human genetic modification and selection. It asked how they thought the genetic modification of human beings ought to be regulated, and offered the following five options:

1. All genetic modification of embryos should be banned.
2. People should be allowed to make their own decisions about what to change in their children.
3. A law should be passed to say what changes can be made to children.
4. Doctors should say what changes can be made to children.
5. A regulatory body such as the HFEA should say what changes can be made to children.

These options allowed for the women to endorse the current legislative position (option 1), or to sanction a complete absence of regulation, allowing women to make their own decisions according to conscience (option 2). They were also able to recommend firm legislative guidelines as to what would be acceptable uses of genetic modification (option 3), or to rely on voluntary codes of conduct and professional standards of practice (option 4). The final option was to support a regulatory body whose role would be defined by statute, but which would have the flexibility to make individual decisions. The response to this final option was also seen as a reflection of the women's opinion as to the HFEA's record of effectiveness in deciding on the use of reproductive technologies, as well as the appropriateness of their decisions.

Overall, the option of a regulatory body was the most popular with 39% of respondents choosing this option (Table 6.1). The passing of a law was the second most popular response, with control going to doctors and parents at 14% and 15% respectively. The least popular option was for all modification of human embryos to be banned, contrary to the current legislative position. It is important to note, however, that the questionnaire was completed under the assumption that the technology would only be available once standards

Table 6.1   Choice of regulation

Option	Frequency	Percentage
(1) All banned	7	5.8
(2) Parents	19	15.7
(3) Law	29	24.0
(4) Doctors	18	14.9
(5) Regulatory body	48	39.7

of safety and efficacy had been met. Even so, the dominant discourses advocating strict legislative controls identify concerns other than those related to safety issues. In view of the women's recognition of these dominant discourses, there is a suggestion that, even with these concerns in mind, the total prohibition of genetic modification is disproportionate to the threat to society.

Despite a complete ban on genetic modification techniques being the least popular of all the options, a liberal stance was also relatively unpopular with the women in this study, with only 19 (15.7%) of the respondents wanting to see the decision lying with women themselves. The controlling factor on the decision would then be the woman's individual conscience:

> 'I suppose the only thing would be that it would be available to everybody and it would be just down to personal choice. And then they would have to live with their conscience . . . even though I don't agree with it, I don't think it's for me to say, "well, I don't want to do it, and you're not going to do it either" because you're forcing your opinions on someone else.' (Lillian)

It is impossible to tell whether those women who spoke in favour of free choice did so because of a real belief in a woman's right to make her own reproductive decisions, or a distrust of outside agencies. Although just 14.9% of the women completing the questionnaire indicated that the decision should lie with medical professionals, the majority of those interviewed felt that the role of women in determining the type of genetic interventions they could use should be in partnership with other agencies outside of the family, particularly with doctors:

> 'As a parent, you'd be guided by the advice you're given by medical services.' (Jackie)
> 'I don't know where to draw the line. I suppose it's up to doctors.' (Jade)
> 'I think the hospitals who know what they're doing should be in charge of it really.'(Otto)

Working in partnership with medical professionals is therefore seen by many women as a legitimate means of controlling the use of human genetic modification. Yet, for others, a tighter regulatory control, in the form of legislative provisions, was felt to be more appropriate. Twenty-four per cent of the women wanted to see genetic modification controlled through legislation; by setting parameters within which women would be able to make their decisions:

> 'I think it should start with a law. Yes. With a law governing what you can and can't do. Then there's hopefully no grey areas about it.' (Helen)
> 'I think there has to be a cut-off point, you know, which is what the regulations would be.'(Debbie)

The strength of legislation in this area was seen to be its certainty. But its role would also be a normative one in that it would distinguish what *can* be done from what *ought* to be done. Yet, these very strengths were also seen by other respondents as weaknesses. There was a concern that a law could be inflexible or interpreted too narrowly, to the detriment of women wanting treatment:

'But if you had a law, then it might be . . . I don't know if there might be some cases that just go over the lines; where it's not cosmetic, but it could be seen as cosmetic. And then what do you do? Then how do you get past it?' (Otto)

'I mean, in an ideal situation, you would hope that it would be a bit more flexible, because, I mean, everyone has individual needs. I suppose, on the whole, there should be set ground rules, but sometimes there would be exceptions to that rule.' (Sarah)

Despite the criticisms levelled at the working of the HFEA and its interpretation of the provisions of the HFE Act, the women demonstrated a great deal of confidence in this model, with nearly 40% of the women choosing this option from the questionnaire. For these women, one of the main attractions of a regulatory body was its membership. The membership of the HFEA spreads across a broad range of academic disciplines and professional specialisms, as well as incorporating a lay element. One of the criticisms levelled at the HFEA during the recent challenges to its decision-making was that the body, once established, ceased to be subject to Parliamentary control, unless its decisions fell within the narrow categories applicable to judicial review (*R (Assisted Reproduction and Gynaecology Centre) v Human Fertilisation and Embryology Authority*, 2002.). Yet several of the women in this study actually favoured the existence of a regulatory body *because* of the lack of Parliamentary, and specifically *political*, intervention.

'It should be monitored by somebody. Not the Government, no. not the Government. Because I wouldn't trust the Government.' (Jack)

'I don't think politics should come into it. Because that should be nothing to do with developing medicine in that way. It's a medical field. It's not something that should be used to win votes, or whatever.' (Wendy)

As the HFEA, the Human Genetics Commission,[37] and its predecessor, the Human Genetics Advisory Commission[38] have all identified, the involvement of the 'public' in the debate over new genetic technologies is extremely important. This is not just an exercise in providing information, but enabling lay people to fully engage with the issues and be active participants in the deliberations. The women in the sample also strongly advocated consultation with a wide section of society:

'[There should be] proper consultation taking place that doesn't just involve just health matters, or just financial matters. It's a combination of so many different things that everyone should be involved.' (Zoë)

'You also need a large cross-section of society. You know, a lot of differ-ent social groups so that they might pick up what the more ordinary people's worries might be.' (Anne)

REGULATING AUTONOMY

The purposes for which laws are conceived and implemented, particularly where their purpose is to control behaviours and enforce morality, results in a separation between those behaviours and mores that may legitimately be subject to state surveillance and control, and those that are 'private' and therefore unregulated. The English legal tradition has always been that pri-vate (intimate) lives should not be subject to legal control unless there is a cogent argument that suggests that great harm will otherwise result. Where regulation impinges on personal decision-making, autonomy is severely compromised, and such an intrusion must be closely examined to determine whether or not it is justified in the interests of the community or for protect-ing the rights of others. As Dworkin states: 'Laws that constrain one man, on the sole ground that he is incompetent to decide what is right for himself, are profoundly insulting.'[39]

Although the dominant discourses identify several instances where harm *might* result, this is not a sufficiently persuasive argument for regulating (and restricting) a woman's reproductive autonomy. The reality is that women's reproductive decision-making is being usurped by 'experts' and profession-als and that women are seen as incompetent to make their own decisions, through being ill-informed, and unable to distinguish between their preju-dices and moral values.[40] Tight legislation and close supervision lead to a sit-uation where the public interest 'trumps' individual rights, placing personal autonomy and state regulatory provision in opposition. With regard to women's reproductive choices, the courts have intervened to protect the state's interest in preserving life, forcing caesarean sections on women (*Re S (adult: refusal of medical treatment)* [1992] 4 All ER 671; *Re AC* 533 A 2d 611 (DC 1987); *Norfolk and Norwich Healthcare Trust v W* [1996] 2 FLR 613), and incar-cerating drug-dependent pregnant women in order to prevent behaviour that may harm the fetus (*Winnipeg Child and Family Services (Northwest Area) v G (DF)* [1997] 2 SCR 925). Indeed 'those who wish to resist such intrusion into personal decisions, will have a hard furrow to plough'.[41] The result of the existing culture of control is that women's autonomy is placed in conflict with state regulatory provision.

In order to diminish, if not fully resolve this conflict within the sphere of intimacy, an alternative paradigm – regulated autonomy – might be adopted.[42] It is argued that intimate decisions are 'entwined with one's strong evaluation regarding the good: with reflection on who one is and wants to be, and how to lead one's life'.[43] This concept of autonomy, pro-tected by the ideal of a private life that is protected by individual rights, most notably the right to privacy, is open to criticism.[44–46] The feminist cri-tique argues that the very reality of an area of existence that is unregulated

leads to an understanding of intimacy as being legally and socially constructed, culturally defined, and the site of power relations, including
oppression and gendered violence.[47] It should be recognised that reproductive decisions are made under material and social conditions that may
severely reduce the number of options that are available to women. These
conditions include gender stereotypes of women as 'mothers' and 'carers',
gendered hierarchies, and patriarchal domination of women – all within a
sphere that is not perceptive to public scrutiny because it is labelled 'private'.
Under a liberal regime, then, the whole discourse of privacy supports legit-
imised domination of women within the family. Conversely, the communitarian paradigm holds that individualised privacy rights, based on flawed
assumptions of personal identity, mores and individualism, undermine
social values. Both these critiques lead to an understanding of privacy that
fails to protect women from the state, gendered power relations, or, indeed,
themselves. Yet it is not the concept of privacy itself that is defective, but the
ideological foundations of the competing paradigms on which the critique of
privacy is based:

> 'The first approach misses the normative symbolic, and empowering
> dimensions of privacy rights because it is preoccupied with unmasking
> the functional role they can play in preserving inequality and hierarchy.
> The second . . . fails to grasp the moral importance of rights guaranteeing
> decisional autonomy and ascribing ethical competence and a sense of
> control over one's identity needs in the domain of intimacy to socialized,
> solidary individuals.'[48]

This is not to say, however, that repro-genetic interventions themselves
should be free from state surveillance and control. Indeed, it is important to
recognise and appreciate the benefits that privacy can bestow, while at the
same time being aware that legal regulation can protect privacy as well as
provide a structure of justice within intimate relationships. Where the sphere
of intimacy is unregulated, this can lead to an assumption that the woman's
role as mother and carer is to care for a child no matter what its physical
condition, while failing to provide the material and social support to fulfil
this task.

While the intimacy and importance of reproductive decision-making
should lead to a strong presumption in favour of freedom of choice, it does
not mean that there should be no external constraints. Total deregulation
ignores the need for legislative guarantees of adequate standards in medical services, and the potential for abuse of power within the realms of
intimacy. Conversely, the total prohibition of genetic modification under-
mines parental autonomy, and is an unnecessary intrusion into intimacy.
Regulatory mechanisms should provide an enabling, supportive framework
for autonomy. They must also provide the opportunity for women *not* to
avoid having a disabled child if that is their choice. For this reason, regulation should act as both protection *of* and protection *within* the arena of reproductive decision-making.

CONCLUSIONS

Existing regulation of assisted reproduction in the UK reflects the state of scientific progress and the ethical debates that existed in the mid-1980s when the Warnock Committee produced the report on human fertilisation and embryology[49] that would later become the Human Fertilisation and Embryology Act 1990. At this time many of the techniques that have since entered common therapeutic practice had not even reached the experimental stage of development, and the possibility that human genetic modification could ever be considered safe and effective was so remote as to justify a prohibitive stance. Since 1990, the science behind assisted reproductive technologies has moved on tremendously, and the HFEA has responded to each new procedure as it has arisen. While this has led to accusations of unethical decision-making and acting outside of its remit, the credibility and legitimacy of the HFEA do not appear to have been damaged by the recent challenges to its decision-making capabilities. The HFEA, or a similar regulatory body modelled on the HFEA, is still the pattern of regulation with which the women in my research were most confident.

Despite the suggestion that women are not in a position to judge reproductive technologies in terms of 'drawing lines in clinical practice and the law', the women in this study demonstrated that they not only understand the social, ethical and legal issues relating to assisted reproduction, but that they are also able to evaluate the issues and make moral and practical judgements based on their evaluations. Women are situated individuals in that they define themselves within a specific context, drawing on the cultural tools, personal relationships and institutional norms in order to form an individual identity. They should therefore not be seen as isolated, self-interested parties, but as interdependent and *responsible* decision-makers.

In the interests of mothers and their babies, proscriptive legislative provisions are essential as long as procedures are unsafe and unpredictable, and therefore existing prohibitions (e.g. Human Fertilisation and Embryology Act 1990; Human Reproductive Cloning Act 2001; Canada's Assisted Human Reproductive Act, Section 5(1)(a)) on human genetic modification and human reproductive cloning are justified. Yet, many assisted reproduction techniques have been shown to be safe and effective, and it is hard to demonstrate that the potential harms are sufficiently probable or severe as to support state encroachment into this intimate area of women's lives. Yet this does not suggest that assisted reproductive technologies should become unregulated, but that care should be taken both to prevent harms and promote autonomous reproductive decision-making within a framework that espouses regulated autonomy.

References

1. Hogan B, Beddington R, Constantini F, et al. Manipulating the mouse embryo: a laboratory manual. 2nd edn. Cold Spring Harbor, NY: Cold Spring Harbor Press; 1994.

2. Rulicke T. Transgenic technology: an introduction. International Journal of Experimental Pathology 1996; 77:243–245.
3. Laurence J. Test-tube baby born to save his sister's life. The Independent 4 October 2000.
4. Shakespeare T. Losing the plot? Medical and activist discourses of contemporary genetics and disability. In: Conrad P, Gabe J, eds. Sociological perspectives on the new genetics. Oxford: Blackwell; 1999.
5. Stock G, Campbell J, eds. Engineering the human germline: an exploration of the science and ethics of altering the genes we pass to our children. Oxford: Oxford University Press; 2000:16.
6. Russo E, Cove D. Genetic engineering: dreams and nightmares. Oxford: Oxford University Press; 1998:212.
7. Wilmut I, Schneike AE, McWhire J, et al. Viable offspring derived from fetal and adult mammalian cells. Nature 1997; 385:810–813.
8. Steinberg DL. Bodies in glass: genetics, eugenics, and embryo ethics. Manchester: Manchester University Press; 1997:117.
9. Reindal SM. Disability, gene therapy and eugenics: a challenge to John Harris. Journal of Medical Ethics 2000; 26(3):89–94, at 92.
10. French S, Swain J. Across the disability divide: whose tragedy? In: Fulford KWM, Murray TH, eds. Healthcare ethics and human values. Oxford: Blackwell; 2002.
11. Muller HJ. The dominance of economics over eugenics: a decade in the progress of eugenics. Baltimore: Williams and Wilkins; 1934.
12. Stacey M. The new genetics: a feminist view. In: Marteau T, Richards M, eds. The troubled helix: social and psychological implications of the new human genetics. Cambridge: Cambridge University Press; 1996:342.
13. Shakespeare T. Losing the plot? Medical and activist discourses of contemporary genetics and disability. In: Conrad P, Gabe J, eds. Sociological perspectives on the new genetics. Oxford: Blackwell; 1999:184
14. Harris J. Is gene therapy a form of eugenics? Bioethics 1993; 7:178–187.
15. Asch A, Geller G. Feminism, bioethics and genetics. In: Wolf SM, ed. Feminism and bioethics: beyond reproduction. Oxford: Oxford University Press; 1996:319.
16. Purdy LM. Genetic diseases: can having children be immoral? In: Arras JD, Roden NK, eds. Ethical issues in modern medicine. 3rd edn. Mount View, CA: Mayfield; 1989.
17. Ettorre E. Reproductive genetics, gender and the body: 'Please Doctor, may I have a normal baby?' Sociology 2000; 34(3):403–420.
18. Stacey M. The new genetics: a feminist view. In: Marteau T, Richards M, eds. The troubled helix: social and psychological implications of the new human genetics. Cambridge: Cambridge University Press; 1996:339.
19. Maher ER, Afnan M, Barratt CL. Epigenic risks related to assisted reproductive technologies: epigenetics, imprinting, AR and icebergs? Human Reproduction 2003; 18(12):2508–2511.
20. Galton DJ, Kay A, Cavanna JS. Human cloning: safety is the issue. Nature Medicine 1998; 4(6):644.
21. Reaves J. The scientists speak: no human cloning. Time 8 January 2002.
22. Genetics and Society (2003) '1998–Early 2000: the first wave of "Designer Baby" coverage'. Online. Available: http://www.genetics-and-society.org/analysis/media/designer.html.
23. Human Genetics Advisory Commission. Cloning issues in reproduction and medicine. London: HMSO; 1998.

24. Fazackerley A. Scientists fear pro-life hijacking of debate. Times Higher Education Supplement 3 February 2004.

25. Pembrey M. In: Scientists fear pro-life hijacking of debate. Times Higher Education Supplement 3 February 2004.

26. Jackson E. Regulating reproduction: law, technology and autonomy. Oxford: Hart; 2001.

27. Human Fertilisation and Embryology Authority. HFEA to allow tissue typing in conjunction with preimplantation genetic diagnosis. 13 December 2001. Online. Available: http://www.hfea.gov.uk/frame.htm.

28. Morgan D, Lee R. Blackstone's guide to the Human Fertilisation and Embryology Act 1990: abortion and embryo research – the new law. London: Blackstone; 1991.

29. Winston R. The IVF revolution: the definitive guide to assisted reproductive technologies. London: Vermillion; 1999:148.

30. Winston R. The IVF revolution: the definitive guide to assisted reproductive technologies. London: Vermillion; 1999.

31. Jackson E. Regulating reproduction: law, technology and autonomy. Oxford: Hart; 2001:9.

32. Jackson E. Regulating reproduction: law, technology and autonomy. Oxford: Hart; 2001:2.

33. Human Fertilisation and Embryology Authority. HFEA to allow tissue typing in conjunction with preimplantation genetic diagnosis. 13 December 2001. Online. Available: http://www.hfea.gov.uk/frame.htm.

34. Jackson E. Conception and the irrelevance of the Welfare Principle. The Modern Law Review 2002; 65(March):2.

35. HFEA. Press release: 'HFEA confirms that HLA tissue typing may only take place when preimplantation genetic diagnosis is required to avoid a serious genetic disorder'. 1 August 2002. Online. Available: http://www.hfea.gov.uk/PressOffice/Archive/43573563.

36. Lee R, Morgan D. Human fertilisation and embryology: regulating the reproductive revolution. London: Blackstone; 2001:12.

37. Human Genetics Commission and Human Fertilisation and Embryology Authority. Outcome of the public consultation on pre-implantation genetic diagnosis. HFEA 2001. Online. Available: www.hfea.gov.uk.business_publications.htm.

38. Human Genetics Commission. Public attitudes to genetic information. London: HMSO; 2001.

39. Dworkin R. Taking rights seriously. London: Duckworth; 1977:297.

40. Harris J. In: Fazackerley A. Scientists fear pro-life hijacking of debate. Times Higher Education Supplement 3 February 2004.

41. McLean S. Reproductive medicine. In: Dyer C, ed. Doctors, patients and the law. Oxford: Blackwell; 1992:104.

42. Cohen J. Regulating intimacy: a new legal paradigm. Oxford: Princeton University Press; 2003:7.

43. Cohen J. Regulating intimacy: a new legal paradigm. Oxford: Princeton University Press; 2003:22.

44. MacKinnon C. Feminism unmodified. Cambridge: Harvard University Press; 1987.

45. Sunstein C. Neutrality in constitutional law. Columbia Law Review 1992; 92:1.

46. Olsen F. A finger to the devil: abortion, privacy and equality. Dissent 1991 (Summer): 337–381.

47. Cohen J. Regulating intimacy: a new legal paradigm. Oxford: Princeton University Press; 2003:23.

48. Cohen J. Regulating intimacy: a new legal paradigm. Oxford: Princeton University Press; 2003:26.
49. Report of the Committee of Inquiry into Human Fertilisation and Embryology (Warnock Report). CMND 9314. London: HMSO; 1984.

Chapter **7**

Preimplantation genetic diagnosis – towards a principled construction of law?

Thérèse Callus

CHAPTER CONTENTS

The laissez–faire approach of
   the Human Fertilisation
   and Embryology Act 1990:
   a social construction
   of law   135
Liberal statutory provisions   136
A purposive judicial
   interpretation   139

Towards a principled
   construction of law?   141
In search of coherence   141
Acknowledging ethical
   imperatives   143
Conclusion   145
References   146

Assisted conception and related techniques involving the use of in vitro embryos continue to provoke debate and disagreement. Quite apart from the controversial nature of the very status of the embryo, each different technique appears to engender new social dilemmas and sensitive ethical and legal challenges. Preimplantation genetic diagnosis is one technique which, although it has been carried out in the UK for over ten years, has brought to the fore the difficulties facing the law in the search for a coherent regulatory framework that can satisfy a two-fold aim. On the one hand, society is anxious to afford protection and respect to the very beginning of human life; on the other, society also wishes to be at the forefront of scientific innovation in the quest to ensure more control of what is perceived to be a healthy, disease-free life. It is not the purpose of this chapter to put into question the very existence of the in vitro embryo which ultimately lies at the heart of assisted conception, and which was accepted by the British legislator in the Human Fertilisation and Embryology Act 1990 (hereafter the 1990 Act). Rather, it is to analyse the current regulation of preimplantation genetic diagnosis, which appears to favour scientific claims that satisfy individual desires over the need to establish a coherent regulatory framework based on consistent ethical principles. Indeed, we are witnesses to an era where scientific prowess is equated with liberated individuals; where technical capabilities are transformed into individual rights. The regulation of preimplantation genetic diagnosis is one example of this trend which, it will be argued, results in the law being subservient to science, dominated by those able to exercise the most pressure on the legislator. The question is whether society is willing to allow a socially constructed law, fuelled predominantly by the scientific lobby (promoting individual choice and more importantly, economic interests), to displace the privileged position of each individual to be respected as an end in himself or herself.

Preimplantation genetic diagnosis is the testing of an embryo created in vitro for certain genetic diseases. Following preimplantation genetic diagnosis, the parents (based on medical advice) may choose which embryos should be transferred to the woman's womb. Embryos deemed 'unsuitable' because they are carriers of certain genetic characteristics may be discarded. In one sense, it is akin to prenatal diagnosis, where the fetus in the womb is tested for identifiable genetic diseases or handicap. The results of prenatal diagnosis may sometimes lead the parents to choose an abortion, which is permitted under Section 1(1)(d) Abortion Act 1967 (as amended by the Human Fertilisation and Embryology Act 1990) in the case of the fetus being diagnosed with a particularly serious handicap. However, although some parallels can be made with prenatal diagnosis,[1] it is clear that preimplantation genetic diagnosis raises novel ethical and legal considerations. For example, upon which criteria will the selection of embryos take place and what will happen to the 'unsuitable' embryos? How can the interests of the child to be born from the selected embryo be protected? Can such issues be addressed within a legal framework?

There are a variety of applications for which preimplantation genetic diagnosis may be suggested:

1. To identify a serious hereditary disease caused by a single gene mutation: e.g. cystic fibrosis, sickle cell, beta thalassaemia and some inherited cancers such as colon cancer.
2. To identify the sex of the embryo which may be required for one of two reasons: (i) to avoid transferring an embryo which carries a genetic sex-linked disease, e.g. haemophilia or Duchenne muscular dystrophy; or (ii) for 'social' reasons – choice of sex of the first offspring or equilibrium of sexes in composition of the family.
3. To carry out tissue typing (human leukocyte antigen – HLA testing) which would identify an embryo as a potential histocompatible donor for an existing sibling suffering from a disease and in need of a bone marrow transplant, for example.
4. To identify a susceptibility to a disease, e.g. by identifying the gene linked to breast cancer.
5. To identify a serious late-onset hereditary disease, e.g. Huntington's, without the parent being told of his potential carrier or sufferer status.

It is evident that the motivation behind each of these reasons differs substantially: it may be in the interests of the embryo (and resulting child) – for example, to avoid the implantation of an embryo carrying a particular genetic disease; or it may be in the interests of a third party – for example, to provide a tissue donor for an existing sick child. Nevertheless, one thing is clear: it is precisely because of the potentiality of the embryo *qua* future child that the diagnosis is of interest.

Despite the potential ramifications of the various applications, preimplantation genetic diagnosis remains very loosely regulated in the UK: the Human Fertilisation and Embryology Act 1990 which governs the provision and extent of services provided by in vitro fertilisation (IVF) clinics is virtually silent on the matter. Consequently, decisions as to the legitimacy of different applications of the technique fall to be assessed on a case-by-case basis by the Human Fertilisation and Embryology Authority (HFEA). The HFEA is a statutory body set up under the 1990 Act to oversee the provision and exercise of both IVF treatment and embryo research.[2] Although at the time of the adoption of the 1990 Act, preimplantation genetic diagnosis was one of the techniques heralded as addressing the need for families to bear children free from identifiable genetic diseases, very little parliamentary debate was actually spent on the ramifications of the technique. If in 1990 the extent of the different applications could not be foreseen, there is clearly a need today to examine their ethical and legal consequences. This chapter seeks to address this need. The first part will examine the laissez-faire approach adopted towards preimplantation genetic diagnosis in the 1990 Act, which leaves to the court the possibility to engage in a purposive construction of the general terms of the Act when faced with extended applications of the technique. The second part will analyse the difficulties with the current law and the ethical inconsistencies which are revealed by the laissez-faire environment. Consequently, it will be suggested that there is a need to establish a principled framework which will allow the various applications of the technique to be evaluated, while at the same time ensuring respect for the autonomy and dignity of each individual concerned.

THE LAISSEZ-FAIRE APPROACH OF THE HUMAN FERTILISATION AND EMBRYOLOGY ACT 1990: A SOCIAL CONSTRUCTION OF LAW

As a technique to prevent the birth of seriously handicapped babies, preimplantation genetic diagnosis may be said to be at the heart of the laissez-faire approach adopted by Parliament in the 1990 Act: 'that IVF could be used to prevent serious disease and acute suffering significantly advanced the case for facilitative regulation'.[3] Yet it is ironic that the term does not appear anywhere in the Act. Indeed, the Act is more concerned with setting out a general framework within which a statutory body, the HFEA, deals with specific applications of different techniques on a case-by-case basis. The Authority has considered requests for licences for a variety of applications of preimplantation genetic diagnosis ranging from the desire by one family to identify the sex of the embryo in order to balance the family composition (the Masterton family sought preimplantation genetic diagnosis accompanied by sex selection in order to conceive a girl: they already had four sons and their only girl had died aged 3 years),[4] to requests by families to carry out tissue typing for compatibility with an existing child who suffers from a debilitating genetic disease. It was in relation to the latter type of request that the Authority granted a treatment licence for the Hashmi family who sought to select embryos that were not only free from beta thalassaemia but also genetically compatible with an existing child who suffers from this hereditary genetic disease.[5] In the light of the general terms of the Act and the ethical difficulties with the proposed application, the Authority's decision was challenged in judicial review proceedings.

Liberal statutory provisions

It is trite to say that when the Human Fertilisation and Embryology Act 1990 was enacted, it was impossible to foresee how the scientific techniques would develop and that the Act would to a certain extent always lag behind the science. Nevertheless, the nature of the Act was intended to allow new techniques to be accommodated within a general framework to achieve the purposes of the Act. It is apparent from the parliamentary debates that the legislation has two aims: (i) 'the regulation of certain types of infertility treatment';[6] and (ii) 'to identify and offer help to people who are at risk of passing on a genetic disorder'.[7] Central to the general framework is the HFEA, which oversees and licenses all activities relating to the creation and use of gametes and embryos in vitro. Thus, Section 3(1)(b) of the Act provides that the keeping and use of an embryo can only be carried out in pursuance of a licence. Further, the Authority is only authorised to license clinics to carry out 'practices designed to secure that embryos are in a suitable condition to be placed in a woman or to determine whether embryos are suitable for that purpose' (Schedule 2, para 1(1)(d)) – provided that they are carried out 'in the course of providing treatment services'. In Section 2(1), the Act defines 'treatment services' as 'medical, surgical or obstetric services provided . . . for the purpose of assisting women to carry children'. It is interesting to note that preimplantation genetic diagnosis is carried out for *treatment* and not research; nevertheless, preimplantation genetic diagnosis is also implicitly referred to in the research provisions of the Act, which provide that a research licence may be granted if the Authority deems it 'necessary or desirable for the purpose of . . . developing methods for detecting the presence of gene or chromosome abnormalities in embryos before implantation' (Schedule 2, para 3). Consequently, it has been assumed that the use of preimplantation genetic diagnosis in treatment (which is the result of such research) must be accepted as authorised under the 1990 Act. Otherwise, there would be no point in allowing research in this area if the fruits of this research were to be abandoned.

Because such an interpretation of the Act implies that preimplantation genetic diagnosis may be carried out in the course of providing treatment services, it follows that a licence is required. Yet not all applications will be

approved. The authorisation of preimplantation genetic diagnosis in one particular case by the HFEA has highlighted the ambiguity of the statutory provisions and the ability of the Authority to make decisions on a case-by-case
basis. The subsequent refusal by the HFEA of a similar application highlights
the uncertain application of the law.

The Hashmi decision

The Hashmi case has provoked much public discussion thanks to mass media
interest in the plight of Zain Hashmi, a 4-year-old suffering from the genetic
disease of beta thalassaemia, who requires a bone marrow transplant in order
to improve his fatal prognosis. His parents sought authorisation for preimplantation genetic diagnosis accompanied by tissue typing. They hoped to
be able to identify embryos that were not carriers of the disease and who
would also provide a tissue match for Zain. If this succeeded, cord blood could
be taken from the mother on the birth of the baby and used in transplantation
for Zain. In this way, the chances of rejection by Zain of the transplanted tissue
would be slim. The HFEA granted a licence subject to a number of conditions:

- the condition of the affected child should be severe or life-threatening, of a
  sufficient seriousness to justify the use of the technique
- the embryos conceived in the course of this treatment should themselves
  be at risk from the condition by which the existing child is affected
- all other possibilities of treatment and sources of tissue for the affected
  child should have been explored
- the techniques should not be available where the intended recipient is a
  parent
- the intention should be to take only cord blood for purposes of the treatment, and not other tissues or organs
- appropriate counselling should be a requirement for couples undergoing
  this type of treatment
- families should be encouraged to participate in follow-up studies and clinics should provide detailed information about treatment cycles and their
  outcomes
- embryos should not be genetically modified to provide a tissue match.

It is apparent that the concern of the Authority was not whether the technique could be said to fall within the statutory definition of treatment (which
was at the heart of the judicial review of the decision, discussed below) but
rather whether the welfare of any child born and of any existing children,
would be considered. This is a statutory requirement under Section 13(5) of
the 1990 Act. In its Opinion, the Ethics Committee of the HFEA stated that it
should not restrict itself to a 'narrow legal perspective' of the welfare of the
child to be born. According to the Committee, it is necessary to consider the
potential moral, psychological, social and physical welfare of the child to be
born (para 3.2). This will include any positive effects on the welfare of any
other children of the family, including the benefit that the future child may

experience from knowing that he has saved his sibling (para 3.4). The welfare of the child is thus merged into the welfare of the family. Consequently, the authorisation of the extended use of preimplantation genetic diagnosis to include tissue typing appears to be based on a very loose interpretation of the best interests of the future child and expressly includes the interests of other existing children. Nevertheless, the HFEA also underlined the need for the embryo itself to be at risk of carrying a serious genetic disease before any other application (in this case, tissue typing) could be envisaged. This is clearly the original justification for the implicit approval of the diagnosis by Parliament. Indeed, this corresponds to the Department of Health's own 'Guiding Principles' on preimplantation genetic diagnosis. Paragraph 1 states that preimplantation genetic diagnosis uses IVF technology 'to enable couples at high risk of passing a serious genetic disorder to their offspring to avoid an affected pregnancy'.[8] The HFEA reiterated this condition in a subsequent decision concerning the Whitaker family.

The Whitaker case[9]

In this case, the Whitaker family requested preimplantation genetic diagnosis in order to select an embryo that would be compatible with an existing sibling who was suffering from a serious, but not hereditary, disease in the hope that the future child would be a suitable tissue donor for the sick sibling. This case differs from the Hashmi case insofar as there was no expected diagnosis of a genetic disease. Thus the preimplantation genetic diagnosis would be carried out for the sole purpose of assisting a sick sibling. The Authority refused to authorise preimplantation genetic diagnosis for tissue typing only, on the basis that this would amount to an instrumentalisation of the future child.

These two decisions illustrate the tensions inherent in implicit regulation which relies on the discretion of a statutory body for its application. However, decisions by statutory bodies can be challenged by way of judicial review by anyone who has an interest in their application (see *R v Secretary of State for Foreign and Commonwealth Affairs, ex parte World Development Movement Ltd* [1995] 1 WLR 386 (the Pergau Dam affair)). The authorisation of preimplantation genetic diagnosis and tissue typing in the Hashmi case thus provided the opportunity to challenge the scope of the laissez-faire regulation. A public interest group, Comment on Reproductive Ethics (CORE) whose purpose is 'to focus and facilitate debate on ethical issues arising from human reproduction and in particular, assisted reproduction' (*R (Quintavalle on behalf of Comment on Reproductive Ethics) v Human Fertilisation & Embryology Authority* [2003] 2 All ER 105, Queen's Bench Division per Kay J at paragraph 5), duly sought judicial review of the Hashmi decision. Upholding the validity of the decision of the HFEA, the Court of Appeal confirmed the appropriateness of a purposive interpretation of the 1990 Act and endorsed the discretionary power of the Authority.

A purposive judicial interpretation

CORE based its claim on the very grounds that preimplantation genetic diagnosis accompanied by tissue typing cannot fall within the statutory definition of 'treatment services'. At first instance, Kay J held that tissue typing of an embryo in the interests of an existing child, could not be said to be performed to assist the woman to carry the child, but rather to assist her to carry a particular child: 'To take the example of the unfortunate family whose problems have given rise to this case – it is not suggested that those problems arise from an impaired ability to conceive or to carry a child through pregnancy to full term and birth. The sole purpose of tissue typing is to ensure that any such child would have tissue compatibility with its older sibling. I do not consider that it can be said to be "necessary or desirable" for the purpose of assisting a woman to carry a child' (para 17). The Authority appealed against this ruling claiming that Schedule 2, paragraph 1 of the Act provides for 'practices which are designed to secure that embryos are in a suitable condition to be placed in a woman or determine whether embryos are suitable for that purpose'; and accordingly, that the diagnosis aimed to establish that the embryos were indeed suitable.

The Court of Appeal dealt with the issue in two parts (R (Quintavalle on behalf of Comment on Reproductive Ethics) v Human Fertilisation & Embryology Authority [2003] EWCA Civ 667, Court of Appeal). First, Lord Philips confirmed the implicit legitimacy of the practice of preimplantation genetic diagnosis resulting from the express statutory authorisation of carrying out research to achieve this end: 'it 'makes little sense for Parliament at the same time, to prohibit reaping the benefit of that research, even under licence' (paragraph 40). Moreover, the fact that the preimplantation genetic diagnosis treatment allows a woman to bear children in the confidence that the child will not suffer from a hereditary disease can be said to fall within the definition of treatment (for the purpose of assisting women to carry children). Thus, the purpose of activities that seek to establish whether the embryo is in a 'suitable condition' includes the *psychological* state of the woman according to the Court of Appeal. This is the first step in recognising that interests external to the embryo may be involved when deciding whether the particular application is lawful under the Act.

The Court of Appeal then considered the question of whether extending preimplantation genetic diagnosis to include tissue typing fell within that purpose of assisting a woman to carry a child. All three judges recognised that once preimplantation genetic diagnosis itself was lawful under the Act subject to licensing conditions, then Parliament had delegated the application of the technique to the HFEA, who retained the discretion whether to grant a licence or not: 'Parliament envisaged the possibility or likelihood of future developments (even though it could not know precisely what they would be) and positively intended to bring all such procedures within the sphere of the HFEA, with the exception of those specifically prohibited' (per Mance LJ at paragraph 44).

Thus, to address the question of whether tissue typing could be said to be for assisting women to carry children, the Court of Appeal referred to the emotional state of the woman. In order for her to pursue a pregnancy in confidence that the baby she was carrying would be a compatible tissue match for an existing child, tissue typing would be acceptable within the licence for preimplantation genetic diagnosis. This appears to be a somewhat stretched interpretation that goes beyond the purpose of the Act. Indeed, the definition of treatment services under the Act states that the woman needs assistance to *carry* a child. The parliamentary debates on the 1990 Act clearly show that the Act was adopted with a view to providing a medical solution to those having difficulty in conceiving, or to avoid transmitting a serious hereditary disease, which may itself threaten the ability of the woman to carry the fetus to term. In this respect, Kay J's approach at first instance has much to recommend it because he recognised that consideration of elements external either to the infertility of the woman or to the health of the embryo itself (in the case of a genetic disease) could not be said to be pursuant to the purpose of treatment services. Whereas preimplantation genetic diagnosis may enable a woman to carry a child free from a serious genetic disease – and as such falls within the definition of 'treatment services', any extended application will not automatically satisfy this condition. Indeed, tissue typing cannot be said to be directly linked to these aims as it is clear that those seeking tissue typing are not necessarily sterile nor do they run the risk of passing on a serious genetic disease – they are merely hoping to conceive a child who may be a potential donor for an existing child. By extending the meaning of 'treatment', the Court of Appeal has moved from consideration of the interests of the embryo being carried to those of the woman, without the decision being justified by reference to fundamental principles. This wide purposive approach thus confirms the mandate of the HFEA to decide on an ad hoc basis which applications of preimplantation genetic diagnosis are lawful. However, it is questionable whether Parliament intended such decisions to be taken in the absence of a clear principled framework and without recourse to public debate (this point has recently been echoed by Brownsword[10]). 'Democracy is not served by unelected quangos taking decisions on behalf of Parliament.'[11] Indeed, it will only be in the case of an interest group seeking judicial review that the legitimacy of any decision will be publicly scrutinised.

The outcome of these cases is two-fold: (i) preimplantation genetic diagnosis is authorised within the statutory framework of the 1990 Act thanks to an ambiguous purposive interpretation of the definition of treatment and suitability of the embryo to be implanted; (ii) the HFEA has been recognised by the court as the legitimate forum in which further applications of the technique may be authorised on a case-by-case basis, even if they are carried out in the interests of a third party. It is this latter factor which poses the most difficult legal and ethical questions that need to be addressed. An examination of the reasoning adopted in the Hashmi and Whitaker cases reveals a number of inconsistencies in the Authority's reasoning and illustrates the inadequacy of the implicit statutory provisions relating to preimplantation genetic diagnosis to address the challenging ethical issues raised. A recent change in policy announced by the HFEA to allow tissue typing as a stand-alone test without the need for the embryo to be screened for a genetic disease clearly attempts to achieve greater consistency.[12] Yet critical analysis of this latest policy merely serves to highlight the inadequacy of the ad hoc approach to the regulation of preimplantation genetic diagnosis in general as it reinforces regulation built upon scientific ability and individual desires, rather than upon sound ethical principle. This social construction of law fails to address the long-term issues engendered by the application of assisted conception techniques in general.

TOWARDS A PRINCIPLED CONSTRUCTION OF LAW?

It is evident that the development of the regulation on preimplantation genetic diagnosis has been dictated by the availability of techniques and their ability to respond to individual needs. As a result, the general terms of the 1990 Act facilitate an ad hoc approach by the regulatory body. Yet this ad hoc approach risks producing inconsistent, not to say incompatible, decisions. Consequently, it is suggested that a more principled framework based on standard ethical principles may be more appropriate to deal with the varied applications of preimplantation genetic diagnosis.

In search of coherence

One criterion figures heavily in the decisions of the HFEA: that of the welfare of the child. Although the concept is subject to limitations and individual interpretation, it is nevertheless a common, albeit complex, concept in English law. The welfare of a hypothetical child expected to be born from an embryo in vitro is even more difficult to articulate and must undoubtedly be the source of arbitrary appreciation. Nevertheless, given that preimplantation genetic diagnosis is carried out in the expectation that the embryo will develop into a child, it is understandable that the welfare of the child to be born appears to be the central principle adopted in the decision of the HFEA in the Hashmi case. However, the Authority's interpretation of this principle is far from watertight as a more in-depth analysis of the Hashmi and Whitaker cases will show. As noted above, the HFEA expressly stated that it intended to give a wide interpretation to the notion of welfare, going beyond the mere consideration of the physical welfare of the embryo and resulting child. Consequently, according to the Authority's appreciation it was in the resulting child's *moral* interests to know that he was conceived to save his sibling. There are three difficulties with this: first, it is merely an assumption of a wider *moral* well-being of the future child, which is particularly difficult to evaluate. Second, it is inconsistent with the Authority's insistence on the need for the embryo to be tested for a genetic disease as a condition to carrying out the extended tissue typing application. Finally, preimplantation genetic diagnosis is founded upon the biopsy of a one or two cells from the embryo. As the chair of the HFEA has accepted, this invasive intervention might prove to be harmful to the development of the embryo and resulting child.[13]

With regard to the first criticism, we can indeed question on what basis it may be said that knowing one was conceived to treat another person is necessarily in the best (moral) interests of the child conceived. The Authority fails to consider the effect on the child and the parent–child relationship once the child born 'to save' the sibling learns of the circumstances surrounding his or her existence: 'To what extent would children resent such an intrusion on their own autonomy? . . . [T]he selection may well come with a stifling set of expectations'.[14] Furthermore, how detrimental might the feeling be on the child of having been born to 'save' a sibling, but perhaps not succeeding? Likewise, the prospect of being asked to donate tissue at a later stage may also be cause for concern. The HFEA indicated that it would not support such a practice (para 3.16 of its Opinion), but it will have no say over what happens to the child once born. It will be a question of whether the parents give consent to the second child donating certain tissue, as with all cases of donation by incompetent minors. Consequently, the child's capacity for autonomy is threatened as he may become a living donor throughout his youth. Thus, although some could suggest that the fact the child once born will be loved for himself means that he is not used merely as an end, we can see that the prospect of being forced or expected to donate may be detrimental. John Harris has suggested that the motives for the creation of a child are irrelevant provided it is in the child's interest to be created (and it must be, because existence is better than non-existence) *and* provided that the individual will have the capacity for autonomy.[15] However, it is precisely the future autonomy of the child born that is in jeopardy if extended use of preimplantation genetic diagnosis is permitted: 'The nature of the act depends not only on the act itself but also on its role in a total human situation over time'.[16] Paradoxically, the risk of instrumentalisation is acknowledged by those who favour allowing tissue typing in conjunction with preimplantation genetic diagnosis for a serious genetic disease but not where the embryo does not run the risk of suffering from a genetic disease.

Thus, the second difficulty lies in reconciling the (assumed) moral welfare of the child to be born in saving his sibling with the decision of the HFEA in the Whitaker case. It will be remembered that the HFEA refused to authorise preimplantation genetic diagnosis accompanied by tissue typing when the embryo to be tested did not run any perceived risk of a genetic disease. Yet if the avoidance of a genetic disease in the embryo is to be the overriding criterion, there is no need to refer to the moral welfare of the child in saving his sibling. There cannot be said to be any link between preventing the implantation of an embryo carrying a genetic disease and implanting an embryo which will also be a tissue match for an existing person. As the first instance judge in the *Quintavalle* case pointed out, treatment to identify an embryo suitable to be implanted may extend to the former but cannot be said to extend to the latter. Yet the moral welfare of that child knowing that he may have saved his sibling is exactly the same, irrespective of whether the embryo has been tested for the existence of a genetic disease in his own right. Likewise, the welfare of the family in saving the sick sibling would also be promoted as it was held to be the case in the Hashmi situation. Clearly, the potential for providing life-saving treatment through the cord blood is the same in both cases and yet the potential benefit to the future child is not deemed to be the primary consideration of the HFEA in this second case.

Finally, it is also important not to deny the relevance of practical consider-ations in such an ethically challenging debate. As well as the already noted possibility that biopsy might damage the development of the embryo and resultant child, selection following diagnosis leads to the destruction of embryos deemed unsuitable.

In the absence of a convincing, reasoned use of the welfare principle, it appears necessary to seek an alternative framework which will ensure that consistent, coherent decisions are made and that the ethical challenges posed by extended applications of preimplantation genetic diagnosis are properly addressed.

Acknowledging ethical imperatives

At the beginning of the third millennium, it is clear that the economic and therefore political, stakes in scientific progress are great. As the analysis of the development of the law relating to preimplantation genetic diagnosis illus-trates, we are experiencing a 'biocracy' rather than a democracy when it comes to assessing the validity and viability of new reproductive techniques and their application. The 1990 Act and its application by the Authority it instigated merely accommodates the exercise of preimplantation genetic diagnosis that existed before then. This approach sits neatly with the overall consumer climate in which assisted conception has developed. Yet it is ques-tionable whether such an approach can be maintained in the light of the very serious issues raised by the increasing instrumentalisation of human life. On what basis then should the law be constructed?

A possible starting point is the fundamental tenet that humanity must always be treated as an end in itself and not merely as a means to an end for another as espoused by Immanuel Kant: 'Act so that you use humanity, in your own person as well as in that of another, always also as an end and never only as a means'.[17] It may be questioned whether Kant's imperative is merely 'empty rhetoric invoking resonant principles with no conceivable or coherent application to the problem at hand'. Harris states: 'If you are inter-ested in the ethics of creating people, then so long as existence is in the cre-ated individual's own best interests, and so long as the individual will have the capacity for autonomy like any other, the motives for which the individ-ual was created are either morally irrelevant or subordinate to other moral considerations.'[18] However, it is crucial to remember that preimplantation genetic diagnosis itself is carried out in the expectation that the embryo will develop into a child. Thus, the basic principle is potentially central to both medical and legal considerations and as such serves as a useful starting point in the debate on the selection of embryos using preimplantation genetic diagnosis.

Yet if we are to invoke this ethical stance, we need to ask whether there is something about preimplantation genetic diagnosis or its extended applications, that prevent the resulting child from being treated as an end in itself ? With regard to preimplantation genetic diagnosis accompanied by tissue typing, an affirmative answer must be forthcoming. As suggested above, this is because the autonomy of the resulting child is limited by the fact that the parents have predetermined that the child will be a suitable and available donor for the sick sibling. Therefore, if we look at the *purpose* of the conception of the embryos (the birth of a child with particular genetic traits) and the *consequence* (using the child born as a donor for a sick sibling), it is possible to suggest that the embryo's very existence is desired for what it will become. The very selection of embryos based on a third party's interest (tissue typing for compatibility with sibling; sex selection of offspring for social reasons) indicates that one category of person is desirable over another and that a third person (parent or doctor or state?) will make a choice. There is then the risk of disrupting the reciprocal respect due between equal individuals in what Habermas has referred to as the 'reversibility' of inter-human relationships: nobody should depend on another in an irreversible manner.[19] The choice of (desirable) genetic characteristics by one person for another person may be perceived as violating the equal status of all individuals. It follows that if the purpose and consequence of the conception is carried out for a third party's interest, then the embryo and resulting child are not respected as ends in themselves, but rather used as an instrument to satisfy the third party's needs or desires. The autonomy of the future child is threatened as they may be required to act as donors for their sick sibling. Such a potential burden leads to the suggestion that a regulatory framework based on the fundamental principle of never treating others merely as a means to another's end is to be preferred.

It follows from the above discussion that preimplantation genetic diagnosis has the potential both to identify and select embryos that are free from genetic disease and to identify and select embryos whose very existence will serve another's end. The difficulty, as recognised by the Human Fertilisation and Embryology Authority, is that it is necessary to distinguish acceptable from unacceptable applications of preimplantation genetic diagnosis. Once it is accepted that the resulting child should not be used merely as a means to an end, as a matter of principle, preimplantation genetic diagnosis should be limited to applications that do not violate this rule.

Consequently, it is suggested that within the confines of the 1990 Act, preimplantation genetic diagnosis should be limited to situations where it may be said to be in the best *clinical* interests of the child to be born from the selected embryo. That is, that preimplantation genetic diagnosis should address one major aim – to assist families who are identified as genetic disease carriers or sufferers to conceive a baby not affected by the same genetic disease. This responds to the very social need of families who experience difficulties in looking after one handicapped child and wish to procreate using the techniques available, to avoid bringing another handicapped child into their family. Moreover, a joint consultation paper in 1999 between the HFEA and the Advisory Committee on Genetic Testing (now the Human Genetics Commission) reinforced this point.[20,21]

There may well be difficulties with identifying what is a serious genetic disorder, but it is suggested that the current reference to Royal College of Obstetricians and Gynaecologists' guidelines is appropriate.[22] These Guidelines apply to decisions to terminate a pregnancy on medical grounds following prenatal diagnosis in utero. For preimplantation genetic diagnosis, it does not seem appropriate for the legislator to lay down an exhaustive list of illnesses which would become ever longer as further advances are made in identifying more genetic diseases. Furthermore, this maintains a certain place for proper clinical judgement as it protects against state intervention in the clinical exercise of the doctor–patient relationship. It also ensures that the future child is at the centre of the equation. There are no considerations for third parties as there may be in the case of tissue typing, or sex selection to suit the parents' wishes. Confining the use of preimplantation genetic diagnosis to the diagnosis of a serious genetic disease in the embryo itself does not undermine the idea of the child as an end in himself. Thus, there is no risk of using that child as a recurrent donor for a sick sibling – unlike the extension of preimplantation genetic diagnosis to include tissue typing which does indeed potentially risk violating respect for that child's physical integrity. Consequently, identifying compatibility for a donor to treat a *genetic* disease is deemed acceptable – because the embryo itself will be screened for the disease.

Such an approach may appear at odds with the overwhelmingly utilitarian nature of the 1990 Act. Yet it would be pure reverie to image that there cannot be any contradictions in such a sensitive area. Nevertheless, this does not mean that society should abstain from constantly questioning the path it has chosen and admitting to the need for change when it can be objectively justified.

CONCLUSION

This need for change has now been recognised and the Government announced in January 2004 that the 1990 Act would be reviewed (see www.doh.gov.uk). We may question whether it would have been opportune for the HFEA to await the outcome of this review before considering any change in policy to the extended use of tissue typing which was announced in July 2004.[12] Given the ramifications of the decisions taken to date on extended uses of preimplantation genetic diagnosis, coupled with an increasing societal awareness of the need for sensitive ethical issues to be fully discussed, it was surely inevitable that democratic debate should be reopened. It is opportune to note that preimplantation genetic diagnosis provides the vehicle by which the very foundations of the current regulatory regime may be evaluated. As alluded to at the beginning of this chapter, it does not appear viable to question the very existence of embryos in vitro: even if a moratorium were to be declared today, there would still exist a number of embryos in vitro the fate of whom would have to be decided. However, preimplantation genetic diagnosis does allow us to reflect upon the implications of the regulatory framework adopted in 1990 on two fundamental points: (i) what sort of society deliberately creates embryos only to discard those not deemed genetically suitable for a third party's interest? and (ii) to what extent is society prepared to allow the instrumentalisation of another human being for a third party's purpose? The first point goes to the heart of eugenic practices, so often condemned by civilised societies and yet so easily couched in acceptable terms: if we can implant an embryo who not only is free from a genetic disease, but who could also provide compatible tissue to save the life of a sibling, what is so grotesque with that? The second point violates the general principle of individual autonomy and the right to respect for the dignity of each human being. If we allow scientific imperatives and individualism to construct the law instead of coherent ethical principles, we run the risk of returning to a society that places biological characteristics above all other considerations. History has shown us that some of the worst humanitarian atrocities were committed when biological criteria form the basis of an individual's position in society. Preimplantation genetic diagnosis may be a far cry from those activities; but unless it is carried out within defined parameters, it may toll the knell for the very basis of civilised societies – respect for each individual member of the human race in his or her own right.

References

1. Holm S. Ethical issues in pre-implantation genetic diagnosis. In: Harris J, Holm S, eds. The future of human reproduction. Oxford: Clarendon Press; 1998:176–190.
2. Lee R, Morgan D. Human fertilisation and embryology: regulating the reproductive revolution. London: Blackstone Press; 2001.
3. Jackson E. Regulating reproduction: law, technology and autonomy. Oxford: Hart; 2001:183.
4. Morgan D. Legal and ethical dilemmas of fetal sex identification and gender selection. In: Morgan D, ed. Issues in medical law and ethics. London: Cavendish; 2001:129–151.
5. Human Fertilisation and Embryology Authority. Ethical issues in the creation and selection of pre-implantation embryos to produce tissue donors: Opinion of the Ethics Committee, 22 November 2001. London: Human Fertilisation and Embryology Authority.
6. Clarke K, Secretary of State for Health. House of Commons Debates vol. 170, 2 April 1990, col. 914. London: Hansard; 1990.
7. Richardson J, MP, House of Commons Debates 23 April 1990, cols. 42–44. London: Hansard; 1990.
8. Department of Health. Preimplantation genetic diagnosis – guiding principles for commissioners of NHS services. London: HMSO; September 2002.
9. Human Fertilisation and Embryology Authority. HFEA confirms that HLA tissue typing may only take place when pre-implantation genetic diagnosis is required to avoid a serious genetic disorder. Press release, 1 August 2002. London: HFEA.

10. Brownsword R. Reproductive opportunities and regulatory challenges. Modern Law Review 2004; 67(2):304.
11. Fourth Report, Science and Technology Committee. Developments in human genetics and embryology. Hansard, House of Commons, session 2001–2002, para 26.
12. Preimplantation Tissue Typing: Human Fertilisation and Embryology Authority Report. Human Fertilisation and Embryology Authority, July 2004. Online. Available: www.hfea.gov.uk.
13. Leather S. Chairman Human Fertilisation and Embryology Authority, Interview on Today Radio 4, 17 June 2003.
14. Botkin JR. Ethical issues and practical problems in pre-implantation genetic diagnosis. Journal of Law, Medicine and Ethics 1998; 26:17–28, at 23.
15. Harris J, Amnesty Lecture: Clones, genes and human rights. In: Burley J, ed. The genetic revolution and human rights. Oxford Amnesty Lectures. Oxford: OUP; 1999.
16. Poplawski N, Gillett G. Ethics and embryos. Journal of Medical Ethics 1991; 17:62–69, at 66.
17. Kant I. Groundwork of the metaphysics of morals, translated HJ Paton. London: Routledge; 1991.
18. Harris J. Cloning and bioethical thinking. Nature 1997; 389:433.
19. Habermas J. Die Zukunft der Menschlichen Natur: Auf dem Weg zu einer liberale Eugenik? (trans. C Bouchindhomme). Paris: Gallimard; 2002:97–98.
20. Human Fertilisation and Embryology Authority, Advisory Committee on Genetic Testing. Consultation document on pre-implantation genetic diagnosis. London: Human Fertilisation and Embryology Authority/ACGT; 1999: para 9.9.
21. Human Fertilisation and Embryology Authority, Human Genetics Commission. Outcome of the public consultation on pre-implantation genetic diagnosis. London: HFEA/HGC; 2001.
22. Royal College of Obstetricians and Gynaecologists. Termination of pregnancy for fetal abnormality. London: RCOG; 1996.

SECTION THREE

Bodies and body parts

SECTION CONTENTS

8. Human bodies, inhuman uses: public reactions and legislative responses to the scandals of bodysnatching   151

9. *Nemo censetur ignorare legem?* Presumed consent to organ donation in France, from Parliament to hospitals   173

Chapter 8

Human bodies, inhuman uses: public reactions and legislative responses to the scandals of bodysnatching

M.E. Rodgers

CHAPTER CONTENTS

Introduction 151
The nineteenth century 152
The twentieth century 153
The public outrage 154
The victims and perpetrators 155
The media response to the
  medical men 157

The medical justification 160
Legislative responses 164
The Anatomy Act 1832 164
The Human Tissue Act 1961
  and the future 167
Conclusion 169
References 169

INTRODUCTION

'Doon the close and up the stair
But an' ben wi' Burke an' Hare
Burke's the butcher
Hare's the thief
Knox the man who buys the beef!'[i]

Burke and Hare rank amongst the best known of Britain's serial killers due to the abhorrent nature of their crimes: murder and profiting from the sale of their victims' bodies. And yet, despite their fame, Burke and Hare were certainly not the only resurrectionists[ii] who committed murder, nor does the evidence indicate that murder was their only means of procuring bodies for sale. However, the public outrage that ensued was such to ensure that their names were branded into the public consciousness to the exclusion of other

---

[i] An extract from a popular song after the Burke and Hare scandal which probably has its origins in the verses commonly published in the penny broadsheets.[1]

[ii] 'Resurrectionists' or 'resurrection men' being the term given to those engaging in the removal of recently buried corpses from the graveyard for the purpose of sale to anatomists and lecturers of anatomy. Frequently the resurrectionists would in fact be medical students themselves.

resurrectionist misdemeanours.[iii] While credit is often given to them as being responsible for the legislative changes regarding the use of corpses for the teaching of anatomy,[2] as will be seen, debate had been continuing for some time on this matter. Legislative change had been contemplated before these crimes came to light, but the new crime of 'Burking',[iv] together with the resulting public panic, increased the pressure to amend the law.

The disgust with which public sentiment regarded these crimes, and the growing public realisation of the precise nature of anatomists' practices, is not something consigned to history. Medical science continues to develop, anatomists continue to need bodies, and bodysnatching, albeit of body parts as opposed to whole corpses, still occurs. The main distinction between the periods is that today's resurrectionists are exclusively the medical men themselves, for example the pathologist at the Royal Liverpool Infirmary, and the practitioners at Bristol Royal Infirmary. Unlike their nineteenth-century peers, today's resurrectionists do not need to resort to murder. The moral outrage surrounding these 'new' resurrectionists is equally strong as that regarding Burke and Hare in the nineteenth century, if not more so, since today we have a developed rights-based culture and a clear expectation of consensual medical practices.

The similarities between the moral panics arising from the bodysnatching scandals in both nineteenth- and twentieth-century Britain will be explored and examined, together with the medical justifications. The legislative consequences will also be considered, since both eras have produced suggestions for reform.

THE NINETEENTH CENTURY

The story of Burke and Hare's unorthodox methods of obtaining bodies for the anatomy lecture halls of Edinburgh broke at the beginning of November 1828. The *Evening Courant* published its account of the affair on 3 November, with broadsides[v] quickly following it up thus:

> 'An account of a most Extraordinary circumstance that took place on Friday night . . ., in a House in the West Port, Edinburgh, where an Old Woman of the name of Campbell is supposed to have been Murdered, and her Body Sold to a Medical Doctor.'[4]

[iii] Note, here the term misdemeanours is not being used in its legal sense.

[iv] See, for example, the comments of Mr O'Connell in the debates in the Commons on the Anatomy Bill in February 1832: '. . . it was much better to risk the chance of some indecencies being committed with respect to dead subjects than to risk the chance of the living being converted into dead subjects by the atrocious practice of Burking'.[3]

[v] Broadsides consisting of a one page 'news' sheet – the accuracy of the news often being in doubt. These broadsides are often referred to as broadsheets, half or quartersides, reflecting the actual size of the paper used. They invariably cost one penny, although the same publishers would often reprint the information, with additional new material in more expensive pamphlets.

Thereafter the press became bored with the affair, with little by way of coverage, until the actual trial of William Burke and his mistress, Helen MacDougal, for murder, with William Hare acting as King's Witness. As stated in the *Glasgow Courier*:

> 'In the absence of any political news of any importance we have devoted a considerable portion of our paper of today in giving a full report of the trial before the High Court of Justiciary, of Burke and Hare.'[5]

The Edinburgh *Evening Courant* ran the report of the trial on 25 December 1828, providing its readers with a full recounting of legal argument and the summing up to the jury.[6] The *Caledonian Mercury* provided two full pages of report on the same day.[vi]

The trial, by the standards of the day, was lengthy, lasting 'above 24 hours' with '55 witnesses called',[7] and resulted in a guilty verdict for Burke and one of not proven for MacDougal. Burke was sentenced to death with his execution date set for 28 January 1829. The remainder of the 'participants' in the crime were set free. When the time came for Burke's public execution he had confessed to at least 16 murders,[vii] although in reality it is likely that the number was somewhat less. Burke's execution was, by all accounts, a particularly popular event. Thousands crowded the streets of Edinburgh to witness his hanging, and when, ironically, his body was publicly dissected, competition for viewing was fierce.

While the mainstream press might have misjudged the public's thirst for knowledge (at least until they ran out of news of the political events in Silestra which had until then dominated the press), the penny broadsides were more than happy to oblige. These popular news-sheets provide an interesting insight into the more mainstream view of the affair, aimed as they were at the less educated of the population who would not read a more traditional newspaper. Frequently these broadsides and subsequent pamphlets took the form of verses and rhymes and they often claimed to be reporting directly from the mouths of the criminals, the victims' relations, or other 'involved' parties. What is interesting, and will be explored below, is the similarity between the nature of the public outcry in the Burke and Hare situation and that evidenced through the media in the Alder Hey scandal over a century later.

THE TWENTIETH CENTURY

The bodysnatching scandal of the modern era is equally well known, concerning as it did, the removal and retention of body parts of children dying in

---

[vi] A collection of cuttings chiefly from Edinburgh newspapers, relating to the Burke and Hare murders (1828–1841) National Library of Scotland Ry.III.a.6(1).
[vii] See, for example, *The Official Confessions of William Burke* (1829 Shillies Library) in National Library of Scotland, West Port Murders, Vol. IV, LC 1573(30), one of the many True or Official Confessions allegedly made by Burke before his execution on 28 Jan 1929.

various NHS hospitals across England and Scotland. The main focus of the scandal was the Alder Hey Hospital in Liverpool, and to a certain extent, the Bristol Royal Infirmary. As with the Burke and Hare case, the initial public realisation of the nature of medical practices following death and post-mortem in these institutions appears somewhat low key. The Bristol Royal Infirmary was, initially, subject to inquiry due to the high mortality rate of children undergoing heart surgery. The surgeons concerned had been referred to the General Medical Council (GMC) with respect to their poor performance, and were found guilty in 1998 of professional misconduct. The complainants, who had precipitated this disciplinary action, were also calling for a Public Inquiry, and an Inquiry was announced on 18 June 1998 (for full terms of reference of the Public Inquiry see the Report[8]). In the GMC hearing evidence was given as to the retention of body parts by the Infirmary but media coverage was not extensive at this stage. It was primarily after the Inquiry and the disclosure by Professor Robert Anderson that Alder Hey was custodian of one of the largest collections of hearts in the UK[9] that the media interest arose, and intensified considerably after an Inquiry into the situation at Alder Hey was announced.[viii] One area of great concern in both cases was the fact that body parts, not restricted to hearts, were being retained and that many parents did not believe they had ever consented to the retention of their child's organs or body parts.[ix] This fact led to some of the most sensationalist coverage in the press, and mirrors the approach in relation to Burke and Hare.

In addition, the relevant inquiries, as supposedly was the case following the Burke and Hare murders, supported the call for amendment of the legislation covering the use of body tissue and organs for medical purposes after death. Before reflecting on the legislative consequences of these scandals, the similarities of the public outrage will be considered.

THE PUBLIC OUTRAGE

The reaction of the media, in both cases the printed press, reflects the nature of the public's perception to these scandals, and demonstrates the repugnance of society to 'unlawful' and 'unnatural' acts being carried out by the

---

[viii] The Inquiry being announced on 3 December 1999 by Lord Hunt, Parliamentary Under Secretary of State. For full details of the term of reference see Chapter 1, para 4.1, the Report of the Royal Liverpool Children's Inquiry.[9]

[ix] It is interesting to note that the majority of parents involved with the Bristol Royal Infirmary Inquiry had indeed completed and signed a consent form. Indeed in the Interim Report, Part II, para 43, the panel states that of the 265 post-mortems 220 'were coroners' post-mortems for which consent and, hence, a signed consent form [was] not required. In relation to the 45 hospital post-mortems, the Inquiry has verified that in all but three cases parents' written consent was given; there was no suggestion in these three cases that consent was not obtained. In a further case, whilst the consent form was missing, the parent recalls giving consent.' What the issue here concerned was the fact that those parents did not understand, or have explained to them, the meaning of the consent documentation that they signed.

medical profession. There are also clear similarities in both cases in relation to the responses by the medical profession itself in justifying its actions and responding to the criticism of medical practices. These similarities will be considered below, focusing on the image created of the victims, the perceptions of the perpetrators, media response to the medical perpetrators, and the justification provided by the medical profession for their acts.

The victims and perpetrators

Despite the difference in numbers of victims between the two affairs, the image of them portrayed in the media is strikingly similar. In the early nineteenth century, where immorality was closely linked to alcohol abuse,[10,11] the description of Burke and Hare's first known victim was of a good, but poor woman, who was in the wrong place at the wrong time. The *Newgate Calendar* cites the evidence of one William Noble, to the effect that Mrs Campbell had on the afternoon before her murder 'begged for charity' and was 'quite destitute' but was also 'sober',[12] suggesting that, although poor, Mrs Campbell had a good moral character. This perception is endorsed in the broadsides, 'the old woman, it is said, *with reluctance* joined in the mirth, and also partook of the liquor' (emphasis added),[4] again suggesting the victim's moral character.

Their second known victim was equally perceived to be of a good moral character, albeit that he was classed as an idiot, and went by the name of 'Daft Jamie'.[x] Jamie (James Wilson) had allegedly been lured to his death after encountering Burke in the Grassmarket when Jamie was seeking the whereabouts of his mother.[13] The description of his character is almost eulogistic:

> 'Jamie was for many years (before he fell a victim) never known to be absent a day, forenoon, afternoon nor evening, (or even at any other time, if he got notice that there were a sermon) from Mr Aikman's Chapel, it was astonishing how regularly he attended that place of worship.'

He was also described as a 'poor, harmless good natured idiot'[14] and was supposedly well known to those medical students who observed his dissection, a fact that caused great concern due to their failure to report the murder: '[I]f any of them had been possessed of the smallest feeling, they would have given notice to the Captain of Police'.[14]

Unlike many of their fellow resurrectionists, Burke and Hare claimed they had never disinterred a body to sell to the anatomists:

> 'You have been a resurrectionist (as it is called) I understand?' 'No. Neither Hare nor myself ever got a body from a churchyard. All we sold

---

[x] Burke and Hare were never charged with the murder of Daft Jamie, but the circumstantial evidence was such that in all likelihood the pair did kill and sell his body to Dr Knox.

were murdered save the first one which was that of the woman who died a natural death in Hare's house . . .'[15]

Hence, if this so called confession is true, the term 'resurrectionist' does not, in reality, apply. However, the purpose of their crime, the sale of a body to an anatomist, highlighted the immoral practice that had been tolerated by the law enforcers until that date:

'So long as the resurrectionists confined their activities to the filching of dead bodies, their illegal acts, although exciting disgust and horror, did not approach the magnitude of crime.'[2]

Thereafter the illegality of 'filching' dead bodies and selling them lost the tacit acceptance of the law enforcers.

The murderers, and also the anatomist Dr Knox, who received and paid for the bodies, were roundly condemned for their immoral behaviour and for their 'monstrous Crimes'.[16] Certain media interests pressed for the prosecution of Dr Knox, the 'learned butcher',[16] as 'a receiver, or accessory after the fact' since without the existence of the trade in bodies, 'we should not hear of these bloody murders and hardened wretches'.[17] Indeed Dr Knox was:

'[In] the eyes of many . . . a greater criminal . . . and outspoken and unthinking people went the length of declaring that these misguided men were but instruments in his hands obeying his behests.'[18]

Despite the lack of legal action against Dr Knox, the public did take matters into their own hands and shortly after the discovery of these 'events', there occurred a 'popular tumoult' whereby an effigy of Dr Knox was hanged from a tree, then burnt, and a riotous crowd assembled outside Knox's premises in Surgeon's Square.[19] Although questions were asked in parts of the media about Knox's involvement, and this small section of the media classing him equally a perpetrator since Knox was seen to be just as much a 'butcher' as Burke and Hare, as will be seen later, the general media coverage of Dr Knox's role was far more circumspect.

The sentiments about the moral worth and harmless innocence of the known victims of Burke and Hare and the insensitivity of the medical profession are echoed in the Bristol Royal Infirmary and Royal Liverpool Children's Hospital inquiries, although here much of the rhetoric is linked to the perceptions of the perpetrators. The fact that the 'victims' were all children increased the level of outrage felt at the desecration of their bodies. While it could be argued that these children were not victims in the Burke and Hare sense, since they all suffered congenital medical difficulties and did not technically die via deliberate killing, the actions of the medical profession are throughout castigated as being 'criminal', hence making the term 'victims' a useful one to use. In the Report of the Royal Liverpool Children's Inquiry, the view of the parents of one of the victims is explained thus:

'They describe the hospital as having stolen their daughter's body which was "as white as driven snow. It was reduced to skin and bone by predators and it must never happen again".'[20]

Another family 'discovered their beautiful daughter's heart had been one of those removed by Birmingham Children's Hospital without consent'.[21]

In the Royal Liverpool Children's Inquiry a parent commented 'Medical research must not be carried out at the expense of *innocent* children'[22] (emphasis added).

There are numerous examples from the media coverage and the Inquiry Reports themselves to support this notion of criminality, and the horror and revulsion the removal of organs caused:

'They are angry at the deceit, grotesqueness and obscenity of removing without their knowledge or consent their daughter's brain, heart and lungs.'[22]

'It is mutilation.'[23]

'Hearts, while medically just wonderful pumps, are the organs to which we attribute love. To steal them from children is repugnant.'[24]

'[The father] has slammed the actions of the doctors in the case as "barbaric". The couple eventually won their legal battle. It is the first case in Scotland where parents have got back a child's "stolen" organ.'[25]

'Their daughter was abused and treated like a piece of meat.'[26]

'This is symptomatic of pathology practice, which was barbaric . . . this is Scotland's holocaust – our children were ripped open and their organs experimented on.'[27]

'In my opinion what they did was barbaric. It is like something out of Burke and Hare.'[25]

As these extracts demonstrate, there are common themes – the revulsion felt due to the theft of body parts, the callousness of the medical profession and the dislike of use of body parts for medical research: themes that all arose in the Burke and Hare era. Not only was the public reaction to the news of the scandals similar, the media vilification (or lack of it) of the medical men concerned, the justification of the medical profession for their actions and the expressed knowledge of the medical profession as to the relevant legislation, all show a striking resonance.

The media response to the medical men

Although the medical men concerned in both eras have come in for criticism through the media, the methods employed and the extent of the vilification have been very limited. While Dr Knox was seen, in some quarters, as being as much a butcher as Burke and Hare, the general approach was to do nothing more than to allude to his involvement, especially in the lead-up to the trial and its immediate aftermath. Even when reporting on the 'popular tumoult' of the Edinburgh public, the reference was to an 'Effigy of a *certain*

Doctor, who has been rendered very obnoxious to the public by recent events'[19] (emphasis added). Elsewhere references are still allusory:

> 'To whom were the bodies so murdered sold?' 'To Dr ————. We took the bodies to his rooms in ———— and then went to his house to receive the money from him.'[28]
>
> 'After a search, the body was found yesterday morning in the lecture room of a *respectable practitioner*.'[4] (Emphasis added.)
>
> 'Against ————, the medical practitioner, who had purchased many of the bodies from Burke and his companions, the curses were loud and deep.'[29]

Despite this latter claim, the curses must have been through means other than the press since the Edinburgh *Weekly Chronicle* was stated to have commented, 'With regard to Dr Knox too much delicacy and reserve have been maintained by . . . the press'.[30] Indeed, the reserve continued into the other means of disseminating information – the broadsides and the songsheets – which referred to his involvement thus:

> 'Men, women, children, old and young
> The sickly and the hale
> Were murder'd, pack'd up, and sent off
> To K————'s human sale.'[31]

Exactly why Knox was rarely named is not clear. For those in Edinburgh, presumably everyone would have known who was being referred to, so there would be no need to name him. But equally, because Knox was known to be the 'respectable practitioner' of the reports, what reason exists to keep his name out of the media? Also, the coverage of Burke and Hare's misdemeanours spread further than Edinburgh alone – with publications from Glasgow and London being common, and also some falling outside of the immediate timescale of events. Arguably, this caution or reserve exists because of Knox's position – he was an eminent surgeon and anatomical lecturer of the day and deserved respect, as did many others of his situation and class. This reverence is something that still persists today, with the ready acceptance of things done and said by the medical profession.

While respect for medical practitioners continues today, the media are less likely to grant an elevated status to their actions and the only circumstance when they are likely to refuse to 'name and shame' is where there is a risk of defamation claims being brought. However, it is interesting to note the paucity of press coverage for the modern day 'bodysnatchers' by reference to the actual perpetrators. As the scandals in Bristol and Alder Hey were unfolding, individual practitioners were not being targeted for criticism – the references are to 'they', 'the doctors', 'the hospital' or 'the pathologists' – even though in some cases the surgeons involved were known and were capable of being named. Even after the respective Inquiry Reports were published, very little individual criticism took place, and interestingly, the Inquiries themselves were reserved in their comments. The Bristol Royal Infirmary Inquiry Interim Report comments thus:

'27... There was, however, a long-standing habit among *pathologists* (emphasis added) of taking and keeping human material, other than that required to establish the cause of death, for other purposes; for example research or education . . . it was common among *pathologists* to keep human material. . . .'
'57... blame has a proper role where there is personal misconduct. But where, as here, it was a system which was responsible, and a system which needs to be changed, blaming any individual is not only unfair and unhelpful; it is positively counter-productive.'[32]

Hence, despite the ability to recognise individuals who were remiss in their practice, for example Mr Dhasmana, who despite being advised in 1992 to seek clarification from the parents of children dying during surgery that tissue could be retained following post-mortem, stated 'lately there has been some oversight on my part to discuss the matter with parents and relatives and therefore consent was not taken by my junior staff'; or Mr Wisheart, who despite receiving and acknowledging the advice given, 'neither accepted the basis of (this advice) nor agreed to vary his conduct',[33] the press did not 'go to town'. The main aspect of press coverage was the fact that the surgeons in question were disciplined for poor surgery, not for their poor communication with parents, or for their failure to comply with guidance issued from their employers that resulted in retention of organs without the knowledge of the deceased's parents.

The Alder Hey scenario was slightly different, in that the evidence to the Inquiry demonstrated that the actions of one pathologist alone contributed to the wholesale removal and retention of body parts, and yet here too, the response of the media was muted. In the Inquiry Report itself it was stated:

'Within a week of taking up the Chair Professor van Velzen issued an instruction in the Unit that there was to be no disposal of human material. The technical staff soon realised that Professor van Velzen's clinical practice in the removal and retention of organs was unlike anything they had seen before. Until now pathologists had retained sections only of the relevant organs and returned everything else to the body except heart/lungs and possibly brains in relevant cases. Professor van Velzen removed every organ in every case and retained every organ in every case.'[34]

As with the Bristol Royal Infirmary Inquiry, the Alder Hey process sought to minimise the 'blame' that could attach to other doctors:

'We heard no evidence from any doctor that parents were ever told that they would be burying the body without the brain or heart. The doctors themselves were *ignorant* of Professor van Velzen's practice of removing all the organs for fixation, so they could not have explained this to the parents.'[34] (Emphasis added.)

Despite this clear recognition of one sole perpetrator, van Velzen, the media was again muted in its response. *The Express* ran the story thus:

> 'The doctor who stripped body parts from dead babies went into hiding last night as the enormity of the horror at Alder Hey hospital was exposed. Professor Dick van Velzen, 51, the man responsible for one of the biggest scandals in British medical history, was dubbed a monster for not expressing a single word of regret.'
>
> 'Now he is facing prosecution after a Government Report branded him a liar and a thief . . .'
>
> '[The Health Secretary] was scathing of van Velzen, who had "lied to parents, lied to other doctors . . . He falsified statistics and reports".'[35]

Despite the inclusion of sensationalist language, the underlying tone is still somewhat respectful and belies the moral panic that was created when the scandal of body part retention first broke. *The Guardian* was even more circumspect, and simply reported the main findings in relation to van Velzen's activities, again despite previous sensationalist reporting during the lead-up to the final report.[36] When van Velzen was suspended by the GMC, *The Guardian* described him as a 'composite of Burke and Hare, with a dash of Hannibal Lecter and a smattering of Mengele thrown in' but still went on to ameliorate such criticism by commenting that

> 'the professor, for all his flaws, is hardly a necromancer. Nor has he killed anyone. In hoarding body parts without consent, he was only doing, albeit on a grander scale, what other doctors did.'[37]

The outrage at van Velzen's activities was short-lived, the press having moved on within a matter of weeks to the next big issue: the seeking of monetary compensation from the hospitals concerned.

Obviously the reasons behind this reluctance to 'name and shame' the relevant medical practitioners can only be guessed at. Regardless of these reasons, it is remarkable that the media in both eras have, by and large, respected the medical profession and published relatively little on their misdeeds. Rather, they have provoked a wide public outrage that is aimed at the actions of 'doctors' in general without specifically targeting the moral panic on those few practitioners who were involved.

THE MEDICAL JUSTIFICATION

In seeking to justify the actions that they took, the medical practitioners in both eras again show surprising similarities, despite the fact that different legal regimes existed, and the nature of medical training between the two time frames was significantly different.

At the time Dr Knox was conducting his anatomy lectures in Edinburgh, the legislation governing the use of corpses for anatomical uses was the Act of Geo. II which directed that 'the bodies of murderers shall be given up to be anatomized'.[38] As a consequence the Select Committee on Anatomy of 1828, established to consider the problems faced by anatomists, found that the number of subjects available via this means was 'so small in comparison to his total wants, that the inconvenience which he would sustain from its repeal would be wholly unimportant'.[38] The numbers claimed necessary for a student to be fully versed in the workings of the human body, and hence to be able to practise competently, varied only slightly from witness to witness. For example, Sir Astley Cooper suggested:

> 'If he be afterwards to practise surgery, I should say three bodies are required, two for anatomical purposes, the other for operations on the dead; less would be insufficient . . .'[39]

whereas William Lawrence Esq. stated:

> 'I should think it desirable that a student who is going through his education as a professional man, more particularly if he is to practise surgery, should be able to employ three or four bodies annually for dissection and other purposes. A smaller number than that might be considered to be barely sufficient.'[40]

Despite these differences as to how many bodies were needed per student, all witnesses were agreed that anatomy, and the study of it, was critical to becoming an effective practitioner, and without anatomy, practitioners would be a danger to their patients:

> '. . . you must employ medical men, whether they be ignorant or informed; but if you have none but ignorant medical men, it is you who suffer from it; and the fact is, that the want of subjects will very soon lead to your becoming the unhappy victims of operations founded and performed in ignorance.'[41]
> '. . . what degree of importance [do] you attach to dissection, both as regards the practise of surgery and of medicine?' 'There can be no knowledge of surgery without it, and very little knowledge of medicine.'[42]
> '[Dissection] is of the highest importance . . . nothing in life, I believe, that can be considered as more important; it is the foundation of all medical knowledge.'[43]

The clear message was that dissection, and the supply of bodies to use for dissection, was crucial for medical education.

As to the level of knowledge of the legal provisions underpinning the supply of bodies, again most of the witnesses showed a surprisingly homogeneous lack of understanding.

> 'The law does not prevent our obtaining the body of an individual if we think proper; for there is no person, let his situation be what it may, whom, if I were disposed to dissect, I could not obtain . . .' 'What

have professional men generally understood to be the law on the subject of receiving into their possession, for the purpose of dissection, the bodies of persons who have been disinterred; have they known that for so doing they were indictable for a misdemeanour?' 'Until I read the charge of Baron Hullock, I did not understand that a surgeon was exposed to any danger from dissection, therefore I have never concealed dissection in my own house . . . I did not then know that I was amenable to the law . . . We did not consider, until of late, that it was a misdemeanour to have a body in our possession.'[xi, 44]

In response to a question of the knowledge of anatomy professors on the legal position of having disinterred bodies in their presence, and the fact that this was a misdemeanour, Caesar Hawkins commented, 'I believe it did not occur, it did not to myself, and probably not to others'.[45]

As for Dr Knox, he also claimed no knowledge of, or breach of, the law. In March 1829 (notably after the Select Committee Report), Knox wrote to the *Caledonian Mercury* with evidence as to his innocence; this evidence being from a 'Committee' established to assess his liability. The report concluded:

'It appears, in evidence, that Dr Knox had formed and expressed the opinion (long prior to any dealing with Burke and Hare) that a considerable supply of subjects for anatomical purposes might be procured by purchase, and without any crime, from the relatives or connections of deceased persons in the lower ranks of society.'
'In forming this opinion . . . the Committee cannot consider Dr Knox to have been culpable. They believe there is nothing contrary to the law of the land in procuring subjects to dissect in that way . . .'[46]

This misconception as to the legal provisions was not confined to the medical men themselves – surprisingly perhaps, even magistrates did not know it was a misdemeanour to possess a body for dissection unless it was the body of a murderer, as was indicated by one Thomas Halls in his evidence to the Select Committee:

'You are one of the police magistrates for Bow-street?' 'Yes.' 'Have you considered the state of the law as it affects persons having possession of dead bodies, whether they are guilty or not of any offence?' 'I should conceive that the mere possession of bodies for the purpose of dissection was not an offence.'[47]

[xi] The reference to Baron Hullock refers to an indictment for conspiracy to procure a disinterred body for the purposes of dissection: *R. v Davies and another*, reported in *The Times*, 19 May 1828 and included in the Appendices to the Select Committee Report.

With this level of knowledge among law enforcers,[xii] it is perhaps not surprising that the medical men carried on their dissections in blissful ignorance of their own misdeeds!

The claims of benefiting medical science and lack of knowledge of the law are to be found in the Bristol Royal Infirmary and Alder Hey reports as justification for the actions of the profession, together with a desire to spare the deceased's relatives additional grief. As indicated earlier, the Interim Report from Bristol highlighted the common practice of retaining human material for a range of purposes and cites one pathologist thus:

> 'Many of these conditions are rare and no two hearts with a given condition are quite the same. So, by keeping quite a large number, a very large number from the perspective of people who are not pathologists, it is possible to provide somebody who wishes to study a particular anomaly a range of examples that would take them many years to see in their own practice.'[49]

The Interim Report goes on to conclude that:

> '. . . taking and using human material were important for medical development, research and education was seen by the medical-scientific community as sufficient justification in itself.'[50]

The Alder Hey report endorses this reasoning for keeping substantial collections of body parts; in Chapter 2 stating, for example:

> 'There can be no doubt that the use of the heart collection has been invaluable in terms of research, education and training . . . Heart specimens have also been used to . . . develop methods of diagnosis in life, to develop operations and techniques . . . [and] the most compelling evidence of the value of the collection was the dramatic reduction in the mortality rate following complex cardiac surgery.'[51]

However, despite these benefits the report points out that 'the value and benefits generally . . . does not in itself justify the collection'.[52]

With regard to legal knowledge, the medical profession were equally lacking, although the lack of clarity of the legal regime itself could be seen to provide some form of excuse. The primary Act called into question, where post-mortem examinations whether for the coroner or for the hospital itself are concerned, is the Human Tissue Act 1961, although the precise details of the Act are not important here. In the Interim Report from Bristol the lawfulness, and legal knowledge of the medical practitioners, was considered in the following manner:

[xii] It is not unreasonable to assume a working knowledge of statutory law for a stipendiary magistrate at this point in time. Although for some time the magistrates attached to the nine police offices in London had no legal background, being aldermen etc., after Robert Peel became Home Secretary in 1822 he adopted the practice of appointing lawyers as police magistrates (see further Bentley[48]).

'As regards the lawfulness of the practices adopted . . ., the overall impression . . . is that, while the law was recognised as having some relevance, it was not clearly understood. . . It is no wonder that a kind of professional folklore developed which served the role of the real law . . . Practice had developed . . . which suited the interests and needs of those involved: the medical professionals. Pathologists and clinicians largely held the view, if they ever gave their mind to it, that the law was something remote, far removed from the realities of their daily practice.'[53]

Equally, the Alder Hey Inquiry was

'. . . surprised at the general ignorance of the medical profession concerning the provisions of the Human Tissue Act 1961. No doctor could remember having read it . . . [N]one had any training in the legal requirements at undergraduate level and nor did they receive any training in their various clinical posts.'[54]

The paternalistic approach of the practitioners in both hospitals, in claiming that detail was not given about post-mortems in order to protect parents from the realities of the examination, and through a desire not to upset the parents any further at a time of grief was noted, but also seen as a reason self-serving to the profession, and was certainly no excuse for failing to comply with the law.

The use of paternalism by the profession, and the concern to ensure the development of medical knowledge in both eras, is not unexpected. However, the disregard of legal provisions is of more concern. In both time periods, the lack of adherence to the law was blatant, whether or not linked to a desire to do good to the greater number, and that ignorance should be used as a justification should only add to the moral panic that these scandals caused.

LEGISLATIVE RESPONSES

The Anatomy Act 1832

'Exposure of [Burke and Hare's] crimes aroused public sentiment to such an extent that the Parliament, which had long ignored the prayers and petitions of anatomists and surgeons for the legalisation of anatomical study, was compelled to act.'[2]

Although this statement by J.M. Ball is a popular view of the consequences of the Burke and Hare case the extent to which it is valid can be questioned. The public outrage at the crimes of Burke and Hare was considerable, as indeed the actions of the public at Burke's hanging illustrates. The fact that the actions of 'true' resurrectionists had been known for some time is evidenced in the 1828 Report of the Select Committee on Anatomy, which highlights the cause of some of the difficulties in procuring suitable bodies:

'To what particular cause do you attribute the present difficulty of obtaining a supply?' 'To the vigilance of the public in watching all the depositories of the dead.'[55]

'To what do you ascribe the increase of the difficulty?' 'In a great measure to the increased severity with which magistrates act in case of any discovery, and partly also because those constant discoveries which take place, increase the prejudices of the people against dissection generally, and cause greater vigilance in endeavours to prevent exhumation.'[56]

Hence, to return to J.M. Ball, the actions of the resurrectionists invited disgust and horror on the part of the public, and whilst not necessarily seen as significant enough to create a moral outrage in themselves, were clearly significant enough to impede the supply of human bodies to anatomists. The increasing need for bodies to dissect was such that the resurrectionists could make a more than decent living from the task, the cost of corpses having risen dramatically as demand outstripped supply. Indeed, anatomists were even paying the fines imposed by the more vigilant magistracy, or supporting the families of convicted bodysnatchers.[xiii] Hence pressure to reform the legislation was coming from two sides, the public who disliked the practice and the anatomists who could not afford the inflated prices, and whose students were commonly studying abroad, where the supply of bodies was less restricted.

The first real sign of action to address the difficulties being experienced was in April 1828 when the Select Committee on Anatomy was established. The Committee was charged with inquiring

'into the manner of obtaining Subjects for Dissection in the Schools of Anatomy, and into the State of Law affecting the Persons employed in obtaining or dissecting Bodies'.[58]

This Select Committee commenced its inquiries on 28 April and the report was published on 22 July 1828: well before the actions of Burke and Hare had been discovered. As has been seen earlier, the Committee was clear that the dissecting of bodies, other than those provided after hanging for murder, was unlawful. However, throughout the Minutes of Evidence, the questions were primarily focused not on the illegality of the anatomists' actions, but on how to improve the supply of bodies, with the options of importing them from abroad, or using unclaimed bodies from workhouses or public hospitals, being the favoured approaches. Despite recommendations for the repeal of the Act of Geo. II which caused 'more evil than good' and for the House to consider if 'it would be expedient to introduce . . . some legislative measure'[59] to increase the supply of bodies via the workhouse, it was some eight months before a proposal was made in the House of Commons to introduce a bill. In so doing, Mr Warburton made reference to what 'had so lately occurred in

---

[xiii] See, for example, the evidence of Sir Astley Cooper and Joseph Henry Green, Esq. contained in the Minutes of Evidence,[57] at pages 17 and 36.

Edinburgh' and the requirement of legislation to exonerate the medical profession and prevent them being implicated by the wrongdoings of 'either
resurrection-men, or a class of villains whose atrocities had been so very
recently brought to light'.[60] Leave to introduce the bill was granted. However,
the bill that was introduced, which made it unlawful to disinter a body,
required licensing of schools of anatomy, and for unclaimed bodies from
workhouses and hospitals to be given up to such schools, did not succeed. In
the Lords, the Archbishop of Canterbury, whilst noting the inconveniences
that resulted from the present state of the law, hoped that it would not proceed further and that a new bill be introduced which was 'less offensive to the
feelings of the community, and therefore less objectionable'.[61] After more
debate the bill was withdrawn by the Lords in June 1829, having successfully
completed its passage through the Commons.

Mr Warburton waited over two years before seeking leave to reintroduce a
Bill for Regulating Schools of Anatomy, with leave being given on 15
December 1831.[62]

This bill differed somewhat from the one introduced in 1829, and when it
finally completed its passage through Parliament, it included provisions of a
similar thrust to parts of the current Human Tissue Act 1961 and Anatomy
Act 1984, but what is perhaps most interesting is the cause that precipitated
the Government's action.

On 5 November 1831, John Bishop and Thomas Williams were appre-
hended and detained on suspicion of murder and subsequent sale of a body
to King's College, London. The inquest into the death of this adolescent heard
evidence from the porter at the dissecting room of King's, who confirmed that
he had been offered a body for the purposes of dissection. The body had been
bought for nine guineas, and on subsequent examination by the anatomist,
signs of an unnatural death were found. Bishop, Williams and another, May,
were tried for murder on 2 December 1831, and were accused not just of the
murder of the boy, but of a woman who was presumed sold for dissection.
The accused were convicted of murder, and Bishop subsequently confessed to
the murders, with Williams alone, for the purpose of sale, but denied murder
in relation to the some other 500/1000 bodies that they had sold for dissection. Bishop and Williams were executed outside Newgate gaol, with May's
sentence being commuted.[44] The fact that 'Burking' had been discovered so
close to home has been suggested as the real reason for introducing the Bill
for Regulating Schools of Anatomy at this time, rather than the events in
Edinburgh three years earlier:

> '. . . the fact remains that Government did nothing for the relief of the
> medical profession or for the furtherance of anatomical study until after
> crimes, like those committed in Edinburgh, had aroused the citizens of
> London'.[63]

The validity of this claim can be seen in the debates in Parliament on
Warburton's new bill:

'Something must be done to put an end to the dreadful practices which had recently occurred.'[64]

'. . . was not the Legislature, therefore, bound to guard against the repetition of such atrocious crimes as had been lately committed, by reducing the temptation to commit them?'[65]

'. . . it [was] a matter of great regret that some bill had not been brought forward to prevent the practice of 'Burking'; a practice which had been carried on of late to such an extent, that he was surprised it had not come under the special notice of Ministers.'[66]

'An ordinary murderer hides the body, and disposes of the property. Bishop and Williams dig holes and bury the property, and expose the body to sale.'[67]

The Bill for Regulating Schools of Anatomy did this time succeed in becoming the Anatomy Act 1832 on 1 August 1832; it required all schools to register and gain a licence to practise, permitted persons in lawful custody of bodies to allow them to undergo anatomical examination after death (unless the nearest known relative objected) and removed any criminal liability of an anatomist who was in possession of a body for the purposes of dissection. Burke and Hare therefore provided a catalyst for the change in the law, but did not precipitate it.

The Human Tissue Act 1961 and the future

As indicated before, both the Inquiries into the scandals of the twentieth century identified a lamentable lack of knowledge of, or concern by, practitioners for the legal provisions governing the practice of removal and retention of body parts. While so doing, the Bristol Royal Infirmary Inquiry did acknowledge that the legislation on this issue was vague and difficult to understand, but did not allow that fact to condone all the practices of the medical practitioners. In both situations, the main concern was the removal and retention of human material without the consent or understanding of the parents of the 'victims' during both coroner's and hospital post-mortems, and this resulted in the moral outrage demonstrated through the media. Both Inquiry Reports called for a review of the legislation, and taken together with the public reaction, the government produced a consultation document in 2002 to consider the options.[68]

With regard to the actual legal provisions in place, post-mortems carried out for the purpose of a coroner's inquiry are covered by the Coroners Act 1988, and those requested by the hospital are covered by the Human Tissue Act 1961. The former category of post-mortem does not rely on the consent or failure to object by a relative; the coroner has a legal duty to act in specified circumstances as laid down by the Act and associated regulations. The latter form of post-mortem, because it is not required by law, is governed by the Human Tissue Act 1961, which again does not rely on consent, but on the objection of the deceased's relatives where there is no clear evidence of the wishes of the deceased.[xiv] In the presence of a rights-based culture, where consent to medical procedures is seen as crucial to validate the actions of the medical practitioner, the scenario where intervention is linked to active objection is seen as problematic. The Bristol Royal Infirmary Interim Report questioned whether the law of consent applies at all, arguing that it should as it is so closely connected to the deceased victims' medical treatment. If it does, the issue is then whether the same level of information provision should apply, i.e. is there a law of informed refusal, and what are the obligations of the medical profession to communicate this information? The Alder Hey Inquiry, while focusing on the issue of what was required of the profession in establishing whether there was an objection, concluded:

> '. . . the wording of the Human Tissue Act 1961 differs from the concept of *informed consent*, in practical terms there had to be informed consent for the next of kin at least for there to have been compliance with the Act in the overwhelming majority of cases;'[69]

and recommended that

> 'The Human Tissue Act 1961 be amended to provide a test of fully informed consent for the lawful post mortem examination and retention of parts of the bodies of deceased persons.'[70]

The Isaacs Report,[71] concerning as it did the unlawful retention of adult brains, also called for amendments to the Human Tissue Act 1961. This Report recommended that the term 'lack of objection' be replaced with the phrase 'with consent of'. Interestingly, however, this Report implies that any existing permission granted by the deceased themselves is irrelevant.

The consultation exercise on the legislation announced in July 2002 has sought to address these concerns and recommendations. The issues for debate include the amendment of the 1961 Act to ensure that consent of parents or relatives is obtained for the retention of organs or tissue following post-mortem, whether the same requirements should apply to the death of an adult, and how consent should inform the use that is actually made of these retained parts of human material. The conclusions from this consultation exercise include the need for adherence to the wishes of the deceased, where known, and where there is no such expression, for consent to removal and retention to be granted by a person nominated by the deceased, or failing that, someone close to the deceased.[72] These conclusions have been reflected in the new Human Tissue Act 2004, the majority of the provisions of which will come into force during 2006. Some of the proposals have been implemented in any event by hospitals changing the structure of the consent forms for post-mortem. However, it is not clear whether such changes would prevent similar scandals in future. The ability of relatives to obtain information and make an informed decision in the aftermath of death will still be questionable – all the parents

---

[xiv] See further Part III to the Bristol Royal Infirmary Inquiry Interim Report for a fuller explanation as to the workings of the legislation and the identified problems.

involved in Bristol were found to have given consent to the post-mortem, but did not know what it meant – and even if informed consent is given, it will not automatically prevent a pathologist acting in the manner of Professor van Velzen. Indeed, it is questionable whether there is in fact any real distinction between the ability to object in the current law, and a requirement to consent. Surely for both to be valid, there has to be the provision of information to enable objection or consent to take place. Amendments to the legislation may provide some reassurance to the public, and assuage the panic of the 1990s, but can only do so if workable and enforceable. Given human sensitivity to death, and particularly the death of a child, informed consent would seem to be storing up problems some of which have already been identified, such as how much information needs to be given and how quickly. In the absence of clear legal requirements this will no doubt produce yet another bodysnatching scandal in the future.

CONCLUSION

It is often said that we learn by experience, and yet, as the above has illustrated, the human experience seems to be one of repeating, or permitting, the same mistakes. In the early nineteenth century, scientific knowledge and the desire to improve medical practice, despite being a laudable goal, was allowed to override popular feeling until it reached the stage where public outrage boiled over. The anatomists were required to admit a lamentable lack of knowledge of the law, and blatant disregard for that law. As a consequence, however, the anatomists eventually got the legislative regime they desired with the implementation of the Anatomy Act 1832. The twentieth-century anatomists and medical practitioners again demonstrated their woeful ignorance of the law, and their adherence to a paternalistic approach to communication with patients and their next of kin. Unlike their peers of yesteryear, they may not get a law they want, since the reforms that are underway remove the scope for paternalism and continue to enforce the patient rights culture in medical practice. But will the changes remove the excuse of 'we didn't understand', and 'medical science necessitated our actions'? Given this illustration of the way in which history repeats itself, the answer must be no.

Acknowledgements

This chapter originally appeared as an article with the same title in *Nottingham Law Journal* (Vol. 12(2), 2003, pp. 1–17). It is reproduced with the kind permission of the Journal.

References

1.   Lyal A. Witchery tales, the darker side of old Edinburgh. Edinburgh: Moubray House Press; 1988.
2.   Ball JM. Sack-'em-up men. Edinburgh: Oliver & Boyd; 1928:72.

3. Hansard 1832: vol. 10, col. 378.

4. Extraordinary Occurrence, and Supposed Murder etc. Edinburgh 3 November 1828. Held in National Library of Scotland: West Port Murders, Vol. IV, Miscellaneous, LC 1573 (1).

5. MacGregor G. The history of Burke and Hare and of the resurrectionist times. Glasgow: Thomas Morrison/London: Hamilton Adams & Co; 1884:114.

6. West Port Murders, Vol. V, Miscellaneous, LC 1574(16).

7. West Port Murders, Vol. IV, Miscellaneous, LC 1573(15).

8. Bristol Royal Infirmary Inquiry. Learning from Bristol: the report of the public inquiry into children's heart surgery at the Bristol Royal Infirmary 1984–1995, Cm 5207. London: The Stationery Office; 2001: Ch 1, para 14.

9. Report of the Royal Liverpool Children's Inquiry. London: The Stationery Office; January 2001: Ch 3, para 1.1.

10. Balfour CL. Women and the temperance reformation. London; 1849.

11. Harrison B. Drink and the Victorians: the temperance question in England 1815–1872. London: Faber and Faber; 1971.

12. The Newgate Calendar, extracted from www.exclassics.org/newgate/ng601.htm on 7 March 2003.

13. A laconic narrative of the life and death of James Wilson, known by the name of Daft Jamie. To which is added a few Anecdotes (1829, published W Smith) held by the National Library of Scotland in West Port Murders, Vol. IV, Miscellaneous, LC 1573(5).

14. Extract from press cutting, The Edinburgh Murders (Further Particulars) in West Port Murders, Miscellaneous, Edinburgh City Library, YRA 637.

15. Life and transactions of murderer Burke and his Associates. National Library of Scotland, RY III a 6 (26), Date unknown.

16. Press cutting, newspaper unknown, 4 January 1829, National Library of Scotland, RY III a 6 (30).

17. Press cutting, newspaper and date unknown, National Library of Scotland, RY III a 6 (30).

18. MacGregor G. The history of Burke and Hare and of the resurrectionist times. Glasgow; 1884:234, 235.

19. Edinburgh Evening Courant, A Full and Particular account of the Riot which took place in Edinburgh on Thursday last, also of the Hoax played off on a Celebrated Doctor, date unknown, National Library of Scotland RY III a 6 (10).

20. Report of the Royal Liverpool Children's Inquiry. London: The Stationery Office; January 2001:421 (Ch 14).

21. Birmingham Post 9 March 2000:13.

22. Report of the Royal Liverpool Children's Inquiry. London: The Stationery Office; January 2001:423 (Ch 14).

23. Daily Mail 8 March 2000:41.

24. Birmingham Evening Mail 11 February 1999:2.

25. Sunday Mail (Scotland) 12 December 1999:9.

26. Report of the Royal Liverpool Children's Inquiry. London: The Stationery Office; January 2001:427 (Ch 14).

27. Sunday Mirror 4 February 2001:4, 5.

28. Life and transactions of murderer Burke and his associates; author and date unknown. National Library of Scotland, RY III a 6 (26).

29. Author unknown, The murders of the close: a tragedy of real life. London: Cowie and Strange; 1829:169.

30. MacGregor G. The history of Burke and Hare and of the resurrectionist times. Glasgow: Thomas D. Morrison/London: Hamilton Adams & Co; 1884.

31. Wag P. A timely hint to anatomical practitioners, and their associates – the resurrectionists, a new song (Tune: Macpherson's Farewell), date unknown, published W. Smith, National Library of Scotland, West Port Murders, Vol. IV, Miscellaneous, LC 1573(12).

32. Bristol Royal Infirmary Inquiry Interim Report: Removal and retention of human material. Bristol: Bristol Royal Infirmary Inquiry; May 2000.

33. Bristol Royal Infirmary Inquiry Interim Report: Removal and retention of human material. Bristol: Bristol Royal Infirmary Inquiry; May 2000: para 40.

34. Report of the Royal Liverpool Children's Inquiry. London: The Stationery Office; January 2001: Ch 10.

35. The Express 31 January 2001:6.

36. The Guardian 31 January 2001:3.

37. The Guardian 4 February 2001. Online. Available: society.guardian.co.uk/ alderhey/comment/

38. Report from the Select Committee on Anatomy, 22 July 1828, House of Commons, London, p. B2.

39. Minutes of Evidence, Report from the Select Committee on Anatomy, 22 July 1828, House of Commons, London; p. 17.

40. Minutes of Evidence, Report from the Select Committee on Anatomy, 22 July 1828, House of Commons, London; p. 33.

41. Minutes of Evidence, Report from the Select Committee on Anatomy, 22 July 1828, House of Commons, London; p. 16

42. Benjamin Collins Brodie, Esq., Minutes of Evidence, Report from the Select Committee on Anatomy, 22 July 1828, House of Commons, London; p. 23.

43. John Abernethy, Esq., Minutes of Evidence, Report from the Select Committee on Anatomy, 22 July 1828, House of Commons, London; p. 28.

44. Sir Astley Cooper, Minutes of Evidence, Report from the Select Committee of Anatomy, 22 July 1828, House of Commons, London; pp. 18, 19.

45. Minutes of Evidence, Report from the Select Committee of Anatomy, 22 July 1828, House of Commons, London; p. 46.

46. Communication from Dr Knox to the Editor of the Caledonian Mercury, dated 17 March 1829, National Library of Scotland, RY III a 6.

47. Minutes of Evidence, The Report of the Select Committee on Anatomy, July 1828, House of Commons, London; p. 93.

48. Bentley D. English criminal justice in the nineteenth century. London: Hambledon Press; 1998.

49. Professor Berry. Bristol Royal Infirmary Inquiry Interim Report: Removal and retention of human material. Bristol: Bristol Royal Infirmary Inquiry; May 2000: para 27.

50. Professor Berry. Bristol Royal Infirmary Inquiry Interim Report: Removal and retention of human material. Bristol: Bristol Royal Infirmary Inquiry; May 2000: para 31.

51. Report of the Royal Liverpool Children's Inquiry. London: The Stationery Office; January 2001: paras 6.1 to 6.6.

52. Report of the Royal Liverpool Children's Inquiry. London: The Stationery Office; January 2001: para 5.1

53. Bristol Royal Infirmary Inquiry Interim Report: Removal and retention of human material. Bristol: Bristol Royal Infirmary Inquiry; May 2000: paras 58, 59.

54. Report of the Royal Liverpool Children's Inquiry. London: The Stationery Office; January 2001: Ch 10, para 7.2.

55. John Abernethy, Esq., Minutes of Evidence, Report from the Select Committee on Anatomy, 22 July 1828, House of Commons, London; p. 30.

56. Caesar Hawkins, Esq., Minutes of Evidence, Report from the Select Committee on Anatomy, 22 July 1828, House of Commons, London; p. 40.

57. Minutes of Evidence, Report from the Select Committee on Anatomy, 22 July 1828, House of Commons, London; pp. 17, 36.

58. Minutes of Evidence, Report from the Select Committee on Anatomy, 22 July 1828, House of Commons, London; p. 3.

59. Minutes of Evidence, Report from the Select Committee on Anatomy, 22 July 1828, House of Commons, London; p. 12.

60. Mr Warburton, Hansard, New Series (Commons) Vol. XX 6 February to 30 March 1829: cols. 998–1000.

61. Hansard, New Series (Lords) Vol. XXI 31 March to 24 June 1829: cols. 1170–1171.

62. Hansard, 3rd Series (Commons) Vol. IX 6 December 1831 to 6 February 1832: cols. 300–307.

63. Ball JM. Sack-'em-up men. Oliver & Boyd, 1928:163.

64. Mr Hunt, Hansard, 3rd Series (Commons) Vol. IX, 6 December 1831 to 6 February 1832: cols. 302–303.

65. Mr Hume, Hansard, 3rd Series (Commons) Vol. IX, 6 December 1831 to 6 February 1832: col. 580.

66. Mr Hunt, Hansard, 3rd Series (Commons) Vol. IX, 6 December 1831 to 6 February 1832:cols. 582–583.

67. Mr Macaulay, Hansard 3rd Series (Commons) Vol. X 7 February to 8 March 1832: col. 834.

68. Human bodies, human choices: the law on human organs and tissue in England and Wales: A consultation report. London: Department of Health; 2002.

69. Report of the Royal Liverpool Children's Inquiry, 30 January 2001. London: The Stationery Office; January 2001: Ch 10, para 10.

70. Report of the Royal Liverpool Children's Inquiry. London: The Stationery Office; January 2001: Ch 10, para 11.1.

71. HM Inspector of Anatomy. Isaacs Report. London: The Stationery Office; May 2003:21.

72. Human bodies, human choices. Summary of responses to the consultation report. London: Department of Health; 2003:35.

Chapter 9

Nemo censetur ignorare legem?
Presumed consent to organ donation in France, from Parliament to hospitals

Graciela Nowenstein

CHAPTER CONTENTS

Introduction   173
The presumption of consent:
   from law to practice   174
Conflicting priorities   178
Professional ethos and the
   law   182

Back to the legislative
   field   185
Conclusion   186
References   187

INTRODUCTION

In 1976, French legislators chose to organise the system of cadaveric organ donation for transplantation around the concept of presumed – as opposed to express – consent.[1] The passing of this law appears in parliamentary discussions, reports and law drafts as a project of legal engineering with the double aim of modifying behaviours in the short term (increasing procurement and donation rates), and attitudes in the middle and long term (increasing the acceptance of organ donation and transplantation by the general population).

The passing of this law was at the time justified by the need to enhance the development of transplantation. This was to be done by fighting against the two factors legislators identified as the main causes of mismatch between the demand and the supply of organs.[2] The first factor was said to be the role that relatives of potential donors were often playing in the donation decision. One can read in parliamentary data that the decision ought to depend on the wishes of each citizen and not on those of their mourning relatives. The second factor identified by legislators as impacting upon the mismatch between supply and demand was that most potential donors died without having left any testimony about their wishes regarding organ donation. Legislators attributed this more to a lack of discussion and reflection among the French general population than to a generalised and conscious opposition to donate. Therefore, the silence of the French could be understood as an unstated wish to donate.

The key elements of the law on presumed consent were (i) moving the family away from the decision about donation by limiting the sphere of divergent interests to a binary tension between those of each citizen and the general interest represented by patients in need of transplantation; (ii) reversing the meaning of silence and thereby giving the community a right to harvest by limiting the right of the deceased to have their corpses preserved. The violence contained in the principle *nemo censetur ignorare legem* was acknowledged and justified as a necessary means to reach positive ends, namely saving lives and enhancing medical progress.[2]

Time has passed, and if one compares the original aims and expectations of this law to what has been its practical fate since 1976, the conclusion invites scepticism to say the least. In particular, the law has not had the intended effect of reducing the role of relatives in decisions about donation. On the contrary, the role of relatives has been reinforced – especially since the early 1990s – by those supposed to be *the arm of the law,* namely by the physicians (intensivists as most cases take place in intensive care units) and nurses (called hospital coordinators) in charge of the decision of harvesting, who do not resort to the presumption of consent as a tool to obtain donation. This chapter will (i) trace the legal evolution of presumed consent since 1976; (ii) describe practice since 1976; and (iii) analyse it from three aspects: one oriented towards the conflicting values and priorities at stake in the donation process; another oriented towards the specific position occupied by the law among other normative spheres informing the situation; and the third going back to the legislative and political fields and to the ambiguity of their action.[i]

THE PRESUMPTION OF CONSENT: FROM LAW TO PRACTICE

Organs for transplantation come from corpses and from living donors. The law of presumed consent obviously only applies to the first – and more specifically to cadavers diagnosed as brain dead. A person is said to be brain dead when her brain has been 'irreversibly' damaged while the vital functions of her body are still active.[3] This occurs most of the time as the result of cranial haemorrhages caused by traffic or cardiovascular accidents.[4] Because the brain-dead body is still functioning, its appearance does not correspond to the traditional image of a cadaver and shows all signs generally identified with life. The ambiguity of this type of death is summarised by the paraphrase that often serves to designate it: 'décès à coeur battant' or 'heart beating death'.[5]

---

[i] The data informing this work comes from that gathered for my PhD dissertation between 1999 and 2004:

- 25 in-depth interviews with hospital coordinators and intensivists in charge of dealing with the donation/harvesting process; a national survey with hospital coordinators; 2 interviews with members of the management of the Etablissement français des Greffes; 6 interviews with hospital directors or vice-directors; regular encounters with hospital coordinators and intensivists between 2000 and 2004.
- Legal texts, parliamentary reports and debates, press articles.

The 1976 law was passed in a rather optimistic atmosphere about the contribution the legal presumption of consent would make to cadaveric transplant rates. The text was concise and stated simply that organs for transplantation could be taken from brain-dead corpses if the physician in charge was not aware of any opposition to donate expressed by the deceased while alive. In 1994 the French Parliament passed the so-called 'Lois de bioéthique',[6] where were included the regulations on organ donation and transplantation. The presumption of consent was confirmed, but the text was completed with two additions.

The first consisted of the creation of a registry where citizens opposed to organ donation could formally register their wishes (Registre National des Refus). The justification of this measure was that individuals opposed to donation should have a formal means to avoid having their organs taken. But it was also expected that the existence of the registry would facilitate by the same token the implementation of the presumption of consent by reinforcing the donor status of those unregistered. The second addition stipulated that if professionals in charge do not have any information about the wishes of the deceased they have to *strive* ('s'efforcer de') to obtain this information by soliciting the next-of-kin.[ii] If this modification formally only put the relatives in the position of being conveyors of information about the wishes of the deceased, some legislators rightly warned during parliamentary discussions that including the family in the law was a way of giving it an active role in the decision process, something that the 1976 version of the law had excluded. Furthermore, they added, this would remove legitimacy from the Registre National des Refus even before it started functioning.[7] The Lois de bioéthique started in 1999 a long process of parliamentary re-examination and evaluation.[8,9,iii] A vote concluded it in 2004 with no significant modification of the presumed consent framework (Loi relative à la bioéthique 2004).

French institutions that were supposed to evaluate the strict legal validity of laws[10,iv] never questioned the presumption of consent,[11,12] which also enjoys moral support from institutions such as the Comité Consultatif National d'Ethique[13,14] and the Commission Consultative des Droits de l'Homme.[15] On the other hand, sustained and regular criticisms about its strict legal and social validity have been addressed by some legal scholars who have insisted on five critical points:

[ii] Art. L. 671–7: '. . . [L]e prélèvement peut être effecuté dès lors que la personne concernée n'a pas fait connaître, de son vivant, son refus d'un tel prélèvement.
Ce refus peut être exprimé par l'indication de sa volonté sur un registre national automatisé prévu à cet effet . . . .
Si le médecin n'a pas directement connaissance de la volonté du défunt, il doit *s'efforcer* de recueillir le témoignage de sa famille.' (Italics are mine.)

[iii] Discussions since 1999 go back to the conflict between the role given to the relatives and the existence of the Registre National des Refus.

[iv] Strict legal validity is here understood within the logic of the legal system and not according to the sociopolitical fate of laws once passed.

1. Presumptions in French law are traditionally in favour of the person whose behaviour or wishes are presumed and not the other way around as with organ donation.[16]
2. The exclusion of the family from the decision of harvesting is in contradiction with the law that has been regulating the fate of corpses and funerals in France since the end of the nineteenth century in which the absence of directives left by the deceased makes her relatives responsible for the fate of her corpse.[16,17]
3. The vocabulary used in the legal text is ambiguous and misleading; it has been noted that it is not coherent to talk about 'donation' when the behaviour at stake does not result from a positive and personal statement but is deduced from silence.[18]
4. The gap between law and practice feeds arguments about the social invalidity of the law.[16]
5. A law resting on the principle *nemo censetur ignorare legem* cannot have its main mechanism ignored by the majority of the population. Even less so when:[19]

   - more than 51% of the general population considers harvesting is only possible in cases of explicit consent by the deceased, and only 17% consider donation is presumed from silence
   - 67% consider that in the absence of information about the wishes of the potential donor it should be up to her relatives to decide.

It is obvious that the 1994 law is formally less clear than the 1976 one. In fact, if the presumption of consent, from what one can infer from parliamentary data, was confirmed by the Lois de bioéthique of 1994, the perspective was no longer one of faithful optimism. Indeed, it was known by this time that the law had not produced the effects expected and that it was not being applied.[20,21]

As a matter of fact, the legislators of 1994 were certainly less convinced about the instrumental possibilities of the law than those of 1976, and if they confirmed the presumption of consent, the introduction of the relatives of potential donors into the text – even if formally only as conveyors of information – was eviscerating the principle.

A confirmation vote took place in 2004[22] within an ever more disenchanted context, with no trace in parliamentary works of any real hopes about the effectiveness of presumed consent as a tool for social engineering in the French sociopolitical context.[8,23,24]

All this having been said, behaviours have not always been so clearly removed from what 1976 legislators seemed to expect; they have in fact evolved from a context of great heterogeneity towards the systematic inclusion of the relatives of the deceased in the decision process. The most constant fact in this evolution is that the presumption of consent has never been systematically applied in France.

Interviews with hospital coordinators (HCs hereafter) and intensivists who were involved in the procurement activity in the early years give a picture of a fairly heterogeneous situation between 1976 and the late 1980s or early

1990s. It appears that in some intensive care units (ICUs hereafter) the next-of-kin were consulted by a nurse or an intensivist who had not followed any specific training and often without any directions from the head of the ICU. In other cases, especially in hospitals where transplantation units existed, it could be that transplantation surgeons would deal directly with the family. The duration and content of the exchange, as well as the physical space where the encounter would occur – the room where the potential donor was, a corridor, the waiting room, etc. – were as a consequence highly variable.[25] But it could also happen that the relatives were simply not informed at all, in which case, the absence of the family next to the body of the potential donor would be taken as a cue to take it to the operating room. Whether a family would be confronted by one or the other of these different patterns depended on the personal orientations and views of the person in charge of the exchange with the family that day, on those of the head of the ICU, on the presence in the hospital of transplantation surgeons, etc.

The beginning of the 1990s confirmed a process of homogenisation consisting of a normalisation of the participation of families in the decision-making process. Health professionals in this field and human scientists[26,27] generally attribute the development of the gap between law and practice to the coexistence of two factors: Firstly, there were the public scandals that showed the media and public opinion could react negatively to cases of harvesting where the next-of-kin had felt abused by the medical staff; and, secondly, the routinisation of the activity and the generalisation of the function of HC fulfilled by nurses brought both a change of orientation regarding the attitude towards the next-of-kin and a standardisation of practices (through among other things standardised training offered to professionals and the creation of the French association of hospital coordinators – AFCH – in 1994).

What does the existence of the continuing gap between law and practice since 1976 mean? Is it interesting to reflect on it? It actually appeared as a rather irrelevant question to the HCs and intensivists interviewed, who seemed after all to consider that, indeed, everyone knows laws are often not applied in practice, and that this is not a very interesting thing to think about. The question is nonetheless relevant. First, because the interviewees' rejection of the issue as irrelevant does not come from an absolute attitude towards law and towards the role it might play in the regulation and organisation of medical activity. For instance, it is in their view of capital importance to have legal texts regulating the diagnosis of brain death and organising organ allocation, and that these are strictly applied by professionals. Second, because whilst the insistence of legislators on supporting and confirming the presumption of consent was common knowledge, it never had the effects expected on behaviour and attitudes, making it interesting to ask what the social role of law is in French society. Finally, the question is interesting as such if one wants to understand how social actors respond to situations where divergent normative schemes are in conflict.

Before going further it is necessary to consider the most obvious hypothesis that could explain the situation of non-application of presumed consent legislation: the ignorance of the legal regulation in question on the part of the health professionals involved.[28] It has been noted that the general population, and thus the relatives that professionals are called to discuss organ donation with, mostly ignore the fact that in the absence of any statement made by an individual the state assumes that person to be a potential organ donor. Nevertheless, the general population's ignorance of the law does not render the law formally inapplicable. Actually, it has been thought to serve especially in this situation. It may be, then, that those supposed to be the arm of the law ignore its existence or are mistaken about its content. HCs and intensivists in charge of the procurement process are well aware of the content of the law. Furthermore, they are aware that this regulation was passed with the expectation that they would use it and that by not resorting to it they are not contributing as expected to an increase in procurement rates.

CONFLICTING PRIORITIES

This having been said, let us now continue with the interviewees' analysis of the situation, which they see as inherently problematic and ambiguous in terms of normative expectations and priorities.

Professionals say the aim of the encounter with the relatives is two-fold. First they have to explain brain death to them. At this stage the main difficulty lies in the fact that both common sense and the senses convey signals to the relatives about the image of their loved one that are in conflict with professionals' discourse stating death. Indeed, a patient who has been diagnosed as brain dead does look alive; her heart beats, she is warm, and she breathes – even if helped by mechanical assistance. In these circumstances, professionals have to convince the relatives of the reality of death even though nothing has changed between before and after the announcement of death. It is in fact the statement made by a physician that in effect transforms a comatose patient into a corpse. The second aim of the encounter is of course organ donation. In this respect professionals say they always try to start the discussion by focusing on the wishes of the deceased regarding organ donation and on the possible knowledge relatives might have about these. The problem is, they note, that most of the time the relatives do not know much about the wishes of the deceased.

In fact, during the whole encounter intensivists and HCs are confronted with contradictory priorities and values. Indeed, evoking the question of brain death implies a constant oscillation between two opposite spheres of meaning: on the one hand, that of biotechnology and 'rational' Western medicine that allows considering a brain-dead body as a corpse and corpses as sources of healing material for other patients; on the other, that of affective, non-dualistic and non-cartesian representations of the body where a body with signs of life is not a corpse and where body parts are not neutral material. The consultation of the family in order to know whether the brain-dead person ever expressed her will not to give her organs for transplantation also implies the confrontation of two contradictory spheres of meaning: On the one side, that of a law embedding solidarity and the utilitarian dominance of the community's well-being upon individual and family autonomy; and, on the other, that of individual, family and affective relations, where the wishes of the deceased – if ever expressed – and the affective needs of the mourning relatives must come above all other things.

If professionals have the impression of being in front of a group of people who seem not to accept the reality of brain death, it is not possible to approach the question of organ donation, since it would amount to proposing to take vital organs from a living body. In these cases there will be no harvesting of organs, and the ICU staff will either wait until the brain-dead person naturally passes to a state of normal death, or hasten this passage by ceasing all external assistance. On the other hand, if brain death seems to have been more or less understood, or at least accepted by the next-of-kin, professionals switch to the question of organ donation, which they more or less introduce as: 'You have probably heard about organ transplantation, do you happen to know whether your mother, father, sister, husband, etc. has ever expressed any opposition to organ donation?' To this question most of the time the answer is 'We do not know, we never talked about it'.

The law of presumed consent has been passed to take advantage of this situation, but this is not what professionals in charge actually do. In fact they do not take it as the end but rather as the beginning of a dialogue with the relatives, which is then generally re-oriented towards the less precise question 'If you do not know what she wanted, what do you think she might have wanted?' But very often there is no clear answer to this question either. At this point, as legal scholar Thouvenin notes,[7] the best the relatives can do is interpret and extrapolate a wish from what they think they know about the deceased. Besides, it is difficult in practice for the interviewers to know in whose name the relatives are talking. Are the relatives able to infer what the wishes of the deceased might have been? Are they talking for themselves although formally in the name of the deceased? HCs and intensivists note that, especially in cases of refusal, the dialogue often slips from the original question to the views of the family, which are frequently expressed with statements such as: 'I can't cope with the idea of her body being opened and emptied', 'I can't imagine her heart beating in somebody else's chest', 'How can you ask *me* such a thing right now?!' etc. They even add they are aware that the next-of-kin can 'lie' quite often; the question about the wishes of the deceased gives them the opportunity to make their own decision while formally talking in the name of the deceased. In a way the law contains the pretext for those participating at the encounter to follow the families' wishes while maintaining the illusion that the wishes of the dead are being respected. One of the interviewees summarised the ambiguity at the essence of the situation at stake. She first tried to quote the law:

'L'équipe médicale doit s'efforcer de recueillir le témoignage du défunt auprès de la famille.' ['The medical team must strive to obtain the testimony of the deceased from his family.']

And then carried on with an explanation about the implications of such text:

'C'est, c'est un peu, c'est un peu, c[e n]'est pas très bien, parce que on laisse porter LA RESPONSABILITE du oui ou du non à la famille, mais d'un autre côté ça leur laisse aussi LA LIBERTE du oui ou du non.' ['It's, it's a little, it's a little, it's not really a good thing, because it is the family who are left to bear THE RESPONSIBILITY to say yes or no, but on the other hand, it also leaves them THE FREEDOM to say yes or no.']

This considered, professionals insist they do not see why they should confront relatives with that, and/or use it as an argument to enforce the application of presumed consent legislation. Actually, the content of the law is most often left out of the discussion, and very seldom utilised as an argument by professionals to obtain donation.

Why is this so? Professionals are aware of not making use of the tool created by legislators with the explicit aim of increasing procurement rates. They note they are regularly confronted by transplantation surgeons who in more or less subtle statements can make them responsible for the death of some of their patients who do not survive the wait for an organ.

They justify their behaviour first with value arguments. Imposing the presumption of consent amounts, in their view, to forcing people in deep emotional distress to lift themselves from their suffering, and asking them to act according to the interests of the community. Interviewees judge that this imposition of a concern for community obligations at this moment implies the breaking of a moral taboo. Furthermore, they consider that if their aim is to obtain organs, this cannot be done at any cost, and they observe that part of their job is to give care to the relatives and to accompany them until they give their own decision.

They complete this value-oriented argument with a more pragmatic one, as they consider it would be counterproductive in the middle and long term to push too much to obtain organ donation and to force it via presumed consent legislation. They think neither the relatives nor the general population are willing to accept this sort of imposition. They also think an authoritarian attitude would provoke negative and outraged reactions, with the immediate risk of increased refusals, and the less immediate one of producing public scandals which would have a damaging effect on procurement rates. Their argument at this level takes the form of very vehement statements such as: 'it is not possible' [to apply the law] 'you cannot do such a thing', 'how could we . . . ?' In that sense, they clearly feel impotent in front of the relatives, and the existence of a law backing them does not seem to be diminishing this feeling of impotence.

Building on this, they complete their presentation of the situation with a historical analysis of the evolution of the doctor–patient (here doctor–family) relationship in France. They all state that it has evolved in the last decades from a paternalistic and authoritarian mode towards one more transparent and equal.[v] Professionals who were involved in the procurement system since the early 1970s note that those among them who were then resorting to the presumption of consent do not feel like doing so now. In other words, what they judged as normal in the 1970s and 1980s – i.e. patronising – is no longer legitimate behaviour in their own view. Indeed, they note, society has changed; families and patients tolerate less paternalism, and the professional ethos is less authoritarian.

The law of presumed consent is clearly in conflict with this trend towards less paternalism. Those working in the field add that the changing trend has taken away part of the power that medical professionals had previously. This means that the presumption of consent is no longer applicable with families that generally and increasingly demand to be informed and to participate in the decision-making and who are ready, they fear, to sue hospitals, doctors and nurses, and to divulge their cases in the media. The non-application of the law of presumed consent appears here therefore as a pragmatic measure that seeks to protect public institutions in general and medical ones in particular.

This pragmatic argument does not seem to reflect a cynical view about how to manage people's reactions. Even if the professionals involved do not always agree with the reasons given by families for accepting or refusing donation, they do consider that the latter have the right to be wrong about this. And that often the decision legitimately belongs to the families because their state of mourning gives them the right to oppose the harvesting of the newly dead.

An analysis in terms of conflicting identities will shed some light here. In fact, their discourses seem to show their conflicting loyalties: they are public health professionals who understand the needs of the health system as those of the community as a whole, but also citizens, fathers, mothers, etc., who identify with the situation the next-of-kin are going through.

They are primarily tempted to behave rather as individuals than as representatives of the 'general interest'. The feeling of being *on the families' side* is very strong in their discourses, and is reinforced by one of guilt. Indeed, as professionals who have not been able to save the potential donor, they are in a situation of failure. The image of their failure is strongly reflected by the next-of-kin's often histrionic exteriorisation of grief in the face of sudden and

---

[v] Of course many authors continue to note that paternalism and authoritarianism have all but disappeared from medical ideology and action.[25] Nevertheless, it is certainly true that the relation has changed in the last decades and that, concerning the presumption of consent, if many units used to proceed to harvest without consultation of the families in the 1970s and the 1980s, such behaviour has today disappeared.

unexpected situations of loss.[vi] After feeling responsible for their grief, it is difficult, they note, to assume the responsibility of imposing on them the painful issue of organ donation and the violence of the presumed consent device.

But this feeling of identification tainted by guilt finds opposition in their attachment in terms of professional identity to certain biomedical and public health principles contained in the law. From this perspective they ideally agree with senator Caillavet, who drafted the first law, who thinks there are no *valid* reasons, namely rational or 'cartesian' reasons,[vii] to oppose organ donation and harvesting. As he declared in 1992, there is in his view a moral obligation to donate one's organs, an obligation no one should try to run away from:

> 'L'être humain a, incontestablement, une dimension morale. Par conséquent, il ne peut pas se dérober lorsqu'il s'agit d'aider son prochain.'[30] ['There is no doubt that the human being has a moral dimension. Therefore, he must not shirk from helping his neighbour.']

In fact, if one of the stronger constraints to the application of the law seems to be the identification by those supposed to apply it with the next-of-kin, this is not to be confused with the sharing of all their reasons, but partly as an immediate identification with, and respect for, the pure suffering the family is going through.

Does the self-conscious non-application of the law have implications in the analysis professionals make about what the ideal legislative framework for organ donation should be?

PROFESSIONAL ETHOS AND THE LAW

The years during which this research has taken place (1999–2004) have coincided with a long process of parliamentary re-evaluation of the Lois de bioéthique, which started in 1999. This allowed me to explore with professionals involved the question of a possible or suitable modification of the law. Although they all admitted and justified the non-use of the law of presumed consent, and even the pragmatic impossibility of utilising it, most of them expressed a rather clear opposition to the possibility of modifying the law in any way, even so that it accorded more with their own behaviour.

[vi] Brain death generally unexpectedly strikes rather young people who were previously in good health. In this context interviewees observe the reactions of their relatives are often much stronger than in situations of 'normal death'.

[vii] '... les réanimateurs peuvent se trouver dans un certain nombre de cas en face de décisions qui échappent à un raisonnement 'cartésien' .... Il apparaît donc que, dans bien des cas, la décision d'accepter ou non le prélèvement n'est pas basée sur des arguments réfléchis ....'[29] [Intensivists can in some cases be confronted with decisions taken outside the cartesian reasoning .... Hence, it appears that the decision to accept or refuse the harvesting is in many cases not based on reflected arguments ....]

They first of all admitted that the law does not correspond to practice, but this was not seen at all as problematic per se, and, furthermore, they thought it would be irrelevant to try to modify it. They indeed saw no reason to change the law if there is no hope that this will have a positive effect on reality, namely by increasing the donation rate. It is clear here how far the concerns of the health professionals are from those of legal scholars interested in the (in)validity and (in)effectiveness of laws,[10] and from those of social scientists interested in the authority of the French state[31] and of the role of legal rules in the regulation of behaviour.[32] Summing up the view of professionals: Families are not complaining and the donation rate is, if not among the highest in the world, still a decent one; and there are now trained professionals familiar with the existing context. In other terms, if rates cannot be improved, it is better not to change a structure that is well known and has results that are not too unsatisfactory. This vision seems to be very much sustained in fact by the idea that laws are not to be respected and applied simply because they are laws, for in fact they do not possess an intrinsic legitimacy – disconnected from their content – to regulate social – or at least medical – activity. In that sense, interviewees feel perfectly comfortable about the situation of non-application because they consider they are doing the right thing in ethical and pragmatic terms.

The importance of personal conscience[viii] as opposed to the external imposition of rules of practice was expressed through a discursive disqualification of the law via the delegitimation of its source, namely legislators. Lawmakers were depicted both as not having enough knowledge about what happens in the field and as, at the same time, having the pretension of imposing their views upon those working in the field. The same lack of consideration also affected the Comité Consultatif National d'Ethique. It is the Committee's and the lawmakers' distance from the field when contrasted to the professional's own closeness that seems to be giving the latter the final legitimacy to direct and orient their action as they personally, or rather as professionals, think it should be.

This being-in-the-field 'privilege' draws much of its strength from the fact that the interviewees consider themselves as very much involved – affectively and in terms of time – in an activity they see as intrinsically difficult. They say their everyday work as intensivists or ICU nurses – HCs are most of the time ICU nurses – often consists of dealing with death, grieving families, and, too often they say, with failure. Furthermore, they have the impression that they are, in the transplantation chain, those who do the 'dirty job' without it being acknowledged: 'nobody invites you on a TV show to talk about grieving families and open corpses', while transplantation surgeons get all the public rewards. All this seems to make them very critical of the legitimacy of

---

[viii] This *conscience clause* privilege is certainly not one non-medical staff enjoy: nurses are not allowed to refuse to participate in a donation process. HCs interviewed were in fact more critical towards intensivists not starting procurement processes. Although this difference did not have any influence on their perception of the law in general.

any comment, criticism, or mere recommendation coming from outside the ICU sphere.

To the extent that they are imbued with this idea that they know better than anyone else what is the appropriate thing to do when facing the families of a potential donor, they tend not to give much consideration to what the law would expect them to do, especially because in their view the law is not adapted to reality. Nevertheless they show a consistent attachment to this law. Why is this so? Why, although they do not show any real concern about the gap between law and practice, would they care about perpetuating the present legal structure? Is their fear that a change would not bring any improvement in donation rates sufficient to oppose any change?

In fact, in the present context, intensivists and HCs do have the option of applying the law: presumed consent as a tool with which to confront the families remains – if only formally – at their disposal. This potential or formal power has been evoked by the interviewees as a good reason for keeping the law as it is. Indeed, if they normally do not use it for all the reasons that have been mentioned above, they note that it can occasionally, albeit very rarely, be used with varied aims. For instance, it can be used to present an unwitting failure to ask the family in a less negative light. It can also be a tool to increase the number of organs in a very specific case, namely, when it has been impossible to reach any members of the family of the deceased. Actually, it is only with potential donors whose corpses professionals think no one will ever claim that the presumption of consent is used. Interviewees noted that if they think there is a risk that relatives could claim for the corpse even after the harvesting had taken place, they do not proceed with harvesting, because this could provoke a scandal. This means that, at the end of the day, it is homeless people who are in practice likely to be submitted to the presumption of consent. The interviewees were conscious that such a selective application of the law meant it would only be able to supply an almost insignificant number of supplemental organs. Yet enough to be viewed as reason enough to keep the law with the selectivity of application not being considered ethically problematic.

This very marginal and unquestioned application actually touches on one of the fundamental principles that seem to be inspiring their attitude towards the law and the families; the harvesting of 'hoboes' is not ethically problematic since no relatives are going to suffer from this decision.

French anthropologist Augé[33] is right when he notes that what counts in many of the social acts surrounding death are the living – the grieving here – rather than the dead. It can indeed be seen with this extreme case of the 'hobo', that one of the most important sources of HCs' and intensivists' behaviour is the management of the suffering they are facing, that of the grieving family. Yet, one could consider, as the law does, that among the living concerned by the situation it is the patients in the waiting list for transplantation who should be the first concern for HCs and intensivists. This being on the grieving families' side rather than on that of potential receivers is a tragic choice professionals are very much aware of. Actually, they do not really see it as a tragic choice, but rather as the only reasonable response they can bring to the situation, both pragmatically and in terms of values.

BACK TO THE LEGISLATIVE FIELD

The position and behaviour of the health professionals working in this field as discussed so far, ambiguous in terms of practice and both the interests and the principles at stake, cannot be completely understood if one remains within the limits of their professional world. Indeed, as Freidson[34] wrote, the autonomy of professions regarding self-regulation is dependent on the outside world, on the network of power relations and structures into which each profession is inserted. More specifically, the autonomy of the medical profession is very much linked to its relation with the state. It is in this respect absolutely clear that neither legislators nor health authorities are putting the professionals supposed to be the arm of presumed consent legislation under pressure so that they apply the law. The law of presumed consent is certainly not applied for all the reasons already mentioned. Yet, things would most probably be different if the authorities were willing to allow less autonomy of action to the health professionals in this field. The hypothesis that the non-application of the law of presumed consent is far from being a problem for legislators and political authorities – or at least something they want to do something about – seems to be pretty much an obvious fact. First of all there is no legal obligation for professionals to apply the presumption of consent since the law foresees no sanction if a decision on harvesting is not taken in the absence of information about the wishes of the potential donor. Second, public information campaigns about the existence of this law based on the principle that *nemo censetur ignorare legem* have been, if not non-existent, at least very limited. Last but not least, professionals are not put under pressure by public authorities to resort to the presumption of consent. Again, as with professionals, one should ask why do legislators show such an attachment to this law, endorsing it with regular votes while they know it is not accomplishing the formal aims it was passed for?

It is important here not to take for granted the instrumentalist postulate that assumes laws are simply passed and/or perpetuated in order to be applied. It is interesting at this point to take some inspiration from studies that have focused on historical cases of regulation for the purpose of analysis of broad power relations in France. Castel's analysis[35] of the legal regulation of madness in France in the nineteenth century, and Foucault's study[36] of the rise of psychiatric expertise in the judicial sphere show how certain laws formally aimed at regulating medical activity and practice can be promulgated not necessarily with the aim of having them applied, but partly as responses from the political field to the pressure or needs of certain groups. Legal regulation of madness, Castel shows, has been at certain periods of French history the result of efforts to endow psychiatry with scientific legitimacy rather than the result of an attempt at properly regulating the treatment of the mentally ill.

The promulgation of a law can in that sense be understood as an aim in itself, whether it will be applied or not.

It would seem that the law of presumed consent belongs, at least since 1994, pretty much to this category. Indeed, it has been noted that the French authorities have been very reticent in the area of public communication on organ donation and in presumed consent. As observed by the interviewees, politicians and legislators cannot expect hospital professionals to do the most unpleasant part of the job – applying presumed consent – if they do not do their own, which consists at least in informing the general population about what might happen to them in hospital.

But one can find other advantages for legislative and political authorities in perpetuating the present situation. The transition to a system of express consent would provoke, almost certainly, protests from transplantation surgeons. Not changing it appeases their lobby without losing much, since the existence of the law of presumed consent is largely ignored by the population, and actual behaviour is organised according to a *deviant* normative structure the content of which seems to be well accepted by most of the general population.

Last but not least, as can be gleaned from parliamentary debates and from interviews with professionals, the existing law tells a pleasant tale of French society as one based on enlightened solidarity, on progress and on rationality. Specifically, this idea that the law has been promulgated as a tool for changing traditional behaviours within the population gives to the members of the legislative corps an image of a group with the responsibility of guiding and educating a population not always responding with cartesian (i.e. rational) reactions to the needs of the community. In a historical context where the French state has less power to regulate behaviours that are now considered to belong more to the private sphere,[31] this law demonstrates, if not the power, at least the aspiration of legislators to regulate certain social behaviours.[37]

CONCLUSION

The attention paid to the formal and practical aspects of this attempt by French authorities at regulating and modifying behaviours and attitudes through a process of legal engineering leads to the conclusion that both political authorities and those who act as the arm of the law are apparently unable to apply it and certainly unwilling to try. The causes seem to be two-fold. Firstly, the lack of legitimacy of political authorities – and of those supposed to apply their regulations – to impose certain behaviours and ethical choices that appear to be too far away from the vision of the world of the population in general. Secondly, there is, at the same time, a mismatch between the role legislators originally wanted medical professionals to play and the one these professionals are in practice willing to play. As a matter of fact, and contrary to the hopes of the lawmakers in 1976, it was not enough to pass a law of presumed consent to obtain a modification of procurement rates. Laws are not effective per se, they are not normative objects dropped in a virgin territory, in a normless land. The content of the law of presumed consent has as a matter of fact been challenged in practice by other sources of normal regulation, and its application by an evolving set of power relations among the social groups called to act in situ.

Acknowledgements

This chapter was written during the author's stay at the Department of Legal Theory of the University of Groningen as a visiting scholar within the programme 'Regulating Socially Problematic Medical Behaviour'.

References

1. Loi Caillavet 76-1181 du 26 décembre 1976.
2. Sénat. Rapport no. 58 Annexe au procès-verbal de la séance du 16 novembre 1976.
3. Circulaire Jeanneney du 24 avril 1968.
4. Etablissement Français des Greffes 2003 Evolution des causes de décès des sujets en état de mort encéphalique prélevés entre 1996 et 2002 Entante 20:3.
5. Carvais R, Sasportes M, eds. La greffe humaine. (In)certitudes ethiques: du don de soi à la tolérance de l'autre. Paris: PUF; 2000.
6. Lois de bioéthique no. 94-654 du 29 juillet 1994.
7. Thouvenin D. L'organisation de l'activité de transplantation d'organes par les règles juridiques. In: Carvais R, Sasportes M, eds. La greffe humaine. (In)certitudes ethiques: du don de soi a la tolérance de l'autre. Paris: PUF; 2000:643–665.
8. Office d'Evaluation des Choix Scientifiques et Technologiques. Rapport sur l'application de la loi no. 94-654 du 29 juillet 1994 relative au don et à l'utilisation des éléments et produits du corps humain, à l'assistance médicale à la procréation et au diagnostic prénatal. 1999. Online. Available: http://www.assemblee-nationale.fr/rap-oesct/bioethique/r1407.asp.
9. Assemblée Nationale. Projet de loi relatif à la bioéthique adopté le 22 janvier 2002. Online. Available www.assemblee-nationale.fr/ta/ta0763.asp.
10. Carbonnier J. Flexible droit: textes pour une sociologie du droit sans rigueur. Paris: Librairie générale de droit et de jurisprudence; 1979.
11. Conseil Constitutionnel. Décision no. 94-343/344 DC du 27 juillet 1994. Online. Available: www.conseil-constitutionnel.fr/decision/1994/94343dc.htm.
12. Conseil d'Etat. Les lois de bioéthique: cinq ans après. 1999. Online. Available: www.conseil-etat.fr/ce/index_ra_li9904.shtml. no. 96-1041 du 2 décembre relatif au constat de la mort préalable au prélèvement d'organes, de tissus et de cellules à des fins thérapeutiques ou scientifiques.
13. CCNE. Avis no. 50 sur le réexamen des lois de bioéthique. 1998. Online. Available: www.ccne-ethique.fr.
14. CCNE. Avis no. 67 sur l'avant-projet de révision des lois de bioéthique. 2001. Online. Available: www.ccne-ethique.fr
15. CCDH. Avis portant sur la révision des lois de 1994 sur la bioéthique. 2000 Online. Available: www.commission-droits-homme.fr.
16. Hennette-Vauchez S. Le consentement présumé du défunt aux prélèvements d'organes: un principe exorbitant mais incontesté. R.R.J. 2001; 1:183–228.
17. Iacub M. La construction de la mort en droit français Enquête 1998; 7:39–54

18. Thouvenin D. De l'éthique biomédicale aux lois 'bioéthiques'. Revue Trimestrielle de Droit Civil 1994; 4:717–736.

19. Carvais R, Hermitte M-A. Les français, attachés au droit commun, réticents à l'égard du droit de la bioéthique. In: Carvais R, Sasportes M, eds. La greffe humaine. (In)certitudes éthiques: du don de soi à la tolérance de l'autre. Paris: PUF; 2000:843–870, at 845.

20. Assemblée nationale. Rapport no. 2600 présenté le 25 mars 1992 par Jean Louis Bianco, Projet de loi relatif au don et à l'utilisation des éléments et produits du corps humain et à la procréation médicalement assistée, et modifiant le code de la santé publique.

21. Assemblée nationale. Rapport fait au nom de la commission mixte paritaire chargée de proposer un texte sur les dispositions restant en discussion du projet de loi relatif au don et à l'utilisation des éléments et produits du corps humain, à l'assistance médicale à la procréation et au diagnostic prénatal, Jean-François Mattei, député, Jean Chérioux, sénateur, annexe au procès verbal de la séance du 9 juin 1994.

22. Loi relative à la bioéthique no. 2004-800 du 6 août 2004.

23. Sénat. Comptes rendus des débats, séance du 20 janvier 1998, Application de la loi sur les prélèvements d'organes.

24. Assemblée nationale. Commission des Affaires Culturelles, Familiales et Sociales, Compte rendu de séance, 18 mars 2003.

25. Waissmann R. Analyse des acceptations et des refus du don d'organes; une analyse de cas en France. Sociologie et Sociétés 1996; 2:109–118.

26. Moatti J-P. Dons d'organes: un révélateur des arbitrages entre l'efficience et l'équité dans le système de santé. In: Carvais R, Sasportes M, eds. La greffe humaine. (In)certitudes éthiques: du don de soi à la tolérance de l'autre. Paris: PUF; 2000:599–628.

27. Campion-Vincent V. Les récits et la légende des vols d'organes, expressions des réticences face à la greffe. In: Carvais R, Sasportes M, eds. La greffe humaine. (In)certitudes éthiques: du don de soi à la tolérance de l'autre. Paris: PUF; 2000:357–372.

28. Aubert V. Some social functions of legislation. Acta Sociologica 1966; 10:98–121.

29. Bonnet F. Aspects techniques et organisationnels. Le point de vue d'un anesthésiste-réanimateur. In: Carvais R, Sasportes M, eds. La greffe humaine. (In)certitudes éthiques: du don de soi à la tolérance de l'autre. Paris: PUF; 2000:305–320.

30. Revue de la mutualité. Présomption de consentement. La loi Caillavet. Un entretien avec son auteur 1992; 148:12–14, at 12.

31. Willaime J-P. Etat, éthique et religion. Cahiers internationaux de sociologie 1990; (janvier–juin):189–213.

32. Commaille J. L'esprit sociologique des lois: essai de sociologie politique du droit. Paris: PUF; 1994.

33. Augé M, ed. La mort et moi, et nous. Paris: Editions Textuel; 1995.

34. Freidson E. Method and substance in the comparative study of professions. Plenary Address by Eliot Freidson, Conference on Regulating Expertise, Paris, 14 April 1994. Online. Available: http://itsa.ucsf.edu/~eliotf/Method_and_Substance_in_Co.html.

35. Castel R. The regulation of madness: the origin of incarceration in France. London: Polity Press; 1988.

36. Foucault M, ed. Moi, Pierre Rivière, ayant égorgé ma mère, ma soeur et mon frère: Un cas de parricide au XIXè siècle. Paris: Gallimard; 1973.

37. Weber M. Economie et société. Paris: Pocket; 1995.

SECTION FOUR

Questionable interventions during life

SECTION CONTENTS

10. The proper limits for medical intervention that harms the therapeutic interests of incompetents   191

11. Infant vaccination: a conflict of ethical imperatives?   213

12. Cyberwoman and her surgeon in the twenty-first century   233

Chapter **10**

The proper limits for medical intervention that harms the therapeutic interests of incompetents

Austen Garwood-Gowers

CHAPTER CONTENTS

Introduction   191
Contemporary legal standards
    relating to medical
    intervention on the
    incompetent   193
Applying a best interests
    approach to interventions
    that harm the therapeutic
    interests of the incompetent
    197
The legal scope for
    interventions on the
    insentient dying person   201

Should the right to bodily
    security of the incompetent
    be treated as absolute
    vis-à-vis the needs of
    others or diluted to aid
    the meeting of those
    needs?   203
Conclusion   209
References   210

INTRODUCTION

The medical tradition of treating the human body as 'predominantly something one does therapy to and only incidentally gets medical benefits from'[1] has been subject to an unprecedented level of dilution over the last century. The value of cadavers in fields like medical education, research and transplantation is now exploited systematically on a mass scale and it has become commonplace for the living to be subject to interventions that harm their therapeutic interests. The circumstances in which it is ethically and legally acceptable to subject a person to such harm have yet to be fully debated and explored.

In relation to the living prospective subject, one of the problems hampering the debate has been a difference in opinion over what harming therapeutic interests means. Most of the discourse orients itself from a therapeutic/non-therapeutic classification of intervention. However, there is no single accepted definition of the terms therapeutic and non-therapeutic. In order to have a shared discourse, we must reject the idea that they mean whatever each medical professional or researcher wants them to mean in favour of the idea that they refer to the objective prospective impact of an intervention. Traditionally, impact has been seen to refer only to direct impact – thus, for example, testing a potentially harmful drug on a healthy volunteer is non-therapeutic as is taking body material from a healthy person in order to transplant it into a sick person. The feature of certain interventions that harm therapeutic interests, these included, is that they may be part of something constructive – with the subject, another person or persons and, in some cases, human society at large benefiting from things that result from the intervention. For example, if a kidney is given to a person with end-stage renal failure it might benefit their quality of life, benefit society by taking a person off the waiting list and benefit the donor in numerous ways such as by enhancing self-esteem and protecting his or her vested interest in the well-being of the community at large along with potentially a stronger vested interest in the well-being of the specific prospective recipient. According to this usage an intervention may be non-therapeutic and yet potentially consistent with what is best for the person who is subject to it. A potent minority of commentators and bodies take an alternative approach where the concept of 'therapy' is conflated with that of what is in a person's interests. Unfortunately, some of these same authorities continue to describe interventions that lack direct benefit as 'non-therapeutic' with the result of this being a false assumption that what is non-therapeutic is not in a person's interests. Naturally, this thinking has had its most powerfully confusing effects in relation to the discourse on use of incompetents.

In an effort to bring some clarity to the field, this chapter will maintain the normative usage of the term non-therapeutic as referring to interventions that for their prospective subject lack direct benefit. It will be demonstrated that not only can some such interventions generate indirect benefit to the person subjected to them but that in some instances they may, even beyond the more obvious living donation context, be consistent with a person's interests overall and hence capable of being performed on an incompetent in jurisdictions that require the best interests of incompetents to be protected.

As a further aid to understanding I will be employing a division between intervention which is therapeutically optimal for the person (in terms of direct benefit) and that which is not. The latter incorporates both interventions that are non-therapeutic and those that are therapeutic but of a lesser therapeutic suitability than that which is (or should reasonably be made) available. On the basis that a person's therapeutic interests is in having what is optimal, such therapeutic but sub-optimal interventions can be grouped together with non-therapeutic interventions as intervention that is actually harmful to therapeutic interests.

This classification system is a useful tool for clarifying what the issues are. In relation to the incompetent they centre on. Firstly, what the test for protection of interests is; secondly, how to apply it in this context; *and,* thirdly whether it is the right test in the first place. In practice the first issue has not just been about identifying what the normal legal standard for protection of the incompetent is, but also about whether the standard applies to situations in which the body of the incompetent can be used to fulfil certain societal needs (such as needs for medical research and body materials) or will be diluted in such a way as to favour meeting these needs.

Assuming that the law is normally aimed at protecting the incompetent's interest in bodily security against such dilution, the second issue becomes one of assessing when an intervention that harms the therapeutic interests of the incompetent has sufficient indirect benefits to be consistent with her interests overall. In the context of English law particularly, part of the problem encountered when making this assessment has been a dispute over what type of benefit can be taken into account. The key aims of the chapter in this context are to bury the misperception that interests can be judged by reference to medical professional/researcher intent and to suggest that indirect benefit cannot be rightfully limited to mental and physical benefit but must also take into account the value of respecting a person irrespective of whether that respect will manifest in physical or mental benefit to her. The latter suggestion has particularly strong implications for how we treat people who are insentient and dying. Some of these implications are explored in the chapter. In particular there is an explanation of when and how far we should take into account what such a person would have wished for in determining whether to perform intervention on them that could not otherwise have been lawfully justified.

In relation to the third issue, it is evident that, for example, certain international instruments appear to allow certain forms of research on the incompetent adult that are inconsistent with her overall interests. English law, judging by the Mental Capacity Act 2005, has followed suit. Advocates of such an approach have attempted to justify it on various grounds, including through arguing that is necessary from the point of view of equality of persons. In this chapter it is suggested that such arguments have no merit whatsoever and that in fact to dilute the protection of bodily security of one class of persons is to fundamentally undermine the principle of equality of persons.

CONTEMPORARY LEGAL STANDARDS RELATING TO MEDICAL INTERVENTION ON THE INCOMPETENT

Debates about what legal standard should govern intervention on the incompetent have largely centred on how best to show him or her respect. This is essentially a question of how much emphasis to give autonomy and how much to give paternalism. Most common law jurisdictions have given pre-eminence to autonomy only to the extent of allowing advance directives and, in some cases, powers of attorney. In the absence of such a directive or power the norm has been to protect the best interests of the incompetent – an approach that tends to give pre-eminence to clinical factors over the incompetent's past or present wishes. (For an advocacy of the main alternative of substituted judgement see, for example, Robertson.[2])

Outside the common law tradition many jurisdictions eschew a best interests approach in favour of specific prescriptions on permissible levels of harm and risk vis-à-vis potential benefit. This is particularly the case, for example, in relation to living donor transplantation.[3] In general the sole aim of such provisions remains protection of the incompetent's interests. However, this is not to say that most or even the majority of jurisdictions always strive to protect the right of bodily security vis-à-vis the needs of others. Indeed, most jurisdictions where there is active medical use of the body after death permit use in certain cases without clear evidence that the deceased would have agreed to it. This is particularly so in the transplant context.[4] Furthermore, some make it mandatory for the living to use their body in life to rescue another in the common accident, danger and emergency situation (albeit not to such an extent that it should put themselves in any significant danger and probably not to the extent of undergoing a medical intervention). Many continental jurisdictions take this approach (for a detailed (though dated) survey see Feldbrugge;[5] for more recent discussion see Calabresi[6]). There is also no getting away from the fact that some international instruments envisage protection of the interests of the incompetent adult being diluted to meet the needs of others in the medical research context. Article 17 of the Convention on Human Rights and Biomedicine, which is entitled 'Protection of persons not able to consent to research', states that:

'1. Research on a person without the capacity to consent as stipulated in Article 5 may be undertaken only if all the following conditions are met:
   i. the conditions laid down in Article 16, sub-paragraphs i to iv, are fulfilled;[i]
   ii. the results of the research have the potential to produce real and direct benefit;
   iii. research of comparable effectiveness cannot be carried out on individuals capable of giving consent;
   iv. the necessary authorisation provided for under Article 6 has been given specifically and in writing; and
   v. the person concerned does not object.

---

[i] These conditions relate to there being no alternative of comparable effectiveness to research on humans, the risks incurred by the subject not being disproportionate to the potential benefits of the research, prior approval by the competent body after independent examination of its scientific merit (including assessment of the importance of the aim of the research, and multidisciplinary review of its ethical acceptability) and the subjects being informed of their rights and the safeguards prescribed by law for their protection.

2. Exceptionally and under protective conditions prescribed by law, where the research has not the potential to produce results of direct benefit to the health of the person concerned, such research may be authorised subject to the conditions laid down in paragraph 1, sub-paragraphs i, iii, iv and v above, and to the following additional conditions:

  i. the research has the aim of contributing, through significant improvement in the scientific understanding of the individual's condition, disease or disorder, to the ultimate attainment of results capable of conferring benefit to the person concerned or to other persons in the same age category or afflicted with the same disease or disorder or having the same condition;

  ii. the research entails only minimal risk and minimal burden for the individual concerned.'

The key provision here is 17(2)(i), which makes it clear that the research does not have to be aimed at (or presumably have the prospect of resulting in) benefit to its subjects if it has a benefit to other persons in the same age category or afflicted with the same disease or disorder or having the same condition. Taken in isolation it would appear that Article 17 allows the interests of the incompetent to be violated in order to meet the needs of others. However, it does not sit easily with Article 2, entitled 'Primacy of the human being', which states that '(t)he interests and welfare of the human being shall prevail over the sole interests of science and society'. At the very minimum, Article 2 would appear to mean that if there is no benefit in a medical intervention for the subject of it, that medical intervention cannot be performed by reference to the interests of science or society. Yet Article 17 envisages just such interventions being performed. A similar problem arises with the Declaration of Helsinki's incompetent adult research provisions (see Principles 24–26) and their relationship with its foundational norms which include an emphasis on considerations related to the well-being of the human subject taking precedence over the interests of science and society (Principle 5 of the Introduction of the Declaration of Helsinki (1964) (as amended most recently in Scotland, October, 2000)). As a matter of construction it could be suggested that specific research norms ought to be interpreted consistently with foundational norms. However, to provide certainty both instruments ought to be reformed. Unfortunately UK legislation, as will later be illustrated (pp. 205–7), has adopted a similar approach.

Common law at least does seem to protect the bodily security of the living as absolute vis-à-vis the needs of others. The classic demonstration of this is the case of *McFall v Shimp* (1978) 10 Pa D & C (3d) 90 (Ct Comm Pl, Pa). The context of this case was that David Shimp had voluntarily undertaken initial tests which showed that he was a bone marrow match for his cousin, Robert McFall, an aplastic anaemia sufferer. When Shimp refused to go any further, McFall applied to the Alleghany County Court to force him to undertake the remaining tests and, if suitable, donate bone marrow.

In rejecting the application, Mr Justice Flaherty stated in no uncertain terms that,

> 'Our society, contrary to many others, has as its first principle, the respect for the individual, and that society and government exist to protect the individual from being invaded and hurt by another . . . For our law to compel the defendant to submit to an intrusion of his body would change every concept and principle upon which our society is founded. To do so would defeat the sanctity of the individual, and would impose a rule which would know no limits, and one could not imagine where the line would be drawn . . . For a society, which respects the rights of *one* individual, to sink its teeth into the jugular vein or neck of one of its members and suck its sustenance for another member, is revolting to our hard-wrought concepts of jurisprudence. Forcible extraction of living body tissue causes revulsion to the judicial mind. Such would raise the spectre of the swastika and the Inquisition, reminiscent of the horrors this portends.'

Around the time this case was being published, Gerald Dworkin was suggesting that the test for infants and young children participating in non-therapeutic research was a 'not against interests' one.[7–9] Dworkin attempted to derive support for this view from Lord Reid's obiter dicta statement in *S v S, W v Official Solicitor* [1970] 3 All ER 107 (HL). His Lordship stated, obiter dicta, that when determining whether a blood test might be performed on a minor to determine paternity

> 'surely a reasonable parent would have some regard to the general public interest and would not refuse a blood test unless he thought that would clearly be against the interests of the child. I cannot assume that in the present cases the husbands are acting in selfish disregard of these children's interests in asking for blood tests.' ([1970] 3 All ER 107 at 111–112)

A 'not against interests' standard was subsequently adopted in *Re X (A Minor)* [1975] 1 All ER 697, where publication of a book was authorised in the interests of freedom of expression despite the fact that the book could cause gross psychological damage to a 14-year-old if she read it, since it described her deceased father's depraved behaviour towards her. The Court of Appeal subsequently used it in *Re H (A Minor) (Blood Tests: Parental Rights)* [1996] 4 All ER 28 to justify blood-testing a minor for purposes of determining paternity. However, such cases are best understood not as authority for diluting protection of the incompetent's interests to meet the needs of others but as an attempt to arrive at a fair solution to a situation in which fundamental rights are in conflict. If this is not of itself obvious it becomes so when one takes into account the recent case of *Re S (A Child) (Identification Restrictions on Publication)* [2004] UKHL 47. Here, in allowing disclosure of the fact that a child's parents were the subject of legal proceedings despite the fact that it would harm the child psychologically, the

House of Lords specifically employed a weighing of rights approach, paving its way to favouring freedom of expression over the child's right to privacy by holding Section 1(1) of the Children Act 1989 to be inapplicable. It is arguably just as well that the courts have begun to eschew the idea of a not against interests approach. There was never a single clear definition of what the test meant in the first place. Price notes that it is typically used to describe interventions that are de minimus in terms of physical harm.[10] However, using the phrase in this way amounts to suggesting that something is not 'bad' for a person if it does not do them much physical harm. In reality, however, even if an intervention were to involve no physical harm it would still have to be classified as harmful to a person's interest in bodily security and therefore against their interests in the absence of conferring a sufficient countervailing benefit upon them.

APPLYING A BEST INTERESTS APPROACH TO INTERVENTIONS THAT HARM THE THERAPEUTIC INTERESTS OF THE INCOMPETENT

Although Kennedy and Grubb state that 'it is fair to state that the inherent notion of "best interests" is that the medical intervention must be therapeutic',[11] their chapter on transplantation does not challenge case law that employs this test but nonetheless supports living donation by the incompetent.[3] However, what both authors and a number of other academics do clearly believe is that the test will not allow incompetents to participate in non-therapeutic research.[12-19] Stauch and Wheat with Tingle go even further in the context of discussing incompetents by doubting 'whether treatment determined on randomised, rather than clinical, grounds in an RCT can ever be in the patient's best interests'.[18] The line of thinking here is not made explicit. However, it seems that the authors are logically extending the conclusion that non-therapeutic research is not in the best interests of the incompetent to sub-optimal therapeutic research. They also appear to be implying that all randomised controlled trials (RCTs) fall into the sub-optimal category, which conflicts with the reality that where there is no existing treatment or no effective treatment, participation in such a trial may be the optimal therapeutic choice. (Even if the control is a placebo this can still be the case because participation still offers a chance of getting treatment.)

Views that non-therapeutic and sub-optimal research are inconsistent with best interests are hard to sustain. There is no reason why such research cannot be in the best interests of the incompetent on some of the occasions where he or she has the prospect of obtaining significant indirect benefits from participation. Indirect benefits in the research context can range from educational and self-esteem benefits obtained through the act of participation, the protection of a vested interest in the community at large and even the benefit, in certain cases, of the investigation having the potential to lead to improvements in the way a condition that one, or someone important to one, has. These benefits are not always trifling and in certain circumstances where the intervention has limited or no adverse impact on the body and mental state of the incompetent they could quite clearly be sufficient to justify intervention where there are no better (e.g. less intrusive) methods for the incompetent to achieve the same levels of benefit. There is also no reason why genetic screening performed for the benefit of family members cannot also be in the interests of the incompetent in certain situations, for example where it involved little harm and risk to the incompetent but protected a significant vested interest he or she had in the well-being of certain relatives. Finally, it is entirely possible that certain interventions on the insentient dying person could be justified purely by reference to what the insentient would have wished.

Misperceptions about the best interests test have prevented these conclusions from being generally accepted. At the centre of the problem in relation to incompetent adults is Lord Brandon's statement in the House of Lords in *Re F (Mental Patient: Sterilisation)* [1990] 2 AC 1, [1989] 2 WLR 1025 that an 'operation or other treatment will be in' the best interests of incompetent adults 'if, but only if, it is carried out in order either to save lives, or to ensure improvement or prevent deterioration in their physical or mental health' (p. 1067). Apparently hanging on to the words 'in order', the Law Commission's report *Mental Incapacity*[19] concludes that non-therapeutic research is not in the best interests of the incompetent adult due to the 'simple fact is that the researcher is making no claim to be acting in the best interests of that individual person and does not therefore come within the rules set out in *Re F*' (para 6.29). Presumably for the same reason, the Commission concluded that genetic screening for the benefit of family members is unlawful (para 6.25). It also simply adopted (para 6.24) the conclusion of the King's Fund Research Report[20] that elective ventilation is unlawful because '(t)he ventilation procedure is clearly being used for the benefit of the recipient of the transplanted organs and not for the patient'.[ii] Not only did the last two conclusions ignore the possibility of these interventions being justified by reference to an advance directive but all of them ignore the legal reality that whether or not an intervention is in the best interests of a person is not dependent on what the medical professional intends but the objective reality of its prospective impact. This is recognised in Lord Bridge's judgment when he states that:

> 'It seems to me to be axiomatic that treatment *which is* necessary to preserve the life, health, or well being of the [incompetent adult] patient may lawfully be given without consent.' (*Re F (Mental Patient: Sterilisation)* (HL) [1989] 2 WLR 1025-1093 at 1064; italics and words in brackets added.)

Lord Goff stated that:

[ii] A section entitled 'The law and elective ventilation' begins with a sentence stating that: However, there is nothing else resembling a reason in the rest of this section or the report as a whole.[21]

'When the state of affairs is permanent or semi-permanent, action *properly* taken to preserve the life, health or well-being of the assisted person may well transcend such measures as surgical operation or substantial medical treatment . . .' (Italics added.)

The word 'properly' here implies that the court is ultimately the arbiter of whether action taken satisfies the relevant test. The judgments do emphasise that a medical professional deciding best interests on behalf of an incompetent adult may escape liability if best interests have been interpreted in a manner that is *Bolam* reasonable, but this is not the same as saying that a subjective approach is taken. Rather, it is saying that the courts are heavily predisposed to viewing a medical professional's assessment of best interests as reasonable if the medical professional can show that such an assessment would be considered reasonable by a responsible body of medical opinion.

However, even if one removes the subjective tint to Lord Brandon's statement his emphasis on the need to ensure improvement or at least preventing deterioration of physical or mental health is preclusive of valuing wishes in their own right within the best interests test. This approach begins to look odd when we realise that the wishes of incompetents are treated as an end in their own right in the enforcement of advance directives. In *Malette v Shulman* (1990) 67 DLR (4th) 321 (Ont CA), for example, an advance directive refusing blood and blood products was deemed to be valid even though the patient would have simply moved from unconsciousness to death had the doctor respected it.

There are a number of other reasons why we should not take Lord Brandon's narrow focus too seriously. Firstly, none of the judges appeared to have considered the question of whether wishes should be considered an end in their own right. Secondly, Lord Brandon's judgment does not even specifically refer to non-therapeutic interventions and his problematic formulation begins with the words 'operation or other treatment', suggesting that he was confining himself to consideration of therapeutic interventions. His approach seems to be coloured by the context he was addressing, i.e. sterilisation, where numerous factors point toward a restrictive approach to best interests. Lastly, whilst necessity is a restrictive concept in general, once it has been determined that (in the absence of an advance directive) intervention on the long-term incompetent is governed by best interests, it makes sense to then include any relevant factors when assessing what 'best interests' means. Wishes would seem to be relevant in their own right in as much as protecting them can form part of treating a person with respect. This point would already seem to be recognised in as much as most societies generally respect (subject to taxation) people's wishes for what they want to do with their property after death.

One of the key authorities in relation to concepts of dignity and respect is *Airedale NHS Trust v Bland* [1993] 1 All ER 821 (HL) where the House of Lords declared it to be lawful to discontinue feeding of Anthony Bland who was in a persistent vegetative state. Lord Mustill suggested that Tony Bland had no interests and hence no interests in having intervention continued ([1993] 1 All ER 821 at 897). Similarly, Lord Keith concluded that, '(i)n the case of a permanently insentient being, who if continuing to live would never experience the slightest actual discomfort, it is difficult, if not impossible, to make any relevant comparison between continued existence and the absence of it. It is, however, perhaps permissible to say that to an individual with no cognitive capacity whatever, and no prospect of ever recovering any such capacity in this world, it must be a matter of complete indifference whether he lives or dies' ([1993] 1 All ER 821 at 856). He favoured the opinion that existence in such a state was not a benefit to the patient. Lord Goff suggested that in withdrawal and withholding cases involving patients in a persistently vegetative state 'there is in reality no weighing operation to be performed' ([1993] 1 All ER 821 at 869). He continued by stressing that treatment in this situation was futile and that this was the justification for its withdrawal. However, his Lordship also concluded that sanctity of life was an important principle ([1993] 1 All ER 821 at 863–864). The important point here is that although intervention is prima facie a battery we all have an interest in our lives being preserved because they are all of intrinsic value whatever our state is. Arguably, the only circumstance in which this interest is insufficient to justify intervention is where an interest in dignity points toward being left to die. None of the judgments in the House of Lords seem to recognise this. Lord Goff did suggest it would be cruel to a person to use medical intervention to prolong their life regardless of the circumstances:

> 'The point was put forcibly in the judgment of the Supreme Judicial Court of Massachusetts in *Superintendent of Belchertown State School v Saikewicz* (1977) 370 NE 2d 417, 428, as follows: "To presume that the incompetent person must always be subjected to what many rational and intelligent persons may decline is to downgrade the status of the incompetent person by placing a lesser value on his intrinsic human worth and vitality".' ([1993] 1 All ER 821 at 865)

His Lordship's use of the term cruel is open to question given that Bland was on the face of things incapable of experiencing life. However, substitute the idea of it being contrary to respect or dignity and one has something reasonable to work with. The judgments given in the Court of Appeal, especially those of Butler-Sloss LJ and Hoffmann LJ, saw the problem with intervention on Tony Bland very much in these terms ([1993] 1 All ER 806 respectively at 820–824 and 826 particularly). Hoffmann LJ stated that the 'fallacy' in the argument that Tony Bland had no interest which suffered from his being kept alive was 'that it assumes that we have no interests in those things of which we have no conscious experience' ([1993] 1 All ER 806 at 829). He continued by observing that

> '(a)t least part of the reason why we honour the wishes of the dead about the distribution of their property is that we think it would wrong them not to do so, despite the fact that we believe that they will never know

that their will has been ignored. Most people would like an honourable and dignified death and we think it wrong to dishonour their deaths, even when they are unconscious that this is happening . . .' ([1993] 1 All ER 806 at 829)

Butler-Sloss LJ commented that mentally incompetent patients as a whole had 'the right to be respected' and that this included 'a right to avoid unnecessary humiliation and degrading invasion of his body for no good purpose' ([1993] 1 All ER 806 at 822).[iii]

THE LEGAL SCOPE FOR INTERVENTIONS ON THE INSENTIENT DYING PERSON

There is a whole range of interventions that a medical professional may wish to perform on an insentient dying person. Most would be interventions that have the prospect of ultimately benefiting third parties, such as: intervention on comatose pregnant women to maintain life so as to facilitate the delivery of viable babies; medical experimentation on long-term coma victims;[22] and interventions on insentient dying persons to facilitate use of their body materials. It is the last category of interventions that is of most concern here. They include use of interventions that preserve the 'quality' of body materials for later use and actual extractions of materials.

One of the key issues is whether the insentient person is actually alive or dead when intervention takes places. Most countries gave up cardiorespiratory approaches to defining death once it became possible to employ a standard based on irreversible loss of function in both the upper and lower brainstem. However, cardiorespiratory approaches are now being employed under certain protocols that are aimed at increasing organ transplantation. One of the pre-eminent examples is the Pittsburgh protocol which stipulates that death occurs after irreversible loss of cardiorespiratory function, which it goes on to define as occurring after 2 minutes loss of respiration and heart beat. However, loss of cardiorespiratory function is at best evidence of death not proof of it and as regards the Pittsburgh protocol specifically the suggestion that loss of function is irreversible after 2 minutes flatly conflicts with the reality that function can spontaneously restart after 2 minutes have passed.[23] The proper approach that the law ought to insist on is one where death is only

---

[iii] By way of an aside, one could also argue that medicine should be understood as having limits which medical professionals should not have to go beyond. As Lord Bingham stated in the Court of Appeal: 'It is relevant to consider the objects of medical care. I think traditionally they have been (1) to prevent the occurrence of illness, injury or deformity (which for convenience I shall together call "illness") before they occur; (2) to cure illness when it does occur; (3) where illness cannot be cured, to prevent or retard deterioration of the patient's condition; (4) to relieve pain and suffering in body and mind. I doubt if it has ever been the object of medical care merely to prolong the life of the insentient patient with no hope of recovery where nothing can be done to promote any of these objects.' [1993] 1 All ER 806 at 809.

pronounced following suitable clinical tests having confirmed irreversible loss of brainstem function. Interventions performed before this stage should thus have to satisfy legal standards pertaining to intervention on the incompetent.

As to these, it is evident that the law protects everyone's interest in not having their bodily security directly and intentionally invaded. Evidence may suggest that insentient dying persons will never be aware of being subject to medical intervention but they are nonetheless protected from being subject to such intervention without lawful justification.[iv] This protection extends all the way up to the law of murder where they have their life purposely shortened and potentially (at the discretion of the jury) where they are merely subject to an act which can be foreseen to be virtually certain to shorten life (*R v Woollin* [1998] 4 All ER 103). Such criminal liability can be avoided where the intervention has been validly consented to in advance by the insentient person or where it is in his or her best interests. However, the structure of these two justifications is such that not all types of intervention are going to be lawful by pure virtue of the fact that the insentient person wished to be subject to them. Consent, given in advance or contemporaneously, is only treated as valid where an intervention is acceptable from a public policy standpoint, meaning that it must not be unreasonable (per Lord Lane in *Attorney General's Reference* [No. 6 of 1980] [1981] 2 All ER 1057, confirmed by the House of Lords in *R v Brown (Anthony)* [1993] 2 All ER 75) or improper (per Lord Mustill in *Airedale NHS Trust v Bland* [1993] 1 All ER 821 at 889). It is not certain what scope this gives to interventions that are therapeutic interest harming but have the prospect of benefiting another or others. Judges might be guided by legislative provisions from other jurisdictions on the issue of the harm and risk to which a living donor may be lawfully subjected. These provisions often include a statement to the effect that organs that are vital to continued life or well-being cannot be removed.[24]

Interestingly, the adverse impacts of vital organ removal on a person are more limited if he or she is insentient and dying because there is an inability to experience what is happening at this point. However, interventions on any person are invasive of bodily security and thus raise issues of dignity and respect. These issues are arguably amplified the more intrusive the intervention is in a general or bodily privacy sense, the more mutilation it involves and, finally, the more it alters the way that the body looks and functions. They are also amplified where intervention has the prospect of foreshortening life and, to a lesser extent, where it has the prospect of drawing life out. In these terms it is quite clear that something like vital organ removal falls into the category of interventions on the insentient that would be hardest to justify as not

---

[iv] This is made explicit within some of the House of Lords judgments in Bland. For example, Lord Lowry stated that, 'if it is not in the interests of an insentient patient to continue the life-supporting care and treatment, the doctor would be acting unlawfully if he continued the care and treatment' [1993] 1 All ER 821 at 877. Lord Goff also emphasised that treatment must be stopped where it no longer in the patient's best interests ([1993] 1 All ER 821 at 869). These views are undoubtedly correct, with the caveat that intervention could still be lawful if justified by a valid advance directive.

intrinsically unreasonable or improper. It not only foreseeably shortens life but is highly intrusive and mutilative. By contrast, interventions such as the administration of heparin, which foreseeably shorten life but are less intrusive and mutilative, might not be intrinsically unreasonable or improper.

There are two reasons why a much more restrictive approach to intervention ought to be taken when evidence of the insentient's wishes does not amount to an advance consent. First, if the evidence did not support an advance consent, it must, as a matter of course, have been weaker. Second, there is less scope to undertake intervention that must be in the best interests of the insentient as opposed to merely reasonable or proper in the overall sense. For example, a measure that foreseeably shortens life could be justifiable where therapeutic (as with the administration of morphine for pain relief) but it is hard to see one that is non-therapeutic (such as administration of heparin to aid organ preservation) being justifiable even where its other impacts on the body are limited and it was both wished for and of potential societal benefit. Equally, interventions that extend life (such as elective ventilation) might be quite hard to justify under a best interests approach, as might interventions that have significant other impacts on the body – such as inserting a catheter and pumping cooling liquid through it. Arguably, at the other end of the spectrum it would fail to respect the dignity of an insentient dying person who had wished to become a cadaveric donor *not to do* extremely minimal interventions (such as taking a blood sample to tissue type) where these are important to the level of success in post-mortem use in transplantation (such as where taking a blood sample helps to find a better matched recipient or at least provide a better time scale for recipient clinical work-up).

Ultimately, whether therapeutic interest-harming interventions that are capable of being acceptable are actually acceptable will depend on the strength of the evidence as to the incompetent's wishes that is presented. The extent to which different types of evidence as to wishes can be relied upon needs to be assessed. From this assessment guidelines should be developed to ensure a more uniform and accurate approach to assessing best interests in this context. Table 10.1 is designed to contribute to this process.

SHOULD THE RIGHT TO BODILY SECURITY OF THE INCOMPETENT BE TREATED AS ABSOLUTE VIS-À-VIS THE NEEDS OF OTHERS OR DILUTED TO AID THE MEETING OF THOSE NEEDS?

There have been a number of proposals to the effect that the needs of one person or society at large are a basis in their own right for supporting medical intervention on another. Proposals to move toward a 'not against interests' approach in relation to intervention on the incompetent must be placed in this category; a not against interests approach has the dressing of a sheep (semantically it means the same thing as a best interests approach) but is actually a wolf (typically being used as a label for proposals to allow intervention that causes no or de minimus physical harm to the incompetent irrespective of whether that intervention is actually consistent with best interests). Advocacy

Table 10.1   Interventions on insentient dying persons; using evidence as to wishes

Type of evidence	The extent to which it should be relied upon in the performance of interventions
Abstracting support for an intervention from an advance directive applying to a different intervention	The problem with abstraction of this kind is that it is essentially a form of guesswork. For example, if we ask what kinds of intervention before death would a person carrying a donor card have wished to be subject to to facilitate use of their body materials the answer might prove very unclear. Perhaps the most one can say is that they would almost certainly have wished to be subject to interventions that had a minimal impact on their body and did not affect the dying process, such as having a blood sample taken for tissue typing. However, there is genuine uncertainty over whether they would want to be subject, say, to something like elective ventilation. Outside the transplant case there is the popularised case of Diane Blood who had her husband's sperm electro-ejaculated when he was in a coma and dying. He had not specifically consented to this and it would be rather dubious to conclude from the fact that he had wanted children with his wife whilst alive that he would wish her to do this to have his children after his death.
Evidence provided by next-of-kin	One issue here is verifiability. If there is no reason to suspect that next-of-kin are lying or that their evidence is otherwise unreliable, then there is no reason in principle why what they say about the wishes of the insentient person should not be taken into account. However, this should be approached with caution and it should be ascertained whether the evidence is direct or merely abstracted from more general things that the insentient said or felt about life. One clinician, for example, recounted how he asked the insentient's next-of-kin what kind of person he was and whether he would have liked to have done things to help others. On the basis that he was a kind person and there was no evidence that he would disagree, the next-of-kin and clinician mutually agreed that intervention should be performed. The problem with this thinking is that it tends to assume that kind people would universally support intervention facilitative of transplantation. Yet quite significant percentages of the population do not even agree with transplantation and it would be wrong to suppose that this was simply meanness on their part. Abstraction of this kind is too speculative to warrant being a basis for intervention given that it is not a question of tipping an evenly balanced scale between non-intervention and intervention in favour of the latter but a question of justifying invasion of a dignity interest in bodily security.

Abstracting what the insentient person might have wanted from what people tend to want in this situation	This form of evidence is even more speculative, meaning that it ought not to be taken into account given the observations above.[a]

[a] It is notable in this respect that in *Bland*, Lord Goff took into account what the general population might think about living in a persistent vegetative state as a factor in assessing whether or not intervention that would keep Tony Bland alive would be consistent with his best interests. However, ultimately it seems that he merely used the fact that most of the public would probably not want intervention to keep them alive in such a state to confirm his existing impression that such intervention was not in Tony Bland's interests.

of a not against interests approach has proved particularly popular in relation to non-therapeutic research on incompetent adults[25,26] and, to a lesser extent, incompetents as a whole.[27]

A variation on the not against interests theme is found in the Law Commission's report *Mental Incapacity*.[28] The Commission jettisoned its commitment to best interests in two contexts. First, it recommended that interventions outside the research context that are not carried out for the benefit of the incompetent but will not cause him or her significant harm and will be of significant benefit to others[29] should be capable of being undertaken where the Secretary of State, after consultation and subject to an affirmative resolution by each House of Parliament, has made an order to this effect. Secondly, it concluded that research 'which is unlikely to benefit a participant, or whose benefit is likely to be long delayed, should be lawful in relation to a person without capacity to consent if (1) the research is into an incapacitating condition with which the participant is or may be affected and (2) certain statutory procedures are complied with.'[30] The procedures referred to include approval of the research by a Mental Incapacity Research Committee which, to paraphrase, must, amongst other things, satisfy itself that the research:

- is desirable in order to provide knowledge of the causes or treatment of, or of the care of persons affected by, mental disability
- has an object which cannot be effectively achieved without the participation of persons who are or may be without capacity to consent
- will not expose such a person participating in the research to more than negligible risk and that what is done in relation to such a person for the purposes of the research will not be unduly invasive or restrictive and will not unduly interfere with his freedom of action or privacy.[31]

Interestingly, Clause 4 of the government's Draft Mental Incapacity Bill (presented to Parliament by the Secretary of State for Constitutional Affairs in June 2002) maintained an emphasis on the best interests test for all but 'excluded decisions' and nothing in Clauses 26–29 which concerned excluded decisions affected the status quo of the law as regards non-therapeutic interventions. However, in June 2004 the draft bill was superseded by the Mental Capacity Bill, the latest version of which was published on 17 March 2005 and given Royal Assent on 7 April 2005. The Mental Capacity Act 2005 allows research that would be unlawful if carried out on a person capable of consenting without his or her consent to be conducted on an incompetent adult provided that various substantive and procedural requirements are met.[v] The key procedural aspect is that the research must be approved by the appropriate body – defined in Section 30(4) as the 'person, committee or other body specified in regulations made by the Secretary of State as the appropriate body in relation to a project of the kind in question'. The key substantive requirements are within Section 31. Section 31(1) states that the appropriate body may only approve the research project if it is satisfied that the following sub-sections are met in relation to 'P' (the incompetent prospective subject):

'(2) The research must be connected with:
   (a) an impairing condition affecting P, or
   (b) its treatment.
(3) 'Impairing condition' means a condition which is (or may be) attributable to, or which causes or contributes to (or may cause or contribute to), the impairment of, or disturbance in the functioning of, the mind or brain.
(4) There must be reasonable grounds for believing that research of comparable effectiveness cannot be carried out if the project has to be confined to, or relate only to, persons who have capacity to consent to taking part in it.
(5) The research must:
   (a) have the potential to benefit P without imposing on P a burden that is disproportionate to the potential benefit to P, or
   (b) be intended to provide knowledge of the causes or treatment of, or of the care of persons affected by, the same or a similar condition.
(6) If the research falls within paragraph (b) of subsection (5) but not within paragraph (a), there must be reasonable grounds for believing:
   (a) that the risk to P from taking part in the project is likely to be negligible, and
   (b) that anything done to, or in relation to, P will not:
      (i) interfere with P's freedom of action or privacy in a significant way, or
      (ii) be unduly invasive or restrictive.
(7) There must be reasonable arrangements in place for ensuring that the requirements of Sections 32 and 33 will be met.'

[v] Clinical trials which are subject to the provisions of clinical trials regulations are excluded (Section 30(3)).

Section 32 goes on to stress the role of carers and others in the process and Section 33 entitled 'Additional safeguards' goes on to stress that in spite of the incompetent not being able to consent:

'(2) Nothing may be done to, or in relation to, him in the course of the research:
  (a) to which he appears to object (whether by showing signs of resistance or otherwise) except where what is being done is intended to protect him from harm or to reduce or prevent pain or discomfort, or
  (b) which would be contrary to:
    (i) an advance decision of his which has effect, or
    (ii) any other form of statement made by him and not subsequently withdrawn,
    of which R is aware.
(3) The interests of the person must be assumed to outweigh those of science and society.
(4) If he indicates (in any way) that he wishes to be withdrawn from the project he must be withdrawn without delay.
(5) P must be withdrawn from the project, without delay, if at any time the person conducting the research has reasonable grounds for believing that one or more of the requirements set out in Section 31(2) to (7) is no longer met in relation to research being carried out on, or in relation to, P.'
(6) But neither subsection (4) nor subsection (5) requires treatment that P has been receiving as part of the project to be discontinued if R has reasonable grounds for believing that there would be a significant risk to P's health if it were discontinued.

None of these provisions specifically guarantee that research will only be conducted if it is in the best interests of the incompetent adult. Nor will their combined effect ensure the protection of best interests in practice. The Act's explanatory notes state that its research clauses are based on 'long-standing international consensus, for example, laid down by the World Medical Association [Declaration of Helsinki] and the Council of Europe Convention on Human Rights and Biomedicine' (para 93). However, the reality is that neither the 'con' or the 'sense' in this consensus is very strong. The Convention, Declaration and Act all have foundational norms which appear to be opposed to diluting protection of the right to bodily security to meet need, making it appear abnormal that their research provisions support such dilution in relation to the incompetent adult. This would imply that it needs to be properly justified. However, the only writers to even properly attempt to ideologically defend it would appear to be Gunn et al and John Harris, and their arguments are almost wholly one-sided. Harris has suggested that:

'It is not plausible to believe that the costs of acting morally fall only on those competent to consent. So long as we ensure that such costs do not fall *more heavily* on those not competent to consent than on others I see no sound argument for exempting them from the demands of morality. They may not be *accountable* in law, if they do wrong, but there is no reason to ensure that they do wrong by exempting them from their moral obligations.'[32]

He later adds that if we can pursue research without the use of incompetent adults so much the better but if the current position:

'jeopardises our capacity to pursue well founded research then perhaps we should remember that free-riding is not an attractive principle; nor is it a moral principle. We should not . . . assume that those incompetent to consent would wish to be free-riders, nor that they be excluded from discharging an obligation of good citizenship which we all share.'[33]

Echoing this concern about free-riding Gunn et al have suggested in their article 'Medical research on incompetent adults', that:

'If one wishes to gain the benefit of medical research, one has the obligation to offer oneself for participation. Otherwise, the person gaining the benefit of the research is a mere parasite on society, taking only the advantages and undertaking no risks.'[34]

Harris goes on to formalise his argument by suggesting that reform is necessary to achieve equality. However, having defined equality in this article as the idea 'that each person is entitled to the same concern, *respect* and protection of society as is accorded to any other person in the community'[32] (italics added), he states in a subsequent article that respect involves 'not just respect for the choices of those competent to make them *but also respect for the best interests or welfare of those who are not*'[35] (italics added). Furthermore, his proposal discriminates in the way that it attempts to prevent free-riding. It would allow researchers to subject incompetents to interventions that are not in their best interests whilst leaving competents free to refuse such interventions. Modifying his proposal to give incompetents the choice of whether or not to participate in interventions that were inconsistent with their best interests would not solve the problem; it would mean they would continue to be at a disadvantage vis-à-vis competents by being left in a position to make decisions that, by definition, they were incapable of making. The current position cannot be described as favouring incompetents simply by allowing competents to participate in interventions that may not be in their best interests. Rather, it simply gives competents the wide scope to express their wishes that the right to self-determination warrants.

The only other argument Harris could make is that incompetents as a group participate less and this of itself justifies diluting protection of their right to bodily security. However, to suggest that individuals should gain less protection by virtue of the simple fact that they happen to belong to an under-performing group is to advocate an arbitrary form of discrimination. History has borne witness many times over to the disturbing consequences of people being treated adversely by virtue of 'belonging' to a particular group.

Such arbitrary discrimination falls foul of a basic notion of equality protected under the rule of law and within basic human rights norms. The only way to avoid it and still link contribution to benefit is to reform the law for *everyone* such that: (1) only contributors can obtain benefits,[vi] or (2) everyone's protection of their right to bodily security is diluted to meet the needs of others in an equal manner. However, the first suggestion, though useful, is fraught with problems. Meanwhile, the second is deeply problematic in a number of ways that need too much elucidation to do them justice here.[vii]

Gunn et al put forward additional justifications for diluted protection that can be summarised as follows:

1. the ability to generalise research outcomes to incompetent adults without participation of some of their number can be limited.[34]
2. the incompetent will not even be involved in research which is largely or wholly for their own benefit as a group.[38]
3. By facilitating participation, a change in the law (i.e. abandoning the best interests approach) would be 'consistent with principles of normalisation and social inclusion. It challenges stereotypes that incompetent adults are a drain on society.'[34]

One problem with all three points is that they exaggerate the case for change by failing to recognise that incompetent adult participation in non-therapeutic research is already possible under the current law. This aside, the first point is valid but hardly a sufficient reason to dispense with a best interests approach. The second point is compromised by the fact that it fails to treat incompetent persons as individuals (when we do, this benefit to the group becomes irrelevant except in so far as it is also a benefit for the individual). Meanwhile, the third point is sophistic; since marking incompetent adults out for special adverse treatment of their right to bodily security is arbitrary discrimination, it is more aptly described as dehumanising and to dehumanise a person is to socially exclude and abnormalise them. If anything, treating them adversely in these ways reinforces the stereotype that they were a drain on society in the first place, whereas the reality is that the assessment of what any one individual, incompetent or otherwise, has taken and given in life is more complex and multi-dimensional.

CONCLUSION

Much of the confusion over the scope for performing interventions on incompetents that harm their therapeutic interests is attributable to misconceptions

---

[vi] For such a suggestion in the transplantation context see Jarvis,[36] who suggests that priority on organ transplant waiting lists should be given to those who register as a potential organ donor.

[vii] The arguments are surveyed in Garwood-Gowers,[37] Here it is concluded both that the right to bodily security is by its nature an absolute one vis-à-vis the needs of others and that, irrespective of this, there are sound pragmatic reasons for treating it as absolute.

about the best interests test and, to a lesser extent, a failure to consider the role of advance directives. Where such interventions have the capacity to benefit others, overly narrow conceptions of the possibility of performing them have added fuel to calls to dilute protection of incompetent interests. Through the Mental Capacity Act 2005, Parliament has heeded these calls in relation to medical research on competent adults. The minister responsible for the Act, David Lammy, has stated that in his view the Act's provisions are convention compliant. However, the Act's research provisions arbitrarily discriminate against the bodily security interest of incompetent adults which is certain to make them incompatible with Article 14 used in conjunction, for example, with Article 8. It is to be hoped that this problem will be addressed by the courts. One possibility is that the elements of the research provisions which are inconsistent with best interests could be struck down given that section 1(5) states that '(a)n act done or decision made, under this Act for or on behalf of a person who lacks capacity must be done, or made, in his best interests.' The argument for such an approach is bolstered by the fact that the courts have a duty to interpret law consistently with convention rights in so far as is possible under section 3 of the Human Rights Act 1998. If this does not work the courts should at least issue a Declaration of Incompatibility under section 4 of the Human Rights Act 1998 with the effect of placing political pressure on the Government for fast track remedial change of the law by ministerial order under section 10. Equally it is to be hoped that the Department of Health's current review of non-heart beating donation[viii] leads to an endorsement of the principle of protecting best interests and guidelines which encourage a balanced application of the principle to interventions on dying persons, insentient or otherwise.

Acknowledgements

My thanks go to Marc Stauch and Kay Wheat for their helpful comments on this chapter at its draft stage.

References

1. Garwood-Gowers A. The right to bodily security vis-à-vis the needs of others. In: Weisstub DN, Pintos, GD, eds. Autonomy and human rights in healthcare. Kluwer Academic Publishing, forthcoming, Ch 27, Introduction.
2. Robertson GB. Organ donation by incompetents and the substituted judgement doctrine. Columbia Law Review 1976; 76:48.
3. Garwood-Gowers A. Living donor organ transplantation: key legal and ethical issues. Aldershot: Ashgate; 1999: Chs 5 and 6.
4. Price D. Legal and ethical aspects of organ transplantation. Cambridge: Cambridge University Press; 2000: Ch 2.

[viii] It recently held a 'Non-heart beating donation open space workshop' on the issue (London, 15 July 2004) where the views of various experts were canvassed.

5. Feldbrugge FJM. Good and bad Samaritans: A comparative survey of criminal law provisions concerning failure to rescue. American Journal of Comparative Law 1966; 14:630–657, at 655–656.
6. Calabresi G. Do we own our own bodies? Health Matrix 1991; 1(5):5–18.
7. Dworkin G. Legality of consent to non-therapeutic research on infants and young children. Archives of Disease in Childhood 1978; 53:443.
8. Skegg PDG. Consent to medical procedures on minors. Modern Law Review 1970; 36:370–381.
9. Skegg PDG. English law relating to experimentation on children. Lancet 1977; ii:754–755.
10. Price D. Legal and ethical aspects of organ transplantation. Cambridge: Cambridge University Press; 2000:355.
11. Kennedy I, Grubb A. Medical law. London: Butterworths, 2000:778.
12. Kennedy I. Research and experimentation. In: Principles of medical law. Oxford: Oxford University Press; 1998: Ch 13, para 13.39
13. Kennedy I, Grubb A. Medical law. London: Butterworths; 2000:1731.
14. Mason J, McCall-Smith RA. Law and medical ethics. London: Butterworths; 1994:362.
15. Kennedy I. Research and experimentation. In: Principles of medical law. Oxford: Oxford University Press; 1998: Ch 13, para 13.42.
16. Grubb A, Pearl D. Sterilisation – courts and doctors as decision makers. Cambridge Law Journal 1989; 380, 382.
17. Kennedy I, Grubb A. Medical law. London: Butterworths; 2000:1731
18. Stauch M, Wheat K, Tingle J. Sourcebook on medical law. London: Cavendish; 2002:574.
19. Law Commission. Mental incapacity. Law Com 231; 1995: paras 6.23–6.29.
20. New B, Solomon M, Dingwall R, McHale J. A question of give and take: improving the supply of donor organs for transplantation. Research Report 18. London: King's Fund; 1994.
21. New B, Solomon M, Dingwall R, McHale J. A question of give and take: improving the supply of donor organs for transplantation. Research Report 18. London: King's Fund; 1994:63.
22. Morton S. Coma victims to replace animals in experiments. The Times 8 April 1996.
23. Price D. Organ transplant initiatives: the twilight zone. Journal of Medical Ethics 1997; 23:170–175.
24. Garwood-Gowers A. Living donor organ transplantation: key legal and ethical issues. Aldershot: Ashgate; 1999: Ch 2.
25. Medical Research Council. The ethical conduct of research on the mentally incapacitated. Medical Research Council; 1991.
26. Gunn M, Wong J, Clare ICH, Holland A. Medical research and incompetent adults. Journal of Mental Health Law 2000; February: 60–72, at 66.
27. Kennedy I. Principles of medical law. Oxford: Oxford University Press; 1998: paras 1340–1345.
28. Law Commission. Mental incapacity. Law Com 231; 1995.
29. Law Commission. Mental incapacity. Law Com 231; 1995: para 6.26.
30. Law Commission. Mental incapacity. Law Com 231; 1995: paras 6.31, 6.36.
31. Law Commission. Mental incapacity. Law Com 231; 1995: para 6.34.
32. Harris J. The ethics of clinical research with cognitively impaired subjects. Italian Journal of Neurological Sciences Supplement 1997; 5:9–13, at 12.
33. Harris J. The ethics of clinical research with cognitively impaired subjects. Italian Journal of Neurological Sciences Supplement 1997; 5:9–13, at 13.

34. Gunn M, Wong J, Clare ICH, Holland A. Medical research on incompetent adults. Journal of Mental Health Law 2000; February: 60–72, at 63.

35. Harris J. Law and regulation of retained organs: the ethical issues. Legal Studies 2002; 22(4):527–549, at 529.

36. Jarvis R. Join the club: a modest proposal to increase availability of donor organs. Journal of Medical Ethics 1995; 21:199–204.

37. Garwood-Gowers A. The right to bodily security vis-à-vis the needs of others. In: Weisstub DN, Pintos GD, eds. Autonomy and human rights in healthcare. Kluwer Academic Publishing, forthcoming; Ch 27.

38. Gunn M, Wong J, Clare ICH, Holland A. Medical research on incompetent adults. Journal of Mental Health Law 2000; February: 60–72, at 61.

Chapter **11**

Infant vaccination: a conflict of ethical imperatives?

Stephanie Pywell

CHAPTER CONTENTS

Introduction   213
Background   214
Empirical studies   215
The Toddler Questionnaire   215
The JABS Questionnaire   216
General considerations   216
The ethical imperatives   217
A government's duty to
   vaccinate   217

Respect for the autonomy
   of decision-makers   218
The doctor's duty to put
   the patient's interests
   first   226
Is patients' trust
   misplaced?   228
Conclusion   229
References   230

INTRODUCTION

The mass vaccination of infants raises several issues of interest to medical ethicists. At an individual level it involves invasive clinical intervention on healthy patients who are too young to express their own views. At a societal level it concerns measures that most people view as being for the good of every member of the population. The purpose of this chapter is to consider the ethical conflict which arises, at least in theory, between the state's duty to protect the health of its citizens and all patients' rights to have their autonomy respected and their individual health regarded by their doctors as being above all other considerations.

The arguments draw, in part, on doctoral research conducted between 1997 and 2001.[1] Because infant vaccination policy is formulated for the welfare of society as a whole, one objective of the research was to ascertain the effects of this policy on individuals. Two surveys involving written questionnaires were conducted: one was given to parents of young children who, it was expected, would have had a 'normal' experience of vaccination; the other was sent to parents who believed their children had been harmed by vaccines.

Both questionnaires received appropriate ethical approval. They are discussed more fully under the heading 'Empirical studies'.

It is recognised that the theoretical issues discussed in this chapter should not necessarily be determinative of public health policy and practice, but it is suggested that changes could be made which would achieve a better balance between the conflicting ethical considerations described above.

BACKGROUND

Vaccination is a process with which most people are familiar, but there are some aspects of it which underlie the arguments in this chapter and which therefore merit specific mention.

Firstly, the purpose of vaccination is to prevent disease by administering to the patient a small amount of an infectious agent, so that the immune system is triggered into a response. When the process is successful, the result is immunisation; the term is not synonymous with 'vaccination'.

Secondly, no vaccinations are compulsory in this country, although they are strongly encouraged. This is not universally known, and is very important to some of the arguments that follow.

Thirdly, it is appropriate to identify the vaccines which were, when the research was conducted, administered to most of the babies and preschool children in this country, via the primary and secondary schedules. Each individual antigen, whether given orally or by injection, is properly considered as a 'dose' of vaccine, even where combinations of antigens are given as a single pharmaceutical product (Dr Norman Begg, then Consultant Epidemiologist, Public Health Laboratory Service: personal contact, 13 July 1999). Table 11.1 therefore shows that, in 2001, most children received 26 doses of vaccine, in 12 pharmaceutical products – nine injections and three oral administrations – before they reached the age of 5 years.

Fourthly, it is received wisdom that the primary object of vaccination is not to protect the individual who has received the vaccine, but to protect the population as a whole from the disease.[2] This wider protection is called 'herd immunity', and its great benefit is that it protects people who cannot, for whatever reason, receive vaccines, as well as those who have been vaccinated.

Table 11.1   Primary and secondary vaccine schedules at the time of the empirical research (2001)

Age	Vaccines administered
2 months	Diphtheria, tetanus, pertussis, Hib, polio, meningitis C
3 months	Diphtheria, tetanus, pertussis, Hib, polio, meningitis C
4 months	Diphtheria, tetanus, pertussis, Hib, polio, meningitis C
13 months	Measles, mumps, rubella
4 years	Diphtheria, tetanus, measles, mumps, rubella

It is therefore arguable that the primary beneficiary of vaccination is the whole population, rather than the individual vaccinee, although each individual vaccinee derives the benefits of living in a society from which preventable infectious diseases have been more or less eliminated. It is arguable that the best course of action for any individual is to be the sole unvaccinated individual in an otherwise fully vaccinated population,[3] although it would be absurd to propose this as a strategy for a population. The difference between the risk/benefit ratio of any of the routine childhood vaccines at individual and population levels has a significant effect on the ethical considerations which should be taken into account when formulating vaccination policies.

EMPIRICAL STUDIES

The Toddler Questionnaire

A questionnaire ('the Toddler Questionnaire') about infant vaccination was completed by parents of pre-school children in and around North Hertfordshire in 1999–2000. In most cases, this survey was completed, after a face-to-face explanation, by parents attending group meetings such as parent-and-toddler groups, playgroups and parental support groups. Where a carer other than the child's parent attended the group, the questionnaire was taken home to the parent, with a letter of explanation about its purpose and a free-post envelope for its return. The survey was conducted anonymously.

Three hundred and sixty-nine questionnaires were completed. The overall response rate of 87% was encouraging. One source suggests that 75–80% is usual for face-to-face surveys, with rates exceeding 85% being rare.[4] Another suggests 65–95%.[5] A third suggests that trained interviewers can achieve rates of almost 100%,[6] but a study involving face-to-face interviews conducted by trained interviewers at subjects' homes achieved, in one case, a response rate of only 64%.[7]

Parents were asked facts about their children's vaccinations, and their opinions about the process. The questionnaires were completed from memory, which means that they may have been subject to recall errors, and no verification was possible. Care was, however, taken to ensure that the wording of all questions was neutral, so that respondents did not feel that certain answers would be more 'helpful' than others. No oral explanations of any terms were given unless specifically requested, and an amanuensis service was offered to all respondents. Of those who took up this offer, most had young children in their arms, but a few appeared uncomfortable at the prospect of reading and writing in a public place, possibly due to problems with basic literacy skills. It was necessary to discard the answers to one question because it was clear that many respondents misunderstood it.

The questionnaire contained a number of questions about demographic factors. Responses were compared with national and county data about ethnicity and social class, which showed that North Hertfordshire was reasonably representative of Great Britain, and respondents were reasonably representative of North Hertfordshire.

Ethical constraints meant that parents could be questioned only in group settings. Despite efforts to visit a wide variety of groups, the age of respondents exceeded the national average age of mothers – there were no respondents under 20, while 6.9% of mothers nationally fall into this age bracket. Anecdotal information from various social services professionals suggested that very young mothers tend to meet informally, deliberately avoiding social settings where they might encounter 'the authorities'. Data collected about the parents' marital status at the time of the youngest child's birth showed that, among respondents, married people were over-represented. The numbers of respondents from both one- and two-adult households whose income was within quintile limits obtained from the Office for National Statistics were, in most cases, close to the expected 20%.

The JABS Questionnaire

JABS is a self-selecting group, in that most of its members believe that vaccinations have damaged their children. The group was formed by parents who suspected that measles, mumps and rubella (MMR) vaccine had damaged their children and 70% (252 out of 360) of respondents believed their children to have been damaged by this vaccine.

The questionnaire was sent, with a JABS Newsletter and endorsement from JABS' coordinator, to all members. Those who responded to the questionnaire were self-selected from the whole group, and there is no way of knowing how, if at all, their experiences and views differ from those of the whole group. The 360 usable responses represented 34.4% of the questionnaires distributed – a rather low response rate for a postal survey, which may be partly explicable by the constant pressures upon parents caring for seriously disabled children. Responses were anonymous, but the postmarks on the prepaid envelopes showed that respondents were widely spread geographically. The anonymity of respondents made it impossible to verify parents' anecdotal evidence about what had happened to their children.

Three other organised groups of people who believe their children were vaccine-damaged were approached, but none consented to take part in the study. The experiences of these people may differ significantly from those of JABS' members, particularly in respect of the vaccines that parents believe caused harm to their children.

General considerations

Both questionnaires ran to 12 sides of A4 paper, including a cover and an explanation sheet. The design incorporated a significant amount of white space, and many questions could be skipped by most respondents. A computerised readability test showed that each questionnaire was within the 'standard document' range. As both questionnaires necessarily included some specialised clinical vocabulary, this suggests that the wording of the questions was straightforward. A pilot version of each questionnaire was tested on about 20 respondents in its target groups, resulting in some minor modifications to wording.

It was not possible to verify whether any respondent to either survey had fully understood the questions. Part of the data entry process involved 'cleaning' the data, which involved discarding an individual's response to one of more questions if there were obvious inconsistencies within the questionnaire.

No financial or other inducement was made to any potential respondent in either survey. Subsequent letters of thanks were sent to toddler group leaders and the JABS coordinator. These people were requested, where possible, to make members aware of the letters, and to offer them access to the findings of the research.

The results of the questionnaires must be read with these limitations in mind, but there is little other published data on parents' experiences and opinions of infant vaccination from which to obtain a 'micro' view of a 'macro' policy.

THE ETHICAL IMPERATIVES

The purpose of this chapter is to consider whether the ethical imperative of preventing preventable disease justifies the arguable violation of two other ethical imperatives: patients' right to autonomy, and doctors' duty to put the health of their patients before other considerations. These are not inherently related, but they may both be infringed by the same thing – the excessive promotion of vaccines to the point where some parents actually believe that vaccination is compulsory.

A government's duty to vaccinate

The eradication of preventable disease via mass vaccination is widely perceived as a positive indicator of public health. Some international agreements suggest that governments have a duty to optimise the health of their citizens:

- The Constitution of the World Health Organization declares that 'the enjoyment of the highest attainable standard of health is one of the fundamental rights of every human being'.[8]
- The Universal Declaration of Human Rights provides that everyone has the right to a standard of living adequate for his family's health, and it affords special care to mothers and children.[9]
- The Convention on the Rights of the Child recognises children's right to the highest attainable standard of health, including developing preventive health care.[10]

- The International Covenant on Economic, Social and Cultural Rights alludes to the 'highest attainable standard of physical and mental health', incorporating '[t]he prevention, treatment and control of epidemic . . . and other diseases'.[11]

Health promotion is widely perceived as a desirable political objective. The fact that MPs of all political parties miss no opportunity to declare their support for mass infant vaccination provides evidence that it transcends traditional political party divisions.

The requirement for governments to promote vaccination as a cost-effective public health measure is accepted as the first ethical imperative. It is not discussed further here because the purpose of this chapter is to offer a research-based critique of a policy whose societal benefits are widely perceived as being beyond doubt. Fundamental objections to the principles of medicalisation, such as those proposed by Ivan Illich,[12] are beyond the scope of this chapter.

Respect for the autonomy of decision-makers

Autonomy may be defined as encompassing intention, understanding and a lack of controlling influences.[13] The first requirement – intention – is straightforward. Understanding requires a real knowledge of the potential risks and benefits of vaccination, and a lack of controlling influences demands a total lack of pressure from any source.

Because routine vaccines are administered to very young children, the decision about whether to accept the vaccine must be taken by adults, usually parents or guardians. It has been argued that the primary ethical framework in such third-party decisions should be patient-centred principles.[14] If patients are competent, their autonomy is regarded as very important. This principle suggests that the autonomy of proxy decision-makers should be respected in the same way that the autonomy of competent adult patients should be respected when they are deciding whether to undergo non-urgent medical treatment. It is therefore appropriate to consider whether parents do indeed make decisions about vaccination in circumstances where they have full understanding and are not subject to any controlling influences.

An understanding of the risks and benefits of vaccines?

No parent can have full understanding of the risks and benefits of vaccines, because these are not known at the moment. Whilst the risks of many innovations are not fully understood, there seems to be little coherent strategy underlying whether governmental caution will be exercised or fears of unproven risks will be officially dismissed. In March 2004 the UK Government banned blood donations from any individual who had received a blood transfusion since 1980, because of what Dr John Reid, the Secretary of

State for Health, termed an 'uncertain but slight risk' of such persons' blood spreading variant-Creutzfeldt–Jakob disease (vCJD, which is discussed further below). This measure will reduce by around 3% the number of donors to a supply already struggling to cope with demand.[15] Fears about the unknown health risks of GM crops and mobile telephones are not, however, taken into account when public policy is formulated, although environmental concerns about GM crops have now led to restrictions on their planting in the UK. Fears about vaccine risks are also dismissed, presumably because of their obvious benefits, and the unequivocal promotion of the childhood vaccination programme continues.

It is at least arguable that the benefits of vaccines are overstated, and the risks understated.

The possible overstatement of benefits from vaccines   One reason why the benefits of vaccines may be overstated is that the vaccine-preventable diseases are now presented to the public as being more dangerous than they were formerly believed by the public to be – this point is discussed further below in respect of measles. Another reason is that vaccines are often presented as being more effective, and having more dramatic effects, than is really the case.

The diseases against which vaccination was, in 2001, routinely offered to young children are listed in Table 11.1. All except one of them – tetanus – are infectious, so there is at least some benefit to someone other than the vaccinee: every person I meet is marginally less likely to contract an infectious disease if I am immune to it. Some of the diseases – like meningitis and tetanus – are widely feared, and it therefore seems sensible to vaccinate against them.

Polio, however, has now been almost eradicated from the developed world – because the vaccine has been so successful – and the majority of cases of polio in this country are now caused by non-immune people catching the disease from live vaccine in the stools of recently vaccinated babies.[16] In England and Wales in 2005, therefore, polio vaccine may be doing more harm than good. The disease has almost, but not quite, been eradicated from the whole world. Until this happens, it is probably appropriate to continue mass vaccination, so as to reduce further the geographic areas where the disease occurs.

Another disease in the routine vaccine schedule is rubella. This disease is so mild that many children contract it with no real symptoms, and it attracted no medical interest until it was discovered that, if caught during the first trimester of pregnancy, it is associated with congenital rubella syndrome (CRS), which manifests itself as a range of birth defects. The disease is, however, harmless to young children, so it is arguable that there is no benefit at all to the vaccinee at the time of the vaccination – or, for male vaccinees, ever. The benefit of rubella vaccine is enjoyed by people who have not been conceived at the time of its administration. The vaccine is offered to all preschool children only because the previous strategy of vaccinating teenage girls had an insufficiently high take-up rate. The wider use of the vaccine has been very successful: there were 70 cases of CRS and a further 700 rubella-related thera-peutic abortions annually before the vaccine was introduced, but only eight reported cases of maternal rubella in 1995.[16]

Measles is a much more serious illness for the person who contracts it, and it can have lasting serious side-effects, including death. Public concern about the safety of MMR vaccine has led to a decline in vaccination coverage, and this is believed to have been the cause of recent outbreaks of the disease, such as that in mid-Ulster in 1999.[17] Measles is now a disease feared by parents – the disease was regarded as 'very serious' by 15% of parents in April 1994, but by 55% in October/November 1994, following a shocking advertising campaign which included television advertisements depicting grieving parents whose child had died from the disease.[18] In former years, however, the disease was not widely feared: it was accepted as 'part of growing up' in the 1960s, 1970s and early 1980s, and parents even held 'measles parties' so that their children could contract the disease at a time of their choosing. People continue to die from measles, especially in the developing world, but some commentators have argued that mortality in the developed world had declined to almost zero before the vaccine became available,[19] and thus the improved prognosis cannot be attributable to the vaccine. Measles can have serious side-effects – such as brain damage – even in developed countries, and the risk of such sequelae must obviously be taken into account when considering the respective risks and benefits of vaccines and the diseases they are designed to prevent.

Diphtheria has now been almost eradicated from England and Wales, so it could be argued that it is pointless for all children to be vaccinated against it unless they propose to travel to a country where it remains endemic. The objective of keeping England and Wales free of the disease could, in theory, if not in political reality, be achieved by compulsory vaccination at entry points for immigrants from countries where the disease still exists. It is often assumed that the vaccine is responsible for the virtual elimination of diph-theria, but some US states without vaccination programmes showed a steep decline in mortality at the time when the vaccine was introduced into England and Wales, suggesting that other factors had at least some effect.[19] Unless, however, there is a well-founded suspicion that the vaccine has serious side-effects, it is probably better to keep it in the routine vaccination schedule.

Whooping cough is a dangerous disease, especially in young babies. The pertussis vaccine has been extremely successful, reducing reported cases in England and Wales from over 100 000 to approximately 2000 annually.[16]

Not all the diseases, therefore, are believed to pose significant risks – in terms of incidence and/or severity of consequences – to young children in twenty-first century England and Wales, yet some official literature implies that parents are irresponsible if they choose not to accept all the standard vac-cines for their children.[i]

---

[i] For example: 'The final decision on immunization is the parents'. But if a child is not immunized, he/she will remain at risk. The child will then rely on other people immuniz-ing their children to avoid becoming infected.'[20]

It is notable that the MMR vaccine that is administered to 4-year-olds is, unlike the contemporaneous diphtheria and tetanus vaccine, not a 'booster', in that it is not administered because the protection afforded by the first dose of the vaccine is believed to have worn off. The second injection of MMR is offered to all children in this age cohort because about 10% of them will not have had the first dose of MMR vaccine at age 13 months and, of those that did have the first dose, at least 10% will not have responded by becoming immune to all three diseases. The second dose is therefore an attempt to immunise those people for the first time – for something like 80% of the people who receive it, it is completely unnecessary. Its administration to all children of this age is officially justified on the grounds that a second dose is even less likely than a first dose to have any adverse effects, because the recipient's immune system does not receive a 'naive challenge' from the second dose (Ms Joanne White, Principal Scientist (Epidemiology), Public Health Laboratory Communicable Disease Surveillance Centre: personal contact, 12 July 2000).

The normal tenets of medical ethics, based on a conventional risk/benefit analysis, would suggest that it is inappropriate to administer any pharmaceutical product that is without benefit to its recipient, because all drugs carry a slight risk of occasional adverse side-effects. The benefit for each person for whom the first vaccine was effective, so far as is known, is nil, so this is inevitably outweighed by the risks – however small – of adverse effects. Forty-eight per cent of 460 health professionals in one survey stated that they had reservations about giving the second dose of MMR, and 3% disagreed with this practice.[21] Although some official literature states that the second injection is of benefit to those who did not respond to the first,[ii] other literature does not use such clear language.[iii,iv] Even the former category does not use the word 'only', and none of the standard literature states that the second injection is believed to be unnecessary for most 4-year-olds. It is therefore questionable whether most parents understand, on the basis of a computerised appointment card, that this vaccine is more likely than not to be of no benefit to their children.

One official view is that the efficacy of vaccines – calculated as the difference in attack rates of the relevant disease between vaccinated and unvaccinated populations (Dr Norman Begg, then Consultant Epidemiologist, Public Health Laboratory Service: personal contact, 13 July 1999) – ranges from 80 to 95%.

[ii] For example: 'The second dose protects anybody who did not respond to the first dose'.[22] (The word 'dose' is used here to denote a triple vaccine, which is different from the use stated by Dr Begg – see text above Table 11.1.)

[iii] For example, there is no mention of the need for the second MMR in 'Immunization: the safest way to protect your child'.[23]

[iv] 'Your child will receive two doses because measles, mumps and rubella vaccines don't always work well enough on the first go. The second MMR immunization makes sure that your child gets the best protection against these three diseases. This also gives a second chance for those children who missed out the first time around. So, you can be sure your child is well protected before they start school.'[24]

Some vaccine publicity leaflets, however, imply that vaccines are always effective, and confer lifelong immunity to diseases.[v] Detailed literature is honest about these matters, but it is likely that multi-page booklets are read by far fewer parents than the leaflets. Many parents are presumably not in possession of this knowledge when they take the decision whether to accept vaccines for their children, and believe that the vaccines will confer complete, lifelong immunity.[20,24] This will, of course, be the case for many recipients; it is certainly reasonable to assume that vaccines which have been widely available since the 1950s and 1960s are effective for 40–50 years, on the basis of the lack of epidemics of preventable diseases amongst people who are now middle-aged. MMR, however, was not widely used in this country until October 1988, and the vaccines for Hib and meningitis C are much more recent. The first cohort of children to receive MMR as babies are now aged around 18, although some people now in their early 20s will have had the vaccine in early childhood as part of a 'catch up' campaign. Research has not revealed any scientific assessment of the immunity of this population although, again, the lack of outbreaks of the diseases among vaccinated individuals suggests that their immunity has not yet waned. It is impossible, however, to predict what the immune status of these people will be when they reach 50. If their immunity declines with age, the consequences could be very serious, because all the diseases tend to be much more acute, and to have more serious and enduring side-effects, in adults than in children.

The possible understatement of risks from vaccines   The risks of most of the vaccines routinely given to children in England and Wales are not known. It is true, as all public health literature states, that there is no reliable evidence that certain of these vaccines cause certain adverse effects. What is also true, but is not stated by such literature, is that there is, in some cases, no reliable evidence that they do not cause such effects.

MMR is a case in point. Even allowing for the fact that it is never possible conclusively to prove a negative, it is notable that there have not been, anywhere in the world, optimally designed, long-term, prospective studies which would have confirmed parents' anecdotal accounts of the kinds of ill-effects suffered by their children after receiving MMR.[vi] A detailed critique of the studies upon which, until 2005, official assurances of MMR's safety were

---

[v] For example: 'Immunization gives protection (immunity) against a disease by giving the child a small dose of the disease';[23] 'MMR vaccine protects your child against measles, mumps and rubella (German measles)'.[22]

[vi] As this book was going to press, an important new study involving over 300 000 Japanese children was published.[46] It found that the reported incidence of autistic spectrum disorders (ASDs) was lower among children who had received MMR than among those who had received single-antigen replacement vaccines. The study concludes that MMR could not have caused autism in children who were born after the vaccine was withdrawn in Japan. Although this study makes an important contribution to the debate about the relative safety of MMR and its components, it does not prove that none of the component vaccines is linked to the rise in ASDs. This could be properly investigated only by measuring the reported incidence of ASDs among an otherwise similar population of children who had received neither MMR nor any of its components.

based is beyond the scope of this chapter, but it is relevant to note that most of them are presented as giving a degree of reassurance that is not justified by the actual findings of the studies.

One example is a Finnish study, funded by Merck USA, which manufactured a vaccine used in all but 2570 of the 3 million doses of vaccine involved.[25] The study lasted 14 years, but individuals were followed up for only 3 weeks after vaccination unless they presented with acute gastrointestinal symptoms within that time. The JABS Questionnaire indicated that, in most cases where children are eventually diagnosed as having a serious illness such as epilepsy or autistic spectrum disorders, the adverse events observed shortly after vaccination are relatively mild and behavioural, such as loss of appetite or a fit from which the child appears to recover completely. More serious symptoms, such as repeated fits or loss of speech, usually become apparent over a period of many months. Any child presenting with only minor, apparently self-limiting symptoms in the first 3 weeks would not have merited inclusion in the longer-term follow-up component of the study. The impression conveyed by the title of the study, however, is that each recipient of the vaccine was followed up for 14 years: this certainly happened to one patient, and may have happened to 169 children whose cases were subjected to 'greater scrutiny', but it certainly did not happen to all the 1.8 million participants in the study.

It is striking that the paper does not mention autism or bowel disorders except in its 'results' and 'discussion' sections. The 'results' about autism and bowel disorders consist of single sentences with footnote references to an earlier paper,[26] yet Dr Elizabeth Miller, then Head of the Immunisation Division at the Public Health Laboratory Service, was quoted as saying 'cases of autism in association with bowel disease would certainly have been detected' by this study.[27] Dr Miller's response appears to attribute to the Finnish study more power than is warranted by its methods and scope.

A later study compared rates of autism and autistic spectrum diseases in over half a million children born in Denmark in 1991–1998.[28] This study was retrospective, and found no significant difference in the incidence of autism among children who had received MMR vaccine and those who were unvaccinated. This study was not funded by any drugs companies, but it faced the unavoidable problem that there was a huge disparity in numbers of vaccinated and unvaccinated children – 82% of the subjects had received the vaccine. This paper describes what appears to be the best-designed published study to date; if it can be replicated in other populations, concern about the safety of MMR vaccine may finally be laid to rest.

There is no evidence that events which are observed shortly after vaccination, and which are later perceived as the beginning of a serious deterioration in a child's health, are caused by vaccination. It is, however, regrettable that the only scientific study to take as its starting point parents' own reports of their children's apparent adverse reactions to vaccines obtained parents' reports on 531 children, but fully investigated only 12 of them, eliminating the remainder because they did not meet at least one of four inclusion criteria:

- medical confirmation of diagnosis or clinically relevant symptoms
- onset of condition occurred within 6 weeks of MMR vaccination
- no pre-vaccination history relevant to the possible adverse event
- no other cause of the possible adverse event.[29]

The stringency of these criteria meant that the study missed the opportunity fully to investigate parents' anecdotal evidence.

Vaccine safety was discussed at the BSE Inquiry, because there was concern that some vaccines cultured from British fetal calf tissue might present a risk of vCJD to vaccinees. A polio vaccine involving such serum was withdrawn in October 2000. The Rt Hon Kenneth Clarke MP, former Secretary of State for Health, admitted that public statements about confidence in vaccines are exaggerated. He alluded to 'the needless death of infants' when 'mothers had been induced not to vaccinate their children' and said that it had been necessary to avert a similar situation: 'the difficulty is if you said, as we all believed, that the risk from vaccine was remote, that unless you say there is absolutely no risk or 110% certain that there is never any risk, it is terribly easy for somebody to go haring off starting another vaccine scare'.[30] This statement shows that, at least on occasions, it is official policy to understate the believed risks of vaccines.

The nature of the MMR safety debate   One issue of concern is the antagonistic nature of the debate about the safety of vaccines. This gives a clear impression of two opposing faiths, as opposed to a common scientific quest for truth. This was very apparent in respect of the paper which suggested that MMR vaccine was inadequately trialled before being licensed.[31] The four referees, whose comments were – unusually – published with the paper, were a former Chair of the Medicines Commission, a former Chair of the Committee on Safety of Medicines, a former Principal Medical Officer in the Department of Health who served as Medical Assessor to the Committee on Safety of Medicines and a consultant neurologist.

The Department of Health's response to the article contains footnotes to 11 studies, as opposed to the 71 references in the article itself. The response takes issue with the referees' supportive comments, remarking that 'it seems that the referees do not have current expertise in vaccines. It is unfortunate that the journal Editor did not seek the views of at least one current expert in vaccinology.'[32]

The journal editor's publication of the referees' names and comments was an indicator of his awareness of the metaphorical heat of the MMR safety debate, and could be interpreted as a provocative departure from normal scientific publication etiquette. The rapid response casting doubt upon the referees' expertise was, perhaps, a manifestation that the Department of Health had risen to the bait. The overall tone of the response is that of a PR document, rather than a scientific paper; the article itself appears to be the former, although the response identifies what it claims are several factual errors – none of which, even if the claims are all true, affect the general message of the paper. The enduring impression given to readers of the article and response is of a verbal battle where each side is desperate to erode the other's credibility.

A lack of controlling influences?

The question of whether parents are subject to external influences when they are deciding whether to accept vaccines for their children was explored using the Toddler Questionnaire.

Out of 369 respondents, 281 – 81% – believed the most important reason for vaccinating children was to protect those children from childhood diseases. Fifty-one had been told that they should accept vaccination to protect the health of their own children. This shows that most parents are unaware that the primary purpose of infant vaccination is officially viewed as herd immunity,[2] so they had accepted vaccination on the basis of at least one false premise. Twelve people had been told by a health professional that it was their social duty to accept vaccines, which is closer to the truth, but such remarks nonetheless constitute an external influence.

Because vaccination is widely perceived as a social duty, some jurisdictions have imposed civil sanctions on children who do not receive all the recommended vaccines. In the USA, unvaccinated children are not allowed to attend publicly funded schools and, in France, child benefit is not paid in respect of any unvaccinated child. These sanctions have the benefit of making it clear that the decision to vaccinate is not one in respect of which parents should take account only of the interests of their own children. If a similar policy were adopted in England and Wales, it would be necessary to consider the approach towards children who eventually receive all the required antigens, but via the non-recommended means of single-antigen vaccines administered privately.

Respondents to the Toddler Questionnaire were asked whether they had ever felt under pressure to accept vaccines for one or more of their children; 92 people – 25% of respondents – answered this question affirmatively. The word 'pressure' was not defined, but the next question asked respondents who had answered 'yes' to describe the pressure. The options for this were as follows:

- partner or family in favour of vaccination
- friends in favour of vaccination
- health visitor (HV) or nurse in favour of vaccination
- family doctor in favour of vaccination
- doctor, HV or nurse told you vaccination was a social duty
- HV or nurse said you should protect your child's health
- family doctor said you should protect your child's health
- family doctor would remove you from his/her list if you refused
- other (please describe).

Options involving GPs, HVs and nurses together accounted for 177 responses from the 92 respondents, indicating that some respondents had felt more than one sort of pressure. These data are wholly subjective, and do not indicate any breach of professional ethics, but the inherent imbalance of power in doctor–patient relationships means that clinicians may inadvertently make patients feel pressurised into agreeing with their own expressed or perceived views. Only one respondent claimed that she had been threatened with removal from the GP's list if she refused to accept vaccines; this is discussed further below.

Some respondents to the Toddler Questionnaire orally remarked that they had believed vaccines were compulsory, although the questionnaire did not seek this information. This information supports the results of a study in which GPs, HVs and practice nurses stated that parents may feel that they have no choice about whether to accept vaccines for their children.[33]

Is the patient's autonomy respected?

The above discussion of vaccine studies and publicity shows that there remains considerable uncertainly about the true extent of the benefits and possible risks of vaccines. To an extent, this applies to all scientific endeavour: science is a quest for truth but the nature of what is believed to be true is constantly changing. If, however, optimally designed studies, aimed at finding the post-vaccine symptoms and diagnoses reported anecdotally by parents, were carried out, there might at least be consensus on some issues. At present, parents' decisions about vaccination are not taken with the highest level of understanding which science could permit.

The quarter of respondents who had felt some form of pressure to accept vaccination for their children had been subject to a mild form of controlling influence, as had the 12 who had been told that accepting vaccines was their social duty. The vaccination of the children of these parents therefore did not follow a decision which had been taken with respect for the parents' autonomy.

The doctor's duty to put the patient's interests first

The second ethical imperative which may be violated by official measures to encourage mass vaccination is GPs' duty to give priority to the welfare of each patient. This is identified as an important aspect of the doctor–patient relationship: 'a physician must not exploit patients for the physician's own gain because the patient's interests come first'.[34]

GPs are paid by a system of fees and allowances which, for over a decade, included significant financial bonuses if they fully vaccinate target percentages of preschool children in specified age groups. Their new contracts, which came into effect in April 2004, designate childhood vaccinations as a Directed Enhanced Service, for which payments are made to general practices, rather than to individual GPs. The detail of the payments is beyond the scope of this article, but the previous principles – that no payment will be made unless at least 70% of the registered child patients in specified age bands receive all vaccinations in the primary and secondary schedules, and that the payment for attaining 90% coverage is significantly higher than that for 70% – remain. Payments are now proportionately increased if the target is exceeded; previously they were paid at a flat rate irrespective of whether targets were met or exceeded.

Such target payments appear to violate some of the key principles of general codes of medical ethics. Two examples of these, with comments, follow.

1. *'Doctors should therefore avoid accepting any pecuniary or material inducement which might compromise, or be regarded by others as likely to compromise, the independent exercise of their professional judgement in prescribing matters.'*[35]

 The incentive payments are intended as a 'pecuniary inducement' to vaccinate babies and young children. This is not morally problematic for GPs who genuinely believe that vaccines are universally beneficial and wholly safe, since the payments would not induce them to act differently from the way they would act if the payments did not exist. The payments may, however, cause GPs who have personal doubts about vaccine safety, or about the necessity or desirability of vaccination for some or all of their child patients, to adopt practices which they would not otherwise follow. The incentive payments were introduced in order to increase vaccine coverage, which amounts to deliberately interfering with clinical practice. Dr David Salisbury, Principal Medical Officer, Communicable Disease Branch, Department of Health, has publicly declared that the payments were 'successful' in increasing vaccine coverage annually from 1991 to 1994.[36] It has been persuasively argued that patients have an expectation of undivided loyalty from doctors, and that this is compromised by collateral profits for GPs if they perform some treatments rather than others. Vaccine payments therefore constitute a 'particularly intrusive' attack on the relationship of trust between doctor and patient.[37]

 It is reported that, in order to meet their vaccine coverage targets, some GPs remove children from their patient lists if their parents do not consent to vaccination.[38–40] This had happened to only one respondent in the Toddler Survey, but two other respondents orally noted that it had happened to friends of theirs. This practice does not appear to be widespread, but it demonstrates a clear failure by a minority of GPs to put the health of their child patients above other considerations.

 There have been press reports that the incentive payments system has led to GPs failing to register child patients whom they treat, but whose parents do not accept vaccination.[41] This is preferable to de-registering children and then refusing to provide healthcare to them; it indicates that some GPs who are unwilling to tolerate a reduction in their incomes are nonetheless conscientious in their care of patients.

 When the idea of a GP contract introducing the vaccine incentive payments was first mooted in 1987[42] it was opposed by 75% of doctors. It was, nevertheless, introduced, but one is left wondering for whose benefit the vaccine payments exist. The suspicion that the incentive payment system may be disliked by GPs is given some credibility by the statement in respect of the new scheme that 'exception reporting, including for informed dissent, does not apply'.[43] Anecdotal evidence suggests that some GPs are fundamentally opposed to vaccine incentive payments – and to all the other payments, such as those for female contraception and cervical smears, which are payable only if doctors perform state-recommended procedures on their patients.

Dr Jane Donegan, a GP, has publicly suggested that this potential conflict of interest could be avoided by making the incentive payment in respect of every patient to whom a GP had explained the full facts about vaccination. Parents could be asked to sign a disclaimer if they decided not to accept vaccination for their children.[44] This would ensure that vaccines were actively promoted, but would remove the temptation for GPs to regard non-accepting patients as problematic obstacles to numerical targets.

2. *'It may be improper for a doctor to accept per capita or other payments from a pharmaceutical firm in relation to a research project such as the clinical trial of a new drug, unless the payments have been specified in a protocol which has been approved by the relevant national or local ethics committee.'*[45]

If the word 'government' is substituted for 'pharmaceutical company', the first part of this extract is a good description of the incentive schemes. It is arguable that the mass administration of many of the vaccines now in widespread use constitutes research, because the present generation of vaccinees is the first to receive them. There are, as yet, no data about what, if any, the effects of vaccines introduced in the 1980s and 1990s will be when the recipients reach middle age. Although there are numerous people who have received the vaccines, and thus a very large group of potential research subjects, there seems to be no attempt to ascertain the long-term possible effects of vaccines.

The second ethical imperative is therefore violated by the former and current systems of administering incentive payments to encourage GPs to vaccinate as many young children as possible.

Is patients' trust misplaced?

The arguable violations of these codes of medical ethics are relevant to two empirical findings: that patients trust doctors, and that most patients are unaware of the vaccine incentive payments.

Nearly 79% (290 out of 369) of respondents to the Toddler Questionnaire did not know that GPs are paid bonuses to encourage vaccination. Of those:

- 168 had sought information about vaccination from their HV or nurses, who are usually attached to general practices and who may, in many cases, share the views of the GPs with whom they work
- 109 had sought information about vaccination from their GPs
- 24 had felt pressure to vaccinate from HVs or nurses
- 40 had felt pressure to vaccinate from GPs.

All these people sought or received advice in ignorance of the vested interest which GPs have in achieving high levels of vaccination coverage. This means that they will not have viewed the information with the caution which should have applied if they had been aware of GPs' conflict of interest. They relied upon healthcare professionals for advice in ignorance of external influences upon the professionals' judgement.

CONCLUSION

On one side of the ethical balance there exists the Government's undisputed duty to optimise the health of the population, so far as it is able to do so. On the other side, there are doctors' duties to respect decision-makers' autonomy and to put patients' interests above all other considerations. Current vaccination practices give greater weight to the societal aim of eradicating diseases than to the principles which should prevail within individual doctor–patient relationships. This priority of 'macro' over 'micro' considerations is reasonable because the policy is society-wide.

The challenge for those who govern us is to restore the balance between these conflicting ethical imperatives. The process will inevitably be a slow one; a good start would be to commission long-term, large-scale, prospective research to investigate whether statistically significant numbers of children manifest, after being vaccinated, the kinds of symptoms anecdotally reported by parents and, if so, whether such symptoms ultimately prove to have been the first indications of more serious adverse consequences. This would facilitate a more accurate assessment of the risks of vaccines, and the publication of results would make parents' decisions more informed.

A further step which could be taken would be the abolition of incentive payments in their present form. If the payments were made upon parents' signed declarations that their GPs had discussed vaccines in detail with them, the inherently unethical financial pressure to vaccinate would be removed.

A number of parents were surprised and concerned to learn from the Toddler Questionnaire that doctors receive vaccine incentive payments. The question from this questionnaire which had to be discarded was whether various recent public health 'scares' – the link between BSE and vCJD, genetically modified food, listeria, etc. – had had any effect on parents' trust in Government information. Many parents wrote (outside the space provided) 'unchanged because I had no confidence to start with'. This made responses to the formal question meaningless, but it shows the importance of transparency in research and policy regarding infant vaccination.

If such transparency could be seen to be achieved, parental confidence in official advice would presumably increase, and a probable result would be an increase in the uptake of vaccines. This would facilitate the attainment of the ultimate aim of vaccination policy: improving children's health.

References

1. Pywell SM. Compensation for vaccine damage. PhD thesis, University of Hertfordshire, 2002.

2. Nokes DJ, Anderson RM. Vaccine safety versus vaccine efficacy in mass immunization programmes. Lancet 1991; 338:1309–1312.

3. Psychoanalytic Institute for Social Research. Ethical, legal and social aspects of vaccine research and vaccination policies. Rome: Centro Stampa d'Ateneo, Università degli Studi di Roma; 2001. (European Commission Research Project Contract Number BMH4 98 3197.)

4. Hoinville G, Jowell R. Survey research practice. London: Heinemann Educational Books; 1978.

5. Czaja R, Blair J. Designing surveys: a guide to decisions and procedures. Thousand Oaks, CA: Pine Forge Press; 1996.

6. Gardner G. Social surveys for social planners. Milton Keynes: The Open University Press; 1978.

7. Genn H. Paths to justice: what people do and think about going to law. Oxford: Hart Publishing; 1999.

8. World Health Organization. Health for all in the twenty-first century. Geneva: World Health Organization; 1998. Online. Available: http://www.who.int/wha-1998/pdf98/ea5.pdf 11 September 2000.

9. United Nations Universal Declaration of Human Rights, Article 25. United Nations Organization; 1948. Online. Available: http://www.magnacartaplus.org/declare/un-univ-right.htm 17 September 2000.

10. United Nations High Commissioner for Human Rights; 1989. Convention on the Rights of the Child, Article 24. Online. Available: http://www.unhchr.ch/html/menu3/b/k2crc.htm 17 September 2000.

11. International Covenant on Economic, Social and Cultural Rights, Article 12(2)(c). United Nations; 1976. Online. Available: http://www.hri.ca/uninfo/treaties/2.shtml 3 January 2001.

12. Illich I. Limits to medicine: medical nemesis – the expropriation of health. London: Marion Boyars; 1976.

13. Faden RR, Beauchamp TL. A history and theory of informed consent. New York: Oxford University Press; 1986.

14. Buchanan A E, Brock DW. Deciding for others: the ethics of surrogate decision making. Cambridge: Cambridge University Press; 1990.

15. Boseley S. Blood donor list slashed to stop vCJD. The Guardian 17 March 2004.

16. Department of Health, Welsh Office, Scottish Office Department of Health and DHSS Northern Ireland. Salisbury D M, Begg N T (eds). 1996 Immunization against infectious disease. London: HMSO; 1996.

17. Uffindell, R. Mumps outbreak prompts warning. The Irish News 7 April 2000.

18. Parliamentary Office of Science and Technology. Vaccines and their future role in public health. London: HMSO; 1995.

19. McKeown T. The medical contribution; 1976. In: Davey B, Gray A, Seale C, eds. Health and disease: a reader. 7th edn. Buckingham: Open University Press; 1995:182–190.

20. MMR immunization factsheet. London: Health Education Authority; 1997.

21. Petrovic M, Roberts R, Ramsay M. Second dose of measles, mumps and rubella vaccine: questionnaire survey of health professionals. BMJ (London) 2001; 322:82–85.

22. MMR the facts. London: Health Promotion England; 2001.
23. Immunization: the safest way to protect your child. London: Health Education Authority; 1998.
24. A guide to childhood immunizations including advice on recognizing meningitis. London: Health Education Authority; 1997.
25. Patja A, Davidkin I, Kurki T, et al. Serious adverse events after measles–mumps–rubella vaccination during a fourteen-year prospective follow-up. Pediatric Infectious Disease Journal 2000; 19:1127–1134.
26. Peltola H, Patja A, Leinikki P, et al. No evidence for measles, mumps and rubella vaccine-associated inflammatory bowel disease or autism in a 14-year prospective study. Lancet 1998; 351:1327–1328.
27. Boseley S. Stop stifling debate, critics warn government. The Guardian 24 January 2001.
28. Madsen KM, Hviid A, Vestergaard M, et al. A population-based study of measles, mumps and rubella vaccination and autism. New England Journal of Medicine 2002; 347:1477–1482.
29. Committee on Safety of Medicines. Report of the Working Party on MMR Vaccine. Online. Available: http://www.open.gov.uk.
30. BSE Inquiry, Day 87 transcript, page 111, lines 2–18. Online. Available: http://www.bse.org.uk/transcripts/tr981127.txt 13 May 1999.
31. Wakefield AJ, Montgomery SM. Measles, mumps and rubella vaccine: Through a glass, darkly. Adverse Drug Reactions and Toxicological Reviews 2000; 19(4):265–283.
32. Department of Health. Combined measles, mumps and rubella vaccines: Response of the Medicines Control Agency and Department of Health to issues raised in papers published in 'Adverse Drug Reactions and Toxicological Reviews, volume 19, no 4, 2000'. 2000. Online. Available: http://www.doh.gov.uk/pdfs/mmrresponse.pdf 1 February 2001.
33. Reflexions Communication Research. Childhood immunisation: the perspective of health professionals. In: Hey V. Immunisation research: a summary volume. London: Health Education Authority; 1998:38–63.
34. Beauchamp TL, Childress JF. Principles of biomedical ethics. New York: Oxford University Press; 1994: 21.
35. General Medical Council. Professional conduct and discipline: fitness to practise. London: General Medical Council; 1983:27.
36. Salisbury D. Speaking at 'Vaccines and Health', held at University of Hertfordshire; 10 December 1999.
37. Bartlett P. Doctors as fiduciaries: equitable regulation of the doctor–patient relation-ship. Medical Law Review 1997; 5: 193–224, at 215–216.
38. Barnett A. GPs ban frightened parents who refuse triple baby jabs. The Observer 29 August 1999.
39. Alderson P, et al. Childhood immunisation: support to health professionals. In: Hey V, ed. Immunisation research: a summary volume. London: Health Education Authority; 1998:19–37.
40. Forrest J. Who calls the shots? An analysis of lay health beliefs about childhood vac-cination. London: South Bank University (Occasional Papers in Sociology and Social Policy); 1995.
41. Wright O. Doctors accused of MMR jab fiddle. The Times 10 February 2003.
42. Department of Health and Social Security. Promoting better health. White Paper on Primary Health Care (Cmd 249). London: HMSO; 1987.

43. Childhood immunizations: specification for a directed enhanced service, April 2003. Online. Available: http://www.bma.org.uk/ap/nsf/Content/DESchildimmunisations 22 July 2003.

44. BBC Radio Four. Woman's Hour. 24 September 1999.

45. Royal College of Physicians. Guidelines on the practice of Ethics Committees in medical research involving human subjects. 2nd edn. London: Royal College of Physicians of London; 1990:40.

46. Honda H, Shimizu Y, Rutter M. No effect of MMR withdrawal on the incidence of autism: a total population study. Journal of Child Psychology and Psychiatry 2005; DOI: 10.1111/j.1469-7610.2005.01425.x

Chapter 12

Cyberwoman and her surgeon in the twenty-first century

Melanie Latham

CHAPTER CONTENTS

Introduction   233
Regulation of cosmetic
   surgery   234
Common law rules   234
Statutory regulation   239

Feminist ethics and cosmetic
   surgery   242
Conclusions   247
References   248

INTRODUCTION

Many invasive surgical procedures performed in Britain today are not carried out on the National Health Service (NHS) for life-threatening illnesses or diseases. A growing number of people are requesting invasive and non-invasive cosmetic surgery procedures for purely aesthetic reasons from private practitioners. They invariably wish to look younger, or just more 'attractive'. They can choose to 'improve' their skin with a chemical peel; augment their lips with collagen; soften wrinkles with Botox injections; 'improve' breast size and shape with silicone implants or reduction; refine nose outlines; enhance brows, eyes and faces with their skin lifted and stapled; or have liposuction to remove fat and reduce waist and hip measurements. They can also have their eyesight corrected permanently with laser treatment to their corneas; and baldness treated with hair transplantation. Cosmetic surgery is also popular: Mintel estimated that 72 000 procedures were carried out in 2002 in the UK alone.[1]

There has been mixed reaction to cosmetic surgery. Those who request it see these new medical procedures as widening consumer choice and only as dangerous as other surgical procedures. Others point out that the risks and dangers of anaesthesia and postoperative complications are only worth taking when surgery is necessitated by illness or disease, '(i)n the face of a growing market and demand for surgical interventions on women's bodies that can and do result in infection, bleeding, embolisms, pulmonary oedema, facial nerve injury, unfavourable scar formation, skin loss, blindness, crippling, and death, our silence becomes a culpable one.'[2] The UK Government, for its part, has seen fit to tighten the regulation of the cosmetic surgery industry recently with the Care Standards Act 2000.

Feminist ethicists have argued that cosmetic surgery could potentially enhance the autonomy of individual women who fulfil their own needs and desires about their bodies. They have questioned, however, the legitimacy of consent when women might feel under pressure to conform to a certain physical ideal.[3] They have also underlined the effect the decisions of individual women might have on other women in the wider community.[4] Feminists have debated the importance for women's condition of the concept of the 'cyborg'. This hybrid of machine and organism might lead to a dissolution of boundaries between male and female genders and between human and machine. It poses questions about what a woman is or might be.[5] The 'cyberwoman' who selects techniques offered by cosmetic surgeons might increase her ability to be autonomous and in control of her own body. A danger inherent in any emphasis on cosmetic surgery, however, is that it is only *beauty* enhancing. Women are surrounded by cultural images of successful and famous 'beautiful people'. But new imagery coming, for example, from such science fiction heroines as the athletic computer game character Lara Croft may offer new role models for women. Should women be discouraged, then, from undergoing non-therapeutic cosmetic surgery? This chapter sets out to discover the legal rights of patients of cosmetic surgery in the UK, and to ascertain its possible implications for feminists and feminist ethicists.

REGULATION OF COSMETIC SURGERY

Plastic surgery has been used since the First World War, particularly for facial reconstruction. It is largely concerned with congenital, traumatic and acquired conditions. Cosmetic surgery is more appropriately used to describe nontherapeutic procedures, which might aesthetically improve the appearance of a physical feature which is essentially healthy. Patients who choose to undergo cosmetic procedures are afforded protection by common law rules and by statute. In consequence, legal rules on consent and negligence apply to cosmetic surgery. Such surgery is invariably carried out by private practitioners, as the NHS restricts the number of non-therapeutic operations it will fund. Regulations governing private practice are therefore of particular relevance.

Common law rules

Consent is a central concept in medical law and in the provision of healthcare services. It is linked to an idea of the autonomy of the patient from the health professional. Emphasis on the autonomy of the patient implies that the patient must be given the opportunity to agree, or 'consent', to the treatment being carried out. This is particularly important in the healthcare context for two reasons. As a result of the power dynamic between health professional and patient – the health professional held in high esteem even today, as an 'expert', by society, and indeed by the law itself – the encounter between them is largely controlled by the professional. The particular nature of healthcare treatment also means that such encounters decide important issues related to the body, illness and matters of life and death.

Under English common law, physical contact is permissible only where the healthcare professional has the patient's consent. Health professionals are also under a duty to provide patients with information about proposed treatment, and alternatives. A cosmetic surgeon must seek a patient's consent before providing treatment. The famous *Bolam* case, almost half a century old now, set out that a health professional is not negligent if he acts in accordance with a practice accepted at the time as proper by a responsible body of medical opinion (*Bolam v Friern Hospital Management Committee* [1957] 2 All ER 118). The recent case of *Bolitho v City and Hackney Health Authority* [1997] 4 All ER 771 has weighted the *Bolam* principle in the patient's favour to some extent by ensuring that the doctor should make a *logical* decision about a treatment. This would entail weighing up the risks and benefits of a particular treatment. The decision he comes to must be logical in the opinion of the court, in order to be held reasonable or responsible, no matter how many medical experts the defendant can find who would have done the same thing.

Following *Sidaway*, the decision to consent to surgery can only be made if information is provided on the risks and benefits of treatment, and alternative methods of treatment (*Sidaway v Board of Governors of the Bethlem Royal and the Maudsley Hospital* [1985] 1 All ER 643, [1985] 1 AC 871, [1985] 2 WLR 480). This was found to be as much as could be expected of a health professional acting in accordance with a competent body of professional opinion as per *Bolam*. Although an enquiring patient should be given all the information they request, it was thus found that the test for disclosure was not subjective but objective – the doctor would decide this, not the patient. This judicial support for doctors was followed in *Gold v Haringey Health Authority* [1987] 2 All ER 888, and *Blyth v Bloomsbury Health Authority* [1993] Med LR 151, whether the treatment was therapeutic or non-therapeutic (as with contraceptive treatment in *Gold*, or thus with cosmetic surgery) or whether or not the patients asked particular questions.

Will it always be the case, then, that it is the cosmetic surgeon who is to decide on how much information on risks that particular patient will need to know, even the enquiring patient? Should she be told about the relatively small risk of loss of sensation in her breast after augmentation, for example? Several cases now suggest that there is an increasing obligation on a surgeon to disclose risks to the patient. In *Smith v Tunbridge Wells Health Authority* [1994] 5 Med LR 334, the failure to warn a 28-year-old man of the relatively small risk that rectal surgery might result in impotence was held to be 'neither reasonable nor responsible'. Such a risk might well have dissuaded the man from undergoing such surgery and the surgeon was therefore found to have been negligent. More meaningfully, perhaps, in *Pearce v United Bristol Healthcare NHS Trust* [1998] 48 BMLR 118, Lord Woolf stated that in the normal course of events a *reasonable* patient should be informed of a *significant* risk, 'if the information is needed so that the patient can determine for him or herself as to what course she should adopt'. Obviously, opinions will differ amongst patients and health professionals as to what constitutes a significant risk, but this does seem to point toward a less conservative attitude toward judicial interpretation of disclosure by clinicians. (It should be noted, however, that judges have remained consistently reluctant to interpret what is reasonable or significant in terms of medical practice. This decision has remained one for clinicians to decide. On this issue see, for example, Jones.[6])

Professional guidelines published periodically by bodies such as the General Medical Council (GMC) do go further than the *Bolam* or even *Bolitho* tests.[7] In fact they advise doctors to err on the side of the 'prudent patient test' seen in Lord Scarman's minority judgment in *Sidaway* and favoured now in Australia and elsewhere. This would entail giving a patient as much information as is requested.[i] These will only be guidelines, however, and the *Bolam* and *Bolitho* tests would invariably be of greater importance in any court. Their significance in court might lie in the fact that they constitute evidence of the current professional standard required by these tests. In its 1998 Guidelines on consent the GMC refers to the issue of withholding information. This it sees as valid only where it would cause serious harm to the patient, '(i)n this context serious harm does not mean the patient would become upset or decide to refuse treatment'. This still leaves the clinical definition of 'significant risk' open to interpretation as it does not state clearly what serious harm does in fact mean, at least to the GMC. It does imply though that it would refer to the sort of psychological or physiological harm that a reasonable patient might not want to run the risk of.

As far as protection of the public is concerned, the GMC is not, theoretically, without teeth. The Medical (Professional Performance) Act 1995 enables the GMC to suspend and ultimately strike off any doctor's name from the Register. Indeed, this has resulted in at least one cosmetic surgeon being removed from the Register (see *Norton v General Medical Council* [2002] UKPC 6, 68 BMLR 169). The GMC is now working closely with the National Care Standards Commission to protect patients of cosmetic surgeons, under the aegis of the Care Standards Act 2000 (see below).

There is also the possibility that the cosmetic surgeon might be subject to a criminal prosecution for assault or battery if he intentionally or recklessly causes injury, particularly if the patient dies, though this is a very rare type of prosecution. The common law of assault is the basis of criminal law offences against the person, under the Offences Against the Person Act 1861. A doctor could be prosecuted under this Act if he masquerades as a health professional; if he carries out treatment without consent; if consent has been forced

---

[i] In Canada and Australia the 'prudent patient' standard has been set as a test of how much information to give an enquiring patient and of how significant a patient might judge such information (*Reibl v Hughes* (1980) 114 DLR (3d) 1); (*Rogers v Whitaker* (1992) 109 ALR 625 (HC of Aust).

from the patient or treatment forced on the patient; if the patient could not have consented through lack of competence; if the patient refused to consent; or if the patient was not properly informed to provide consent. Of course, if the person giving treatment, health professional or otherwise, causes or inflicts *serious* harm (GBH) or wounding to the patient, knowing that the treatment will cause harm to the patient, *and* the patient did not consent, then he will be convicted for a much more serious offence. It is the consent that is the key here. Consent to that *particular* treatment and consent to being treated by a professional. If surgery is being consented to, then the 'surgeon' must not by law be a student or a nurse. That is not what has been consented to. In a similar vein, a patient cannot consent to being harmed or treated *unnecessarily*, for reasons of public policy. Any individual who inflicts harm on another person cannot say that this other person requested it, that they consented. (For example, in *R v Brown* [1993] 2 All ER, 65 adults could not lawfully consent to sado-masochistic sex.) You can consent, however, to 'proper medical treatment', no matter if it is invasive or even life-threatening (*Airedale NHS Trust v Bland* [1993] 1 All ER 821.) The term reasonable is also used in a number of cases; see, for example, *R v Brown* [1993] 2 All ER, 65.

So what does the law mean exactly by competence in the area of consent? Who has the capacity to consent? What of the mentally ill person who demands a particular procedure? How far is a cosmetic surgeon able to make a psychological assessment of such a patient? The test for capacity to consent to or to refuse treatment was set out by Thorpe J in *Re C (Refusal of Medical Treatment)* [1994] 1 FLR 31. In this case an elderly man suffering from paranoid schizophrenia refused to have his gangrenous leg amputated. Such a refusal threatened his life, yet he was found to be competent and allowed to refuse treatment. The test that Thorpe J applied in this case was based on the evidence of a psychologist, Dr E. It divided analysis and decision-making into three stages: (being able to) comprehend and retain treatment information; believing that information; and (being able to) weigh it in the balance to arrive at a choice. In 1995 the Law Commission[ii] defined capacity based around this test and it forms the basis of the decision-making test at the heart of the Mental Capacity Act 2005 (section 3).

If the patient is deemed competent and none of the exceptions are present, then the health professional must obtain consent. Such consent can be written, oral, or even 'implied'. But this consent must also be an informed consent. The patient must have been informed 'in broad terms' of the nature of the treatment to be given (*Sidaway v Board of Governors of the Bethlem Royal and the Maudsley Hospital* [1985] 1 All ER 643, [1985] 1 AC 871, [1985] 2 WLR 480). *Re T (Adult: Refusal of Medical Treatment)* [1992] 3 WLR 782 concerned a case where a Jehovah's Witness was found to have had undue influence during a conversation with her daughter, who subsequently refused to consent to a life-saving blood transfusion. Lord Donaldson MR expressed his concern that

---

[ii] Cf. Law. Com. 231 on Mental Capacity and Draft Mental Incapacity Bill Cm. 5859-I, Clause 3.

consent must not be the result of pressure from others but must have been decided by the patient herself. It must be remembered that cosmetic aesthetic enhancement can be the result of wider social, even familial pressure (for example, from someone influential in a relationship, such as a spouse). A wife bundled into a clinic by a husband demanding liposuction would not be operated on by any responsible cosmetic surgeon.

Numerous cases have been brought by patients of cosmetic surgery against their surgeons. These have involved, inter alia, allegations of lack of proper informed consent; negligence; misleading information; and a lack of a full explanation of risks involved.

In *Christine Williamson v East London and the City Health Authority & ORS* [1998] 41 BMLR 85, the claimant sought damages for medical negligence. She needed several operations after silicone breast implants leaked. A second cosmetic surgeon, Mrs Neill, operated to replace the prosthesis. On examining the claimant preoperatively, Mrs Neill decided she might have to perform a mastectomy. However, she did not inform the patient of this or have her sign a new consent form for this more extensive operation. This negligent failure to acquire a full and informed consent resulted in the claimant being awarded £20 000 in damages.

In the case of *Norton v General Medical Council* [2002] UKPC 6, 68 BMLR 169, Dr Thomas Norton appealed against the finding of serious professional conduct by the General Medical Council and his removal from the Medical Register. He had carried out elective liposuction. Non-medical staff had seen the patients preoperatively. Dr Norton had also failed to take an adequate history, not performed an adequate physical examination, had not given his patients full explanations of the operations and the pain and risk involved or anaesthesia to be used, and had thus not obtained informed consent from them. He had also failed to provide adequate pain-relief or postoperative care, and had not kept proper records. Taken together this made him a danger to the public. His appeal failed. However, after 5 years a practitioner in Dr Norton's position is still able to apply for restoration under the Medical Act (Amendment) Order 2000.

In *O'Keefe v Harvey-Kemble* [1999] 45 BMLR 74, the Court of Appeal agreed with the trial judge that the defendant's preoperative consultations had fallen below the requisite standard, having heard the testimonies of several expert witnesses on both sides. The surgeon had not informed the claimant of the risks associated with breast implants, most notably the very high risk of encapsulation which in fact ensued.[iii] Had she been so informed it was found to be more than probable that she would not have chosen to undergo the original operation. She would not then have had to undergo a further seven

---

[iii] In this case smooth shell implants were used instead of textured implants and contrary to the usual medical practice at that time. The risk of encapsulation of smooth shell silicone implants is put at 30–35%. For textured shell implants this reduces dramatically to 6–8%. (A.D. Karidis MD. FRCS, cosmetic surgeon, Capsular Contraction, nipntuck.co.uk.)

painful and distressing operations. Nor did he assess the aspirations of the patient as to outcome or give proper written advice for her to study at a later date about risks. Her award of damages stood at approximately £25 000. The appeal by the surgeon was therefore dismissed by Swinton Thomas and Potter LJJ.

Statutory regulation

A patient seeking cosmetic surgery will invariably engage a private surgeon for her treatment. That private surgeon will contract to provide treatment to that patient. The surgeon will be expected to exercise reasonable skill and care as per the usual standard expected of any doctor under the *Bolam* test. Despite the existence of a contract, any surgeon is not able to or liable to guarantee any specific result. This will depend on the physiology of the patient. In any negligence case where the patient is alleging that she would not have gone ahead with the operation had the risks of the subsequent failure been explained to her, however, a private patient needs to be able to pinpoint exactly which individual out of those involved in the operating team acted negligently. That is unless the clinic or hospital offers a 'package' of treatment to the patient as then that clinic will be liable for the actions of its employees.[8]

The Unfair Contract Terms Act 1977 expresses the liability of the cosmetic surgeon contracting to treat his patient to exercise reasonable skill and to be responsible for negligent death or personal injury. The Supply of Goods and Services Act 1982 also contains implied terms which are relevant to the cosmetic surgery patient in that services must be carried out with due care and skill. Goods must also, 'meet the standard that a reasonable person would regard as satisfactory' (Sale and Supply of Goods Act 1994, s.1). In addition, should a patient be supplied with a defective product, such as a faulty breast implant, she may be able to claim for resultant harm under the tort of negligence or the Consumer Protection Act 1987. The latter makes the producer of a product, such as the manufacturer, liable for defects without proof of fault unless the manufacturer can come up with a relevant defence, such as the state of scientific knowledge at the time it put the product into circulation not being such as to enable the existence of the defect to be discovered.

Otherwise a claim of negligence may lie against the surgeon with the usual provisos of the *Bolam* test. The Medical Devices Agency, part of the Medicines and Healthcare products Regulatory Agency, oversees the conformity of breast implants to European safety standards set out in Directive 03/12/EC and the Medical Devices (Amendment) Regulation 2003. This places the onus principally on the manufacturers of medical devices such as breast implants to ensure these are safe and fit for the purpose.

As a result of the evidence of negligence in cosmetic surgery cases, the Government responded gradually in the late 1990s with a statutory response which attempted to resolve the many issues raised, particularly in relation to consent and medical qualifications. The Care Standards Act 2000, which came into force on 1 April 2002, is a wide-ranging statute which sets out to regulate private and voluntary health and social care. It replaced the Registered Homes Act 1984, Part II of which had covered the inspection of the facilities of independent acute hospitals by Local Health Authorities, though it had not regulated clinical standards, which were invariably low and inconsistent across the UK. This meant in effect that at least 80% of private cosmetic surgery was completely unregulated and could be carried out by unqualified surgeons. This contrasted with NHS plastic surgery, which was carried out by surgeons with 6 years relevant training and who were listed on the General Medical Council's specialist register in plastic surgery.[9] Part I, Section 6, of the Care Standards Act establishes a new independent regulatory body and registration authority, the National Care Standards Commission (NCSC), whose function is set out as regulating private healthcare services (alongside residential care and nursing homes); informing and advising the Secretary of State; supporting consumers through the provision of information; and encouraging the development of better services. Section 2(4) defines an independent clinic as being where medical practitioners provide services, whether or not on the premises. NHS services are excluded. 'This will bring private primary care premises, where prescribed, within the regulatory framework for the first time' (Explanatory notes to Care Standards Act 2000, s.30).

The Act introduces national minimum standards for clinics which are enforced by the NCSC who will inspect clinics annually, impromptu where necessary. Clinic Registered Managers must operate clinical governance procedures. All practitioners must be appropriately recruited, trained and qualified clinicians. Patients must be interviewed preoperatively by the consultant surgeon and provided with written and verbal information about results and risks. They must also be offered counselling and a 2-week 'cooling-off' period before treatment. All private hospitals and clinics must have a formal complaints procedure. Advertising, including promotional literature, must comply with BMA and Advertising Standards Authority guidelines as regards accuracy and clarity of information.[9]

The tightening of standards regarding cosmetic surgery was essential and is to be welcomed. The Act is not without its critics, however. Nightingale and Kay,[9] the latter an NHS cosmetic surgeon, make several important comments about the Act. In relation to clinical practice they have observed that the new standards are very minimal; existing unqualified practitioners are not forced to adhere to these new standards, only those registering to work in private practice after 1 April 2002; no single body yet regulates standards across the cosmetic surgery profession; and only two organisations – the British Association of Plastic Surgeons (BAPS) and the British Association of Aesthetic Plastic Surgeons (BAAPS) – ensure that practitioners are trained in the relevant cosmetic surgery procedures. In relation to patients themselves, Nightingale and Kay pointed out that patients may opt out of the 'cooling-off' period and are thus still under pressure to undergo procedures. Additionally, complainants may only have their complaints heard and investigated: they are not necessarily entitled, under the Act, to have more treatment or compensation. It is also still possible for clinics to mislead patients over consultants' qualifications and experience, even given Advertising Standards Authority standards. Ultimately, they argue, the Care Standards Act is less likely to be effective without a universal set of standards of qualification imposed and regulated by a single umbrella body such as the Royal College of Surgeons.

The first comprehensive inspection of 22 small clinics providing cosmetic surgery in Central London was carried out by the NCSC in March/April 2003.[10] The Report catalogued the extent to which the majority of these establishments were not adhering even to the minimum standards set by the Care Standards Act. Many of the criticisms made in the Report echo those put forward by Nightingale and Kay, amongst others. Care of patients was less than adequate with a lack of written guidance to clinic procedure; misleading advertisements about the potential success of treatments; and informal and undocumented complaints' procedures. For those patients who underwent clinical procedures they were unable to rely on the qualifications of practitioners, as clinics were not able to provide documentary evidence about their clinical employees, even those on a Specialist Register. Moreover, there were too few available members of clinic staff with knowledge of life support procedures, and medical records held on patients were found to be inadequate. Finally, in relation to clinical governance, establishments were not monitoring the quality of their clinical activity and adverse incidents were not being recorded.

This Report demonstrates a serious lack in the standards offered to cosmetic surgery patients. Even given the apparent force of law, some of the surgeons in this Report who are offering such inherently dangerous and risky procedures as liposuction and face lifts appear unprofessional, even dangerous. The lack of even a minimum standard of clinical care in too many of these establishments appears to be matched by a lack of patient provision generally. Unfortunately, it is more than likely that evidence of bad practice in London is mirrored elsewhere in the UK. This will not resolve the current issues of patient dissatisfaction or accusations of negligence. Following publication, the NCSC recommended new self-assessment tools for specific procedures to assist clinics to monitor their own performance. Sir Liam Donaldson, Chief Medical Officer, talked of the Report constituting the beginnings of scrutiny and that it was hoped that a full review of cosmetic surgery would be carried out across England by the NCSC.[11]

A lack of explanations of medical risks to patients making such important decisions might appear to lessen the chance of ascertaining clearly the expectations of those patients as to outcome. Research has been carried out by French ethicists into the connection between claims for compensation after cosmetic surgery and the expectations those particular patients had.[12] The authors examined the case notes of 20 patients who had sought compensation for injuries in the French courts in 1999. What interested the authors of the study was that, in these particular cases, injury was found ultimately to be minimal or non-existent but that patients were left dissatisfied enough to seek compensation through the courts. In fact, 15 patients complained that the results of the operation were unsatisfactory, 2 that the operation had affected another medical condition, and 3 that they had been given insufficient information about the procedure being carried out. There were six cases of minor psychiatric illness amongst the patients and this may have contributed to their feelings of disappointment. There were also, however, six cases of alleged unprofessional conduct by the health professionals involved. The authors speculated that these were also tangible reasons behind the complaints. Ultimately they argue that the risks and benefits to individual patients are not being sufficiently assessed by surgeons. This raises ethical problems in relation to informed consent and autonomous decision-making.

FEMINIST ETHICS AND COSMETIC SURGERY

Common law rules on consent and negligence have been the subject of numerous ethical debates, and medical law is rarely discussed separately from its ethical counterpart.

Conventional ethical theories, such as utilitarianism, can offer useful insights into questions about the ethics of cosmetic surgery. The calculation of the relative risks and benefits of surgery that is likely to be painful, dangerous, and which carries risks for mental health, might need to emphasise potential psychological, social or financial benefits, in addition to clinical ones. Cosmetic surgeons are under an obligation to inform their patients of the relevant risks, but are unlikely to be qualified to carry out any comprehensive assessment of the possible psychological consequences of a treatment. On the other hand, what price might we put on the value of autonomy in informed consent? The value of a patient making up her own mind about what happens to her body is high.[13]

Such issues of choice have been among the many medico-legal issues subject to debate and criticism from feminist quarters, most notably in this arena from feminist ethicists.[14–17] It is the perspective of such feminist ethicists which is particularly salient in any discussion of a medical treatment carried out more particularly on women's bodies, and, it has to be said, for the most part by male surgeons.[iv]

Feminist ethicists have concentrated particularly on the power relationship between patient and doctor and the effect of that on issues of autonomy and choice.[17] The presence of this relationship in the medico-legal context has potentially serious consequences for the female patient.[15,16] There might be varying views as to the amount of information a patient seeking cosmetic surgery would need, for example, on risks of surgery that are not medical but cosmetic. Another possible non-medical risk is that the patient might fail to achieve her physical aspirations. The patient may have psychological needs

---

[iv] That is not to say that feminist ethics is only relevant to issues concerning women and health. Its emphasis on context rather than the individual is of relevance across the spectrum of decision-making around health.

that are not investigated by the surgeon and which put her mental health at risk should such dissatisfaction arise or should the procedure then result in the need for further corrective treatments. Ideally, counselling may be needed to explore fully the reasons for surgery and the expectations of the patient. Whether such thorough counselling is routinely available is open to question.

These issues are especially salient where private treatment is being offered for non-therapeutic reasons. Similarities abound with the practice of assisted conception where the majority of the treatment available is offered on a private basis. In this context, many commentators have raised the issue of the motivations of private clinics being to profit from the number of procedures performed.[18] Unsuitable patients and inappropriate treatments are much more likely to be seen at private clinics offering assisted conception treatment, and, by extension, at those offering cosmetic surgery.

Ideas about what constitutes 'feminist ethics' are usually traced back to work done by Carol Gilligan in the early 1980s.[19] Her six-stage theory (which included three levels of development) about what constituted moral development arose as a criticism of Lawrence Kohlberg's perspective on justice.[20] According to Kohlberg, people making moral decisions passed through various stages of moral development. These went from deferring to authority to operating from self-chosen, universal principles of justice. Abstract ethical theories such as these emphasise that people are antagonistic and operate according to their own individual needs. Here people are seen as other and different with their individual rights deserving respect. Their highly independent moral spaces must be respected and negotiated with.

Gilligan applied Kohlberg's stages to female research subjects and found that they, as opposed to male research subjects, were more inclined to appeal to a set of connections and relationships underpinned by communication, than to more hierarchical value systems. Gilligan therefore suggested that women speak in a different voice, though not a *deficient* voice. In her own six-stage analysis of moral development, a person moves upwards from having a preoccupation for survival; being wholly self-sacrificial; embracing a principle of care for self and others; not having tension between self and others; having participation and interaction in relationships; and finally, to choosing the principle of care based on a person's context. This would mean that interdependence of self and others is recognised, and exploitation and hurt are condemned. Rights are not abandoned, but take a back seat to *care*.

This takes into account the *context* and actual experience of women. These vary greatly across ethnicities, classes, cultures, sexual orientation, physical abilities, educational backgrounds, and ages. Thus feminist ethics differs from medical ethics in that it realises that the perspective and needs of a woman from an ethnic minority, such as Black or Asian or even Irish Catholic, may well differ from the needs of the white person in the context of healthcare.

Susan Sherwin and others have further developed the ethic of care, 'in my view, feminist ethics must recognize the moral perspective of women; insofar as that includes the perspective described as an ethics of care, we should expand our moral agenda accordingly[v] ... [and] determine when caring should be offered and when it should be withheld.'[21]

More particularly, *context* has been emphasised by Sherwin as a central issue:

> 'Moral analysis needs to examine persons and their behaviour in the context of political relations and experiences, but this dimension has been missing so far from most ethical debates ... In its appeal to contextual features, feminist ethics resists the model of traditional ethics, wherein the principal task is to define a totalising or universal theory that prescribes rules for all possible worlds. Feminist ethics focuses instead on the need to develop a moral analysis that fits the actual world in which we live ... That is not to say that feminist ethics involves no concern with principles. It encompasses theories that are committed to concerns about social justice, because it demands criticism of the various patterns of dominance, oppression and exploitation of one group of persons by another.'[22]

In relation to cosmetic surgery this raises questions around the care that is taken about each individual patient, and the extent to which cosmetic surgeons should be taking into account the context or background of that patient before deciding to offer treatment. Are financial incentives given more prominence in private clinics than they should be? Are both clinical and moral obligations toward patients, and reflections about the effect surgery might have on them, taking a back seat to financial considerations? Moreover, women's moral decisions on their health are not, necessarily, made in a vacuum as they are situated within the general oppression of women and the social disadvantage of women. Should women choosing to have cosmetic surgery consider the effect of their choice on the position of their fellow women in society? Should women, surgeons, even regulators, take this into account when weighing up the risks and benefits of surgery? Should cosmetic surgery increase in popularity amongst women, will all women then be further exposed to the 'culturally imposed physical standard' that is the 'beauty myth'?[23]

Kathryn Pauly Morgan has written at length about the social norms which women conform to as opposed to freely choose. She emphasises that this is in fact an essential ingredient for the success of those women. 'For virtually all women, as women, success is defined in terms of interlocking patterns of compulsion: compulsory attractiveness, compulsory motherhood, and compulsory heterosexuality, patterns that determine *the legitimate aims of attraction and motherhood.*'[24] (Italics added.)

This compulsion is driven and enabled by biotechnology and surgery. Critics of medical technology have observed that pressures to achieve norms of motherhood and fertility have led to women choosing to undergo assisted conception. Similarly, pressures to achieve norms of womanhood and heterosexuality have persuaded women to undergo cosmetic surgery. Morgan refers

---

[v] Feminist ethicists and others have recognised the risks of associating the female gender with care.[21]

to the, 'pressure to achieve perfection through technology' and the 'double pathologizing of women's bodies'.[25] Morgan and others refer to the mythical ability of biotechnology to achieve flawless reproduction persuading many women to attempt to improve on what were in fact their own normal reproductive processes. Misogynist beliefs about the imperfections, inferiority and deformity of the female body have been seen to be behind the development of technical attempts to improve upon it. At the same time, Western medicine has been criticised for equating women's bodies with machines to be improved upon. Women have been encouraged to use technology at all stages of motherhood and this has been seen to be to their detriment.[26] Morgan links this use of technology to the rise in cosmetic surgery, particularly in the West: 'Now technology is making obligatory the appearance of youth and the reality of "beauty" for every woman who can afford it. Natural destiny is being supplanted by technologically grounded coercion, and the coercion is camouflaged by the language of choice, fulfilment and liberation.'[27] She criticises clinicians who categorise normal female physique as abnormal, with technology offered as a remedy. Hence, in cosmetic surgery literature, normal female body shape is described as if it had deformities, diseases or illnesses. Morgan also points out that objectification and women's assimilation of it are not new. In 1792 in *A Vindication of the Rights of Woman*, Mary Wollstonecraft remarked, '(ta)ught from infancy that beauty is woman's sceptre, the mind shapes itself to the body and roaming round its gilt cage, only seeks to adorn its prison'.[28]

Links have also been made between the context of women's lives and social and cultural pressures for body modification in non-Western countries. Lois Bibbings, for example, has underlined the similarities in relation to such cultural and social pressures between cosmetic surgery and genital surgery.[29] She does acknowledge differences in pressure being put even on adult women who undergo genital surgery, however, and the health risks involved in any such surgery for a woman's reproductive functions. Such cultural pressures as religious requirements and economic survival are not as great for the Western woman as they are for her non-Western counterpart. Nonetheless, these links are noteworthy.

Cultural and social pressures on Western women which might persuade them to undergo cosmetic surgery are certainly not insignificant. Arguments were put forward by Michel Foucault on 'the docile body', 'that may be subjected, used, transformed and improved'.[30] His arguments rose out of his observations of soldiers and prisoners who are disciplined and controlled until they submit themselves to the authority of the army or the prison. Women patients submit their docile bodies to the hands of cosmetic surgeons who dismantle and then rebuild them.

Kathy Davis points out that women get used to the idea of the objectification of their bodies by our culture and then objectify their bodies themselves.[31] At the same time, they are dissatisfied with the portrayal of themselves as nothing but a body. They are left feeling uneasy about themselves and their bodies. Davis can then understand why women allow their bodies to be surgically manipulated. Women's use of cosmetic surgery demonstrates their objectification of their own bodies, and their struggle to be inside and in control of (the image of) their own body, 'to be embodied subjects rather than mere bodies'. In short, women are attempting to be their own bodies and to control their own identities: 'I can treat women's ongoing struggles to justify a contradictory practice like cosmetic surgery as a resource for developing a feminist response which speaks to women's experiences rather than simply reiterating the correct line on women's involvement in the beauty system.'[32]

Feminist ethical understanding of the context of individual women thus makes a neutral stance on cosmetic surgery possible, even essential. Davis is critical of feminist theory on the oppressiveness of the beauty industry, which portrays women as, 'cultural dopes': 'In doing so they fail to acknowledge the extent to which women know the risks and limitations of body modification.'[33] In a similar vein, Susan Bordo observes that racism, sexism and narcissism in Western society dictate a particular but sure route to economic and personal success. People are not necessarily 'dopes' if they follow these.[34] Women are prepared to undergo pain and risk in order to access the power that eludes them elsewhere. What is more they can choose how to transform themselves, which gives them at least a moderate amount of self-determination. These women feel they have chosen their own identity:[35] '(a)nd under those circumstances, it may not be possible for her to register her resistance in the form of refusal. The best one can hope for is a heightened sense of the nature of the multiple double-binds and compromises that permeate the lives of virtually all women and are accentuated by the cosmetic surgery culture.'[36]

Interestingly, Morgan sees as paradoxical the choice women make to use cosmetic surgery and assisted conception as these do not in fact lead to full womanly autonomy but lead instead to dependence on experts who are usually men.[37] On the other hand, this may not be such a paradoxical choice. Male cosmetic surgeons are much more likely to know the exact surgery patriarchal society will most approve of and give that to these women, ensuring their ultimate success as 'women' in that society.

This use of technology to create the perfect body can be taken further, feminists have argued, to create the 'cyberwoman'. These new imagined individuals, part human, part machine, challenge binary and oppositional discourses such as male/female, human/machine, human/animal. Donna Haraway's *A Manifesto for Cyborgs* is seen as the precursor of this debate.[5] In her Manifesto, Haraway saw the cyborg as the solution to problems produced by gender inequality. Feminist theorists would not find a time or place where structural inequality was not the norm. There was no Garden of Eden, no mythical organic *natural* place. The cyborg was an example of technoscience, and it was this which had the ability to address and redraw boundaries between human beings, animals and machines – between natural and artificial. Natural bodies and artificial bodies. Natural humans and artificial humans. As a cyborg a woman could be anything she wanted. The cyborg or cyberwoman would enable women to reinvent the category woman, to question the limits put on the definition of womanhood by society. This was a prospect for the future, not the past.

Morgan refers to a 'robowoman'.[38] She too refers to the liberating potential of technology and the idea of the cyborg:

'we have arrived at the stage of regarding ourselves as both technological subject and object, transformable and literally creatable through biological engineering ... Given the oppressive consequences of associating women with the Natural in capitalist, racist, patriarchal cultures.'[39]

More significantly still, she goes on to affirm that, 'it is not surprising that women themselves should envision access to technological control as a way of severing this connection.'[40] In other words, cosmetic surgery itself can be seen as having liberating potential for women. It could be argued that the woman who chooses to transform herself through cosmetic surgery is thus a manifestation of a cyberwoman. She might be appropriating cosmetic surgery for her own moral and political purposes. Moreover, cosmetic surgery is just one example of how the human body is created by the culture in which we live. Indeed, Morgan has suggested that cosmetic surgery could be used for a feminist political agenda which wanted to dispel the beauty myth and 'revalorise the domain of the "ugly" '. Feminists could do this by having cosmetic surgery to make themselves unattractive, 'if we cringe from this alternative, this may, in fact, testify (so to speak) to the hold that the beauty imperative has on our imagination and our bodies.'[41]

CONCLUSIONS

Cosmetic surgery is becoming increasingly popular, whether as a result of individual choice or social pressure. Legal protection in the UK has now been substantially improved by the Care Standards Act 2000. Shortcomings of the Act have been highlighted and vigilant monitoring of cosmetic surgery in private practice will be essential. Feminist ethicists have emphasised the importance in any healthcare context of treatment decisions being made by patient and cosmetic surgeon alike with context and care in mind. The effects of invasive and dangerous treatments cannot be ignored, particularly when the surgery is essentially for aesthetic purposes. These effects might be seen on the wider community of women as well as on the woman patient herself. That said, it is essential to realise that patients who choose cosmetic surgery may be fully aware of their reasons and the risks involved. They may only be choosing to utilise the rewards on offer after transforming themselves. Are they choosing to be cyberwomen? What are the future possibilities of cybersurgery for patient autonomy? A future is possible where patients as cyberwomen might increasingly ask surgeons for specific procedures for themselves and be empowered by that. The chances of a return to a natural non-technological world are slim and not necessarily in women's favour. Most women benefit from medical advances, providing they are in a position to consent autonomously to them.[vi] Sense- or mind-enhancing surgery that is defined by

---

[vi] There are many examples of how women's autonomy, particularly their reproductive autonomy, has benefited from technological revolutions which have produced, for example, the contraceptive pill, the vacuum method of abortion, and the abortion pill RU 486. The technologies themselves are not necessarily harmful to women. It is medical control of these technologies that is more likely to make them so.[18]

the possibilities of technology rather than the cultural pressures for *beauty* might be possible in the not-too-distant future. What is essential is professional organisation of cosmetic surgery, closely regulated by the state. This can ensure high standards and the safe administration of treatments, whatever they might turn out to be, and whether women choose to request them or not.

References

1. Short A. The iVillage guide to cosmetic surgery. iVillage.co.uk 25 March 2003.
2. Morgan KP. Women and the knife: cosmetic surgery and the colonization of women's bodies (Hypatia 1991; 6(3) Fall). In: Sherwin S, Parish B, eds. Women, medicine, ethics and the law. Aldershot: Ashgate; 2002:28.
3. Sherwin S. Ethics, 'feminine' ethics, and feminist ethics. In: Shogan D, ed. A Reader in feminist ethics. Toronto: Canadian Scholar Press; 1993:16–23.
4. Callahan JC, ed. Reproduction, ethics and the law: feminist perspectives. Bloomington: Indiana University Press; 1995.
5. Haraway D. A manifesto for cyborgs: technology and socialist feminism in the 1980s. In: Nicholson LJ, ed. Feminism/Postmodernism. London: Routledge, 1990.
6. Jones M. Informed consent and other fairy stories. Medical Law Review 1999; 7:103–134.
7. General Medical Council. Seeking patients' consent: the ethical considerations, November 1998.
8. Brazier M. Medicine, patients and the law. 3rd edn. Harmondsworth: Penguin; 2003:180.
9. Nightingale K, Kay S. Cosmetic surgery receives a face lift. Law Society Gazette 2002; 99(10):37.
10. National Care Standards Commission. Report to the Chief Medical Officer for England on the findings of inspectors of private and cosmetic surgery establishments in Central London during March/April 2003. June 2003.
11. The Guardian 8 July 2003.
12. Meningaud JP, Servant JM, Herve C, Bertrand JC. Ethics and aims of cosmetic surgery: a contribution from an analysis of claims after minor damage. Medicine and Law 2000; 19(2):237–252.
13. Harris J. The value of life. London: Routledge; 1985.
14. Bridgeman J, Millns S, eds. Law and body politics: regulating the female body. Aldershot: Dartmouth; 1995.
15. Sheldon S, Thomson M. Feminist perspectives on health care law. London: Cavendish; 1998.
16. Morris A, Nott S. Well women: the gendered nature of health care provision. Aldershot: Ashgate; 2002.
17. Sherwin S, Parish B, eds. Women, medicine, ethics and the law. Aldershot: Ashgate; 2002.
18. Latham M. Regulating reproduction: a century of conflict in Britain and France. Manchester: Manchester University Press; 2002.
19. Gilligan C. In a different voice. Psychological theory and women's development. Cambridge, MA: Harvard University Press; 1982.
20. Callahan JC, ed. Reproduction, ethics and the law: feminist perspectives. Bloomington: Indiana University Press; 1995.
21. Sherwin S. Ethics, 'feminine' ethics, and feminist ethics. In: Shogan D, ed. A reader in feminist ethics; Toronto: Canadian Scholar's Press; 1993:16.

22. Sherwin S. Ethics, 'feminine' ethics, and feminist ethics. In: Shogan D, ed. A reader in feminist ethics; Toronto: Canadian Scholar's Press; 1993:16–23.

23. Wolf N. The beauty myth. New York: Vintage; 1990:12.

24. Morgan KP. Women and the knife: cosmetic surgery and the colonization of women's bodies (Hypatia 1991; 6(3) Fall). In: Sherwin S, Parish B, eds. Women, medicine, ethics and the law. Aldershot: Ashgate; 2002:32.

25. Morgan KP. Women and the knife: cosmetic surgery and the colonization of women's bodies (Hypatia 1991; 6(3) Fall). In: Sherwin S, Parish B, eds. Women, medicine, ethics and the law. Aldershot: Ashgate; 2002:39.

26. Corea G. The mother machine. Reproductive technologies from artificial insemination to artificial wombs. London: Women's Press; 1985.

27. Morgan KP. Women and the knife: cosmetic surgery and the colonization of women's bodies (Hypatia 1991; 6(3) Fall). In: Sherwin S, Parish B, eds. Women, medicine, ethics and the law. Aldershot: Ashgate; 2002:40.

28. Morgan KP. Women and the knife: cosmetic surgery and the colonization of women's bodies (Hypatia 1991; 6(3) Fall). In: Sherwin S, Parish B, eds. Women, medicine, ethics and the law. Aldershot: Ashgate; 2002:34.

29. Bibbings L. Female circumcision: mutilation or modification? In: Bridgeman J, Millns S, eds. Law and body politics: regulating the female body. Aldershot: Dartmouth; 1995.

30. Foucault M. Discipline and punish: the birth of the prison. New York: Vintage; 1977:136.

31. Davis K. Reshaping the female body: the dilemma of cosmetic surgery. London: Routledge; 1995:58–64.

32. Davis K. Reshaping the female body: the dilemma of cosmetic surgery. London: Routledge; 1995:60.

33. Davis K. Reshaping the female body: the dilemma of cosmetic surgery. London: Routledge; 1995:40.

34. Bordo S. Unbearable weight: feminism, Western culture and the body. Berkeley: University of California Press; 1995:30.

35. Morgan KP. Women and the knife: cosmetic surgery and the colonization of women's bodies (Hypatia 1991; 6(3) Fall). In: Sherwin S, Parish B, eds. Women, medicine, ethics and the law. Aldershot: Ashgate; 2002:42.

36. Morgan KP. Women and the knife: cosmetic surgery and the colonization of women's bodies (Hypatia 1991; 6(3) Fall). In: Sherwin S, Parish B, eds. Women, medicine, ethics and the law. Aldershot: Ashgate; 2002:43.

37. Morgan KP. Gender rites and rights: the biopolitics of beauty and fertility. In: Sumner LW, Boyle J, eds. Philosophical perspectives on bioethics. University of Toronto Press; 1996:226–233.

38. Morgan KP. Women and the knife: cosmetic surgery and the colonization of women's bodies (Hypatia 1991; 6(3) Fall). In: Sherwin S, Parish B, eds. Women, medicine, ethics and the law. Aldershot: Ashgate; 2002:30.

39. Morgan KP. Gender rites and rights: the biopolitics of beauty and fertility. In: Sumner LW, Boyle J, eds. Philosophical perspectives on bioethics. University of Toronto Press; 1996:224.

40. Morgan KP. Gender rites and rights: the biopolitics of beauty and fertility. In: Sumner LW, Boyle J, eds. Philosophical perspectives on bioethics. University of Toronto Press; 1996:225.

41. Morgan KP. Women and the knife: cosmetic surgery and the colonization of women's bodies (Hypatia 1991; 6(3) Fall). In: Sherwin S, Parish B, eds. Women, medicine, ethics and the law. Aldershot: Ashgate; 2002:46.

SECTION FIVE

The end of life

SECTION CONTENTS

13. Legal recognition of the right to die   253

14. Regulating active voluntary euthanasia: what can England and Wales learn from Belgium and the Netherlands?   269

Chapter **13**

Legal recognition of the right to die

Heleen Weyers

CHAPTER CONTENTS

Three processes of legal
   change 254
The Netherlands 254
Belgium 256
Denmark 258

Changes in value
   orientations 259
Political opportunities 262
To conclude 265
References 266

For the people and organisations who work for and against the legalisation of euthanasia,[i] the year 2002 was remarkable. Both the Netherlands and Belgium legalised termination of life on request by doctors provided they meet certain requirements of careful practice.[ii] The processes of legal change in the Netherlands and Belgium have been extensively documented,[1–6] but the question why euthanasia has been legalised in these countries and not elsewhere is hardly ever asked.

In this chapter, I seek to contribute to answering this question. My starting point will be that the legalisation of euthanasia is a manifestation of two larger processes of legal change that are taking shape in all Western countries: the development of individual rights of patients,[iii] and the removal of

---

[i] I use the term euthanasia to refer to termination of life or assistance with suicide on request by a doctor. Whenever quotation marks are used – 'euthanasia' – the meaning of the word is different or less clear.

[ii] For the record, four states (the Netherlands, Belgium, Switzerland and Oregon, USA) now have laws that permit termination of life at the patient's request. Since the 1980s, the Swiss have had a practice of regulated assistance with suicide by lay persons. In legal terms, Swiss law provides that assistance with suicide is liable to punishment only if done for self-interested reasons. Since 1997, in Oregon, terminally ill patients have had the possibility of doctor-assisted suicide.

[iii] The expression 'individual rights of patients' is used to cover both the legalisation of advance directives in which treatment is refused and the legalisation of euthanasia. I note that the Dutch and Belgian laws do not provide the inhabitants of the two countries with an individual right to euthanasia but give doctors protection against prosecution.

religion-based prohibitions from the Criminal Code. Recognition of a patient's right to refuse treatment is an example of the first; eliminating the prohibition of termination of life on request is an example of the second.

I do not claim to be able to give a final answer to the question. However, I am convinced that an explanation can only be found by an international comparison. Eligible countries for comparison are those where either euthanasia or advance directives or both have been legalised. Euthanasia has been legalised in the Netherlands and Belgium; in addition to these two countries, three other countries in the European Union have a law recognising advance directives: Denmark, Finland and Spain.[iv] In this chapter, besides the Netherlands and Belgium, special attention is paid to Denmark.[v] I will examine the processes of legal change regarding individual rights of patients, the cultural values that might be important in relation to this legal change, and features of political systems that may be relevant.

THREE PROCESSES OF LEGAL CHANGE

The Netherlands, Belgium and Denmark are in many important aspects alike. All three are small, relatively rich countries with a rather well-developed social security system. With respect to politics, the three are countries with a consensus model of democracy. Some important features of this model are: executive power shared in broad coalition cabinets; balance of power between the executive and the legislative; a multi-party system; proportional representation; and interest group corporatism.[7]

The Netherlands[vi]

Since the end of the 1960s, euthanasia has been a subject of public debate in the Netherlands. In the 1970s several people had to defend themselves in court on charges of helping a member of the family to die. The most famous of these cases is *Postma* (*Nederlandse Jurisprudentie* 1973, no. 183) in which the defendant, a general practitioner, stood trial for ending the life of her mother. The first formulations of what later came to be known as the 'requirements of careful practice' are articulated in these law cases.

In those years, the right of dying patients to be informed about their condition and their right to refuse treatment was an important subject of discussion too. The organisations which worked hard for the legalisation of euthanasia (the Dutch Association for Voluntary Euthanasia and the Foundation for Voluntary Euthanasia) formulated models for advance directives and distributed them

---

[iv] In the United Kingdom advance directives are legally recognised but not provided for by statute.

[v] There is hardly any information in English on the Finnish legalisation of 1993 and legal recognition in Spain is very recent (2003).

[vi] Terminating life on request and assistance with suicide are prohibited in Articles 293 and 294 of the Dutch Criminal Code. The maximum sentences are 12 years and 3 years.

widely. The legislator, too, was active. At the end of the 1970s, the Commission on Patients' Rights was set up to advise on a change in the law. In 1982 the Constitution was changed by the introduction of an article guaranteeing the right of inviolability of the human body. The explanatory memorandum made it clear that medical treatment is only allowed after permission has been given by the patient or a person entitled to make decisions on behalf of the patient. The Commission on Patients' Rights suggested that the doctor–patient relationship is a contractual one in which the patient decides after being informed whether or not to be treated. This proposal became law through a change in the Civil Code in 1994.[vii]

In the 1980s, the process of legal change with respect to euthanasia gained momentum. The prosecutor's office decided not to prosecute provided the doctor fulfilled the requirements of careful practice established in judicial decisions. Rulings of the Supreme Court held that euthanasia could be justifiable, under Article 40 of the Criminal Code,[viii] in effect legalising euthanasia by a doctor. Another result of the rulings of the Supreme Court was more clarity regarding the content of the requirements of careful practice.

The process of legal change also developed rapidly in another way. In 1984, the year of the first ruling of the Supreme Court, the Executive Board of the Royal Dutch Medical Association stated that euthanasia was an issue to be dealt with within the doctor–patient relationship. The Board stressed that only doctors should be allowed to engage in actions that terminate life. The Board considered euthanasia performed by a doctor acceptable if the doctor had taken adequate steps to conform to the requirements of careful practice.[ix] A third development in 1984 was the introduction in Parliament of a bill in which euthanasia performed by a doctor who conforms to the requirements of careful practice was made an exception to the prohibition of euthanasia. In 1985, a State Commission on Euthanasia issued advice in which the majority pressed for a change in the law.

It took until 2002 before the legal change resulting from the rulings of the Supreme Court in the 1980s was reflected in legislation. In the meantime, the issue of euthanasia never disappeared from the public and political agendas. In particular, debate was stimulated by the national surveys of 1990 and 1995 on the frequency and quality of life-ending and life-shortening behaviour of doctors.

[vii] In this Law on Contracts for Medical Treatment advance directives were given legal status.

[viii] A doctor confronted with on the one hand the duty to relieve the suffering of a patient and on the other hand the duty to obey the norm of Article 293 of the Criminal Code finds himself in a state of necessity. If, in this state of necessity, the doctor acts according to scientific opinion and according to norms applied in medical ethics, he is entitled to the justification of necessity.

[ix] The first ruling on euthanasia of the Supreme Court came after the new policy of the Executive Board of the Medical Association was formulated. It is thought that the position of the Board functioned as an amicus curiae brief in support of the Supreme Court's decision.

That the legislative process took so long is partly due to the Christian Democratic Party. The Christian Democrats, opponents of euthanasia, figured in all governments between 1917 and 1994. However, the first cabinet in which the Christian Democrats were not represented did not change the law on euthanasia either. That government did not want to offend the Christian Democrats and the dissenting members of the coalition parties. It took the position that before enacting changes the reporting rate of euthanasia had to be higher. Its hand was forced by a bill that quickly won a majority; the second cabinet without Christian Democrats ultimately proposed a bill in which Articles 293 and 294 of the Criminal Code were amended to allow euthanasia and assistance with suicide by doctors. This proposal was accepted in Parliament and the new law was enacted in 2002.

Belgium[x]

In Belgium in the 1970s and 1980s, neither euthanasia nor patients' rights in general were much debated.[xi] There was one exception: abortion. In those years Belgium was entangled in a tumultuous, difficult process of legal change on this subject. In 1990, this dossier was finally closed with a law legalising abortion which was supported by an 'exchange majority'[xii] in Parliament, a change that could only become law through a temporary abdication of the king.[xiii]

In the 1980s, private members' bills to legalise euthanasia were regularly put forward. None of these proposals reached the final stages of the legislative process. Initiative bills hardly ever succeed without the support of government and these initiatives could not receive this support as long as the Christian Democrats were at the centre of power. After 1990, the Christian Democrats required as a basis for coalition agreements an explicit ban on 'exchange majorities' on ethical matters.

Civil society was rather silent regarding euthanasia but not completely.[xiv] Between 1985 and 1987 a so-called 'National Colloquium on Bioethics in the

---

[x] This part is based on articles by Adams and Geudens.[1-3] The Belgian Criminal Code has no articles on killing on request or assistance with suicide. Killing on request can be prosecuted as homicide or poisoning. Assistance with suicide is not a criminal offence because suicide is not.

[xi] In Belgium, as in other countries, there were a few prosecutions of family members of the patient for killing on request or out of compassion.

[xii] A majority formed by parties of the Government and parties of the opposition.

[xiii] According to Witte,[8] the process of legal change on abortion was very different from other processes of legal change in Belgium. She deems the following features in the case of abortion to be special: a sexual problem becoming a subject of public debate; failure to pacify the problem; the subject being shifted to Parliament instead of arranged by Government; a compromise cutting through the political parties; and of course the way in which the bill finally became law.

[xiv] A Flemish and a Walloon 'Right-to-die society' were formed in the 1980s.

1990s' provided a stimulus for debate. Furthermore, developments in the Netherlands were followed closely, especially by the Flemish part of the country.

In 1992 the Belgian Medical Association adopted a new version of the Rules of Conduct for the medical profession.[xv] This code excludes active termination of life but also 'therapeutic stubbornness'.[xvi] By excluding the latter the Belgian Medical Association accepted abstaining from treatment even if this hastens death. However, this did not mean that the Belgian Medical Association was in favour of the principle of the autonomy of the patient: the Association had a negative view of advance directives, holding that a doctor is not obliged to comply with an advance refusal of treatment.

The middle of the 1990s showed a shift with respect to the process of legal change regarding euthanasia. In 1994 the Chair of the Medical Association in Ghent pleaded for research similar to that in the Netherlands.[xvii] However, the most important incentive for a change regarding self-determination with respect to the end of life came with the establishment of the Advisory Committee for Bioethics. In 1997, this committee delivered its first advice, which was on the desirability of legalising euthanasia. The advice consists of four different possibilities, some going further to legalise euthanasia than others.

In 1999, after the 'purple-green coalition' came to power, developments in Belgium picked up speed. This coalition, in which no Christian Democratic party was represented, made clear from the beginning that it would welcome bills on euthanasia. Shortly after the Government took office, members of the Senate submitted proposals based on the different options put forward by the Advisory Committee for Bioethics. The governing parties rather quickly arrived at a compromise proposal. The Government's proposal led not only to debate in Parliament but also to a more general public debate. In 2002 the enactment of the new law on euthanasia took place and in the same year for the first time a doctor was prosecuted for killing a patient at the patient's request.

Somewhat separately from the process of legal change regarding euthanasia, but at the same time, a process of legal change with respect to advance directives took place. In 2002 advance directives were legally recognised as a legal tool to secure patient self-determination.

[xv] Unlike the Dutch Medical Association, the Belgian Association is responsible for medical disciplinary law.

[xvi] Article 95 of the Code reads: 'The physician may not intentionally cause the death of one of his or her patients or help them to take their own life' (Adams,[2] p. 30).

[xvii] From earlier small-scale research it appeared that Belgian physicians did perform 'euthanasia' (De Groot,[9] p. 71). Research similar to the Dutch research was done in Flanders at the end of the 1990s. This research showed that Belgian doctors sometimes do terminate a patient's life.[10]

Denmark[xviii]

In the 1970s, the Danes discussed the 'right to a dignified death'.[xix] The debate was about the right to be protected from life-prolonging treatment and the right of the patient to be informed. In 1976 the association 'Mit Livtestamente' (my living will) was founded to fight for these rights. 'Mit Livtestamente' published forms which patients could use to describe their wishes concerning pain relief and refusal of treatment.[xx]

Advance directives concerning the ending of life were also debated in other circles. In 1976, the Director General of the National Board of Health stated that an advance directive might well be an important tool to help a doctor decide on medical treatment. The judicial authorities held the same view. At the same time, the National Board of Health stressed that abstaining from treatment and pain relief 'even though this has an unpremeditated effect might invoke a risk that death occurs slightly earlier' can be justified (Vestergaard,[12] p. 80).

In 1987, the Minister of Justice established a working group to look into whether advance directives should be legalised.[xxi] From the 1989 report it became clear that all members of the working group except the representatives of 'Mit Livtestamente' recommended only a modest change in law. They proposed to clarify the principle of informed consent and give it statutory status. However, a vast majority in Parliament supported the ideas of 'Mit Livtestamente'. In 1992, they enacted a set of provisions on aid in dying such as the duties of the physician in connection with advance directives as amendments to the Physicians' Act. 'Mit Livtestamente' dissolved as its mission was successfully completed.

In 1998, after a new report by the National Ethical Council, the provisions on informed consent were clarified and moved to a new, comprehensive Patients' Rights Act. Although the law allows a terminally ill patient to refuse

---

[xviii] Articles 239 and 240 of the Danish Criminal Code prohibit killing on request and assistance with suicide. The offence of Article 239 carries a maximum punishment of 3 years. The offence of Article 240 carries a fine or lenient imprisonment, but if the assistance is given out of selfish motives, the punishment is imprisonment up to 3 years.

[xix] This part is based on articles by Vestergard.[11,12] In Denmark there have been a few cases of termination of life in which relatives were involved. In two cases professionals were charged with killing on request. In 1974 a nurse was convicted and given 2 years on probation for ending the life of an almost completely paralysed patient at his request. Five years later a doctor was prosecuted for manslaughter after assisting a patient with acute leukaemia to die. The doctor was acquitted.

[xx] In a short time 25 000 members filled in a form although the legal status of such a document was not clear.

[xxi] The Danish public debate on a dignified death is embedded in a broader public debate on bioethical issues. Typical of the Danish debate on issues of health law is its public character. The Danish National Ethical Council not only advises but also initiates public debates. Characteristically, both doctors and patients participate in these debates and consensus leading to new law is an explicit aim (Rendtorff and Kemp[13], p. 163). The same authors conclude that there has been a shift in the Danish debate from a rather positivistic and pragmatic approach to regulating biomedical issues in a more moralistic way.

treatment which only postpones the moment of death, it does not provide for a right to refuse treatment if this refusal provokes a death that is not imminent. As before, the refusal of treatment can be set down in an advance directive. Both the Ministry of Health and the National Board of Health issued a form for advance directives. Patients have to send their filled-in form to the Living Will Data Bank and subsequently they will receive a receipt. Three weeks later the advance directive comes into effect. If a patient's condition is covered by the provisions in the law and the responsible physician is considering life-prolonging treatment, the physician is obliged to check with the data bank.[xxii] A doctor who treats a patient against his or her will can be prosecuted.[xxiii]

Euthanasia is not a subject of public debate in Denmark. Almost all of the 17 members of the Danish Ethical Council have recommended maintaining the prohibitions and looking for improvement of palliative care. Euthanasia is deemed inconsistent with human dignity, a 'death without care'. Furthermore, the Ethical Council is of the view that the possibility of euthanasia would weaken the prohibition of killing (Rendtorff and Kemp,[13] p. 169). No influential Danish politician and no political party or organisation campaigns for legalisation of euthanasia. Medical associations and nurses' organisations and representatives of denominations regularly speak out against euthanasia. In recent years no physician has been prosecuted for performing euthanasia.

CHANGES IN VALUE ORIENTATIONS[xxiv]

One explanation for these developments in patients' rights in some countries might be found in the opinions of the inhabitants of those countries. In his well-known books on value orientations Inglehart concludes that there is a correlation between prosperity and value orientation. People who grow up without a threat to their livelihood tend to think of values such as freedom, self-expression and improvement of the quality of life as more important than

---

[xxii] Hardly anything is known about the effectiveness of the law. In November 1999, 73 772 people had filed advance directives with the National Living Will Data Bank and on a daily basis some 10–20 people file advance directives. On a weekly basis, physicians contact the data bank only a few times.

[xxiii] The law states that 'an irreversibly dying patient may receive analgesic, or similar remedies, which are necessary to alleviate the patient's plight, even if that might effect an acceleration of the moment of death'. From a medical disciplinary law case, it became clear that to carry out an automatic and continuous increase in morphine medication is illegal. However, a vehement debate is going on about the exact boundaries of pain relief and about the possibility of professional guidelines on the issue.

[xxiv] Since the 1970s, data on values have been collected three times by the so-called European Values Study. Although the studies take a couple of years, I will refer to them as the study of 1980, the study of 1990 and the study of 2000. The findings from the second study – 1990 – are published in Inglehart et al;[14] the findings of the third study in Halman.[15] The results are recorded in different ways in the various books. In the last book on the findings[15] the means of the scores in countries are given. To make a comparison possible I asked WORC/EVS Tilburg University for the relevant means of the study of 1980 and 1990.

values such as social security and personal safety. Inglehart speaks about a shift from a 'materialistic value orientation' to a 'post-materialistic value orientation'.[16] A correlation between a growth in prosperity and a growth in the number of inhabitants that think of 'post-materialist values' as important has in fact been found in almost all European countries. In the early 1990s, the Netherlands and Denmark are special because in these two countries for the first time people with a 'post-materialistic value orientation' outnumber people with a 'materialistic value orientation'.[17]

In what follows I will limit the discussion to findings in the three European values studies about changes in values regarding self-determination with respect to one's body.[xxv] According to Elchardus et al the answers to questions on suicide, abortion, homosexuality, 'euthanasia' and divorce are important with respect to the value of 'bodily self-determination'.[18] The European values studies show that countries with a high score on post-materialism in general – the Netherlands and Denmark – are among the countries in which most people think of 'bodily self-determination' as important.[xxvi] Finland had a rather high score in the second study (1990)[xxvii] but in the third study (2000) the country was overtaken in many respects by other countries.[xxviii] The other

---

[xxv] The relevant questions asked are: 'Please tell me for each of the following statements whether you think it can always be justified, never be justified or something in between'. The researcher then shows words such as homosexuality, abortion, divorce, 'euthanasia' (defined as 'terminating the life of the incurable sick') and suicide.

[xxvi] Whenever the order between countries changes because of a decline in the mean I will mention this explicitly. Therefore with one exception the reader can take for granted that a change in the order of countries does not signify a decline in the mean. The exception concerns Denmark. In Denmark all the relevant figures of the second research are lower than those of the first one. However, in 2000 the Danes have a higher score than in the first study. The Netherlands has the highest score on homosexuality in all three surveys; with respect to suicide it was in third position in 1980 and in first position in 1990 and 2000; regarding 'euthanasia' in second position in 1980 and 1990 and in first position in 2000; with respect to abortion and divorce the country does not have a very high position: the score on abortion is fourth position in 1980, third in 1990 and fifth in 2000; with respect to divorce this is successively: ninth, third and fifth positions.

The Danes found themselves with respect to homosexuality in second position in 1980, third in 1990 and fourth in 2000. With respect to abortion the Danes moved from first position in 1980 to second position in 2000 (the Danish score in the 1990 research is not known); with respect to divorce they held second position in 1980 and 2000, and fifth in 1990; regarding 'euthanasia' they moved from first in 1980 to third in 1990 and second in 2000. The Danes score relatively low with respect to suicide (second in 1980, seventh in 1990 and eighth in 2000).

[xxvii] Figures from the study of 1980 do not exist for Finland.

[xxviii] In the second study (1990) the Finns had a high score on nearly all items: first on divorce, abortion and 'euthanasia'; second on suicide and sixth regarding homosexuality. From the figures of 2000 it is clear that the Finns are moving in a different direction from the inhabitants of most other European countries: With respect to divorce they held third position (a decline in the mean was found); regarding abortion fourth position (also with a declining mean); regarding 'euthanasia' seventh position; regarding suicide ninth position (a decline in the mean again) and regarding homosexuality sixth position.

countries in which self-determination around the end of life has found some recognition – Belgium, Spain and the UK – have a rather low score on all five questions. The conclusion must be that there is no direct connection between the legal recognition of advance directives and euthanasia on the one side and opinions concerning 'bodily self-determination' on the other. This conclusion is strengthened by the case of Sweden. Although Sweden has a high score on 'bodily self-determination',[xxix] neither advance directives nor euthanasia are legalised.

If we want to find indicators of the emergence of patients' rights with respect to the end of life, it seems obvious to look for them in the answers regarding 'euthanasia' and suicide. However, in doing so it must be noted that opinions about what is called 'euthanasia' in the European Values Study do not necessarily amount to opinions about intentionally ending a patient's life on request because the meaning of the word 'euthanasia' in the research is rather vague.[xxx] A similar remark has to be made in relation to opinions about suicide. Many people's opinions might be affected by whether they are thinking of young persons who impulsively end their life or elderly persons who after long deliberation decide that for them life has no value anymore. But the Values Study makes no such distinction.

A more precise look at the results shows that the Dutch have a high score in particular on homosexuality, suicide and 'euthanasia'. The Danes have a high score regarding all subjects except suicide. In 1990, the Finns had a high score on 'euthanasia' and suicide but in 2000 they only had a high score on two issues which at first sight have no relation with the legal recognition of individual rights of patients regarding the end of life (divorce and abortion). In 2000, Belgians had changed their opinions regarding 'euthanasia' and suicide. More Belgians than before think of these as permissible.[xxxi] In other words: the countries where advance directives are legalised had a high score on the permissibility of 'euthanasia' during the period of legalisation of advance treatment refusals. It seems that the answers regarding 'euthanasia'

[xxix] In 2000 the Swedes had the highest score on abortion and on divorce (with respect to abortion they held second position in 1980 and 1990; with respect to divorce they held third position in 1980 and second position in 1990). Also, on the other items the Swedes have a rather high score: second position with respect to homosexuality (in 1990 they held fourth position and in 1980 third position on this issue); third position regarding suicide (in 1990 the Swedes also held third position, in 1980 fourth position) and fourth position with respect to 'euthanasia' (in 1990 sixth position and in 1980 fifth position).

[xxx] In the European Values Study no distinction is made between actively ending life and shortening life by abstaining from treatment or as a side effect of pain relief. Furthermore, no distinction is made between termination of life on request and termination of life without an explicit request.

[xxxi] With respect to these two issues they are in fifth position in 2000; regarding 'euthanasia' this was already the case in 1990 whereas in 1980 they had had a rather low score. With respect to suicide the Belgians had a rather low score both in 1990 and in 1980. Regarding the other three issues the Belgians have a low score in the past and they still do.

in the European Values Study give an indication for the legal recognition of advance directives.

Furthermore, the results make clear that acceptance of 'euthanasia' has grown in all countries in the past decades. With respect to suicide such a trend is less visible. In some countries, in particular Denmark and Finland, fewer people than in the past consider suicide permissible. In other countries a (relatively) high score regarding 'euthanasia' goes together with a high score with respect to suicide. The Netherlands and Belgium, the two countries in which terminating a life on request has been legalised, are examples of this relationship. A difference between these two countries is that the Netherlands has had a high position regarding these two issues in all three surveys whereas Belgium has only had a high score in 2000 and even then it was lower than the Dutch score. A high score on both questions may be an indicator for the legalisation of euthanasia and assistance with suicide. Countries which have high scores on 'euthanasia' and suicide but in which termination of life on request has not yet been legalised are France,[xxxii] Sweden[xxxiii] and Luxembourg.[xxxiv]

POLITICAL OPPORTUNITIES

From the three descriptions given above, the processes of legal change appear to have been rather different in the Netherlands, Belgium and Denmark. In this part I try to answer the question whether, from the perspective of the political opportunity structure of the three countries, the different courses the legalisation process took were to be expected. I will look in particular at whether in the process of legal change, unexpected events occurred. Unexpected events are those that do not fit into the political structure. Political scientists[19] consider the following conditions as favouring the success of new social movements: the healing of former political dividing lines; a decentralised state; a strong civil society; a multi-party system; room for judicial activism; and a decisive establishment.

Whether new issues such as individual rights of patients enter the political agenda depends, among other things, on the healing of old dividing lines. The more that older divisive conflicts are healed, the more room there is for new issues on the political agenda and the more the competition of political parties will be directed toward such new issues. In Denmark and the Netherlands old

---

[xxxii] The French were in second position on suicide in 1980, third in 1990 and again second in 2000. With respect to 'euthanasia' the French were twice in fourth position and the last time in third place.

[xxxiii] With respect to 'euthanasia' the Swedes had a fifth, a sixth and a fourth position; regarding suicide they were twice in fourth position and once in third.

[xxxiv] We do not know in which directions the inhabitants of Luxembourg are moving because they were not involved in the studies of 1980 and 1990. In 2000 the Luxembourgers had a score between the Belgians and the Dutch on most issues. This does not hold for the question on 'euthanasia'. On this issue they had a lower score than the Belgians (sixth position).

dividing lines over the distribution of wealth and religion have not played an important role for many years. Until recently Belgium was seriously divided by political and regional oppositions between Flemings and Walloons and the country was strongly segregated. It is only since the 1990s that these deep-seated conflicts have subsided.

Centralised states are often considered unconducive to new social movements. In a central state such a movement has to manifest itself in national politics and the national level is supposed to be less sensitive to changes in societal opinions. Furthermore, if a movement fails on the national level hardly any opportunity on a lower level is left open. The Netherlands and Denmark are both centralised states and recognition of the individual rights of patients had to take place in parliament. Probably the length of the processes of legal change is influenced by this characteristic. However, this feature was not decisive in the sense that it made change impossible. The same goes for Belgium. Although a federal state, the Belgian legalisation of patients' rights had to be realised at the national level.[xxxv]

A well-developed civil society capable of bringing pressure to bear on political institutions is supposed to be favourable to new social movements. In this regard, we can distinguish three types of countries in Europe. The Netherlands and the Scandinavian countries are characterised by a highly organised civil society. On the other side we see France and the southern-European countries which have a low level of organisation among the public. Other West European countries such as Belgium are somewhere in between. Furthermore, it seems to be important what kinds of organisations attract people. This requires us to distinguish between Denmark, the Netherlands and Belgium. Denmark and Belgium are countries in which traditional organisations such as political parties, trade unions and denominations have many members, whereas other organisations are not strongly developed.[20] In the Netherlands, by contrast, relatively few people are members of traditional organisations. The country is characterised by a large sector of other non-governmental organisations such as environmental organisations, human rights organisations and patients' organisations.[xxxvi] In countries in which a (forceful) civil society consists of traditional organisations the call for individual rights of patients and even more so the call for the legal possibility of euthanasia might not find an audience because traditional organisations aim at other goals or have strong objections to self-determination with respect to the end of life (this applies for many denominations).

[xxxv] It might be that the rather unexpected legalisation of advance directives in Spain resulted from the advantages of decentralisation. The legalisation started in semi-autonomous parts of the country and was only in a later phase taken over by the Spanish Government.

[xxxvi] The difference between the Netherlands and Belgium can be illustrated by the membership figures of right-to-die-societies. In 1997 the Flemish organisation 'Recht op waardig sterven' [right to a dignified death] had 2700 members whereas the Dutch Association for Voluntary Euthanasia had 95 000 members (population figures: Flanders roughly 5 000 000; the Netherlands roughly 16 000 000).

Political scientists suggest furthermore that the accessibility of the political system for new issues such as individual rights of patients is determined by the relation between the legislative power and the executive power. If parliament has a strong position, then organised citizens have more opportunities to influence decisions. Political parties represented in parliament are considered more sensitive to the views of 'outsiders' than the legislative and the judiciary. This is even more the case if many parties are represented in parliament. The Netherlands, Belgium and Denmark are countries in which many parties bid for the goodwill of the voters and therefore countries in which the voters have maximum chance to make their voice heard.

Arguably, the possibility of legal development by judicial decision is favourable for political change in the domain of individual rights. The most obvious example of this is the case of the legalisation of abortion by the Supreme Court of the USA (*Roe v Wade* 410 US 113 (1973)). With respect to this characteristic, common law countries such as the United Kingdom are thought to offer greater opportunities than countries on the European continent.[xxxvii] However, in the Netherlands the judges and the prosecuting authorities played a leading role in the process of legal change with respect to euthanasia. The Dutch process is special in two respects. First, perhaps surprisingly, Dutch judges appeared to be receptive to new issues. Secondly, Dutch prosecuting authorities did use the prosecution of doctors to explore the boundaries of the law. In hardly any other country in the world is there case law regarding termination of life by doctors. The exceptional position of the Netherlands in this regard is striking because the Dutch prosecuting authorities are known for their reluctance to prosecute.

The absence of prosecutions in other countries is not a result of an absence of euthanasia. It is known that not only Dutch and Belgian doctors but also Danish doctors perform euthanasia.[22] However, where the Dutch prosecuting authorities, subject to directions of the Minister of Justice, have actively sought to accomplish legal developments and clarification by bringing prosecutions the prosecuting authorities of other countries have thought it wise not to bring known cases to court.[xxxviii]

A last important characteristic of political structure, as far as the capacity to embrace a new social movement is concerned, is the decisiveness of the decision-making process. Political scientists who study new social movements suggest that political processes in multi-party systems last longer and therefore run the risk that politicians lose interest. The Netherlands, Belgium and Denmark have multi-party systems. In the Netherlands as well as in

---

[xxxvii] In the UK advance directives have achieved legal recognition in this way.[21]

[xxxviii] It is thus not the Dutch prosecuting authorities who have most vigorously used their discretion not to prosecute but those of other countries. The Belgian and Danish solution of simply not prosecuting doctors has been defended in the Netherlands too. In the first case that came to the Supreme Court the Procurator-General Remmelink was of the opinion that prosecutorial discretion not to prosecute offers an adequate way of dealing with 'honourable' doctors.

Denmark the processes of legal change are very long. In the Netherlands it took almost twenty years before the change in law offered by judges was enacted into law by Parliament. The legalisation of advance directives took more than a decade. In Denmark we see the same thing: a lengthy process of legal change. However, the case of Belgium shows us that a short period is possible.

I conclude that the enactment of advance directives in the Netherlands and Denmark took place in the way that is to be expected from the political structure of the two countries. The issue lost its contentious overtones and the favourable characteristics of a multi-party system in a country with a strong civil society are clearly recognisable.

A similarity between Belgium and the Netherlands with respect to euthanasia and the processes of legal change is the absence in the Government of Christian Democrats at the time of the enactment. In the Netherlands their absence did not lead immediately to a change in law; in Belgium it did. The Belgian case shows that even in a multi-party system an adroit coalition can radically change the whole field of patients' rights.

An important difference between Belgium and the Netherlands is that the legalisation of euthanasia in Belgium forms the starting point of a debate whereas in the Netherlands the legalisation was one of the last phases of the process of legal change. As seen, in the Netherlands the judiciary played a decisive role. Legalising an issue by the judicial process is only possible if two conditions are met. First, the prosecuting authorities have to be willing to prosecute and secondly, judges have to be willing to use the legal room for manoeuvre offered by doctrines such as the defence of justification.[xxxix]

In the Netherlands it was not only the judiciary but also the medical association that was active. From what I have described above it is clear that Dutch civil society is rather special because of its strength and because it consists of many non-traditional organisations. It is possible that only in a country with such a civil society would a medical association take a position such as the KNMG (Royal Dutch Medical Association) did. On the other hand, the Belgians show that the collaboration of a medical association is not a necessary condition for the legalisation of euthanasia.

TO CONCLUDE

I have tried above to answer the question why euthanasia has been legalised in some countries and not in others in two different ways. It is obvious that this quest for explanation does not lead to a firm conclusion.

[xxxix] Necessity, the justification accepted in the Netherlands, is in principle on hand in other countries. Already in 1957 Glanville Williams pointed to this justification in relation with euthanasia. However he cleverly added that he did not expect British judges to follow this road (Glanville Williams,[23] p. 322). In 1996 Velaers predicted the same for Belgian judges (Velaers,[24] p. 554).

The European Values Study shows that the Netherlands is special because 'bodily self-determination', in particular with respect to shortening and termination of life, has been seen as permissible for many years. Denmark and Belgium do not share this characteristic. From the discussion of the results of the value studies it is furthermore clear that opinions regarding 'euthanasia' might be an indicator for the legalisation of advance directives refusing treatment.

The Danish and Dutch processes of legal change regarding advance directives show that the legalisation of advance directives does not pose major political problems. It is to be expected that countries which produce similar value indicators over a considerable period will undergo the same processes of legal change. France and Sweden are countries that come into mind.

If a high position on both 'euthanasia' and suicide were an indication for the legalisation of euthanasia, then this would have been expected in France and Sweden, and not in Belgium or Denmark. From the Belgian example it becomes clear that a long-term high score regarding the permissibility of euthanasia and suicide is not a necessary condition for the enactment of euthanasia. Probably its proximity to the Netherlands played a more important role in the Belgian change of law than the long-term development of value orientations.[xl] If this surmise is true then a change of law in Luxembourg would not come as a big surprise.

The only marked similarity between the Dutch and the Belgian processes of legal change with respect to euthanasia lies in the formal characteristic that in both countries there was a divergence from what was to be expected from the political opportunity structure. In the Netherlands the judiciary played an unusually active role and in Belgium the new coalition showed a decisiveness that is unusual in a consensual state. In the near future more research must be done to discover under which conditions such deviation from the usual way of coping can be expected.

Acknowledgements

A Dutch version of the argument is also available. (Weyers, H. Wettelijke erkenning van het recht om te sterven. In: Adams M, Griffiths J, den Hartogh G Euthanasie. Nieuwe Knelpunten in een voorgezette discussie. Kampen: Kok 2003: 19–37.)

References

1. Adams M. Recht en ethiek in een plurale en democratische samenleving: casus België. Nederlands Tijdschrift voor Rechtsfilosofie en Rechtstheorie 2000; 29:105–112.
2. Adams M. Euthanasia: the process of legal change in Belgium. Reflections on the parliamentary debate. In: Klijn A, Otlowski M , Trappenburg M, eds. Regulating physician-negotiated death. s-Gravenhage: Elsevier; 2001:29–48.

[xl] The Values Study of 2000 showed, however, that the Belgian Government had the right intuition regarding changed public opinion on 'euthanasia' and suicide.

3. Adams M, Geudens G. De regulering van euthanasie in België. Principiële beschouwingen naar aanleiding van een aantal recente wetsvoorstellen. Rechtskundig weekblad 1999-2000; 63:793–818.

4. Griffiths J, Bood A, Weyers H. Euthanasia and law in the Netherlands. Amsterdam: Amsterdam University Press; 1998.

5. Kennedy J. Een weloverwogen dood. Euthanasie in Nederland. Amsterdam: Bert Bakker; 2002.

6. Weyers H. Euthanasie: het proces van rechtsverandering. Amsterdam: Amsterdam University Press; 2004.

7. Lijphart A. Patterns of democracy. Government forms and performance in thirty-six countries. New Haven and London: Yale University Press; 1999:42–45.

8. Witte E. Twintig jaar politieke strijd rond de abortuswetgeving in België (1970–1990). Res Publica 1990; 32:427–488.

9. De Groot E. Leven tot in de dood. Omtrent euthanasie. Brussels: VUB Press; 1997.

10. Deliens L, Mortier F, Bilsen J, et al. End-of-life decisions in medical practice in Flanders, Belgium: a nationwide survey. Lancet 2000; 356:1806–1811.

11. Vestergaard J. Medical aid in dying under Danish law: mainly regarding living wills and other forms of renouncing life-prolonging treatment. European Journal of Health Law 2000; 7:405–426

12. Vestergaard J. Danish law concerning medical aid in dying. In: Dameno R, Autodeterminarsi nonostante. Genoa: Guerini e associati; 2002:77–104.

13. Rendtorff JD, Kemp P. Basic ethical principles in European bioethics and biolaw. Vol. I Autonomy, dignity, integrity and vulnerability. Barcelona; 2000.

14. Inglehart R, Basañez M, Moreno A. Human values and beliefs: A cross-cultural sourcebook. Political, religious, sexual and economic norms in 43 societies: findings from 1990–1993 world values survey. Ann Arbor: University of Michigan Press; 1998.

15. Halman L. The European Values Study: a third wave. Source book of the 1990/2000 European values study surveys. Tilburg: WORC; 2001.

16. Inglehart R. The silent revolution. Princeton: Princeton University Press; 1977:28.

17. Inglehart R. Modernization and postmodernization. Cultural, economic and political change in 43 societies. Princeton: Princeton University Press; 1997:139.

18. Elchardus M, Chaumont J-M, Lauwers S. Morele onderzekerheid en nieuwe degelijkheid. In: Dobbelaere K et al. Verloren zekerheid. De Belgen en hun waarden, overtuigingen en houdingen. Lannoo, Tielt 1992: 153–192, at 154–155.

19. Duyvendak J W, van der Heiden H A, Koppmans R, Wijmans L. Tussen verbeeld-ing en macht. 25 jaar nieuwe sociale bewegingen in Nederland, Amsterdam: SUA; 1992.

20. Sociaal Cultureel Planbureau. Sociaal en cultureel rapport 2000. The Hague: Nederland in Europa; 2000:139–140.

21. Faden RR, Beauchamp TL. A history and theory of informed consent. New York and Oxford: Oxford University Press; 1986.

22. Folker AP, Holtug N, Jensen AB. et al. Experiences and attitudes towards end-of-life decisions amongst Danish physicians. Bioethics 1996; 10:233–249.

23. Williams G. The sanctity of life and the criminal law. New York: Alfred A. Knopf; 1957.

24. Velaers J. Het leven, de dood en de grondrechten. Juridische beschouwingen over zelfdoding en euthanasie. In: Velaers J, ed. Over zichzelf beschikken? Juridische en ethische bijdragen over het leven, het lichaam en de dood. Antwerp: MAKLU; 1996:469–755.

Chapter 14

Regulating active voluntary euthanasia: what can England and Wales learn from Belgium and the Netherlands?[i]

Samantha Halliday

CHAPTER CONTENTS

Introduction   269
Why legislation legalising AVE
   is desirable in England
   and Wales   270
The Dutch law   274
The due care criteria   276
The notification
   requirement   281
The Belgian law   283
The conditions for lawful
   euthanasia   285
The notification
   requirement   289
What can England and
   Wales learn from the
   Netherlands and
   Belgium?   290

The absolute requirement of a
   voluntary, informed request
   for termination of life   291
The patient must be
   experiencing unbearable
   suffering without prospect
   of improvement   294
Consultation requirements   295
The requirement of due
   care   296
Review committees and the
   notification requirement   296
Conscientious objection   298
The need for an investment
   in palliative care   298
Conclusion   298
References   299

INTRODUCTION

The process of dying has become medicalised to the extent that death is now often the result of human choice – the choice to withhold or withdraw medical treatment; to administer pain-relieving drugs in order to alleviate suffering, in the knowledge that by so doing the patient's death is likely to be hastened; or indeed to actively cause death. The law in England and Wales, the Netherlands and Belgium recognises that a competent patient

---

[i] A version of this paper was presented to the SLSA Annual Conference 2003 at Nottingham Trent University. Many thanks to the participants at that event for their helpful comments.

has the right to refuse medical treatment, even life-sustaining treatment[ii] and that doctors acting in contravention of that refusal will commit a trespass to the person.[iii] Similarly, each of the jurisdictions accepts that doctors may lawfully withhold and/or withdraw life-sustaining medical treatment and even hasten death as an unintended consequence of pain relief. However, whilst in English law the active termination of life at the patient's request will constitute murder, both the Dutch and the Belgian Parliaments have recently enacted legislation enabling doctors to perform active voluntary euthanasia (AVE) in certain circumstances without fear of prosecution.

Although the performance of euthanasia[iv] is permissible in both jurisdictions, significant differences exist between the two pieces of legislation, not least that whilst the Belgian law decriminalises the performance of euthanasia by a doctor, the Dutch law merely exempts doctors from criminal liability. This chapter will briefly outline the primary reasons why similar legislation legalising euthanasia in England and Wales is desirable, before focusing upon the regulatory approaches adopted by the Dutch and Belgian Acts. Whilst it is not suggested that either Act could be imported wholesale into English law, not least because both countries have different legal systems and legal cultures from that of England and Wales, the final section of this chapter will consider the safeguards that should be part of any legislation seeking to legalise AVE, considering what can be learnt from the Dutch and Belgian experiences.

WHY LEGISLATION LEGALISING AVE IS DESIRABLE IN ENGLAND AND WALES

As a direct result of improvements in medical science and increasing therapeutic possibilities people are living longer. However, this increased longevity is not necessarily a benefit to the affected individual; indeed it may be death, rather than life, that is being prolonged. As Justice Scalia recognised in the case of *Cruzan v Director, Missouri Department of Health*, science is making continu-

---

[ii] In *Re T. (Adult: Refusal of Treatment)* [1993] Fam. 95, per Lord Donaldson MR at 102; *Airedale NHS Trust v Bland*, [1993] AC 789, per Lord Keith at 857; *St George's Healthcare NHS Trust v S* [1998] 3 All ER 673, per Judge LJ at 685; *Re MB (Medical Treatment)* [1997] 2 FLR 426, per Butler-Sloss LJ at 432; Article 450 Dutch Civil Code; Article 8 §4 Belgian Law Relating to the Rights of the Patient, 2002; Article 5 Convention for the Protection of Human Rights and Dignity of the Human Being with Regard to the Application of Biology and Medicine: Convention on Human Rights and Biomedicine (Oviedo, 4 April 1997).

[iii] In *Re T. (Adult: Refusal of Treatment)*, per Lord Donaldson MR at 102; *Airedale NHS Trust v Bland*, per Lord Mustill at 891; *B v An NHS Hospital Trust* [2002] 2 All ER 449. Moreover, treatment given in contravention of a valid refusal will constitute a breach of Art. 8 ECHR (the right to respect for private and family life), *X v Austria* (1980) 18 DR 154.

[iv] Throughout this chapter when reference to the Dutch and Belgian law is made, 'euthanasia' will be used in the Dutch/Belgian sense, that is in relation to the active termination of an individual's life at her request, categorised as AVE in the Anglo-American literature.

ous strides in keeping 'the human body alive for longer than any reasonable person would want to inhabit it' (110 S Ct 2841 (1990), at 2859, US Supreme Court). The increasing emphasis placed upon autonomy, coupled with the decreasing influence of the church in what is now an essentially secular society, has led to the recognition of the significance of the patient's quality of life. Although in its traditional form the sanctity of life doctrine suggests that *all* life is inherently valuable, it has long been accepted that this principle is not absolute and the contemporary view of the doctrine stresses the importance of the *quality* rather than the *quantity* of life that may be preserved. Therefore, there is increasing acceptance of the view that biological life (what the House of Lords referred to as existence in *Bland*[v]) is not as important as the ability to pursue a biographical life, a life where the patient retains the ability to experience her[vi] life with what she perceives to be an acceptable quality of life.

In England and Wales AVE will constitute murder, with the attendant mandatory life sentence; as Lord Goff stressed in *Bland*, 'Euthanasia is not lawful at common law'.[vii] The courts have attempted to mitigate the harshness of this rule by recognising that life-prolonging medical treatment may legitimately be withheld and/or withdrawn (so-called passive euthanasia) from a patient in accordance with her best interests.[viii] However, this crucial distinction between killing and allowing to die has been largely discredited on the basis that it is illogical and that acts and omissions are morally equivalent.[ix,1,2] Indeed, as Lord Mustill acknowledged in *Bland*, the categorisation of the withdrawal of artificial nutrition and hydration, undertaken with the aim of terminating the patient's life, as an omission and thus as lawful, as distinct from an unlawful active step taken with the aim of terminating the patient's life, has left the law 'morally and intellectually misshapen'.[x]

Another mechanism adopted by the courts in their attempt to allow socially acceptable behaviour to take place within the confines of the law is the doctrine of double effect, which entails a distinction being drawn between foreseeing an undesirable outcome and intending it. The courts have accepted that this doctrine enables a doctor to give a patient pain-relieving medication with the intention of relieving her pain, despite recognising that it is also likely to hasten her death.[xi] The application of the doctrine relies upon the fact that although the doctor foresees death as the likely result of increasing doses of pain relief (the unintended consequence of the medication), she only intends to relieve pain (the good effect of the medication).

---

[v] *Airedale NHS Trust v Bland;* see, for example, per Lord Keith, at 856.

[vi] The use of feminine pronouns in this chapter is intended to encompass both genders.

[vii] *Airedale NHS Trust v Bland* [1993] AC 789, at 865.

[viii] *Airedale NHS Trust v Bland* [1993] AC 789, per Lord Goff at 868.

[ix] *Airedale NHS Trust v Bland* [1993] AC 789, per Lord Goff at 865; per Lord Mustill at 887; and per Lord Browne-Wilkinson at 885.

[x] *Airedale NHS Trust v Bland* [1993] AC 789, per Lord Goff at 887.

[xi] *Airedale NHS Trust v Bland* [1993] AC 789, per Lord Goff at 868; *Re J (A Minor) (Wardship: Medical Treatment)* [1991] Fam 33, per Lord Donaldson at 46; *R v Adams* H. Palmer, 'Dr Adams' Trial for Murder' [1957] Crim LR 365, per Devlin J.

However, the tenability of the doctrine was wholly undermined by the House of Lords' decision in *R v Woollin* [1999] 1 AC 82, which conflated foresight with intention. Lord Steyn stated that:

> 'Where a man realises that it is for all practical purposes inevitable that his actions will result in death or serious harm, the inference may be irresistible that he intended that result, however little he may have desired or wished it to happen.' ([1999] 1AC 82, at 93)

Therefore, it would appear that by foreseeing death as the likely effect of the medication, the doctor may be taken to have intended that result and would thus have the necessary *mens rea* for murder. However, as Ashworth has pointed out, Lord Steyn stipulated that the inference of intention *may* be irresistible; thus he has argued that 'if the courts are only "entitled" to find intention in these cases, then they might lawfully decide not to find intention despite foresight of virtual certainty'.[3] Moreover, whilst it has been suggested that doctors are equally subject to the same law as everyone else in relation to murder,[xii] it may be possible for the courts to formulate a medical exception to the test set out in *Woollin*. Thus for example in *Re A* Brooke LJ suggested that the extended meaning of intention provided by the House of Lords in *Woollin* was inappropriate when considering whether the separation of the conjoined twins constituted intentional killing of Mary (*Re A (Children) (Conjoined Twins: Surgical Separation)* [2001] Fam 147, at 238). A similar distinction has been drawn in relation to non-treatment decisions such as the turning off of a life-support machine. In *Bland* Lord Goff recognised that whilst such an action might be lawful if performed by a doctor in accordance with the patient's best interests, it would be murder if a non-doctor were to perform the same action as that 'interloper' would actively intervene 'to stop the doctor from prolonging the patient's life, and such conduct cannot possibly be categorised as an omission' ([1993] AC 789, at 866). Thus it may be possible for the court to formulate a medical exception to the extension of the meaning of intention, but until that is done, considerable uncertainty exists about whether the doctrine of double effect can still apply to doctors administering pain relief with the intention of relieving pain, but in the knowledge that death is likely to be hastened thereby.[xiii]

More than a decade ago Lord Mustill pointed to the need for legislation relating to euthanasia, stating:

> 'The whole matter cries out for exploration in depth by Parliament and then for the establishment by legislation not only of a new set of ethically and intellectually consistent rules, distinct from the general criminal law, but also of a sound procedural framework within which the rules can be applied to individual cases. The rapid advancement of medical technology makes this an ever more urgent task and I venture to hope that Parliament will soon take it in hand.' ([1993] AC 789, at 891)

[xii] See for example *R v Arthur* (1981) 12 BMLR 1.
[xiii] For an excellent discussion of the impact of *Woollin* see Williams.[4]

Similarly, in *R (Pretty) v Director of Public Prosecutions* [2002] 1 AC 800, the House of Lords reiterated that any repeal of the prohibition of assisted suicide should be undertaken by the legislature rather than by judicial creativity.[xiv] However, as these two cases demonstrate, the competent terminally ill patient is treated with less respect than the incompetent patient suffering no pain and with no real likelihood of imminent death. Whilst Pretty could make an autonomous choice that she wanted to die, Bland could not make the same choice, yet his existence was deemed futile[5] and medical treatment was withdrawn leading to his death. By contrast, Pretty was condemned to die in exactly the way she had feared due to a prohibition of assisted suicide.[xv]

Following *Bland* the Walton Committee rejected the proposal to create a separate offence of mercy killing, such as that found in the Dutch Penal Code (Article 293), to distinguish between murder and AVE. However, it did suggest that the mandatory life sentence for murder should be abolished in order to introduce some flexibility into sentencing so that account could be taken of the defendant's motive and the circumstances of the case.[7] Nevertheless the Government rejected this recommendation[8] and the courts have continued to rely upon the dubious distinction between killing and allowing to die and the doctrine of double effect in order to mitigate the harshness of the law.

Nevertheless, there is some evidence that AVE does take place in England and Wales, albeit without the safeguards set out in the Dutch and Belgian Acts.[xvi] Therefore, it is argued that the maintenance of an absolute legal prohibition of AVE and assisted suicide does not constitute effective control; it merely forces euthanasia underground so that it takes place in an unregulated manner without supervision or safeguards.[xvii,11,12] The resulting semi-clandestine practice of euthanasia leads to the risk of idiosyncratic decision-making without accountability. As Otlowski has persuasively argued, 'This approach to euthanasia appears to create an environment where unauthorised practices, performed other than at the explicit request of the patient flourish.'[14]

Keown has argued that many criminal laws are regularly broken, but that this does not constitute a good reason for repealing the laws that are being so contravened.[15] Whilst it is suggested that he is correct in arguing that rape should continue to be prohibited, despite its all too frequent commission, that does not mean that the same principle should apply to the legalisation of AVE. Unlike rape, AVE enjoys a significant amount of public support[xviii] and

---

[xiv] [2002] 1 AC 800, per Lord Steyn at 834; per Lord Hobhouse at 852.

[xv] See also M. Freeman,[6] at 253–4.

[xvi] See, for example, Ward and Tate,[9] reporting that 12% of the surveyed GPs and consultants who had received a request for AVE had complied with that request. Recently Biggs[10] estimated that at least 18 000 terminally ill people are helped to die by doctors every year. However, it should be noted that these figures are likely to include non-treatment decisions and cases where death is hastened as a by-product of pain relief.

[xvii] For an excellent discussion of the Australian experience, where AVE also constitutes murder, see R. Magnusson.[13]

[xviii] For example during the second reading of his Bill, Lord Joffe cited public opinion surveys showing that more than 80% of the general public support medical assistance in dying for the terminally ill.[16]

thus it is argued that when society has evolved to the extent that prohibited conduct is regarded as desirable, the law should be changed to reflect social reality. Therefore, it is submitted that contrary to suggestions that legalising AVE would lead to involuntary euthanasia,[xix] the absolute prohibition of AVE provides greater scope for abuse, scope that could be minimised if a legislative framework for the performance of AVE were to be introduced, bringing with it much needed transparency in medical decision-making at the end of life. Moreover, it is unknown how often passive euthanasia is performed without the knowledge or consent of the patient, but the introduction of legislation to regulate AVE would emphasise the fundamental importance of the patient's request for euthanasia, reinforcing the prohibition of involuntary euthanasia.

As Lord Hobhouse recognised in *Pretty*, if the prohibition of assisted suicide (and it is argued here also AVE) is to be repealed, 'suitable safeguards of an appropriate rigour and specificity' must be included ([2002] 1 AC 800, at 853). Therefore the remainder of this chapter will consider the safeguards contained in the Dutch and Belgian Acts, considering what England and Wales could learn from both pieces of legislation.

THE DUTCH LAW

Unlike the law in England and Wales, the Dutch Penal Code distinguishes between killing upon request (Article 293 Penal Code) and murder (Article 289 Penal Code). Prior to amendment by the 2001 Act,[xx] Article 293 stated:

'A person who takes the life of another person at that other person's express and earnest request is liable to a term of imprisonment of not more than twelve years or a fine of the fifth category.'

By contrast the penalty for murder (Article 289 Penal Code) is a term of imprisonment of not more than twenty years or a fifth category fine. In 1985 the State Commission on Euthanasia drew explicitly upon Article 289 in defining euthanasia as 'intentionally terminating another person's life at the person's request'.[18, xxi] As this definition of euthanasia makes clear, the Dutch concept of euthanasia is limited to what Anglo-American jurisprudence would term AVE. Thus in the Dutch sense of the word, euthanasia requires the request of the individual concerned and entails an active, intentional termination of the individual's life rather than the withdrawal/withholding of medical treatment or the use of pain-relieving drugs that might hasten death. Furthermore, in both the Netherlands and England and Wales, assisting suicide is a crime; however, whereas such assistance may result in imprisonment for up to 14 years in England and Wales (Suicide Act 1961, s.2), in the

---

[xix] The empirical slippery slope argument, see for example Keown.[17]
[xx] Termination of Life on Request and Assisted Suicide (Review Procedures) Act 2001.
[xxi] This definition has been adopted by the Dutch courts, the medical profession and the legislature.

Netherlands the penalty is much more moderate, consisting of a maximum term of three years imprisonment or a fine (Article 294 Penal Code).

Thus in both jurisdictions, the performance of AVE and the assistance of suicide will constitute a crime. Nevertheless, in contrast to the situation in England and Wales, for more than thirty years Dutch doctors have been able to actively terminate life, at the individual's request, or to assist suicide, without incurring a criminal penalty by relying upon the justification of necessity (*overmacht*, Article 40 Penal Code).[xxii] The Supreme Court held that a doctor could rely upon the justification in cases where responsible medical opinion would consider her to be in a situation of necessity, due to the conflict between her duty to preserve life and her duty to do everything possible to relieve her patient's unbearable and hopeless suffering (*Chabot* case, *Nederlandse Jurisprudentie* 1994, no. 656 (Supreme Court), at 3154). In a series of cases the Dutch courts set out the criteria which would allow a doctor to rely on the justification of necessity and these criteria were developed further by the KNMG[xxiii] in their guidelines for careful practice. Indeed, as Griffiths has argued, the KNMG was instrumental in the development of the criteria for permissible euthanasia and physician-assisted suicide (PAS) and in establishing a notification procedure.[19] The Dutch Termination of Life on Request and Assisted Suicide (Review Procedures) Act 2001 effectively codified the most important requirements set out in the existing guidance and case law.[xxiv]

The 2001 Act did not legalise either euthanasia or PAS – both remain crimes, subject to the same penalties as mentioned above. Nevertheless, the Act did amend the Penal Code so that a doctor who fulfils the due care criteria and complies with the notification procedure will be exempt from criminal liability, Article 20, obviating the need for reliance upon the justification of necessity. However, it should be noted that only doctors are exempt from criminal liability and that this exemption does not apply to associated healthcare professionals, including nurses,[xxv] or suicide counsellors.[xxvi]

[xxii] *Schoonheim* case, *Nederlandse Jurisprudentie* 1985, no. 106 (Hoge Raad). Whilst it had been suggested that the medical exception might be applied in cases of euthanasia and assisted suicide so that doctors could not be guilty of either offence, the Supreme Court held that this defence could not succeed in *Pols* (*Nederlandse Jurisprudentie* 1987, no. 607 (Hoge Raad)). Similarly the defence of 'absence of substantial violation of the law' was rejected in *Wertheim* (*Nederlandse Jurisprudentie* 1982, no. 63 (District Court of Rotterdam)), confirmed by the Supreme Court in *Schoonheim*. Thus, the only justification open to a doctor who had performed euthanasia or assisted a suicide was held to be that of necessity.

[xxiii] *Koninklijke Nederlandsche Maatschappij tot bevordering der Geneeskunst*, the Royal Dutch Medical Association.

[xxiv] Whilst a detailed examination of the development of these requirements falls outside the scope of this chapter, relevant case law will be considered in relation to the operation of the current Act. For an excellent discussion of the case law and professional guidelines leading up to the Act see Griffiths.[20]

[xxv] See, for example, *Nederlandse Jurisprudentie* 1996, no. 61 where the Leeuwarden Court of Appeals held that the justification of necessity could only apply to doctors.

[xxvi] See for example the case of Willem Muns, reported in Henley.[21]

The due care criteria

The due care criteria are set out in Article 2 and comprise a mixture of substantive and procedural rules. The first requirement is that the doctor must be satisfied that the patient has made a voluntary and carefully considered request.[xxvii] This request is clearly the key requirement, as without it the doctor would be liable to prosecution for murder; thus the Act is clearly limited to AVE and PAS. Significantly, unlike the KNMG guidance (1995)[22] the Act does not contain an explicit requirement that the request is repeated and durable, nor is a statutory cooling-off period established. However, the report submitted by the doctor after the termination of life must specifically state when the patient first requested euthanasia and when she repeated her request. Thus there is a presumption that more than one request should be made and that a reasonable amount of time for reflection must pass before the euthanasia is performed. Nevertheless, as the Act requires only *a* request, the fact that it had not been repeated would not in itself mean that the doctor had not complied with the due care criteria and thus forfeited the statutory exemption from criminal liability; it might, however, lead to disciplinary action. The lack of a cooling-off period takes account of the situation where the patient is expected to die shortly and where it would be impractical to deny that patient assistance on the basis that she must wait until it can be shown that her request is truly durable. Nevertheless, it is clear that the request cannot simply reflect a mere fleeting desire.[23] More surprisingly the Act does not require a written request, despite the KNMG's recommendation that the patient's request should be written, or where that is impossible, that the oral request should be recorded. However, the Regional Review Committees' Annual Report for 2002 stressed that wherever possible the patient should submit a written request for euthanasia.[24]

Whilst the KNMG's guidance and the majority of the case law preceding the Act related to adult patients, the Act enables minors to request euthanasia in certain circumstances. In its original formulation the Bill contained a provision which followed the example of other Dutch Acts relating to consent to medical treatment, allowing a minor over the age of 11, who is capable of making a reasonable appraisal of her own interests (similar to the concept of *Gillick*-competence), to request euthanasia or PAS without parental consent.[xxviii] However, this clause proved to be too controversial and was withdrawn. Nevertheless, the Act does enable a minor to request the termination of her life from the age of 16, provided that she is deemed capable of making a reasonable appraisal of her own interests and her parents or guardian are consulted, although they are not required to give their consent, Article 2(3). In relation to younger children, Article 2(4) allows minors between the ages of 12 and 16 to request termination of their lives, provided

---

[xxvii] Cf. the wording of Article 293(1) Penal Code, which refers to the individual's 'express and earnest request'.
[xxviii] Clause 2(4), TK 1998–1999, 26691 no. 2 at 2.

that their parents/guardian consent. Any doctor who terminated such a minor's life without such consent, or who terminated the life of a minor under the age of 12, could not comply with the due care criteria because such minors lack the capacity to make an effective request and the Act does not empower anybody else to make a request on their behalf. In such cases the doctor would have to rely on the justification of necessity as in the case of *Prins* (*Nederlandse Jurisprudentie* 1996, no. 113), where the doctor successfully relied upon the justification after terminating the life of a young baby at her parents' request.

Moreover, the Act explicitly recognises the concept of precedent autonomy, providing that a competent patient of 16 and over can execute an advance euthanasia directive, requesting that her life be terminated in specified circumstances if she becomes incompetent, Article 2(2). Thus the Act recognises the validity of an anticipatory request for euthanasia or PAS, although just as in the case of a contemporaneous request, the doctor is under no duty to accede to that request. However, Article 2(2) states that the due care criteria are equally applicable to anticipatory and contemporaneous requests and it is difficult to see how the doctor can assure himself that the patient's request was voluntary and well considered in the former situation, unless the doctor was involved in the drafting of the directive and the patient was able to foresee how her condition would develop in the future with some degree of accuracy. Thus the Regional Review Committee's 2002 Annual Report stressed the need for doctors and patients to discuss the content and implications of anticipatory requests in good time.[25]

It is also remarkable that there is no requirement that the anticipatory request be renewed or confirmed after a lapse of time. Thus it appears that a request would remain valid regardless of how many years have passed since it was drafted, although this would presumably be a factor that the doctor would take into account in assessing whether the due care criteria could be fulfilled and in determining whether or not to comply with the request. An advance euthanasia directive will only come into force once the patient is incapable of expressing her wishes. However, the Dutch Act makes no provision for the appointment of a proxy decision-maker, leaving the doctor to determine when (if ever) the anticipatory request should be actioned.

The second due care criterion consists of two cumulative requirements: the doctor must be satisfied that the patient's suffering was both unbearable and without prospect of improvement. Therefore, this criterion requires the doctor to make a subjective assessment, that the patient is suffering unbearably, and an objective assessment, that the patient's suffering is hopeless. The first assessment, that the patient is enduring unbearable suffering, was the subject of detailed consideration in the *Chabot* case (1994) where the Supreme Court held that unbearable suffering is not limited to suffering during the terminal stage of illness and that such suffering need not be physical in nature. Thus the Supreme Court recognised that psychiatric suffering could constitute unbearable suffering and that the psychiatric nature of the suffering did not preclude a voluntary and well-considered request for termination of life.

Nevertheless, the Supreme Court recognised that in such cases doctors must exercise exceptional care because 'It is more difficult to objectively establish the fact of suffering and particularly its gravity and lack of prospect of improvement' (*Nederlandse Jurisprudentie* 1994, no. 656, at 3155). Whilst the guidelines of careful practice required the attending doctor to consult an independent doctor about the case, there was no requirement that the independent doctor actually examine the patient. However, in *Chabot*, the Supreme Court held that the requisite exceptional care would necessitate an independent doctor actually examining the patient, rather than merely discussing the patient's situation with the attending doctor as had occurred in this case. Thus the court stressed the need for extreme caution in the case of psychiatric suffering and indeed the inclusion of non-physical suffering has proved to be very controversial, not least with psychiatrists, and the statistics show that very few such cases result in either euthanasia or PAS each year.

During the parliamentary debates the Minister of Justice reiterated the decision of the Supreme Court in *Schoonheim*, confirming that unbearable suffering might take the form of degradation of personal dignity and the loss of the opportunity to die with dignity; however, he stressed that it could not encapsulate the situation where a person is simply 'tired of life'.[xxix] Whilst the exclusion of existential suffering is not apparent in the Act, the Supreme Court has recently clarified that unbearable suffering is not so flexible a concept that it can include such non-somatic suffering. Thus in the case of *Sutorius*[xxx] the Supreme Court held that just because the patient was tired of life and socially isolated, that did not mean that he was suffering unbearably. It stressed that unbearable suffering must have a somatic origin, that is it must be caused by either a diagnosable physical or psychiatric illness. Whilst this clarification is to be welcomed, it is unlikely to put an end to the debate, not least because in cases where the patient is 'tired of life' that same patient may also be suffering from some physical disease that might cause the patient distress. Indeed in the *Sutorius* case itself the patient (former Senator Brongersma) was suffering from a number of physical ailments and it could be suggested that if the attending doctor had focused upon the suffering derived from those ailments, that suffering might well have been sufficient to constitute 'unbearable suffering'.

As stated above, the doctor must also comply with the due care criteria in the case of an anticipatory request for euthanasia. Thus the doctor must be satisfied that the incompetent patient is suffering unbearably. However, as Dame Butler-Sloss recognised in *NHS Trust A v M; NHS Trust B v H*, an insensate patient in a persistent vegetative state cannot be said to be in a state of physical or mental suffering. ([2001] Fam. 348, at 363.) In the 2003 Annual Report, the Regional

---

[xxix] TK 2000–2001, 26691 no. 22, at 60; the majority of the upper chamber agreed with this assessment, see EK 26691, no. 137b at 32, 34, 42.

[xxx] HR 00797/02, 24/12/2002;[26] full text available at: http://www.rechtspraak.nl/uitspraak/frameset.asp?ljn=AE8772.

Review Committees suggested that in extreme circumstances a comatose patient might be considered to be suffering unbearably, particularly if she were only semi-comatose and showed signs of distress.[27] Nevertheless, this requirement is likely to severely restrict the cases in which euthanasia may be performed pursuant to an anticipatory request.

In addition to classifying the patient's suffering as unbearable, the doctor must also be satisfied that the suffering is without prospect of improvement, i.e. that it is hopeless. As the Supreme Court recognised in the *Schoonheim* case, this is an objective assessment and thus dependent upon medical opinion. Nevertheless, as the Supreme Court pointed out in the case of *Chabot*, whilst a competent patient may refuse any medical treatment, Article 450 Civil Code, if the patient rejects a realistic alternative to termination of life that could alleviate her suffering, the doctor will be unable to conclude that the suffering is unbearable and without any prospect of improvement (Nederlandse Jurisprudentie 1994, no. 656, at 3155). Thus the question arises whether or not a patient must exhaust all treatment avenues prior to requesting termination of life – what will constitute a realistic alternative? During the parliamentary debates the Minister of Justice and the Minister of Health, Welfare and Sport suggested that a realistic alternative must take the form of a curative (rather than palliative) treatment, that responsible medical opinion would not consider to impose burdens disproportionate to the likely improvement in the patient's situation. Therefore, it is clear that the requirement of hopeless suffering is a relatively flexible, objective medical assessment.

The third requirement obliges the doctor to inform the patient about her situation and prospects. Indeed without such information the patient will be in no position to make the requisite well-considered request. Noticeably, however, there is no explicit requirement that the doctor discuss palliative care options with the patient. As will be discussed below, this is a clear point of contrast with the Belgian Act and arguably serves to diminish the patient's ability to make a well-informed request. The fourth criterion amplifies the requirement that the doctor be satisfied that the patient's suffering is hopeless by insisting that both the doctor and the patient must have concluded that there is no reasonable alternative to euthanasia or PAS in the light of the patient's situation. Thus, euthanasia and PAS are portrayed as a last resort.

In the *Chabot* case the Supreme Court held that whilst an independent doctor must be *consulted* in cases of physical suffering if the doctor is to comply with the procedural aspects of the requirements of careful practice, the need for extreme caution in relation to psychiatric suffering dictated that the consulted doctor should actually *examine* the patient. Significantly, the Act removed this distinction between physical and psychiatric suffering by requiring that the consulted doctor must actually examine the patient in all cases. The consulted doctor must be independent, that is should not be related to either the patient or the attending doctor, belong to the same practice as the attending doctor, be part of the patient's treatment team or be a

subordinate of the attending doctor.[28,29,xxxi] If the consulted doctor cannot confirm that the requirements of due care have been fulfilled the attending doctor may approach a second doctor. However, this should not continue *ad
infinitum* and the KNMG advise that should the second doctor also conclude
that the requirements have not been met, the attending doctor should reconsider her own decision.[xxxii]

A cause for concern is that the Act does not require the doctor consulted to
be a specialist in the patient's condition.[xxxiii] Nevertheless, the KNMG guidance (1997) stated that in the case of psychiatric suffering the consulted doctor must be a psychiatrist[31] and it is likely that failure to seek such a specialist
opinion would render the attending doctor liable to disciplinary proceedings.
In 1985 the State Commission on Euthanasia suggested that the Minster of
Health, Welfare and Sport should identify doctors capable of acting as
euthanasia consultants. Although the Ministry has not adopted this proposal,
it has supported the creation of the so-called SCEN project, the Support and
Consultation on Euthanasia in the Netherlands[xxxiv] network. This network
consists of doctors who have been specially trained to act as independent
euthanasia consultants, nevertheless attending doctors remain free to select
their own independent consultant and are not required to enlist the services
of a SCEN doctor.

The consulted doctor must submit a written report, confirming that she is
satisfied that the due care criteria (a–d) are fulfilled. Thus the requirement
that an independent doctor be consulted may be argued to operate as a form
of *a priori* peer review. However, it is submitted that as the doctor need not be
a specialist in the patient's pathology this is a particularly weak form of control. Indeed the 1999 and 2000 Annual Reports of the Regional Review
Committees criticised the quality of consultation, with the exception of that
provided by SCEA[xxxv] consultants.[32] Thus it remains questionable whether
the consultation requirement in its current formulation can provide a real
check upon the performance of euthanasia and PAS, or whether it is simply a
rubber-stamping exercise.

Finally, the due care criteria require the doctor to perform euthanasia or
PAS with due medical care and attention. This requirement would certainly
include the doctor being under a duty to administer an appropriate drug in
the correct dosage to terminate the patient's life. However, it may also entail
the doctor remaining with the patient during the dying stage or at least being
available during that stage. Whilst that is unlikely to be problematic in the
case of euthanasia, in the case of PAS, particularly cases where the doctor

---

[xxxi] In the Schoonheim case the Court Appeals heald that the defendant's assistant could
not give an objective independent opinion because of the working relationship between
himself and the defendant.
[xxxii] KNMG Guidance (1995), discussed by Griffiths et al.[30]
[xxxiii] See also *Admiraal* case (1985) *Nederlandse Jurisprudentie* 1985, no. 709.
[xxxiv] *Steun en Consultatie bij Euthanasie in Nederland.*
[xxxv] The Amsterdam forerunner of the national SCEN network.

merely supplies the patient with a lethal drug to take at some later date, such a requirement would be much less practicable and more problematic. Nevertheless, in 2003 the Regional Review Committees found that two doctors had not complied with the due care criteria because they had not remained with their patients whilst they took the lethal drugs, despite the fact that both were contactable if required.[33]

Therefore, the Dutch Act includes a number of safeguards that aim to protect the patient from abuse. However, a number of the pre-existing requirements of careful practice have not been included. For example, the Health Council recommended that the patient's family should be involved in the decision-making process, unless the patient had a serious and well-founded objection (in the view of the attending and consulted doctor) to this course of action.[34] This recommendation was adopted in the KNMG's guidance (1995), but forms no part of the due care criteria. Nevertheless, the model report that is completed by the attending doctor after the termination of life makes it clear that there is an expectation that family members will have taken part in the decision-making process.[xxxvi] A similar expectation is evident in the model report in relation to consultation with other members of the patient's treatment team, although the Act does not require the doctor to seek the views of anyone other than the patient and the independent doctor. Therefore, the due care criteria represent only a minimum standard and compliance with the due care criteria (and the notification requirement discussed below) will only exempt doctors from criminal liability; should they fail to observe the other requirements imposed by professional guidelines they may still face a medical disciplinary tribunal.

The notification requirement

In addition to complying with the due care criteria, in order to be able to rely upon the exemption from criminal liability the doctor must comply with the notification requirements imposed by the Act. One of the key aims of the Act was to increase the incidence of reporting. The 1990, 1995 and 2001[35-38] studies commissioned by the Dutch Government showed that reporting levels were unacceptably low, with reporting rates amounting to only 18% of all medical end-of-life decisions[xxxvii] in 1991, rising to 41% in 1995 and to 54% in 2001, prior to the entry into force of the current Act. The reporting procedure set out in the Act is the culmination of a series of different approaches adopted to encourage reporting within the last decade. After performing euthanasia or PAS, the attending doctor must submit her report detailing compliance with the due care criteria to the municipal pathologist, who performs a post-mortem before forwarding the report, together with her own

---

[xxxvi] Model Report Part II, 13a–c.
[xxxvii] Medical end-of-life decisions include not only the performance of euthanasia and the assistance of suicide, but also non-treatment decisions and the hastening of death as a by-product of pain relief.

and any annexes (for example an anticipatory request for euthanasia), to one of the regional review committees (ss.7–10 Burial & Cremation Act, as amended by the 2001 Act).

The five regional committees[xxxviii] have a minimum of three members – a legal expert, an ethicist and a doctor – each of whom is appointed by the Ministers of Justice and Health, Welfare and Sport for a renewable term of six years. Their role is to review the reported cases of euthanasia and PAS and to determine whether the attending doctor acted in accordance with the due care criteria. The committee must inform the attending doctor of its findings, giving reasons, within six weeks of receiving the report, although this deadline may be extended to twelve weeks. If the majority of the committee conclude that the doctor did not act in accordance with the due care criteria it must notify the Board of Procurators General of the Public Prosecution Service and the regional health care inspector, Article 9. However, if a majority of the committee considers that the doctor complied with the due care criteria that is the end of the matter; the case will not be referred to the public prosecutor, because the doctor is exempt from criminal liability, Article 293(2) Penal Code. This is a significant policy change from the 1998 reporting procedure under which the committees played only an advisory role, advising the public prosecutor whether the doctor had complied with the requirements of careful practice. The public prosecutor was under no obligation to accept the committee's recommendation and thus the doctor remained liable to prosecution notwithstanding the committee's view that she had complied with the then requirements of careful practice. Thus the Act has enhanced the role of the regional review committees, so that their role is no longer merely advisory and compliance with the reporting requirement will no longer automatically trigger a criminal investigation. However, it is still possible for the public prosecutor or the Medical Inspectorate to commence proceedings of their own accord, as might happen, for example, if a member of the health-care team or the deceased's family made a complaint about the attending doctor's conduct. In such a situation, the regional review committee is required to provide the public prosecutor with all the information she may require, Article 10.

The revised notification procedure aims to increase the rate of reporting by removing the public prosecutor from the equation, at least in those cases in which the commission decides that the doctor has fulfilled the due care criteria. It is hoped that explicit recognition of an exception to the offences of killing upon request and assisted suicide, together with the exceptional,[xxxix] rather than automatic, criminal investigation will increase doctors' willingness to

---

[xxxviii] Gronigen, Friesland and Drenthe; Overijssel, Gelderland, Utrecht and Flevoland; North Holland; South Holland and Zeeland; North Brabant and Limburg.

[xxxix] During the first year of the Act's operation (2002) the regional review committees referred only 5 of the reported 1882 reports of euthanasia/PAS to the public prosecutor and Health Inspectorate after concluding that the doctors concerned had not acted in accordance with the due care criteria.[24]

report the performance of euthanasia or PAS. Nevertheless, the problem remains that it is those cases where the doctor has not complied with the criteria, especially those cases where no request for termination of life was made, that are unlikely to be reported. In addition to assessing the doctor's compliance with the due care criteria, the committees are responsible for compiling an annual report providing detailed statistics about the number of reported cases of euthanasia and PAS, the nature of those cases, the committees' findings and reasons.

It is clear that the Act is doctor rather than patient orientated. It does not give patients the right to demand either euthanasia or PAS; rather the Act is intended to enable doctors to perform euthanasia or assist a suicide without incurring criminal sanction in certain circumstances.[xxxx] When that factor is taken into account, it is not surprising that the Act does not contain a conscientious objection clause, as there is no duty to provide this 'service' to patients. However, the KNMG's 1995 guidance did suggest that in cases of conscientious objection there should be a duty to refer the patient on to another doctor and indeed this sentiment was also expressed during the parliamentary debates that led to the Act,[xxxxi] although no such duty is set out in the Act itself.

The Act was intended to codify the requirements of careful practice in order to provide legal certainty for doctors and to encourage reporting. In reality the Act is nothing more than a framework that changes little of the Dutch law relating to end-of-life decision-making. The Act's significance lies in its explicit recognition that a doctor will be exempt from criminal liability for performing euthanasia or PAS provided that she complies with the due care criteria and the notification requirement, largely removing the need for doctors to rely upon the politically expedient justification of necessity. Nevertheless, it must be recognised that the Act's requirements represent only a minimum standard of behaviour with which the doctor must comply in order to obtain exemption from criminal liability. The professional guidelines are much further reaching and even if the doctor complies with the Act, disciplinary proceedings may still be initiated by the Medical Inspectorate if she has not complied with the professional guidance.

THE BELGIAN LAW

Just over a year after the Dutch Parliament enacted the Termination of Life on Request and Assisted Suicide (Review Procedures) Act, the Belgian Parliament followed suit, passing the Law Relating to Euthanasia 2002. Whilst the Belgian Act clearly draws upon the Dutch experience, there are significant differences, both between the two Acts, but also in the genesis of the Acts. Whilst the Dutch Act is little more than a codification of the Dutch

---

[xxxx] A similar legislative intent underlies the regulation of abortion in England and Wales, Abortion Act 1967.
[xxxxi] See for example TK 2000–2001, 26691 no. 9, at 22.

case law and guidance issued by the KNMG relating to careful practice, the Belgian Act can be conceptualised as an innovation of the legislature. Indeed, as the vice-chair of the Belgian Order of Physicians (ODMB)[xxxii] stated during the Senate Committee hearing: '[the association] is neither for nor against legislation, but neither is it asking for it'.[xxxiii]

Unlike the Dutch Penal Code the Belgian Penal Code does not recognise euthanasia as a separate category of homicide. Instead 'mercy killing' could constitute murder (Article 394 Penal Code), manslaughter (Article 393 Penal Code), or fatal poisoning (Article 397 Penal Code.) Assisting suicide is not a crime per se. However, it may contravene Article 422*bis* Penal Code, the offence of failing to assist a person in grave danger, or, depending upon the nature of the assistance given, the offence of fatal poisoning; (Penal Code Article 397). Nevertheless, as Deliens' study[40,41] showed, in 1998 euthanasia was practised place to approximately the same extent as in the neighbouring Netherlands, despite the fact that euthanasia was absolutely prohibited in Belgium and that neither the courts nor the prosecutorial authorities had indicated that they would tolerate euthanasia.

In 1997 the Belgian Advisory Committee for Bioethics (BACB) delivered its Opinion concerning the desirability of adopting legislation relating to euthanasia,[42] setting out four alternative views.[xxxiv] According to the first view, euthanasia performed by a doctor should, subject to certain conditions, be decriminalised; the second and third views suggested that euthanasia should remain a crime, but that doctors should be able to perform euthanasia in certain circumstances and thereafter rely upon justification of necessity. Both views considered that the doctor's actions should be subject to procedural review, but whilst the second view favoured the Dutch approach, procedural control *after* the fact, the third view considered that the performance of euthanasia should be subject to prior approval. The final view was that the absolute prohibition of euthanasia should be maintained. In fact the 2002 Act adopted legislation along the lines envisaged by the first view, coupled with a post-euthanasia procedural review similar to that suggested in the second. Thus unlike its Dutch counterpart, the Belgian Act does not merely exempt doctors who perform euthanasia from criminal liability, instead, provided that the requirements of the Act are complied with, no offence will be committed, Article 3.[xxxv] Moreover, unlike the Dutch Act, the Belgian Act makes no provision for amendment to be made to the Penal Code, thus emphasising that euthanasia will constitute a crime, other than in the exceptional circumstances set out in the Act.

The Belgian Advisory Committee for Bioethics defined euthanasia in the same terms as the Dutch State Commission, namely as an 'act performed by

---

[xxxii] Ordre des médecins – Belgique.

[xxxiii] Quoted in Adams. [39]

[xxxiv] The commission is not permitted to indicate how much support the various views reported enjoy.

[xxxv] There is considerable debate about which specific offence the doctor would commit if she does not comply with the requirements set out in the Act.[43]

a third party which intentionally ends the life of a person at the latter's request'.[42] This definition was adopted by the Act, Article 2. Whilst the definition refers only to a third party, as Article 3(1)(a) makes clear, only euthanasia performed by a doctor has been decriminalised. Moreover, as this definition and the subsequent articles suggest, the Belgian Act only regulates euthanasia, unlike the Dutch Act which regulates the performance of both euthanasia and PAS.[xxxvi]

In most respects the requirements set out in the Belgian Act 2002 for lawful euthanasia are similar to those found in the Dutch Act. However, the Belgian Act is noticeably more detailed, which is at least partly because it is not supplemented by detailed professional guidelines. One of the key differences between the two Acts is that the Belgian Act imposes differing criteria depending upon whether the patient is conscious or unconscious, terminally ill or non-terminally ill, whereas the Dutch Act seeks to apply the same criteria to all requests for termination of life.

The conditions for lawful euthanasia

Chapter II of the Act sets out the conditions and procedure applicable to conscious patients. The primary requirement is that the patient must request euthanasia. The doctor must be satisfied that the patient has made a voluntary, well-considered and repeated request without external pressure, Article 3 §1.[xxxvii] Moreover, the doctor is required to inform her patient of her state of health and life expectancy, as well as the therapeutic and palliative care measures available to her, Article 3 §2(1). Thus the central requirement of both the Dutch and Belgian Acts is that the patient make a voluntary, informed and well-considered request for active euthanasia. However, unlike the Dutch Act, the Belgian Act explicitly requires the doctor to discuss potential palliative care measures and their consequences with the patient; a factor that is arguably necessary if the patient's request is to be considered fully informed, and certainly a factor that is likely to result in requests being better considered. Significantly the Law Relating to Palliative Care was introduced in conjunction with the Law Relating to Euthanasia, guaranteeing every patient the right to palliative care (Loi relative aux soins palliatifs (2002), Art. 2). Thus the Belgian Act emphasises that lack of access to palliative care should not be grounds for euthanasia; nevertheless, a refusal of palliative care would not exclude a patient's request for euthanasia. Moreover, the National Council of the ODMB has emphasised the considerable role to be played by palliative

---

[xxxvi] Adams and Nys[43] have argued that the exclusion of PAS could constitute discrimination contrary to Articles 10 and 11 of the constitution, at 357.

[xxxvii] The Dutch Act does not include a requirement that the doctor be satisfied that the patient's request is made without external pressure. However, it is submitted that such pressure would lead to the conclusion that the request was not truly voluntary and thus that such a requirement is superfluous.

care at the end of life, arguing that properly administered palliative care could constitute an adequate response to certain requests for euthanasia; could reduce the number of requests made; and could create the opportunity to discuss other ways of ending the patient's life, thus reducing the need for euthanasia.[44]

Although the KNMG guidance stresses the importance of a written request, the Dutch Act does not require the patient's request to be made in written form. By contrast the Belgian Act requires a written request in all circumstances, Article 3 §4. Similarly, whilst the KNMG guidance states that the patient's request should be enduring, the Dutch Act does not contain any such limitation, whereas the Belgian Act stipulates that the patient must make a 'repeated' request. Although the Act does not specify how many times the patient must request euthanasia, it does state that the doctor must have several conversations with the patient, spread out over a reasonable period of time, in order to ensure the durable nature of the patient's request, Article 3 §2(2), and requires that '*all* the requests formulated by the patient' be noted in the patient's medical record, Article 3 §5. Thus it is clear that the patient must make a number of euthanasia requests. However, it is submitted that this requirement will mean that those close to death will be unable to show that their request is sufficiently durable unless requests are made in quick succession or, more controversially, in anticipation of the fact that the patient may wish to request euthanasia in the future. Unlike the Dutch Act, the Belgian Act draws a crucial distinction between patients who are expected to die within a short period of time and those that are not, with additional requirements being imposed upon the latter case. A mandatory cooling-off period is imposed in the case of patients not expected to die shortly, requiring that at least one month must elapse between the submission of a written request by the patient and the performance of euthanasia. Moreover, a second, more rigorous, consultation requirement, discussed below, is applied to cases involving such patients.

In order to make a valid request the patient must be either a competent adult or an emancipated minor, that is a married minor, or a minor who is at least 15 years old who has been emancipated by judicial declaration (Article 476 Civil Code). According to the Belgian Law Relating to the Rights of the Patient, minors who are considered capable of a reasonable appreciation of their interests may exercise the rights set out in that Act, including the right to refuse treatment, and if the minor is not considered competent, her parents or guardian can exercise the rights on her behalf (La loi relative aux droits du patient (2002), Art. 12 §§1,2). However, the Law Relating to Euthanasia does not permit the unemancipated, but competent, minor to request euthanasia, nor does it enable her parents to do so on her behalf. Therefore, in practice the Belgian Act is likely to be much more restrictive than the Dutch Act as a minor will only very rarely be able to make a valid request for euthanasia and thus will essentially be reliant upon the withdrawal/withholding of treatment or the hastening of death as a by-product of pain relief.

In common with the Dutch Act, the Belgian Act requires the doctor to be satisfied that the patient is in a hopeless, rather than terminal, condition[xxxxviii] and that the patient's constant unbearable physical or mental suffering cannot be alleviated (Article 3 §1). As noted above in relation to the Dutch Act, the inclusion of mental suffering is very controversial. Nevertheless, whilst the Belgian Act clearly states that the patient's suffering may be of either a psychiatric or physical nature, it does limit this broad conception of suffering by stating that the suffering must emanate from a serious and incurable disorder, caused by either illness or accident, thus excluding existential suffering of the type encountered in the *Sutorius* case.

Moreover, the Act requires the doctor and the patient to conclude together that there is no other reasonable solution to the patient's situation (Article 3 §1(1)). However, the guidance issued by the National Council of the ODMB in 2003 is much more restrictive than the Act, stating that the doctor and patient must conclude that no other medical decision relating to the end of life offers a reasonable alternative to the active termination of life. Thus, like the Belgian legislature, the ODMB has emphasised that euthanasia is a last resort. However, in so doing it also expressed a clear preference for the hastening of death via either a non-treatment decision or as a by-product of pain relief. As discussed above, many have argued that there is no morally relevant difference between acts and omissions, or indeed between a pain-relieving drug that hastens death as a by-product of relieving pain and a lethal injection. Nevertheless, despite the fact that euthanasia has been legalised in Belgium, the ODMB has adopted the position that doctors should not take active steps to terminate the patient's life, unless the alternative mechanisms for achieving the same result are considered to be unreasonable.

In addition to ensuring that both the patient's request and her suffering are enduring, the attending doctor must obtain a second opinion from an independent[xxxxix] doctor confirming the serious and incurable nature of the patient's condition, Article 3 §2(3). Somewhat surprisingly, in the case of a terminally ill patient, the consulted doctor is not required to confirm that the patient's request is voluntary, well considered, durable and free of external pressure; thus in such cases the consulted doctor plays a much more limited role than her Dutch counterpart, being required only to confirm the medical aspects of the case. Moreover, whilst the consulted doctor must be competent to give an opinion about the patient's pathological condition, she is not required to be a specialist. However, where patients are not expected to die in

---

[xxxxviii] By contrast, in its Opinion of 17/11/2001 the National Council of the ODMB recommended that euthanasia should not be available to patients who were unlikely to die shortly.[45]

[xxxxix] Within the Flemish speaking medical community LEIF, a network similar to the Dutch SCEN network, has been established and attending doctors are encouraged to seek a consultant from this network.

the short term an additional consultation with a second independent doctor is required. This second consultation requirement is likely to be much more rigorous than the first consultation because it must be undertaken by either a psychiatrist or a specialist in the patient's condition, which should ensure a higher quality second opinion. Moreover, whilst the first doctor consulted must only confirm that the patient is enduring constant, unbearable and unrelievable suffering, the second consulted doctor is required to confirm that the patient's request is well considered, voluntary and persistent in addition to confirming the medical aspects of the case. Just as in the case of the first consulted doctor, the second doctor must be independent of both the attending doctor and the patient; however, the second doctor must also be independent of the first consulted doctor. Thus, the Act envisages a much more rigorous form of peer review in the case of a patient who is unlikely to die shortly.

In addition to obtaining a second opinion from at least one other doctor, the Belgian Act requires the attending doctor to consult other interested parties to a greater extent than its Dutch counterpart. The attending doctor is required to discuss the patient's request with nursing staff that have regular contact with the patient, reflecting the reality that in many cases nursing staff will know the patient better than the doctor and thus should be better able to assess the voluntary and enduring nature of her request. However, the view(s) of the nursing staff is not determinative, the doctor merely has to consult them. Additionally, the doctor is required to ensure that the patient has had the opportunity to discuss her request with whomever she wanted, and, if the patient so wishes, the doctor should discuss the patient's request with those she designates as being close to her. Whilst it is clear that those individuals do not have a veto right, they may well be able to influence the doctor's decision as to whether or not to comply with the patient's request.

A further significant difference between the Dutch and Belgian Acts concerns the manner in which they apply to adults lacking capacity. Both Acts foresee the possibility of an adult[l] being able to draft an anticipatory request for euthanasia. However, the Dutch Act does not distinguish between an anticipatory request and a contemporaneous request, applying the same requirements to the two very different types of request. As the Belgian Act makes clear, a specific anticipatory request for euthanasia is required; a more general advance directive will not suffice, although it could require the withholding or withdrawal of medical treatment.[li] Unlike its Dutch counterpart, the Belgian Act stipulates that the request must have been drafted or

---

[l] Additionally the Belgian Act permits emancipated minors to draft such a request, whilst the Dutch Act allows any minor over the age of 16 to make an anticipatory request for euthanasia or PAS.

[li] Chapter 4 of the Loi relative aux droits du patient (2002) deals with the validity of advance directives and the ability of the patient to appoint a healthcare proxy.

confirmed less than five years before the onset of incapacity,[lii] and provision is made for the attending doctor and the healthcare proxy appointed by the patient to determine together when the request should be executed, rather than the timing simply being a matter for the doctor's discretion as in the Netherlands. However, the anticipatory request will only become effective if the patient is unconscious and suffering from a serious and incurable accidental or pathological condition that is considered to be irreversible in the current state of medical science. Therefore, the Belgian approach avoids the problems outlined in relation to the Dutch Act's stipulation that the doctor must be satisfied that the anticipatory request was voluntary and well considered; and that the patient must be suffering unbearably. However, it only envisages the execution of an anticipatory request, in cases of unconsciousness, thus excluding cases such as dementia. This is a significant omission as many would argue that a patient may endure unbearable suffering due to dementia, whereas an unconscious patient is not usually considered to be suffering at all.

One element that is clearly lacking from the Belgian Act is a requirement that the doctor performing euthanasia should do so with 'due care'.[liii] However, the National Council of the ODMB have stated that the attending doctor must have a thorough knowledge of the relevant drugs so that she can ensure that her patient dies peacefully without suffering.[liv] It is suggested that this must be correct and that even if the Act does not explicitly require due care in the performance of euthanasia, a failure to meet the required standard of professional conduct would result in disciplinary proceedings.

The notification requirement

Following the example of the Dutch Act, the Belgian Act relies primarily on an *a posteriori* review of euthanasia, requiring the attending doctor to submit a detailed report to the Federal Commission of Control and Evaluation (FCCE) within four days of the performance of euthanasia. Unlike the Dutch regional review committees, the Belgian committee operates at a federal level. It is made up of sixteen members: eight doctors, four lawyers and four members from 'environments entrusted with the problems of patients suffering from an incurable disease', typically a hospice or hospital environment. Thus although the membership is larger than the Dutch regional review committees, its composition could not be said to be broader; 50% of its members are medical practitioners or professors of medicine, making up the largest group within the committee, and ethicists are excluded unless they happen to also fall into one of the three named categories.

[lii] Article 4 §1; Arrêté royal fixant les modalités suivant lesquelles la declaration anticipée relative à l'euthanasie est rédigée, reconfirmée, révisée ou retirée (Royal decree laying down the manner in which the anticipated declaration relating to the euthanasia is written, reconfirmed, revised or withdrawn), 02/04/2003 Article 3. Available at: http://www.health.fgov.be/AGP/fr/euthanasie/DeclarationAnticipe.htm.

[liii] Cf. Article 2(1)(f) Dutch Act 2001.

[liv] Avis no. 100;[44] see also views 2 and 3 of the BACB opinion 1997.[42]

The FCCE is allotted a maximum of two months for its deliberations and if a two-thirds majority concludes that the doctor has not acted in accordance with the law it must submit a report to the public prosecutor. Additionally, it is responsible for preparing a biannual report comprising a statistical report based upon the information provided in the report submitted by the attending doctor (including, for example, information about the serious and incurable, accidental or pathological condition suffered by the patient); a report describing and evaluating the implementation of the Act and, if applicable, setting out recommendations that may lead to legislative initiatives and or other measures concerning the implementation of the Act. Thus unlike the Dutch regional review committees, the FCCE does not merely have a reporting function, rather it enjoys a political mandate to evaluate the current law and formulate recommendations.[lv]

Thus the Belgian Act is very similar to its Dutch predecessor. However, it is more detailed, at least in part due to the lack of relevant case law and professional guidance preceding the Act. In certain respects it is more conservative than the Dutch Act; for example, it applies only to euthanasia, excluding the possibility of lawful PAS, although as discussed below the dividing line between the two may be very difficult to draw. Moreover, the ability of minors to request euthanasia is severely restricted and anticipatory requests may only be acted upon in the case of an unconscious patient. Essentially the Act adopts the same pragmatic response evident in the Dutch legislation. In recognising that euthanasia was being performed despite the prohibition contained in the Penal Code, the Belgian legislature enacted a series of procedural and substantive safeguards designed to protect patients from abuse. In common with its Dutch counterpart, the Act does not give patients a right to euthanasia; it merely enables doctors to perform euthanasia in certain circumstances without committing a criminal offence. The fact that doctors act as the gatekeepers to euthanasia is emphasised by the inclusion of a conscientious objection clause (Article 14). Nevertheless, if the doctor relies upon the conscientious objection clause she is required to refer the patient on to another doctor.

WHAT CAN ENGLAND AND WALES LEARN FROM THE NETHERLANDS AND BELGIUM?

In 1994 the Walton Committee concluded that:

> 'It would not be possible to frame adequate safeguards against non-voluntary euthanasia if voluntary euthanasia were to be legalised. It would be next to impossible to ensure that all acts of euthanasia were truly voluntary and that any liberalisation of the law was not abused.'[46]

However, as discussed above, it appears that doctors do perform AVE and assist suicide in the United Kingdom, although they do so without the benefit of a regulatory framework or safeguards designed to protect the patient

---

[lv] Chapter V, Arts 6–9.

from abuse, and more particularly to ensure that the euthanasia is voluntary. Therefore, it is submitted that legislation should be enacted to legalise AVE and PAS, incorporating appropriate safeguards to protect patients from abuse. Drawing upon the experience of the Netherlands and Belgium some suggestions may be made as how this might be achieved.

In relation to the permissible forms of euthanasia the Dutch approach of permitting both AVE and PAS should be followed; as the Dutch Health Council recognised, 'The context in which the treatment takes places seems far more important than the form assumed by the assistance in a specific case.'[47] The doctor plays an active and necessarily causal role in the patient's death in both AVE and PAS,[48] but PAS is generally regarded as less controversial than AVE, particularly because it emphasises the voluntary nature of the termination of life and increases the patient's control of her death.[lvi] However, a number of studies have shown that efficacy problems are quite frequently encountered with PAS and that it may not lead to the 'gentle and easy' death desired.[lvii] Moreover, it may be very difficult to accurately draw the line between AVE and PAS; for example, if a patient were physically unable to place the lethal drugs in her mouth and at her request the doctor inserted the tablets in her mouth for her to swallow, would the doctor's action constitute PAS or would she have crossed the Rubicon into the realm of AVE? Therefore, it is suggested that both forms of intervention should be legalised, but only in relation to doctors as medical expertise will be required in order to ensure the avoidance of unnecessary suffering and to fulfil the necessary safeguards. Moreover, the Belgian approach should be adopted, distinguishing both between the competent patient and incompetent patient, and between the terminally ill patient and patients who are not expected to die shortly.

The absolute requirement of a voluntary, informed request for termination of life

In both the Netherlands and Belgium 'euthanasia' is defined as the active termination of an individual's life *at that person's request*,[42,18] whereas the House of Lords' Select Committee defined euthanasia as 'a deliberate intervention undertaken with the express intention of ending a life to relieve intractable suffering',[51] making no distinction between voluntary and involuntary euthanasia. The primary safeguard in any legislation that legalises AVE and PAS must be to ensure that the termination of life only takes place at the request of the patient. The attending doctor should assure herself that the competent patient's request is voluntary, fully informed, well considered and enduring. Therefore requests should be made to the patient's GP, at least in the first instance, as the GP is likely to be well acquainted with the patient's situation and thus be in a better position to consider the voluntariness of the request.[lviii]

[lvi] See for example KNMG 1995.[45]
[lvii] See for example Groenewoud.[50]
[lviii] In the Netherlands euthanasia is most frequently performed by the patient's GP.[52,53]

The competent adult patient

In order to constitute a valid request, the request should not only be voluntary (free of undue influence and not the result of treatable clinical depression), but should also be made after the patient has been fully informed of her condition. She should receive information about her prognosis, about the likely development of her condition and about all the available options to combat her distress and pain. As required by the Belgian Act, information about pain relief and palliative care options must be included in that information. However, as recognised by the ODMB[44] the average doctor lacks sufficient knowledge about the current possibilities and objectives of palliative care, a branch of medicine that remains underfunded in the UK. If the requirement that the patient is to be given palliative care information is to serve more than a merely notional purpose, such information should be provided by someone who is experienced in that specialism, rather than the patient's GP or a specialist in the patient's pathology. The incorporation of a palliative care filter into the consultation requirement, considered below, is significant as it will emphasise that requests for AVE or PAS should not be motivated by inadequate palliative care.

Moreover, the request should be well considered and durable. This requirement does not mean that a set number of requests must be made. However, the doctor should be satisfied that the request is well considered and is not merely a fleeting response to a bad day. The Belgian example of distinguishing between terminally ill patients, and those patients who are unlikely to die shortly, should be followed, with more safeguards being applied to the latter category. Whilst it would be unrealistic to impose a cooling-off period in the case of a terminally ill patient, the same is not true of the patient who is not expected to die shortly, and in such cases a mandatory cooling-off period should be imposed. If the cooling-off period is too long, there is a real risk that patients will request AVE/PAS before they really want to die, in an effort to avoid having to wait too long for their request to be fulfilled. Nevertheless, sufficient time must be allowed for the attending doctor to obtain the necessary second opinions and the prior approval of the regional review committee, discussed below, and so a one-month cooling-off period appears to be appropriate.

As required by the Belgian Act, in determining whether the request is voluntary, fully informed and well considered, the attending doctor should consult any other members of the patient's treatment team. Provision should also be made for the doctor to consult those close to the patient, with the patient's consent, although those individuals should not be able to veto the patient's request. Finally, as required by the Belgian Act and recommended by the KNMG, the request must be formalised in writing, providing strong evidence that the patient's life was terminated at her request. The written request should be witnessed by two individuals who will not benefit from the patient's death and who are not responsible for her treatment or affiliated with any treatment facility that is responsible for her care; ideally one of the witnesses should be the patient's solicitor. In cases where the patient is unable to draft the request herself, another individual fulfilling the aforementioned criteria could draft the request on her behalf, in the presence of the two witnesses. Furthermore, prior to the termination of the patient's life, the request should be renewed orally.

Incompetent patients

Clearly neither AVE nor PAS can take place without a request from the patient concerned. However, provision should be made for requests made by minors and anticipatory requests made in advance of incapacity. In the case of a minor, s.8(1) of the Family Law Reform Act 1969 enables a minor of 16 years and above to give a valid consent to medical treatment. Moreover, children under the age of 16 have a common law right to consent to medical treatment provided that they are '*Gillick* competent', that is that they are capable of understanding the treatment proposed and are able to express their own views (*Gillick v Wisbech AHA* [1986] AC 112). However, the courts have made clear in a number of cases that a refusal of treatment deemed to serve her best interest by both a *Gillick*-competent or 16 to 17-year-old child may be overridden by someone with parental responsibility or the court exercising its wardship jurisdiction.[lix] Nevertheless, there appears to be no good reason why a child suffering unbearably should be ineligible for either AVE or PAS. Therefore, an approach modelled upon the Dutch Act could be adopted, enabling the *Gillick*-competent child or minor over the age of 15 to request termination of life, provided that someone with parental responsibility for the minor is involved in the decision-making process. The involvement of a parental responsibility holder should not, however, include the power of veto. In other cases life-prolonging treatment could be withheld or withdrawn in accordance with the patient's best interests.

Both the Belgian and the Dutch Acts foresee the possibility of a competent patient drafting an anticipatory euthanasia request. It is submitted that a sufficiently recent and specific advance euthanasia request, as distinct from a more general advance directive, could represent a valid request for termination of life after the onset of incompetence. However, as stipulated by the Dutch Act, the attending doctor should be satisfied that the request was voluntary, well considered, informed and durable at the time it was drafted. In practice this will mean that the patient will need to discuss her anticipatory request with her GP and a note of the discussion should be kept on the patient's medical record. Moreover, as in Belgium, an anticipatory request should designate a proxy decision-maker who, together with the attending doctor, should determine when the time has come for the request to be actioned.

[lix]   See for example, *Re W (a minor) (medical treatment : court's jurisdiction)* [1992] 4 All ER 627; *South Glamorgan County Council v W and B* [993] 1 FLR 574.

The patient must be experiencing unbearable suffering without prospect of improvement

Both the patient and the attending doctor should be satisfied that the patient's suffering is unbearable and without prospect of improvement. The Belgian and Dutch Acts differ from the Oregon Death with Dignity Act (1994) and the short-lived Northern Territory's Rights of the Terminally Ill Act (1995) in permitting assistance in dying when the patient is not terminally ill. The Dutch statistics show that the majority of patients assisted in dying are terminally ill and that the average shortening of life is just 1–2 weeks. Nevertheless, AVE and PAS should not be restricted to the terminally ill; the non-terminally ill patient may be considered to be suffering unbearably, but may live for a considerable amount of time without the active termination of her life. However, any legislation adopted should follow the example of the Belgian Act by applying additional safeguards in the case of requests made by patients who are not expected to die shortly.

As envisaged by both the Dutch and Belgian Acts, the suffering could be of either a physical or a psychiatric nature. However, in common with the Dutch Supreme Court's ruling in *Sutorius* and the Belgian Act, the suffering should have some somatic basis, thus excluding cases of existential suffering. The inclusion of psychiatric suffering is much more controversial than that of a physical nature, although as Burgess and Hawton have persuasively argued, suicidal wishes expressed by individuals suffering from mental illness are not necessarily merely symptoms of that mental illness.[54] Whilst mental illnesses are generally treatable, to at least some extent, many have a chronic or remitting course[55] and the treatment for some mental illnesses, and side effects thereof, can be extremely unpleasant, constituting a significant burden for the patient. Thus there appears to be no good reason for excluding the possibility of AVE, or more probably PAS, in the case of a patient who is enduring unbearable psychiatric suffering, providing that the patient is considered to have the requisite capacity to make the request.

Moreover, it is recognised that suicide is one of the main causes of premature death in people with mental illness[56,57] and it has been suggested that 15% of people suffering from major depression, together with 10% of schizophrenics, commit suicide.[58] Thus it could be argued that by enabling such people to request assistance in dying, an opportunity would be provided to offer both them and their family support, regardless of whether the request were acceded to or not. Doctors would be required to discuss alternative treatments available and to ensure that the patient had made a well-considered request. Clearly a psychiatric evaluation would be required, not only to determine capacity, but also to ensure that the patient's wish to die is an expression of her autonomy rather than merely a symptom of her illness.

In the case of a previously competent patient who has drafted an anticipatory request for termination of life, the requirement of unbearable suffering should not be applied. As discussed above, the Dutch Act requires such patients to be suffering unbearably, despite the fact that few patients in a coma or a persistent vegetative state are thought to suffer at all. Avoiding this problem, the Belgian Act requires that the incompetent patient be unconscious, thus excluding for example, cases of dementia. Thus in both jurisdictions there are likely to be patients who have drafted anticipatory requests, but whose requests fall outside the scope of the Acts. One of the primary aims of precedent autonomy is that a competent patient should be able to determine at what point her quality of life will reach an unacceptable level in advance of becoming incompetent. Therefore, provided that the other conditions are fulfilled and the patient has appointed a proxy decision-maker to verify that the patient would have wanted her life to be terminated at this point, the anticipatory request should be honoured.

In addition to establishing that the patient's suffering is unbearable, the attending doctor must also conclude that there is no prospect of improvement in the patient's situation. As mentioned above, the patient's request must be fully informed, that is she must be aware of all treatment possibilities that might alleviate her suffering, including palliative care measures. However, the conclusion that her suffering is without prospect of improvement does not mean that the patient should be obliged to exhaust all the therapeutic measures available. However, if a curative, rather than merely palliative, treatment is available, that would at least substantially alleviate the patient's suffering, without imposing a disproportionate burden on her, the patient's suffering cannot be classified as without prospect of improvement.

Consultation requirements

A form of peer review should be instituted via a consultation requirement. In order to constitute an effective safeguard, two consultations should take place, the first by an independent doctor specialising in palliative care, the second by an independent doctor specialising in the patient's condition. Both doctors should examine the patient and be given full access to her medical records, before confirming that: her request is voluntary, fully informed, well considered and enduring; the patient's prognosis and the treatment options available to her; and that she is enduring unbearable suffering without prospect of improvement. However, where the suffering is purely psychiatric in nature, both consultations should be conducted by independent psychiatrists.

In the case of an anticipatory request the two consultations should take place at the time that the request is made, confirming that the patient's request is voluntary, fully informed, well considered and enduring; her prognosis and the treatment options likely to be available to her. A further independent doctor specialising in the patient's condition should be consulted when it appears appropriate to action the request, confirming that the patient's condition is hopeless and that the terms of her request are such that termination of life should occur. In order to ensure the independence of consultants, a network similar to the SCEN and Leif networks should be created to provide the necessary consultants, with the relevant specialist knowledge, throughout the country.

The requirement of due care

Any termination of life must be conducted in accordance with the standards of good medical practice. Thus the doctor must ensure that the appropriate drugs are used in sufficient quantities to ensure that death ensues without causing the patient any unnecessary pain and distress. The medical professional bodies should work together with the Royal Pharmaceutical Society of Great Britain to draw up guidance relating to the most appropriate drugs, method of administration and dosage required in order to achieve the desired result. Moreover, the attending doctor should personally administer the drugs in cases of AVE, staying with the patient until she dies. Whilst PAS may not necessitate the attendance of the doctor, given the reported problems with the efficacy of PAS, it would appear essential that the attending doctor should be available at all times, if not actually present.

Review committees and the notification requirement

The patient who is not expected to die shortly and anticipatory requests for euthanasia

Both the Dutch and Belgian Acts rely upon a procedural review taking place *after* the termination of life has occurred. Whilst such an *a posteriori* review is likely to be the only reasonable option in the case of a terminally ill patient, due to the short time frame in which a decision must be taken, the same is not true of patients who are not expected to die shortly or in the case of an anticipatory request. Although the Dutch and Belgian review committees are interdisciplinary in composition, the decision to terminate a life upon request or to assist suicide remains essentially a medical decision as the review only takes place after the event. Therefore, whilst the procedure for independent consultation outlined above will constitute an important safeguard, prior approval for the termination of life should be sought from a regional review committee in cases where the patient is not expected to die shortly or where the patient's request was formulated in advance of her becoming incompetent.

The regional committees should be interdisciplinary in nature being made up of at least four members, including a lawyer (acting as the chair), a doctor, an ethicist and a palliative care expert. After the consulting doctors have compiled their reports they should be forwarded, together with the report of the attending doctor, a copy of the patient's written request for termination of life and a copy of the patient's medical records to a regional review committee. The committee should review the request for termination of life on the basis of the documentary evidence submitted and approve or reject the request, notifying the attending doctor and the patient within ten days of receiving the documentation. If the committee were to require further information it could require the attending doctor, the consulted doctors and/or the competent patient to give evidence in person, or to submit further written evidence.

Should the committee refuse to grant prior approval, it should provide full reasons for its decision and indicate that the patient has a right of appeal to the national review committee.

Within three working days of terminating the patient's life the attending doctor should notify the national review committee in accordance with the procedure outlined below, appending a copy of the certificate of approval from the regional committee to her report, whereupon the national committee should determine whether the attending doctor has complied with the legal requirements and professional guidelines.

The terminally ill

Where the patient is terminally ill and likely to die shortly, it would be unfeasible to seek prior approval from a regional review committee. Therefore, in such cases the termination of life should be subject to an *a posteriori* review by a national committee established to review cases of AVE and PAS, determining whether the attending doctor acted in accordance with professional guidelines and the law. Within three working days of the termination of life, the attending doctor should notify the national review committee of her actions, submitting copies of her report; the reports of the consulting doctors; the patient's request; and the patient's medical record. The national review committee should be made up of the chairs of three of the regional review committees (lawyers); a consultant oncologist;[ix] a consultant in palliative care; a member of the British Medical Association; and a representative of a patient's organisation. After determining whether the attending doctor has complied with the applicable law and professional guidelines, the committee should notify the attending doctor of its decision within six weeks of the termination of life, although in exceptional circumstances this could be extended to a maximum of three months. If a majority of the committee considered that the doctor had not complied with the legal requirements, it would be obliged to forward the documents to the police; in the case of non-compliance with professional guidance, the documents should be forwarded to the General Medical Council for investigation.

Moreover, the national committee should be required to publish annual reports detailing the number of lives terminated and statistics relating to, for example, the nature of the suffering, the patient's age and gender; and the likely life expectancy of the patient at the time the request was made. However, unlike the Dutch committees, the national review committee should also play a policy-making role, not merely describing how the law is operating, but also how it could be improved and evaluating whether the safeguards appear to be providing adequate protection from abuse. In

---

[ix] If the experience in the United Kingdom were to reflect that of Belgium and the Netherlands, cancer is likely to represent the largest cause of suffering;[52] 88.5% of all reported terminations of life during 2003 concerned cancer patients.[23]

considering what improvements could be made, the committee should consult with the medical professional bodies. It would also be responsible for formulating national guidance for the prior review of requests by the regional committees.

Conscientious objection

It is clear that both the Dutch and Belgian Acts empower the patient to request euthanasia, but neither Act requires the doctor to comply with that request. As in Belgium, the right to conscientious objection should be expressly recognised. However, the Act should also state that if a doctor wishes to avail herself of the right to conscientious objection, she is under a duty to refer the patient on to another practitioner who is not known to object to the active termination of life. Moreover, as the ODMD has recognised, the doctor should inform the patient in good time of her views of the different possibilities at the end of life, avoiding the need for a patient in the advanced stages of terminally illness having to find another doctor who does not have a conscientious objection to euthanasia.[44]

The need for an investment in palliative care

Any Act legalising the termination of life should be accompanied by invest-ment in palliative care. Palliative care is still not well developed in England and Wales and provision varies depending where the patient lives. However, an inability to access adequate palliative care should never be a reason for requesting the termination of life and thus any legislation legalising AVE and PAS should be accompanied by a commensurate investment both in palliative care in general, but particularly in hospice care.

CONCLUSION

Studies conducted in each of the three jurisdictions have shown that the pro-hibition of AVE, either by way of murder or a separate offence of killing on request, does not constitute effective control. This is particularly so given the reluctance to prosecute and/or convict doctors who are suspected of per-forming AVE or PAS. There is little doubt that in England and Wales some doctors actively terminate their patients' lives at their request, or provide PAS. However, the legal situation does not recognise the social reality, mak-ing communication between doctors and patients more difficult, leaving patients vulnerable to abuse and doctors liable to prosecution. Whilst it must be admitted that it would never be possible to prevent all forms of abuse, given the potential for abuse that currently exists, it is argued that that the time has come to regulate AVE and PAS; as Otlowski argues 'There is no scope for control in circumstances where the practice remains hidden.'[11] By drawing upon the Dutch and Belgian experience it would be possible to legalise AVE and PAS, framing adequate safeguards to protect patients from abuse and avoiding the slippery slope to involuntary euthanasia. As the French National Consultative Ethics Committee for Health and Life Sciences stated in 2000, 'It is never healthy for a society to experience situations where discrepancy between rules as they are laid down and real life is too glaring.'[59]

References

1.   Rachels J. The end of life: euthanasia and morality. Oxford: OUP; 1986; Chs 7 and 8.
2.   Harris J. The value of life. London: Routledge; 1985: Ch 2.
3.   Ashworth A. Principles of criminal law. 3rd edn. Oxford: OUP; 1999:180.
4.   Williams G. The principle of double effect and terminal sedation. Medical Law Review 2001; 9:41.
5.   Keown J. Restoring moral and intellectual shape to the law after Bland. Law Quarterly Review 1997; 113:482–503 at 495.
6.   Freeman M. Denying death its dominion: thoughts on the Diane Pretty case. Medical Law Review 2002; 245–270, at 253–4.
7.   Report of the House of Lords Select Committee on Medical Ethics. HL paper 21 (1993–4), para 260–261.
8.   Government Response to House of Lords Select Committee on Medical Ethics, 1994, Cm 2553, at 5.
9.   Ward BJ, Tate PA. Attitudes among NHS doctors to requests for euthanasia. BMJ (London) 1994; 308:332.
10. Doward J. The Observer 19 September 2004.
11. Otlowski M. The effectiveness of legal control of euthanasia: lessons from comparative law. In: Klijn A, et al (eds) Regulating physician-negotiated death (special issue of Recht der Werklijkheid). Elsevier; 2001; 137, at 153.
12. Dutch Health Council. Euthanasie. Advies inzake euthanasie uitgebracht door de Gezondheidsraad aan de Minister en de Staatssecretarie van Volksgezondheid en Milieuhygiëne [Euthanasia: Advice concerning euthanasia from the Health Council to the Minister and the Secretary of State for Public and Environmental Health]. The Hague: Staatsuitgeverij; 1982:86–88.
13. Magnusson R. Angels of death: exploring the euthanasia underground. Melbourne: Melbourne University Press; 2002.
14. Ottlowski M. The effectiveness of legal control of euthanasia: lessons from comparative law. In: Klijn A, et al (eds) Regulating physician-negotiated death (special issue of Recht der Werklijkheid). Elsevier; 200; 137, at 151.
15. Keown J. Euthanasia ethics and public policy: An argument against legalisation. Cambridge: CUP; 2002:63.
16. Hansard HL 6 June 2003: Column 1587.
17. Keown J. Euthanasia ethics and public policy: An argument against legalisation. Cambridge: CUP; 2002: Ch 7.
18. State Commission on Euthanasia. Rapport van der Staatscommissie Euthanasie [Report of the State Commission on Euthanasia]. Vol. 1. The Hague: Staatsuitgeverij; 1985:26.
19. Griffiths J, Bood A, Weyers H. Euthanasia and law in the Netherlands. Amsterdam: Amsterdam University Press; 1998: Ch 6.
20. Griffiths J, Bood A, Weyers H. Euthanasia and law in the Netherlands. Amsterdam: Amsterdam University Press; 1998; Ch 2.
21. Henley J. 'This is not a life. I can lead it no more'. The Guardian 27 October 2003; 14.

22. KNMG. Standpunt hoofdbestuur inzake euthanasie [Position statement of the Governing Board on Euthanasia]. Utrecht; 1995.

23. Regional Review Committees. Annual Report 2003, May 2004, at 22. Available at: http://www.toetsingscommissieseuthanasie.nl/pdf/jaarverslag-2003.pdf.

24. Regional Review Committees. Annual Report 2002, April 2003, at 21. Available at: http://www.toetsingscommissieseuthanasie.nl/pdf/jaarverslag-2002.pdf. A summary of this report is available in English at http://www.toetsingscommissieseuthanasie. nl/pdf/jaarverslag2002_engels.pdf.

25. Regional Review Committees. Annual Report 2002, at 20.

26. Sheldon T. Being 'tired of life' is not grounds for euthanasia. British Medical Journal 2003; 326:71.

27. Regional Review Committees. Annual Report 2003, at 21.

28. Klijn A. Will doctors' behaviour be more accountable under the new Dutch regime? In: Klijn A, et al, eds. Regulating physician-negotiated death (special issue of Recht der Werklijkheid). Elsevier; 2001: 159, at 160.

29. Regional Review Committees. Annual Report 2003, at 23.

30. Griffiths J, Bood A, Weyers H. Euthanasia and law in the Netherlands. Amsterdam: Amsterdam University Press; 1998:105.

31. KNMG. Medisch handelen rond het levenseinde bij wilsonbekwame patiënten [Medical practice at the end of life in relation to incompetent patients]. Houten/Diegem: Bohn Stafleu Van Loghum; 1997.

32. Klijn A. Will doctors' behaviour be more accountable under the new Dutch regime? In Klijn A, et al, eds. Regulating physician-negotiated death (special issue of Recht der Werklijkheid). Elsevier; 2001:159, at 176.

33. Regional Review Committees. Annual Report 2003, at 27–28.

34. Dutch Health Council. Advies inzake zorgvuldigheidseisen euthanasie [Advice concerning the requirements of careful practice for euthanasia]. The Hague: Ministry of Public and Environmental Health; 1987:6.

35. Van der Maas PJ, Van Delden JJ, Pijnenborg L, Loumann CW. Euthanasia and other medical decisions concerning the end of life. Lancet 1991; 338:669–674.

36. Van der Maas PJ, Van der Wal G, Haverkate I, et al. Euthanasia, physician-assisted suicide and other medical practices involving the end of life in the Netherlands, 1990–1995. New England Journal of Medicine 1996; 335:1699–1705.

37. Van der Wal G, van der Maas PJ, Bosma JM, et al. Evaluation of the euthanasia notification procedure in the Netherlands. New England Journal of Medicine 1996; 335:1706–1711.

38. Onwuteaka-Philipsen B, van der Heide A, Koper D, et al. Euthanasia and other end-of-life decisions in the Netherlands in 1990, 1995 and 2001. Lancet 2003; 362:395–399.

39. Adams M. Euthanasia: the process of legal change in Belgium. In: Klijn A, et al, eds. Regulating physician-negotiated death (special issue of Recht der Werklijkheid). Elsevier; 2001:46.

40. Deliens L, Mortier F, Bilsen J, et al. End-of-life decisions in medical practice in Flanders, Belgium: a nationwide survey. Lancet 2000; 356:1806–1811.

41. Mortier F, Bilsen J, Vander Stichele RH, et al. Attitudes, sociodemographic characteristics, and actual end-of-life decisions of physicians in Flanders, Belgium. Medical Decision Making 2003; 502.

42. Belgian Advisory Committee for Bioethics. Opinion Number 1, 12/05/1997, Concerning the desirability of a legal regulation of euthanasia. Available at: http://www.health.fgov.be/bioeth/fr/avis/avis-n01.htm.

43. Adams M, Nys H. Comparative reflections on the Belgian Euthanasia Act 2002. Medical Law Review 2003; 11:353–376, at 360.

44. National Council of the ODMB. Avis no. 100: Avis relatif aux soins palliatifs, à l'euthanasie et à d'autres décisions médicales concernant la fin de vie [Opinion relating to palliative care, euthanasia and other medical decisions relating to the end of life]. 22 March 2003, Bulletin du Conseil National no. 100: 6. Available at: http://www.ordomedic. be/web-Fr/fr/a100/a100006f.htm.

45. National Council of the ODMB. Opinion of 17/11/2001. 'Euthanasie' Bulletin 94: 2. Available at: http://www.ordomedic. be/web-Fr/fr/a94/a094007f.htm.

46. Report of the House of Lords Select Committee on Medical Ethics. HL paper 21 (1993–4), para 238.

47. Dutch Health Council. Euthanasie. Advies inzake euthanasie uitgebracht door de Gezondheidsraad aan de Minister en de Staatssecretarie van Volksgezondheid en Milieuhygiëne [Euthanasia: Advice concerning euthanasia from the Health Council to the Minister and the Secretary of State for Public and Environmental Health]. The Hague: Staatsuitgeverij; 1982:15.

48. Brock DW. Life and death. Cambridge: CUP; 1993:55.

49. KNMG. Vision on euthanasia. Utrecht: KNMG; 1995.

50. Groenewoud JH, van der Heide A, Onwuteaka-Philipsen B, et al. Clinical problems with the performance of euthanasia and physician-assisted suicide in the Netherlands. New England Journal of Medicine 2000; 342:551.

51. Report of the House of Lords Select Committee on Medical Ethics. HL paper 21 (1993–4), para 20.

52. Onwuteaka-Philipsen B, van der Heide A, Koper D, et al. Euthanasia and other end-of-life decisions in the Netherlands in 1990, 1995 and 2001. Lancet 2003; 362: 395–399, at 397.

53. Regional Review Committees. Annual Report 2003, at 3.

54. Burgess S, Hawton K. Suicide, euthanasia and the psychiatrist. Philosophy, Psychiatry & Psychology 1998; 5(2):113.

55. Nolen WA, et al. Assisted suicide in psychiatry: clinical issues. European Psychiatry 1996; 11:198.

56. Department of Health. National suicide prevention strategy for England 2002, at 3.

57. Harris EC, Barraclough B. Suicide as an outcome for mental disorders. A meta-analysis. British Journal of Psychiatry 1997; 170:205.

58. Burgess S, Hawton K. Suicide, euthanasia and the psychiatrist. Philosophy, Psychiatry and Psychology 1998; 5(2):122.

59. French National Consultative Ethics Committee for Health and Life Sciences. Avis no. 63, 2000. End of life, ending life, euthanasia, part 4. Online. Available: http://62.160.32.15/english/pdf/avis063.pdf.

Index

A

Abortion
  anti-abortion group *see* CORE
    (Comment on Reproductive
    Ethics)
  legislation, 122
  preimplantation genetic diagnosis, 134
  women's rights, 121
Abuse, medical
  and medico-crime, 95, 96, 97, 105
  see also Medico-crime (UK)
Acetylarsan (arsenical compound)
  negligence allegations (case law),
    86–87
Act of Geo. II
  and bodysnatching, 160–161, 165
Advertising Standards Authority
  cosmetic surgery, 240, 241
Advisory Committee for Bioethics
  Belgium, 257, 284
Advisory Committee on Genetic Testing,
  145
AFCH (French association of hospital
  coordinators), 177
'Age of Hospitals', eighteenth century as,
  56
Agency for Healthcare Research and
  Quality
  United States, 23
Alberti, K G M M, 58, 73
Alder Hey Hospital
  body parts scandal, 7, 153, 154
  Inquiry, 159, 163, 164, 167, 168
  justifications for actions, 163
  see also Bristol Royal Infirmary; Royal
    Liverpool Children's Hospital
Alliance for Democracy
  United States, 30

Allitt, Beverly, 97
AMA (American Medical Association),
  21
American Medical Association (AMA), 21
Anaesthetics, establishment (1846), 57
Anatomists, sales of bodies to *see*
  Bodysnatching scandals;
  Resurrectionists
Anatomy Act 1832
  bodysnatching scandals, 164–167
Anderson, Robert, 154
Aneurysm, bursting of
  medical negligence case law, 85–86
Antibiotics
  negligent withdrawal of treatment
    (case law), 81–82
Antiseptic surgery, establishment (1865),
  57
Appeal Panel
  National Institute for Clinical
    Excellence, 43
Appraisal Committee
  National Institute for Clinical
    Excellence, 41, 43, 48
Area Health Authorities
  removal, 59
Artificial nutrition and hydration
  withdrawal, 271
Assault
  criminal prosecution of cosmetic
    surgeons, 236
Assisted reproduction *see* PGD
  (preimplantation genetic diagno-
  sis); Reproductive technologies
Assisted suicide
  absolute legal prohibition (Dutch law),
    274, 275
  Belgium, 284
Audit, medical, 61

Augé, M, 184
Australia
  Bolam principle, rejection, 4, 79, 84–86
Autism
  alleged link with MMR vaccine, 222, 223
Autonomy
  clinical, rise of prior to 1948, 57–58
  defined, 218
  euthanasia debate, 9, 10, 277
  incompetent, intervention on, 193
  intimacy, in, 121
  paternalism and, 9
  professionalism, main feature of, 96–97
  psychological, 6
  regulation, reproductive technologies, 126–127
  resulting sibling, preimplantation genetic diagnosis, 142, 144
  self-regulation of medical profession, 103
  vaccination of infants, 218–226
AVE (active voluntary euthanasia)
  autonomy and, 9, 10, 277
  Belgium, 270
  legislation in England and Wales
    absolute requirement of voluntary, informed consent, 292
  advantages, 270–274, 290–291
  as murder, 271, 273
  Netherlands, 270
  public support for, 273
  see also Euthanasia; PAS (physician-assisted suicide)
Ayling, Clifford: intimate examinations by, 96, 97, 98, 102, 106, 108
  Channel 4 documentary, 99
  chaperones and, 107

B

BAAPS (British Association of Aesthetic Plastic Surgeons), 240
Baillie, David, 97
Ball, J M, 164, 165
BAPS (British Association of Plastic Surgeons), 240
Battery
  criminal prosecution of cosmetic surgeons, 236
Begg, Norman, 214, 221–222
Belgian Medical Association, 257

Belgium, right to die debate, 256–257
  euthanasia
    lawful, conditions for, 285–289
    notification requirement, 289–290
  lessons for England and Wales, 290–293
Berger, Peter, 16, 29
Best interests approach
  medical intervention, 197–201
Beta-interferon (multiple sclerosis treatment)
  appraisal of, 3, 44, 45, 46, 47
Bevan, Aneurin, 58
Birmingham Children's Hospital
  removal of child's heart at, 157
Bishop, John, 166
Black Report (1980)
  healthcare inequality (UK), 25
Blair Government
  language of risk, avoiding, 68
  resource allocation, 37, 40, 50
Bland, Anthony, 199–200
Blood donations
  banning when, 218–219
Blue Cross (United States), 21
Blue Shield (United States), 21
Bodily security issues
  incompetents, 194, 195, 202, 203–209
    diluted protected justifications, 193, 208–209
Bodysnatching scandals, 7, 151–172
  nineteenth century, 152–153
  twentieth century, 153–154
  Anatomy Act 1832, 164–167
  Human Tissue Act 1961, 167–169
  media responses, 152, 153, 157–160
  medical justification, 160–164
  public outrage, 154–160
  victims and perpetrators, 155–157
Bolam principle (medical negligence cases), 79–92
  attitude, change of, 81–83
  Australia, rejection of principle in, 4, 79, 84–86
  background/decision, 80–81
  clinical risk and, 59, 64
  commonwealth jurisdiction, 79, 91
  cosmetic surgery, 235, 239
  in Malaysia, 4, 79, 86–91
  reasonableness standard, 79–80, 89
  standard of care, 79–80
Bordo, Susan, 246
Bowel disorders
  alleged link with MMR vaccine, 222, 223
Bradley, David, 58

Brain death
    conflicting priorities, 178–179
    definition, 174
    in young people, 182
Bristol Royal Infirmary
    justification for actions, 163
    Kennedy Report into events at, 47
    paediatric cardiac services failures at,
        40, 68, 154
    Public Inquiry (1998), 154, 156, 158,
        159, 167
        Interim Report, 159, 163–164, 168
    resurrectionists at, 152
    see also Alder Hey Hospital; Royal
        Liverpool Children's Hospital
British Association of Aesthetic Plastic
    Surgeons (BAAPS), 240
British Association of Plastic Surgeons
    (BAPS), 240
British Medical Journal
    Supplement 1943, 58
Broadsides
    defined, 152
Brownsword, R, 140
BSE enquiry, 224
Building a safer NHS for Patients
    (Department of Health), 71
'Bureau-professionalism', 58
Burke, William, 151, 152, 154, 155–156, 165
    Burking, crime of, 152, 166
    trial and hanging of, 153, 164

C

Cadavers, role in medical education, 191
Caillavet (senator), 182
Calabresi, G, 194
Caledonian Mercury, 153, 162
Canada
    health insurance system, 27
Castel, R, 185
Cervical smears, negligence screening of,
    83
CHA (Canada Health Act), 27–28
CHAI (Commission of Healthcare Audit
    and Inspection)
    CHI, superseding of, 67
    clinical governance reviews, 68
Chaperone use
    crime prevention, 107, 108
CHI (Commission for Health
    Improvement)
    annual report on NHS (2003), 69
    clinical governance reviews, 68

establishment, 67
Chief Medical Officer see CMO (Chief
    Medical Officer)
Christian Democratic Party
    Netherlands, 256
CHST (Canada Health and Social
    Transfer), 27
Churches, hospitals in, 56
Citizens Council
    National Institute for Clinical
        Excellence, 43, 49
Civil Code
    Netherlands, 255
Clarke, Kenneth, 224
Clinical governance
    Clinic Registered Managers, 240
    defined, 67–68
Clinical Negligence Scheme for Trusts
    (CNST), 65, 66, 67
Clinical risk, English hospitals see
    Hospitals, ownership of clinical risk
    (England)
Clinic Registered Managers
    clinical governance procedures, 240
Cloning (somatic cell nuclear transfer), 116
CMO (Chief Medical Officer)
    and clinical governance, 67, 68
CNST (Clinical Negligence Scheme for
    Trusts), 65, 66, 67
Cobb, Paul, 97
Comité Consultatif National d'Ethique,
    175, 183
Comment on Reproductive Ethics see
    CORE (Comment on Reproductive
    Ethics)
Commission Consultative des Droits de
    l'Homme, 175
Commission for Health Improvement see
    CHI (Commission for Health
    Improvement)
Commission on Patients' Rights
    Netherlands, 255
'Commitment to Quality, a Quest for
    Excellence' (Department of Health),
    70
Commodity
    health as (in USA), 21–22
Competence of patients
    euthanasia, 292–293
    incompetence, euthanasia, 293
    incompetents, medical intervention see
        Incompetents, medical interven-
        tions harming therapeutic inter-
        ests of
    right to refuse medical treatment, 270

Congenital rubella syndrome (CRS), 219
Conscience clause privilege
    organ donation, 183
Conscientious objections
    euthanasia, 298
Consensus management
    demise of, 59
    introduction, 59
Consent
    capacity to, meaning, 237
    cosmetic surgery regulation, 234, 237
    lack of, cosmetic surgery, 237, 238
    presumption of, organ donation
        (France), 173, 174–178, 179, 181,
        184, 185, 186
Conservative Government (UK)
    cost-containment, 63
    supply-side efficiency, 39
Consultation requirement
    euthanasia, 295
Controls assurance
    defined, 69
Convention on the Elimination of All
        Forms of Discrimination Against
        Women
    and reproductive rights, 121
Convention on Human Rights and
        Biomedicine
    Council of Europe, 194, 207
Convention on the Rights of the Child
    vaccination of children and, 217
Cooper, Astley, 161
CORE (Comment on Reproductive
        Ethics)
    preimplantation genetic diagnosis, 119,
        120
    Whitaker case, 138, 141
Corpses
    conflicting priorities, 178
Cosmetic surgery
    Advertising Standards Authority, 240,
        241
    assault or battery, criminal prosecu-
        tions of surgeons, 236
    beauty industry, oppressiveness, 246
    Bolam principle, 235, 239
    case law, 238
    common law rules, 234–239
    consent, lack of, 237, 238
    disclosure of risk information, 235–236
        inadequate, 238, 241
    feminist ethics, 242–247
    liability of surgeons, 239
    misleading information, 238
    negligence, 238, 239

personal injury, 239
plastic surgery, NHS regulation, 240
private surgeons, 239
    unregulated, 240
'prudent patient test', 236
reactions to, 233–234
regulation, 234–242
    statutory, 239–242
risks and benefits, consideration, 235
skill and care requirement, 239
Cost-containment, 63
Costs of medical care
    United States, 22–23
Council of Europe
    Convention on Human Rights and
        Biomedicine, 194, 207
Council for Science and Society
    Report of Working Party (1977), 62
CPS (Crown Prosecution Service)
    medico-crime, 106
Crime prevention
    medico-crime, 106
Criminal Code, 254
Criminal doctors
    clinically incompetent doctors distin-
        guished, 94, 102–103
    see also Doctors; Medico-crime (UK)
Crown Immunity
    and health and safety risks, hospitals,
        59, 60, 61
CRS (congenital rubella syndrome), 219
Cyberwoman, creation, 234, 246, 247
Cyborg, concept of, 234, 246–247
Cystic fibrosis, 116
Cytoscreeners
    defined, 83

D

Dainton, C, 56
Danish Ethical Council, 259
Davis, Kathy, 245–246
Declaration of Helsinki
    World Medical Association, 195, 207
Declaration of Incompatibility, 210
Degeling, P, 72
Deliens, L, 284
Denmark
    right to die debate, 258–259
Department of Health
    beta-interferon funding, 45
    Building a safer NHS for Patients, 71
    'Commitment to Quality, a Quest for
        Excellence', 70

MMR safety debate, 224
non-heart beating donation, review of, 209
preimplantation genetic diagnosis, 'Guiding Principles', 138
Designer babies, 115, 120–122
Dhasmana, Janardan, 159
Diamorphine
    lethal injection (Shipman case), 94
Diphtheria, 220
Disabled people
    and genetic modification techniques, 116–117, 118
Dobson, Frank, 60
Doctor–patient relationship
    dominance of doctors, 95
    scope for abuse, 96
Doctors
    crimes committed by see Medico-crime (UK)
    criminal see Criminal doctors
    medical dominance, culture of, 58–59, 95
    payment of GPs, 226–228
    'problem', management of, 99–100, 101–102, 103, 104–105
    sexual assault by see Sexual assault by doctors
    striking off, 236
Donaldson, Liam, 67, 241
Donegan, Jane, 228
Double effect doctrine
    euthanasia debate, 271–272
Drug companies see Pharmaceutical industry
Drugs and Therapeutics Bulletin, 45
Du Bois, W, 29
Due care requirement
    euthanasia, 296
        Dutch law, 276–281
Due process
    and legitimacy, 42–44
Dutch Association for Voluntary Euthanasia, 254–255
Dworkin, Gerald, 196
Dworkin, R, 126

E

Economic concentration
    United States, 18–19
Economic and Social Research Council, 118
ECT (electroconvulsive therapy)
    and Bolam case, 80

Edwards, N, 72
Egyptians
    healthcare, 56
Elchardus, M, 260
Ely Hospital
    standard of care inquiry (1969), 60
Ethics
    feminist, and cosmetic surgery, 6, 234, 242–247
    preimplantation genetic diagnosis, 143–145
    rationing decisions, 49
    vaccination of infants, 217–228
Ethnic groups
    healthcare system inequalities, 24–25
Eugenics, 117
European Convention on Human Rights
    reproductive rights, 121
European Values Study
    right to die debate, 261, 262
Euthanasia, 269–301
    active voluntary see AVE (active voluntary euthanasia)
    anticipatory requests for, 278–279
    Belgian law, 283–290
        lessons for England and Wales, 9, 290–293
    competent adult patients, 292–293
    conscientious objections, 298
    consultation requirement, 295
    definition, 253, 284–285, 291
    due care requirement, 296
    Dutch law, 274–283
        lessons for England and Wales, 9, 290–293
    as homicide, 284
    incompetent patients, 293
    intention and foresight, 272
    killing/allowing to kill distinguished, 271, 273
    legalisation in Netherlands/Belgium, 254
    mercy killing, offence of, 273
    palliative care, need for investment in, 298
    review committees see Review committees (euthanasia)
    suffering
        non-somatic, 278
        psychiatric, 278, 279, 287
        unbearable, 277, 278, 279
        without prospect of improvement requirement, 294–295
    terminal illness, 297–298

Euthanasia (*contd*)
  voluntary, informed request for termination of life, absolute requirement, 291–293
  see also Belgium, right to die debate; Netherlands, right to die debate; Right to die
Evening Courant, 152, 153
Everyday crime
  medico-crime distinguished, 94
Evidence
  reproductive technologies, 122–126
'Exemplar operational risk management strategy' (NHS Estates) 1997, 66, 70
Expert opinion
  determinants of medical liability, 81, 82–83
Express, the, 160
Exxon-Mobil, 18

F

Families USA, 29
FCCE (Federal Commission of Control and Evaluation)
  Belgium, 289, 290
Federalism
  United States, 17–18
Fee-for-service systems
  United States, 23
Feldbrugge, F J M, 194
Feminism
  cosmetic surgery, 6, 234, 242–247
  reproductive technologies, 117
Financial assurance, role, 69–70
Finland
  right to die debate, 260
First Class Service: Quality in the new NHS (1998), 40
Ford Corporation, 18
Foucault, Michel, 185, 245
Foundation for Voluntary Euthanasia
  Netherlands, 254–255
France
  National Consultative Ethics Committee for Health and Life Sciences, 299
  organ donation *see* Organ donation (France)
  power relations, 185
  unvaccinated children, sanctions against, 225
Free-from-restraint access
  medico-crime, 95

Freidson, E, 185
Fry, Elizabeth, 57

G

Gamete intra-fallopian transfer (GIFT), 120
GDP *see* Gross domestic product (GDP)
General Medical Council *see* GMC (General Medical Council)
General Motors, 18
General practitioners *see* GPs (general practitioners)
Genetic cleansing
  disabled people, 116–117
Genetic diseases
  examples, 116
  and preimplantation genetic diagnosis, 134, 142
    see also Preimplantation genetic diagnosis
Genetic exceptionalism, 116
Genetic modification techniques, 117, 118
  ban on, option of, 124
    see also PGD (preimplantation genetic diagnosis); Reproductive technologies
Geographical inequalities
  rationing of healthcare resources, 39
German measles, 219
GIFT (gamete intra-fallopian transfer), 120
Gilligan, Carol, 243
Glasgow Courier, 153
GMC (General Medical Council)
  Bristol Royal Infirmary scandal and, 154
  cosmetic surgery guidelines, 236
  crime control and, 98, 105
  criticism of, and Shipman murders, 98, 100, 103
  database of crime, failure to keep, 104
  establishment, 57
  investigations, lack of enforcement, 297
  patient satisfaction questionnaire, development, 107
  plastic surgery, specialist register, 240
  regulation of standards, 96
GM crops, unknown health risks, 219
Godden, Jacqui, 96
GPs (general practitioners)
  payment of, 226–228
    see also Doctors
Grave-robbing *see* Resurrectionists

Great Depression
    and United States, 21
Green, Peter, 102
Greer, S L, 73
Griffiths Inquiry into NHS management
    (1983), 59
Griffiths, J, 275
Gross domestic product (GDP)
    United States, 22
Grubb, A, 197
Guide to Good Medical Practice
    and revalidation, 107
Gunn, M, 207–209

H

Habermas, J, 144
Halls, Thomas, 162
Ham, C, 58, 73
Handicap
    and preimplantation genetic diagnosis,
        134
Haraway, Donna (*Manifesto for Cyborgs*),
    246
Hare, William, 151, 152, 153, 154, 155–156,
    164, 165
Harris, John, 143, 207, 208
Hashmi case
    Human Fertilisation and Embryology
        Act 1990, 136, 137–138, 140, 141,
        143
Haslam, Michael, 97, 102
Hawkins, Caesar, 162
HCs (hospital coordinators)
    organ donation (France), 174, 176–177,
        178, 179, 184
Health
    as commodity (USA), 21–22
    definition of, 5, 20
    healthcare inequity, 23–27
    as public issue (USA), 27–29
Healthcare Commission *see* CHAI
    (Commission of Healthcare Audit
        and Inspection)
Healthcare inequity
    United States, 23–27
Healthcare resources *see* Resources for
    healthcare, allocation
Health Service Ombudsman, 3
Health Services Commission
    Oregon, 48
Healy, Timothy, 97
Herd immunity
    defined, 214

Hereditary diseases
    and preimplantation genetic diagnosis,
        134
    see also Preimplantation genetic
        diagnosis
HFEA (Human Fertisation and
    Embryology Authority), 8–9, 117
    Ethics Committee, 137
    preimplantation genetic diagnosis, 119,
        121–122, 135, 142, 144
        Hashmi decision, 136, 137–138, 140,
            141, 143
    reproductive technologies, effective-
        ness in deciding on, 123
    tissue typing, permitting, 122
HGAC (Human Genetics Advisory
    Commission), 117, 125
Hib vaccine, 222
Higgins, J, 60
Hippocratic tradition, 38–39
Homicide
    euthanasia as, 284
Hospital coordinators *see* HCs (hospital
    coordinators)
Hospitals, ownership of clinical risk
    (England), 55–57
    pre-1948, 56–58
    1948–1990s, 58–61
    1990s, 63–71
    twenty-first century, 71–72
    active/passive ownership, 74
    case law
        Bolam, 71
        Bolitho, 70–71
    clinical autonomy, origins, 57
    non-clinical risk, and, 55–56, 57, 59, 61,
        62–63, 65, 73–74
House of Commons
    Science and Technology Committee, 117
Human Fertilisation and Embryology Act
    1990
    Hashmi case, 136, 137–138, 140, 141, 143
    liberal provisions, 136–138
    preimplantation genetic diagnosis,
        135–141
    'treatment services', defined, 136, 139,
        140
    Warnock Report and, 128
    Whitaker case, 138–139, 141
Human genetic modification, 116
Human Genetics Advisory Commission
    (HGAC), 117, 125
Human Genetics Commission, 125, 145
Human leukocyte antigen (HLA) testing
    see Tissue typing

Human Rights Act 1998, 210
Human Tissue Act 1961
   bodysnatching scandals, 167–169
Human Tissue Act 2004, 1, 168–169
Huntington's disease, 116

I

ICSI (intracytoplasmic sperm injection),
   120
ICUs (intensive care units)
   nurses, 183
   and organ donation (France), 177, 184
Imhotep (ancient healer), 56
Incentive payments
   vaccination of infants, 227, 228
Incompetence, professional
   medico-crime distinguished, 94,
      98–102, 103, 104, 108
Incompetents, medical interventions
      harming therapeutic interests of, 6,
      191–211
   best interests approach, applying, 193,
      197–201
   bodily security issues, 194, 195, 202,
      203–209
      diluted protection justifications,
         193, 208–209
   contemporary legal standards, 193–197
   dignity and respect, 199–200
   dying person (insentient), legal scope
      for interventions on, 201–203,
      204–205
   needs of others and, 203–209
   'not against interests' standard, 203
      case law, 196–197
   therapeutic/non-therapeutic,
      meaning, 191–192
   vital organ removal, adverse impacts,
      202–203
Indemnity, NHS, 61
Individualism doctrine
   United States, 19, 29
Infant mortality
   United States, 24
Inflation, healthcare
   United States, 22–23
Influenza treatment
   zanamivir, appraisal of, 3, 44–45, 46, 47
Inglehart, R, 260
Institute for the Study of Genetics,
      Biorisks and Society
   genetic modification techniques, 118
Integrity rights, 121

Intensive care units see ICUs (intensive
   care units)
Intensivists, and organ donation (France),
   176–177, 178, 179, 183, 184
'Internal market'
   National Health Service, 39, 40, 63
International Covenant on Economic,
      Social and Cultural Rights
   reproductive rights, 121
   vaccination of children, 218
Intimacy obligation
   medical examinations, 95
Intracytoplasmic sperm injection (ICSI),
   120
Invitation to Sociology (P Berger), 29
In vitro embryos, assisted conception, 133
   see also Preimplantation genetic
      diagnosis
Irvine, Sir Donald, 58
Isaacs Report
   unlawful retention of adult brains
      (2003), 168
IVF (in vitro fertilisation) clinics
   and preimplantation genetic diagnosis,
      8, 135

J

JABS Questionnaire
   vaccination of infants, 216, 223
Jackson, E, 118–119, 120
Judicial review
   health rationing, 39

K

Kant, Immanuel, 143
Kay, S, 240, 241
Kennedy, I, 197
Kennedy Report
   Bristol Royal Infirmary, events at, 47
Keown, J, 273
Kerr, William, 102
King's Fund study
   medical audit (1991-92), 61
KNMG (Royal Dutch Medical
      Association)
   right to die debate, 265, 275, 280, 281,
      283, 284, 286, 292
Knox, Robert (anatomist)
   sale of bodies to, 7, 155, 156, 157–158,
      162
Kohlberg, Lawrence, 243

L

Laissez-faire economics
  United States, 19
Lammy, David, 209
Law
  and structure/culture of society, 15–16
Law Commission
  capacity to consent, meaning, 237
  Mental Incapacity report, 205
Lawrence, William, 161
Lazar-houses (thirteenth-century hospitals), 56
Ledward, Rodney, 5
Legitimacy
  and due process, 42–44
  intersubjective reasoning process, 48
  problem of, and health rationing, 2–3,
      37, 38, 40, 41–42, 43–44, 50
Liabilities to Third Parties Scheme, 65
Life expectancy
  in United States, 24
Light, D W, 20
Living donor transplantation, 194, 202
Living Will Data bank
  Denmark, 259
'Lois de bioéthique'
  French organ donation legislation, 175,
      176, 182
Lowrance, W, 62

M

Magnusson, R, 273
Malaysia, *Bolam* principle in, 4, 79, 86–91
Malpractice suits
  United States, 23
'Managed' care, 31
Manifesto for Cyborgs (D. Haraway), 246
Market efficiency
  United States, 25
Marshall, M, 72
Mason, Ronald, 97
Masterton family
  preimplantation genetic diagnosis,
      135–136
Materialistic value orientation
  right to die debate, 260
MacDougal, Helen, 153
Measles, 219, 220
Measles, Mumps and Rubella *see* MMR
      (Measles, Mumps and Rubella)
      vaccine

Media responses
  bodysnatching scandals, 152, 153,
      157–160
  rationing, 39
Medicaid (United States), 26–27
Medical Defence Union, 58, 59, 60
Medical Devices Agency, 239
Medical dominance, culture of, 58–59, 95
Medical history, failure to ask
  negligence case law, 87
Medical-industrial complex
  United States, 26
Medical interventions
  incompetents, for *see* Incompetents,
      medical interventions harming
      therapeutic interests of
Medical negligence
  Bolam principle *see Bolam* principle,
      medical negligence cases
  cosmetic surgery, 238, 239
  Medical Defence Union and, 59
Medicare (United States), 26–27
Medications, pain-killing
  likely to hasten death, 271–272
Medicines and Healthcare Products
      Regulatory Agency, 239
Medico-crime (UK), 93–111
  causes, 95–98
  chaperone use, 107, 108
  CPS protocol, 106
  crime prevention, 106
  database, need for, 104
  definition of 'medico-crime', 93, 94–95
  everyday crime distinguished, 94
  free-from-restraint access, 95
  'harm done', 97
  health professions, 105
  legislation, 106
  medico-patient crime/medico-professional crime sub-categories, 94
  National Framework, 106
  police involvement, 105
  privileges of professionals facilitating,
      94–95, 96–97
  'problem doctors', managing, 99–100,
      101–102, 103, 104–105
  professional incompetence distinguished, 94, 98–102, 103, 104, 108
  public re-education, 103–104, 106
  reform recommendations, 104–108
  revalidation and, 107–108
  self-regulation, 96, 98–99, 108
    resistance to change, 100–102
  statistics, and monitoring, 104–105
  status quo, preserving, 102–104

Mens rea
  euthanasia debate, 272
Mental Capacity Act 2005, 1, 7, 193,
  206–207, 209–210, 237
Mental Incapacity report
  Law Commission, 205
Mental Incapacity Research Committee,
  205
Mercy killing *see* Euthanasia; Right
  to die
Merrett Health Risk Management
  Limited, 64
Miller, Elizabeth, 223
Mills, C W, 19
Mit Livtestamente (Danish organisation),
  258
MMR (Measles, Mumps and Rubella)
  vaccine
  reduction in uptake, 5
  safety debate, 220, 221, 222–225
Monasteries, hospitals in, 56
Moran, G, 25
Morgan, Kathryn Pauly, 244–245, 246
Mortality rates
  United States, 24
Multiple sclerosis
  beta-interferon treatment, appraisal of,
  3, 44, 45, 46, 47
Multiple Sclerosis Society, 45, 46
Murders of patients
  active voluntary euthanasia, 271, 273
  see also Shipman, Harold: murders of
  patients by
Muscular dystrophy, 116

N

NAO (National Audit Office), 3
Nash, Adam, 116
National Audit Office (NAO), 3
National Board of Health
  Denmark, 258
National Care Standards Commission *see*
  NCSC (National Care Standards
  Commission)
National Clinical Assessment Authority
  (NCAA), 105
National Colloquium on Bioethics
  Belgium, 256–257
National Consultative Ethics Committee
  for Health and Life Sciences
  France, 299
National Ethical Council
  Denmark, 258

National Framework for Medico-Crime
  Advisory Committee, 106
National health insurance system
  Canada, 27
National Institute for Clinical Excellence
  see NICE (National Institute for
  Clinical Excellence)
National Patient Safety Authority *see*
  NPSA (National Patient Safety
  Agency)
National Physicians for National Health
  Plans
  United States, 29
National Reporting and Learning System,
  creation (2003), 71
National Service Frameworks (NSFs), 40,
  67
Navarro, Vincent, 26
NCAA (National Clinical Assessment
  Authority), 105
NCSC (National Care Standards
  Commission)
  cosmetic surgery, 240
  cosmetic surgery inspection (2003), 241
'Need' factor
  as rationing principle, 38
Negligence *see Bolam* principle, medical
  negligence cases; Medical negli-
  gence
Nemo censetur ignorare legem principle
  organ donation (France), 7, 174, 185
Netherlands, right to die debate, 254–256
  Christian Democratic Party, 256
  Civil Code, 255
  Commission on Patients' Rights, 255
  Criminal Code, 255
  European Values Study, 266
  euthanasia, 274–283
    due care criteria, 276–281
    notification requirement, 281–283
    Regional Review Committees, 276,
    277, 279, 280, 281, 282
  KNMG (Royal Dutch Medical
    Association), 265, 275, 280, 281,
    286, 292
  lessons for England and Wales,
    290–293
  SCEN project, 280, 295
  State Commission on Euthanasia, 274,
    280, 284
Newgate Calendar, 155
'New managerialism', 59, 64
New NHS: Modern, Dependable (1997), 40
Next-of-kin
  and organ donation, 175, 179, 181–182

NHS Estates
  'Exemplar operational risk management strategy' 1997, 66, 70
NHS Executive
  controls assurance, 69
NHS indemnity
  introduction (1990), 61, 64–65
NHSLA (NHS Litigation Authority)
  and clinical risk, 65, 66, 70
NHS (National Health System)
  complaints procedures, and medico-crime, 105
  creation (1948), 55, 58
  indemnity see NHS indemnity
  'internal market', 39, 40, 63
    reform, 40
  Litigation Authority see NHSLA (NHS Litigation Authority)
  'modernisation' agenda, 72
  plastic surgery, regulation of, 240
  rationing of resources, modes of, 38–40
    see also Rationing of healthcare resources
  risks (1948-1990s), 58–61
  supply-side efficiency, enhancing of, 39
  trusts see NHS Trusts
NHS trusts
  clinical governance reviews, 68
  establishment, 61, 63
  NHS indemnity, introduction (1990), 64–65
  ownership of clinical risk, 61
  risk strategies, 64
  see also CNST (Clinical Negligence Scheme for Trusts)
NICE (National Institute for Clinical Excellence)
  Appeal Panel, 43
  Appraisal Committee, 41, 43, 48
  beta-interferon, evaluation of, 3, 44, 45, 46, 47
  Citizens Council, 43, 49
  establishment, 37, 40–42, 67
  evaluating, 38, 44–47
  evidence, open design of, 43
  guidance of, 40
  independence, perceived lack of, 46
  legitimacy problem, 2, 37, 38, 40, 41–42, 43–44, 50
  methodology, 41–42
  Partners' Council, 43
  rationing of healthcare by, 41
  reform, 47–50
  role, 2, 40–41
  as Special Health Authority, 40, 67

  transparency, alleged lack of, 46
    reform proposals, 48
  zanamivir, evaluation of, 3, 44–45, 46
Nichol, Sir Duncan, 64
Nightingale, Florence, 57, 60
Nightingale, K, 240, 241
Normansfield Hospital
  standard of care inquiry (1978), 60
Notes on Hospitals (F. Nightingale), 57
NPSA (National Patient Safety Agency)
  creation as Special Authority (2001), 71
  risk assurance process promoted by, 71–72
NSFs (National Service Frameworks), 40, 67
Nurses
  criminal actions by, 97
  ICU, 183

O

ODMB (Ordre des médecins)
  Belgian Order of Physicians, 284, 292
    and conscientious objection, 298
  National Council, 285–286, 287
Opisthotonos
  definition (case law), 84
Organ donation (France), 7, 173–188
  conflicting priorities, 178–182
  consent, presumption of, 173, 174–178, 179, 181, 184, 185, 186
  corpses, consideration of, 178–179
  grieving and, 184–185
  'heart beating death', 174
  hospital coordinators, 174, 176–177, 178, 179, 184
  intensivists, 176–177, 178, 179, 183, 184
  legislation, 185–186
  'Lois de bioéthique', 175, 176, 182
  nemo censetur ignorare legem principle, 7, 174, 185
  next-of-kin, 175, 179, 181–182
  professional ethos/law, 182–185
  registration of opposition, 175
  relatives of potential donors, role of, 173, 174, 176, 177, 179, 180
  transplantation units, 177

P

Palin, Henry, 98
Palliative care, 279, 285–286
  need for investment in, 298

Parenti, M, 18–19
Partners' Council
    National Institute for Clinical
        Excellence, 43
PAS (physician-assisted suicide)
    right to die debate, 275, 279, 290, 292,
        293
Paternalism, medical
    autonomy and, 9
    bodysnatching, 164
    clinical risk, ownership, 64
    incompetent, intervention on, 193
    medico-crime, 95
    presumed consent, law of, 181
    soft, 9
'Patient'
    meaning, 95
Patient satisfaction questionnaire, devel-
        opment
    General Medical Council, 107
Patients First (White Paper) 1979, 59
Pergau Dam affair
    preimplantation genetic diagnosis, 138
Persistent vegetative state (PVS), 199–200,
        279
Personal injury
    cosmetic surgery, 239
PGD (preimplantation genetic diagnosis),
        8, 116, 133–146
    applications, 134
    case law
        Hashmi, 136, 137–138, 140, 141, 143
        Masterton, 135–136
        Whitaker, 138–139, 141
    clinical interests of child, 144
    definition, 134
    ethical imperatives, acknowledging,
        143–145
    Human Fertilisation and Embryology
        Act 1990 see Human Fertilisation
        and Embryology Act 1990
    Human Fertilisation and Embryology
        Authority see under HFEA
        (Human Fertilisation and
        Embryology Authority)
    legal difficulties, 133
    Pergau Dam affair, 138
    purpose of conception of embryos,
        144
    purposive judicial interpretation,
        139–141
    regulation, 133, 134
    tissue typing see Tissue typing
    'treatment services', defined, 136, 139,
        140

Pharmaceutical industry
    zanamivir, refusal to recommend by
        NICE, 45, 46
Physician-assisted suicide (PAS) see PAS
        (physician-assisted suicide)
Physicians for a National Health Program
    United States, 30
Police involvement
    medico-crime (UK), 100, 105, 108
Polio, 219, 224
'Postcode prescribing', 39, 40
Post-materialism
    right to die debate, 260
Post-mortems
    legislative provisions, 167–168
Poverty
    United States, 31
Preimplantation genetic diagnosis see
        PGD (preimplantation genetic diag-
        nosis)
Prescription drugs
    pricing of (USA), 21
Primary Care Groups
    creation, 67
Priority-setting in healthcare
    and resource allocation, 37, 49
    in Oregon, 48
Privacy rights
    autonomy concept, 126–127
    reproductive freedom, 120–121
Privatisation of social services
    American model, 16–17
Professional incompetence see
        Incompetence, professional
Property Expenses Scheme, 65
'Prudent patient test'
    cosmetic surgery, 236
Puerperal fever
    medical negligence case law, 81–82
'Purple-green coalition'
    Belgium, 257
PVS (persistent vegetative state), 199–200,
        279

Q

QALY (quality adjusted life year), 46
Quality of care
    defined, 66
Quality control principle
    reproductive rights, 122
Quality Journey: A Guide to Total Quality
        Management in the NHS (NHS
        Management Executive), 59

R

Randomised controlled trials (RCTs), 197
Rationing of healthcare resources
    ability to pay (USA), 23
    clinical autonomy and, 58
    definition of rationing, 2
    deliberative approach to decision-
        making, 48
    'need' factor, 38
    NHS, 38–40
    NICE, 41
    as political process, 42
    'postcode prescribing', 39, 40
    priority-setting, 37, 48, 49
    rationality, 41
    'technical' factors, 42
RCGP (Royal College of General
        Practitioners)
    Guide to Good Medical Practice, 107
    regulation of standards, 96
RCTs (randomised controlled trials), 197
Reasonable care
    test of, 82
Reflective practice model
    healthcare services, 3, 72
Reform
    medico-crime, 104–108
    National Institute for Clinical
        Excellence, 47–50
Registre National des Refus
    organ donation opposition registry
        (France), 175
Regulating Schools of Anatomy Bill
        (1831), 166, 167
Reid, John, 218–219
Relaxant drugs, failure to give
    Bolam case, 80
Reproductive technologies, 115–131
    designer babies, 115, 120–122
    discourses, 116–117
    empirical evidence, 122–126
    feminism, 117
    regulation of reproduction, 119–120
        autonomy regulation, 126–127
        choice, 123
    women, 118
Resources for healthcare, allocation, 37–54
    legitimacy
        and due process, 42–44
        problem of, 2–3, 37, 38, 40, 41–42,
            43–44, 50
    NHS, rationing modes, 38–40
        see also Rationing of healthcare
            resources

NICE see NICE (National Institute for
    Clinical Excellence)
Resurrectionists
    Burke and Hare as, 155–156
    defined, 151, 165
    historical comparisons, 152
Retinopathy, 116
Revalidation
    limitations of, 107–108
Reversibility, inter-human relationships
    Habermas on, 144
Review committees (euthanasia)
    Belgium, 289–290
    Netherlands, 276, 277, 279, 280, 281,
        282
    patient not expected to die shortly,
        296–297
    terminally ill patients, 297–298
Right to die, 253–267
    death as human choice, 269
    legal change, processes of
        Belgium, 256–257
        Denmark, 258–259
        Netherlands, 254–256
    political opportunities, 262–265
    value orientations, changes in,
        259–262
    see also AVC (Active Voluntary
        Euthanasia; Euthanasia; PAS
        (physician-assisted suicide)
Risk
    clinical, ownership of see Hospitals,
        ownership of clinical risk
        (England)
    non-clinical, 55–56, 57, 59, 61, 62–63,
        65, 73–74
    awareness of (1990s), 63–71
    disclosure of, cosmetic surgery, 235–236
        inadequate, 238, 241
    grammatical use of term, 62
    literature on, 63
Risk management
    introduction into NHS on 'systems'
        basis, 73
Risk Management Manual (CNST), 65
Risk Management Manual (NHS
        Executive), 64, 67, 70
Risk Pooling Scheme for Trusts (RPST),
        65, 66
'Risk-sharing' policy
    beta-interferon funding, 45, 46
Robert Wood Johnson Foundation
    United States, 29
'Robowoman', 246
Roman Empire, fall of, 56

Royal College of General Practitioners *see* RCGP (Royal College of General Practitioners)
Royal College of Obstetricians and Gynaecologists
preimplantation genetic diagnosis, 145
Royal Dutch Medical Association (KNMG) *see* KNMG (Royal Dutch Medical Association)
Royal Hospitals, 56
Royal Liverpool Children's Hospital Public Inquiry, 156–157, 158
see also Alder Hey Hospital
Royal Liverpool Infirmary for Children resurrectionists at, 152
Royal Pharmaceutical Society of Great Britain, 296
Royal Society Study Group
Report (1983), 62
Report (1992), 63
RPST (Risk Pooling Scheme for Trusts), 65, 66
Rubella, 219

S

St Bartholemew's Hospital, 56
St Thomas's Hospital, 56
Salisbury, David, 227
Salisbury, Jane, 227
Salter, B, 57
SCEN project (Support and Consultation on Euthanasia in the Netherlands), 280, 295
Science and Technology Committee House of Commons, 117
Scientific bureaucratic model healthcare services, 3, 72
Scotland healthcare delivery in, 73
Secretary of State for Health NICE, accountability to, 40
Select Committee on Anatomy (1828), 161, 162, 165
Minutes of Evidence, 165
Report, 164
Select Committee on Health NICE, evaluation of, 44, 46–47, 48, 50
Self-regulation, medical profession, 96, 98–99, 108–109
purpose, 102
resistance to change, 100–102
Septicaemia medical negligence case law, 81–82

Sexual assault by doctors professional misconduct, as, 105
see also Ayling, Clifford: intimate examinations by
Sherwin, Susan, 243–244
Shipman, Harold: murders of patients by, 5, 94, 97, 101, 102
GMC, criticism for failure to prevent, 100
homicide rate, effect on, 104
initial police investigation, 99, 105
methods, 94
Shipman Inquiry, 98, 103, 107
Sigmoidoscopic examinations general anaesthesia, 87–88
Simpkin, M, 25
Skill and care requirement cosmetic surgery, 239
Smith, Dame J, 107
Smith, D I, 99
Sociologists role, 28, 29–30
Sociology business of, 2, 16
Somatic cell nuclear transfer (cloning), 116
Special Health Authority NICE as, 40, 67
NPSA as, 71
Standard of care *Bolam* principle, 79–80
failures, 70
skill of individual doctor, dependant on, 100–101
Stanley Royd hospital (Wakefield) food poisoning outbreak at (1984), 60
Starr, Paul, 23
State Commission on Euthanasia Netherlands, 274, 280, 284
Statements of Internal Control required from chief executives, 69
Stauch, M, 197
Stimpson, A, 16
Stimpson, J, 16
Subarachnoid haemorrhage medical negligence case law, 84–85
Suffering non-somatic, 278
psychiatric, 278, 279, 287
unbearable, 277, 278, 279
without prospect of improvement, 277–278, 294–295
Swan, Michael, 62
Sympathetic ophthalmia medical negligence case law (Australia), 84

T

Therapeutic/non-therapeutic, meaning, 192
Thouvenin, D, 179
Tingle, J, 197
Tissue typing
    definition, 134
    Hashmi case, 138
    HFEA, permitting by, 122
    Masterton family case, 135–136
    purpose, 139
    Whitaker case, 138
Toddler Questionnaire
    vaccination of infants, 215–216, 225–226, 228, 229
TQM (total quality management), 59, 64

U

United Kingdom
    active voluntary euthanasia, 290–291
    assisted suicide, 290–291
    Black Report (1980), 25
    hospitals *see* Hospitals, ownership of clinical risk (England)
    managed competition, 31
    medico-crime *see* Medico-crime (UK)
    serial killers *see* Burke, William; Hare, William; Shipman, Harold
United States
    African-Americans, 24, 25
    changing health laws/policies, 29–31
    corporations, 18, 22
    costs, controlling, 2, 22–23
    democracy, façade of, 17–18
    federalist system, 17–18
    foundation for social change, estab-lishing, 30
    GDP, 22
    health
        as commodity, 21–22
        as public issue, 27–29
    healthcare inequity, 2, 23–27
    healthcare system, 16, 18, 20–21
    health law, 2, 15–36
    health programmes, 26–27
    Hispanics, 24, 25
    individualism, 19
    inequality, and maintenance of status quo, 18–20
    laissez-faire economics, 19
    life expectancy, 24
    'medical model', 20
    national health insurance system, 27
    poverty in, 31
    privatisation of social services, 16–17
    social change, implementing, 30–31
    social context, 17, 28
    social programmes/policies, 19–20
    sociologists, role, 29–30
    unvaccinated children, sanctions against, 225
    wealth, 18
    wealthfare system, 27
Universal Declaration of Human Rights
    and reproductive rights, 121
    vaccination of children and, 217
Utilitarianism, 242

V

Vaccination of infants, 213–231
    autonomy of decision-makers, 218–226
    background, 214–215
    benefits
        possible overstatement, 219–222
        risks and, 218–224
    civil sanctions, unvaccinated children, 225
    definition, 214
    Directed Enhanced Service, as, 226
    doctor's duty, 226–228
    empirical studies
        general considerations, 216–217
        JABS Questionnaire, 216, 223
        Toddler Questionnaire, 215–216, 225, 226, 228, 229
    ethical imperatives, 217–228
    external influences, 225–226
    government's duty, 217–218
    incentive payments, 227, 228
    JABS Questionnaire, 216, 223
    MMR safety debate, 224
    primary/secondary schedules, *214*
    purpose, 214
    risks
        benefits and, 218–224
        possible understatement of, 222–224
    Toddler Questionnaire, 215–216, 225, 226, 228, 229
    trust of patients, misplacement, 228
Van Velzen, Dick, 7, 159, 160, 169
vCJD (variant-Creutzfeldt-Jakob disease), 219, 224
Viagra
    rationing of, 39

Vicarious liability
    NHS bodies, 61
Vindication of the Rights of Women
        (M. Wollstonecraft), 245

W

Walsh, K, 60
Walton Committee
    on mercy killing, 273, 290
Warburton, Mr
    anatomy regulation, 165–167
Warnock Committee
    Report of the Committee of Inquiry
        into Human Fertilisation and
        Embryology (1984), 128
Wealthfare system
    United States, 27
Weekly Chronicle (Edinburgh), 158
Welfare principle
    reproductive rights, 122
Welsh Assembly
    NICE, accountability to, 40
Wheat, K, 197
Whitaker case
    Human Fertilisation and Embryology
        Act 1990, 138–139, 141
White, Joanne, 221

Whooping cough, 220
WHO (World Health Organization)
    Constitution, 217
    health, definition of, 5, 20
    NICE, evaluation of, 44, 46–47, 48
Williams, Thomas, 166
Wilson, James ('Daft Jamie')
    death of, 155
Wisheart, James, 159
Wollstonecraft, Mary, 245
Women
    reproductive technologies, 118
Working for Patients (Department of
        Health), 61
World Medical Association
    Declaration of Helsinki, 195, 207

X

X-rays, establishment (1896), 57

Z

Zanamivir (influenza treatment)
    appraisal of, 3, 44–45, 46, 47